MYSTERIES OF THE SCRIPTURES REVEALED

Shattering the Deceptions Within Mainstream Christianity
Deciphering and Revealing End Times Prophecies
Making a Straight Path for the End Times Saints

GEORGE B. LUJACK

MYSTERIES OF THE SCRIPTURES REVEALED

ISBN: 978-0-9983-5250-3 (sc)
ISBN: 978-0-9983-5251-0 (e)

Because of the dynamic nature of the Internet, any web addresses or links contained in this book may have changed since publication and may no longer be valid. The views expressed in this work are solely those of the author and do not necessarily reflect the views of the publisher, and the publisher hereby disclaims any responsibility for them.

Any people depicted in stock imagery provided by Thinkstock are models, and such images are being used for illustrative purposes only. Certain stock imagery © Thinkstock.

Scripture taken from the New King James Version®. Copyright © 1982 by Thomas Nelson. Used by permission. All rights reserved.

Scripture taken from the King James Version of the Bible.

Tree of Life (TLV) Translation of the Bible. Copyright © 2015 by The Messianic Jewish Family Bible Society.

THE HOLY BIBLE, NEW INTERNATIONAL VERSION®, NIV® Copyright © 1973, 1978, 1984, 2011 by Biblica, Inc.® Used by permission. All rights reserved worldwide.

Scripture taken from the Halleluyah Scriptures (HSV) is freely distributed and used by permission. HSV Scripture quotes are Bereshith (Genesis) 1:1-2,28; Wayyiqra (Leviticus) 11:13-19; Debarim (Deuteronomy) 14:12-18; Iyob (Job) 38:14,25; Yeshayahu (Isaiah) 18:1; Romiyim (Romans) 10:4, Yohanan 1 (1 John) 5:7-8.

Lulu Publishing Services rev. date: 7/21/2017

CONTENTS

4. DOCTRINES, HOLIDAYS, AND PRACTICES

5. THEOLOGICAL QUESTIONS ANSWERED

6. DIET AND HEALTH

7. THE SABBATH

8. DEATH AND RESURRECTION

9. HEAVEN AND HELL

10. SCIENCE AND SCRIPTURE

11. CATHOLICISM AND PROTESTANTISM REFUTED

12. END TIMES PROPHECY REVEALED

INTRODUCTION

By George Lujack

Greetings in the name of Elohim (God) the Father Almighty, Yeshua Messiah (Jesus Christ), and the Ruach HaKodesh (Holy Spirit)!

ACKNOWLEDGEMENTS

ELOHIM (GOD)

This book is dedicated to the glory of God and His coming kingdom. It is God, first and foremost, who has inspired the writing of this book. It was a deep desire instilled within me, from the time of my teenage years, to do a great work inspired by God; namely to uncover the falsehoods of organized denominational Christianity, reveal many of God's unknown mysteries, and to fully decipher all pertinent Scripture prophecy for believers living in the end times. The Spirit of God has guided my efforts in this endeavor during the past fifteen years, culminating in the completion of my life's greatest work, *"Mysteries of the Scriptures Revealed."*

JULIE BORIK, EDITOR AND CONTENT CONTRIBUTOR

Julie Borik is a godsend, an answer to prayer. Having realized that the task at hand was much bigger than me, I called upon God in prayer for assistance to help me make my book become a reality. I soon afterward came into contact with Mrs. Julie Borik through a religious discussion group forum in a mutual effort to secure justice for an imprisoned Christian evangelist, Kent Hovind. Julie was a woman searching for spiritual answers - genuine Scripture verifiable truths. Having come out of the Catholic Church and all of its deceptions, Julie found herself scratching her head over many of the doctrines and Scripture explanations of mainstream Christianity. Then, as fate would have it, our paths crossed. Julie appreciated my articulate, easy to understand, Scripture-based explanations. So, she kept asking questions. Some questions were already addressed in articles that I had previously written, but there were many questions I had not yet addressed. Impressed with my work and my goal to publish the greatest Scripture explanation help book of all time, Julie offered her editor services, correcting many of the grammar and punctuation mistakes in my articles.

As Julie became more involved with my project, theological objections and questions arose from her mainstream Christian associates, which were presented to me. Many of these topics addressed would wind up becoming articles for the book. Julie also suggested a few topic ideas that became articles for the book. Julie became a valuable content contributor for the book and Julie remains a close spiritual confidant and friend. Together we have co-founded Scripture Truth Ministries.

HERBERT W. ARMSTRONG

Herbert W. Armstrong (1892-1986) was an early spiritual influence. Armstrong was the founder of the Worldwide Church of God and a televangelist whose teachings were unlike any that I had heard in church. Mr. Armstrong showed me that God's dietary laws were perpetual and that the holidays associated with mainstream Christianity were not God's holy days, but were pagan in origin and were even condemned in Scripture.

After Mr. Armstrong died, ravenous wolves (Matthew 7:15) took over the ministry he started and sought to destroy all the work that he had done in proclaiming the eternal nature of God's laws and exposing the deceptions of mainstream Christianity. Some today like to point out the errors, shortcomings, and sins of Mr. Armstrong, but his ministry was well known and respected the world over. Many of Armstrong's teachings made a lasting impression and helped shape my faith and understanding of the Scriptures.

KENT HOVIND

Kent Hovind is an ordained Baptist minister and founder of Creation Science Evangelism. Hovind is perhaps the greatest refuter of Evolution Theory who has ever lived. Watching Hovind's videos of him debating the greatest evolutionary 'scientific' minds of our time, making them look absurd and unintelligent, was both amusing and instructive. Hovind would always humbly introduce himself by saying, "Hello. My name is Kent Hovind. I was a high school science teacher for 15-years and now I have been doing seminars all over the world on creation, evolution, and dinosaurs." Hovind helped inspire this former police officer of 20-years by asking, "What are you doing for the Lord? Get busy! Find something to do."

OTHERS

Special thanks to 119 Ministries for their online teaching videos that contributed to some of the articles in this book and to Blake Daniel, whose science and Scripture social media posts contributed to the *Science and Scripture* article in this book. Thank you Caiden Cowger, for providing a website platform for me to begin posting my articles and for being an inspirational young man of great character, integrity, and strong moral values.

ABOUT THE AUTHOR GEORGE LUJACK

Born in 1965, I was raised as a Lutheran Protestant (protesting Catholic), but rejected the faith of my upbringing and became a non-denominational, biblical Christian. Modified my faith to being an independent Messianic believer in 2012, at the age of 47. Declared myself an independent, non-ordained, Messianic minister on Jan. 02, 2016 at the age 50.

Career: Police officer with the New York City Police Department for 20-years, serving from 1987-2007. International police officer employed by the State Department for the United Nations International Police Task Force in Croatia from 1996-1997 and in Kosovo from 2000-2001. Managing editor for CowgerNation. com, a conservative political and religious content online news network from 2014 to present.

Twenty years of writing police reports prepared me for writing the articles contained within this book. I took the same approach in composing topical Scripture articles as when writing a report at a crime scene. I listened to the witnesses (doctrines), gathered the relevant evidence (Scripture verses), looked for discrepancies (eliminated falsehoods), and based on all the available information wrote up a report of what occurred (composed the articles).

Upbringing and travels: Born in Queens, then moved to Island Park, Long Island, New York at the age of five. Grew up in the suburbs of the South Shore of Long Island between the Island Park and Long Beach area towns till the age of forty-three. Moved to New Port Richey, Florida in 2008-2012, and purchased first home in Apollo Beach, Florida in 2012, where I currently reside. Stateside travels include most states in America. World travels include Albania, Bosnia and Herzegovina, Brazil, Canada, Colombia, Czech Republic, Croatia, France, Germany, Greece, Hungary, Israel, Jamaica, Japan, Kosovo, Macedonia, Mexico, Poland, Serbia, Slovakia, Slovenia, Switzerland, Uganda, and Ukraine.

Ministry: I am an independent, non-ordained, Messianic minister. Being non-ordained and unattached to any denominational church, ministry, or synagogue organization and its requisite teachings, other than my own Scripture Truth Ministries, which was founded on January 2, 2016, has afforded me the flexibility and freedom to present God's word without any hindrance or interference from others, whose organization - if I was beholden to through ordination, might not doctrinally approve of every truth presented in my writings and could hamper them from being presented. My ministry and my writings are dedicated to presenting the truth of God's written word, without any organized religious interference. Unlike other ordained ministers, I am not dependent upon a ministry salary. Ordination can be a stumbling block for God's word to be proclaimed and for it to be presented truthfully. No one should be impeded from proclaiming the truth of the Scriptures and the true gospel of Yeshua Messiah (Jesus Christ) (Mark 9:38-39; Luke 9:49-50).

MATTHEW 28:18-20 (NKJV):

And Yeshua (Jesus) came and spoke to them, saying, "All authority has been given to Me in heaven and on earth. Go therefore and make disciples of all the nations, baptizing them in the name of the Father and of the Son and of the Holy Spirit, teaching them to observe all things that I have commanded you; and lo, I am with you always, even to the end of the age."

Knowledge and wisdom attained through a comprehensive study and understanding of the Scriptures, along with declaration of proclaimed faith through adult baptism, is ordination enough for anyone who wishes to go and teach people to observe all things Yeshua (Jesus) commanded.

ABOUT THE BOOK

The truth concerning many Scripture topics remains a mystery to many, as thousands of years of erroneous doctrines continue to be widely taught by ministers in denominational churches along with many new deceptive Scripture teachings. This book is written for Messianics, Christians, Jews, and anyone else seeking true answers and explanations of God's word. As the articles address both Messianics and Christians, the Hebraic Messianic and the (Greek Christian) names for the Son of God, Yeshua (Jesus), and Messiah (Christ) are often written together as such throughout the book.

DANIEL 12:4 (NKJV):

"But you, Daniel, shut up the words, and seal the book until the time of the end; many shall run to and fro, and knowledge shall increase."

PROVERBS 10:17 (NKJV):

He who refuses correction goes astray.

PROVERBS 11:30 (NKJV):

The fruit of the righteous is a tree of life, and he who wins souls is wise.

Technological knowledge has increased *and* Scripture knowledge has increased as well. The very purpose of this book is to correct doctrinal errors of faith, to win souls for salvation, and minds for truth. This Scripture explanation helps book will equip believers with in-depth explanations of doctrines and the prophecies of our end times. Every doctrinal topic covered in the articles of this book discloses ALL the relevant Scripture verses related to the subject matter. People who preach or write on doctrinal matters, but only use supporting verses to make their doctrinal case, while intentionally omitting verses that refute their argument, are being disingenuous. The articles contained in this book do not do that.

MATTHEW 7:13-14 (NKJV):

"Enter by the narrow gate; for wide is the gate and broad is the way that leads to destruction, and there are many who go in by it. Because narrow is the gate and difficult is the way which leads to life, and there are few who find it."

Four elements of true faith that are key to developing a right relationship with God and a proper understanding of Scripture will be emphasized throughout this book:

1. One must have a fear of God. The fear of YHWH 'the Lord' is the beginning of knowledge and wisdom (Psalm 111:10; Proverbs 1:7, 9:10).

2. One must believe in the ultimate authority of God. We are not our own authority (1 Corinthians 6:19). He is King of kings, Sovereign of sovereigns, and has authority over the entire universe, over all His creation, and over us (1 Timothy 6:15; Revelation 17:14).

3. One must know and follow God's commands and believe that His words, including His commands, shall not pass away (Matthew 24:35; Mark 13:31; Luke 21:33).

4. One needs to truly believe in eternal life and have faith reflective of that. This enables us to get through this life without feeling we are 'missing out' on things, strengthens us to avoid sin, and reminds us that this world will pass away. Our hope and our eternal destiny await us in the world that is yet to come, as sons and daughters in the kingdom of God (Romans 8:18; 2 Corinthians 6:18).

2 THESSALONIANS 2:7 (NKJV):

For the mystery of lawlessness is already at work...

This book is dedicated to explaining the doctrinal deceptions and errors of organized Christianity, many of which are designed to lead believers into lawlessness; declaring God's truths; and revealing His end times prophesies to prepare the saints for His return.

I open up to take a look into the bright and shiny book;
Into the open scheme of things
Book of brilliant things
Oh, book of brilliant things
- Excerpt from the song, "Book of Brilliant Things," Simple Minds, 1984

Prepare to take a fresh look at the Scriptures from a new perspective.
Prepare to be amazed by the book of brilliant things...

GOD LOVES THE RIGHTEOUS MORE THAN HE HATES THE WICKED

By George Lujack

In 1692, the city of Port Royal, Jamaica, literally slid into the sea when it was struck by a massive earthquake. Port Royal was a city of prostitution and sin. Many had predicted that this corrupt city of pirates and cutthroats would one day suffer God's judgment. Therefore, the earthquake disaster that came upon the city was not a surprise. One righteous man, Lewis Galdy, who had fled Protestant persecution in Europe and recently arrived in Port Royal, was shocked at the freely sinning people all around him. When the earthquake struck, Galdy was buried alive in the first shock wave. He remained conscious and understood what had happened. In prayer, he resigned his fate to the will of God. A few moments later, another earthquake threw Galdy high in the air and out into the sea. He landed unhurt in the water and swam until a boat picked him up.[1][2]

Many believers in these end times go through anxiety and grave concern (tribulation) over the future as they experience and eyewitness society degenerating all around them, becoming more corrupt year after year and generation after generation. Many feel disheartened, hopeless, and powerless to stop society's slide into lawlessness and sin. We fear not only for society, but that we may get caught and trapped in God's wrath along with the evil, godless, hard-hearted, secular, sin-filled people who surround us.

Faithful believers shouldn't needlessly worry about God's upcoming wrath upon an evil wicked society that they may happen to be living amongst, but instead continue to focus on living righteously, according to God's word, and doing His will. God once flooded the Earth in judgment, but righteous Noah found grace in the eyes of YHWH (the Lord), and God saw to it that Noah and his family, a total of eight persons, were spared from the floodwaters on the ark (Genesis 6:8; 1 Peter 3:20). God once promised Abraham that He would not destroy Sodom for the sake of ten righteous persons (Genesis 18:22-33). God did not destroy Sodom before He warned Lot and his family to flee from the city and to not look back upon it (Genesis 19:15). God cares more for protecting the righteous than He does for punishing the wicked. God will provide an escape exit or a shield for His saints when He brings forth His judgment and wrath upon the wicked.

DOES GOD LOVE US UNCONDITIONALLY?

By George Lujack

I AM LOVED UNCONDITIONALLY - Romans 5:8.

Is that really what Romans 5:8 says?

ROMANS 5:8 (NKJV):

But God demonstrates His own love toward us, in that while we were still sinners, Messiah (Christ) died for us.

Romans 5:8 does not proclaim that God loves us unconditionally, but rather that God loved us so, that Yeshua Messiah (Jesus Christ) died in our place to satisfy God's CONDITION that sin be punished by death – so that we could be saved. If God loved us unconditionally, there would have been no need for Yeshua (Jesus) to die on the cross to atone for our sins. All sinners would go to heaven if God loved us unconditionally and Yeshua (Jesus) dying for us on the cross would have been unnecessary.

UNCONDITIONAL = WITHOUT CONDITIONS

God does not love us unconditionally. This poisonous doctrine known as "God's Unconditional Love" is what many believers proclaim. The word "unconditional," or the phrase, "unconditional love," do not appear anywhere in Scripture.

When God created Adam and Eve, they were not loved unconditionally. YHWH (the Lord) God gave Adam and Eve just one command (a condition): to not eat of the fruit of the tree of the knowledge of good and evil, for if they did, they would surely die (Genesis 2:16). Adam and Eve broke God's command (condition) (Genesis 3:6) and YHWH (the Lord), being righteous and a keeper of His word, did not unconditionally love and forgive Adam and Eve. God kicked them out of the Garden of Eden (Genesis 3:22-24) and they died, as He promised they would (Genesis 5:5).

DEUTERONOMY 11:26-28 (NKJV):

Behold, I set before you this day a blessing and a curse; A blessing, if you obey the commandments of the LORD your God, which I command you this day: And a curse, if you will not obey the commandments of the LORD your God...

There are three basic conditions for us to be accepted and loved by God: repentance, obeying God's Commandments, and accepting Yeshua Messiah (Jesus Christ) as our personal Lord and Savior. Repentance is a condition. Commandments are conditions. Accepting Yeshua Messiah (Jesus Christ) as Lord and Savior is a condition. To say that God loves us unconditionally is scripturally inaccurate and is an emotionally driven false doctrine.

DOES RECEIVING GOD'S GRACE REQUIRE ANY ACTION ON OUR PART?

HEBREWS 10:26-28 (NKJV):

For if we sin willfully after we have received the knowledge of the truth, there no longer remains a sacrifice for sins, but a certain fearful expectation of judgment, and fiery indignation which will devour the adversaries. Anyone who has rejected Moses' law dies without mercy on the testimony of two or three witnesses.

HEBREWS 10:29 (NKJV):

Of how much worse punishment, do you suppose, will he be thought worthy who has trampled the Son of God underfoot, counted the blood of the covenant by which he was sanctified a common thing, and insulted the Spirit of grace?

Believers are deceiving themselves if, after receiving grace, they think that God will continue to unconditionally love them if they willfully sin after receiving the knowledge of God's truths (1 Corinthians 6:9-10; Galatians 6:7-8).

JOHN 14:15 (NKJV):

Yeshua (Jesus) said, "If you love Me, keep My commandments."

GOD LOVES THE SINNER, BUT HATES SIN...

Some may say that God loves the sinner, but hates sin. Without repentance, God cannot separate the sin from the sinner. Yeshua (Jesus) died to atone for our sins with the condition that we first repent and then accept His free salvation gift. One needs to repent or otherwise the message that you are telling God is that you enjoy sin and that you reject God's ways. Sinners, along with their unrepentant sins, will be cast into hell. God will only forgive the sins of those who repent, not the sins of those who refuse to repent. God will not force anyone to repent and one must repent and obey God of his or her own free will.

God loves us and is not permissive concerning sin. God wouldn't properly love us if He were an enabler of sin. If God did not correct our sin, but allowed us to sin freely and then enter His kingdom without conditions, this would not be love, but enabling.

"God is love." In the same manner in which people take a verse out-of-context, so too do many believers take this verse out of the entirety of the Scriptures. Many believers preach, "God is love," and refuse to proclaim the rest of the Scriptures concerning God. The Scriptures say that God is love, but this is only a partial description of God's nature.

God is described by many adjectives besides love:

-God is holy (Joshua 24:19)

-God is gracious and merciful (2 Chronicles 30:9; Psalm 116:5; Joel 2:13)

-God is a jealous God (Exodus 20:5, 34:14, Deuteronomy 4:24, 5:9, 6:15; Joshua 24:19; Ezekiel 39:25; Nahum 1:2)

-God is love (1 John 4:8)

-God is righteous (Deuteronomy 32:4; Ezra 9:15; Psalm 116:5; Daniel 9:14)

-And is many other wonderful things…

Want unconditional love? Get a puppy. Yet even a dog will not unconditionally love if it is physically abused. A mistreated dog will not love, but fear its owner.

PROVERBS 13:24-25 (NKJV):

He who spared his rod hates his son, but he who loves him disciplines him promptly.

Should a father unconditionally love his child? Those who say that they should are proclaiming that they should accept, allow, enable, and love sin. God commands us to rebuke sinners, not love them unconditionally (Leviticus 19:17). Unrepentant sinners will not inherit the kingdom of God (1 Corinthians 6:9-10).

There is nothing more repulsive than to hear a 'believer' say, "I love my gay son / daughter." That is an enabling, no need to repent, remain just as you are, unconditional love statement. It is like saying, "I love my adulterous, physically abusive husband." A sane person doesn't say that. It would be proper to say, "I love my son / daughter, but I do not accept or condone his / her abominable homosexual lifestyle."

"Unconditional love" of a person with sexually depraved behavior or any other egregious sin, close relative or not, is not what God would have us proclaim. God calls upon us to rebuke sin, not accept and condone it. When a person accepts and condones the sins of others, instead of righteously rebuking them, they share in their sin.

LEVITICUS 19:17 (NKJV):

You shall surely rebuke your neighbor, and not bear sin because of him.

1 CORINTHIANS 6:20 (NKJV):

For you were bought at a price; therefore glorify God in your body and in your spirit, which are God's.

God's love for mankind is not unconditional or free. For God to be able to love us we had to be purchased at a great cost. Yeshua (Jesus) paid a terrible price to redeem us, and through His sacrifice we are healed and reconciled to God (Isaiah 53).

REFINER'S FIRE: PURIFIER OF SILVER

By George Lujack

This article will discuss how God's Spirit and His words, when applied in our lives, refine us to be a reflection of Him.

PSALM 12:6 (NKJV):

The words of YHWH (the Lord) are pure words, like silver tried in the furnace of earth, refined seven times.

The words of Yeshua Messiah (Jesus Christ) are pure words. His words in the gospel were spoken to us carefully, flawlessly, genuinely, perfectly, precisely, purposefully, and truthfully. All of His commandments were well thought out before He ever issued them to us.

MATTHEW 24:35, MARK 13:31, LUKE 21:33 (NKJV):

"Heaven and earth will pass away, but My words will by no means pass away."

God is good, holy, and righteous, but we are desperately wicked and our righteousness is like filthy rags compared to Him.

ISAIAH 64:6 (NKJV):

But we are like an unclean thing and our righteousnesses are like filthy rags.

JEREMIAH 17:9 (NKJV):

The heart is deceitful above all things and desperately wicked.

Yeshua (Jesus) came into the world to pay the penalty for our unrighteousness, the just for the unjust.

1 PETER 3:18 (NKJV):

For Messiah (Christ) also suffered once for sins, the just for the unjust, that He might bring us to God, being put to death in the flesh but made alive by the Spirit.

There is only one way for us to be brought before God and that is through the righteousness of Yeshua (Jesus).

JOHN 14:6 (NKJV):

Yeshua (Jesus) said to him, "I am the way, the truth, and the life. No one comes to the Father except through Me."

ACTS 4:12 (NKJV):

Nor is there salvation in any other, for there is no other name under heaven given among men by which we must be saved.

In order to go to the Father we must go through the Son. We must come to Him of our own free will, repent of our sins, and obey His commandments.

MATTHEW 4:17, MARK 1:15 (NKJV):

From that time Yeshua (Jesus) began to preach and to say, "Repent, for the kingdom of heaven is at hand."

1 JOHN 2:4 (NKJV):

He who says, "I know Him," and does not keep His commandments, is a liar, and the truth is not in him.

YESHUA (JESUS) REFINES US AS A SILVERSMITH REFINES SILVER

MALACHI 3:2-3 (NKJV):

For He is like a refiner's fire and like launderer's soap.
He will sit as a refiner and purifier of silver.

To refine silver, a silversmith heats up a furnace and sits in front of the fire while holding the silver over it to refine it. Silver is held in the middle of the fire where the flames are hottest to burn away the infirmities. The silversmith needs to sit and watch the silver refining process, keeping his eyes on the silver the entire time that it is in the fire. If the silver is left too long in the flames, it can be destroyed. The silver is fully refined and removed from the fire when the silversmith sees his image reflected in it.

2 CORINTHIANS 6:18 (NKJV):

"I will be a Father to you, and you shall be My sons and daughters," says YHWH (the Lord) Almighty.

Yeshua (Jesus) is our Silversmith, refining us to be like a reflection of Him. If we repent, seek Him, and obey His commandments, He will refine us. He will present us before the Father to become the sons and daughters of Almighty God.

THE MYSTERY OF THE BLINDNESS OF THE JEWS

By George Lujack

For millennia, Christians have often asked, "Why won't the Jews just accept Jesus as their Lord and Savior?" This article will examine Romans 11 and discuss why the Jews, God's original chosen people, have been blinded from accepting their Messiah.

ROMANS 11:1-2 (NKJV):

I say then, has God cast away His people? Certainly not! For I also am an Israelite, of the seed of Abraham, of the tribe of Benjamin. GOD HAS NOT CAST AWAY HIS PEOPLE WHOM HE FOREKNEW.

For thousands of years, many righteous-living Jews have lived and died, not knowing that Yeshua (Jesus) was their true Messiah, having rejected Him. Have they perished, never to see life again? Are (Yeshua / Jesus) Messiah-denying Jews destined to be cast into hell in God's judgment? NO!!! Righteous Jews who have died will be resurrected to life and will stand before Yeshua the Messiah (Jesus the Christ) *and then they will know* He is their Lord and Messiah and then they will accept Him (Ezekiel 37).

ROMANS 11:7-12 (NKJV):

What then? Israel has not obtained what it seeks; but the elect have obtained it, and the rest were blinded. Just as it is written:

"God has given them a spirit of stupor, eyes that they should not see and ears that they should not hear, to this very day.

And David says:

"Let their table become a snare and a trap, a stumbling block and a recompense to them.

Let their eyes be darkened, so that they do not see, and bow down their back always."

I say then, have they stumbled that they should fall? Certainly not!

BUT THROUGH THEIR FALL, TO PROVOKE THEM TO JEALOUSY, SALVATION HAS COME TO THE GENTILES. Now if their fall is riches for the world, and their failure riches for the Gentiles, how much more their fullness!

How has salvation come to the Gentiles through the fall of the Jews? First and foremost, it was required that Yeshua (Jesus) would die to atone for the sins of mankind. Had the Jews received Yeshua (Jesus) as their

Messiah and had not conspired with the Romans to execute Him, there would be no atonement sacrifice for the salvation of the Gentiles.

The Jews are somewhat jealous of the elects' (Gentiles') Savior, commonly known as Jesus Christ, but they will not accept Jesus Christ as their Messiah. The Jews, God's original chosen people, will not accept a Messiah who is one-third of a polytheistic triune 3-branch god, a Messiah who changed the perpetual Sabbath day from the seventh day of the week to the first day, a Messiah who allows statues to be made of Himself, a Messiah who is honored through pagan holidays such as Christmas and Easter, a Messiah who allows people to eat pork, shellfish, and all other kinds of unclean creatures, or a Messiah who goes by the non-Hebraic, Hellenized name of 'Jesus' (Gee-Zeus).

The blindness that has happened to the Jews concerning accepting their Messiah is a direct result of the false gospel that has been proclaimed by the Babylonian / Greek / Roman-inspired Christian churches for thousands of years. In these end times, spiritual knowledge has increased (Daniel 12:4).

Thanks to the Internet, social media sites, and a spiritual awakening occurring in these end times, God's true word, His perpetual laws, His perpetual Sabbaths, His holy festivals, and His true gospel message is being made known to the Gentiles. Jews are truly driven to jealously of the Gentiles when Gentiles become Torah (law) observant, accepting the unchanging, Hebraic Yeshua the Messiah and forsake the lawless, pagan, Babylonian / Greek / Roman Jesus the Christ. In these end times, as more and more Christians come out of mainstream Christianity and become Torah-observant Messianic believers, the Jews' jealousy will intensify.

ROMANS 11:13-18 (NKJV):

For I speak to you Gentiles; inasmuch as I am an apostle to the Gentiles, I magnify my ministry, if by any means I may provoke to jealousy those who are my flesh and save some of them. For if their being cast away is the reconciling of the world, what will their acceptance be but life from the dead?

For if the firstfruit is holy, the lump is also holy; and if the root is holy, so are the branches. And if some of the branches were broken off, and you, being a wild olive tree, were grafted in among them, and with them became a partaker of the root and fatness of the olive tree, do not boast against the branches. But if you do boast, remember that you do not support the root, but the root supports you.

The Jews' non-acceptance of Yeshua their Messiah has given the Gentiles time to come out of Babylon (confused religion), receive truth, worship Him in spirit and truth, live righteously, and be rightly grafted into God's kingdom.

ROMANS 11:19-22 (NKJV) [WITH INTERPRETATION]:

You will say then, "Branches were broken off that I might be grafted in." Well said. BECAUSE OF UNBELIEF THEY [THE JEWS] WERE BROKEN OFF, AND YOU [GENTILES] STAND BY FAITH. Do not be haughty, but fear. For if God did not spare the natural branches [THE JEWS], He may not spare you [GENTILES] either. Therefore consider the goodness and severity of God: on those [JEWS] who fell, severity; but toward you [GENTILES], goodness, IF YOU CONTINUE IN HIS GOODNESS [IF YOU OBEY HIS COMMANDMENTS]. Otherwise you also will be cut off.

ROMANS 11:23-24 (NKJV) [WITH INTERPRETATION]:

And they [JEWS] also, if they do not continue in unbelief [OF YESHUA BEING THEIR MESSIAH], will be grafted in, for God is able to graft them [THE JEWS] in again. For if you [GENTILES] were cut out of the olive tree which is wild by nature, and were grafted contrary to nature into a cultivated olive tree, how much more will these [THE JEWS], who are natural branches, be grafted into their own olive tree?

As the Jews, the natural branches, have been cut off for their disbelief in their Messiah, and are in danger of losing their salvation if they ultimately do not accept Him, the Gentiles, the wild branches, have been accepted by faith, BUT many of the Gentiles have NOT continued in His goodness as a result of rejecting His commandments and thus are in danger of being cut off and losing their salvation. The Jews need to accept Yeshua the Messiah in order to be grafted into God's kingdom and the Gentiles need to accept His Torah (laws) or they will be in danger of being cut off from God's kingdom.

ROMANS 11:25 (NKJV):

For I do not desire, brethren, that you should be ignorant of this mystery, lest you should be wise in your own opinion, that blindness in part has happened to Israel until the fullness of the Gentiles has come in.

The Jews have been blinded to allow time for the FULLNESS of the Gentiles to come in.

What is the 'fullness of the Gentiles' that is spoken of? It is the fullness truth which must come to Gentile Christian believers regarding obedience to His laws and His holy day festivals, so that the Gentiles can be grafted into God's kingdom, live righteously, and serve God in spirit and truth. This act of God, allowing the Jews to remain in blindness, demonstrates His love for the Gentile peoples of the world.

JOHN 3:16 (NKJV) [WITH INTERPRETATION]:

"For God so LOVED THE WORLD [NOT ONLY THE JEWS] that He gave His only begotten Son, that whoever believes in Him should not perish but have everlasting life."

Yeshua (Jesus) could have proven Himself to the Jews, but for the sake of the Gentiles, He has not done so - yet. Yeshua (Jesus) left the Jews, His chosen people, in a state of confusion, proclaiming to them that they would not see Him again until they, in their darkest hour, call upon Him to save them.

MATTHEW 23:38-39; LUKE 13:35 (NKJV) [WITH INTERPRETATION]:

"Your house is left to you desolate; for I say to you, you shall see Me no more till you say, *'Blessed is He* [YESHUA THE MESSIAH] *who comes in the name of* [YHWH] *the Lord!'"*

Consider the sorry state of confusion of the Gentile Christian churches. When Yeshua (Jesus) returns to Earth, He is coming to judge the Earth and rule over it with a rod of iron (Psalm 96:13, 98:9; Revelation 19:15). If Yeshua (Jesus) were to return to the Earth today, many Gentiles, including lawless Gentile *professing* Christians, relying on God's perpetual grace while living comfortably in sins, would perish (1 Corinthians 6:9-10; Galatians 5:19-21; Ephesians 5:5-6; Revelation 21:7-8).

EZEKIEL 33:11 (NKJV):

"As I live," says YHWH (the Lord) GOD, "I have no pleasure in the death of the wicked, but that the wicked turn from his way and live. Turn, turn from your evil ways!"

The fact that the Jews are blinded to Yeshua being the Messiah is a benefit to the Gentile Christian peoples of the world, who have been blinded by a false gospel message and are living lawlessly. The blindness of the Jews gives the Gentiles time to accept the fullness of the truth of God's word and reject the false gospel that the Christian churches have preached for thousands of years.

ROMANS 11:26-32 (NKJV) [WITH INTERPRETATION]:

And so all Israel [SPIRITUAL ISRAEL - JEWS AND GENTILES] will be saved, as it is written:

"The Deliverer will come out of Zion, and He will turn away ungodliness from Jacob; for this is My covenant with them, when I take away their sins."

Concerning the gospel they [THE JEWS] are enemies for your sake, but concerning the election they [THE JEWS] are beloved for the sake of the fathers. For the gifts and the calling of God are irrevocable. For as you [GENTILES] were once disobedient to God [GOD'S COMMANDMENTS], yet have now obtained mercy through their [THE JEWS'] disobedience [TO YESHUA THE MESSIAH], even so these [JEWS] also have now been disobedient, that through the mercy shown you [GENTILES] they [JEWS] also may obtain mercy. For God has committed them all [JEWS AND GENTILES] to disobedience, that He might have mercy on all.

Jews and Gentiles need to be grafted in, as spiritual Israel, to God's kingdom. Jews need to accept Yeshua as their Messiah to be grafted back into the kingdom and Gentiles need to repent and obey God's commandments in order to obtain God's mercy.

EPHESIANS 3:1-6 (NKJV):

For this reason I, Paul, the prisoner of Messiah Yeshua (Christ Jesus) for you Gentiles - if indeed you have heard of the dispensation of the grace of God which was given to me for you, how that by revelation He made known to me the mystery (as I have briefly written already, by which, when you read, you may understand my knowledge in the mystery of Messiah (Christ)), which in other ages was not made known to the sons of men, as it has now been revealed by the Spirit to His holy apostles and prophets: THAT THE GENTILES SHOULD BE FELLOW HEIRS, OF THE SAME BODY, and partakers of His promise in Messiah (Christ) through the gospel.

REVELATION 17:14 (NKJV):

"These will make war with the Lamb, and the Lamb will overcome them, for He is Lord of lords and King of kings; and those who are with Him are called, CHOSEN, and faithful."

Jews are no longer God's *only* chosen people, as Gentiles are fellow heirs of God's kingdom.

2 PETER 3:9 (NKJV):

The Lord is not slack concerning His promise, as some count slackness, but is longsuffering toward us, not willing that any should perish but that all should come to repentance.

REVELATION 12:12 (NKJV):

"Woe to the inhabitants of the earth and the sea! For the devil has come down to you, having great wrath, because he knows that he has a short time."

The age of grace will expire and the Jews will not be blinded to the fact that Yeshua is their Messiah forever. Gentile Christians who accept Yeshua (Jesus), but live lawlessly are in far graver danger of losing their salvation than righteous-living Jews who currently are blinded to the identity of their true Messiah. The mystery of the blindness of the Jews is a demonstration of God's love of all the Gentile peoples of the world. Gentiles have been afforded time, at the Jews' expense, to come out of Babylon (confused religion) and receive salvation. But the time is short. Repent now and worship God in spirit and truth!

THE FALSE DOCTRINE OF THE TRINITY: WHY THE HOLY SPIRIT IS NOT A PERSON

By George Lujack

The Holy Spirit (Ruach HaKodesh) is not a person, not a being, and not a God of a Trinity. God is biunial, not triune. This article will present 17-reasons why the Holy Spirit is not a person / being and will explain many of the reasons why the belief in a Triune God is a false doctrine.

1. THE HOLY SPIRIT IS THE SPIRIT 'OF' GOD, NOT THE SPIRIT GOD

2. GOD (ELOHIM / YHWH / YESHUA / THE LORD) HAS A SPIRIT

3. THE HOLY SPIRIT IS NOT A PERSON, THE HOLY SPIRIT IS AN 'IT'

4. GOD CONSISTS OF FATHER AND SON. THE HOLY SPIRIT IS NOT CALLED GOD, AS A PERSON, THROUGHOUT SCRIPTURE. GOD IS BIUNIAL, NOT TRIUNE

5. THE HOLY SPIRIT HAS NO THRONE IN HEAVEN

6. OUR BODIES ARE TEMPLES OF THE HOLY SPIRIT

7. THE HOLY SPIRIT HAS NO IMAGE

8. GOD'S SPIRIT IS NOT A PERSON APART FROM GOD

9. 'TRINITY' AND THE PHRASES 'HOLY TRINITY' AND 'GOD THE HOLY SPIRIT' DO NOT APPEAR IN SCRIPTURE

10. THE FAMILY STRUCTURE OF GOD; GOD IS NOT A CO-EQUAL TRINITY

11. BLASPHEMY AGAINST THE HOLY SPIRIT IS WORSE THAN BLASPHEMY AGAINST MESSIAH OR THE TEACHINGS OF GOD

12. THE HOLY SPIRIT DOES NOT HAVE ITS OWN AUTHORITY TO SPEAK; IT ONLY SPEAKS WHAT IT HEARS FROM GOD

13. THE HOLY SPIRIT BEARS WITNESS, AS DO OTHER NON-PERSONS

14. THE HOLY SPIRIT GRIEVES, COMFORTS, HELPS, AND TEACHES, AS DO OTHER NON-PERSONS

15. YESHUA (JESUS) IS THE ONLY BEGOTTEN SON OF GOD

16. GOD USES HIS SPIRIT TO BE OMNIPRESENT, TO PROJECT AND SHARE HIS POWER WITH SPIRIT-FILLED BELIEVERS

17. WE ARE COMMANDED TO HAVE NO OTHER GODS

1. THE HOLY SPIRIT IS THE SPIRIT 'OF' GOD, NOT THE SPIRIT GOD

The Holy Spirit is never referred to as the Spirit God or God the Holy Spirit throughout Scripture. In the Hebrew language and texts, the phrase Ruach HaKodesh is properly translated to Holy Spirit and refers to the Spirit of YHWH. The Holy Spirit is referred to throughout Scripture as the Holy Spirit of God, the Spirit of YHWH, the Spirit of God, the Spirit of the Lord, My Spirit, His Spirit, Ruah of ha'Mashiah, Ruah of Elohim, etc., but NEVER referred to as the Spirit God.

The word 'of' is a preposition, expressing the relationship between a part and a whole. When we say the Spirit 'of' God, this indicates that the Spirit is a part of God that belongs to the whole of God. This would be in the same manner as if we were to say, "the right hand of God." God's Spirit and His right hand are 'of' God, but are NOT a God. Neither God's Spirit, nor His right hand, are a person apart from God.

We are commanded by Scripture to not add to it, nor take away from it (Deuteronomy 4:2, 12:32; Proverbs 30:6; Revelation 22:18-19). The Trinity doctrine takes away 'of' in reference to the Spirit 'of' God to create the Spirit God, a person.

2. GOD (ELOHIM / YHWH / YESHUA / THE LORD) HAS A SPIRIT

GENESIS 6:3 (NKJV):

And YHWH (the Lord) said, "MY SPIRIT shall not strive with man forever..."

1 JOHN 4:13 (NKJV):

By this we know that we abide in Him, and He in us, because He has given us of HIS SPIRIT.

YHWH (the Lord) claims the Spirit as belonging to Him when He declares the Spirit to be "My Spirit" and "His Spirit" (Genesis 6:3; Numbers 11:29; Job 26:13, 34:14; Psalm 106:33; Isaiah 30:1, 34:16, 42:1, 44:3, 48:16, 59:21; Ezekiel 36:27, 37:14, 39:29; Joel 2:28-29, Haggai 2:5; Zechariah 4:6, 6:8, 7:12; Matthew 12:18; Acts 2:17-18; Romans 8:11; 1 Corinthians 2:10, Ephesians 3:16; 1 John 4:13). If the Spirit was an individual, it would not be a part of YHWH (the Lord), and He wouldn't say it was "My Spirit" and Scripture wouldn't declare "His Spirit."

3. THE HOLY SPIRIT IS NOT A PERSON, THE HOLY SPIRIT IS AN 'IT'

ROMANS 8:16 (KJV):

The Spirit ITSELF bears witness with our spirit that we are the children of God.

The Spirit itself (NOT Himself) bears witness, declares Scripture. Subsequent revisions of the King James Bible have retranslated Romans 8:16 from "The Spirit itself" to "The Spirit Himself," based on the doctrinal belief that the Spirit is a person, ignorant of the truth that the Holy Spirit is an attribute of God that pertains to God.

JOHN 14:26 (NKJV):

"But the Helper, the Holy Spirit, whom the Father will send in My name, He will teach you all things, and bring to your remembrance all things that I said to you."

The Holy Spirit is often referred to as a 'He' in Scripture. While it is possible to describe a masculine attribute allegorically as a 'He,' it is NOT possible to allegorically describe a person as an 'it.' One could say the following: "America celebrated her 200th birthday in 1976." "She is a fine sailing ship." Describing a country or a ship using the pronouns 'her' or 'she,' does not mean that a country or a ship are persons. It would NEVER be proper to allegorically use the word 'it' to describe a person or God.

EXAMPLE:

DEUTERONOMY 4:39 (NKJV):

Therefore know this day, and consider it in your heart, that YHWH (the Lord) HIMSELF is God in heaven above and on the earth beneath; there is no other.

DEUTERONOMY 4:39 (NKJV):

Therefore know this day, and consider it in your heart, that YHWH (the Lord) ITSELF is God in heaven above and on the earth beneath; there is no other.

Inserting 'itself' in place of 'Himself,' when speaking of a person or God doesn't work. It is appropriate grammatically to say, "The Spirit itself…" Furthermore, the Holy Spirit does not have a proper name, making it a thing, but not a person. It is not grammatically correct to preface the name of a person with the word 'the.' One does not refer to the Son of God as "the Yeshua (Jesus)." The Holy Spirit is a thing, and we preface things with the word 'the,' and that's why we call God's Spirit 'the' Holy Spirit.

4. GOD CONSISTS OF FATHER AND SON. THE HOLY SPIRIT IS NOT CALLED GOD AS A PERSON THROUGHOUT SCRIPTURE. GOD IS BIUNIAL, NOT TRIUNE

JOHN 1:1-3 (NKJV):

In the beginning was the Word, and the Word was with God, and the Word was God. He was in the beginning with God. All things were made through Him, and without Him nothing was made that was made.

COLOSSIANS 2:2-3 (NKJV):

To the knowledge of the mystery of God, BOTH of the Father and of Messiah (Christ), in whom are hidden all the treasures of wisdom and knowledge.

God consists of both the Father and Yeshua (Jesus). Anyone who declares that the Holy Spirit is a being, that the Holy Spirit is God and not an attribute of God, adds to Scripture. From a reading of Scripture, we can know with all certainty that there are two individual beings who are referred to as being God - not three. The Father and Son make up God and the Holy Spirit is their Spirit that emanates from them, that makes them omnipresent.

The Word (Yeshua / Jesus) was with God (the Father) and was God also (John 1:1-3). Both (two beings, not three) the Father and the Messiah (Christ) are God (Colossians 2:2-3).

5. THE HOLY SPIRIT HAS NO THRONE IN HEAVEN

MARK 13:32 (NKJV):

"But of that day and hour no one knows, not even the angels in heaven, nor the Son, but only the Father."

Matthew 13:32 declares who currently resides in heaven: The Father, the Son, and the angels. There is no mention of a being known as the Holy Spirit residing there. The Holy Spirit does not sit on a throne in heaven, nor is mentioned as dwelling in heaven at all. The Son of God sits at the Father's right hand, but the Holy Spirit is not mentioned as sitting with God at His left hand or dwelling anywhere at all with God. The Holy Spirit does not exist as a dove hovering above Father and Son in heaven either, as is depicted in some artist renderings. The Holy Spirit is God's Spirit. God's Spirit is indwelling in God, Father and Son, in heaven, but does not have a throne to sit upon as the Father and Son do. The Holy Spirit is not a person, but is a part of God, the Spirit of God, God's Spirit.

6. OUR BODIES ARE TEMPLES OF THE HOLY SPIRIT

GENESIS 2:7 (NKJV):

And YHWH (the Lord) God formed man of the dust of the ground, and breathed into his nostrils the breath of life; and man became a living being.

JOHN 20:22 (NKJV):

And when He had said this, He breathed on them, and said to them, "Receive the Holy Spirit..."

YHWH (the Lord) God Yeshua (Jesus) breathes His Spirit into us to give us life, to indwell in us, and to create (Genesis 2:7; Job 33:4; Psalm 33:6; John 20:22; Acts 2:1-4; Romans 8:11; Galatians 4:6; Ephesians 3:16; 1 Peter 1:11; 1 John 4:13). The Holy Spirit is God's own Spirit, which He literally breathes, gives, and shares by indwelling in believers, so that they may receive His holiness and power.

1 CORINTHIANS 6:19 (NKJV):

Or do you not know that your body is the temple of the Holy Spirit who is in you, whom you have FROM GOD, and you are not your own?

Our own bodies are temples of the Holy Spirit, God's Spirit (1 Corinthians 3:16, 6:17,19).

If the Holy Spirit was a person, He could not indwell simultaneously and separately in believers worldwide. The Holy Spirit is God's Spirit, is from God, and connects us to God.

7. THE HOLY SPIRIT HAS NO IMAGE

GENESIS 1:26-27 (NKJV):

Then God said, "Let Us make man in Our image, according to Our likeness;" ... So God created man in His own image; in the image of God He created him; male and female He created them.

GENESIS 9:6 (NKJV):

For in the image of God He made man.

We are made in God's image. A Spirit that is shapeless and dwells in believers worldwide simultaneously and separately does not have an image. The Holy Spirit, God's Spirit, can hover above the waters or manifest itself and take on an image, such as a dove, but the Holy Spirit does not have a fixed image of its own (Genesis 1:2, Matthew 3:16, Mark 1:10, Luke 3:22, John 1:32).

8. GOD'S SPIRIT IS NOT A PERSON APART FROM GOD

Man is a living spirit (Genesis 2:7) and God is a Spirit Being (John 4:24). We are made in the image and likeness of God. God's Spirit is not a person apart from Himself just as our human spirits are not persons apart from us.

9. 'TRINITY' AND THE PHRASES 'HOLY TRINITY' AND 'GOD THE HOLY SPIRIT' DO NOT APPEAR IN SCRIPTURE

The word 'Trinity' or phrase 'Holy Trinity' do not appear anywhere in the Scriptures from Genesis through Revelation. "In the name of the Father and of the Son and of the Holy Spirit," appears in Scripture (Matthew 28:19), but the phrase, "God the Father, God the Son, and GOD THE HOLY SPIRIT," does NOT appear in Scripture. We are commanded not to add to Scripture (Proverbs 30:6) and anyone who proclaims or teaches 'Trinity,' 'Holy Trinity,' or 'God the Holy Spirit,' is ADDING to Scripture.

10. THE FAMILY STRUCTURE OF GOD; GOD IS NOT A CO-EQUAL TRINITY

JOHN 14:28 (NKJV):

"My Father IS GREATER than I."

JOHN 15:26 (NKJV):

"But when the Helper comes, whom I SHALL SEND TO YOU from the Father, the Spirit of truth who *proceeds from* the Father, He will testify of Me."

The Trinity doctrine FALSELY proclaims that the Father, Son, and Holy Spirit are 3-CO-EQUAL beings who together make up a Triune God. The Godhead is structured like a kingdom, a top-down kingdom. Almighty God the Father is ruler over all. Yeshua Messiah (Jesus Christ) is God and has been granted all authority from God the Father (Matthew 28:18). Only in matters of ultimate authority and in regards to the throne of the kingdom of heaven is God the Father greater than God the Son. Yeshua the Messiah (Jesus the Christ), seated on His heavenly throne, is positioned at the Father's right hand and NOT as an equal at His side. Yeshua (Jesus) acknowledges the Father's supremacy over Him and declares throughout Scripture that He was sent from the Father in heaven and came to do His Father's will on Earth. Yeshua (Jesus) has sent us His Spirit from the Father (John 15:26). The Father has sent the Son and the Son has sent the Spirit. He who sends IS GREATER THAN He who is sent (John 13:16). Therefore the Trinity Doctrine, the belief that God is a CO-EQUAL threesome, is proven false through Scripture's declaration of the different positions of authority that the Father, Son, and Spirit have.

According to the belief in the Trinity, the Father does not mean a real Father, the Son does not mean a real Son, and the Spirit does not mean a real Spirit. The relationship of God the Father, Son, and Holy Spirit, according to the Trinity, is not literal, but metaphorical. If the persons of the Godhead are completely the same co-equals, then there cannot literally be a Father, Son, and Spirit existence, negating literal Scripture which says that Yeshua (Jesus) was the only begotten Son of the Father, and the Spirit is the Spirit 'of' God.[3]

11. BLASPHEMY AGAINST THE HOLY SPIRIT IS WORSE THAN BLASPHEMY AGAINST MESSIAH OR THE TEACHINGS OF GOD

Blasphemy against the Holy Spirit WILL NOT be forgiven, but blasphemy against Messiah WILL BE forgiven (Matthew 12:31-32). This is a PROBLEM if one maintains that God is a co-equal Trinity. Something is NOT EQUAL when sins against one person of the Trinity (the Messiah) WILL BE forgiven, but sins against another person of the Trinity (the Holy Spirit) WILL NOT be forgiven. The reason blasphemy against the Son of God will be forgiven, but NOT against the Spirit of God, has to do with witnessing a miracle from God using His Spirit. The Pharisees had witnessed such a miracle when they saw Yeshua (Jesus) cast demons out from a blind-mute man and heal him. Yeshua (Jesus) then warned the Pharisees that blaspheming the Holy Spirit POWER, which He used to heal the man, calling this power of Beelzebub (Satan), would not be forgiven (Matthew 12:22-32). Blasphemy against the Holy Spirit as something not being forgivable illustrates that the Holy Spirit is God's Spirit and power.

12. THE HOLY SPIRIT DOES NOT HAVE ITS OWN AUTHORITY TO SPEAK; IT ONLY SPEAKS WHAT IT HEARS FROM GOD

JOHN 16:13 (NKJV):

"However, when He, the Spirit of truth, has come, He will guide you into all truth; FOR HE WILL NOT SPEAK ON HIS OWN AUTHORITY, BUT WHATEVER HE HEARS HE WILL SPEAK; and He will tell you things to come."

The Holy Spirit has no authority to speak on its own. Contrast that with Yeshua Messiah (Jesus Christ) who has been given all authority on heaven and on Earth (Matthew 28:18). If the Holy Spirit is a person, is a God of a Trinity, why then does He have no authority to speak, but only speaks what He hears and is told to speak? God's Spirit, the Holy Spirit, speaks through God, just as a telephone receiver 'speaks' to a person on the other end of a telephone call. The receiver's speaker only 'speaks' what it 'hears,' by what it is told to speak by the person talking into the phone. The Holy Spirit, as an extension of God, is far more complex and greater than a telephone receiver; the telephone analogy is merely used to illustrate.

13. THE HOLY SPIRIT BEARS WITNESS, AS DO OTHER NON-PERSONS

ROMANS 8:16 (NKJV):

The Spirit itself bears witness with our spirit that we are children of God...

God's Spirit, which is of God (not a separate person) bears witness with our spirit, which is of our self (not a separate person). We are made in the image and likeness of God. If our spirit is not a separate person from our self, then neither is God's Spirit a separate person from Himself.

1 JOHN 5:6 (NKJV):

And it is the Spirit who bears witness, because the Spirit is truth.

How can the Holy Spirit not be a person if it bears witness? As an extension of God, His Spirit is omnipresent, seeing and recording all things.

GENESIS 4:10 (NKJV):

And He said, "What have you done? The voice of your brother's blood cries out to Me from the ground."

God's Spirit bore witness to YHWH (the Lord) and informed Him that Cain slew Abel. In a similar manner, a video recording can bear witness to an incident or a crime. The ability to bear witness does not indicate personhood.

14. THE HOLY SPIRIT GRIEVES, COMFORTS, HELPS, AND TEACHES, AS DO OTHER NON-PERSONS

EPHESIANS 4:30 (NKJV):

And do not grieve the Holy Spirit of God, by whom you were sealed for the day of redemption.

The Holy Spirit, as an extension of God, can grieve. When a Holy Spirit-filled believer does not do the will of God, the Holy Spirit within is 'grieved.' We are commanded therefore to do the will of God and to not grieve the Holy Spirit within us.

JOHN 14:26 (NKJV):

"But the Comforter (Helper), the Holy Spirit, whom the Father will send in My name, He will teach you all things, and bring to your remembrance all things that I said to you."

Something that comforts or helps us is not confirmation of personhood. A pet dog can be a 'he' and he can comfort his owner, but is not a person. Modern appliances comfort and help us, yet no one would say that they are persons. A teacher is a person who teaches us, but again a teacher does not necessarily have to be a person. A book, computer program, or a learning course can teach us and they are not persons. There is, of course, intelligence behind any teaching aide as there is intelligence behind the Holy Spirit and that intelligence is God. God comforts, helps, and teaches us *through* His Spirit.

15. YESHUA (JESUS) IS THE ONLY BEGOTTEN SON OF GOD

The Holy Spirit is NOT a begotten Child or Son of God, NOT a distinct person / being, but God's Spirit. If the Holy Spirit, the Spirit of God, were a person, then the Holy Spirit would have had to been begotten of God. If one believes that the Holy Spirit is a person, then he or she cannot believe that Yeshua (Jesus) is the ONLY begotten Son of God (John 1:18, 3:16-18; Hebrews 1:5; 1 John 4:9), but MUST believe that the Holy Spirit is ALSO a begotten Son of God. That is unscriptural. If one believes that the Holy Spirit was not a person BEGOTTEN from God, yet still a person, the only other way that this could be is if the Holy Spirit was always in existence apart from God the Father and united with the Father. That belief would also be unscriptural as Scripture proclaims the Holy Spirit is the Spirit of God, not a separate being apart from

God the Father. If one believes that the Holy Spirit is not a begotten Son, but instead a begotten Spirit of God, this is again unscriptural. Nowhere does Scripture indicate that the Holy Spirit was begotten of God, but Scripture does say that the Holy Spirit is the Spirit of God, God's Spirit.

16. GOD USES HIS SPIRIT TO BE OMNIPRESENT, TO PROJECT AND SHARE HIS POWER WITH SPIRIT-FILLED BELIEVERS

GENESIS 1:2 (NKJV):

And the Spirit of God was hovering over the face of the waters.

GENESIS 4:9-10 (NKJV):

Then YHWH (the Lord) said to Cain, "Where is Abel your brother?" He said, "I do not know. Am I my brother's keeper?" And He said, "What have you done? THE VOICE OF YOUR BROTHER'S BLOOD CRIES OUT TO ME FROM THE GROUND."

The first mention in Scripture of the Holy Spirit is in Genesis 1:2, when God uses His Spirit to move upon the face of the waters. YHWH (the Lord) was not personally present when Cain slew Abel, but His Spirit is omnipresent. Blood does not speak, but YHWH's (the Lord's) Spirit does. The Spirit is an extension of YHWH (the Lord) that spans every particle of His creation and speaks to YHWH (the Lord), allowing Him to know and record all things.

MATTHEW 18:20 (NKJV):

"For where two or three are gathered together in My name, I am there in the midst of them."

Yeshua (Jesus) does not make a personal appearance every time two or three believers are gathered together in His name, but He is present through His Spirit when two or three believers are gathered in His name.

LUKE 24:49 (NKJV):

"Behold, I send the Promise of My Father upon you; but tarry in the city of Jerusalem until you are endued WITH POWER from on high."

ACTS 1:8 (NKJV):

"But you shall RECEIVE POWER WHEN THE HOLY SPIRIT HAS COME UPON YOU; and you shall be witnesses to Me in Jerusalem, and in all Judea and Samaria, and to the end of the earth."

ACTS 10:38 (NKJV):

God anointed Yeshua (Jesus) of Nazareth WITH THE HOLY SPIRIT AND WITH POWER, who went about doing good and healing all who were oppressed by the devil, for God was with Him.

Yeshua (Jesus), upon His resurrection, commanded His disciples to remain in Jerusalem until they were filled with the power from on high, which is the power of the Holy Spirit, His Spirit. God does good works and heals through the power of His Holy Spirit.

17. WE ARE COMMANDED TO HAVE NO OTHER GODS

EXODUS 20:2-3 (NKJV):

I am YHWH (the Lord) your God; You shall have no other gods before Me.

JUDE 1:20 (KKJV):

But you, beloved, building yourselves up on your most holy faith, praying IN the Holy Spirit, keep yourselves in the love of God…

When a believer elevates God's Spirit, an attribute of God, to being God, he or she breaks the First Commandment of God. Some might consider it a stretch to imply that worshiping God's Spirit is having 'another god,' but technically this is true. We are to pray 'in' the Holy Spirit, NOT 'to' the Holy Spirit. God's Spirit is not an individual, a third part of a Trinity, but is a part of Him that He shares with His Spirit-filled believers. Referring to the Holy Spirit as God might initially seem like a harmless thing, but many believers have been led astray by this teaching. Many have worshiped the Spirit as God, in place of God and His word in the Scriptures.

GALATIANS 5:18 (NKJV):

But if you are led by the Spirit, you are not under the law.

Many have embraced Galatians 5:18 and have misunderstood it to mean that since they are led by the Spirit, they do not need to obey the law, instead of properly understanding that if they are led by the Spirit, they are not under the curse for having broken the law.

1 JOHN 4:1 (NKJV):

Beloved, do not believe every spirit, but test the spirits, whether they are of God; because many false prophets have gone out into the world.

The danger of the Trinity doctrine, of worshiping God's Spirit as God, is that some believe that they can be led exclusively by the Spirit while disregarding God's laws as not applying to them, because they are "led by the Spirit and are not under law." A person can believe that he or she is being led by the Spirit and be deceived by an evil spirit of deception or the desires of the heart. Many modern day believers have been deceived by worshiping the Holy Spirit as God, falsely worshiping 'a spirit that guides them,' negating Scripture and God's laws written in Scripture, which they nullify by claiming that they are led by the Spirit and not by the law. We must test the spirits that guide us, and the only way to test any spirit is through the word of God, in Scripture. God's Spirit would never lead anyone to break any of His laws, so any spirit that causes a person to act contrary to Scripture or His laws is not of God.

The apostles never taught the Trinity Doctrine. It was a concept that was adopted into Christianity through the 'Universal' Roman Catholic Church in the fourth century. Babylonian-inspired Roman Catholicism often borrows concepts from pagan religions and mixes them together with true Scripture, resulting in Babylonian confusion.

God's Spirit is not a person, but is an attribute part of Him that He shares with His believers. The Holy Spirit is the power of God and the Spirit of life eternal (2 Timothy 1:7).[4] We who believe and are faithful can experience the goodness, the holiness, and the power of the Holy Spirit (Ruah HaKodesh) indwelling within us.

GOD: TRIUNE OR BIUNIAL?

By George Lujack

The Trinity doctrine has been promoted as infallible and unquestionable truth throughout most of Christian history and has even made its way into many Messianic organizations. This article will show that God consists of two persons, not three, united as one. This article will also expose the corrupted Scripture verses that supposedly proclaim a triune God, which many Trinitarians have based their faith on.

biunial:

Combining two in one.[5]

triune:

Three in one.

Of or relating to the Trinity <the triune God>.

Consisting of three parts, members, or aspects.[6]

God the Father is God, the all-powerful being, and He has one begotten Son, the Lord Yeshua the Messiah (Jesus the Christ). These two beings, these two persons, are united as one God. There is no trinity of three beings or persons. The Spirit of God is 'of' God, NOT a god, nor a being, nor a person. The Spirit of God, the Holy Spirit, is God's Spirit. The belief in a triune God is not Scriptural. The words 'trinity,' and 'triune' do not appear in Scripture. The triune nature of God was not something spoken of by the Apostles.

The Roman Catholic Church imposed God as being a trinity in one of its adopted creeds, the Athanasian Creed. The Athanasian Creed contradicts itself by first declaring the Holy Spirit to be a person, then declaring the Holy Spirit is NOT a person.

EXCERPT FROM THE ATHANASIAN CREED (Contradictions in CAPS):

For like as we are compelled by Christian truth to acknowledge EVERY PERSON BY HIMSELF to be both God and Lord; so are we forbidden by the Catholic religion to say, there be three Gods or three Lords. So the Father is God, the Son God, and THE HOLY SPIRIT GOD; and yet not three Gods but one God. So the Father is Lord, the Son Lord, and THE HOLY SPIRIT LORD; and yet not three Lords but one Lord. For like as we are compelled by Christian truth to acknowledge EVERY PERSON BY HIMSELF to be both God and Lord; so are we forbidden by the Catholic religion to say, there be three Gods or three Lords.

The Father is made of none, neither created nor begotten. The Son is of the Father alone, not made nor created but begotten. THE HOLY SPIRIT IS OF THE FATHER AND THE SON, NOT MADE NOR CREATED NOR BEGOTTEN *BUT PROCEEDING*. So there is one Father not three Fathers, one Son not three Sons, and Holy Spirit not three Holy Spirits. And in this Trinity there is nothing before or after, nothing greater or less, but the whole three Persons are coeternal together and coequal.

The Athanasian Creed incorrectly calls the Holy Spirit a God, a Lord, and a person, then goes on to correctly describe the Holy Spirit as being *of the Father and Son*, something that *proceeds from both of them*. A person does not proceed from another two persons. Something that proceeds from a person is a part of the whole of the person, not a separate entity or person. The Athanasian Creed describes the different positions of the Father, Son, and Holy Spirit, then goes on to say that they are the same and are coequal.

JOHN 14:28 (NKJV):

"My Father IS GREATER than I."

-Yeshua Messiah (Jesus Christ)

Scripture declares that there are two unequal beings who are united as one biunial God. There are not three coequal beings, or persons, who are united as a triune God.

JOHN 1:1-3 (NKJV):

In the beginning was the Word, and the Word was with God, and the Word was God. He was in the beginning with God. All things were made through Him, and without Him nothing was made that was made.

Yeshua (Jesus) was the Word, and the Word was with God (the Father), and the Word was God. So God was with God, a union of two, not three.

COLOSSIANS 2:2-3 (NKJV):

To the knowledge of the mystery of God, BOTH OF THE FATHER AND OF MESSIAH (CHRIST), in whom are hidden all the treasures of wisdom and knowledge.

God is 'both,' a biunial Father and Son, not a 'tri,' a triune Father, Son, *and* Holy Spirit.

both:

Used to refer to two people or things, regarded and identified together.[7]

JOHN 10:30 (NKJV):

"I and My Father are one."

My 'Father' and 'I' indicate two persons, not three persons, united as one God.

JOHN 5:19 (NKJV):

Then Yeshua (Jesus) answered and said to them, "Most assuredly, I say to you, THE SON CAN DO NOTHING OF HIMSELF, but what He sees the Father do; for whatever He does, the Son also does in like manner."

JOHN 5:30 (NKJV):

"I can of Myself do nothing."

Although Yeshua (Jesus) is rightly called God, and is directly begotten of God, and is a person, and is a being, He is not God apart from God the Father, nor can He be. All godly power and authority comes from the Father. All authority on heaven and Earth has been given to the Son (Matthew 28:18), but the Father remains greater in authority than the Son is (John 14:28). If the Father and Son were always coequals, then how could the Father grant the Son authority?

THE CORRUPT ADDED SHORT CLAUSE OF TRINITARIANS: 1 JOHN 5:7-8

The solitary verses in Scripture in some bibles that can be genuinely used to support the belief in God being a 3-in-1 trinity are 1 John 5:7-8. Trinitarians corruptly [INSERTED] a deceptive trinity clause into the text of Scripture. Widely known amongst Scripture scholars as the 'Comma Johanneum,' some person or persons in centuries past were so zealous to proclaim support for their belief in the trinity that they literally added a trinity-supporting passage to the holy Scriptures. The scholarly consensus is that this short clause is a Latin corruption that was inserted onto some Greek manuscripts, but is absent from thousands of other manuscripts, and is the handiwork of representative(s) of the Roman Catholic Church.[8]

The majority of Greek B'rit Hadashah (New Testament) manuscripts read differently from the KJV and NKJV English translations. The words added onto 1 John 5:7-8, which shouldn't be in the KJV and NKJV text, were inserted as follows [IN CAPS]:

1 JOHN 5:7-8 (NKJV) [WITH COMMA JOHANNEUM CLAUSE]:

For there are three that bear witness: [IN HEAVEN: THE FATHER, THE WORD, AND THE HOLY SPIRIT; AND THESE THREE ARE ONE. AND THERE ARE THREE THAT BEAR WITNESS ON EARTH] the Spirit, the water, and the blood; and these three agree as one.

Correctly translated Greek to English texts:

1 JOHN 5:7-8 (HSV):

Because there are three who bear witness: The Ruah, and the water, and the blood. And the three are in agreement.

1 JOHN 5:7-8 (TLV):

For there are three that testify - the Spirit, the water, and the blood - and these three are one.

This is how 1 John 5:7-8 should read, without the Comma Johanneum added clause, in the KJV and NKJV English texts:

1 JOHN 5:7-8 (NKJV) [WITHOUT COMMA JOHANNEUM CLAUSE]:

For there are three that bear witness: the Spirit, the water, and the blood; and these three agree as one.

WHY DOES SATAN WANT PEOPLE TO WORSHIP GOD'S SPIRIT AS GOD?

Trinity is a signature mark of Satan. The trinity equilateral triangle consists of three coequal 60-degree angles, which is a 666 mark of Satan. The trinity symbol, the interlaced triquetra, also contains three looping sixes making a 666.

Satan is a deceiver. Believers, please do not believe in the triune God based on a couple of corrupted verses in some of the English translated Scriptures. Satan wishes for people to believe in and pray to God's Spirit as God, for he can then appear as a spirit of truth and deceive believers into doing evil (2 Corinthians 11:14; Ephesians 6:12).

Always test any spirit guiding you, through Scripture, which is the only way to test the spirits (1 John 4:1). The Holy Spirit would never guide any believer to break any law, small or great, of Scripture. The Holy Spirit is God's Spirit, is holy, and since God cannot sin, neither can His Spirit advise any believer to sin against His word. If any spirit compels anyone to break any of God's laws, then it is NOT the Holy Spirit. Hold fast to the biunial true God, Father and Son, and be led by Their true Holy Spirit.

TEST THE SPIRITS; ARE YOU BEING LED BY THE HOLY SPIRIT, EVIL SPIRITS, OR BY YOUR OWN HEART?

By George Lujack

There are many Christian believers who profess to being led by the Spirit. On a daily basis they speak in such a manner as to say, "God told me to do this today" or "The Spirit told me to do this for you." This article will address whether this is the kind of faith 'walking in the Spirit' believers are supposed to have and will warn on the dangers of being misled by evil and false spirits.

1 JOHN 4:1 (NKJV):

Beloved, do not believe every spirit, but TEST THE SPIRITS, whether they are of God; because many false prophets have gone out into the world.

The 'spirits' 1 John 4:1 refers to are living spirits: ministers. Many false prophets (teachers) are in the world, so we are commanded to test them. The test for angelic spirits, demonic spirits, or living beings is the same. The proper way to test the spirits, whether they are living beings or celestial spirit beings, is through Scripture.

GALATIANS 1:6-9 (NKJV):

I marvel that you are turning away so soon from Him who called you in the grace of Messiah (Christ), to a different gospel, which is not another; but there are some who trouble you and want to pervert the gospel of Messiah (Christ). But even if we, or an angel from heaven, preach any other gospel to you than what we have preached to you, let him be accursed. As we have said before, so now I say again, if anyone preaches any other gospel to you than what you have received, let him be accursed.

Today, just as in the Apostle Paul's time, there are many who possess the Scriptures, but they are turned away to a different gospel, to a gospel and belief system that is far different than the written word contained in the Scriptures. Many are turned to a perverted gospel salvation message through the false teachings of many false prophets. Paul instructs us to not listen to the preaching from an angel of heaven or even himself* if what is preached is a message that goes against the Scriptures.

*Many ministers twist Paul's words to overturn the laws of Scripture (2 Peter 3:16).

ISAIAH 30:9-10 (NKJV):

Children who will not hear the law of YHWH (the Lord);

Who say to the seers, "Do not see," and to the prophets, "Do not prophesy to us right things; Speak to us smooth things, prophesy deceits."

MATTHEW 7:15 (NKJV):

"Beware of false prophets, who come to you in sheep's clothing, but inwardly they are ravenous wolves."

There are many false prophets who, like extremely hungry wolves, make a living catering to Christian children who will not hear the law of YHWH (the Lord) or are misleading the ignorant, lost, and naïve who are genuinely searching for the truth. Mainstream Christianity has, to a greater or lesser extent - depending on the denomination, rejected God's laws. A believer seeking God's true ways is not likely to learn about them in most mainstream Christian congregations today.

Test today's end-time ministers, through the Scriptures, to see whether they are of God, because many of them are false prophets.

BEING LED BY THE HOLY SPIRIT, THE SPIRIT OF GOD

ROMANS 8:14 (NKJV):

For as many as are led by the Spirit of God, these are sons of God.

FRIVOLOUSLY BEING LED

There are many today who proclaim that the Spirit is leading them in just about all activities during the course of their daily lives. "God told me to order this for lunch" or "The Spirit led me to ask you this question…" are not uncommon statements by people claiming to be led by the Spirit.

The problem with this type of being 'Spirit-led' is that people seem to be turning off their God-given brains, of which God gave us free will to make choices and decisions in our lives, and they claim to be completely submitting to the will of the Holy Spirit. The truth is, God doesn't really want to control every aspect of our life, as long as we live within His commandments. Many Christians, who believe that God's commandments have been abolished as a burdensome yoke, take on a much more extreme form of bondage, a mindless servitude mentality, losing all sense of identity, independence, and individuality, believing that the Holy Spirit commands and guides their every activity throughout the course and routine of their daily lives. When believers constantly talk by saying, "God told me to do this" or or "The Spirit led me to ask you this," what they may actually be doing is speaking with empty words and / or breaking the third commandment: to not take God's name in vain (Exodus 20:7; Deuteronomy 5:11; Ephesians 5:6).

This is not to say that God's Spirit does not lead persons to do things, great things, but His Spirit likely doesn't tell most people to brush their teeth in the morning. That's why God gave us brains.

BEING LED BY FALSE SPIRITS, BY ONE'S OWN HEART, AGAINST THE LAW

GALATIANS 5:18 (NKJV):

But if you are led by the Spirit, you are not under the law.

When Galatians 5:18 is taken out of context, many have understood it to mean that if the Spirit leads them, they do not need to comply with the commandment laws of God. The Spirit of God is 'of' God and God cannot lead any believer to break any of His laws. What law then, are those who are led by the Spirit not under? The various laws of the lusts of the flesh that sinners are imprisoned under (in bondage to)...

ROMANS 8:12-13 (NKJV):

Therefore, brethren, we are debtors - not to the flesh, to live according to the flesh. For if you live according to the flesh you will die; but if by the Spirit you put to death the deeds of the body, you will live.

GALATIANS 5:16-21 (NKJV) [WITH INTERPRETATION]:

I say then: WALK IN THE SPIRIT, AND YOU SHALL NOT FULFILL THE LUST OF THE FLESH. For the flesh lusts against the Spirit, and the Spirit against the flesh; and these are contrary to one another, so that you do not do the things that you wish. But if you are led by the Spirit, you are not under the law [OF THE LUST OF THE FLESH].

Now the works of the flesh are evident, which are: adultery, fornication, uncleanness, lewdness, idolatry, sorcery, hatred, contentions, jealousies, outbursts of wrath, selfish ambitions, dissensions, heresies, envy, murders, drunkenness, revelries, and the like; of which I tell you beforehand, just as I also told you in time past, that those who practice such things will not inherit the kingdom of God.

There are many who have deceived themselves into believing that they are led by the Spirit and are no longer under the commandment laws of God. Such 'believers' marry divorced women in adultery, commit fornication, pray over unclean creatures before consuming them, and engage in many other lawless acts of the flesh, some of which could bar them from inheriting the kingdom of God (1 Corinthians 6:9-10).

LED BY THE SPIRIT OR DECEIVED BY THE HEART?

PROVERBS 28:26 (NKJV):

He who trusts in his own heart is a fool.

JEREMIAH 17:9 (NKJV):

The heart is deceitful above all things, and desperately wicked; who can know it?

Oftentimes believers will proclaim that the Spirit led them to do something that is unscriptural. God's Spirit will never cause believers to break God's laws, so either an evil spirit is leading them or their wicked heart is leading them.

THE APOSTLE PETER TESTED THE HOLY SPIRIT

ACTS 10:10-14 (NKJV):

Then he became very hungry and wanted to eat; but while they made ready, he fell into a trance and saw heaven opened and an object like a great sheet bound at the four corners, descending to him and let down to the earth. In it were all kinds of four-footed animals of the earth, wild beasts, creeping things, and birds of the air. And a voice came to him, "Rise, Peter; kill and eat." BUT PETER SAID, "NOT SO, LORD! FOR I HAVE NEVER EATEN ANYTHING COMMON OR UNCLEAN."

ACTS 11:7-8 (NKJV):

And I heard a voice saying to me, 'Rise, Peter; kill and eat.' BUT I SAID, 'NOT SO, LORD! FOR NOTHING COMMON OR UNCLEAN HAS AT ANY TIME ENTERED MY MOUTH.'

Peter knew God's dietary laws, put the vision he received to the test, and was not 'led by the Spirit' to break God's dietary laws. Peter never ate anything unclean as a result of receiving this vision, did not break any dietary command, and came to understand that God cleansed the Gentile people of the world. Peter recognized that God used unclean creatures as a metaphor for the Gentiles in his vision (Acts 10:28,34-35,43).

FALSE APOSTLES, DECEITFUL WORKERS, AND EVIL SPIRITS

2 CORINTHIANS 11:13-14 (NKJV):

For such are false apostles, deceitful workers, transforming themselves into apostles of Messiah (Christ). And no wonder! For Satan himself transforms himself into an angel of light.

2 THESSALONIANS 2:13 (NKJV):

God from the beginning chose you for salvation through sanctification by the Spirit *and* belief in the truth.

The Holy Spirit is NOT the Spirit God and believers should not pray to God's Spirit as God. The Holy Spirit is the Spirit 'of' God, and believers should pray to God alone. Satan has always wanted believers to believe in the trinity, to believe that God's Spirit is God, so his demons could masquerade as angels of light, or as the Holy Spirit, and deceive God's people from believing in the truth of His laws and His word.

EZEKIEL 36:26-27 (NKJV):

I will give you a new heart and put a new spirit within you; I will take the heart of stone out of your flesh and give you a heart of flesh. I will put My Spirit within you and cause you to walk in My statutes, and you will keep My judgments and do them.

God's Spirit, when dwelling within Spirit-filled believers, causes them to walk in His statutes, obey His commandments, and not live contrary to them (1 John 2:3-6). If any believer thinks that he or she is being led by the Holy Spirit to break any of God's laws, then he or she should understand that this is NOT the Holy Spirit, but an evil spirit. Test the spirit(s)!

IS YESHUA (JESUS) GOD?

By George Lujack

Is Yeshua the Messiah (Jesus the Christ) Elohim (God)? This question has puzzled theologians and Scripture scholars for millennia. This article will offer a definitive answer to this doctrinal question through a comprehensive and logical examination of Scripture.

YESHUA (JESUS) IS THE SON OF GOD

Yeshua (Jesus) Himself confirms and Scripture repeatedly declares that Yeshua (Jesus) is the Son of God.

JOHN 9:35-37 (NKJV):
Yeshua (Jesus) … said to him, "Do you believe in the Son of God?" He answered and said, "Who is He, Lord, that I may believe in Him?" And Yeshua (Jesus) said to him, "You have both seen Him AND IT IS HE WHO IS TALKING WITH YOU."

Yeshua (Jesus), during His trial, was accused of being the divine Son of God to which He replied that indeed He was.

LUKE 22:70 (NKJV):
Then they all said, "Are You then the Son of God?"
So He said to them, "You RIGHTLY say that I am."

DOES BEING THE SON OF GOD EQUATE TO BEING GOD?

This is the crux of the matter. Yeshua (Jesus) Himself and Scripture declare that He is the Son of God. Does being the Son of God mean that Yeshua (Jesus) is God?

Scripture declares that there are two beings, the Father and Son, who are the Creators and are called God.

GENESIS 1:26 (NKJV):
Then God said, "Let Us make man in Our image, according to Our likeness…"

God (Us-plural) created mankind in God's (Our-plural) image and likeness.

ACTS 13:33 (NKJV):

God has fulfilled this for us THEIR children, in that He has raised up Yeshua (Jesus).

God has fulfilled this for us (Their-plural) children, not (His-singular) children.

PSALMS 40:17 (NKJV):

Yet YHWH (the Lord) thinks upon me. You are my help and my deliverer. Do not delay, O my God.

Yeshua (Jesus) is the prophesied Deliverer AND God.

PROVERBS 8:22-31 (NKJV):

YHWH (the Lord) possessed Me at the beginning of His way, before His works of old. I have been established from everlasting, from the beginning, before there ever was an earth. When there were no depths I was brought forth, when there were no fountains abounding with water. Before the mountains were settled, before the hills, I was brought forth; while as yet He had not made the earth or the fields, or the primal dust of the world. When He prepared the heavens, I was there, when He drew a circle on the face of the deep, when He established the clouds above, when He strengthened the fountains of the deep, when He assigned to the sea its limit, so that the waters would not transgress His command, when He marked out the foundations of the earth, then I was beside Him as a Master Craftsman; and I was daily His delight, rejoicing always before Him, rejoicing in His inhabited world, and My delight was with the sons of men.

JOHN 1:1-3 (NKJV):

In the beginning was the Word, and the Word was with God, and the Word was God. He was in the beginning with God. All things were made through Him, and without Him nothing was made that was made.

JOHN 1:10 (NKJV):

He was in the world, and the world was made through Him, and the world did not know Him.

EPHESIANS 3:9 (NKJV):

God who created all things through Messiah Yeshua (Jesus Christ).

COLOSSIANS 1:15-18 (NKJV):

He is the image of the invisible God, the firstborn over all creation. For by Him all things were created that are in heaven and that are on earth, visible and invisible, whether thrones or dominions or principalities or powers. All things were created through Him and for Him. And He is before all things, and in Him all things consist. And He is the head of the body, the church, who is the beginning, the firstborn from the dead, that in all things He may have the preeminence.

The Word (Yeshua / Jesus) was with God (the Father) AND was God. All things were made through Yeshua (Jesus) and by Him. Yeshua (Jesus) was and is the Master Craftsman.

JOHN 20:28 (NKJV):

And Thomas answered and said to Him, "My Lord and my God!"

After His resurrection, Yeshua (Jesus) was directly called "My God" by the Apostle Thomas (John 20:28) and was not corrected or rebuked by Yeshua (Jesus) (John 20:28).

EVE WAS BEGOTTEN OF ADAM

GENESIS 2:21-23 (NKJV):

And YHWH (the Lord) God caused a deep sleep to fall on Adam, and he slept; and He took one of his ribs, and closed up the flesh in its place. Then the rib, which YHWH (the Lord) God had taken from man, He made into a woman, and He brought her to the man.

And Adam said:

"This is now bone of my bones and flesh of my flesh; She shall be called Woman, because she was taken out of Man."

1 CORINTHIANS 11:7-12 (NKJV):

For a man indeed ought not to cover his head, since he is the image and glory of God; but woman is the glory of man. For man is not from woman, but woman from man. Nor was man created for the woman, but woman for the man. For this reason the woman ought to have a symbol of authority on her head, because of the angels. Nevertheless, neither is man independent of woman, nor woman independent of man, in the Lord. For as woman came from man, even so man also comes through woman; but all things are from God.

Woman was begotten and created from man to be the glory of man and to be one with man. Man and woman together comprise MANKIND.

YESHUA (JESUS) WAS BEGOTTEN OF GOD THE FATHER

JOHN 3:16 (NKJV):

"For God so loved the world that He gave His ONLY BEGOTTEN SON, that whoever believes in Him should not perish but have everlasting life."

JOHN 16:28 (NKJV):

"I came forth *from* the Father and have come into the world."

HEBREWS 1:5,8-9 (NKJV) (HSV†):

For to which of the angels (†messengers) did He ever say:

"You are My Son, today I have begotten You?"...

But to the Son He says:

"Your throne, O God, is forever and ever...

Therefore God, Your God, has anointed You."

God the Father begat His Son Yeshua (Jesus) out of Himself and calls His Son 'God.' Scripture clearly states that Yeshua (Jesus) was NOT a created being, nor an angel, nor a man who was born into existence. Yeshua (Jesus) is a unique being, distinguished from all the created beings: the angels, messengers, and man in that He is the ONLY BEGOTTEN SON of God the Father (Psalm 2:7; John 1:14,18, 3:16,18; 1 John 4:9, 5:1). Life reproduces after its own kind (Genesis 1:11-12,21,24-25). Man begets mankind. God the Father begat only one Son, Yeshua the Messiah (Jesus the Christ). Can any being beget a being not of his or her own kind? If Yeshua (Jesus) is truly begotten (taken from) and reproduced directly from God the Father, then He is the direct offspring and substance of God and is God. The Son of God was begotten from God the Father, to give glory to the Father, and to be one with the Father. The Father and Son are comprised of the same substance. The Father and Son together comprise the GOD-KIND.

YESHUA (JESUS) WAS NOT BORN INTO EXISTENCE AS OTHER MEN ARE

JOHN 8:58 (NKJV):

Yeshua (Jesus) said to them, "Most assuredly, I say to you, BEFORE Abraham was, I AM."

JOHN 17:5 (NKJV):

"And now, O Father, glorify Me together with Yourself, with the glory that I had with You BEFORE the world was."

Yeshua (Jesus) did not come into existence at birth as other men do. Yeshua (Jesus) was in paradise with the Father, was SENT to Earth, FROM heaven - by the Father, to be born, take on human flesh, live a righteous life, and be the perfect atonement sacrifice for the sins of mankind (John 5:30,36-37, 6:39,44,57, 8:16,18,29,42, 12:49, 17:21,25, 20:21).

ONE GOD UNITED, ONE UNITED GOD

A dilemma for some believers who do not accept Yeshua (Jesus) as being God, or divine, is that they believe that there is one God and therefore ONLY one being who can be called God. If God the Father and Yeshua (Jesus) are both God, then there are two Gods, they reason. There are other people who believe that Yeshua (Jesus) and the Father are the same person. A literal reading of the following verses is how some people reason that there is only one being who is God:

MARK 12:32; ROMANS 3:30; 1 CORINTHIANS 8:6; 1 TIMOTHY 2:5; JAMES 2:19 (NKJV):

... there is one God ...

1 CORINTHIANS 8:4 (NKJV):

... there is no other God but one.

How should believers view the seeming contradiction that there are two beings called God, the Father and Yeshua (Jesus) the Son, yet Scripture declares that there is one God?

There is more than one definition for the word 'one.'

1. A single individual, being, object, thing, or item rather than two or more.

2. Existing, acting, or considered as a single unit, entity, or individual. Of the same or having a single kind, nature, or condition. United as one. (We belong to one team. We are of one resolve).

In light of all Scripture, believers should accept definition number two as applicable when Scripture refers to God as 'one God' and that 'God is one.'

JOHN 14:9-11 (NKJV):

Yeshua (Jesus) said to him, "Have I been with you so long, and yet you have not known Me, Philip? He who has seen Me has seen the Father; so how can you say, 'Show us the Father'? Do you not believe that I am in the Father, and the Father in Me? The words that I speak to you I do not speak on My own authority; but the Father who dwells in Me does the works. Believe Me that I am in the Father and the Father in Me."

Scripture is speaking poetically and allegorically when it declares that there is one God. God, Father and Son, are united as one. Yeshua (Jesus) allegorically declares that He and the Father are one, yet they are two distinct individual beings.

JOHN 10:30 (NKJV):

"I and My Father are one."

JOHN 17:20-23 (NKJV):

"I do not pray for these alone, but also for those who will believe in Me through their word; that they all may be one, as You, Father, are in Me, and I in You; that they also may be one in Us, that the world may believe that You sent Me. And the glory which You gave Me I have given them, that they may be one just as We are one: I in them, and You in Me; that they may be made perfect in one, and that the world may know that You have sent Me, and have loved them as You have loved Me."

'I,' and 'My Father,' indicate two separate individuals being united as one in 'Us' and 'We.' The United States is one country, yet there are fifty individual states within this one country. A man and woman are two distinct separate individuals, yet when married, as husband and wife, they are to be considered one flesh (Matthew 19:6; Mark 10:8). God is one family and one kingdom comprised of two individuals.

IS YESHUA (JESUS) GOOD?

MATTHEW 19:17; MARK 10:18; LUKE 18:19 (NKJV):

So He [Yeshua (Jesus)] said to him, "Why do you call Me good? No one is good but One, that is, God…"

Some may be confused by Yeshua's (Jesus') question, asking, "Why do you call Me good?" and statement saying, "No one is good but One, that is, God." It may initially sound as if Yeshua (Jesus) were being extremely humble by saying that He is not good, only God is good, and He is not God.

A young man asked Yeshua (Jesus), "Good Teacher, what good thing shall I do to inherit eternal life (Matthew 19:16; Mark 10:17; Luke 18:18)?" Yeshua (Jesus) responded with a rhetorical question, "Why do you call Me good?" to the young man with great possessions.

The purpose of this question posed to the young man was to test his faith, to see if He knew who Yeshua (Jesus) was, to see if he knew Yeshua (Jesus) was God.

Yeshua (Jesus) then said, "No one is good but One, that is, God..."
Yeshua (Jesus) did not say that He was not good or that He was not God.
Yeshua (Jesus) and the Father are One, are united as One God (John 10:30).

YESHUA (JESUS) DECLARED THAT HE IS THE GOOD SHEPHERD

JOHN 10:11-13 (NKJV):

"**I AM THE GOOD SHEPHERD. THE GOOD SHEPHERD gives His life for the sheep. But a hireling, he who is not the shepherd, one who does not own the sheep, sees the wolf coming and leaves the sheep and flees; and the wolf catches the sheep and scatters them. The hireling flees because he is a hireling and does not care about the sheep.**

JOHN 10:14-18 (NKJV):

I AM THE GOOD SHEPHERD; and I know My sheep, and am known by My own. As the Father knows Me, even so I know the Father; and I lay down My life for the sheep. And other sheep I have which are not of this fold; them also I must bring, and they will hear My voice; and there will be one flock and one shepherd.

"**Therefore My Father loves Me, because I lay down My life that I may take it again. No one takes it from Me, but I lay it down of Myself. I have power to lay it down, and I have power to take it again. This command I have received from My Father.**"

Yeshua (Jesus) knew no sin and gave His life to pay for our sins (2 Corinthians 5:21). Yeshua (Jesus) lived a perfect sinless life. He is good.

The totality of Scripture declares that Yeshua (Jesus) was Creator and God, who was with God (the Father) (John 1:1-3), existing in glory with Him before the world was (John 17:5). The Father is greater than the Son in regards to authority, glory, and the throne of heaven (Matthew 28:18; John 10:29, 14:28). It is not for believers to reason away, reinterpret, or retranslate Scripture to make Scripture fit in with their worldview of God existing as one being in the Father, therefore excluding the Son as God, -or- of God as an all-in-one-being in which the Father and Son are one, not two, distinct beings, or a trinity of three co-equal beings.

God is one united Father and Son, one united family, and one united kingdom. God is comprised of two individuals, the Father and Son. The Father is God and Yeshua (Jesus) the Son is God. The Father and Son are indivisible, united as one in family, kingdom, and purpose.

COLOSSIANS 2:2-3 (NJKV):

The knowledge of the mystery of God, BOTH of the Father and of Messiah (Christ), in whom are hidden all the treasures of wisdom and knowledge.

BOTH God the Father and the Son of God Yeshua (Jesus), are God.

YESHUA MESSIAH (JESUS CHRIST) IS KING OF KINGS AND LORD OF LORDS

By George Lujack

These will make war with the Lamb, and the Lamb will overcome them, for He is Lord of lords and King of kings.
-Revelation 17:14 (NKJV)

Many who live in this generation have fallen away from the truth and are actively waging a spiritual war with the Lamb of God, Yeshua Messiah (Jesus Christ). This war is being fought on a cultural, educational, intellectual, judicial, media, political, social, and spiritual level.

We are living in the end times, when evil is called good and good is called evil (Isaiah 5:20). Atheistic Darwinian evolution is called science and the Genesis account of creation is called a fairy tale. Infanticide murder is called abortion of an unborn fetus (pro-choice), and live babies in the womb do not have rights and can be chopped up and sold for body parts. The traditional husband and wife family unit has long been under assault from feminist propaganda and homosexuals seeking 'marriage' with one another.

How quickly the Judeo-Christian countries (America and the Westernized nations) have spiritually fallen!

Scripture records an oft-repeated cycle of Israel believing upon God, then falling into national sin and forgetting their God. This cycle is not limited to national Israel, but all nations that have believed in the God of Scripture.

PSALM 33:12 (NKJV):
Blessed is the nation whose God is YHWH (the Lord).

2 CHRONICLES 7:14 (NKJV) [WITH INTERPRETATION]:
If My people who are called by My name ['Christ'–ians] will humble themselves, and pray and seek My face, and turn from their wicked ways, then I will hear from heaven, and will forgive their sin and heal their land.

Believers should always fight for the cause of righteousness, but need to be prepared and understand that the land where they are living will not necessarily repent of their national evils.

It is incumbent for a believer to repent, to come out of the wicked ways of this world, and be separate (2 Corinthians 6:17).

When two angelic messengers visited Lot's house in Sodom, they were accosted by the men of the city who sought to (homosexually) rape them. God blinded the evil men of Sodom to protect Lot, his household, and his guests. God's grace upon the wickedness of Sodom expired and the appointed time of Sodom's judgment had come. God destroyed Sodom the very next day (Genesis 19).

The institutionalization and widespread acceptance of homosexuality is generally the final national sin tolerated by God before He acts in judgment against a nation. America passed the tipping point when the U.S. Supreme Court declared sodomy-based homosexual marriage a Constitutional right on June 26, 2015.

Judeo-Christian tolerant (of sin) nations often forget the lessons of Scripture. God's blessings and grace are prophesied to one day expire upon America and the other 'Christian' nations that have embraced and institutionalized sin in these end times. God will raise the Gentile nations against His own Christian spiritually wicked rebellious nations (Ezekiel 30:3). America will be destroyed for embracing the national sin of homosexuality in the same manner as Sodom and Gomorrah were (Jeremiah 49:18,50:40).

1 JOHN 2:18 (NKJV):
Little children, it is the last hour; and as you have heard that the Antimessiah (Antichrist) is coming, even now many antimessiahs (antichrists) have come, by which we know that it is the last hour.

There are many antimessiahs (antichrists) of this world who speak against the teachings of Messiah (Christ) and Scripture. These would include abortion 'healthcare' providers, atheists, business leaders, college professors, co-workers, employers, false prophets, family, friends, judges, legislators, pagan religions, politicians, reporters, scientists, secularists, teachers, and others.

MATTHEW 12:30 / LUKE 11:23 (NKJV):
"He who is not with me is against Me..."
-Yeshua Messiah (Jesus Christ)

JOHN 14:6 (NKJV):
"I am the way, the truth, and the life. No one comes to the Father except through Me."
-Yeshua Messiah (Jesus Christ)

Those who claim to be pro-choice Christians, gay Christians, or Christians who support abortion rights and / or gay marriage are not Christians at all. They are not with Messiah (Christ), but against Him and are thus antimessiahs (antichrists). This is true of all people, politicians, judges, presidents, kings, and rulers.

1 JOHN 2:4 (NKJV):
He who says, "I know Him," and does not keep His commandments, is a liar, and the truth is not in him.

THE FEAR OF YHWH (THE LORD) IS:

Clean, enduring forever (Psalm 19:9);

The beginning of wisdom (Psalm 111:10; Proverbs 9:10);

The beginning of knowledge (Proverbs 1:7);

To hate evil (Proverbs 8:13);

Strong confidence (Proverbs 14:26);

A fountain of life (Proverbs 14:27);

The instruction of wisdom (Proverbs 15:33);

And by the fear of YHWH (the Lord) one departs from evil (Proverbs 16:6).

Many people of these end-time generations do not fear YHWH (the Lord). Many seek to fulfill sinful pleasures personally and are accepting and tolerant of sin in society. Secular judges and politicians are actively legislating immorality. Few are working out their own salvation with fear and trembling (Philippians 2:12).

YHWH (the Lord) has killed sinners. He has the righteous authority to kill sinners in judgment and He has exercised that authority (Genesis 38:7,10).

YHWH (the Lord) once wiped out all flesh from the face of the Earth with a global flood, save Noah and those with him on the ark (Genesis 7:23).

MATTHEW 10:28 (NKJV):

"And do not fear those who kill the body but cannot kill the soul. But rather fear Him who is able to destroy both soul and body in hell."

-Yeshua Messiah (Jesus Christ)

A popular slogan is that God loves the sinner, but hates the sin. Yet a person is what he or she does and God does not accept or tolerate sin. God hopes that the sinner will repent, as He does not want anyone to perish, but unrepentant sinners will be cast into hell together with their sins.

2 PETER 3:9 (NKJV):

The Lord is not slack concerning His promise, as some count slackness, but is longsuffering toward us, not willing that any should perish but that all should come to repentance.

ACTS 17:30-31 (NKJV):

Truly, these times of ignorance God overlooked, but now commands all men everywhere to repent, because He has appointed a day on which He will judge the world in righteousness by the Man whom He has ordained.

One day the age of grace will expire at an appointed time.

The following unrepentant sinners will not inherit the kingdom of heaven:

1 CORINTHIANS 6:9-10 (NKJV) (HSV†):

Do you not know that the unrighteous will not inherit the reign of Elohim (kingdom of God)? Do not be deceived. Neither fornicators, nor idolaters, nor adulterers, nor effeminate, nor homosexuals, nor thieves, nor covetous (†greedy of gain), nor drunkards, nor revilers, nor swindlers will inherit the kingdom of God (†reign of Elohim).

Yeshua (Jesus) will not arbitrate, nor will He strive with man forever (Genesis 6:3; Isaiah 47:3).

There are many people who question God, His morality, and His wisdom. Many argue they were born a certain way; or if God doesn't accept me as I am then He is a bigot; or that if God exists then why doesn't He reveal Himself to me. These arguments come from faithless people who do not fear YHWH (the Lord) and are unwise fools who follow their own morality - having made themselves their own god.

God's kingdom is not a democracy; it is a kingdom ruled by a Sovereign King. The subject does not tell the King how to run His kingdom, nor does the creature have greater authority, knowledge, morality, understanding, or wisdom than the Creator.

ISAIAH 29:16 (NKJV):

Surely you have things turned around! Shall the potter be reckoned as the clay? Should what is made say of its Maker, "He did not make me?" And what is formed say of Him who formed it, "He has no understanding?"

PROVERBS 3:5-7 (NKJV):

Trust in YHWH (the Lord) with all your heart, and lean not on your own understanding; In all your ways acknowledge Him, and He shall direct your paths. Do not be wise in your own eyes. Fear YHWH (the Lord) and depart from evil.

Yeshua Messiah (Jesus Christ) is Judge of judges, King of kings, Lord of lords, Ruler of rulers and Sovereign of sovereigns. His thoughts are higher than our thoughts and His ways are higher than our ways (Isaiah 55:9). His judgments, laws, rulings, and statutes are wiser than any supreme court, unrighteous law, or ruling of man.

YESHUA (JESUS) IS NOT A GIRLIE-MAN!

By George Lujack

Throughout millennia, Yeshua (Jesus) has very often been depicted as an overly feminized, gentile, soft, weak-willed man. This article will show that Yeshua (Jesus) was not only the gentle Lamb of God, but is also a very fierce, manly, rugged, strong-willed man, a Lion of God.

YESHUA (JESUS) DRIVES OUT THE MERCHANTS AND MONEY CHANGERS FROM THE TEMPLE OF GOD IN JERUSALEM

MATTHEW 21:12-13 (NKJV):

Then Yeshua (Jesus) went into the temple of God and drove out all those who bought and sold in the temple, and overturned the tables of the money changers and the seats of those who sold doves. And He said to them, "It is written, *'My house shall be called a house of prayer,'* but you have made it a *'den of thieves.'*"

MARK 11:15-17 (NKJV):

So they came to Jerusalem. Then Yeshua (Jesus) went into the temple and began to drive out those who bought and sold in the temple, and overturned the tables of the money changers and the seats of those who sold doves. And He would not allow anyone to carry wares through the temple. Then He taught, saying to them, "Is it not written, *'My house shall be called a house of prayer for all nations'*? But you have made it a *'den of thieves.'*"

JOHN 2:13-16 (NKJV):

Now the Passover of the Jews was at hand, and Yeshua (Jesus) went up to Jerusalem. And He found in the temple those who sold oxen and sheep and doves, and the money changers doing business. When He had made a whip of cords, He drove them all out of the temple, with the sheep and the oxen, and poured out the changers' money and overturned the tables. And He said to those who sold doves, "Take these things away! Do not make My Father's house a house of merchandise!"

YESHUA (JESUS) CONFRONTED THE HIGH PRIESTS AND PHARISEES, CALLED THEM NAMES, AND OUTWITTED THEM

MATTHEW 12:34 (NKJV):

"Brood of vipers! How can you, being evil, speak good things?"

MATTHEW 23:13-17,19,23,25,27,29,33 (NKJV):

"But woe to you, scribes and Pharisees, hypocrites! ...

Woe to you, scribes and Pharisees, hypocrites! ...

Woe to you, scribes and Pharisees, hypocrites! ...

Woe to you, blind guides, ... Fools and blind! ... Fools and blind! ...

Woe to you, scribes and Pharisees, hypocrites! ...

Blind guides, who strain out a gnat and swallow a camel! ...

Woe to you, scribes and Pharisees, hypocrites! ... Blind Pharisee, ...

Woe to you, scribes and Pharisees, hypocrites! For you are like whitewashed tombs, which indeed appear beautiful outwardly, but inside are full of dead men's bones and all uncleanness. Even so you also outwardly appear righteous to men, but inside you are full of hypocrisy and lawlessness.

Woe to you, scribes and Pharisees, hypocrites! ...

Serpents, brood of vipers! How can you escape the condemnation of hell?"

MATTHEW 22:15-22 (NKJV):

Then the Pharisees went and plotted how they might entangle Him in His talk. And they sent to Him their disciples with the Herodians, saying, "Teacher, we know that You are true, and teach the way of God in truth; nor do You care about anyone, for You do not regard the person of men. Tell us, therefore, what do You think? Is it lawful to pay taxes to Caesar, or not?"

But Yeshua (Jesus) perceived their wickedness, and said,

"Why do you test Me, you hypocrites? Show Me the tax money."

So they brought Him a denarius.

And He said to them, "Whose image and inscription is this?"

They said to Him, "Caesar's."

And He said to them, "Render therefore to Caesar the things that are Caesar's, and to God the things that are God's." When they had heard these words, they marveled, and left Him and went their way.

Overturning tables, driving out merchants with a whip, calling the religious leaders of the time evil and all other sorts of offending descriptive names are the sort of things only bold, driven, strong-willed men do.

YESHUA (JESUS) VOLUNTARILY GAVE HIS LIFE FOR US

JOHN 10:17-18 (NKJV):

"Therefore My Father loves Me, because I lay down My life that I may take it again. NO ONE TAKES IT FROM ME, BUT I LAY IT DOWN OF MYSELF. I have power to lay it down, and I have power to take it again. This command I have received from My Father."

Yeshua (Jesus) was not merely a helpless victim of circumstance doing His Father's will in being sacrificed for mankind. No one took His life against His will. He could have said, 'No.' Yeshua (Jesus) laid down His life of His own free will, to be tortured and killed, which was the only way to save us. Yet He still had the option to refuse to lay down His life.

YESHUA (JESUS) WAS THE LAMB, BUT IS RETURNING AS A LION

It has been said that the Jews were desiring a Lion for their Messiah, but instead got a Lamb, and that many Christians are expecting a Lamb to return, but instead will get a Lion.

JOHN 19:30 (NKJV):

Yeshua (Jesus) said, "It is finished!" And bowing His head, He gave up His spirit.

With those words, Yeshua's (Jesus') work as the suffering Shepherd Messiah, who came to atone for the sins of mankind, was finished. There will be no more sacrifices for sin (Hebrews 7:27).

He is returning to rule the Earth as a King, with fierceness and with a rod of iron.

REVELATION 19:15-16 (NKJV) (HSV†):

Out of His mouth goes a sharp sword, that with it He should strike the nations. And He Himself will rule them with a rod of iron. He Himself treads the winepress of the fierceness and wrath of Almighty God. And He has on His robe and on His banner written:

KING OF KINGS AND LORD OF LORDS (†SOVEREIGN OF SOVEREIGNS AND MASTER OF MASTERS).

DOES YESHUA (JESUS) HAVE TWO NATURES, A DIVINE NATURE AND A HUMAN NATURE?

By George Lujack

The concept of Yeshua (Jesus) being one person with two natures is derived from the doctrine of the hypostatic union that states Yeshua (Jesus) has two natures: a divine nature and a human nature. This article will present the two natures of Yeshua (Jesus) Hypostatic Union doctrine as not being of Scripture and declare the doctrine as a made up false teaching of the Catholic Church.

Catholicism's Jesus is often depicted in idolatrous graven art and statue images holding out two fingers indicating His two supposed natures: divine and human. There is no verse in Scripture that declares that Yeshua (Jesus) ever held up two fingers indicating His divine and human natures, nor does Scripture ever proclaim that He is one person with two natures.

The error in the 'Jesus two natures Hypostatic Union' doctrine is that it confuses Yeshua's (Jesus') state or form of being with His nature. Yeshua (Jesus) is the only being who has ever crossed over and existed as both a spiritual being - the Son of God and as a human being - the Son of Man.

JOHN 1:1 (NKJV):

In the beginning was the Word, and the Word was with God, and the Word was God.

JOHN 17:5 (NKJV):

"And now, O Father, glorify Me together with Yourself, with the glory that I had with You before the world was."

Yeshua (Jesus) existed as the Word, as God with God the Father, before the world existed.

1 JOHN 4:9-10 (NKJV):

In this the love of God was manifested toward us, that God has sent His only begotten Son into the world, that we might live through Him. In this is love, not that we loved God, but that He loved us and sent His Son to be the propitiation for our sins.

Yeshua (Jesus) was sent down to Earth from heaven, by God the Father, to be born into human flesh, live a perfect sinless life, and to suffer and die to atone for the sins of mankind.

nature:

The fundamental qualities of a person or thing; identity or essential character.[9]

TWO FORMS, NOT TWO NATURES

Yeshua (Jesus) has existed *in two forms*: in His spirit form and in His human flesh form. To say that Yeshua (Jesus) has a 'human nature' stands in contradiction to His holy sinless nature. Yeshua (Jesus) has a divine nature.

SCRIPTURE PROCLAIMS THAT YESHUA (JESUS) HAS A DIVINE NATURE AND DOES NOT SAY THAT HE HAS A HUMAN NATURE

JOHN 14:9 (NKJV):

"He who has seen Me has seen the Father…"

2 PETER 1:2-4 (NKJV):

Grace and peace be multiplied to you in the knowledge of God and of Yeshua (Jesus) our Lord, as His divine power has given to us all things that pertain to life and godliness, through the knowledge of Him who called us by glory and virtue, by which have been given to us exceedingly great and precious promises, that through these you may be partakers of the DIVINE NATURE…

To say Yeshua (Jesus) has two natures, a divine nature *and* a human nature, because He has existed as the Son of God and as the Son of Man, is wrong. Fallen man has two natures: a good righteous nature and an evil wicked nature. Declaring Yeshua (Jesus) to have two natures is an attack on His divinity and holiness. Yeshua (Jesus) had and maintained one divine nature, in His human form, all throughout His life on Earth as the Messiah - the Son of Man.

FORERUNNERS...
OF YESHUA MESSIAH (JESUS CHRIST)

By George Lujack

Throughout Scripture history, there have lived righteous saints whose lives reflect the character, life, and nature of Yeshua (Jesus). This typology compilation compares *some* of the parallel events of the lives of saints who were forerunners of Yeshua (Jesus), pointing to Him as the Messiah (Christ). The life of Yeshua (Jesus) is in **bold**, in the typology comparisons, for clarity.

<u>HEBREWS 6:20 (NKJV)</u>:

Yeshua (Jesus) has entered as a forerunner for us, having become High Priest forever.

Messiah (Christ) is our forerunner who showed us how to live righteously and He has preceded us into the kingdom of heaven.

ABRAHAM

Abraham offered his only begotten son of promise to be sacrificed (Genesis 21:12, 22:16, Hebrews 11:17-19).

Yeshua (Jesus) was God's only begotten Son who God offered as a sacrifice with a promise of eternal life to all who believed upon Him (Joel 2:32; John 3:16; Acts 2:21; Romans 5:9-10, 10:13).

Abraham offered his son as a sacrifice on a mountain in Moriah, Jerusalem (Genesis 22:2-10).

Yeshua (Jesus) was offered as a sacrifice by His Father on Mt. Calvary, Jerusalem (Matthew 16:21-23, 27:35; Luke 23:33; John 3:16-17, 12:27, 19:17-18).

Abraham was prepared to sacrifice his only son by binding him, laying him upon wood, piercing him with a knife, and shedding his blood without breaking a bone of his body (Genesis 22:9-10).

Yeshua (Jesus), the only begotten Son of God, was prepared by His Father to be a sacrifice by being bound, laying Him crucified upon the wood of the cross, piercing His side with a spear, and shedding His blood without having any bone of His body broken (Matthew 27:2,35; Mark 15:24-25; Luke 23:33; 24:20; John 18:12, 19:18-37 Acts 2:23).

Abraham, although he was prepared to go and sacrifice his son, had faith that his son would return with him after God resurrected him (Genesis 22:5).

Yeshua (Jesus), although He was prepared to lay down and sacrifice His life, had faith that He would be resurrected (Matthew 27:63; Mark 8:31; Luke 9:22; John 2:19-21).

Through Abraham, God multiplied his descendants as the stars of heaven and the sand of the seashore, and blessed all the nations of the Earth (Genesis 22:17-18; Galatians 3:7-8).

Through Yeshua (Jesus), God saved many and blessed all the nations of the Earth and of His kingdom there will be no end (Matthew 20:28, 25:32, 26:28; Mark 10:45; Mark 14:24; Luke 1:33; Galatians 3:14).

ADAM

Adam, who was in the garden (Genesis 3:6), was tempted by Satan, the serpent (Genesis 3:1-5).

Yeshua (Jesus) who was in the wilderness, was tempted by Satan (Matthew 4:1-10; Mark 1:12-13; Luke 4:1-13).

Adam was among the beasts when Satan tempted him (Genesis 3:1).

Yeshua (Jesus) was among the beasts when Satan tempted Him (Mark 1:13).

Adam was tempted by Satan with food (Genesis 3:5).

Yeshua (Jesus) was tempted by Satan with food (Matthew 4:3; Luke 4:3).

Adam was visually tempted by a tree, which was pleasant to the eyes (Genesis 3:6).

Yeshua (Jesus) was visually tempted with all the kingdoms of the world, which He was shown (Matthew 4:8-9; Luke 4:5-7).

Through Adam, all have sinned and died (Romans 5:12-14; 1 Corinthians 15:21-22).

Through Yeshua (Jesus), all who have sinned can be made righteous and receive salvation (1 Corinthians 15:21-22,45).

DAVID

David was anointed to be king over the Jews of Israel (1 Samuel 2:1-12; 2 Samuel 23:1; Psalm 84:9, 89:20).

Yeshua (Jesus) was born and anointed to be King of the Jews and King of kings (Matthew 2:2, 27:11,29; Mark 15:2-18; Luke 4:18, 23:3,37; John 18:33-39, 19:3,21; Acts 10:38; 1 Timothy 6:13-16; Revelation 17:14).

David was with the Spirit of God (1 Samuel 18:28; 2 Samuel 23:2).

Yeshua (Jesus) was with the Spirit of God (Luke 4:18).

David was a man after God's own heart and did His will (1 Samuel 13:14; Acts 13:22).

Yeshua (Jesus) was a Man after God's own heart and did His Father's will (Luke 22:42; John 5:30, 6:38, 10:30, 12:49-50, 14:9).

ELIJAH

Elijah rebuked the people and the religious leaders of Israel for their idolatry (1 Kings 18:21).

Yeshua (Jesus) rebuked the scribes, Pharisees, and religious leaders of Israel for misleading the people (Matthew 23).

Elijah was given power from God to control the rain (1 Kings 17:1).

Yeshua (Jesus) was given power from God and controlled a windstorm (Mark 4:35-41; Luke 8:22-25).

Elijah spoke the word of YHWH (the Lord) and multiplied the food supply of flour and oil, so that it would not run out for a starving widow and her son (1 Kings 17:12-16).

Yeshua (Jesus) multiplied the five barley loaves and two small fishes that He and the disciples had and fed the multitude of about five thousand people with it (Matthew 14:13-21; Mark 6:37-44; Luke 9:10-17; John 6:1-14).

Elijah called on God and resurrected a child from death (1 Kings 17:17-24).

Yeshua (Jesus) resurrected children and others from death (Mark 5:35-42; Luke 7:11-15; John 11:1-44).

ELISHA

Elisha resurrected a child from the dead (2 Kings 4:32-35).

Yeshua (Jesus) resurrected a child from the dead (Mark 5:35-42).

Elisha multiplied oil into much oil (2 Kings 4:2-7) and served a group of a hundred men with a small amount of food, and they ate and there was food left over (2 Kings 4:41-44).

Yeshua (Jesus) multiplied bread and fish into much bread and fish and fed 4,000 and 5,000 people and there was food left over (Matthew 14:15-21; 16:8; Mark 6:36-44, 8:17-20; Luke 9:12-17; John 6:5-14).

Elisha cured Naaman of leprosy (2 Kings 5:1-14).

Yeshua (Jesus) cured ten lepers (Luke 17:11-19).

Elisha made an iron axe float on water (2 Kings 6:5-7).

Yeshua (Jesus) walked on water and made Peter walk on water (Matthew 14:25-29; John 6:19-20).

ISAAC

Isaac was the only begotten son of his father Abraham and mother Sarah (Genesis 22:2; Hebrews 11:17).

Yeshua (Jesus) was the only begotten Son of His Father God (Psalm 2:7; John 1:14,18, 3:16,18; 1 John 4:9, 5:1).

Isaac was the son (born of genealogy line) of Abraham (Genesis 21:3, 22:2).

Yeshua (Jesus) was the Son (born into the genealogy line) of Abraham (Matthew 1:1).

Isaac was offered as a sacrifice by his father on a mountain in Moriah, Jerusalem (Genesis 22:2-10).

Yeshua (Jesus) was offered as a sacrifice by His Father on Mt. Calvary, Jerusalem (Matthew 16:21-23, 27:35; Luke 23:33; John 3:16-17, 12:27, 19:17-18).

Isaac carried the wood for his own sacrifice, was bound, and was placed atop the wood (Genesis 22:6,9).

Yeshua (Jesus) carried the wood cross for His own sacrifice, was bound, and was placed atop the wood cross (Matthew 27:2; Luke 23:26; John 18:12, 19:17-18).

Isaac was prepared for sacrifice and three days later he was relieved from the grave as a ram caught in a thicket (thorn bush) took his place (Genesis 22:4,13).

Yeshua (Jesus) was sacrificed wearing a crown of thorns and three days later He was resurrected from the grave, which could not hold Him (Matthew 12:40, 16:21, 17:22-23, 20:19, 27:29; Mark 9:31, 10:34, 15:17; Luke 9:22, 24:7, 24:46; John 19:2,5; Acts 10:40; 1 Corinthians 15:4).

JACOB

Jacob had twelve sons, who were the patriarchs of the twelve tribes of Israel (Genesis 35:22; Acts 7:8).

Yeshua (Jesus) had twelve apostles, who will judge the twelve tribes of Israel (Luke 22:30).

Jacob had one beloved son, Joseph, who pleased him (Genesis 37:3).

Yeshua (Jesus) is the beloved Son of God, in whom His Father is well pleased (Matthew 3:17, 17:5; Mark 1:11; Luke 3:22).

Jacob received His father's blessing (Genesis 27:26-29).

Yeshua (Jesus) received His Father's blessing (Matthew 28:18).

JEPHTHAH'S DAUGHTER

Jephthah's unnamed daughter honored her father who, as a commander of Israel, made a rash vow requiring him to sacrifice his only begotten daughter or break his vow made to Almighty God.

Yeshua (Jesus) honored His Father who, as God the Father Almighty, sent His only begotten Son as a sacrifice to atone for the sins of mankind, so that whoever believes in Him should not perish but have everlasting life (John 3:16; Colossians 1:19-20).

Jephthah's daughter honored her father and agreed to lay down her life as a burnt offering, so that her father would not break his word and would be reconciled to God.

Yeshua (Jesus) honored His Father and agreed to be sent into the world to lay down His life as an offering, so that man could be reconciled to God (John 10:18, 12:27).

Jephthah's daughter wandered the mountains for two months, to mourn, then returned and voluntarily laid down her life for her father, though she was a virgin and had done no wrong (Judges 11:30-39).

Yeshua (Jesus) wandered in the wilderness for forty days, before returning and then voluntarily laid down His life for His Father, though He was without sin and had done no wrong (Matthew 4:1-11; Mark 1:12-13; Luke 4:1-13; 2 Corinthians 5:21).

JOHN (THE BAPTIST)

John was sent from God to bear witness of the Light (John 1:6-8).

Yeshua (Jesus), the Light, was sent from God to bear witness to the truth (John 18:37).

An angel appeared to John's father Zacharias to tell him not to be afraid, that his wife would bear a son, and was told to call his name John, who would be filled with the Holy Spirit, and will turn many people to the Lord their God (Luke 1:13-16).

An angel appeared to Yeshua's (Jesus') father Joseph to tell him not to be afraid to take Mary as his wife, that his wife would bear a Son, and was to call His name Yeshua (Jesus), who was conceived in Mary of the Holy Spirit, and He will save their people from their sins (Matthew 1:20-21).

Zacharias asked the angel who appeared to him how he could have a son being that his wife was well advanced in years (Luke 1:18).

Mary asked the angel who appeared to her how she could have a Son being that she was a virgin and did not know a man (Luke 1:34).

John was brought forth by a miraculous birth as the first-born son to a barren mother (Luke 1:7,57).

Yeshua (Jesus) was brought forth by a miraculous birth as the first-born Son to a virgin mother (Matthew 1:25; Luke 2:6-7).

John was circumcised on his eighth day and was then named John (Luke 1:59-63).

Yeshua (Jesus) was circumcised on His eighth day and then was named Yeshua (Jesus) (Luke 2:21).

John baptized his followers with water (Matthew 3:11; Luke 3:16; Acts 1:5, 19:4).

Yeshua (Jesus) baptized with the Holy Spirit (Matthew 3:11; Luke 3:16; John 20:22; Acts 1:5-8).

John was the most righteous man born of a woman who ever lived (Matthew 11:11; Luke 7:28).

Yeshua (Jesus) was the only Man born of a woman who ever lived without ever sinning (2 Corinthians 5:21; 1 Peter 2:22; 1 John 3:5).

JONAH

Jonah was called on by God to preach repentance to the people of Nineveh (Jonah 1:1-2, 3:1-2).

Yeshua (Jesus) was called on by God (the Father) to preach repentance to the world (Matthew 3:2, 4:17, 28:18-20; Luke 13:3-5).

Jonah was willing to sacrifice his life to save his shipmates (Jonah 1:12).

Yeshua (Jesus) was willing to sacrifice His life to save the people of the world (Matthew 20:28; Mark 10:45; John 1:29, 10:17-18; 1 Timothy 2:6).

Jonah was entombed in the belly of a great fish for three days and afterward the fish vomited him out (Jonah 2).

Yeshua (Jesus) was entombed in the heart of the Earth for three days and three nights He walked out from it (Matthew 12:40, 27:60; Mark 6:29; Luke 23:53).

After coming out from the 'grave' of the great fish (Jonah 2:2), Jonah preached to the people of Nineveh and warned them that God would destroy Nineveh in forty days if the people did not repent (Jonah 3:4).

After His resurrection Yeshua (Jesus) preached to His disciples for forty days before His Ascension (Matthew 28:16-20; Mark 16:12-20; Luke 24; John 20-21; Acts 1). Yeshua (Jesus) preached that people would perish if they did not repent (Luke 13:3-5).

JOSEPH (OF EGYPT)

Joseph was one of twelve brothers of whom his father Jacob (Israel) loved above all the others (Genesis 37:3).

Yeshua (Jesus) loved John, one of the twelve disciples, above all the others (John 19:26, 20:2, 21:7,20).

Joseph's brothers conspired together to kill him (Genesis 37:18).

Yeshua's (Jesus') countrymen, the high priests and Pharisees, conspired together to kill Him (Matthew 12:14, 27:1; Mark 3:6, 9:31, 10:33-34; Luke 18:32-33, 22:2-6; John 5:16-18, 7:1, 11:53).

Joseph was betrayed by his brothers and sold for twenty pieces of silver (Genesis 37:28).

Yeshua (Jesus) was betrayed by one of His disciples and sold for thirty pieces of silver (Matthew 26:15).

Joseph was stripped of his multicolored tunic that was dipped in the innocent blood of a goat and his tunic was torn (Genesis 37:31).

Yeshua (Jesus) was stripped of His garments, which absorbed His innocent blood and His garments were torn and divided (Matthew 27:35; Mark 15:24; Luke 23:34; John 19:23-24).

Joseph overcame temptation (Genesis 39:7-12).

Yeshua (Jesus) overcame temptation (Matthew 4:1-10).

Joseph was falsely accused (Genesis 39:17-18).

Yeshua (Jesus) was falsely accused (Matthew 26:59-61).

Joseph was punished with two other men; one was saved and the other perished (Genesis 40).

Yeshua (Jesus) was punished with two other men; one was saved and the other perished (Luke 23:32-43).

Joseph was believed to be dead (Genesis 42:13,21-22,32,36,38, 44:20,28).

Yeshua (Jesus) was believed to be dead (Luke 24:3-7; John 20:1-9,13,25).

Joseph was later discovered to be alive, but he wasn't recognized and some did not believe at first (Genesis 42:6-8, 45:3-4,26-28).

Yeshua (Jesus) was later discovered to be alive, but He wasn't recognized and some did not believe (Matthew 28:17; Mark 16:11-14; Luke 24:9-11,13-39; John 20:14-15,24-29).

Joseph was thirty years old when Egypt's Pharaoh made him governor of Egypt, ruler over all.

Yeshua (Jesus) was thirty years old when He began his ministry (Luke 3:23) and He was made governor of all creation, ruler over all, upon His resurrection (Matthew 28:18).

Only in regards to the throne of Egypt was Pharaoh greater than Joseph (Genesis 41:40-46).

Only in regards to the throne of the kingdom of heaven is God the Father greater than Yeshua (Jesus) (John 14:28).

Joseph was sent by God as a deliverer to Egypt to save the world from famine and made Joseph ruler over Egypt (Genesis 45:7-8).

Yeshua (Jesus) was sent by God as the Deliverer into the world to save the world from sin and made Yeshua (Jesus) Ruler of kings (John 3:16-17; Revelation 17:14).

LAZARUS

The chief priests plotted together to kill Lazarus (John 12:10).

The high priests and Pharisees plotted together to kill Yeshua (Jesus) (Matthew 12:14, 27:1; Mark 3:6, 9:31, 10:33-34; Luke 18:32-33, 22:2-6; John 5:16-18, 7:1, 11:53).

Lazarus was resurrected from a tomb after being dead for four days (John 11:38-44).

Yeshua (Jesus) was resurrected from a tomb after having been dead for three days (Luke 24:1-7).

MOSES

The Pharaoh of Egypt ordered all newborn Hebrew males to be slaughtered, but Moses survived by fleeing to Egypt (Exodus 1:22-2:10).

King Herod of Israel ordered all Hebrew males two years old and under to be slaughtered, but Yeshua (Jesus) survived by fleeing to Egypt (Matthew 2:13-16).

Moses delivered his people from the bondage of slavery and lifted up a bronze serpent on a pole so that people would look upon the serpent and live (Numbers 21:8-9).

Yeshua (Jesus) delivered His people from the bondage of sin and was lifted up on the cross, so that whoever believes in Him should not perish, but have eternal life (John 3:14-15).

SAMSON

An angel of God appeared to Samson's mother, who was barren, and prophesied that she would conceive and bear a son (Judges 13:3).

An angel of God appeared to Yeshua's (Jesus') mother Mary, who was a virgin, and prophesied that she would conceive and bear a Son (Luke 1:26-31).

Samson was a Nazirite who began to deliver his people from the hands of the Philistines (Judges 13:5).

Yeshua (Jesus) was a Nazarene who delivered His people from their sins (Matthew 1:21).

Sampson was arrested and bound by the Philistine authorities and was mocked by them (Judges 16:21-25).

Yeshua (Jesus) was arrested and bound by the Jewish and Roman authorities and was mocked by Jewish elders, high priests, and the Roman soldiers (Luke 23:36; John 18:12, 19:1-3).

Samson outstretched his arms against the temple pillars, and brought down the temple. Samson killed more people in his death than he had killed in his life (Judges 16:26-30).

Yeshua (Jesus) outstretched His arms on the cross where He was crucified and upon His death, the veil of the Jewish temple was torn in two (Matthew 27:51; Mark 15:38; Luke 23:45). Yeshua (Jesus) saved more people through His death and resurrection than He had saved in His life (Romans 10:9).

CLEAN ANIMALS

Sacrifices and offerings of unblemished clean animals were a forerunner of the Perfect Sacrificial Offering. Mammals and birds distinguished as being 'clean' symbolized that they were holy; being 'without blemish' signified that they were physically perfect without injury. Lambs, the blood of clean animals, were sacrificed to temporarily atone for man's sins.

Yeshua Messiah (Jesus Christ) was the Perfect Sacrificial Offering, taking away the first; a foreshadowing of sanctification through animal sacrifices, to establish the second, everlasting sanctification through the sacrificed body of Messiah (Christ) (Hebrews 10:9-10). Yeshua Messiah (Jesus Christ), whose life was holy and without sin, met the qualifications to permanently take away the sins of the world. Yeshua (Jesus) permanently paid for the remission of sin, therefore there are to be no more animal sacrifices or offerings for sin, as Messiah's sacrifice was offered once and forever to atone for man's sins (Hebrews 10:1-18). Yeshua (Jesus) was distinguished as the only man who ever lived a clean, holy life without blemish, illness, injury, or sin. Yeshua (Jesus), the Lamb of God, gave His life as the once-and-forever substitute sacrificial offering for man's sins (1 Peter 1:19). Yeshua's (Jesus') blood was shed to permanently atone for man's sins.

CONCLUSION

Throughout Scripture we are provided with examples of forerunners of Yeshua (Jesus), saints who lived righteous lives. Although the righteous saints of Scripture were not without sin, nor lived perfect lives, nonetheless they provide an example for all believers as to how we should strive to live.

1 JOHN 2:3-6 (NKJV):

Now by this we know that we know Him, if we keep His commandments. He who says, "I know Him," and does not keep His commandments, is a liar, and the truth is not in him. But whoever keeps His word, truly the love of God is perfected in him. By this we know that we are in Him. He who says he abides in Him ought himself also to walk just as He walked.

1 JOHN 3:10 (NKJV):

In this the children of God and the children of the devil are manifest: Whoever does not practice righteousness is not of God.

Forerunner saints of Yeshua Messiah (Jesus Christ) serve as examples for believers to emulate.

Believers are commanded to live righteously, to practice righteousness, as forerunners of Messiah (Christ), who came before us, lived. Believers are to live like Messiah (Christ), to be like Him, to walk as He walked.

CALLING UPON THE TRUE NAME OF YHWH (THE LORD)

By George Lujack

ZEPHANIAH 3:9 (NKJV):

For then will I restore to the people a pure language, that they may all call upon the name of YHWH (The Lord), to serve him with one accord.

Messianics and Christians often engage in debate over the true name of YHWH as being Yeshua, Yahuah, Yahweh, Yahshua, Yahusha, Yahushua, Jesus, Iesous, etc. Many Messianics and Christians needlessly get themselves hung up on the correct pronunciation of His name: YHWH. Some get so hung up and divisive over this topic that they actually proclaim this to be a salvation issue and only those who properly pronounce His name correctly will be saved.

No one knows for sure the true pronunciation of His name and can only 'best guess' by adding vowels of which His name, as recorded YHWH, does not contain.[10]

Hebraic scholars differ in their opinion as to the pronunciation and vowel insertion concerning His name. How then, if Hebrew scholars cannot agree on the pronunciation of His name, can Messianic English-speaking persons, some who claim to have studied Hebrew, say with all certainty that they know for sure how His name is pronounced?

The notion that a mispronunciation of His name can land a believer in hell is a terribly misguided belief. Do we serve a God who will cast the righteous, those who obey His commandments, to hell, because they do not know the true pronunciation of His name? There are many reasons unrighteous persons will not inherit the kingdom of God, but mispronunciation of His name is not listed as one of them.

1 CORINTHIANS 6:9-10 (NKJV) (HSV†):

Do you not know that the unrighteous will not inherit the reign of Elohim (kingdom of God)? Do not be deceived. Neither fornicators, nor idolaters, nor adulterers, nor effeminate, nor homosexuals, nor thieves, nor covetous (†greedy of gain), nor drunkards, nor revilers, nor swindlers will inherit the kingdom of God (†reign of Elohim).

GALATIANS 5:19-21 (NKJV) (HSV†):

Now the works of the flesh are evident, which are: adultery, fornication, uncleanness, lewdness, idolatry, drug sorcery, hatred, quarrels, jealousies, fits of rage, selfish ambitions, dissensions, heresies, envy, murders, drunkenness, revelries, and the like; of which I tell you beforehand, just as I also told you in time past, that those who practice such things will not inherit the kingdom of God (†reign of Elohim).

REVELATION 21:7-8 (NKJV):

He who overcomes shall inherit all things, and I will be his God and he shall be My son. The cowardly, untrustworthy, abominable, murderers, sexually immoral, drug sorcerers, idolators, and all liars shall have their part in the lake which burns with fire and brimstone, which is the second death.

Some caution against using the word 'Lord' as His name, but fail to understand that Lord is stated as a title, not a name. The word 'Lord' is pagan in origin and is derived from the false god Baal, so it is proper to point these things out, but no one is going to hell for calling YHWH 'My Lord.'

HOSEA 2:16 (NKJV):

"And it shall be, in that day," says the Lord, "That you will call Me 'My Husband,' and no longer call Me 'My Master,'"

The NKJV and other similar texts do not quite reveal the significance of Hosea 2:16, as when read from the Hebraic translation.

HOSEA 2:16 (HSV):

"And it shall be, in that day," declares YHWH, "that you call Me 'My Husband,' and no longer call Me 'My Ba'al.'"

Ba'al or Baal is a name or title meaning Lord and is of pagan origin. 'Baal' is what the word 'Lord' is derived from. No one calls YHWH 'My Ba'al,' so by using a little reasoning we can surmise that when YHWH returns, no one will call Him, 'My Lord.' Ba'al = Lord.

'Jesus' is not a Hebrew name and was surely not the name the Son of God went by. 'Jesus' is a Hellenized Greek transliteration of His name. Some believe that 'sus' is derived from the Greek god 'Zeus' and 'Je-sus' equates to the phrase, "Hail Zeus," while others dispute that claim. What cannot be disputed is that 'Jesus' is a common Latin / Spanish name that is pronounced, "Hey Zeus."

Many believers only know or have known His name as Jesus Christ, and have gone to their graves not knowing the Hebrew to Latin transliterated 'YHWH' or His proper Hebraic name. YHWH (the Lord) is not going to send millions of believers to hell for calling Him 'Jesus' or 'Lord.' YHWH (the Lord) will correct the masses that call Him 'Lord' upon His return as prophesied in Hosea 2:16.

THE UNFORGIVABLE SIN;
WHAT IS BLASPHEMY AGAINST THE HOLY SPIRIT?

By George Lujack

MATTHEW 12:31-32 (NKJV):

"Therefore I say to you, every sin and blasphemy will be forgiven men, but the blasphemy against the Spirit will not be forgiven men. Anyone who speaks a word against the Son of Man, it will be forgiven him; but whoever speaks against the Holy Spirit, it will not be forgiven him, either in this age or in the age to come."

Many read this statement from Messiah (Christ) out-of-context and declare, "How can the Holy Spirit not be God if blasphemy against the Holy Spirit will not be forgiven?"

BLASPHEMY AGAINST THE HOLY SPIRIT IS PROOF THAT GOD IS NOT A GOD OF A TRINITY, THAT THE HOLY SPIRIT IS NOT AN INDIVIDUAL BEING, BUT IS AN ATTRIBUTE PART OF GOD.

Notice how Yeshua (Jesus) said that blasphemy against the Son of Man (Himself) WILL BE forgiven... Yeshua (Jesus) is the Son of God, and God, so why will blasphemy against the Son be forgiven, but not blasphemy against the Holy Spirit? Is the Holy Spirit a greater God than Messiah (Christ)? No. Yeshua (Jesus) commands and sends the Holy Spirit. He who sends is greater than He who is sent (John 13:16).

The Holy Spirit is not God. The Holy Spirit is the Spirit 'of' God. The Holy Spirit, or the Spirit of God, is not the Spirit God. The Spirit 'of' God is the Holy Power that comes from God that also makes Him omnipresent.

Matthew 12:31-32 MUST be read in the FULL CONTEXT in which it was spoken.

MATTHEW 12:22-24 (NKJV):

Then one was brought to Him who was demon-possessed, blind and mute; and He healed him, so that the blind and mute man both spoke and saw. And all the multitudes were amazed and said, "Could this be the Son of David?" Now when the Pharisees heard it they said, "This fellow does not cast out demons except by Beelzebub, the ruler of the demons."

MATTHEW 12:25-32 (NKJV):

But Yeshua (Jesus) knew their thoughts, and said to them: "Every kingdom divided against itself is brought to desolation, and every city or house divided against itself will not stand. If Satan casts out Satan, he is divided against himself. How then will his kingdom stand? And if I cast out demons by Beelzebub, by whom do your sons cast them out? Therefore they shall be your judges. But if I cast out demons BY THE SPIRIT OF GOD, surely the kingdom of God has come upon you. Or how can one enter a strong man's house and plunder his goods, unless he first binds the strong man? And then he will plunder his house. He who is not with Me is against Me, and he who does not gather with Me scatters abroad. "Therefore I say to you, every sin and blasphemy will be forgiven men, but the blasphemy against the Spirit will not be forgiven men. Anyone who speaks a word against the Son of Man, it will be forgiven him; but whoever speaks against the Holy Spirit, it will not be forgiven him, either in this age or in the age to come."

The Pharisees accused Yeshua (Jesus) of casting out demons by the power of Satan (Beelzebub). Yeshua (Jesus) asked, "Why would Satan cast out Satan?" (Matthew 12:26). Then, in Matthew 12:28, Yeshua (Jesus) says, "But if I cast out demons by the Spirit of God..." Here we have a definitive statement. Yeshua (Jesus) said 'I' cast out demons. How did Yeshua (Jesus) cast them out? Yeshua (Jesus) cast out demons and healed people by the Spirit of God, by His OWN Spirit power. Yeshua (Jesus) is God and the Holy Spirit is 'of' God (Himself). We then come to the statement in which Yeshua (Jesus) says that blasphemy against Him will be forgiven, but blasphemy against the Holy Spirit WILL NOT be forgiven.

Why? What did Messiah (Christ) mean by this?

Yeshua (Jesus) said this to and about the Pharisees, AFTER THE PHARISEES JUST BLASPHEMED THE HOLY SPIRIT!

How did the Pharisees blaspheme the Holy Spirit?

The Pharisees just witnessed a miracle of God. They just witnessed Yeshua (Jesus) cast demons out from a blind-mute man and heal him, so that the blind-mute man could now see and speak. Rather than getting on their knees and praising Yeshua (Jesus) as the Son of God, what did they do? They blasphemed Yeshua's (Jesus') Holy Spirit power that He used to heal the demon-possessed blind-mute man and said this POWER that Yeshua (Jesus) used came from Satan.

That, in a nutshell, is blasphemy against the Holy Spirit.

Why will blasphemy against the Holy Spirit not be forgiven?

God can never trust a person who calls His holy power evil. If one witnesses a righteous miracle performed by Yeshua (Jesus) using His Holy Spirit power, as the Pharisees did, and then calls God's holy power evil, then that person blasphemes the holy power of God. If God performs a miracle and one witnesses and acknowledges the miracle then blasphemes it, saying it comes from Satan, God can never trust that person.

We believe in God through faith. The angels believed and knew God through proof. They were with God in heaven and witnessed the creation and the power of His Holy Spirit. Satan convinced 1/3rd of the angels to rebel. Since Satan and the fallen angels knew God through proof, they can never be forgiven. Fallen angels or demons can never be forgiven, because they rebelled against God - blaspheming His Holy Spirit, as they were eyewitnesses to the creation and many other wonders of God's spiritual power.

In order to blaspheme the Holy Spirit one would have to witness Yeshua (Jesus) use His Holy Spirit power, then call that miracle evil or witness some other miraculous manifestation of the Holy Spirit and call it evil. We won't see Yeshua (Jesus) again until He returns at His coming at the final trumpet, but His Holy Spirit is with us.

YESHUA MESSIAH (JESUS CHRIST) IS THE SAME YESTERDAY, TODAY, AND FOREVER (AND SO ARE HIS TIMES AND LAWS)

By George Lujack

AN UNCHANGING GOD; NO CHANGES IN GOD'S COMMANDMENTS

When discussing God's commandments, confirming them as sound doctrine, it is imperative to understand that God is holy and unchangeable. Scripture repeatedly and exhaustively characterizes and establishes that God is both holy and unchangeable. Since God is holy, we can know with assurance that what He says is true and that He will keep His word. Since God is unchanging, we know that God will not change His word or His commandments. If God were a God who was inclined to change His word or His commandments, it would render Him unholy and changeable. God repeatedly reminds us that He is holy and unchanging, so we can rely on Him and trust Him. If God were inclined to not keep His word, our very salvation would be forever at risk. God could simply change His mind about mankind and destroy us at any moment in time.

Yeshua (Jesus) did not die on the cross to alleviate us from His laws (Matthew 5:17-19, 11:30). Yeshua (Jesus) suffered and died to atone for our sins, to pay the penalty for sins we have already committed, not so we could sin freely and perpetually, but that we should repent and live righteously (Acts 17:30; Romans 6:15-23; Hebrews 10:26-31; 1 John 2:3-6).

Scripture reveals in clear simple language that God and God's laws have not, nor will ever change. God does not change. Why is it then that people believe that they can relax some or all of God's commandments when Scripture teaches us not to relax any of them?

DEUTERONOMY 4:2, 12:32 (NKJV):

You shall not add to the word which I command you, nor take from it, that you may keep the commandments of YHWH (the Lord) your God which I command you. ...

Whatever I command you, be careful to observe it; you shall not add to it nor take away from it.

PSALM 102:27, 111:7-8, 119:160 (NKJV):

But you are the same and your years shall have no end. …

All His commandments are sure. They stand fast forever and ever and are done in truth and uprightness. … Your word is true from the beginning and every one of your righteous judgments endures forever.

PROVERBS 24:21, 30:6 (NKJV):

My son, fear the Lord and the king; Do not associate with those given to change. …

Do not add to His words, lest He rebuke you and you be found a liar.

ISAIAH 24:5, 40:8 (NKJV):

The earth is also defiled under its inhabitants, because they have transgressed the laws, changed the ordinance, broken the everlasting covenant. …

The grass withers, the flower fades; but the word of our God shall stand forever.

MALACHI 3:6 (NKJV):

I am the Lord, I do not change.

MATTHEW 5:17-19 (NKJV) [WITH INTERPRETATION]:

"Do not think that I came to destroy the Law or the Prophets. I did not come to destroy [THE LAW] but to fulfill [WHAT THE PROPHETS WROTE ABOUT ME]. For assuredly, I say to you, till heaven and earth pass away, not an iota, not a dot, will pass from the law till all is fulfilled. Whoever therefore breaks one of the least of these commandments, and teaches men so, shall be called least in the kingdom of heaven; but whoever does and teaches them, he shall be called great in the kingdom of heaven."

MATTHEW 24:35; MARK 13:31; LUKE 21:33 (NKJV):

"Heaven and earth shall pass away, but My words shall not pass away."

LUKE 16:17, 21:33 (NKJV):

"It is easier for heaven and earth to pass, than one tittle of the law to fail." …

"Heaven and earth will pass away, but My words will by no means pass away."

HEBREWS 13:8 (NKJV):

Yeshua Messiah (Jesus Christ) is the same yesterday, today, and forever.

JAMES 1:17 (NKJV):

Every good gift and every perfect gift is from above, and comes down from the Father of lights, with whom is no variableness, neither shadow of turning.

1 PETER 1:25 (NKJV):

But the word of the Lord endures forever. And this is the word by which the gospel is preached unto you.

WHO CHANGED GOD'S ETERNAL LAWS?

It is not God who changes any of His commandments; it is man. Man's rebellion against the word of God has a long history. Man declaring God's laws have changed has also had a long history.

<u>ISAIAH 30:9-10 (NKJV)</u>:

That this is a rebellious people, lying children, children who will not hear the law of YHWH (the Lord); Who say to the seers, "Do not see," and to the prophets, "Do not prophesy to us right things; Speak to us smooth things, prophesy deceits.

<u>DANIEL 7:25 (NKJV)</u>:

He shall speak pompous words against the Most High, shall persecute the saints of the Most High, and shall intend to change times and law.

The officeholder known as the Catholic Pope, all of them, have fulfilled the Daniel 7:25 prophecy. Scripture says, "He shall *intend* to change times and law." All Catholic popes have either INTENDED to change God's laws or have upheld the intended changes of Catholic popes who came before them. Catholic popes CANNOT change God's times or laws, though that is their intention. God's appointed times and eternal laws REMAIN as God originally commanded them.

WAS THE TORAH (LAW) GIVEN TO THE GENTILES OR TO THE JEWS ONLY?

By George Lujack

Many Christians proclaim that the Torah (law) was never given to the Gentiles, but to the Jews only, so the Gentiles are not bound to obey it. This article will challenge that proclamation, declare it to be untrue, and affirm that the law was indeed given to the Gentiles and that the Jews and Gentiles are both bound to obey it.

ALL THINGS CAME TO THE JEWS FIRST, THEN TO THE GENTILES

MATTHEW 10:5-7 (NKJV):

These twelve Yeshua (Jesus) sent out and commanded them, saying: "DO NOT GO INTO THE WAY OF THE GENTILES, AND DO NOT ENTER A CITY OF THE SAMARITANS. But go rather to the lost sheep of the house of Israel. And as you go, preach, saying, 'The kingdom of heaven is at hand.'"

MATTHEW 15:22-24 (NKJV):

Then Yeshua (Jesus) went out from there and departed to the region of Tyre and Sidon. And behold, a woman of Canaan came from that region and cried out to Him, saying, "Have mercy on me, O Lord, Son of David! My daughter is severely demon-possessed."

But He answered her not a word.

And His disciples came and urged Him, saying, "Send her away, for she cries out after us."

But He answered and said, "I WAS NOT SENT EXCEPT TO THE LOST SHEEP OF THE HOUSE OF ISRAEL."

ROMANS 1:16 (NKJV) [WITH INTERPRETATION]:

For I am not ashamed of the gospel of Messiah (Christ), for it is the power of God to salvation for everyone who believes, for the Jew first and also for the Greek [GENTILE].

Yeshua (Jesus) did not come to preach to the Gentiles, but to the Jews. With few exceptions, Yeshua (Jesus) did preach exclusively to the Jews. Yeshua (Jesus) commanded His disciples to not preach to the Gentiles, but instead to the Jews only. Yeshua (Jesus) did not come to start a new religion called 'Christianity,' but to be the Messiah (Christ) of the already established faith. God offered both the Torah (law) and the gospel of the Messiah (Christ) to the Jew first, then after to the Gentiles.

ROMANS 2:5-11 (NKJV) [WITH INTERPRETATION]:

God, *"will render to each one according to his deeds"* eternal life to those who by patient continuance in doing good seek for glory, honor, and immortality; but to those who are self-seeking and do not obey the truth, but obey unrighteousness - indignation and wrath, tribulation and anguish, on every soul of man who does evil, of the Jew first and also of the Greek [GENTILE]; but glory, honor, and peace to everyone who works what is good, to the Jew first and also to the Greek [GENTILE]. For there is no partiality with God.

The Gentiles were given the Torah (law) and not only the gospel. God promises to judge the Jew and the Gentile equally, without partiality - by their deeds, according to the Torah (law).

HEATHEN AND PAGAN GENTILES THROUGHOUT THE WORLD DO NOT HAVE THE LAW OR THE GOSPEL

ROMANS 2:12-16 (NKJV):

For as many as have sinned without law will also perish without law, and as many as have sinned in the law will be judged by the law (for not the hearers of the law are just in the sight of God, but the doers of the law will be justified; for when Gentiles, who do not have the law, by nature do the things in the law, these, although not having the law, are a law to themselves, who show the work of the law written in their hearts, their conscience also bearing witness, and between themselves their thoughts accusing or else excusing them) in the day when God will judge the secrets of men by Yeshua Messiah (Jesus Christ), according to my gospel.

1 CORINTHIANS 9:19-23 (NKJV):

For though I am free from all men, I have made myself a servant to all, that I might win the more; and to the Jews I became as a Jew, that I might win Jews; to those who are under the law, as under the law, that I might win those who are under the law; to those who are without law, as without law (not being without law toward God, but under law toward Messiah (Christ), that I might win those who are without law; to the weak I became as weak, that I might win the weak. I have become all things to all men, that I might by all means save some. Now this I do for the gospel's sake, that I may be partaker of it with you.

Some have argued that ALL Gentiles do not have the law, as Romans 2:12-16 and 1 Corinthians 9:19-23 might suggest. This is simply not the truth. Paul is referring to heathen or pagan Gentiles who do not have the law or the gospel, who might be living in remote parts of the world, who have neither heard of the law or the gospel of Yeshua Messiah (Jesus Christ), but still obey the law through their hearts and conscience.

All Christians have been given the Torah (law). The Tanakh (Old Testament) Scriptures were in circulation among the Gentiles, who sought wisdom through the Jews, before the Good News gospel was preached.

When the printing press became available and the Scriptures were printed in books, the Gentiles were given the Torah (law) in the Tanakh (Old Testament), *along with* the gospel of Yeshua Messiah (Jesus Christ) in the B'rit Hadashah (New Testament). The Gentiles were not given the B'rit Hadashah (New Testament) Scriptures exclusively, without the Tanakh (Old Testament) included.

The Jews currently reject Yeshua Messiah (Jesus Christ) and the Scriptures that they possess do not include the B'rit Hadashah (New Testament) gospel. In the English language, the Tanakh (Old Testament) is more properly termed the First Covenant and the B'rit Hadashah (New Testament) is more properly named the Renewed Covenant.

Many will bemoan and groan that they cannot possibly keep all the so-called 613 laws of the Torah (law) that God commands. Governments issue literally thousands of civil, criminal, tax code, and vehicle traffic laws, which must be obeyed. The truth is that no single person needs to follow every law written in Scripture, just as no one person needs to obey every governmental law that does not apply to him or her. If you are a male, it will never be required for you to obey female menstrual cycle laws, farming laws (unless you are a farmer), or Levitical priest laws (unless you are a Levite priest). Many of the applicable laws of God are common sense laws, which are obeyed by most anyway.

MATTHEW 28:18-20 (NKJV):

And Yeshua (Jesus) came and spoke to them, saying, "All authority has been given to Me in heaven and on earth. Go therefore and make disciples of ALL THE NATIONS, baptizing them in the name of the Father and of the Son and of the Holy Spirit, TEACHING THEM TO OBSERVE ALL THINGS THAT I HAVE COMMANDED YOU; and lo, I am with you always, even to the end of the age."

Yeshua (Jesus) commanded His Jewish disciples not to preach to the Gentiles and He Himself, with few exceptions, didn't preach to the Gentiles during His Messianic mission (Matthew 10:5-7). It was after Yeshua (Jesus) died and was resurrected that He commanded His disciples to preach to all the nations, to teach them (the Gentiles) to observe all things that He commanded His Jewish disciples to observe.

PROVERBS 28:26 (NKJV):

He who trusts in his own heart is a fool, but he who WALKS WISELY will be delivered.

1 JOHN 2:6 (NKJV):

He who says he abides in Him ought himself also to WALK JUST AS HE WALKED.

1 PETER 1:13-16 (NKJV):

Be sober, and rest your hope fully upon the grace that is to be brought to you at the revelation of Yeshua Messiah (Jesus Christ); as obedient children, not conforming yourselves to the former lusts, as in your ignorance; but as He who called you is holy, you also be holy in all your conduct, because it is written, *"Be holy, for I am holy"* (Leviticus 11:44-45, 19:2, 20:7).

1 PETER 2:8 (NKJV) [WITH INTERPRETATION]:

They [GENTILE BELIEVERS] stumble, being disobedient to the word [THE LAW], to which they also were appointed [GIVEN TO OBEY].

Yeshua (Jesus) did not come to abolish the law (Matthew 5:17) and He obeyed it perfectly. He wants Gentiles and well as Jews to keep His commandments, to walk as He walked (1 John 2:3-6). It is not possible for Gentiles to walk as He walked if they do not strive to keep His commandments. Message to the Gentiles, to those who believe they were not given the law, "Open your bibles! The law has been given to the Gentiles!"

The commandments, all of them, were given to the Gentiles along with the gospel message.

ECCLESIASTES 12:13 (TLV):

A final word, when all has been heard:

Fear God and keep His commands! For this applies to ALL mankind.

ONE LAW – THE SAME LAW FOR JEWS AND GENTILES

EXODUS 12:49 (NKJV):

ONE LAW shall be for the native-born and for the stranger who dwells among you.

LEVITICUS 24:22 (NKJV):

You shall have the SAME LAW for the stranger and for one from your own country; for I am YHWH (the Lord) your God.

NUMBERS 15:16 (NKJV):

ONE LAW and one custom shall be for you and for the stranger who dwells with you.

Mainstream Judaism has accepted the Torah (law), but has rejected Yeshua (Jesus).

Mainstream Christianity has accepted Yeshua (Jesus), but has rejected the Torah (law).

The mainstream Messianic faith has rightly accepted Yeshua (Jesus) *and* has accepted the Torah (law).

DID YESHUA (JESUS) FULFILL THE LAW?

By George Lujack

MATTHEW 5:17-19 (NKJV):

Do not think that I came to destroy the Law or the Prophets. I DID NOT COME TO DESTROY BUT TO FULFILL. For assuredly, I say to you, till heaven and earth pass away, one jot or one tittle will by no means pass from the law till all is fulfilled. Whoever therefore breaks one of the least of these commandments, and teaches men so, shall be called least in the kingdom of heaven; but whoever does and teaches them, he shall be called great in the kingdom of heaven.

DID YESHUA (JESUS) FULFILL THE LAW?

Answer: No. Yeshua (Jesus) only fulfilled the law in the sense that He fulfilled *the requirements* of the law by being obedient to it. We as believers are advised to walk just as He walked, obeying His commandments *in obedience to the law*, fulfilling the requirements of the law, which are not abolished.

1 JOHN 2:4-6 (NKJV):

He who says, "I know Him," and does not keep His commandments, is a liar, and the truth is not in him. But whoever keeps His word, truly the love of God is perfected in him. By this we know that we are in Him. He who says he abides in Him ought himself also to walk just as He walked.

DID YESHUA (JESUS) FULFILL THE LAW, SO THAT WE DON'T NEED TO OBEY IT?

ROMANS 13:8 (NKJV):

Owe no one anything except to love one another, for he who loves another HAS FULFILLED THE LAW.

2 CORINTHIANS 10:4-6 (NKJV):

Bringing every thought into captivity *to the obedience* of Messiah (Christ), and being ready to punish all disobedience *when your obedience* IS FULFILLED.

GALATIANS 5:14 (NKJV):

FOR ALL THE LAW IS FULFILLED in one word, even in this: "You shall love your neighbor as yourself."

The most basic flawed false teaching and misunderstanding in all of mainstream Christianity is that Yeshua (Jesus) both fulfilled and thus abolished the law, so we no longer need to obey it. Those who proclaim Yeshua (Jesus) fulfilled the law and therefore we don't need to obey it, through ignorance and/or deceptive intent, incorrectly equate the words 'fulfill' with 'abolish' and 'destroy.' Yeshua (Jesus) cannot fulfill the law for believers. Believers must repent and obey the law for themselves.

FULFILL, ABOLISH, and DESTROY are NOT synonymous words.

fulfill:

- Bring to completion or reality; achieve or realize (something desired, promised, or predicted).
- Carry out (a task, duty, or role) as required, pledged, or expected.[11]

abolish:

Formally put an end to (a system, practice, or institution).[12]

destroy:

Put an end to the existence of (something) by damaging or attacking it.[13]

Christians who proclaim that Yeshua (Jesus) 'fulfilled' the law, in implication and application, declare that the Torah (law) was in need of modification and Yeshua (Jesus) changed or abolished it. They are declaring that God's laws were impossible to follow and Yeshua (Jesus) 'fulfilled' them, so we no longer need to obey them.

Yeshua (Jesus) didn't fulfill any laws. Laws don't need fulfilling, unless they are written incompletely and God laws weren't.

To 'fulfill' a law would be like saying that a local government had put up speed limit signs, but it left out the actual mile-per-hour speed limit. Then the people of the local government elected a governor, who fulfilled the speed limit law by either entering in a mile-per-hour speed limit figure or abolishing the speed limit altogether by tearing down (destroying) the speed limit signs. Sounds ridiculous, doesn't it? This is exactly what mainstream Christianity proclaims when it declares Yeshua (Jesus) fulfilled the law, so we do not need to obey it.

Yeshua (Jesus) rendered some measures and ordinances for breaking the law obsolete, such as animal sacrifice measures to atone for sin, but that is not a fulfillment - it is a replacement with a new superior atonement: His blood as a once and forever substitute to atone for sin (Hebrews 10).

Another erroneous Christian belief is that 'parts' of the 'Mosaic' law have changed, or were rescinded, when Yeshua (Jesus) fulfilled them. Most Christians adhere to eight or nine of the Ten Commandments (which are Mosaic law). Christians don't actually believe that laws against murder and stealing are no longer in effect. Many Christians however, falsely believe that God's perpetual Torah laws that were not specifically repeated in the B'rit Hadashah (New Testament) were fulfilled, meaning they were abolished, changed, and / or rescinded through Yeshua (Jesus).

Three of God's laws that many Christians believe have been changed or abolished, as a result of Yeshua (Jesus) fulfilling them are:

The Sabbath day, God's dietary laws, and circumcision.

perpetual:
1. Never ending or changing.
2. Occurring repeatedly; so frequent as to seem endless and uninterrupted.[14]

SATURDAY SABBATH OR SUNDAY SABBATH: DOES IT MATTER?

EXODUS 31:12-17 (NKJV):

And YHWH (the Lord) spoke to Moses, saying, "Speak also to the children of Israel, saying: 'Surely My Sabbaths you shall keep, for it is a sign between Me and you throughout your generations, that you may know that I am the Lord who sanctifies you. You shall keep the Sabbath, therefore, for it is holy to you. Everyone who profanes it shall surely be put to death; for whoever does any work on it, that person shall be cut off from among his people. Work shall be done for six days, but the seventh is the Sabbath of rest, holy to YHWH (the Lord). Whoever does any work on the Sabbath day, he shall surely be put to death. Therefore the children of Israel shall keep the Sabbath, to observe the Sabbath throughout their generations as a PERPETUAL covenant. It is a sign between Me and the children of Israel FOREVER; for in six days YHWH (the Lord) made the heavens and the earth, and on the seventh day He rested and was refreshed.'"

It is not improper to worship God on Sunday or on any day of the week. The Sabbath entails more than mere church attendance and / or worship. It is a day of rest and recuperation, of doing no work, of not employing people to do work, and a day of no buying and selling. The Sabbath cannot be observed on every day of the week and is not to be observed on a day of our choosing. The day does matter. The seventh day Saturday Sabbath is not for the Jews only, but for everyone who wishes to be grafted into Israel and be God's people. The Sabbath is observed from Friday sundown through Saturday sundown. The Sabbath is PERPETUAL, meaning that the day cannot be changed, nor is there any Scripture to support that the Sabbath day was changed to the first day, Sunday. Yeshua (Jesus) cannot 'fulfill' or change something that YHWH (the Lord), through Scripture, declares is PERPETUAL and that lasts FOREVER.

DIETARY LAWS: ABOLISHED -OR- PERPETUAL AND REMAINING?

LEVITICUS 3:17, 11:10-11 (NKJV):

It shall be a PERPETUAL STATUTE for your generations throughout all your dwellings, that you shall eat neither fat nor blood. …

Anything in the seas or the rivers that do not have fins and scales, of the swarming creatures in the waters and of the living creatures that are in the waters, is an abomination to you. They SHALL BE (remain, stay) an abomination to you; of their flesh you shall not eat and their carcasses you shall have in abomination.

Yeshua (Jesus) declared in Matthew 5:17 that He did not come to destroy or change any of His laws. He did not 'fulfill' His dietary laws. The dietary laws were put in place to protect us from the various ailments, diseases, feebleness, and premature death that Christians often suffer as a result of eating unclean creatures. The dietary laws were not put in place as some type of temporary restriction to be rescinded later on. Pork and shellfish were always unclean and unhealthy for human consumption. God's dietary laws are PERPETUAL STATUTES and it SHALL BE (remain, stay) an abomination to consume pork, shellfish, and other Scripture-declared unclean creatures. There is no example of any saint in all Scripture, in the Tanakh or B'rit Hadashah (Old or New Testaments), eating any unclean creature. Peter never did eat anything unclean in Acts chapter 10. Yeshua (Jesus) cannot 'fulfill,' meaning abolish, dietary laws that Scripture declares are PERPETUAL and SHALL BE (remain, stay) so.

IS CIRCUMCISION OPTIONAL NOW?

GENESIS 17:9-14 (NKJV):

And God said to Abraham: "As for you, you shall keep My covenant, you and your descendants after you throughout their generations. This is My covenant that you shall keep, between Me and you and your descendants after you: Every male child among you shall be circumcised; and you shall be circumcised in the flesh of your foreskins, and it shall be a sign of the covenant between Me and you. He who is eight days old among you shall be circumcised, every male child in your generations, he who is born in your house or bought with money from any foreigner who is not your descendant. He who is born in your house and he who is bought with your money must be circumcised, and My covenant shall be in your flesh for an EVERLASTING COVENANT. And the uncircumcised male child, who is not circumcised in the flesh of his foreskin, that person shall be cut off from his people; he has broken My covenant."

LEVITICUS 12:1-3 (NKJV):

Then YHWH (the Lord) spoke to Moses, saying, "Speak to the children of Israel, saying: 'If a woman has conceived, and borne a male child, then she shall be unclean seven days; as in the days of her customary impurity she shall be unclean. And on the eighth day the flesh of his foreskin shall be circumcised.'"

Genesis 17:13 declares that circumcision is to be done on male children on their eighth-day and this will be an EVERLASTING COVENANT. Yeshua (Jesus) cannot and did not abolish what God has established as EVERLASTING. The law of circumcision remains, as this is an EVERLASTING COVENANT. What then, of the circumcision discussion among the apostles and statement by Peter in Acts 15:24, in which Peter declared that there is no commandment to circumcise new adult converted men?

ACTS 15:1-3 (NKJV):

And certain men came down from Judea and taught the brethren, "Unless you are circumcised according to the custom of Moses, you cannot be saved." Therefore, when Paul and Barnabas had no small dissension and dispute with them, they determined that Paul and Barnabas and certain others of them should go up to Jerusalem, to the apostles and elders, about this question. So, being sent on their way by the church, they passed through Phoenicia and Samaria, describing the conversion of the Gentiles; and they caused great joy to all the brethren.

ACTS 15:4-6,24 (NKJV):

And when they had come to Jerusalem, they were received by the church and the apostles and the elders; and they reported all things that God had done with them. But some of the sect of the Pharisees who believed rose up, saying, "It is necessary to circumcise them, and to command them to keep the law of Moses."

Now the apostles and elders came together to consider this matter. ...

Since we have heard that some who went out from us have troubled you with words, unsettling your souls, saying, "You must be circumcised and keep the law"—to whom we gave no such commandment...

Peter, under the influence of the Holy Spirit, was correct. There is no commandment to circumcise *adult men*. God commands circumcision to be performed on male children on the eighth day AND ONLY ON THE EIGHTH DAY, according to the law (Genesis 17:12; Leviticus 12:3).

There is no law in Scripture to circumcise adult males. A male child is perfectly geared for circumcision on the eighth day, as science now confirms that the eighth day is the optimal day for circumcision, as it's the exact day when vitamin K and prothrombin levels are at their peak in infants, which causes blood coagulation that aids in any surgical procedure.

Were the elders' objection concerning circumcision for new uncircumcised male Gentile converts without merit? Not exactly. The elders who were calling for adult male converts to be circumcised were concerned with Scripture:

GENESIS 17:14 (NKJV):

And the uncircumcised male child, who is not circumcised in the flesh of his foreskin, that person shall be cut off from his people; he has broken My covenant.

Why didn't God require newly converted Gentile adult males to be circumcised? Why didn't God "cut them off from His people"?

Yeshua (Jesus) died to pay the penalty for mankind's transgression of the law. He didn't die to abolish the law or nail the law to the cross; He nailed the ordinances or penalties for breaking the law to the cross. In the case of circumcision, if parents didn't have their male child circumcised, either through neglect or lack of knowledge of the law of circumcision, that child was to be cut off from God's people unless he became circumcised as an adult male. Yeshua (Jesus) has saved the uncircumcised - as well as all sinners, bearing our iniquities and shortcomings, and those shortcomings of our parents for us as well.

Yeshua (Jesus) took away the ordinance for not being circumcised, which was to be cut off from His people, yet the circumcision law for 8-day-old male children remains an everlasting covenant.

YESHUA (JESUS) WAS CIRCUMCISED

LUKE 2:21 (NKJV):

And when eight days were completed for the circumcision of the Child, His name was called Yeshua (Jesus), the name given by the angel before He was conceived in the womb.

Yeshua (Jesus) followed the law perfectly, even in His infancy. God (the Father), in His infinite wisdom, chose Mary and Joseph to raise Yeshua (Jesus), as the Father knew that they would properly circumcise Yeshua (Jesus) on the appointed eighth day. Hypothetically speaking, if Mary and/or Joseph had rebelled against God and chose not to have Yeshua (Jesus) properly circumcised, the Father most certainly would have sent angels down from heaven to make sure His only begotten Son was rightly circumcised. In a similar manner, as Yeshua (Jesus) is the Rock, Scripture declared that not one of His bones would be broken (John 19:36). If one of the Roman guards, or anyone else, attempted to break the legs or any of the other bones of Yeshua (Jesus) after He had died, God the Father would have moved heaven and Earth to protect Him, not allowing any of His bones to be broken.

1 CORINTHIANS 7:18-20 (NKJV):

Was anyone called while circumcised? Let him not become uncircumcised. Was anyone called while uncircumcised? Let him not be circumcised. Circumcision is nothing and uncircumcision is nothing, but keeping the commandments of God is what matters. Let each one remain in the same calling in which he was called.

The law of circumcision remains an EVERLASTING COVENANT. Parents, according to God's law, are required to circumcise their male children on their eighth day. Adolescent or adult males whose parents did not have them circumcised cannot go back to their eighth day and properly obey the law. Circumcision becomes optional for men after their eighth day.

If an uncircumcised adult male chooses not to be circumcised in adulthood, he will not be cut off from God's people, as Yeshua (Jesus) has paid the ordinance penalty for the lack of proper eighth day circumcision. Uncircumcised men can be grafted into and welcomed to God's family through grace and faith.

WHAT DID YESHUA (JESUS) MEAN WHEN HE SAID HE CAME TO FULFILL?

Matthew 5:17 is a two-part statement referring to the law AND the prophets.

MATTHEW 5:17 (NKJV):

Do not think that I came to destroy the Law or the prophets. I did not come to destroy but to fulfill.

Matthew 5:17 should be understood in the following contextual manner:

MATTHEW 5:17 (NKJV) [WITH INTERPRETATION]:

Do not think that I came to destroy the Law or the prophets. I did not come to destroy [THE LAW] but to fulfill [THE PROPHETS - WHAT THEY WROTE OF CONCERNING ME].

WHAT DID YESHUA (JESUS) FULFILL?

Yeshua (Jesus) did not come to fulfill (abolish, alter, change, or destroy) the law. Matthew 5:18 proclaims that the law will remain until heaven and Earth pass away. Heaven and Earth will not pass away, as a new heaven and a new Earth will replace them, so they will never actually pass away (Revelation 21:1). God's laws and words will by no means pass away (Luke 21:33). Yeshua (Jesus) fulfilled what the prophets had written about Him, concerning the Messiah, which were often duel-prophesies concerning things related to Him.

MATTHEW 1:22-23 (NKJV):

So all this was done THAT IT MIGHT BE FULFILLED which was spoken by YHWH (the Lord) through the prophet, saying: "Behold, the virgin shall be with child, and bear a Son, and they shall call His name Immanuel," which is translated, "God with us."

ISAIAH 7:14 (NKJV) (*FULFILLED*):

Therefore YHWH (the Lord) Himself will give you a sign: Behold, the virgin shall conceive and bear a Son, and shall call His name Immanuel.

MATTHEW 2:14-15 (NKJV):

When he arose, he took the young Child and His mother by night and departed for Egypt, and was there until the death of Herod, THAT IT MIGHT BE FULFILLED which was spoken by YHWH (the Lord) through the prophet, saying, "Out of Egypt I called My Son."

HOSEA 11:1 (NKJV) (*FULFILLED*):

And out of Egypt I called My Son.

MATTHEW 2:16-18 (NKJV):

Then Herod, when he saw that he was deceived by the wise men, was exceedingly angry; and he sent forth and put to death all the male children who were in Bethlehem and in all its districts, from two years old and under, according to the time which he had determined from the wise men. THEN WAS FULFILLED what was spoken by Jeremiah the prophet, saying:

"A voice was heard in Ramah, lamentation, weeping, and great mourning - Rachel weeping for her children, refusing to be comforted, because they were no more."

JEREMIAH 31:15 (NKJV) (*FULFILLED*):

Thus says YHWH (the Lord):

"A voice was heard in Ramah, lamentation and bitter weeping – Rachel weeping for her children, because they were no more."

MATTHEW 2:23 (NKJV):

And he came and dwelt in a city called Nazareth, THAT IT MIGHT BE FULFILLED, which was spoken by the prophets, "He shall be called a Nazarene."

JUDGES 13:7 (NKJV) (*FULFILLED*):

And He said to me, "Behold, you shall conceive and bear a son. Now drink no wine or similar drink, nor eat anything unclean, for the child shall be a Nazirite to God from the womb to the day of his death."

MATTHEW 4:12-14 (NKJV):

Now when Yeshua (Jesus) heard that John had been put in prison, He departed to Galilee. And leaving Nazareth, He came and dwelt in Capernaum, which is by the sea, in the regions of Zebulun and Naphtali, THAT IT MIGHT BE FULFILLED which was spoken by Isaiah the prophet, saying:

MATTHEW 4:15-16 (NKJV):

"The land of Zebulun and the land of Naphtali, by way of the sea, beyond the Jordan, Galilee of the Gentiles: The people who sat in darkness have seen a great light, and upon those who sat in the region and shadow of death Light has dawned."

ISAIAH 9:1 (NKJV) (*FULFILLED*):

Nevertheless the gloom will not be upon her who is distressed, as when at first He humbled the land of Zebulun and the land of Naphtali, and afterward more heavily oppressed her, by way of the sea, beyond the Jordan, in Galilee of the Gentiles.

MATTHEW 8:14-17 (NKJV):

Now when Yeshua (Jesus) had come into Peter's house, He saw his wife's mother lying sick with a fever. So He touched her hand, and the fever left her. And she arose and served them.

When evening had come, they brought to Him many who were demon-possessed. And He cast out the spirits with a word, and healed all who were sick, THAT IT MIGHT BE FULFILLED which was spoken by Isaiah the prophet, saying:

"He Himself took our infirmities and bore our sicknesses."

ISAIAH 53:4 (NKJV) (*FULFILLED*):

Surely He has borne our sicknesses and carried our pains.

MATTHEW 12:14-21 (NKJV):

Then the Pharisees went out and plotted against Him, how they might destroy Him.

But when Yeshua (Jesus) knew it, He withdrew from there. And great multitudes followed Him, and He healed them all. Yet He warned them not to make Him known, THAT IT MIGHT BE FULFILLED which was spoken by Isaiah the prophet, saying:

"Behold! My Servant whom I have chosen, My beloved in whom My soul is well pleased! I will put My Spirit upon Him, and He will declare Right-Ruling to the Gentiles. He will not quarrel nor cry out, nor will anyone hear His voice in the streets. A bruised reed He will not break, and smoking flax He will not quench, till He sends forth Right-Ruling forever; and in His name the nations will trust."

ISAIAH 42:1-4 (NKJV) (*FULFILLED**):

"Behold! My Servant whom I uphold, My Chosen One in whom My soul delights!

I have put My Spirit upon Him; He will bring forth justice to the nations.

He will not cry out, nor raise His voice, nor cause His voice to be heard in the street.

A bruised reed He will not break, and smoking flax He will not quench; He will bring forth Right-Ruling in accordance with truth. He will not fail nor be discouraged, till He has established justice in the earth; and the coastlands wait for His law (Torah)."

*Yeshua (Jesus) will establish justice and rightly rule the nations with a rod of iron as King of kings upon His return to Earth (Psalm 2:9; Revelation 2:27, 12:5, 19:15).

MATTHEW 13:10-15 (NKJV):

And the disciples came and said to Him [Yeshua (Jesus)], "Why do You speak to them in parables?"

He answered and said to them, "Because it has been given to you to know the mysteries of the kingdom of heaven, but to them it has not been given. For whoever has, to him more will be given, and he will have abundance; but whoever does not have, even what he has will be taken away from him. Therefore I speak to them in parables, because seeing they do not see, and hearing they do not hear, nor do they understand. And in them THE PROPHECY OF ISAIAH IS FULFILLED, which says:

'Hearing you will hear and shall not understand, and seeing you will see and not perceive; for the heart of this people has become dull. Their ears are hard of hearing, and their eyes they have closed, lest they should see with their eyes and hear with their ears, lest they should understand with their hearts and turn, so that I should heal them.'"

ISAIAH 6:9-10 (NKJV) (*FULFILLED*):

And He said, "Go and tell this people, 'Hearing you hear, but do not understand; and seeing you see, but do not perceive.' Make the heart of this people dull, and their ears heavy, and shut their eyes; lest they see with their eyes, and hear with their ears, and understand with their heart, and shall turn and be healed.

MATTHEW 13:34-35 (NKJV):

All these things Yeshua (Jesus) spoke to the multitude in parables; and without a parable He did not speak to them, THAT IT MIGHT BE FULFILLED which was spoken by the prophet, saying:

"I will open My mouth in parables; I will utter things kept secret from the foundation of the world."

PSALM 78:2 (NKJV) (*FULFILLED*):

I will open my mouth in a parable; I will utter riddles of old.

MATTHEW 21:1-5 (NKJV):

Now when they drew near Jerusalem, and came to Bethphage, at the Mount of Olives, then Yeshua (Jesus) sent two disciples, saying to them, "Go into the village opposite you, and straightaway you will find a donkey tied, and a colt with her. Loose them and bring them to Me. And if anyone says anything to you, you shall say, 'The Lord has need of them,' and immediately he will send them."

All this was done THAT IT MIGHT BE FULFILLED which was spoken by the prophet, saying:

"Tell the daughter of Zion, 'Behold, your King is coming to you, lowly, and sitting on a donkey, a colt, the foal of a donkey.'"

ZECHARIAH 9:9 (NKJV) (*FULFILLED*):

"Rejoice greatly, O daughter of Zion! Shout, O daughter of Jerusalem! Behold your King is coming to you; He is righteous and having salvation, lowly and riding on a donkey, a colt, the foal of a donkey."

MATTHEW 26:52-56 (NKJV):

But Yeshua (Jesus) said to him, "Put your sword in its place, for all who take the sword will die by the sword. Or do you think that I cannot now pray to My Father, and He will provide Me with more than twelve legions of angels? How then could THE SCRIPTURES BE FULFILLED, that it must happen thus?"

In that hour Yeshua (Jesus) said to the multitudes, "Have you come out, as against a robber, with swords and clubs to take Me? I sat daily with you, teaching in the temple, and you did not seize Me. But all this was done THAT THE SCRIPTURES OF THE PROPHETS MIGHT BE FULFILLED."

ISAIAH 53:7 (NKJV) (*FULFILLED*):

He was led as a lamb to the slaughter, and as a sheep before its shearers is silent, so He opened not His mouth.

MATTHEW 27:6-10 (NKJV):

But the chief priests took the silver pieces and said, "It is not lawful to put them into the treasury, because they are the price of blood." And they consulted together and bought with them the potter's field, to bury strangers in. Therefore that field has been called the Field of Blood to this day.

THUS WAS FULFILLED what was spoken by Jeremiah the prophet, saying, "And they took the thirty pieces of silver, the value of Him who was priced, whom they of the children of Israel priced, and gave them for the potter's field, as YHWH (the Lord) directed me."

JEREMIAH 32:6-9 (NKJV) (*FULFILLED*):

And Jeremiah said, "The word of YHWH (the Lord) came to me, saying, 'Behold, Hanamel the son of Shallum your uncle will come to you, saying, "Buy my field which is in Anathoth, for the right of redemption is yours to buy it."' Then Hanamel my uncle's son came to me in the court of the prison according to the word of YHWH (the Lord), and said to me, 'Please buy my field that is in Anathoth, which is in the country of Benjamin; for the right of inheritance is yours, and the redemption yours; buy it for yourself.' Then I knew that this was the word of YHWH (the Lord). So I bought the field from Hanamel, the son of my uncle who was in Anathoth, and weighed out to him the money, seventeen shekels of silver.

MATTHEW 27:35 (NKJV):

Then they crucified Him, and divided His garments, casting lots, THAT IT MIGHT BE FULFILLED which was spoken by the prophet:

"They divided My garments among them, And for My clothing they cast lots."

PSALM 22:18 (NKJV) (*FULFILLED*):

They divide My garments among them, and for My clothing they cast lots.

MARK 14:48-49 (NKJV):

Then Yeshua (Jesus) answered and said to them, "Have you come out, as against a robber, with swords and clubs to take Me? I was daily with you in the temple teaching, and you did not seize Me. But the SCRIPTURES MUST BE FULFILLED."

ISAIAH 53:7 (NKJV) (*FULFILLED*):

He was led as a lamb to the slaughter, and as a sheep before its shearers is silent, so He opened not His mouth.

MARK 15:27-28 (NKJV):

With Him [Yeshua (Jesus)] they also crucified two robbers, one on His right and the other on His left. So THE SCRIPTURE WAS FULFILLED which says, "And He was numbered with the transgressors."

ISAIAH 53:12 (NKJV) (*FULFILLED*):

And He was numbered with the transgressors...

LUKE 4:16-19 (NKJV):

So He [Yeshua (Jesus)] came to Nazareth, where He had been brought up. And as His custom was, He went into the synagogue on the Sabbath day, and stood up to read. And He was handed the book of the prophet Isaiah. And when He had opened the book, He found the place where it was written:

"The Spirit of YHWH (the Lord) is upon Me, because He has anointed Me to preach the Good News to the poor. He has sent Me to heal the broken-hearted, to proclaim liberty to the captives and recovery of sight to the blind, to set at liberty those who are oppressed, to proclaim the acceptable year of YHWH (the Lord).

ISAIAH 61:1-2 (NKJV) (*FULFILLED*):

The Spirit of YHWH (the Lord) God is upon Me, because YHWH (the Lord) has anointed Me to bring good news to the poor. He has sent Me to heal the broken-hearted, to proclaim liberty to the captives, and the opening of the prison to those who are bound, to proclaim the acceptable year of YHWH (the Lord)...

LUKE 24:44-47 (NKJV):

Then He said to them, "These are the words which I spoke to you while I was still with you, that ALL THESE THINGS MUST BE FULFILLED which were written in the Law of Moses and the Prophets and the Psalms *concerning Me*." And He opened their understanding, that they might comprehend the Scriptures.

Then He said to them, "Thus it is written, and thus it was necessary for the Messiah (Christ) to suffer and to rise from the dead the third day, and that repentance and remission of sins should be preached in His name to all nations, beginning at Jerusalem."

JOHN 12:37-41 (NKJV):

But although He [Yeshua (Jesus)] had done so many signs before them, they did not believe Him, THAT THE WORD OF ISAIAH THE PROPHET MIGHT BE FULFILLED, which he spoke:

YHWH (Lord), who has believed our report? And to whom has the arm of YHWH (the Lord) been revealed?"

Therefore they could not believe, because Isaiah said again:

"He has blinded their eyes and hardened their hearts, lest they should see with their eyes, lest they should understand with their hearts and turn, so that I should heal them.

These things Isaiah said when he saw His glory and spoke of Him.

ISAIAH 6:10, 53:1 (NKJV) (*FULFILLED*):

Make the heart of this people dull, and their ears heavy, and shut their eyes; lest they see with their eyes, and hear with their ears, and understand with their heart, and shall turn and be healed. ...

Who has believed our report? And to whom has the arm of YHWH (the Lord) been revealed?"

JOHN 13:18 (NKJV):

"I do not speak concerning all of you. I know whom I have chosen; but THAT THE SCRIPTURE MAY BE FULFILLED, 'He who eats bread with Me has lifted up his heel against Me.'

PSALM 41:9 (NKJV) (*FULFILLED*):

Even my own familiar friend in whom I trusted, who ate my bread, has lifted up his heel against me.

JOHN 15:23-25 (NKJV):

"He who hates Me [Yeshua (Jesus)] hates My Father also. If I had not done among them the works which no one else did, they would have no sin; but now they have seen and also hated both Me and My Father. But this happened THAT THE WORD MIGHT BE FULFILLED which is written in their law, 'They hated Me without a cause.'"

PSALM 69:4 (NKJV) (*FULFILLED*):

Those who hate me without a cause are more than the hairs of my head...

JOHN 19:24 (NKJV):

Then the soldiers, when they had crucified Yeshua (Jesus), took His garments and made four parts, to each soldier a part, and also the tunic. Now the tunic was without seam, woven from the top in one piece. They said therefore among themselves, "Let us not tear it, but cast lots for it, whose it shall be," THAT THE SCRIPTURE MIGHT BE FULFILLED which says:

"They divided My garments among them, and for my clothing they cast lots."

PSALM 22:18 (NKJV) (*FULFILLED*):

They divide My garments among them, and for My clothing they cast lots.

JOHN 19:28-29 (NKJV):

After this, Yeshua (Jesus), knowing that all things were now accomplished, THAT THE SCRIPTURE MIGHT BE FULFILLED, said, "I thirst!" Now a vessel full of vinegar was sitting there; and they filled a sponge with vinegar, put it on hyssop, and put it to His mouth.

PSALM 69:21 (NKJV) (*FULFILLED*):

And for my thirst they gave me vinegar to drink.

JOHN 19:31-37 (NKJV):

Therefore, because it was the Preparation Day, that the bodies should not remain on the cross on the Sabbath (for that Sabbath was a high day), the Jews asked Pilate that their legs might be broken, and that they might be taken away.

Then the soldiers came and broke the legs of the first and of the other who was crucified with Him. But when they came to Yeshua (Jesus) and saw that He was already dead, they did not break His legs. But one of the soldiers pierced His side with a spear, and immediately blood and water came out. And he who has seen has testified, and his testimony is true; and he knows that he is telling the truth, so that you may believe. For these things were done THAT THE SCRIPTURE SHOULD BE FULFILLED, "Not one of His bones shall be broken." And again ANOTHER SCRIPTURE SAYS, "They shall look on Him whom they pierced."

EXODUS 12:43-46; NUMBERS 9:12 (NKJV) (*FULFILLED*):

And YHWH (the Lord) said to Moses and Aaron, "This is the ordinance of the Passover: … nor shall you break one of its bones."

PSALM 34:20 (NKJV) (*FULFILLED*):

He guards all his bones; not one of them is broken.

PSALM 22:17 (NKJV) (*FULFILLED*):

They look and stare at Me.

ZECHARIAH 12:10 (NKJV) (*YET TO BE FULFILLED**):

"And I will pour on the house of David and on the inhabitants of Jerusalem the Spirit of grace and supplication; then they will look on Me whom they pierced…"

*Will be fulfilled on the day when Yeshua (Jesus) returns (Zechariah 12:7-9).

ACTS 1:15-17 (NKJV):

And in those days Peter stood up in the midst of the brethren (altogether the number of names was about a hundred and twenty), and said, "Men and brethren, THIS SCRIPTURE HAD TO BE FULFILLED, which the Holy Spirit spoke before by the mouth of David concerning Judas, who became a guide to those who arrested YESHUA (Jesus); for he was numbered with us and obtained a part in this ministry."

ACTS 1:18-20 (NKJV):

(Now this man purchased a field with the wages of iniquity; and falling headlong, he burst open in the middle and all his entrails gushed out. And it became known to all those dwelling in Jerusalem; so that field is called in their own language, Akel Dama, that is, Field of Blood.)

"For it is written in the Book of Psalms:

'Let his dwelling place be desolate, and let no one live in it; and

'Let another take his office.'"

PSALM 69:25, 109:8 (NKJV) (*FULFILLED*):

Let their dwelling place be desolate; let no one live in their tents.

…

And let another take His office.

ACTS 3:18 (NKJV):

But those things which God foretold by the mouth of all His prophets, that the Messiah (Christ) would suffer, HE HAS THUS FULFILLED.

ISAIAH 53:4-5 (NKJV) (*FULFILLED*):

Yet we esteemed Him stricken, smitten by God, and afflicted. But He was wounded for our transgressions, He was bruised for our wickedness; The chastisement for our peace was upon Him, and by His stripes we are healed.

ACTS 13:26-27 (NKJV):

"Men and brethren, sons of the family of Abraham, and those among you who fear God, to you the word of this salvation has been sent. For those who dwell in Jerusalem, and their rulers, because they did not know Him, nor even the voices of the Prophets which are read every Sabbath, HAVE FULFILLED THEM IN *condemning Him*.

ACTS 13:28-35 (NKJV):

And though they found no cause for death in Him they asked Pilate that He should be put to death. Now when THEY HAD FULFILLED all that was written *concerning Him*, they took Him down from the tree and laid Him in a tomb. But God raised Him from the dead. He was seen for many days by those who came up with Him from Galilee to Jerusalem, who are His witnesses to the people. And we declare to you glad tidings - that promise which was made to the fathers. God HAS FULFILLED THIS for us their children, in that He has raised up Yeshua (Jesus). As it is also written in the second Psalm:

'You are My Son, today I have begotten You.'

And that He raised Him from the dead, no more to return to corruption, He has spoken thus:

'I will give you the sure mercies of David.'

Therefore He also says in another Psalm:

'You will not allow Your Holy One to see corruption.'

PSALM 2:7 (NKJV) (*FULFILLED*):

YHWH (the Lord) has said to Me, 'You are My Son, today I have begotten You.' (Matthew 3:17, 17:5; Mark 1:11; 2 Peter 1:17).

ISAIAH 55:3 (NKJV) (*FULFILLED*):

I will make an everlasting covenant with you, the sure mercies of David.

PSALM 16:10 (NKJV) (*FULFILLED*):

For you will not leave my soul in the grave, nor will You allow Your Holy One to see corruption.

THE FOLLOWING IS A BRIEF LISTING OF SOME OF THE OVER 300-PROPHESIES FULFILLED BY YESHUA (JESUS):

1. Messiah would be born of a woman. (Gen 3:15; Matt 1:20; Gal 4:4).

2. Messiah would be born in Bethlehem. (Mic 5:2; Matt 2:1; Luke 2:4-6).

3. Messiah would be born of a virgin. (Isa 7:14; Matt 1:22-23; Luke 1:26-31).

4. Messiah would come from the line of Abraham. (Gen 12:3, 22:18; Matt 1:1; Rom 9:5).

5. Messiah would come from the line of Isaac. (Gen 17:19, 21:12; Luke 3:34).

6. Messiah would come from the line of Jacob. (Num 24:17; Matt 1:2).

7. Messiah would come from the tribe of Judah. (Gen 49:10; Luke 3:33; Heb 7:14).

8. Messiah would be heir to King David's throne. (2 Sam 7:12-13; Isa 9:7; Luke 1:32-33; Rom 1:3).

9. Messiah's throne will be anointed and eternal. (Psa 45:6-7; Dan 2:44; Luke 1:33; Heb 1:8-12).

10. Messiah would be called Immanuel. (Isa 7:14; Matt 1:23).

11. Messiah would spend a season in Egypt. (Hos 11:1; Matt 2:14-15).

12. A massacre of children would happen at Messiah's birthplace. (Jer 31:15; Matt 2:16-18).

13. A messenger would prepare the way for Messiah. (Isa 40:3-5; Luke 3:3-6).

14. Messiah would be rejected by His own people. (Psa 69:8; Isa 53:3; John 1:11, 7:5).

15. Messiah would be a prophet. (Deut 18:15; Acts 3:20-22).

16. Messiah would be preceded by Elijah. (Mal 4:5-6; Matt 11:13-14).

17. Messiah would be declared the Son of God. (Psa 2:7; Matt 3:16-17).

18. Messiah would be called a Nazarene. (Judges 13:7; Matt 2:23).

19. Messiah would bring light to Galilee. (Isa 9:1-2; Matt 4:13-16).

20. Messiah would speak in parables. (Psa 78:2-4; Isa 6:9-10; Matt 13:10-15, 34-35).

21. Messiah would be sent to heal the brokenhearted. (Isa 61:1-2; Luke 4:18-19).

22. Messiah would be a priest after the order of Melchizedek. (Psa 110:4; Heb 5:5-6).

23. Messiah would be called King. (Psa 2:6; Zech 9:9; Matt 27:37; Mark 11:7-11).

24. Messiah would be praised by little children. (Psa 8:2; Matt 21:16).

25. Messiah would be betrayed. (Psa 41:9; Zech 11:12-13; Luke 22:47-48; Matt 26:14-16).

26. Messiah's price money would be used to buy a potter's field. (Zech 11:12-13; Matt 27:9-10).

27. Messiah would be falsely accused. (Psa 35:11; Mark 14:57-58).

28. Messiah would be silent before His accusers. (Isa 53:7; Mark 15:4-5).

29. Messiah would be spat upon and struck. (Isa 50:6; Matt 26:67).

30. Messiah would be hated without cause. (Psa 35:19, 69:4; John 15:24-25).

31. Messiah would be crucified with criminals. (Isa 53:12; Matt 27:38; Mark 15:27-28).

32. Messiah would be given vinegar to drink. (Psa 69:21; Matt 27:34; John 19:28-30).

33. Messiah's hands and feet would be pierced. (Psa 22:16; Zech 12:10; John 20:25-27).

34. Messiah would be mocked and ridiculed. (Psa 22:7-8; Luke 23:35).

35. Soldiers would gamble for Messiah's garments. (Psa 22:18; Luke 23:34; Matt 27:35-36).

36. Messiah's bones would not be broken. (Exo 12:46; Psa 34:20; John 19:33-36).

37. Messiah would be forsaken by God. (Psa 22:1; Matt 27:46).

38. Messiah would pray for His enemies. (Psa 109:4; Luke 23:34).

39. Soldiers would pierce Messiah's side. (Zech 12:10; John 19:34).

40. Messiah would be buried with the rich. (Isa 53:9; Matt 27:57-60).

41. Messiah would resurrect from the dead. (Psa 16:10, 49:15; Matt 28:2-7; Acts 2:22-32).

42. Messiah would ascend to heaven. (Psa 24:7-10; Mark 16:19; Luke 24:51).

43. Messiah would be seated at God's right hand. (Psa 68:18, 110:1; Mark 16:19; Matt 22:44).

44. Messiah would be a sacrifice for sin. (Isa 53:5-12; Rom 5:6-8).

With a proper in-context understanding of Matthew 5:17-19 and understanding of the differences in the meanings of the words 'destroy' and 'fulfill,' it becomes evident that Yeshua (Jesus) did NOT fulfill the law in any sense other than obeying it; He fulfilled Scripture prophecy. Yeshua (Jesus) fulfilled what the prophets had written about Him in Scripture, fulfilling the prophecies and the role of the foretold Messiah (Luke 24:44-47; Acts 3:18).

WE ARE NOT UNDER THE LAW, BUT UNDER GRACE (ROMANS 6:14); WHAT DOES NOT LIVING UNDER THE LAW REALLY MEAN?

By George Lujack

Many Christian ministers preach that the Mosaic law or all of the laws of God are abolished based on Romans 6:14, which declares that we are no longer under the law, but under grace. This article will clarify and define what the Apostle Paul really meant when he wrote that "you are not under the law, but under grace."

ROMANS 6:14 (NKJV):

For sin shall not have dominion over you, for you are not under law but under grace.

Although many lawless-minded preachers proclaim that Romans 6:14 implies that the law is abolished and done away with, it does not actually declare that it is. Romans 6:14 states that we are not 'under' the law, but in the context of the very next verse it is clear that the law remains.

ROMANS 6:15 (NKJV):

What then? Shall we sin because we are not under law but under grace? Certainly not!

If the law was abolished, we could not possibly sin, because without law there is no sin. Paul hypothetically asks, "What then? Shall we SIN because we are not under law, but under grace? CERTAINLY NOT!"

Since sin still exists, therefore so does the law. And we should not sin, even though we are under grace, for God will judge us one day for our sins.

ROMANS 6:16-19 (NKJV):

Do you not know that to whom you present yourselves slaves to obey, you are that one's slaves whom you obey, whether of sin leading to death, or of obedience leading to righteousness? But God be thanked that though you were slaves of sin, yet you obeyed from the heart that form of doctrine to which you were delivered. And having been set free from sin, YOU BECAME SLAVES OF RIGHTEOUSNESS. I speak in human terms because of the weakness of your flesh. For just as you presented your members as slaves of uncleanness, and of lawlessness leading to more lawlessness, SO NOW PRESENT YOUR MEMBERS AS SLAVES OF RIGHTEOUSNESS FOR HOLINESS.

When Paul wrote, "sin will not have dominion over you," he was not saying that sin will not have dominion over you *because* the law is abolished. Paul was declaring that we, as believers, are to overcome sin through faithful obedience to the law by living holy in righteousness.

2 PETER 3:15-16 (NKJV):

Our beloved brother Paul, according to the wisdom given to him, has written to you, as also in all his epistles, speaking in them of these things, in which are some things hard to understand, which untaught and unstable people twist to their own destruction, as they do also the rest of the Scriptures.

Lawless-minded Christians twist and use Paul's words to deceive themselves and others into believing God's eternal and unchanging laws are abolished.

WHAT DOES NOT UNDER THE LAW BUT UNDER GRACE MEAN?

ROMANS 6:14 (NKJV) [WITH INTERPRETATION]:

For sin shall not have dominion over you, for you are not [LIVING] under [THE ORDINANCES FOR BREAKING THE] law but under grace [IN THIS AGE - TO TURN AND COME TO REPENTANCE].

GALATIANS 3:13-14 (NKJV):

Messiah (Christ) has redeemed us from the curse of the law, having become a curse for us (for it is written, *"Cursed is everyone who hangs on a tree"*), that the blessing of Abraham might come upon the Gentiles in Messiah Yeshua (Christ Jesus), that we might receive the promise of the Spirit through faith.

Most Christians fully understand what it would mean to live under Islamic Sharia law, but seem to become willfully ignorant to the fact that living under God's laws means virtually the same thing. In Islam, they stone adulteresses and harshly punish people for other sin violations of Islamic law. Similarly, living under the ordinances of the Tanakh (Old Testament) laws of God called for the death penalty for adultery, homosexuality, Sabbath breaking, and many other sins that were capital offenses.

Messiah (Christ) has redeemed us from the CURSE of the law, not the law itself. The curse of the law, for disobeying it, is death. The law remains and is perpetual. The New Covenant is Messiah (Christ) taking death for us, so we can be redeemed, repent, and live righteously through faith in Him.

EZEKIEL 33:11 (NKJV):

'As I live,' says YHWH (the Lord) GOD, 'I have no pleasure in the death of the wicked, but that the wicked turn from his way and live. Turn, turn from your evil ways!

Paul wrote that we are not to live *under the ordinances* for breaking the law, but grace, so that we can willingly turn from sin to live holy and righteously in this age of grace. God will surely judge us over our faithfulness to the law and for our sins. So then, is the law abolished? CERTAINLY NOT!

WHAT WAS NAILED TO THE CROSS?

By George Lujack

It is widely believed by many mainstream Christians that Yeshua (Jesus) nailed the law to the cross, so that the law itself has been abolished. This article will analyze the Colossians 2:14 verse which states that Yeshua (Jesus) nailed the handwriting of ordinances (requirements) that were against us to the cross and declare that these ordinances (requirements) were not the law itself, but the ordinances (requirements) against us for breaking the law.

COLOSSIANS 2:13-14 (NKJV):

And you, being dead in your trespasses and the uncircumcision of your flesh, He has made alive together with Him, having forgiven you all trespasses, having wiped out the HANDWRITING OF REQUIREMENTS that was against us, which was contrary to us. And He has taken it out of the way, having nailed it to the cross.

The law itself was not 'against us,' but the ordinances (requirements) that were contained within the law, for violating the law, is that which was against us.

EPHESIANS 2:14-16 (NKJV):

For He Himself is our peace, who has made both one, and has broken down the middle wall of separation, having abolished in His flesh the enmity, that is, the law of commandments contained in ordinances, so as to create in Himself one new man from the two, thus making peace, and that He might reconcile them both to God in one body through the cross, thereby putting to death the enmity.

Messiah (Christ) died for us, to pay the ordinance penalty required of us for breaking God's laws. Yeshua (Jesus) wiped out the charges that were against us for violating His laws. He took them upon Himself and nailed them to the cross. It is the record of our sins, which are against us, that was nailed to the cross, not the law, which many Christians believe.

The ordinance requirements that stood against us are partially listed in Leviticus 20, but all are descendants of original sin, which required death.

GENESIS 2:17 (NKJV):

And YHWH (the Lord) commanded the man, saying, "Of every tree of the garden you may freely eat; but of the tree of the knowledge of good and evil you shall not eat, for in the day that you eat of it you shall surely die."

ROMANS 3:23 (NKJV):

For all have sinned and fall short of the glory of God.

ROMANS 5:12 (NKJV):

Therefore, just as through one man sin entered the world, and death through sin, and thus death spread to all men, because all sinned.

The ordinance requirement for original sin was death; all men have sinned, all have fallen short of the glory of God, and all are appointed to die once.

JOHN 1:29 (NKJV):

John saw Yeshua (Jesus) coming toward him, and said, "Behold! The Lamb of God who TAKES AWAY THE SIN OF THE WORLD!"

HEBREWS 9:26-28 (NKJV):

He has appeared to put away sin by the sacrifice of Himself. And as it is appointed for men to die once, but after this the judgment, so Messiah (Christ) was offered once to BEAR THE SINS of many.

1 JOHN 3:4-5 (NKJV):

Whoever commits sin also commits lawlessness, and sin is lawlessness. And you know that He was manifested TO TAKE AWAY OUR SINS.

Yeshua (Jesus) bore our sins and took away *the sin* of the world, not *the law* of the world, by nailing it to the cross.

ACTS 10:43 (NKJV):

All the prophets witness that, through His name, whoever believes in Him will receive remission of sins.

remission:
The cancellation of a debt, charge, or penalty.[15]

Yeshua (Jesus) cancelled our charges, debts, and penalties that we owed, as required by the ordinances of the law, by nailing them to the cross.

IS GOD'S LAW (TORAH) BONDAGE?
DID MESSIAH (CHRIST) DIE TO FREE US FROM HIS LAWS?

By George Lujack

Many in these end times who preach lawlessness often cite various verses from the Apostle Paul to justify their faith. Some of these verses, on the surface, may seem to suggest that God's eternal laws (Torah) were bondage that Yeshua (Jesus) came to free us from. This article will examine and analyze some of these verses and reveal the proper viewpoint on them.

<u>**MATTHEW 5:17-18 (NKJV):**</u>

"DO NOT THINK that I came to destroy the Law or the Prophets. I did not come to destroy but to fulfill. For assuredly, I say to you, till heaven and earth pass away, one jot or one tittle WILL BY NO MEANS PASS FROM THE LAW…"

<u>**LUKE 16:17 (NKJV):**</u>

"It is easier for heaven and earth to pass away than for one tittle of the law to fail."

In spite of what Yeshua (Jesus) clearly commanded concerning the law, many lawless advocates want believers to think that He came to destroy the law and free us from it. They proclaim that the law itself was a terrible yoke of bondage that He gave to us and then He freed us from the requirement of having to obey the very law that He once proclaimed to us.

WHAT IS THE YOKE OF BONDAGE?

<u>**GALATIANS 4:8-10 (NKJV):**</u>

But then, indeed, when you did not know God, you served those which by nature are not gods. But now after you have known God, or rather are known by God, how is it that you turn again to the weak and beggarly elements, to which you desire again TO BE IN BONDAGE? You closely observe days and months and seasons and years.

GALATIANS 5:1-6 (NKJV):

Stand fast therefore in the liberty by which Messiah (Christ) has made us free, and do not be entangled again with a YOKE OF BONDAGE. Indeed I, Paul, say to you that if you become circumcised, Messiah (Christ) will profit you nothing. And I testify again to every man who becomes circumcised that he is a debtor to keep the whole law.

You have become estranged from Messiah (Christ), YOU WHO ATTEMPT TO BE JUSTIFIED BY LAW; you have fallen from grace. For we through the Spirit eagerly wait for the hope of righteousness by faith. For in Messiah Yeshua (Christ Jesus) neither circumcision nor uncircumcision avails anything, but faith working through love.

Paul, in Galatians 4:8-10 and 5:1-6, addresses law-keeping Messianic Jews, who were not regarding the righteousness of Messiah (Christ), which is righteousness by faith, and were *solely* seeking to establish (justify) their own righteousness through Sabbath observance, annual calendar festivals, circumcision, and through various law-keeping. Paul was addressing the point that these observances of the law do not make one justified before God and that we are justified by the righteous blood of Yeshua (Jesus).

ROMANS 10:1-3 (NKJV):

Brethren, my heart's desire and prayer to God for Israel is that they may be saved. For I bear them witness that they have a zeal for God, but not according to knowledge. For they being ignorant of God's righteousness, and seeking to establish their own righteousness, HAVE NOT SUBMITTED TO THE RIGHTEOUSNESS OF GOD.

Paul knew that circumcision was an everlasting covenant (Genesis 17:13) and he circumcised Timothy who opted to be circumcised as an adult…

ACTS 16:1-3 (NKJV):

And behold, a certain disciple was there, named Timothy, the son of a certain Jewish woman who believed, but his father was Greek. He was well spoken of by the brethren who were at Lystra and Iconium. Paul wanted to have him go on with him. AND HE TOOK HIM AND CIRCUMCISED HIM…

The 'yoke of bondage,' spoken of by Paul in Galatians 5:1 is further shown NOT to be the 'yoke of the law,' when continuing to read through Galatians 5 to verses 19-21…

GALATIANS 5:19-21 (NKJV) (HSV†):

Now the works of the flesh are evident, which are: adultery, fornication, uncleanness, lewdness, idolatry, drug sorcery, hatred, quarrels, jealousies, fits of rage, selfish ambitions, dissensions, heresies, envy, murders, drunkenness, revelries, and the like; of which I tell you beforehand, just as I also told you in time past, that those who practice such things will not inherit the kingdom of God (†reign of Elohim).

The yoke of bondage that Messiah (Christ) freed us from is the bondage of corruption and sin, which we were once slaves to, but now He has called upon us to be slaves of righteousness and His laws.

2 PETER 2:18-22 (NKJV) [WITH INTERPRETATION]:

For when they [LAW-IS-DONE-AWAY-WITH LAWLESS PREACHERS] speak arrogant words of emptiness, they allure through the lusts of the flesh, through lewdness, the ones who have actually escaped from those who live in error [SIN]. While they promise them liberty, they themselves are SLAVES OF CORRUPTION; for by whom a person is overcome, by him also he is brought into bondage. For if, after they have escaped the pollutions of the world through the knowledge of the Lord and Savior Yeshua Messiah (Jesus Christ), they are again entangled in them and overcome [BY SIN], the latter end is worse for them than the beginning. For it would have been better for them not to have known the way of righteousness [GOD'S LAWS], than having known it, to turn from the holy commandment delivered to them. But it has happened to them according to the true proverb:

"A dog returns to his own vomit," and, *"a sow, having washed, to her wallowing in the mire."*

ROMANS 6:15-23 (NKJV):

What then? Shall we sin because we are not under law but under grace? Certainly not! Do you not know that to whom you present yourselves slaves to obey, you are that one's slaves whom you obey, WHETHER OF SIN LEADING TO DEATH, OR OF OBEDIENCE LEADING TO RIGHTEOUSNESS? But God be thanked that though you were SLAVES OF SIN yet you obeyed from the heart that form of doctrine to which you were delivered. And having been SET FREE FROM SIN, you became SLAVES OF RIGHTEOUSNESS. I speak in human terms because of the weakness of your flesh. For just as you presented your members as SLAVES OF UNCLEANNESS AND OF LAWLESSNESS leading to more lawlessness, so now present your members as SLAVES OF RIGHTEOUSNESS FOR HOLINESS. For when you were SLAVES OF SIN, you were free in regard to righteousness. What fruit did you have then in the things of which you are now ashamed? For the end of those things is death. But now having been SET FREE FROM SIN, and having become SLAVES OF GOD, you have your fruit to holiness, and the end, everlasting life. For the wages of sin is death, but the gift of God is eternal life in Messiah Yeshua (Christ Jesus) our Lord.

ROMANS 8:20-21 (NKJV):

For the creation was subjected to futility, not willingly, but because of Him who subjected it in hope; because the creation itself also will be delivered from the BONDAGE OF CORRUPTION into the glorious liberty of the children of God.

Yeshua's (Jesus') yoke is not a yoke of bondage, His yoke is a yoke of righteousness and His yoke is light.

MATTHEW 11:30 (NKJV):

"For My yoke is easy and My burden is light."

1 JOHN 2:3-6 (NKJV):

Now by this we know that we know Him, if we keep His commandments. He who says, "I know Him," and does not keep His commandments, is a liar, and the truth is not in him. But whoever keeps His word, truly the love of God is perfected in him. By this we know that we are in Him. He who says he abides in Him ought himself also to walk just as He walked.

MATTHEW 22:37-40; MARK 12:29-31 (NKJV):

Yeshua (Jesus) said to him, "*'You shall love the Lord your God with all your heart, with all your soul, and with all your mind.'* This is the first and great commandment. And *the* second is like it: *'You shall love your neighbor as yourself.'* On these two commandments hang ALL THE LAW and the Prophets."

JOHN 13:34 (NKJV):

"A new commandment I give to you, that you love one another; as I have loved you, that you also love one another."

Yeshua's (Jesus') law of love sums up all of His law (Torah), which is good, was given in love, is eternal, and is righteous.

JOHN 7:16-19 (NKJV):

Yeshua (Jesus) answered them and said, "My doctrine is not Mine, but His who sent Me. If anyone wills to do His will, he shall know concerning the doctrine, whether it is from God or whether I speak on My own authority. He who speaks from himself seeks his own glory; but He who seeks the glory of the One who sent Him is true, and no unrighteousness is in Him. DID NOT MOSES GIVE YOU THE LAW, YET NONE OF YOU KEEPS THE LAW?

Yeshua's (Jesus') 'law of love' did not free us from His law (Torah), or the laws of Moses, as He rebuked many of the wicked Jews of His time for not obeying the law.

THE LAW WAS OUR SCHOOLMASTER. DID MESSIAH (CHRIST) END THE LAW?

By George Lujack

This article will clarify the meanings behind some of the verses from Paul's letters to the Galatians and to the Romans that are often taken out-of-context and used by law-is-done-away-with false ministers to promote lawlessness.

GALATIANS 3:24-25 (NKJV) (KJV*) (HSV†):

Therefore the law was our tutor (*schoolmaster) (†trainer) to bring us to Messiah (Christ), that we might be justified by faith. But after faith has come, we are no longer under a tutor (*schoolmaster) (†trainer).

ROMANS 10:4 (NKJV):

For Messiah (Christ) is the end of the law for righteousness to everyone who believes.

Many falsely proclaim that the Torah (law) of God, (or Moses), is bad and that Messiah (Christ) came to end the law for us. All that is required of Christians is to believe and have faith in Yeshua (Jesus). The law, our former schoolmaster, has come to an end now.

After faith has come, is the law abolished? NO! The belief that after faith comes the law is abolished, is the wrong answer, the wrong assumption, and the wrong conclusion.

MATTHEW 5:17 (NKJV):

"Do not think that I came to destroy the Law…"

In his epistle to the Galatians, the Apostle Paul goes on to write that the law remains in effect and those who practice lawlessness will not inherit the kingdom of God.

GALATIANS 5:19-21 (NKJV) (HSV†):

Now the works of the flesh are evident, which are: adultery, fornication, uncleanness, lewdness, idolatry, drug sorcery, hatred, contentions, jealousies, outbursts of wrath, selfish ambitions, dissensions, heresies, envy, murders, drunkenness, revelries, and the like; of which I tell you beforehand, just as I also told you in time past, that those who practice such things will not inherit the kingdom of God (†reign of Elohim).

Ah, say the lawless, but Paul never mentions the dietary commands or Sabbath-keeping, so surely we do not need to obey *those* commands.

Messiah (Christ) declared that the lesser laws remain in effect also.

MATTHEW 5:18-19 (NKJV):

"For assuredly, I say to you, till heaven and earth pass away, ONE JOT OR ONE TITTLE will by no means pass from the law till all is fulfilled. Whoever therefore breaks one of THE LEAST OF THESE COMMANDMENTS, and teaches men so, shall be called least in the kingdom of heaven; but whoever does and teaches them, he shall be called great in the kingdom of heaven."

The law was indeed a tutor for us, and Messiah (Christ) has come, but this does NOT mean that the law is abolished.

Teachers give their students study guides, so that students can study and learn on their own. When the teacher arrives in the classroom, the students are no longer under the tutoring of their study guides; they now have their teacher present to instruct them.

The teacher does not abolish the study guides, nor does the teacher tell his or her students to disregard everything that they learned from their study guides. The teacher further instructs the students, expanding upon what they learned on their own from the knowledge and wisdom contained within their study guides.

Our Teacher, Yeshua (Jesus), likewise did not abolish His law, but further explained the law to deepen our understanding of it.

MATTHEW 5:21-22 (NKJV) (MURDER - FURTHER EXPLAINED):

"You have heard that it was said to those of old, *'You shall not murder,* and whoever murders will be in danger of the judgment.' But I say to you that whoever is angry with his brother without a cause shall be in danger of the judgment."

MATTHEW 5:27-32 (NKJV) (ADULTERY - FURTHER EXPLAINED):

"You have heard that it was said to those of old, *'You shall not commit adultery.'* But I say to you that whoever looks at a woman to lust for her has already committed adultery with her in his heart. If your right eye causes you to sin, pluck it out and cast it from you; for it is more profitable for you that one of your members perish, than for your whole body to be cast into hell. And if your right hand causes you to sin, cut it off and cast it from you; for it is more profitable for you that one of your members perish, than for your whole body to be cast into hell.

"Furthermore it has been said, 'Whoever divorces his wife, let him give her a certificate of divorce.' But I say to you that whoever divorces his wife for any reason except fornication causes her to commit adultery; and whoever marries a woman who is divorced commits adultery."

DOES YESHUA (JESUS) MEAN THE END OF OBEYING THE LAW?

ROMANS 10:4 (NKJV):

For Messiah (Christ) is the end of the law for righteousness to everyone who believes.

The English word 'end' in this context means the ending or the finishing of the law. Yeshua (Jesus) is the COMPLETION of the law. The completion and fullness of the law is grace.

JOHN 1:16-17 (NKJV):

And of His fullness we have all received, and grace for grace. For the law was given through Moses, *but* grace and truth came through Yeshua Messiah (Jesus Christ).

ROMANS 10:4 (NIV):

Messiah (Christ) is the culmination of the law so that there may be righteousness for everyone who believes.

ROMANS 10:4 (HSV):

Messiah (Christ) is the goal of the Torah (law) unto righteousness for everyone who believes.

THE CHIEF CORNERSTONE OF SALVATION AND OF THE LAW

ACTS 4:11-12 (NKJV) [WITH INTERPRETATION]:

"This is the *'stone which was rejected by you builders* [THE JEWS], *which has become the chief cornerstone.'* Nor is there salvation in any other, for there is no other name under heaven given among men by which we must be saved."

—*The Apostle Peter, speaking to the rulers and elders of Israel*

1 PETER 2:7-8 (NKJV) [WITH INTERPRETATION]:

Therefore, to you who believe He is precious; but to those who are disobedient, *"The stone which the builders rejected has become the chief cornerstone,"* and *"A stone of stumbling and a rock of offense."*

They [THE GENTILE BELIEVERS] stumble, being disobedient to the word [THE LAW], to which they also were appointed [TO OBEY].

-*The Apostle Peter, speaking to believers in Pontus, Galatia, Cappadocia, Asia, and Bithynia.*

Yeshua (Jesus) is the chief cornerstone whose salvation message was rejected by the Jews and whose laws were rejected by many mainstream Christians. The Gentiles were given the Torah (law) along with the Gospel message of Yeshua Messiah (Jesus Christ). Messiah (Christ) is not the end (abolishment) of the law; He is the chief cornerstone of the law.

"MY YOKE IS EASY;"
IS MERE BELIEF IN YESHUA (JESUS) ALL THAT IS NECESSARY FOR SALVATION?

By George Lujack

Yeshua (Jesus) spoke of an easy yoke of which He commanded all to come to Him and take. What is this yoke? This article will discuss His easy yoke and address the question as to whether or not mere belief in Yeshua (Jesus) is sufficient for salvation.

MATTHEW 11:30 (NKJV):

"For My yoke is easy and My burden is light."

What is His yoke and what is the burden associated with it? Yeshua's (Jesus') statement, in context and [INTERPRETED]:

MATTHEW 11:28-30 (NKJV) [WITH INTERPRETATION]:

"Come to Me, all you who labor and are heavy laden [WITH SINS], and I will give you rest [FROM THEM]. Take My yoke [WAY] upon you and learn [WISDOM] from Me, for I am gentle and lowly in heart, and you will find rest for your [TROUBLED] souls. For My yoke [WAY] is easy and My burden [CROSS] is light."

Yeshua (Jesus) does give us a way to live by, a cross to bear in this age.

MATTHEW 10:38 (NKJV):

"And he who does not take his CROSS *and follow* after Me is not worthy of Me."

JOHN 14:6 (NKJV):

Yeshua (Jesus) said, "I am THE WAY, the truth, and the life."

What is this cross (burden) we must bear and how shall we follow after Him to be worthy of Him? What way is His way?

1 JOHN 2:3-6 (NKJV):

Now by this we know that we know Him, if we keep His commandments. He who says, "I know Him," and does not keep His commandments, is a liar, and the truth is not in him. But whoever keeps His word, truly the love of God is perfected in him. By this we know that we are in Him. He who says he abides in Him ought himself also to walk just as He walked.

1 JOHN 5:3-4 (NKJV):

For this is the love of God, that we keep His commandments. And His commandments ARE NOT BURDENSOME. For whatever is born of God overcomes the world.

Yeshua's (Jesus') yoke, His burden, is obedience to His commandments. Many end times false prophets are teaching that God's commandments are burdensome and impossible to keep. Scripture directly refutes this falsehood. God never issued commands to man that were impossible to follow. Although we have all sinned and fallen short of the glory of God (Romans 3:23), going forward in our lives we are called upon to repent or else perish.

EZEKIEL 33:11 (NKJV):

'As I live,' says YHWH (the Lord) GOD, 'I have no pleasure in the death of the wicked, but that the wicked turn from his way and live. Turn, turn from your evil ways! For why should you die?'

LUKE 13:3,5 (NKJV):

"I tell you, no; but unless you repent you will all likewise perish."

ACTS 26:19-20 (NKJV):

"Therefore, King Agrippa, I was not disobedient to the heavenly vision, but declared first to those in Damascus and in Jerusalem, and throughout all the region of Judea, and then to the Gentiles, that THEY SHOULD REPENT, turn to God, and DO WORKS BEFITTING REPENTANCE.

- The Apostle Paul

To repent is to feel regret and sorrow over sin, to turn from sin, and to live dedicated to amending one's life. Repentance is a lifestyle change from living in some manner of lawlessness and sin and turning to live in righteousness and in obedience to the commandments of God. Repentance itself is not 'works.' Good deeds and charity are works *befitting* repentance.

Yeshua's (Jesus') death on the cross to atone for our sins saves us. Repentance does not save, but refusing to repent – clinging to certain sins, considering it unnecessary 'work' to repent from them, can condemn someone professing to be a believer of Yeshua (Jesus). Therefore do not be deceived and repent!

1 CORINTHIANS 6:9-10 (NKJV) (HSV†):

Do you not know that the unrighteous will not inherit the reign of Elohim (kingdom of God)? Do not be deceived. Neither fornicators, nor idolaters, nor adulterers, nor effeminate, nor homosexuals, nor thieves, nor covetous (†greedy of gain), nor drunkards, nor revilers, nor swindlers will inherit the kingdom of God (†reign of Elohim).

GALATIANS 5:19-21 (NKJV) (HSV†):

Now the works of the flesh are evident, which are: adultery, fornication, uncleanness, lewdness, idolatry, drug sorcery, hatred, quarrels, jealousies, fits of rage, selfish ambitions, dissensions, heresies, envy, murders, drunkenness, revelries, and the like; of which I tell you beforehand, just as I also told you in time past, that those who practice such things will not inherit the kingdom of God (†reign of Elohim).

REVELATION 21:7-8 (NKJV):

He who overcomes shall inherit all things, and I will be his God and he shall be My son. The cowardly, untrustworthy, abominable, murderers, sexually immoral, drug sorcerers, idolators, and all liars shall have their part in the lake which burns with fire and brimstone, which is the second death.

Yeshua's (Jesus') call to repent is consistent throughout Scripture. As these end times unfold, repent, for the kingdom of God will soon be at hand again.

MATTHEW 4:17 (NKJV):

Yeshua (Jesus) preached and to said, "Repent, for the kingdom of heaven is at hand."

ACTS 17:30-31 (NKJV):

Truly, these times of ignorance God overlooked, but now commands all men everywhere to repent, because He has appointed a day on which He will judge the world in righteousness by the Man whom He has ordained.

REVELATION 3:19 (NKJV):

"Be zealous and repent."

Many end-time false prophets proclaim that it is impossible to repent, repentance is not needed for salvation, and repentance is 'works-based salvation.' Scripture directly refutes this falsehood.

IS MERE BELIEF IN YESHUA (JESUS) SUFFICIENT FOR SALVATION?

ACTS 16:31 (NKJV):

"Believe on the Lord Jesus Christ, and you will be saved…"

Mere belief in Yeshua's (Jesus') existence, that He is the Son of God, is insufficient for salvation. Taking one solitary verse and applying one's own standard – one's own definition of 'belief' to it, while disregarding other verses that show what 'belief' actually entails is deceitful. With belief comes obedience. Without obedience, belief is not acceptable. If one truly believes in Yeshua (Jesus), then one will obey His commandments. Anyone who merely says that he or she believes in Him, but does not keep His commandments is a liar and untruthful (1 John 2:3-6).

JAMES 2:19 (NKJV):

You believe that there is one God. You do well. Even the demons believe - and tremble!

The demons believe in God, they tremble in His presence, and have lost their salvation.

A YOKE THAT MANY ARE UNABLE TO BEAR

The Apostle Peter spoke of a yoke that is very difficult to bear.

ACTS 15:10 (NKJV):

Now therefore, why do you test God by putting a yoke on the neck of the disciples which neither our fathers nor we were able to bear?

Was Peter speaking of the Torah (law) in general? NO! He was speaking specifically of the law of circumcision, in regards to the yoke of *adult* circumcision.

ACTS 15:5 (NKJV) [WITH INTERPRETATION]:

But some of the sect of the Pharisees who believed [IN YESHUA (JESUS)] rose up, saying, "It is necessary TO CIRCUMCISE THEM, and to command them to keep the [CIRCUMCISION] law of Moses."

ACTS 15:6-11 (NKJV) [WITH INTERPRETATION]:

Now the apostles and elders came together to consider this matter. And when there had been much dispute, Peter rose up and said to them: "Men and brethren, you know that a good while ago God chose among us, that by my mouth the Gentiles should hear the word of the gospel and believe. So God, who knows the heart, acknowledged them by giving them the Holy Spirit, just as He did to us, and made no distinction between us [CIRCUMCISED JEWS] and them [UNCIRCUMCISED GENTILES], purifying their hearts by faith.

Now therefore, why do you test God by putting a yoke [ADULT CIRCUMCISION] on the neck of the disciples which neither our fathers nor we were able to bear? But we believe that through the grace of the Lord Yeshua Messiah (Jesus Christ) we [CIRCUMCISED JEWS] shall be saved in the same manner as they [UNCIRCUMCISED GENTILES]."

Circumcision is an everlasting law of God that should be performed on male infants on their eighth day (Genesis 17:9-14). If a male believer has not been circumcised, he is no longer cut off from God. Yeshua (Jesus) paid the penalty for sin, but did not come to abolish the law itself. (Matthew 5:17-19). Circumcision is optional in adulthood, not required.

WAS IT NECESSARY FOR YESHUA (JESUS) TO REPEAT THE LAW?

Many end-time false prophets teach that if Yeshua (Jesus) didn't repeat His commands in the B'rit Hadashah (New Testament), then they no longer apply. Yeshua (Jesus) did not come to repeat His commandments and clearly stated that He did not come to destroy the law or any part of it (Matthew 5:17-19).

Imagine if people applied the 'law must be repeated in the B'rit Hadashah (New Testament) standard' to driving an automobile. A motorist gets on a highway and sees a 70 miles per hour sign and, after some time passes, the motorist crosses a state border and sees no more speed limit signs. So the motorist believes that the speed limit must have been abolished and decides to travel at 120 miles per hour, before getting pulled over by a highway patrolman. The motorist's excuse that the speed limit sign was not constantly repeated will not get the man out of trouble with the highway patrol and the driver will be duly summonsed for speeding.

God gave the law to the Gentiles, as well as the Jews. The law was first given to the Jews at Mount Sinai and later given to the Gentiles after the resurrection of Yeshua (Jesus) through the Tanakh (Old Testament) Scriptures.

Yeshua's (Jesus') yoke, obeying His commandments, is not impossible to do, or He never would have issued them. Obeying His commands, in this world – in this time period before He returns to establish His kingdom on Earth and rule with a rod of iron may be inconvenient, a small burden, a light yoke, but it is not impossible.

1 PETER 3:13-17 (NKJV) [WITH INTERPRETATION]:

And who *is* he who will harm you if you become followers of what is good? But even if you should suffer for righteousness' sake, you are blessed. *"And do not be afraid of their threats, nor be troubled."* But sanctify the Lord God in your hearts, and always be ready to give a defense to everyone who asks you a reason for the hope that is in you, with meekness and fear; having a good conscience, that when they defame you as evildoers, those who revile your good conduct [COMMANDMENT KEEPING] in Messiah (Christ) may be ashamed. For it is better, if it is the will of God, to suffer for doing good than for doing evil.

Many end-time false prophets teach that those who obey God's commandments are evildoers and they revile the good conduct of Torah-abiding (law-abiding) believers. God's laws are good (1 Timothy 1:8). It can be somewhat inconvenient to not go to a restaurant or shopping at the mall on the Sabbath, when everyone else is going, but it is not impossible. It is a small burden to eat proper food, to refuse to eat non-food unclean creatures, but it is not impossible. It may seem like a burden to remain sexually pure, when many are sexually promiscuous, but it is not impossible. It may seem like a heavy burden when people, even professing Christian believers, defame, mock, revile, ridicule, and threaten you for your good conduct, for being obedient to God's commandments, but it is better to suffer for doing good than it is to do evil.

PHILIPPIANS 2:12-13 (NKJV):

Work out your own salvation with fear and trembling; for it is God who works in you both to will and to do for His good pleasure.

REVELATION 14:12 (NKJV):

Here is the patience of the saints; here are those who keep the commandments of God and the faith of Yeshua (Jesus).

Mere belief, without repentance, is insufficient for salvation. Yeshua's (Jesus') yoke is light, but it is not that light! We are to WORK out our own salvation with fear and trembling and God will work in us to bring us to righteousness and to do His will. The light yoke that Yeshua (Jesus) asks His believers to bear is to obey His commandments while patiently putting up with the evils and resisting the temptations of the world.

DO YOU WANT TO BE KNOWN AS 'GREAT' OR 'LEAST' IN THE KINGDOM OF HEAVEN?

By George Lujack

Many mainstream Christians practice and preach that the lesser parts of the law, or the 'Mosaic laws,' have been done away with and no longer need to be observed. Yeshua (Jesus) plainly stated otherwise. This article's purpose is to serve notice to lawless-minded Christians to carefully examine the words of Yeshua (Jesus) regarding the least of His commandments and to reconsider the widespread false teaching that His lesser laws have been abolished and are done away with.

MATTHEW 5:17-19 (NKJV) [WITH INTERPRETATION]:

"Do not think that I came to destroy the Law or the Prophets. I did not come to destroy but to fulfill. For assuredly, I say to you, till heaven and earth pass away, one jot or one tittle will by no means pass from the law till all is fulfilled. Whoever [JEW OR GENTILE] therefore breaks one of the least of these commandments, and teaches men so, shall be called least in the kingdom of heaven; but whoever [JEW OR GENTILE] does and teaches them, he shall be called great in the kingdom of heaven."

LUKE 16:17 (NKJV):

"It is easier for heaven and earth to pass away than for one tittle of the law to fail."

MATTHEW 24:35; MARK 13:31; LUKE 21:33 (NKJV):

"Heaven and earth shall pass away, but My words shall not pass away."

When heaven and Earth do eventually pass away (which has not happened yet), and we have a new heaven and a new Earth (Revelation 21:1), Yeshua's (Jesus') words (which include His commandments - all of them), shall not pass away.

1 CORINTHIANS 6:9-10 (NKJV) (HSV†):

Do you not know that the unrighteous will not inherit the reign of Elohim (kingdom of God)? Do not be deceived. Neither fornicators, nor idolaters, nor adulterers, nor effeminate, nor homosexuals, nor thieves, nor covetous (†greedy of gain), nor drunkards, nor revilers, nor swindlers will inherit the kingdom of God (†reign of Elohim).

GALATIANS 5:19-21 (NKJV) (HSV†):

Now the works of the flesh are evident, which are: adultery, fornication, uncleanness, lewdness, idolatry, drug sorcery, hatred, quarrels, jealousies, fits of rage, selfish ambitions, dissensions, heresies, envy, murders, drunkenness, revelries, and the like; of which I tell you beforehand, just as I also told you in time past, that those who practice such things will not inherit the kingdom of God (†reign of Elohim).

REVELATION 21:7-8 (NKJV):

He who overcomes shall inherit all things, and I will be his God and he shall be My son. The cowardly, untrustworthy, abominable, murderers, sexually immoral, drug sorcerers, idolators, and all liars shall have their part in the lake which burns with fire and brimstone, which is the second death.

Most Christians do not properly observe the Sabbath, do not obey God's dietary commands, and do not observe other lesser parts of the law that they believe are no longer applicable or required to be complied with. Christians often teach others that God's lesser 'Mosaic' commands have been abolished and done away with. Fortunately for Christians, who are living righteously and are not committing the sins listed in 1 Corinthians 6:9-10, Galatians 5:19-21, and Revelation 21:7-8, they are under God's grace in regards to the lesser parts of the law and will inherit the kingdom of God.

Yeshua (Jesus) proclaimed that those who break the least of His commandments and teach others to do likewise, they will be called 'least,' and those who practice all His lesser laws and teach others to do them, they will be called 'great' in the kingdom of heaven.

Disobeying God's lesser commandments and teaching others to disobey them, both carry eternal consequences. Many mainstream Christians who disregard God's perpetual Sabbath (Exodus 31:16), eat unclean creatures in disobedience to God's dietary commands (Leviticus 11; Deuteronomy 14), and disobey other lesser laws will need to be corrected before entering the kingdom of heaven. Lesser-law disregarding Christians will be called 'least' in the kingdom of heaven and will be treated as such in matters of authority and stature. Those who obey all of God's lesser laws, and teach others to do them, will be called 'great' in the kingdom of heaven. As is the case in all kingdoms, the great enjoy authority, power, and privilege over the least.

God's laws are eternal. If convicted by the truth that all of God's laws, including the least of His commandments are eternal, then start learning them, do them, and teach others about them. Those who practice and teach others about the least of God's commandments will be called 'great' in the kingdom of heaven.

THE LESSER PARTS OF THE TORAH (LAW) *EXPLAINED*

By George Lujack

The lesser parts of the Torah (law) have been declared as burdensome and obsolete by mainstream Christians and have often been used as an excuse to declare that all of God's 'Mosaic laws' are abolished. In these end times, some Christian ministers have been saying that God's Ten Commandments need to be done away with also. This article will discuss some of the lesser parts of God's laws, explain how they apply to us today, and address how some of these laws have been misinterpreted and incorrectly practiced.

HEAD SHAVING

LEVITICUS 19:27 (NKJV):
You shall not shave around the sides of your head ...

LEVITICUS 21:5 (NKJV):
They shall not make any bald place on their heads...

Tonsure is known as the practice of shaving most of the male scalp and leaving a ring of hair around the head. This was a specific practice within medieval Catholicism, which was abandoned by a papal order in 1972. Tonsure is still practiced today by some religious orders within Catholicism, the Eastern Orthodox Church, Buddhist monks, Islamists, and Hindus.

The purpose of the tonsure head shaved hairstyle is to show a renunciation of worldliness, display humbleness, and demonstrate devotion to one's religious order.

God has commanded man to not shave around the sides of his head. God does not accept this form of piousness for obvious spiritual reasons. Shaving around the scalp and the sides of the head gives a man a halo image. God's law does not allow for a false image of holiness, a halo effect to be projected upon a man, which constitutes a form of idolatry.

Today, many gay men and lesbian women shave one or both sides of their head to declare their perverted sexual lifestyle and to be identifiable as gay or lesbian by other gay and lesbian prospective lovers.

BEARD TRIMMING

LEVITICUS 19:27 (NKJV):

You shall not shave around the sides of your head nor shall you disfigure the edges of your beard.

LEVITICUS 21:5 (NKJV):

They shall not make any bald place on their heads, nor shall they shave the edges of their beards...

Orthodox Judaism made a ruling on what the sides of the head and edges of the beard were, and declared in their Talmud that it was the sideburns of a man, the hair in front of the ears extending beneath the cheekbone, on level with the nose. It became a custom in certain Jewish circles to let the hair in front of the ears grow and hang down in curls or ringlets, which became known as the payot (peyot).

As the Talmud has erred in many of its teachings, its interpretation of Leviticus 19:27 and 21:5 is also incorrect. Scripture does not command the Jews, or Gentiles, to *grow* the sideburn hair into long ringlet curls or not cut or trim sideburn hair. Scripture states that man should not *shave* (bald) around the sides of the head (*round* the corners of the head) or disfigure the *edges* of the beard (destroy the *corners* of the beard).

EZEKIEL 44:20 (NKJV):

They shall neither shave their heads, *nor let their hair grow long*, but they shall keep their hair *well trimmed*.

Growing long payot (peyot) ringlet curls is actually in opposition to the command of Scripture given to Levite priests to keep their hair 'well trimmed.' It is neither a requirement for Jews, or Gentiles, to grow their sideburns into long ringlet curls, nor is it a requirement for Jews, or Gentiles, to grow and maintain a beard.

What then of the Leviticus laws that state not to shave the edges of a beard?

In order to shave the edges of a beard, a man must first have a beard. If a man does not have a beard, the command against shaving the edges of a beard does not apply, just as the command is inapplicable to women. But if a man does have a beard, then the command does apply. The command against not shaving the edges of the beard equates to not sporting a goatee style beard. The command against not shaving the head also applies to men.

Many cultures throughout history have practiced head shaving while simultaneously sporting goatee style beards. Egyptian men, whom the Hebrews fled from in the Exodus, commonly had this shaved head and goatee style beard arrangement. In the end times, a common look is for men to shave their heads bald and grow goatee beards.

Satan is often depicted in artistic images with a shaved head and goatee style beard. It is unknown what Satan's appearance actually is, or why God forbids head shaving and goatee beards, but His commands are eternal and should be obeyed.

A SIGN ON THE HAND AND FRONTLETS BETWEEN THE EYES

DEUTERONOMY 6:6-8 (NKJV):

And these words, which I command you today shall be *in your heart*. You shall teach them diligently to your children, and shall talk of them when you sit in your house, when you walk by the way, when you lie down, and when you rise up. You shall bind them *as a sign on your hand* and they shall be *as frontlets between your eyes.*

DEUTERONOMY 11:18 (NKJV):

Therefore you shall lay up these words of mine *in your heart* and in your soul, and bind them *as a sign on your hand*, and they shall be *as frontlets between your eyes.*

Some religious Orthodox Jews in Israel wear phylactery, a small cube container with Scripture verses strapped to their foreheads and another strapped to their arm, during weekly morning prayers. Deuteronomy 6:6 states, "And these words which I command you today shall be *in your heart*," and 11:18 says, "Therefore you shall lay up these words of mine *in your heart*." While Orthodox Jews wear phylactery on their foreheads and arms, if they truly want to be consistent with a literal adherence of the commands of Deuteronomy 6:6-8 and 11:18, they should undergo open heart surgery and insert a phylactery cube in or near their hearts.

Yeshua (Jesus) addressed the Jews who engaged in public displays of phylactery wearing.

MATTHEW 23:5 (NKJV):

But all their works they do to be seen by men. They make their phylacteries broad and enlarge the borders of their garments.

Phylactery-wearing Orthodox Jews have taken the figurative commands of Deuteronomy 6:6-8 and 11:18 and have attached literal applications to them, resulting in the ritual practice of morning phylactery prayers.

EXODUS 13:16 (NKJV):

It shall be as a sign on your hand and as frontlets between your eyes, *for by strength of hand the Lord brought us out of Egypt.*

God's command for us to have a sign on our hand and frontlets between our eyes are figurative, not literal commands, as Exodus 13:16 shows. God's commandments (and deeds) shall be *as* (like) a sign on our hand (our works), and *as* (like) frontlets between our eyes (our minds). Scripture never recorded Yeshua (Jesus) as having worn any type phylactery, further showing this practice to be pointless. We, as believers in Yeshua (Jesus), are to walk as He walked (1 John 2:6) and if He never wore phylactery, then we don't need to either.

TZITZITS

DEUTERONOMY 22:12 (NKJV):

You shall make tassels on the four corners of the clothing with which you cover yourself.

NUMBERS 15:37-40 (NKJV):

YHWH (the Lord) spoke to Moses, saying, "Speak to the children of Israel: Tell them to make tassels on the corners of their garments throughout their generations, and to put a blue thread in the tassels of the corners. And you shall have the tassel, that you may look upon it and remember all the commandments of YHWH (the Lord) and do them, and that you may not follow the harlotry to which your own heart and your own eyes are inclined, and that you may remember and do all My commandments, and be holy for your God.

Tzitzits are specially knotted blue and white fringes or tassels. Tzitzits are traditionally attached to the four corners of a prayer shawl. Recent tzitzit applications have been designed as belt loops that many Messianic and Jewish believers wear when coming together for service at synagogues.

YARMULKES, SKULLCAPS, KIPPAH, BEANIES, WOMEN'S HEAD COVERINGS

The yarmulke (also known as skullcap, kippah, beanie) is a brimless cap commonly worn by Jewish men to cover their heads during prayer and worship as a sign of respect towards God, acknowledging that God is above them. Wearing the yarmulke is a custom of Judaism, not a commandment of God, and in fact goes against Scripture tradition instruction.

1 CORINTHIANS 11:2-7 (NKJV):

Now I praise you, brethren, that you remember me in all things and KEEP THE TRADITIONS just as I delivered them to you. But I want you to know that the head of every man is Messiah (Christ), the head of woman is man, and the head of Messiah (Christ) is God. Every man praying or prophesying, HAVING HIS HEAD COVERED, dishonors his head. But every woman who prays or prophesies WITH HER HEAD UNCOVERED dishonors her head, for that is one and the same as if her head were shaved. For if a woman is not covered, let her also be shorn. But if it is shameful for a woman to be shorn or shaved, let her be covered. For a man indeed OUGHT NOT TO COVER HIS HEAD, since he is the image and glory of God; but woman is the glory of man.

Women should cover their heads with a head covering when praying or prophesying, according to Scripture tradition, but not men. It is important to note that Scripture traditions do not necessarily fall under the category of Scripture commandments. Instructions for head coverings are not found in the Torah (law) commandments, but are instructions of custom and tradition, which Paul wrote to his congregation of believers in Corinth to keep and observe.

MODERN DAY APPLICATIONS

None of the lesser parts of the Torah (law) discussed in this article are salvation issues. Obedience to the lesser parts of the Torah (law) are something the more religiously faithful typically practice out of devotion. Yeshua (Jesus) said that not a jot or tittle will pass from even the least of His commandments and whoever does the least of His commandments and teaches others to do them will be called great in the kingdom of heaven (Matthew 5:18-19). A believer who wishes to live more righteously for the sake of the kingdom of heaven should not shave his head bald, either side of his or her head bald, or sport a goatee style beard.

DO YOUR BEST TO PRESENT YOURSELF TO GOD AS ONE APPROVED

By George Lujack

As believers living in these end times, the urgency is upon all to repent and live righteously as the end of this age quickly approaches. The age of grace will soon expire. The great tribulation will soon be upon the world and it will catch many unaware who are unprepared for it. All will one day have to stand before the presence of Yeshua (Jesus) the Lord. There are far too many Christians and others who have become content with sin, being lukewarm about the critical necessity to repent from it and live righteously. This article will advise and warn believers to not be complacent about sin in their lives, encourage them to repent from their sins, live righteously, and prepare to present themselves before God as one approved.

MATTHEW 4:17 (NKJV):

From that time Yeshua (Jesus) began to preach and say, "Repent, for the kingdom of God is at hand."

When Yeshua (Jesus) came to fulfill His role as the Messiah (Christ), He instructed people to repent, for the kingdom of God was at hand. He Himself was the representative of the kingdom of God who was at hand.

MATTHEW 24:11-12 (NKJV):

Many false prophets will rise up and deceive many. And because lawlessness will abound, the love of many will grow cold.

Many ministers in mainstream Christian churches in these end times are deceiving many, teaching their flock to not repent, that the law is done away with, and that it is impossible for believers to live righteously.

MATTHEW 11:20 (NKJV):

Then He [YESHUA (JESUS)] began to rebuke the cities in which most of His mighty works had been done, because they did not repent.

MATTHEW 13:41-43 (NKJV):

The Son of Man will send out His angels, and they will gather out of His kingdom all things that offend, and those who practice lawlessness, and will cast them into the furnace of fire. There will be wailing and gnashing of teeth. Then the righteous will shine forth as the sun in the kingdom of their Father.

Refusing to repent, living lawlessly (not keeping His commandments), and relying on His endless eternal grace that will one day expire, is not the way to prepare to stand before the kingdom of God.

REVELATION 2:21, 3:3,19 (NKJV):

"And I gave her time to repent of her sexual immorality, and she DID NOT REPENT.".…

"Remember therefore how you have received and heard; hold fast AND REPENT. Therefore if you will not watch, I will come upon you as a thief, and you will not know what hour I will come upon you.".…

"Be zealous AND REPENT."

In the end times, many sins that 'believers' refuse to repent of are carnal sins, sexual sins of the flesh. Gays, fornicators, and adulterers (those who cheat on their spouses and those who have married in adultery), who were once widely considered disgraceful, are now embraced by many as normal and acceptable. Sexual norms may change throughout the decades, but Yeshua (Jesus) is the same yesterday, today, and forever (Hebrews 13:8).

1 CORINTHIANS 6:9-10 (NKJV) (HSV†):

Do you not know that the unrighteous will not inherit the reign of Elohim (kingdom of God)? Do not be deceived. Neither fornicators, nor idolaters, nor adulterers, nor effeminate, nor homosexuals, nor thieves, nor covetous (†greedy of gain), nor drunkards, nor revilers, nor swindlers will inherit the kingdom of God (†reign of Elohim).

GALATIANS 5:19-21 (NKJV) (HSV†):

Now the works of the flesh are evident, which are: adultery, fornication, uncleanness, lewdness, idolatry, drug sorcery, hatred, quarrels, jealousies, fits of rage, selfish ambitions, dissensions, heresies, envy, murders, drunkenness, revelries, and the like; of which I tell you beforehand, just as I also told you in time past, that those who practice such things will not inherit the kingdom of God (†reign of Elohim).

EPHESIANS 5:5-6 (NKJV):

For this you know, that no fornicator, unclean person, nor covetous man, who is an idolater, has any inheritance in the kingdom of Messiah (Christ) and God. Let no one deceive you with empty words, for because of these things the wrath of God comes upon the sons of disobedience.

REVELATION 21:7-8 (NKJV):

He who overcomes shall inherit all things, and I will be his God and he shall be My son. The cowardly, untrustworthy, abominable, murderers, sexually immoral, drug sorcerers, idolators, and all liars shall have their part in the lake which burns with fire and brimstone, which is the second death.

A faithful, law-keeping believer once rebuked a lawless-minded, sin-excusing, "if God exists He loves everyone, don't judge me," type agnostic. The agnostic said to the faithful believer, "You seem to know the book of the Lord, but do you know the Lord of the book?" The intention of the question was to suggest that the book of the Lord, the Scriptures, contained a holy, righteous, sin-hating God, but the Lord of the book was somehow different: a non-judgmental, permissive, perpetually-forgiving, sin-tolerating God.

The faithful believer pondered the rhetorical question for a few moments and replied. "The Lord of the book is the exact same Lord written about in the book of the Lord."

In these end times, many people do not know the book of the Lord and therefore do not know the Lord of the Scriptures. Many believe that Yeshua (Jesus) died so we can live in sin perpetually, and that He will accept us in His kingdom just as we are. People often try to make Yeshua (Jesus) into a God of their liking, dismissing the Scripture account of who Yeshua (Jesus) is.

It has been said that when the Messiah (Christ) came, the Jews were expecting a Lion, but got a Lamb, and when Yeshua (Jesus) returns, Christians will be expecting a Lamb, but will get a Lion. Yeshua (Jesus) fulfilled His sacrificial role as the Lamb and He is returning as the Lion of Judah (Revelation 5:5).

LUKE 13:2-5 (NKJV):

And Yeshua (Jesus) answered and said to them, "Do you suppose that these Galileans were worse sinners than all other Galileans, because they suffered such things? I tell you, NO; BUT UNLESS YOU REPENT YOU WILL ALL LIKEWISE PERISH. Or those eighteen on whom the tower in Siloam fell and killed them, do you think that they were worse sinners than all other men who dwelt in Jerusalem? I tell you, NO; BUT UNLESS YOU REPENT YOU WILL ALL LIKEWISE PERISH."

Luke 13:2-5 conveys a correlated message for sinners of these end times:

Do you suppose that the homosexuals of Sodom were worse than all other homosexuals, because they suffered such things (the destruction of Sodom - Genesis 19:24-25, Luke 17:29)? Yeshua (Jesus) *would tell you* NO; BUT UNLESS YOU REPENT YOU WILL ALL LIKEWISE PERISH.

To the fornicators and adulterers of these end times, do you think that the unrestrained Hebrew sinners, who fled Egypt in the Exodus, were worse unrestrained sinners than you, because about three thousand of them died for their sins (Exodus 32:25-28)? Yeshua (Jesus) *would tell you* NO; BUT UNLESS YOU REPENT YOU WILL ALL LIKEWISE PERISH.

CONSEQUENCES

For believers and others who are ignorantly living in deadly sins (1 Corinthians 6:9-10, Galatians 5:19-21, Ephesians 5:5-6, Revelation 21:7-8), the minimal consequence for such persons will be rejection from reigning with Yeshua (Jesus) during the Millennium Kingdom. For those who intentionally and ultimately reject God's laws, refuse to repent, and sin freely, the punishment will be the second death in hell.

HOSEA 4:6 (NKJV):

My people are destroyed for lack of knowledge. Because you have rejected knowledge, I also will reject you from being priest for Me; Because you have forgotten the law of your God.

COLOSSIANS 2:18 (NKJV):

Let no one cheat you of your reward, taking delight in false humility and worship of angels.

REVELATION 20:6 (NKJV):

Blessed and holy is he who has part in the first resurrection. Over such the second death has no power, but they shall be priests of God and of Messiah (Christ), and shall reign with Him a thousand years.

PROTOCOL AND ETIQUETTE BEFORE ROYALTY AND RULERS

Before being presented before earthly royalty, proper etiquette and protocol guidelines are prescribed to those invited to meet a king, queen, president, or other ruler. These directives vary between various providences and kingdoms, but there are always rules that must be followed.

PRESENTING ONESELF TO THE KING OF KINGS

2 TIMOTHY 2:15 (NKJV):

Be diligent to present yourself approved to God, a worker who does not need to be ashamed, rightly dividing the word of truth.

To best present oneself before God, these are a few recommendations to do in preparation for that meeting: accept Yeshua (Jesus) as Lord and Savior, believe and study upon His word as recorded in the Holy Scriptures, repent of all sin, get baptized as a public declaration of faith, live righteously through obeying His commandments as best as possible, enjoy fellowship with fellow believers, do good deeds, and pray to God daily to experience a personal relationship with Him.

JOHN 14:21 (NKJV):

"He who has My commandments AND KEEPS THEM, it is he who loves Me. And he who loves Me will be loved by My Father, and I will love him and manifest Myself to him."

JAMES 1:12 (NKJV):

Blessed is the man who endures temptation; for when he has been approved, he will receive the crown of life which the Lord has promised to those who love Him.

1 JOHN 3:10 (NKJV):

In this the children of God and the children of the devil are manifest: Whoever does not practice righteousness is not of God, nor is he who does not love his brother.

REVELATION 22:14-15 (NKJV):

Blessed are those WHO DO HIS COMMANDMENTS, that they may have the right to the tree of life, and may enter through the gates into the city. But outside are dogs and sorcerers and sexually immoral and murderers and idolaters, and whoever loves and practices a lie.

Do not be deceived with false teachings and empty words of not needing to repent or not needing to keep the commandments of God. Do your best to present yourself to God as one approved.

WORKS-BASED SALVATION:
IS BEING OBEDIENT TO GOD'S COMMANDMENTS AN ATTEMPT TO EARN SALVATION THROUGH THE LAW?

By George Lujack

This article will address the topic of works-based salvation, of which many people incorrectly imply that obeying God's commandments is an act of futility and anyone who keeps His laws is trying to earn his or her salvation through the law.

GALATIANS 3:3-5 (NKJV):

Are you so foolish? Having begun in the Spirit, are you now being made perfect by the flesh? Have you suffered so many things in vain - if indeed it was in vain? Therefore He who supplies the Spirit to you and works miracles among you, does He do it by the works of the law, or by the hearing of faith?

When read alone and out of context, Paul's admonishment to the Galatians can seem like an indictment of the law itself; that anyone who keeps the law is foolish and does not have faith. That is not exactly what Paul said.

The whole context [WITH INTERPRETATION]:

GALATIANS 3:1-4 (NKJV) [WITH INTERPRETATION]:

O foolish Galatians! Who has bewitched you that you should not obey the truth, before whose eyes Yeshua Messiah (Jesus Christ) was clearly portrayed among you as crucified? [THE TRUTH BEING THAT SALVATION COMES THROUGH MESSIAH (CHRIST) NOT THROUGH KEEPING THE LAW]. This only I want to learn from you: Did you receive the Spirit by the works of the law, or by the hearing of faith? [THE HOLY SPIRIT IS RECEIVED IN BELIEVERS BY FAITH, NOT BY KEEPING THE LAW]. Are you so foolish?

Having begun in the Spirit, are you now being made perfect by the flesh? [HAVING BEGUN IN REALIZING THAT SALVATION COMES THROUGH YESHUA (JESUS), ARE YOU NOW FORGETTING THAT FACT AND NOW SEEKING PERFECTION THROUGH YOURSELVES?]. Have you suffered so many things in vain - if indeed it was in vain? [HAVE YOU SUFFERED SO MANY THINGS FOR MESSIAH (CHRIST) IN VAIN, WAS IT IN VAIN - HAVE YOU FORGOTTEN HIM?]

GALATIANS 3:5-9 (NKJV) [WITH INTERPRETATION]:

Therefore He who supplies the Spirit to you and works miracles among you, does He do it by the works of the law, or by the hearing of faith? [DOES YESHUA (JESUS), WHO HAS PERFORMED MIRACLES BY THE HOLY SPIRIT THROUGH YOU, DO THEM BY THE LAW, OR BY FAITH IN HIM?] - just as Abraham *"believed God, and it was accounted to him for righteousness."* Therefore know that only those who are of faith are sons of Abraham. And the Scripture, foreseeing that God would justify the Gentiles by faith, preached the gospel to Abraham beforehand, saying, *"In you all the nations shall be blessed."* So then those who are of faith are blessed with believing Abraham.

GALATIANS 3:10-14 (NKJV) [WITH INTERPRETATION]:

For as many as are of the works of the law are under the curse; for it is written, *"Cursed is everyone who does not continue in all things which are written in the book of the law, to do them."* But that no one is justified by the law in the sight of God is evident [NO ONE CAN BE SAVED BY KEEPING THE LAW], for *"the just shall live by faith."* Yet the law is not of faith, but *"the man who does them shall live by them."* [THE LAW, APART FROM GOD, IS NOT FAITH].

Messiah (Christ) has redeemed us from the curse of the law, having become a curse for us (for it is written, *"Cursed is everyone who hangs on a tree"*), [THE 'CURSE' OF THE LAW IS DEATH. MESSIAH (CHRIST) DIED IN OUR PLACE TO REDEEM AND SAVE US FROM THE CURSE. THE LAW ITSELF IS NOT A CURSE] that the blessing of Abraham might come upon the Gentiles in Messiah Yeshua (Christ Jesus), that we might receive the promise of the Spirit through faith. [THE PROMISE OF THE HOLY SPIRIT IS GIVEN TO THE GENTILES THROUGH FAITH, NOT THROUGH BEING DIRECT DESCENDANTS OF ABRAHAM].

GALATIANS 3:19-22 (NKJV) [WITH INTERPRETATION]:

What purpose then does the law serve? It was added because of transgressions, till the Seed [YESHUA (JESUS)] should come to whom the promise was made; and it was appointed through angels by the hand of a mediator. Now a mediator does not mediate for one only, but God is one.

Is the law then against the promises of God? Certainly not! [THOSE WHO OBEY THE LAW - GOD'S COMMANDMENTS, ARE NOT AGAINST GOD'S PROMISES, BUT ARE OBEDIENT IN FAITH]. For if there had been a law given which could have given life, truly righteousness would have been by the law [NO ONE CAN ATTAIN SALVATION OR BE MADE PERFECTLY RIGHTEOUS BY THE LAW ITSELF]. But the Scripture has confined all under sin [ALL ARE DESCENDED FROM ADAM AND INHERIT ORIGINAL SIN - ROMANS 5:12, AND ALL HAVE SINNED AND HAVE FALLEN SHORT OF THE GLORY OF GOD - ROMANS 3:23], that the promise by faith in Yeshua Messiah (Jesus Christ) might be given to those who believe [THE PROMISE OF SALVATION IS GIVEN TO US BY FAITH IN YESHUA (JESUS), NOT BY KEEPING THE LAW].

In his epistle to the Galatians, Paul was addressing the many Jews who lived among them. These Jews, whose eyes had seen the crucified and resurrected Messiah (Christ) (Galatians 3:1), began to believe in their own righteousness and in making themselves perfect through the law (Galatians 3:3). They had forgotten that their righteousness and their salvation was not a matter of doing the works of the law, but through faith in Messiah (Christ).

Paul reminded the Galatians that miracles performed among them through the Holy Spirit were not manifested as a result of keeping the law, but were supplied by God through faith in Him (Galatians 3:5). Only by having faith in God can prayers be answered, faith healings occur, mountains (obstacles) be moved, and miracles occur. Only by faith in God can we attain salvation.

Should believers discard the law, and rely solely on faith for salvation? Believers should rely solely on faith to attain salvation, but should not discard the law, for in doing so they risk losing their salvation.

MATTHEW 7:21-23 (NKJV) [WITH INTERPRETATION]:

"Not everyone who says to Me, 'Lord, Lord,' shall enter the kingdom of heaven, but he who does the will [OBEYS THE COMMANDMENTS] of My Father in heaven. Many will say to Me in that day, 'Lord, Lord, have we not prophesied in Your name, cast out demons in Your name, AND DONE MANY WONDERS IN YOUR NAME?' And then I will declare to them, 'I never knew you; DEPART FROM ME, YOU WHO PRACTICE LAWLESSNESS!'"

Yeshua (Jesus) proclaims that through faith, many will prophesy, cast out demons, and do many wonders in His name, but because they had 'faith only' and neglected to keep His commandments, He will call them lawless, declare He never knew them, and command them to depart from His presence.

Keeping the law through obeying His commandments does not demonstrate a lack of faith *unless* in doing so one forgets Messiah (Christ). We should never seek to attain perfection in the flesh by keeping the law, as Galatians 3:3 alludes to, but we should keep the law to be as perfect as we can be.

ISAIAH 64:6 (NKJV):

All our righteousnesses are like filthy rags.

MATTHEW 5:48 (NKJV):

"Therefore you shall be PERFECT, just as your Father in heaven is perfect."

1 JOHN 2:4-5 (NKJV):

He who says, "I know Him," and does not keep His commandments, is a liar, and the truth is not in him. But whoever keeps His word, truly the love of God is PERFECTED in him.

Faith and the law are not in conflict with one another, *unless* through self-righteous law keeping, a person negates faith in Messiah (Christ) or if by relying on faith only, a person neglects the law. Faith and law go together.

ROMANS 3:31 (NKJV):

Do we then make void the law through faith? Certainly not! On the contrary, we establish the law.

Works-based salvation has been practiced historically by law-keeping, Messiah-denying Jews and sacrificing, self-suffering Catholics, both of whom err in their motivation in trying to do work for their salvation.

PHILIPPIANS 2:12-13 (NKJV):

WORK OUT YOUR OWN SALVATION with fear and trembling; for it is God who works in you both to will and to do for His good pleasure.

We are commanded to *work out* our salvation. How? By repenting of sin and practicing righteousness through keeping His commandments.

Many end-time lawless ministers have extended the span of those who seek salvation through works by saying that anyone who keeps the law does not have faith and is therefore practicing works-based salvation.

REVELATION 22:12,14 (NKJV):

"And behold, I am coming quickly, and My reward is with Me, to give to every one according to his work. ... Blessed are those who do His commandments, that they may have the right to the tree of life, and may enter through the gates into the city."

The law keepers, those who have faith in Messiah (Christ), will be rewarded for practicing His commandments, for doing good works and they will enter His kingdom. Many non-law keepers who say they have faith in Him and do many wonders in His name, they will be told to depart from Him, because they practice lawlessness (Matthew 7:21-23).

CALL NO MAN RABBI OR FATHER

By George Lujack

Most Messianic Judaism and Catholic religious organizations have spiritual teachers who go by the titles 'Rabbi' and 'Father.' This article will analyze Yeshua's (Jesus') statement against calling anyone by these titles, will examine other titles, and will address the practical application of His words.

MATTHEW 23:8-10 (NKJV):

"But you, do not be called 'Rabbi'; for One is your Teacher, the Messiah (Christ), and you are all brethren. Do not call anyone on earth your father; for One is your Father, He who is in heaven. And do not be called leaders*; for One is your Leader, the Messiah (Christ)."

*Some Scripture translations use the word 'teacher,' but the proper translation is 'leader.' Those who preach and teach God's word are teachers; teachers are obviously those who teach.

MATTHEW 5:19 (NKJV):

Whoever therefore breaks one of the least of these commandments, and TEACHES men so, shall be called least in the kingdom of heaven; but whoever does and TEACHES them, he shall be called great in the kingdom of heaven.

Yeshua (Jesus) said, "Do not call any man on earth 'father,' or 'rabbi.'"

father:

Often as a title or form of address, a priest.[16]

rabbi:

A person appointed as a Jewish religious leader.[17]

Judaism currently rejects their Messiah, Yeshua (Jesus) and His teachings, so it is understandable that they continue to persist in calling their teachers 'rabbis.' Messianics and Catholics, who have accepted Yeshua (Jesus) and His teachings, are without excuse in calling their religious teachers 'rabbi' and 'father.' When Yeshua (Jesus) spoke against calling no man rabbi, father, or leader, He was speaking in the context of calling no *religious male teacher* a rabbi, father, or leader, for we are all brethren and we are all under One Father, God, and One Leader, Messiah (Christ).

CATHOLIC OBJECTIONS

Catholics call their spiritual teacher priests 'father,' and have come up with many excuses for doing so, in spite of the words Yeshua (Jesus) spoke.

"A male parent is called 'father,' the same way we call our priests 'father.'"

"Scripture speaks of Abraham being the 'father' of many nations."

GENESIS 17:4-5 (NKJV):

As for Me, behold, My covenant is with you, and you shall be a father of many nations. No longer shall your name be called Abram, but your name shall be Abraham; for I have made you a father of many nations.

Catholics who defend using the term 'father' to address their priests are intentionally disobeying Yeshua (Jesus) by using an out of context application of what He was saying. Of course we can call our biological dads 'father,' for they are our earthly biological fathers. We can call Abraham the father of Israel, for he is the biological father of Israel, from whom the whole nation sprang. We can call America's founders the Founding 'Fathers,' for they were fathers of the new nation called America. Yeshua (Jesus) clearly spoke of not calling any *spiritual teacher* father, rabbi, or leader. While Yeshua (Jesus) didn't speak against calling anyone 'reverend,' the same principles from His statements apply.

reverend:

used as a title or form of address to members of the clergy.[18]

Origin: Late Middle English, Old French, or Latin: 'person to be revered.'

We should not call anyone reverend, for there is One to be revered, God. What then should we call spiritual teachers and what title should they go by? 'Brother,' 'Minister,' or 'Teacher' is sufficient.

brother:

A male fellow Christian or member of a religious order.[19]

minister:

A member of the clergy.[20]

Origin: Middle English, Old French, Latin: 'servant.'

pastor:

A minister of a church.[21]

teacher:

A person who teaches; causes another to learn through explanation, information, and instruction.[22][23]

THE MARRIAGE COVENANT

MARRIAGE, VOWS, ANNULMENTS, DIVORCE, FORNICATION, ADULTERY, REMARRIAGE, AND OTHER SEXUAL UNIONS

By George Lujack

This article will discuss the marriage covenant and all the associated issues regarding marriage and other sexual unions: vows, annulments, divorce, fornication, adultery, polygamy, and abominable sex - homosexuality.

GOD MADE US MALE AND FEMALE TO BE HUSBAND AND WIFE

GENESIS 2:18,21-24 (NKJV) [WITH INTERPRETATION]:

And YHWH (the Lord) God said, "It is not good that man should be alone; I will make him a helper comparable to him." ...

And YHWH (the Lord) God caused a deep sleep to fall on Adam, and he slept; and He took one of his ribs, and closed up the flesh in its place. Then the rib, which YHWH (the Lord) God had taken from man He made into a woman, and He brought her to the man.

And Adam said:

"This is now bone of my bones and flesh of my flesh;

She shall be called Woman, because she was taken out of Man."

Therefore a man shall leave his father and mother and be joined to his wife, and they shall become one flesh [THROUGH SEXUAL INTERCOURSE]. And they were both naked, THE MAN AND HIS WIFE, and were not ashamed.

THE LAW OF MARRIAGE

DEUTERONOMY 22:13-21 (NKJV) [WITH INTERPRETATION]:

If any man takes a wife, and goes in to her, and detests her, and charges her with shameful conduct, and brings a bad name on her, and says,

'I took this woman, and when I came to her I found she was not a virgin,' then the father and mother of the young woman shall take and bring out the evidence of the young woman's virginity to the elders of the city at the gate. And the young woman's father shall say to the elders, 'I gave my daughter to this man as wife, and he detests her. Now he has charged her with shameful conduct, saying, "I found

DEUTERONOMY 22:13-21 (NKJV) [WITH INTERPRETATION] - continued:

your daughter was not a virgin," and yet these are the evidences [BLOOD-STAINED BEDSHEET] of my daughter's virginity.' And they shall spread the cloth [BLOOD-STAINED BEDSHEET] before the elders of the city. Then the elders of that city shall take that man and punish him; and they shall fine him one hundred shekels of silver and give them to the father of the young woman, because he has brought a bad name on a virgin of Israel. And she shall be his wife; he cannot divorce her all his days.

But if the thing is true, and evidences of virginity are not found for the young woman, then they shall bring out the young woman to the door of her father's house, and the men of her city shall stone her to death with stones, because she has done a disgraceful thing in Israel, to play the harlot in her father's house. So you shall put away the evil from among you.

DEUTERONOMY 24:1-4 (NKJV) [WITH INTERPRETATION]:

When a man takes [HAS SEXUAL INTERCOURSE WITH] a [BETROTHED] wife and marries her, and it happens that she finds no favor in his eyes because he has found some uncleanness in her [SHE WAS NOT A VIRGIN - DEUTERONOMY 22:14], and he writes her a certificate of divorce, puts it in her hand, and sends her out of his house, when she has departed from his house, and goes and becomes another man's wife, if the latter husband detests her and writes her a certificate of divorce, puts it in her hand, and sends her out of his house, or if the latter husband dies who took her as his wife, then her former husband who divorced her must not take her back to be his wife after she has been defiled; for that is an abomination before YHWH (the Lord), and you shall not bring sin on the land which YHWH (the Lord) your God is giving you as an inheritance.

THREE TYPES OF DIVORCE:
- FOR FORNICATION WITH THE RIGHT TO REMARRY
- FOR ADULTERY AND ALL OTHER CAUSES
- REPENTANT DIVORCE FROM AN UNLAWFUL UNION

DIVORCE FOR FORNICATION (A CANCELLED MARRIAGE)

fornication:

Sexual intercourse between people not married to each other.[24]

God's standard for a proper marriage is much greater and purer than what marriage has become under the laws of man. In sexually 'liberated' (sexually sinning) Westernized cultures, premarital sex (fornication) has been normalized. Young couples preserving their virginity until their marriage day is the extreme exception, not the norm. Cultural, moral, and societal norms may change, but God does not change (Hebrews 13:8).

When a man exchanges marriage vows with his betrothed wife (fiancée) and then consummates the marriage through sexual intercourse and takes her virginity, he cannot divorce her (for the purposes of becoming another man's wife - Deuteronomy 24:1-2) all the days of his life. She will be his wife all the days of his life.

When a man exchanges marriage vows with his betrothed wife (fiancée) and then consummates the marriage through sexual intercourse, believing that his betrothed wife (fiancée) was a virgin, but he discovers through initial sexual intercourse that she deceived him and she was not a virgin, then he may divorce her (annul the marriage vow) and both he and his divorced betrothed wife (fiancée) are free to marry someone else (Deuteronomy 24:1-2).

Obviously, if a man knows that his betrothed wife (fiancée) is not a virgin, because he himself has committed fornication (premarital sex) with her or if she has confessed to him that she was not a virgin, then when he exchanges marriage vows with his betrothed wife (fiancée) and then consummates the marriage through sexual intercourse, he cannot divorce her (cancel the marriage vow), because he knew she was not a virgin when he took her to be his wife.

The betrothal (espousal) period for a marriage varies, as there is no set time for it. Typically it can last a few months to a year, but it can go longer. Jacob agreed to be a servant for Leban for seven years, in an agreement to have Leban's daughter Rachel become his wife, so their betrothal (espousal) period was seven years and a week (Genesis 29:18-28).

Under the law, if a man's betrothed wife (fiancée) was discovered to have engaged in fornication (premarital sexual intercourse) with another man, before or during the betrothal period, the man had the right to either stone to death his betrothed wife (fiancée), give her a certificate of divorce, or forgive her virginity deception and keep her to be his wife.

Since we are not living under the law during this current age of grace, the ordinances for breaking the law - the death penalty, would obviously not be permissible today. A man is not to stone his betrothed wife (fiancée) if he discovers that she engaged in fornication (premarital sex) with another man during their betrothal period or if he discovers through initial sexual intercourse that she was not a virgin. Yet today, in some Muslim countries, they still practice stoning women for fornication and adultery.

JOSEPH WAS GOING TO DIVORCE MARY FOR FORNICATION

<u>MATTHEW 1:18-25 (NKJV) [WITH INTERPRETATION]:</u>

Now the birth of Yeshua Messiah (Jesus Christ) was as follows: After His mother Mary was betrothed to Joseph, before they came together [THROUGH SEXUAL INTERCOURSE], she was found with child of the Holy Spirit. Then Joseph her husband, being a just [MERCIFUL] man, and not wanting to make her a public example [BY STONING HER – DEUTERONOMY 22:20-21], was minded to put her away secretly [GIVE HER A CERTIFICATE OF DIVORCE - DEUTERONOMY 24:1-2]. But while he thought about these things, behold, an angel of the Lord appeared to him in a dream, saying, "Joseph, son of David, do not be afraid to take to you Mary your wife, for [SHE IS STILL A VIRGIN AND] that which is conceived in her is of the Holy Spirit. And she will bring forth a Son, and you shall call His name Yeshua (Jesus), for He will save His people from their sins."

So all this was done that it might be fulfilled which was spoken by the Lord through the prophet, saying: *"Behold, the virgin shall be with child, and bear a Son, and they shall call His name Immanuel,"* **which is translated, "God with us."**

Then Joseph, being aroused from sleep, did as the angel of the Lord commanded him and took to him his wife, and did not know her [CARNALLY THROUGH SEXUAL INTERCOURSE] till she had brought forth her firstborn Son [YESHUA (JESUS)].

Joseph believed that Mary not only fornicated (had premarital sex with another man) during their betrothal, but that she was also pregnant with the child of another man. After this discovery, he had no intention of still marrying Mary and raising some other man's child, nor did he want to see her stoned, so he sought to quietly divorce her for her sin of fornication and send her on her way. An angel of the Lord informed Joseph, through a dream, that Mary was not guilty of the sin of fornication, was still a virgin, and that which was conceived in her was of the Holy Spirit. Mary was to be a surrogate mother and give birth to the Savior of the world and Joseph was instructed to take her to be his wife. Joseph knew Mary carnally as his wife *after* Yeshua (Jesus) was born.

YESHUA'S (JESUS') EXCEPTION CLAUSE FOR FORNICATION

MATTHEW 5:32 (KJV) [WITH INTERPRETATION]:

"But I say unto you, that whoever shall put away his wife, saving for the cause of fornication [PREMARITAL SEX], causes her to commit adultery: and whosoever shall marry her that is [OTHERWISE] divorced [FOR ADULTERY OR ANY REASON OTHER THAN FORNICATION] commits adultery."

MATTHEW 19:9 (KJV) [WITH INTERPRETATION]:

"And I say unto you, whoever shall put away his wife, except it be for fornication [PREMARITAL SEX], and shall marry another [WOMAN], commits adultery: and whoever marries her which is put away [FOR ADULTERY OR ANY REASON OTHER THAN FORNICATION] does commit adultery."

Subsequent English translations have watered down Yeshua's (Jesus') exception clause, changing 'fornication' to 'sexual immorality.' The exception is for fornication only (premarital sex) and a marriage must be cancelled, *if it is to be cancelled*, on the day the vow was made according to the law of marriage (Deuteronomy 22:13-21, 24:1-4) and the law of vows (Numbers 30; Deuteronomy 23:21-23).

THE LAW OF VOWS

A marriage is consecrated by a vow, a solemn oath witnessed by God. God is omnipresent. He sees everything we do (Psalm 33:13-14) and hears every word that is uttered from our lips. We will give account for every word we speak. We will be justified by our words and we will be condemned by them (Deuteronomy 23:21-23; Zechariah 8:17; Matthew 12:36-37; Romans 3:4).

IF A VOW IS CANCELLED, INCLUDING THE MARRIAGE VOW, IT MUST BE CANCELLED ON THE DAY IT WAS MADE OR IT STANDS

In order for a vow to be cancelled, so that one is released from the vow, it MUST be cancelled on the day it was made. This is true of all vows, including the marriage vow. There is an exception for the marriage vow for which it CANNOT be cancelled. A marriage vow may be cancelled for fornication, BUT it CANNOT be cancelled if a man marries a virgin and he takes her virginity. Obviously, if a man takes a woman's virginity, he cannot give it back to her, so he CANNOT cancel a marriage vow after he takes his wife's virginity. If a man marries a wife and then takes her virginity, she will be his wife ALL THE DAYS OF HIS LIFE and he cannot then cancel the marriage vow that he has made with her (Deuteronomy 22:19).

DEUTERONOMY 23:21-23 (NKJV):

When you make a vow to YHWH (the Lord) your God, you shall not delay to pay it; for YHWH (the Lord) your God will surely require it of you, and it would be sin to you. But if you abstain from vowing, it shall not be sin to you. That which has gone from your lips you shall keep and perform, for you voluntarily vowed to YHWH (the Lord) your God what you have promised with your mouth.

NUMBERS 30:2-5 (NKJV):

If a man makes a vow to YHWH (the Lord), or swears an oath to bind himself by some agreement, he shall not break his word; he shall do according to all that proceeds out of his mouth.

Or if a woman makes a vow to YHWH (the Lord), and binds herself by some agreement while in her father's house in her youth, and her father hears her vow and the agreement by which she has bound herself, and her father holds his peace, THEN ALL HER VOWS SHALL STAND, and every agreement with which she has bound herself SHALL STAND.

But if her father OVERRULES HER ON THE DAY HE HEARS, THEN NONE OF HER VOWS NOR HER AGREEMENTS BY WHICH SHE HAS BOUND HERSELF SHALL STAND; and YHWH (the Lord) WILL RELEASE HER, because her father overruled her.

NUMBERS 30:6-8 (NKJV):

If indeed she takes a husband, while bound by her vows or by a rash utterance from her lips by which she bound herself, and her husband hears it, AND MAKES NO RESPONSE TO HER ON THE DAY THAT HE HEARS, THEN HER VOWS SHALL STAND and her agreements by which she bound herself SHALL STAND. But if her husband OVERRULES HER ON THE DAY THAT HE HEARS IT, HE SHALL MAKE VOID HER VOW which she took and what she uttered with her lips, by which she bound herself, and YHWH (the Lord) WILL RELEASE HER.

According to the law of marriage and the law of vows, the ONLY way that a man and woman can be released from a marriage vow, to have that vow cancelled with the right of both of them to marry another, is if a man marries a wife who he believed was a virgin, goes into her through initial sexual intercourse and discovers that she was not a virgin, then he can cancel the marriage vow ON THE DAY IT WAS MADE for fornication (premarital sex).

NUMBERS 30:10-12 (NKJV) [WITH INTERPRETATION]:

If she vowed in her husband's house, or bound herself by an agreement with an oath, and her husband heard it, and made no response to her and did not overrule her, then all her vows shall stand [INCLUDING THE MARRIAGE VOW], and every agreement by which she bound herself SHALL STAND.

But if her husband truly made them [OR THE MARRIAGE VOW] VOID ON THE DAY HE HEARD THEM, then whatever proceeded from her lips concerning her vows or concerning the agreement binding her, it SHALL NOT STAND; her husband has made them void, and YHWH (the Lord) will release her [FROM HER VOWS, INCLUDING THE MARRIAGE VOW].

A marriage vow may be cancelled by a husband, but only for fornication (premarital sex) and then it must be cancelled on the day it was made or the marriage vow stands.

DIVORCE FOR ADULTERY AND ALL OTHER CAUSES

adultery:

Voluntary sexual intercourse between a married person and a person who is not his or her spouse.[25]

There are some who believe that divorce is never permissible under any circumstance and others believe that a divorce on the grounds of adultery gives the victim of adultery the right to dissolve the marriage and remarry someone else. A married woman is bound to the marriage vow that she made with her husband and she cannot lawfully, under God's law, divorce or be divorced from him and marry someone else as long as he is alive. Even if a husband commits adultery, leaves his wife, marries another woman, and has nothing more to do with his former wife, the divorced woman is STILL under the marriage vow and cannot remarry. If she does remarry, or if she has sexual intercourse while her original husband lives, she is committing adultery with whoever she has sexual relations with. The marriage vow is not conditional based on the actions of a spouse.

MATTHEW 5:32 (KJV) [WITH INTERPRETATION]:

"But I say unto you, That whoever shall put away his wife, saving for the cause of fornication [PREMARITAL SEX], CAUSES HER TO COMMIT ADULTERY: and whosoever shall marry her that is [OTHERWISE] divorced [FOR ANY REASON OTHER THAN FORNICATION] commits adultery."

A man who divorces his wife CAUSES HER TO COMMIT ADULTERY, because she will be committing adultery with whoever she has sexual intercourse with, whether through remarriage or not, if she has sex with any man while her husband lives. She will be breaking her vow that she made, *'till death do us part,'* (not till divorce do us part), and she will stand as a covenant breaker and an adulteress before God in her judgment.

ROMANS 7:1-4 (NKJV):

Or do you not know, brethren (for I speak to those who know the law), that the law has dominion over a man as long as he lives? For the woman who has a husband IS BOUND BY THE LAW TO HER HUSBAND AS LONG AS HE LIVES. But if the husband dies, she is released from the law of her husband. So then if, while her husband lives, she marries another man, SHE WILL BE CALLED AN ADULTRESS; but if her husband dies, she is free from that law, so that she is no adulteress, though she has married another man.

A divorced woman who gets married to another man while her original husband lives, in this age, is generally called a 'remarried' woman. A divorced woman who marries another man while her original husband lives, in her judgment before God, will be called an adulteress.

1 CORINTHIANS 7:10-11 (NKJV):

Now to the married I command, YET NOT I BUT THE LORD: A wife is not to depart from her husband. But even if she does depart, LET HER REMAIN UNMARRIED or be reconciled to her husband. And a husband is not to divorce his wife.

It is a DIRECT COMMAND FROM THE LORD that if a woman is married and she does depart (due to adultery, financial neglect, physical abuse, or for any other reason), SHE IS TO REMAIN UNMARRIED or be reconciled to her original husband. Remarriage, after a divorce from a lawful valid marriage, is NOT an option for a woman while her original husband lives.

1 CORINTHIANS 7:39 (NKJV):

A wife is bound by law as long as her husband lives; but if her husband dies, she is at liberty to be married to whom she wishes, only in the Lord.

A wife is bound by the law of marriage and the vow that she has made, as long as her husband lives - until the death of either herself or her husband. If she marries another man while he lives, regardless of what her original husband has done or whether he has divorced her and went on to marry someone else himself, she commits adultery every time she engages in sex in a remarriage or with anyone else who is not her original husband.

MARRIAGE IS A COVENANT, NOT A CONTRACT THAT CAN BE DISSOLVED

PROVERBS 6:32 (NKJV):

Whoever commits adultery with a woman lacks understanding; He who does so destroys his own soul.

COVENANT BREAKERS

The one covenant that most people enter into sometime during their lives is the marriage covenant.

MALACHI 2:14 (NKJV):

YHWH (the Lord) has been witness between you and the wife of your youth, with whom you have dealt treacherously; Yet she is your companion and wife BY COVENANT.

ROMANS 1:31 (KJV):

Without understanding, COVENANT BREAKERS, without natural affection, implacable, unmerciful.

A man who divorces his wife to marry other woman is a covenant breaker who not only commits adultery with another woman, but *he causes* his original wife to break her covenant and commit adultery if she ever has sex with a man who is not her original husband or has sexual intercourse in a remarriage. A man who puts away his wife through divorce to marry another woman deals treacherously with the covenant wife of his youth and will not be held guiltless for his original wife's adultery *that he causes* if she engages in sex with other men or gets remarried.

Men also deal treacherously with the wives of their youth when they commit adultery against their wives with mistresses and then return home to their wives, and wives deal treacherously with their husbands when they commit adultery against their husbands with other men and then return home to their husbands.

Even if a husband does not keep his marriage covenant, the covenant remains and a woman is obligated to keep her covenant vow to him and not get married to another man while he lives.

MARK 10:11-12 (NKJV):

Yeshua (Jesus) said to them, "Whoever divorces his wife and marries another commits adultery against her. And if a woman divorces her husband and marries another, she commits adultery."

A woman who divorces her husband to marry another man commits ongoing adultery in either her remarriage or by whomever else she has sexual relations with.

FORNICATION VS. ADULTERY

fornication:
Sexual intercourse between people not married to each other.

adultery:
Voluntary sexual intercourse between a married person and a person who is not his or her spouse.

When a man or woman goes to court to divorce his or her spouse, and it is due to infidelity, an appeal is made to the court to divorce on the grounds of adultery, not on the grounds of fornication. Once fully lawfully married, a husband or wife cannot commit fornication, but can only commit adultery.

Many who divorce on the grounds of adultery by their spouse claim the godly right to remarry, calling a divorce over adultery a 'biblical divorce' with the right to lawfully remarry before God, but such a right does not exist. Adultery does NOT cancel a marriage. Husband and wife, once lawfully married, are husband and wife till the death of either spouse. The right to cancel a marriage is restricted for one reason and one reason only: fornication, that is if a man believes he is marrying a virgin, but discovers she is not a virgin during the betrothal (espousal) period or during initial sexual intercourse.

The right to divorce and remarry has been expanded since the Protestant reformation in the 1500's to include adultery, but this is NOT God's law. Any woman who marries after a valid marriage of which her original husband is still living commits adultery and any man who marries a divorced woman commits adultery with the divorced woman he marries.

A woman who is put away, separated, or divorced, is the put away, separated, or divorced wife of her original husband. With this in mind, marriage should be viewed as a permanent state of being, and a divorced woman should be viewed as the divorced spouse of her original husband, who is not free to remarry, unless her original husband dies. Therefore terms such as 'ex-husband,' or 'ex-wife,' do not appear in Scripture, as one cannot have an ex-spouse any more than one can have an ex-brother, ex-sister, ex-father, or ex-mother. One can only have a deceased spouse through death. As a spouse lives there are no such things as ex-husbands or ex-wives, as marriage remains till death.

CHURCHES DO NOT HAVE AUTHORITY TO ANNUL MARRIAGES

Notably, the Catholic Church takes the position that it has authority over the Scriptures and that it has the authority to annul marriages. Its position is that any marriage outside of the Catholic Church can be considered invalid and can therefore be annulled. Additionally, marriages within the Catholic Church can be annulled, as if they had never taken place. Of course there is corruption involved in such annulments made within the Catholic Church, as the husband typically pays a large fee to the Catholic Church to have his lawful marriage annulled.

DIVORCE BY ANOTHER NAME, 'ANNULMENT,' IS STILL DIVORCE

It is not the Catholic Church, or any other church, that brings together and sanctifies a marriage; God does. A marriage is a marriage when there is a marriage vow made and it is consecrated through sexual intercourse.

Ideally, a man marries a virgin and after exchanging marriage vows, goes into her carnally through sexual intercourse, breaks her hymen, and the husband and wife seal their marriage in blood. Any annulment of a lawfully consecrated marriage, by the Catholic Church or any other church or institution, is still a divorce.

MATTHEW 19:4-6 (NKJV):

And Yeshua (Jesus) answered and said to them, "Have you not read that He who made *them* at the beginning *'made them male and female,'* and said, *'For this reason a man shall leave his father and mother and be joined to his wife, and the two shall become one flesh'*? So then, they are no longer two but one flesh. Therefore what God has joined together, let not man separate."

A man or woman in a bad marriage may not believe they were joined together by God, but once the marriage is valid, it cannot be undone or annulled. This is one reason that a man or woman is commanded to not be unequally yoked, in marriage or other relationships, with unbelievers. If a man or woman is lawfully married to an unbeliever, that marriage is valid and cannot be cancelled.

EXCUSES, EXCUSES, EXCUSES...

Not everyone has the right, under God's laws, to lawfully marry. Children cannot marry, brothers and sisters cannot marry, a divorced woman cannot marry another man while her husband lives, a man cannot marry a divorced woman, a married man cannot divorce his wife to marry another woman, a man cannot marry a man, and a woman cannot marry a woman. Many will twist Scripture to justify remarriage and many women who find themselves divorced cannot accept the truth of the permanency of marriage, which is until death, and will seek remarriage. It is understandable that a woman who is a victim of a bad marriage, who finds herself free from it and divorced, will seek another marriage with another man for emotional / financial support and to enjoy the intimacy of sex. Yet it is a command of God that a woman can have only one husband at a time, that she cannot divorce her husband or be divorced from her husband and marry another man while her original husband lives.

1 CORINTHIANS 7:12-16 (NKJV):

But to the rest I, NOT THE LORD, say: If any brother has a wife who does not believe, and she is willing to live with him, let him not divorce her. And a woman who has a husband who does not believe, if he is willing to live with her, let her not divorce him. For the unbelieving husband is sanctified by the wife, and the unbelieving wife is sanctified by the husband; otherwise your children would be unclean, but now they are holy. But if the unbeliever departs, let him depart; a brother or a sister is not under bondage in such cases. But God has called us to peace. For how do you know, O wife, whether you will save your husband? Or how do you know, O husband, whether you will save your wife?

Many have read and twisted the words of Paul in 1 Corinthians 7:12-16 to mean that if a husband or wife has an unbelieving spouse, and the unbelieving spouse departs, then the believer who has been departed from can divorce, is not under the 'bondage' of marriage, and is free to remarry.

The Apostle Paul cannot contradict or overrule Yeshua (Jesus) who said that WHOEVER (believer or unbeliever) divorces his wife, except for fornication, CAUSES HER to commit adultery AND WHOEVER (believer or unbeliever) marries her who is divorced commits adultery (Matthew 5:32). Although marriage can feel like bondage, it is not, and marriages between believers and unbelievers are valid. If a husband or a wife is in a bad marriage to an unbeliever who wishes to depart the marriage, the husband or wife is not bound to stay in such a marriage. BUT, the wife who is unbound from a bad marriage MUST REMAIN SINGLE (1 Corinthians 7:10-11) and is NOT FREE TO REMARRY (Romans 7:1-3; 1 Corinthians 7:39).

1 CORINTHIANS 7:12-16 (NKJV) [WITH INTERPRETATION]:

But to the rest I [MY ADVICE], NOT THE LORD, say: If any brother has a wife who does not believe, and she is willing to live with him, let him not divorce her. And a woman who has a husband who does not believe, if he is willing to live with her, let her not divorce him. For the unbelieving husband is sanctified [THROUGH MARRIAGE] by the wife, and the unbelieving wife is sanctified [IN MARRIAGE] by the husband [THE MARRIAGE OF AN UNBELIEVER WITH A BELIEVER IS SANCTIFIED]; otherwise your children would be unclean [BASTARDS - CHILDREN BORN OUT OF WEDLOCK], but now they are holy [BORN OF UNEQUALLY YOKED, BUT LAWFULLY MARRIED PARENTS]. But if the unbeliever departs, let him depart; a brother or a sister is not under bondage [UNDER RESPONSIBILITY TO TRACK DOWN A FLEEING SPOUSE] in such cases. But God has called us to [LIVE IN] peace. For how do you know, O wife, whether you will save your husband? Or how do you know, O husband, whether you will save your wife? [HOW DO YOU KNOW O HUSBAND OR WIFE, THAT BY CHASING AFTER YOUR FLEEING SPOUSE YOU WILL SAVE YOUR MARRIAGE?]

Nowhere does Paul proclaim that a wife who is "not under bondage" (1 Corinthians 7:15) is free to remarry. She is not under bondage to remain in a bad marriage, and can live peaceably as one single (1 Corinthians 7:10-11), but she cannot marry another man unless her departed unbelieving husband dies (1 Corinthians 7:39).

1 CORINTHIANS 7:39 (NKJV):

A wife is bound by law as long as her husband lives; but if her husband dies, she is at liberty to be married to whom she wishes, only in the Lord.

A woman who is lawfully married is 'bound' by the marriage law as long as her husband lives and is only free to marry again if he dies.

IS REMARRIAGE ACCEPTABLE FOR DIVORCE, BUT NOT 'PUT AWAY' SEPARATION?

There are some King James Version only proponents who cite Matthew 19:9 and take a magnifying glass to the law of marriage, saying that if you marry a woman who is "put away," this is adultery, but a woman who is properly divorced with divorce papers, she has a God-approved right be remarried and this is not adultery.

MATTHEW 19:9 (KJV):

And I say unto you, "Whosoever shall PUT AWAY his wife, except it be for fornication, and shall marry another, committeth adultery: and whoso marrieth her WHICH IS PUT AWAY doth commit adultery."

The KJV in another verse disputes the falsehood being concocted by the King James only crowd:

MATTHEW 5:31-32 (NKJV):

"It hath been said, Whosoever shall PUT AWAY his wife, let him GIVE HER A WRITING OF DIVORCEMENT: But I say unto you, That whosoever shall put away his wife, saving for the cause of fornication, causeth her to commit adultery: and whosoever shall marry her that is DIVORCED committeth adultery."

So in either case, whether a man marries a woman who is put away (separated) from her husband without divorce papers, or a man marries a divorced woman with divorce papers, he enters a forbidden adulterous marriage and commits adultery with her.

CAN A SPOUSE OF A BINDING MARRIAGE LAWFULLY DIVORCE?

DEUTERONOMY 22:19,29 (NKJV):

And she shall be his wife; he cannot divorce her all his days. …

he shall not be permitted to divorce her all his days.

MALACHI 2:16 (NKJV):

"For YHWH (the Lord) God of Israel says that He hates divorce, for it covers one's garment with violence," says YHWH (the Lord) of hosts. "Therefore take heed to your spirit, that you do not deal treacherously."

Although God hates divorce, divorce is permissible for certain reasons. Although God hates divorce, He stopped short of calling all divorce sin. There often are very valid reasons for divorce. A husband or wife of a lawful valid marriage is never to divorce for a frivolous or selfish reason, which would be dealing treacherously with a spouse, but only for reasons of self-preservation, when danger to one's self becomes evident and obvious.

ISAIAH 50:1 (NKJV) [WITH INTERPRETATION]:

Thus says YHWH (the Lord):

"Where is the certificate of your mother's [ISRAEL'S] divorce, whom I have put away? … And for your transgressions your mother [ISRAEL] has been put away."

JEREMIAH 3:8-9 (NKJV):

Then I saw that for all the causes for which backsliding Israel had committed adultery, I had put her away and given her a certificate of divorce; yet her treacherous sister Judah did not fear, but went and played the harlot also. So it came to pass, through her casual harlotry, that she defiled the land and committed adultery with stones and trees.

YHWH (the Lord) Himself divorced Israel for spiritual adultery, idolatry with carved images of stone and wood. YHWH (the Lord) is a jealous God and He could not stand to see His chosen people Israel making idols of stone and wood in spiritual adultery against Him, so He divorced them.

If a husband or wife has a cheating spouse who is committing adultery and becomes aware of the adultery and confronts the spouse over it, and the spouse continues in adultery AND wishes to continue in sexual relations with his or her spouse as well, this is a cause for separation and / or divorce. A husband or wife cannot accept the adultery of a spouse. A husband or wife should not share in the adultery of a cheating spouse, nor share in the possible sexually transmitted diseases acquired by the cheating spouse.

If a wife is married to a husband who is a serial abuser, who likes to beat up and control his wife in unwarranted jealousy fits of rage, then the abused wife should separate, divorce, and seek safety for her physical protection.

If a husband is married to a deceitful wife, who plans to have him murdered to collect his life insurance, then for the safety of his life the husband should separate, divorce, and seek safety from his murderous-minded wife. If a husband is married to a wife who wants out of the marriage, and is willing to bear false witness against her husband, falsely claiming he hits her, the children, or sexually abuses the children, then the husband should separate before he gets into legal trouble through false allegations. If a wife is married to a husband and she discovers that he is a pedophile and is sexually molesting their own children, then she should flee, separate, and divorce for the safety of her children.

HEBREWS 13:4 (NKJV):

Marriage is honorable among all, and the bed undefiled; but fornicators and adulterers God will judge.

Persons who divorce for these valid reasons of safety will not be held accountable for divorcing their spouses, but the adulterers and abusers who did not honor their marriage will answer to God for dealing treacherously with their spouses. Yet women with legitimate valid reasons to divorce are still under their marriage vow and are not free to remarry, even if they are victims of abuse or adultery.

CAN DIVORCED MEN REMARRY?

A divorced woman definitely cannot remarry while her original husband lives, according to God's marriage law, and if she does she will be judged by God to be an adulteress, as this is repeatedly confirmed throughout Scripture. A question arises as to whether or not divorced men can remarry.

Scripture is clear in stating that whoever marries a divorced woman commits adultery, but what about whoever marries a divorced man? Is this always adultery as well? This is a grayer part of the marriage law that will be explained.

MATTHEW 19:9 (KJV) [WITH INTERPRETATION]:

"And I say unto you, whoever shall put away his wife, except it be for fornication [PREMARITAL SEX], and shall marry another [WOMAN], commits adultery..."

MARK 10:11 (NKJV):

Yeshua (Jesus) said to them, "Whoever divorces his wife and marries another commits adultery against her."

LUKE 16:18 (NKJV):

"Whoever divorces his wife and marries another commits adultery."

A man CANNOT divorce his wife *for the purpose* of marrying another woman or for hoping to marry another woman in the future. If he does, this is adultery *and* he causes his original wife to sin if she ever has sex with another man while he, her original husband, lives.

WHAT IF a wife departs from her husband and *she* marries another man, or if she just divorces him and wishes to not continue in the marriage with him? In this case, is the divorced man free to remarry?

1 CORINTHIANS 7:26-28 (NKJV) [WITH INTERPRETATION]:

I suppose therefore that this is good because of the present distress - that it is good for A MAN to remain as he is: Are you bound [MARRIED] to a wife? Do not seek to be loosed [DIVORCED]. Are you loosed [DIVORCED] from a wife? Do not seek a [NEW] wife. But even if you do marry [SOMEONE ELSE], YOU HAVE NOT SINNED;

A man, if he in good conscience has done no wrong to his wife and has done all that he can to prevent an adulterous-minded or covenant-breaking wife from departing from him, then it will not be a sin for him to marry another wife. However, the wife who is divorced from him IS STILL HIS WIFE and will remain his wife till death, even if she marries another man. In the case that she marries another man, she is still his wife who is living in adultery with another man.

The standards for men and women in marriage are different. Men and women are not equals in marriage, which explains the permissiveness of polygamy in Scripture.

POLYGAMY

It is written in God's law that a man could have more than one wife at a time, but a woman could only be married to one husband at a time. It would simply be inconceivable if, hypothetically speaking, some of the saints in Scripture had wives who were able to flee from them or divorce them, that these men would have remained celibate for the rest of their lives. Men of Scripture often had numerous wives simultaneously and God NEVER condemned polygamy as adultery. Polygamy is NOT adultery, because God is the same yesterday, today, and forever (Hebrews 13:8). If polygamy were adultery today, then it would also have been adultery yesterday, in Scripture times past.

DEUTERONOMY 21:15-17 (NKJV):

If a man has two wives, one loved and the other unloved, and they have borne him children, both the loved and the unloved, and if the firstborn son is of her who is unloved, then it shall be, on the day he bequeaths his possessions to his sons, that he must not bestow firstborn status on the son of the loved wife in preference to the son of the unloved, the true firstborn. But he shall acknowledge the son of the

DEUTERONOMY 21:15-17 (NKJV) - continued:

unloved wife as the firstborn by giving him a double portion of all that he has, for he is the beginning of his strength; the right of the firstborn is his.

If polygamy were adultery, then God needs to correct His law. Deuteronomy 21:15-17 should therefore read: *If a man has two wives, the first wife is his wife and the second woman who he calls his wife he commits adultery with.* Scripture DOES NOT SAY THAT!

Polygamy is still practiced throughout the world, mostly in Middle East and African nations, but has been outlawed in most Western Christian nations.

GENESIS 29:31 (NKJV):

When YHWH (the Lord) saw that Leah was unloved, He opened her womb; but Rachel was barren.

Jacob married two sisters, Leah and Rachel (Genesis 29:21-28). God never said a word about Jacob being in a polygamous marriage, but He did punish Jacob for not loving Leah, by blessing Leah with more children than Rachel. Jacob, as well as Abraham, King David, and Moses - the prophet formally given God's laws, all had multiple wives in polygamy. It is not God's laws that forbid polygamy, but man's laws.

"And the two shall become one flesh" - Genesis 2:24, is often cited as a verse to oppose polygamy, as the two (not three) shall become one flesh. What the phrase actually means is that the two, a husband and wife, shall become one flesh (through sexual intercourse), not spiritually one flesh. So the men in Scripture who had two or more wives, would go into them and become one flesh (have sexual intercourse) with one wife, then afterward go into wife number two, etc., and become one flesh physically (have sexual intercourse) becoming one flesh with each of his wives, one at a time.

KING SOLOMON'S MULTIPLE WIVES

DEUTERONOMY 17:17 (NKJV):

Neither shall he multiply wives for himself, lest his heart turn away; nor shall he greatly multiply silver and gold for himself.

1 KINGS 11:3-4 (NKJV):

And he [KING SOLOMON] had seven hundred wives, princesses, and three hundred concubines; and his wives turned away his heart. For it was so, when Solomon was old, that his wives turned his heart after other gods; and his heart was not loyal to YHWH (the Lord) his God, as was the heart of his father David.

A restriction to polygamy that God did command against was multiplying (not adding) wives. It is obvious that King Solomon, with his seven hundred wives, could not possibly love or control them all. They turned his heart away from God. King Solomon disobeyed the command for kings to not multiply wives unto themselves. Even if King Solomon were capable of having sexual relations twice a day, skipping the Sabbath day to rest, and each time with a different wife until he went through all seven hundred of them, it would have taken him over a year to have sex (become one flesh) with each of his wives. King Solomon was obviously collecting wives like a man collects and hordes cash, gold and silver, treasure that he would never be able to appreciate, spend, or use. King Solomon was the wisest man alive, but his wives turned his heart away from YHWH (the Lord).

MARRIAGE ESTABLISHED, AS ARE OTHER UNIONS, AT THE CREATION SCALE

LEVITICUS 19:19 (NKJV):
You shall not sow your field with mixed seed.

While Leviticus 19:19 concerns farming, the universal application of God and His creation remains, which helps explain why polygamy was acceptable under God's laws. A man is the sower of seed, a woman is the field or garden where the seed gets planted. A man, as a sower, can sow his seed in different gardens, but a woman, as a garden, cannot have different seeds from different men sown in her.

Many people believe that polygamy does not legally exist any longer in the Westernized nations, but will be surprised to find out that marriages do not end in divorce. Therefore, a man who had a wife who left and divorced him, and he then went on to marry another woman, is actually a polygamist whether he knows it or not.

This article is NOT advocating a cultural return to polygamy in this age, as it is quite evident that the current state of society in keeping a marriage together between just one man and one woman is challenging enough and is something that people as a whole are failing at dismally.

YESHUA (JESUS) DIVORCED ISRAEL, BUT REMAINED FAITHFUL TO ISRAEL

Yeshua (Jesus) is our High Priest and as such He remained faithful to backsliding, sinning Israel and did not align Himself (marry) with another nation after He divorced Israel (Jeremiah 3:8).

MATTHEW 10:5-6 (NKJV):
These twelve Yeshua (Jesus) sent out and commanded them, saying: "Do not go into the way of the Gentiles, and do not enter a city of the Samaritans. But go rather to the lost sheep of the house of Israel."

When Yeshua (Jesus) came to Earth as the Messiah (Christ), He came exclusively for the Jews. He was honoring His 'marriage' covenant with them even though the Jews had committed spiritual adultery (served other gods) against Him.

MATTHEW 28:18-20 (NKJV):
And Yeshua (Jesus) came and spoke to them, saying, "All authority has been given to Me in heaven and on earth. Go therefore and make disciples of ALL THE NATIONS, baptizing them in the name of the Father and of the Son and of the Holy Spirit, teaching them to observe all things that I have commanded you; and lo, I am with you always, even to the end of the age."

Death ends a covenant made by a vow, including the marriage covenant. Upon His death, Yeshua's (Jesus') exclusive covenant with the Jews ended and He was free to make a covenant with ALL THE NATIONS.

1 TIMOTHY 3:1-5,12 (NKJV) [WITH INTERPRETATION]:

This is a faithful saying: If a man desires the position of a bishop [OVERSEER / CONGREGATIONAL MINISTER], he desires a good work. A bishop [OVERSEER / CONGREGATIONAL MINISTER] then MUST be blameless, THE HUSBAND OF ONE WIFE, temperate, sober-minded, of good behavior, hospitable, able to teach; not given to wine, not violent, not greedy for money, but gentle, not quarrelsome, not covetous; one who rules his own house well, having his children in submission with all reverence (for if a man does not know how to rule his own house, how will he take care of the church of God, the assembly of Elohim?); ... Let church attendants be the husbands of one wife, ruling their children and their own houses well.

TITUS 1:5-9 (NKJV) [WITH INTERPRETATION]:

You should set in order the things that are lacking, and appoint elders in every city as I commanded you - if a man is blameless, THE HUSBAND OF ONE WIFE having faithful children not accused of dissipation or insubordination. For a bishop [OVERSEER / CONGREGATIONAL MINISTER] must be blameless, as a steward of God, not self-willed, not quick-tempered, not given to wine, not violent, not greedy for money, but hospitable, a lover of what is good, sober-minded, just, holy, self-controlled, holding fast the faithful word as he has been taught, that he may be able, by sound doctrine, both to exhort and convict those who contradict.

A man who is a congregational minister, or a congregational assembly attendant, is to be the husband of one wife. Congregational ministers and assistants are not permitted to have multiple wives. Therefore, hypothetically, if in the current culture a congregational minister had a wife who departed and divorced him, the congregational minister would still be permitted to preach, but if he were to marry another wife, he should then step down in his church assembly position, as he would have two wives, the first who divorced him, and the second who he married afterward.

FEMINISM

Men and women were not intended to have equal roles in marriage. Equality-minded feminist women have done much harm to the institution of marriage.

1 CORINTHIANS 11:3,8-9 (NKJV):

The head of every man is Messiah (Christ), the head of woman is man, and the head of Messiah (Christ) is God. ... For man is not from woman, but woman from man. Nor was man created for the woman, but woman for the man.

Countless marriages have gone through needless hardship and have ended in divorce, because feminist-minded wives refused to accept their role as being a helpmate to their husbands. Often wives choose poor husbands to marry to lead them, but once a marriage is lawfully consecrated it cannot be undone.

Feminism goes against a woman's natural desire to be led by a man. A wife instinctively wants to look up to her husband, which is why women seek men who are taller than they are. In a marriage, there is nothing more revolting and unnatural than to observe a husband being controlled, led, ordered around, and being submissive and subservient to his wife.

Equality of authority in a marriage doesn't work well. A marriage is like a ship and if a ship has two co-equal captains, both captains wishing to manage the ship in the direction of their choosing, constantly vying to take control from the other captain, it will not be long before the two captains come to blows. There can be only one leader of the ship, and one of the captains must submit authority to the other captain, which at sea is usually done by seniority, or whoever is better qualified to captain the ship due to experience with the vessel. The family ship is no different. If husband and wife act as two co-equal partners, the wife being unwilling to submit ultimate authority to her husband in matters concerning the family ship, then conflict in the family ship will likely be the norm.

GOD COMMANDS HOSEA TO MARRY A WHORING WOMAN

HOSEA 1:2-3 (NKJV):

When YHWH (the Lord) began to speak by Hosea, YHWH (the Lord) said to Hosea:

"Go take for yourself a wife of harlotry and children of harlotry, for the land has committed great harlotry by departing from YHWH (the Lord)."

So he went and took Gomer the daughter of Diblaim...

It is uncertain if Gomer was an actual prostitute, but she was certainly a promiscuous woman, a non-virgin. It may seem extremely unfair that God would allow a promiscuous, whoring woman to marry, but would restrict a righteous divorced woman from remarrying. People have wondered why a whoring woman can marry, but a divorced woman, according to Scripture, cannot. The reason is that the divorced woman is under a covenant vow till the death of her spouse, but the promiscuous whoring woman is not under a covenant vow, could repent, and marry.

GOD IS HOLY AND CANNOT GO BACK ON HIS WORD

All throughout Scripture, it is repeated and emphasized that our God is holy. God keeps His covenants, He keeps His vows, and cannot go back on His word. He, therefore, expects us to keep our covenants and keep our vows. We are made in His image and were created to be like Him. The fact that God is holy is the reason that He will not allow spouses out of the lawful vows that they have made and why He will not allow divorced women to remarry.

HOMOSEXUALITY / CROSS DRESSING

LEVITICUS 18:22 (NKJV):

You shall not lie with a male as with a woman. It is an abomination.

LEVITICUS 20:13 (NKJV):

If a man lies with a male as he lies with a woman, both of them have committed an abomination. They shall surely be put to death. Their blood shall be upon them.

DEUTERONOMY 22:5 (NKJV):

A woman shall not wear anything that pertains to a man, nor shall a man put on a woman's garment, for all who do so are an abomination to YHWH (the Lord) your God.

ROMANS 1:26-27 (NKJV):

For this reason God gave them up to vile passions. For even their women exchanged the natural use for what is against nature. Likewise also the men, leaving the natural use of the woman, burned in their lust for one another, men with men committing what is shameful, and receiving in themselves the penalty of their error which was due.

The due penalty that men often receive for engaging in the vile sex act of homosexuality is HIV and AIDS. Homosexual men are largely responsible for spreading HIV and AIDS throughout America and the rest of the world. That is not homophobia; it is a homo-fact and Scripture prophecy fulfilled.

EREMIAH 13:23 (NKJV):

Can the Ethiopian change his skin or the leopard its spots?

Any man or woman who has undergone an operation to change the appearance of his or her gender is a living, breathing, walking, talking abomination. There is no such thing as a sex change operation. One cannot change his or her gender any more than a person can change his or her skin or a leopard can change its spots. Anal intercourse is an abominable sex act between two men or between a man and woman. No court of man can overturn the laws of God. The United States Supreme Court legalized sodomy through gay 'marriage' on June 26, 2015. This is a decision that America will pay the ultimate price for: its own destruction.

MAINTAINING AND REPAIRING A MARRIAGE

Marriage, once lawfully entered into, is a state of permanency that cannot be dissolved except through death. Divorce does not end a legitimate valid marriage. In societies that encourage and promote easy divorce, and permit remarriage, the land has been defiled by adultery. The state of marriage and broken families in America and the Western nations attest to this reality. If people understood the permanent sacred status of marriage, they would bear with it, for better or worse, in sickness and in health, till death, as they have vowed to do so before a holy and righteous God who bears witness.

ADULTEROUS AND GAY MARRIAGES

1 CORINTHIANS 6:9-10 (NKJV) (HSV†):

Do you not know that the unrighteous will not inherit the kingdom of God (†reign of Elohim)? Do not be deceived. Neither FORNICATORS, nor idolaters, nor ADULTERERS, nor EFFEMINATE, nor HOMOSEXUALS, nor thieves, nor covetous (†greedy of gain), nor drunkards, nor revilers, nor swindlers will inherit the reign of Elohim (kingdom of God).

GALATIANS 5:19-21 (NKJV) (HSV†):

Now the works of the flesh are evident, which are: ADULTERY, FORNICATION, UNCLEANNESS, lewdness, idolatry, drug sorcery, hatred, quarrels, jealousies, fits of rage, selfish ambitions, dissensions, heresies, envy, murders, drunkenness, revelries, and the like; of which I tell you beforehand, just as I also told you in time past, that those who practice such things will not inherit the kingdom of God (†reign of Elohim).

REVELATION 21:7-8 (NKJV):

He who overcomes shall inherit all things, and I will be his God and he shall be My son. The cowardly, untrustworthy, ABOMINABLE, murderers, SEXUALLY IMMORAL, drug sorcerers, idolators, and all liars shall have their part in the lake which burns with fire and brimstone, which is the second death.

Fornication, adultery, and homosexuality, if unrepented of, will cause a person to lose his or her inheritance of the kingdom or God, the millennium reign of Yeshua (Jesus). Being married into adultery or homosexuality only makes matters worse, as now the sin is compounded by an unlawful vow.

Many believers today would argue that homosexuals who are in gay marriages should repent of their homosexuality and come out of their abominable marriage and repent of their unlawful vow, and rightly so. However, most would not take such a strong stance against those who are divorced and remarried, against a man who married a divorced woman. Homosexuality is indeed a worse sin than adultery, because homosexuality is a perverted unnatural sex act, whereas heterosexual sexual intercourse between a man and woman is a natural act, but both of these sins unrepented of will equally keep a person from inheriting God's Millennium Kingdom.

IGNORANCE OF THE LAW IS NO EXCUSE TO CONTINUE IN SIN

2 CHRONICLES 7:14 (NKJV) [WITH INTERPRETATION]:

If My people who are called by My name [CHRIST-IANS] will humble themselves, and pray and seek My face, and turn from their wicked ways, then I will hear from heaven, and will forgive their sin and heal their land.

HOSEA 4:6 (NKJV) [WITH INTERPRETATION]:

My people [CHRISTIANS] are destroyed for a lack of knowledge. Because you have rejected knowledge, I will also reject you for being priest for Me [IN THE MILLENNIUM KINGDOM]; Because you have forgotten the law of your God, I will also forget your children.

Some who are remarried will argue that they did not know that it was against God's marriage law to divorce and remarry. Many will say that their church or pastor permitted it. The lack of knowledge excuse may be true, but it will not spare the unlawfully remarried from the judgment of God.

REPENTANCE OF AN UNLAWFUL ADULTEROUS MARRIAGE

It is not a pleasant thing to call for the remarried to repent of an adulterous marriage, but it is a requirement to rightfully rebuke such unions, as John the Baptist did, so that those who are in unlawful remarriages are made aware to come out of them, so as to prevent them from continuing in adultery.

EZEKIEL 33:11 (NKJV):

'As I live,' says YHWH (the Lord) GOD, 'I have no pleasure in the death of the wicked, but that the wicked turn from his way and live.

LUKE 13:3,5 (NKJV):

"But unless you repent you will all likewise perish."

When God commands a man not to do something, in this case divorce and remarriage, and a man does it anyway - even if through ignorance and lack of knowledge, then he will be judged and punished by God. If the man comes to the knowledge of God's word, *after* he has sinned, but repents and corrects his ways, that man can avoid the judgment and punishment of God, because he has repented and chosen to live rightly.

MATTHEW 14:3-4; MARK 6:17-18 (NKJV):

For Herod had laid hold of John and bound him, and put him in prison for the sake of Herodias, his brother Philip's wife. Because John had said to him, "It is not lawful for you to have her."

John the Baptist was the greatest prophet who ever lived according to Yeshua (Jesus) (Matthew 11:11; Luke 7:28). John knew the law of marriage and knew that King Herod married a divorced woman, his brother's wife. John didn't ask about and likely didn't know the circumstances of why Herodias left her husband, as it did not matter. John only knew God's marriage law, which was that is was unlawful for King Herod to have Herodias, a divorced woman, as his wife. John wound up losing his life for rebuking King Herod over his adulterous marriage to Herodius.

The adulterous remarried might say that they are living just fine, they love each other, they may or may not have children together, they cannot financially afford to break apart their marriage, and are not going to break up their remarriage and family based on God's law. These issues are difficult ones to deal with, for sure, but it would be better to deal with them immediately, rather than wait on God to act in judgment, punishment, and wrath.

EZRA 9:10-12 (NKJV):

And now, O our God, what shall we say after this? For we have forsaken Your commandments, which You commanded by Your servants the prophets, saying, 'The land which you are entering to possess is an unclean land, with the uncleanness of the peoples of the lands, with their abominations which have filled it from one end to another with their impurity. Now therefore, do not give your daughters as wives for their sons, nor take their daughters to your sons; and never seek their peace or prosperity, that you may be strong and eat the good of the land, and leave it as an inheritance to your children forever.'

The Hebrews, when they were originally given the land of Israel to possess, were commanded by God through the prophets to drive out its inhabitants and to not give their daughters to marry the local inhabitants, nor take women from the people to make them wives. Many Hebrew men disobeyed God in this matter and married pagan wives.

EZRA 10:2-4 (NKJV) [WITH INTERPRETATION]:

And Shechaniah the son of Jehiel, one of the sons of Elam, spoke up and said to Ezra, "We have trespassed against our God, and have taken pagan wives from the peoples of the land; yet now there is hope in Israel in spite of this. Now therefore, let us make a covenant with our God TO PUT AWAY [DIVORCE] ALL THESE WIVES AND THOSE WHO HAVE BEEN BORN TO THEM, according to the advice of my master and of those who tremble at the commandment of our God; and let it be done according to the law. Arise, *for this matter is your responsibility.* We also are with you. Be of good courage, *and do it.*"

Men who have married divorced women, and in many cases have born children with them, have knowingly or unknowingly disobeyed the commands of God to not marry a divorced woman. It is the responsibility of every man who realizes that he is in an adulterous marriage to put away (divorce) in repentance from it, and do it.

Ezra 9-10 is Scripture's example of a massive putting away (divorce) for repentance. Many people say that God forced the divorce on the men of Israel, because they married foreign pagan wives. That is not exactly correct. In this SPECIFIC instance, at this SPECIFIC time in Israel's history, God gave a SPECIFIC command to the Hebrews, while they came to possess the land, that they were not to marry the people of the land.

God's law allowed foreign women to be grafted into Israel through marriage, such as Ruth and other women (Deuteronomy 21:10-14).

CAN A PERSON WHO REPENTS OF AN ADULTEROUS MARRIAGE GET MARRIED AGAIN?

If a man married a divorced woman, but realized afterward that his marriage was unlawful, then repents and puts her away in a divorce, can he then seek a wife? An unlawful marriage vow is not one that should be upheld, but one to be repented of. If the man's marriage is adulterous, according to God, then it is NOT a marriage, but it is a sin. Therefore, a man can repent of his unlawful marriage sin of adultery, put away the divorced wife of another man who he had married, and seek an available unmarried woman or widow, if he desires a wife and can find one.

1 CORINTHIANS 6:9-11 (NKJV) (HSV†):
Neither fornicators, nor idolaters, nor ADULTERERS, nor effeminate, nor homosexuals, nor thieves, nor covetous (greedy of gain), nor drunkards, nor revilers, nor swindlers will inherit the reign of kingdom of God (†reign of Elohim). AND SUCH WERE SOME OF YOU. But you were washed, but you were sanctified, but you were justified in the name of the Lord Yeshua (Jesus) and by the Spirit of our God.

1 CORINTHIANS 7:2 (NKJV):
Nevertheless, because of sexual immorality, let each man have HIS OWN WIFE, and let each woman have HER OWN HUSBAND.

If a man repents of adultery, even an adulterous marriage, he repents of the unlawful marriage, comes out of it, and has repented of adultery. The man did not leave or divorce *his wife* of a *valid marriage*, and he is free to marry. Likewise if two men are in a homosexual 'marriage,' then this marriage is an abomination. If a man repents of a homosexual marriage, and is able to change his sexual orientation to heterosexual chastity, then he has repented of homosexuality, not a valid marriage, and he is free to lawfully marry a single woman or a widow.

1 CORINTHIANS 7:1 (NKJV):
It is good for a man not to touch a woman.

Paul wrote that it is good for a man not to touch a woman. Fornication is a serious sin and fornication, adultery, and other unlawful sexual union are sins that can cause a person to acquire a sexually transmitted disease.

What about touching a woman without having sexual intercourse with her?

1 CORINTHIANS 7:8-9 (NKJV):

But I say to the unmarried and to the widows: It is good for them if they remain even as I am; but if they cannot exercise self-control, let them marry. FOR IT IS BETTER TO MARRY THAN TO BURN WITH PASSION.

If a couple is dating and having sex, Scripture calls this fornication and they should either marry or break off the relationship immediately. Fornicators will not inherit the kingdom of God (reign of Elohim).

Popular Western culture greatly promotes the touching of women. It may seem extremely prudish, but there was a time when kissing, French-tongue making out type kissing, was reserved for husbands and wives. When an unmarried man and woman engage in tongue kissing they become one flesh through their mouths, by exchanging bodily fluids - saliva, even though this is not sexual intercourse.

After a wedding vow is made, the man marrying the groom says to him, "You may now kiss the bride." What is meant by that statement is that she is now your wife and you may now *lawfully* kiss her. Prolonged kissing leads to sexual arousal, causes thoughts of lust, makes many to lose self-control, and leads many to burn with passion and satisfy their passion through fornication or masturbation. One can get a sexually transmitted disease (mononucleosis - mono) from kissing alone, which indicates that God does punish this lighter form of sexual expression outside of marriage, as well as the greater sins of sexual immorality.

PORNOGRAPHY, MASTURBATION, ONANISM, AND VOYEURISM

MATTHEW 5:27-30 (NKJV):

"You have heard that it was said to those of old, 'You shall not commit adultery.' But I say to you that whoever LOOKS AT A WOMAN TO LUST for her has already committed adultery with her in his heart. If your right eye causes you to sin, pluck it out and cast it from you; for it is more profitable for you that one of your members perish, than for your whole body to be cast into hell. And if your RIGHT HAND CAUSES YOU TO SIN, cut it off and cast it from you; for it is more profitable for you that one of your members perish, than for your whole body to be cast into hell."

Many have falsely proclaimed that if a man merely looks at a passing attractive woman, that Yeshua (Jesus) calls this adultery. This is not true and would make beauty itself a sin. Yeshua (Jesus) addresses the sins of pornography and masturbation through voyeurism in Matthew 5:27-30. If a man views pornographic images of a woman engaged in sex, for the intent purpose TO LUST, he commits adultery with her in his heart. A man then typically uses his RIGHT HAND to masturbate, committing adultery with his right hand.

GENESIS 38:8-10 (NKJV) [WITH INTERPRETATION]:

And Judah said to Onan, "Go in to your brother's wife and marry her, and raise up an heir to your brother." But Onan knew that the heir would not be his; and it came to pass, when he went in to his brother's wife, that he EMITTED [HIS SEMEN] ON THE GROUND, lest he should give an heir to his brother. And the thing which he did displeased YHWH (the Lord); therefore He killed him also.

YHWH (the Lord) once killed Onan for emitting his semen to the ground. How many millions of people casually watch pornography through videos or the Internet and masturbate to them without any fear of God?

Yeshua (Jesus) said that it would be better for a man who views pornography and habitually masturbates, to pluck out his eyes and chop off his right hand, rather than to keep his members and continue in these sins and be cast into hell. Therefore, any believer trapped in the habitual sin of pornography and masturbation MUST work to repent of these serious sins for the sake of his or her very soul (Philippians 2:12).

REMAINING CELIBATE FOR SAKE OF THE KINGDOM OF HEAVEN

MATTHEW 19:9-12 (NKJV) [WITH INTERPRETATION]:

And I say to you, whoever divorces his wife, except for fornication [PREMARITAL SEX] and marries another, commits adultery; and whoever marries her who is divorced commits adultery."

His disciples said to Him, "If such is the case of the man with his wife, it is better not to marry." But He said to them, "All cannot accept this saying, but only those to whom it has been given: For there are eunuchs who were born thus from their mother's womb, and there are eunuchs who were made eunuchs by men, and there are eunuchs who have made themselves eunuchs for the kingdom of heaven's sake. He who is able to accept it, let him accept it."

In these end times, in this age of marriage and rampant divorce, there are some men who will choose NOT to marry, as finding a righteous available woman who has not been divorced to wed is something that is not easy.

PROVERBS 31:10 (NKJV):

Who can find a virtuous wife?

Most men don't actually castrate themselves for the sake of the kingdom of heaven (Yeshua / Jesus was speaking figuratively here), though there have been reported cases of men who have.

There are men who will obey God's commands to not marry a divorced woman and therefore they will not otherwise find a desirable righteous woman to marry. These righteous single men will not engage in adultery, fornication, masturbation, or otherwise have sex, and will remain celibate (like a eunuch) living sexually pure and righteous lives for the sake of the kingdom of heaven.

There are men who will find themselves in an adulterous marriage, having realized through God's word that they are living in sin, repent and put away (divorce) the divorced woman who they married, and then live celibate (like a eunuch) by not engaging in adulterous sex any longer for the sake of the kingdom of heaven.

BUT GOD WANTS US TO BE HAPPY

LEVITICUS 11:44 (NKJV):

For I am YHWH (the Lord) your God. You shall therefore consecrate yourselves, and you shall be holy; for I am holy.

2 PETER 3:11-12 (NKJV):

Therefore, since all these things will be dissolved, what manner of persons ought you to be in holy conduct and godliness, looking for and hastening the coming of the day of God.

God does want for us to be happy, but not at the expense of holiness. If a woman is divorced and her husband lives, God does not permit her to marry another man for the sake of her happiness. God wants us first to be holy and secondly to be happy. God wants us to be holy, and will reward us in His coming kingdom for being holy, even if it means unhappiness in this life.

THE FUTURE OF MARRIAGE IN GOD'S COMING KINGDOM

What will become of marriage in the future, when the saints are living in God's kingdom?

MATTHEW 22:30; MARK 12:25 (NKJV):

"For in the resurrection (when they rise from the dead) they neither marry nor are given in marriage, but are like angels of God in heaven."

Many have read the statements of Yeshua (Jesus) concerning marriage after the resurrection with alarm. Yeshua (Jesus) didn't reveal everything about how we will live after the resurrection or how the angels live in heaven. Many have assumed that we will live solitarily, not in family units, and there will be no intimacy in heaven, but there otherwise will be joy.

There are a few things that a believer must understand...

Marriage is until death. Since there will be no death in heaven, any marriage would be *for eternity*. Therefore, marriage may be given a new name in heaven, if men and women are destined to cohabitate within God's kingdom.

SOUL MATES?

A problem is that if the two soul mates become unhappy with one another in heaven throughout eternity, then what? Be stuck with someone for all eternity? Mankind does not have a great track record of remaining together till death on Earth or remaining faithful within an earthly marriage. Yet the thought of remaining in solitary quarters throughout all eternity is not appealing to many either.

THERE WILL BE CHILDREN BORN AFTER THE RESURRECTION

Historically, in Scripture times and up until the Christian reformation of the 1500's, many divorced women did not remarry and remained childless. Scripture prophecy states that these women, who remained faithful to their wedding vow *after* being divorced, will give birth to many children. Isaiah 54 has comforted many childless divorced women throughout the generations.

ISAIAH 54:1-8 (NKJV) [WITH INTERPRETATION]:

"Sing, O barren, you who have not borne [CHILDREN]! Break forth into singing and cry aloud, you who have not labored with child! For more are the children of the deserted [DIVORCED WOMAN] than the children of the married woman [OF THIS AGE]," says YHWH (the Lord).

"Enlarge the place of your tent, and let them stretch out the curtains of your dwellings; do not spare. Lengthen your cords, and strengthen your stakes. For you shall expand to the right and to the left, and your DESCENDANTS will inherit the nations, and make the desolate cities [OF THE EARTH - AFTER THE GREAT TRIBULATION] inhabited.

Do not fear, for you will not be put to shame, nor hurt, you shall not be humiliated. For you will forget the shame of your youth, and will not remember the reproach of your widowhood any longer. For your Maker is your husband, YHWH (the Lord) of hosts is His name, and your Redeemer is the Holy One of Israel. He is called the God of all the earth. For YHWH (the Lord) has called you like a woman forsaken and grieved in spirit, like a youthful wife when you were refused [PUT AWAY - DIVORCED], says your God.

"For a mere moment [A LIFETIME COMPARED TO ETERNITY IS A MERE MOMENT - ROMANS 8:18] I have forsaken you, but with great mercy I shall gather you [IN THE AGE TO COME].

With a little wrath [DUE TO YOUR SIN] I hid may face from you for a moment [DURING THIS LIFE], but with everlasting kindness I will have compassion on you," says YHWH (the Lord), your Redeemer.

ISAIAH 54:13,17 (NKJV):

All YOUR CHILDREN shall be taught by YHWH (the Lord), and great shall be the peace of YOUR CHILDREN…

This is the heritage of the servants of YHWH (the Lord), and their righteousness is from Me, says YHWH (the Lord).

Isaiah 54:5 proclaims that our Maker, YHWH (the Lord), will be our husband and that there will be children born to women of the resurrection, *after* the resurrection. Who will be the fathers of those children?

JEREMIAH 31:31-34 (NKJV):

"Behold, the days are coming, says YHWH (the Lord), when I will make a new covenant with the house of Israel and with the house of Judah - not according to the covenant that I made with their fathers in the day that I took them by the hand to lead them out of the land of Egypt, My covenant which they broke, though I was a husband to them, says YHWH (the Lord). But this is the covenant that I will make with the house of Israel after those days, says YHWH (the Lord): I will put My law in their minds, and write it on their hearts; and I will be their God, and they shall be My people. No more shall every man teach his neighbor, and every man his brother, saying, 'Know YHWH (the Lord),' for they all shall know Me, from the least of them to the greatest of them, says YHWH (the Lord). For I will forgive their iniquity, and their sin I will remember no more."

HOSEA 2:16 (NKJV):

"And it shall be, in that day, says YHWH (the Lord), "That you will call me 'My Husband,' and no longer call Me 'My Master (Lord)'"

HEBREWS 8:7-12 (NKJV):

For if that first covenant had been faultless, then no place would have been sought for a second. Because finding fault with them, He says: *"Behold, the days are coming, says the Lord, when I will make a new covenant with the house of Israel and with the house of Judah - not according to the covenant that I made with their fathers in the day when I took them by the hand to lead them out of the land of Egypt; because they did not continue in My covenant, and I disregarded them, says the Lord.*

For this is the covenant that I will make with the house of Israel after those days, says the Lord: I will put My laws in their mind and write them on their hearts; and I will be their God, and they shall be My people. None of them shall teach his neighbor, and none his brother, saying, 'Know the Lord,' for all shall know Me, from the least of them to the greatest of them. For I will be merciful to their unrighteousness, and their sins and their lawless deeds I will remember no more."

REVELATION 19:7-9 (NKJV):

"Let us be glad and rejoice and give Him glory, for the marriage of the Lamb has come, and His wife has made herself ready." And to her it was granted to be arrayed in fine linen, clean and bright, for the fine linen is the righteous acts of the saints.

Then he said to me, "Write: 'Blessed are those who are called to the marriage supper of the Lamb!'"

REVELATION 21:2-3 (NKJV):

Then I, John, saw the holy city, New Jerusalem, coming down out of heaven from God, prepared as a bride adorned for her husband. And I heard a loud voice from heaven saying, "Behold, the tabernacle of God is with men, and He will dwell with them, and they shall be His people. God Himself will be with them and be their God."

The marriage of God and man will be an everlasting covenant marriage. This renewed covenant will be similar to the original covenant God made with the Hebrews, that He would be their God and they would be His chosen people, but the new covenant with God and the resurrected saints will not be broken. The resurrected saints will be regenerated, renewed into incorruptible, righteous beings (Matthew 19:28; Romans 8:21-23; 1 Corinthians 15:51-53) and will forever be with God (Revelation 20:6). God will live and dwell with us, protect us from harm, and provide for us, as a good husband takes care of his wife.

Yet what of the children born to the women of Isaiah 54? Who will be the fathers of those children?

Yeshua (Jesus) will be the Husband of the saints. The children born of women of the resurrection will *probably* be fathered by male saints of the resurrection, *who come in the name* of YHWH (the Lord). It will be the resurrected male saints, with all the righteousness of God within them, who will likely be the fathers of the children of the resurrection.

All the resurrected, both male and female saints, will be made righteous by God in the regeneration of their bodies, which will occur in the twinkling of an eye (Matthew 19:28; Romans 8:21-23; 1 Corinthians 15:51-53).

ISAIAH 4:1 (NKJV) [WITH INTERPRETATION]:

And in that day [OF THE RESURRECTION] seven women will take hold of one [RIGHTEOUS] man saying, "we will eat our own food and wear our own apparel; only let us be called by your name, to take away our reproach."

In God's coming kingdom, the righteousness and the works done by the saints on Earth will be rewarded. Those who have lived righteously, did good works, and served God well will be rewarded and will be rich in His kingdom (Matthew 16:27). There will be many in His kingdom who did very little works and they will not be rewarded as well in His kingdom (Matthew 5:18-19). Many women will approach the most righteous men and seek to be greater through the righteousness of these men.

Though seven women will take hold of a righteous man, this does not necessarily mean that the righteous man will accept them all, as wives, in polygamy.

MATTHEW 22:30; MARK 12:25 (NKJV):

For in the resurrection (when they rise from the dead) they neither marry nor are given in marriage, but are like angels of God in heaven.

Yeshua's (Jesus') words must also be considered concerning whether or not there will be any kind of 'marriage' in His coming kingdom. Marriage is until death, but after the resurrection of the righteous saints there will be no more death for them. God hates divorce (Malachi 2:16), so he cannot have His resurrected saints marrying for eternity, then complaining and filing for divorce sometime during eternity.

There will be children born to women of the resurrection (Isaiah 54) and seven women will take the hand of a righteous man to be called by his name (Isaiah 4:1), yet there will not be marriage in God's kingdom *as man has commonly known marriage.*

1 CORINTHIANS 2:9 (NKJV):

But as it is written:

"Eye has not seen, nor ear heard, nor have entered into the heart of man the things which God has prepared for those who love Him."

Something is coming to replace marriage and it will be superior to the earthly institution of marriage that man has known. What that something is remains a mystery that will one day be revealed to the saints of God.

THE LAW OF LIBERTY

By George Lujack

This article will discuss the Scripture phrase known as *the law of liberty* found in the book of James.

JAMES 1:22-25 (NKJV):

But be doers of the word, and not hearers only, deceiving yourselves. For if anyone is a hearer of the word and not a doer, he is like a man observing his natural face in a mirror; for he observes himself, goes away, and immediately forgets what kind of man he was. But he who looks into the perfect LAW OF LIBERTY and continues in it, and is not a forgetful hearer but a doer of the work, this one will be blessed in what he does.

The law of liberty spoken of in the James 1:22-25 passages refer to the Torah (God's laws). God's laws have never been abolished and the law of liberty references obedience to Torah (law) as the means of living freely in liberty from the bondage of sin.

The James 1:22-25 Scripture verses correspond with Romans 2:13.

ROMANS 2:13 (NKJV):

For not the hearers of the law are just in the sight of God, but the doers of the law (Torah) will be justified.

James 2:12-13 speaks of the Torah (law) also, but adds a mercy component in being judged by the Torah (law).

JAMES 2:12-13 (NKJV):

So speak and so do as those who will be judged by the LAW OF LIBERTY. For judgment is without mercy to the one who has shown no mercy. Mercy triumphs over judgment.

The capstone of the law itself is the mercy shown sinners by the atonement sacrifice of Yeshua Messiah (Jesus Christ). Yeshua Messiah (Jesus Christ) paid the penalty for our sins so that we may receive grace, for past sins - upon repentance, not so that we have the liberty to sin freely. Yeshua (Jesus) is the capstone of the Torah (law) of liberty that granted grace and mercy to sinners. Yeshua's (Jesus') atonement sacrifice for us on the cross was His mercy that triumphed over the judgment that was due to all sinners.

ACTS 4:11-12 (NKJV) [WITH INTERPRETATION]:

"This is the 'stone [GRACE THROUGH THE ATONEMENT SACRIFICE OF MESSIAH (CHRIST)] which was rejected by you builders [THE JEWS], which has become the chief cornerstone [OF THE LAW. WITHOUT YESHUA (JESUS), NO ONE CAN BE SAVED BY THE LAW ITSELF].' Nor is there salvation in any other, for there is no other name under heaven given among men by which we must be saved."

1 PETER 2:7-8 (NKJV) [WITH INTERPRETATION]:

Therefore, to you who believe He is precious; but to those who are disobedient, "The stone [GRACE THROUGH THE ATONEMENT SACRIFICE OF MESSIAH (CHRIST)] which the builders rejected has become the chief cornerstone [OF THE LAW. WITHOUT YESHUA (JESUS), NO ONE CAN BE SAVED BY THE LAW ITSELF]," and "A stone of stumbling and a rock of offense." They [THE GENTILE BELIEVERS] stumble, being disobedient to the word [THE LAW], to which they also were appointed [TO OBEY].

Christian churches have historically taught that aspects of the Torah (law) do not apply to Gentiles, but to the Jews only. This error has been the failure of the great commission.

MATTHEW 28:18-20 (NKJV):

And Yeshua (Jesus) came and spoke to them, saying, "All authority has been given to Me in heaven and on earth. Go therefore and make disciples of ALL THE NATIONS, baptizing them in the name of the Father and of the Son and of the Holy Spirit, TEACHING THEM TO OBSERVE *ALL THINGS* THAT I HAVE COMMANDED YOU; and lo, I am with you always, even to the end of the age."

The Gentiles have been either ignorantly or willfully disobedient to the Torah (law) and have stumbled (sinned) due to this disobedience, which is the mystery of lawlessness (2 Thessalonians 2:7).

JAMES 2:13 (NKJV):

For judgment is without mercy to the one who has shown no mercy. Mercy triumphs over judgment.

James 2:13 corresponds to what Yeshua (Jesus) said concerning judgment and mercy.

MATTHEW 7:1-2 (NKJV):

"Judge not, that you be not judged. For with what judgment you judge, you will be judged; and with the measure you use, it will be measured back to you."

LUKE 6:37 (NKJV):

"Judge not, and you shall not be judged. Condemn not, and you shall not be condemned. Forgive, and you will be forgiven."

A non-judgmental person who sins freely, but never judges anyone, will still be judged.

It is an *error in judgment* for a person to believe he or she could willfully break God's laws (sin), never repent, and not be judged. If a person sins freely and willfully, knowing it is sin and refuses to repent, that person will be judged by the law (Romans 2:12).

The law of liberty is not an abolishment of the law, giving us freedom to sin. The law of liberty is obedience to God's law, which gives us liberty from the bondage of sin.

DENOMINATIONALISM;
PLACING THE MESSENGER BEFORE THE MESSIAH

By George Lujack

It is said that there are 43,000 or so denominations of Christianity and every one of them is engaged in the promotion of their particular denominational teachings through the philosophy of their foundational spiritual leader, or spiritual concept, placing that leader or concept before the Messiah (Christ). This article will encourage believers to become independent of denominationalism, to identify themselves through declared faith in Yeshua Messiah (Jesus Christ), and to worship God in spirit and truth.

<u>**EXODUS 20:2-3; DEUTERONOMY 5:7 (NKJV):**</u>
I am YHWH (the Lord) your God ... You shall have no other gods before Me.

When believers declare themselves hyphenated-Christians, they are putting their messenger or concept before God. They are having their 'god' before God.

Many would object to the notion that they are having their spiritual leader, or concept, as 'a god' before God in violation of the First Commandment.

<u>**PSALM 82:6 (NKJV):**</u>
I said, "You are gods, and all of you are children of the Most High."

<u>**JOHN 10:34 (NKJV):**</u>
Yeshua (Jesus) answered them, "Is it not written in your law, 'I said, "You are gods?"'"

We are made in the image and likeness of God (Genesis 1:26). Yeshua (Jesus) said that we *are* gods. We are not all-powerful, almighty Gods; we are God's children, created gods who share certain likenesses with God. Yeshua (Jesus) refers to mankind, His creation made in His likeness and image, as gods. There are no other supernatural gods besides God and man-made idols are not gods. Denominational hyphenated-Christians, who declare their Christian faith through their spiritual leader or concept before Messiah (Christ), are breaking the First Commandment by having another god before God. Even if believers think that they are placing their messenger or concept before God, and not necessarily 'a god' before God, they are still putting a man or an idea before God. Gay-Christians, for example, declare, honor, and prioritize their sin before God, placing their sin before the Messiah (Christ).

JOHN 3:30 (NKJV):

"He must increase, but I must decrease."

- John the Baptist

John the Baptist has *increased* with some before Yeshua (Jesus). Believers who are Baptist-Christians, who refer to themselves as 'Baptists,' are disobeying John the Baptist's testimony that Messiah (Christ) must increase and he (John the Baptist) must decrease. Baptists are declaring faith in the messenger crying in the wilderness, placing him before the Messiah (Christ).

JOSHUA 24:15 (NKJV):

As for me and my house, we will serve YHWH (the Lord).

Believers who refer to themselves as Calvinists, Lutherans, Mennonites, Wesleyans, or any other denominational faith named after a spiritual leader, are honoring their messenger before the Messiah (Christ). Is faith in John Calvin, Martin Luther, Menno Simmons, and John Wesley to be declared before, or in place of, pronounced faith in Yeshua Messiah (Jesus Christ)?

Believers who refer to themselves as Anglicans, Catholics, Episcopalians, Jehovah's Witnesses, Methodists, Mormons, Pentecostals, Presbyterians, Protestants, or any other denominational faith named after a concept or tradition, are honoring their concept or tradition before the Messiah (Christ). Is faith in the Anglican Church of England, the Universal Catholic Church, the Episcopalian American Protestant-Catholic Church, the witnesses of Jehovah (instead of Jehovah), Methodism, Mormonism, Pentecostalism, Presbyterianism, and Protestantism (protesting Catholics) to be declared before, or in place of, pronounced faith in Yeshua Messiah (Jesus Christ)? Pentecost is the festival celebrating the descent of the Holy Spirit on the disciples of Yeshua (Jesus) after His Ascension. Pentecostals have placed a festival of God, which celebrates an event, before God.

WHAT SHOULD BELIEVERS CALL THEMSELVES?

If it were to be suggested that believers who agree with the teachings and writings of George Lujack should henceforth proclaim themselves to be 'Lujackarians,' this would rightly be criticized and rejected as giving undue honor, praise, and worship to a messenger of God in place of the Messiah (Christ). Yet many people do exactly that with other messengers when they declare themselves to be Baptists, Calvinists, Lutherans, Mennonites, and Wesleyans, giving undue honor, praise, and worship to these messengers of God in place of Messiah (Christ).

ACTS 11:26 (NKJV):

And the disciples were first called Messianics (Christians) in Antioch.

ACTS 26:28 (NKJV):

Then Agrippa said to Paul, "You almost persuade me to become a Messianic (Christian)."

1 PETER 4:16 (NKJV):

Yet if anyone suffers as a Messianic (Christian), let him not be ashamed, but let him glorify God in this matter.

There are no hyphenated-Christians in Scripture. Believers in Yeshua Messiah (Jesus Christ) should simply declare themselves to be Messianics or Christians. If pressed to be more specific, believers should claim to be non-denominational, Scripture-believing Messianics or Christians. Believers should not place a messenger, concept, festival, or tradition as a hyphenated declared faith before the Messiah (Christ).

1 CORINTHIANS 1:11-15 (NKJV):

For it has been declared to me concerning you, my brethren, by those of Chloe's household, that there are contentions among you. Now I say this, that each of you says,

"I am of Paul," or "I am of Apollos," or "I am of Cephas," or "I am of Messiah (Christ)." Is Messiah (Christ) divided? Was Paul crucified for you? Or were you baptized in the name of Paul?

I thank God that I baptized none of you except Crispus and Gaius, lest anyone should say that I had baptized in my own name.

The Apostle Paul rebuked sharply those who called themselves by his name. He made it perfectly clear that he didn't want to have anyone saying that they were 'of Paul,' but instead that they were 'of Messiah (Christ).'

1 CORINTHIANS 1:17 (NKJV):

For Messiah (Christ) did not send me to baptize, BUT TO PREACH THE GOSPEL, NOT WITH WISDOM OF WORDS, lest the cross of Messiah (Christ) should be made of no effect.

Paul emphasized that it was not his wisdom of words that should be praised, but rather Messiah (Christ) should be praised who sent him to preach the gospel.

JOHN 4:25 (NKJV):

The woman said to Him, "I know that Messiah is coming" (who is called Christ).

Believers in Yeshua Messiah (Jesus Christ) were first called by the Hebraic term 'Messianics' and later on by the Greek Hellenized term 'Christians,' as the Gentiles separated and distinguished themselves from the Jews who rejected Messiah.

EXODUS 34:14 (NKJV):

For you shall worship no other god, for YHWH (the Lord), whose name is Jealous, is a jealous God.

DENOMINATIONALISM: VARIOUS WINDS OF DOCTRINE

denomination:

A recognized autonomous branch of the Christian Church.[26]

denomination synonyms:

sect, church, cult, faith community, body, persuasion, religious persuasion.

EPHESIANS 4:14-15 (NKJV):

We should no longer be children, tossed to and fro and carried about with every wind of doctrine, by the trickery of men, in the cunning craftiness of deceitful plotting, but, speaking the truth in love, may grow up in all things into Him who is the head -Messiah- (-Christ-).

Believers must worship God in spirit and in truth (John 4:24), not in groupthink lockstep through the unscriptural denominational teachings of any messenger. Believers in Yeshua Messiah (Jesus Christ) must call themselves by His name, not by the name of His messengers, His festivals, concepts, or traditions.

Do not put anything or any person before God. God is a jealous God and one of His names is Jealous. Do not make God jealous!

NO PRIVATE INTERPRETATION;
DOES SCRIPTURE PROCLAIM THAT NO INDIVIDUAL CAN INTERPRET PROPHECY?

By George Lujack

Christian institutions and individuals who defend denominational church teachings, throughout millennia, have proclaimed superior knowledge and wisdom over the individual questioning the flawed doctrines of any particular Christian group, often citing 2 Peter 1:20, which states in part that *"no prophecy of Scripture is of any private interpretation."* This article will address 2 Peter 1:20, a verse which many people use to silence the critic, questioner, or messenger, and will explain the true meaning of the verse.

2 PETER 1:20 (NKJV):

No prophecy of Scripture is of any private interpretation.

When read alone and out of context, it may appear that the individual person does not have any authority or wisdom to interpret Scripture or prophecy. This would mean, of course, that only a collective group of persons or an organization could explain and understand Scripture and prophecy.

This is not so, and Peter himself provides examples which demonstrate that this is not the case at all.

MATTHEW 16:15-17 (NKJV) [WITH INTERPRETATION]:

He [YESHUA (JESUS)] said to them, "But who do you say that I am?"

Simon Peter answered and said, "You are the Messiah (Christ), the Son of the living God."

Yeshua (Jesus) answered and said to him, "Blessed are you, Simon Bar-Jonah, FOR FLESH AND BLOOD [PERSONS] HAS NOT REVEALED THIS TO YOU, BUT MY FATHER WHO IS IN HEAVEN."

God the Father revealed the answer of who Yeshua (Jesus) was to Peter.

ACTS 10:28 (NKJV):

"God has shown me that I should not call *any man* common or unclean…"

Peter had a vision to kill and eat, in Acts chapter 10, which unlike many false teachings provided by various mainstream Christian groups, he individually interpreted the true meaning himself, through God. The unclean creatures shown to him were not meant to be killed and eaten, to abolish God's dietary laws, but were used as a metaphor representing the non-Jewish people, that Peter should no longer consider Gentiles common or unclean.

We are commanded to study the Scriptures for ourselves (2 Timothy 2:15, 3:16-17). Studying the Scriptures would be pointless if we could not receive individual revelation of truths on a personal level from the Scriptures themselves, but could only receive knowledge and wisdom of Scripture and prophecy through groups.

ORDINATION: A PREREQUISITE THROUGH SEMINARY SCHOOL?

MATTHEW 28:18-20 (NKJV):

And Yeshua (Jesus) came and spoke to them, saying, "All authority has been given to Me in heaven and on earth. Go therefore and make disciples of all the nations, baptizing them in the name of the Father and of the Son and of the Holy Spirit, teaching them to observe all things that I have commanded you; and lo, I am with you always, even to the end of the age."

What Yeshua (Jesus) did not say to His disciples was to go out and make disciples of all nations, baptizing *and ordaining* them. Baptism itself *is ordination*! A man should not go out preaching on complex doctrinal issues, unless he is prepared, being well studied and versed on the topic, but to believe that only those who are officially ordained can teach God's word flies in the face of all Scripture, as most saints had no such formal seminary training or ordination, except perhaps the high priests, Pharisees, and scribes, who were often scolded by Yeshua (Jesus) for their erroneous doctrines.

1 CORINTHIANS 1:27-28 (NKJV):

God has chosen the foolish things of the world to put to shame the wise, and God has chosen the weak things of the world to put to shame the things which are mighty; and the base things of the world and the things which are despised God has chosen, and the things which are not, to bring to nothing the things that are.

Fisherman and tax collectors, laborers and civil servants by today's comparison, were Yeshua's (Jesus') disciples. Yeshua (Jesus) did not choose the mighty, the scholarly, or the wealthy, but instead chose the common man to change the world, to spread the gospel message, to confound the wisdom of the scholars of this world, and bring to nothing their false teachings.

Many of the teachings offered in seminary schools are the false doctrines that have been passed down for hundreds or thousands of years, which are used to indoctrinate the ordained scholars of this age. Most often these teachings do not withstand the truth test of Scripture (1 Thessalonians 5:21). Most often the seminary student is not permitted to question the teachings of his seminary school, but is instructed and trained to obey them as unquestionable truths.

THE WORLD RESPECTS DEGREES AND ORGANIZATIONS, BUT HATES THE MESSENGERS OF TRUTH PROCLAIMING GOD'S WORD IN THE SCRIPTURES

The Scripture PhD's, the seminary scholars, and their kind all have one thing in common: they expect people to value their opinion because they have obtained some type of Christian theological degree. Many believers in the world often respect a Christian organization or an individual, who possesses a degree from a Christian education establishment, as a bona fide source of wisdom. Sadly, most believers are misguided into worldly standards of thinking, not realizing the great source of wisdom is in their very homes: the Holy Scriptures, which often goes unstudied in an earnest desire for truth, without preconceived denominational or personal misconceptions.

All handed down denominational teachings sprang forth from an individual, then were adopted by a group, then became institutionalized and unchallengeable doctrine. Christian denominational churches, no matter how bad or unscriptural their doctrines may be, typically stand by their incorrect, easily proven false doctrines.

To proclaim that no individual, but only a group or a council can determine truth is easily refuted by basic common sense. There are numerous different Christian denominations worldwide, each with varying different doctrines. These separate groups or divisions of Christian theology cannot all be correct, as there can be only one truth on any particular topic. So, since Christian church organizations have not been successful with collective groupthink interpretations of Scripture or prophecy, anyone who proclaims that the individual cannot privately interpret Scripture is refuted by the fact that organizations collectively cannot interpret Scripture or prophecy with any certainty either.

NO PROPHECY OF SCRIPTURE IS 'OF' ANY PRIVATE INTERPRETATION

Does Peter actually proclaim that no individual can privately interpret Scripture or Scripture prophecy? No, not at all! Peter is declaring that no prophecy of Scripture, no prophecy *contained in Scripture* came by man's interpretation or origin. Prophecy, which has been written and recorded in Scripture, did not come to the prophets who wrote of them by their own will or intellect, but as they were directed, inspired, and moved by the Holy Spirit.

To better understand the words of Peter, one must read them in their full context...

2 PETER 1:20-21 (NKJV) [WITH INTERPRETATION]:
Knowing this first, that no prophecy of Scripture [WHICH IS IN SCRIPTURE] is of any private interpretation [IS OF ANY PRIVATE ORIGIN APART FROM GOD], for prophecy [RECORDED IN SCRIPTURE] never came by the will of man [NO PROPHET RECORDED HIS OWN PROPHECIES IN SCRIPTURE], but holy men of God spoke as they were moved by the Holy Spirit.

When carefully analyzing the meaning of Peter's words, they do not proclaim that an individual cannot interpret Scripture prophecy. What is actually written is that no Scripture prophecy (which is in Scripture, otherwise it could not be called *Scripture prophecy*) is 'of' any private interpretation, meaning that no Scripture prophecy recorded in the Scriptures is of, or originates from, any man's private thoughts, apart from revelation received from God.

When an individual properly explains a Scripture position or prophecy interpretation, without having expressed preconceived doctrinal or personal bias, correctly using all precept upon precept Scripture related verses to assert an opinion or to refute a doctrine, this is not a 'private' interpretation, but a Scripture-based one.

REVELATION 1:1-3 (NKJV):

The Revelation of Yeshua Messiah (Jesus Christ), which God gave Him to show His servants - things which must shortly take place. And He sent and signified it by His angel TO HIS SERVANT JOHN, WHO BORE WITNESS TO THE WORD OF GOD, and to the testimony of Yeshua Messiah (Jesus Christ), TO ALL THE THINGS THAT HE SAW.

John did not write the prophecies of the book of Revelation by His own will, but wrote them according to all the visions he saw. That is, the book of Revelation was not John's private interpretation. John was a holy man of God who wrote what he saw in the visions that were shown to him as the Holy Spirit moved him.

JEREMIAH 23:25-27 (NKJV) [WITH INTERPRETATION]:

I have heard what the prophets have said who prophesy lies in My name, saying, 'I have dreamed, I have dreamed!' How long will this be in the heart of the prophets who prophesy lies? Indeed they are prophets of the deceit of their own heart, who try to make My people forget My name by their dreams which everyone tells his neighbor, as their fathers forgot My name for Baal [LORD].

REVELATION 22:18-19 (NKJV):

For I testify to everyone who hears the words of the prophecy of this book: If anyone adds to these things, God will add to him the plagues that are written in this book; and if anyone takes away from the words of the book of this prophecy, God shall take away his part from the Book of Life, from the holy city, and from the things which are written in this book.

Properly discerning and interpreting Scripture is not prophesying lies. A warning is issued to not add or take away from the end time prophecies written in the book of Revelation. This warning coincides with Peter's writings proclaiming that no prophecy of Scripture is of any private interpretation, meaning that no Scripture prophecy is of any private origin.

GRAFTED IN, NOT REPLACED

By George Lujack

Did the Christian Church replace Israel or do believers still need to be grafted into Israel? Replacement Theology teaches that the Jews are no longer God's covenant chosen people and that the Church, originally the Catholic Church and now the Christian Church in general, has replaced Israel as the 'new Israel.' This article will reveal what Scripture says about the Jews as being God's chosen people, and will expose Replacement Theology as a deception conjured up and promulgated by the early Christian Church leaders.

Replacement Theology was promoted and taught by early Christian Church teachers such as Justin Martyr, Ignatius, Tertullian, Origen, Eusebius, John Chrysostom, Jerome, Augustine, and Martin Luther. All these men, motivated by hatred of the Jews and a desire to separate Christianity from them, taught that God's covenant with the Jews was no longer valid and that the Christian Church has now replaced the Jews as God's chosen people.

The Catholic Church to this day teaches that it is the kingdom of God on Earth - the new Israel, its pope is God's prime minister, the Vatican is the new temple built over the tomb of Peter ("Upon this rock I will build My church" - Matthew 16:18), and the Eucharist has replaced the Passover Meal.

JOHN 4:22 (NKJV):

"You worship what you do not know; we know what we worship, for salvation is of the Jews."

Yeshua (Jesus) said that salvation was of the Jews. In this He meant that everything concerning salvation came forth from the Jews: the Torah (law), the prophets, the Scriptures (Tanakh and B'rit Hadashah / Old and New Testaments), the apostles, and He Himself - the Messiah (Christ).

ISRAEL, THE FIG TREE

MATTHEW 21:19 (NKJV):

And seeing a fig tree by the road, Yeshua (Jesus) came to it and found nothing on it but leaves, and said to it, "Let no fruit grow on you ever again." Immediately the fig tree withered away.

MARK 11:13-14 (NKJV):

And seeing from afar a fig tree having leaves, Yeshua (Jesus) went to see if perhaps He would find something on it. When He came to it, He found nothing but leaves, for it was not the season for figs. In response Yeshua (Jesus) said to it, "Let no one eat fruit from you ever again."

MARK 11:20-21 (NKJV):

Now in the morning, as they passed by, they saw the fig tree dried up from the roots. And Peter, remembering, said to Him, "Rabbi, look! The fig tree which You cursed has withered away."

LUKE 13:6-9 (NKJV):

Yeshua (Jesus) also spoke this parable: "A certain man had a fig tree planted in his vineyard, and he came seeking fruit on it and found none. Then he said to the keeper of his vineyard, 'Look, for three years I have come seeking fruit on this fig tree and find none. Cut it down; why does it use up the ground?' But he answered and said to him, 'Sir, let it alone this year also, until I dig around it and fertilize it. And if it bears fruit, well. But if not, after that you can cut it down.'"

National Israel, the Jews, are represented as the fig tree throughout Scripture. Yeshua (Jesus) did curse a fig tree, and in doing so symbolically cursed the Jews of national Israel, whom He knew were destined to reject Him as their Messiah. He proclaimed that no spiritual fruit would ever come forth from national Israel again (in this age).

No spiritual fruit has come forth from Israel, as Yeshua (Jesus) stated. The Good News of the Gospel of Yeshua Messiah (Jesus Christ), first proclaimed by the Jewish apostles, this fruit has been spread throughout the world by the Gentiles. The fact that Gentile Christians have spread the gospel message throughout the world does not mean that the Christian Church has replaced the Jews as God's chosen people.

THE HEBRAIC JEWS OF ISRAEL, GOD'S CHOSEN PEOPLE

DEUTERONOMY 7:6 (NKJV):

YHWH (the Lord) your God has chosen you to be a people for Himself, a special treasure above all the peoples on the face of the earth.

THE COVENANT PROMISE TO ABRAHAM

GENESIS 17:7 (NKJV):

I will establish My covenant between Me and you and your descendants after you in their generations, FOR AN EVERLASTING COVENANT, TO BE GOD TO YOU AND YOUR DESCENDANTS AFTER YOU.

ALL BELIEVERS, JEWS AND GENTILES, ARE SPIRITUAL ISRAEL ACCORDING TO THE COVENANT PROMISE MADE TO ABRAHAM

GALATIANS 3:26-29 (NKJV):

For you are all sons of God through faith in Messiah Yeshua (Christ Jesus). For as many of you as were baptized into Messiah (Christ) have put on Messiah (Christ). There is neither Jew nor Greek, there is neither slave nor free, there is neither male nor female; for you are all one in Messiah Yeshua (Christ Jesus). And if you are Messiah's (Christ's), THEN YOU ARE ABRAHAM'S SEED, AND HEIRS ACCORDING TO THE PROMISE.

ZECHARIAH 2:11 (NKJV):

Many [GENTILE] nations shall be joined to YHWH (the Lord) in that day, and they [GENTILES] *shall become* **My people.**

Gentile believers will be joined - grafted into spiritual Israel as Abraham's spiritual seed and shall become God's people through faith, not through being descendants of Abraham, and are heirs to God's kingdom according to the covenant promise God made to Abraham.

RUTH, GRAFTED HERSELF INTO NATIONAL AND SPIRITUAL ISRAEL - GOD'S KINGDOM

RUTH 1:16 (NKJV):

Ruth said: For wherever you go, I will go; and wherever you lodge, I will lodge; Your people shall be my people, and your God, my God.

THE JEWS WERE BROKEN OFF FROM SPIRITUAL ISRAEL, GOD'S KINGDOM, AND THE GENTILES WERE GRAFTED INTO SPIRITUAL ISRAEL

ROMANS 11:17-32 (NKJV) [WITH INTERPRETATION]:

And if some of the branches were broken off [JEWS], and you [GENTILES], being a wild olive tree [A SEPARATE GENTILE TREE], were grafted in among them [SPIRITUAL ISRAEL], and with them [SPIRITUAL ISRAEL] became a partaker of the root and fatness of the olive tree [GOD'S KINGDOM], do not boast against the branches [JEWS]. But if you do boast, remember that you do not support the root [YESHUA (JESUS)], but the root [YESHUA (JESUS)] supports you [GENTILES]. You [GENTILES] will say then, "Branches [JEWS] were broken off that I [A GENTILE] might be grafted in." Well said. Because of unbelief they [JEWS] were broken off, and you [GENTILES] stand by faith. Do not be haughty, but fear [GOD]. For if God did not spare the natural branches [JEWS], He may not spare you [GENTILES] either. And they [JEWS] also, if they [JEWS] do not continue in unbelief, will be grafted in, for God is able to graft them [JEWS] in again. For if you [GENTILES] were cut out of the olive tree [BABYLON] which is wild by nature, and were grafted contrary to nature into a cultivated olive tree [GOD'S KINGDOM], how much more will these [JEWS], who are natural branches [NATURAL DESCENDANTS OF ABRAHAM], be grafted [BACK] into their own olive tree [SPIRITUAL ISRAEL – GOD'S KINGDOM]? For I do not desire, brethren, that you should be ignorant of this mystery, lest you should be wise in your own opinion, that blindness in part has happened to Israel [JEWS] until the fullness of the Gentiles has come in [BEEN GRAFTED INTO GOD'S KINGDOM]. And so all Israel [JEWS AND GENTILES] will be saved, as it is written: "The Deliverer [YESHUA / JESUS] will come out of Zion [JERUSALEM], And He will turn away ungodliness from Jacob [JUDEA]. For this is My covenant with them, when I take away their sins." Concerning the gospel they [JEWS] are enemies for your sake, but concerning the election [THE CHOSEN PEOPLE] they [THE JEWS] are beloved for the sake of the fathers [ABRAHAM, ISAAC, AND JACOB]. For the gifts and the calling of God are irrevocable. For as you [GENTILES] were once disobedient to God, yet have now obtained mercy through their [JEWS'] disobedience, even so these [GENTILES] also have now been disobedient [TO THE TORAH (LAW)], that through the mercy shown you [GENTILES] they [JEWS] also may obtain mercy. For God has committed them [JEWS] all to disobedience, that He might have mercy on all [JEWS AND GENTILES].

Concerning the election, the Messiah-denying Jews (God's chosen elect) are beloved for the sake of the fathers of Israel: Abraham, Isaac, and Jacob (Romans 11:28).

THE JEWS HAVE BEEN DENIED THE TRUTH ABOUT THEIR MESSIAH

The two branches of Mystery Babylon will not prevail against the word of God being revealed to His people. During the Dark Ages (500-1500 A.D.), the Roman Catholic Church forbade people from possessing their own bibles and reading from the Scriptures. The Catholic Church burned bibles along with anyone who possessed one. Pharisaic Talmudic Judaism forbids Jews from reading from the B'rit Hadashah (New Testament). As Roman Catholicism failed to prevent the printed Scriptures from being distributed to the Gentile peoples, so too will Talmudic Judaism fail to prevent the Jewish population from discovering their Messiah through the B'rit Hadashah and through Messianics who are presenting the truth of their Messiah to them.

THE JEWS OF NATIONAL ISRAEL ARE GOD'S LOST SHEEP

MATTHEW 15:24 (NKJV):

But Yeshua (Jesus) answered and said, "I was not sent except to the lost sheep of the house of Israel."

JOHN 10:11-16 (NKJV) [WITH INTERPRETATION]:

"I am the good shepherd; and I know My sheep [JEWS], and am known by My own. As the Father knows Me, even so I know the Father; and I lay down My life for the sheep [JEWS]. And other sheep [GENTILES] I have which are not of this fold [JEWS]; them also I must bring, and they [GENTILES] will hear My voice; and there will be one flock [JEWS AND GENTILES] and one shepherd [YESHUA (JESUS)]."

The Jews, the natural branches, will be grafted back into the olive tree (spiritual Israel - God's kingdom), when they call upon Yeshua (Jesus) in their darkest hour, when the armies of the world descend upon national Israel and He returns to save them from annihilation.

MATTHEW 24:21-22; MARK 13:19-20 (NKJV) [WITH INTERPRETATION]:

"For then there will be great tribulation, such as has not been since the beginning of the world until this time, no, nor ever shall be. And unless those days were shortened, no flesh would be saved; but for the elect's [JEWS'] sake those days will be shortened."

LUKE 13:35 (NKJV) [WITH INTERPRETATION]:

"See! Your house [ISRAEL] is left to you desolate; and assuredly, I say to you [JEWS], you [JEWS] shall not see Me until the [END] time comes when you [JEWS] say, *'Blessed is He [YESHUA (JESUS)] who comes in the name of YHWH (the Lord)!'*"

The story of Ruth serves as an example that God's chosen people - the Jews, are not to be replaced, but joined (Ruth 1:16). The early Christian Church separated itself from the Jews, but did not replace the Jews as God's new chosen people and are not the New Israel. Yeshua (Jesus) didn't come to start a new religion: Christianity, He came to be the Messiah of the already established faith.

Christian believers are destined to join with Jewish believers and be grafted in together as one flock into spiritual Israel - God's kingdom (John 10:16). All believers are spiritual Israel and heirs of God's kingdom through the covenant promise given to Abraham (Galatians 3:29). Gentiles are the wild branches grafted into the olive tree (spiritual Israel - God's kingdom), the root of which is Yeshua (Jesus). The natural branches, the Jews, will be grafted back into the olive tree when they eventually come to accept Yeshua (Jesus) as their Lord and Savior (Luke 13:35).

THE FREE GRACE AND HYPER-GRACE THEOLOGY DECEPTION

By George Lujack

A widely-held Christian view of salvation, known as Free Grace theology or Hyper-grace theology, states that eternal life is received by a person the moment he or she declares belief in Jesus Christ as personal Lord and Savior. Free grace / hyper-grace negates the need to follow Messiah (Christ) and obey His commandments. This article will define grace, discuss the dangers of Free Grace / Hyper-grace theology, and examine what God's grace means for us today.

JAMES 2:19-20 (NKJV):

You believe that there is one God. You do well. Even the demons believe - and tremble! But do you want to know, O foolish man, that faith without works is dead?

To merely believe in Yeshua Messiah (Jesus Christ) as Lord and Savior is insufficient for salvation. Faith (in Him) without works (of the law - obeying His commandments and doing good works) is dead faith.

2 PETER 2:4 (NKJV):

God did not spare the angels who sinned, but cast them down to hell and delivered them into chains of darkness, to be reserved for judgment.

The angels who sinned and became demons believed in Him; they are not saved and are awaiting judgment.

grace:

1. (In Christian belief) the free and unmerited favor of God, as manifested in the salvation of sinners and the bestowal of blessings.

2. A period officially allowed for payment of a sum due or for compliance with a law or condition, especially an extended period granted as a special favor.[27]

Free grace and hyper-grace adherents focus on definition number one and ignore definition number two in the aforementioned definition of 'grace.'

JOHN 1:17 (NKJV):

For the law was given through Moses, but grace and truth came through Yeshua Messiah (Jesus Christ).

Many free and hyper-grace adherents believe that Moses gave us the law and Yeshua (Jesus) abolished it through grace, by an incorrect twisted application and understanding of John 1:17, which should be understood as follows:

JOHN 1:17 (NKJV) [WITH INTERPRETATION]:

For the law was given [BY GOD] through Moses, but grace [MERCY] and truth [CONCERNING A GREATER UNDERSTANDING OF THE LAW] came through Yeshua Messiah (Jesus Christ).

Grace from God existed before Yeshua (Jesus) was born into the world. Noah found grace in the eyes of YHWH (the Lord), because he was living righteously, obeying the commands of God.

GENESIS 6:8 (NKJV):

Noah found grace in the eyes of YHWH (the Lord).

Yeshua (Jesus) paid the atonement ransom payment for all sinners by suffering and dying on the cross in place of us (Hosea 13:14; Matthew 20:28; Mark 10:45; 1 Timothy 2:6). After He was resurrected, He commanded His disciples to teach others all [COMMANDMENTS] that He had taught them and to make [OBEDIENT] disciples of people of all the nations (Matthew 28:19-20).

ROMANS 6:14 (NKJV):

For sin shall not have dominion over you, for you are not under law but under grace.

Yeshua (Jesus) commanded, through the Apostle Paul, that His believers were not to live under the penalties for breaking the law, but live under grace. What many mainstream believers do not understand, nor seem to want to understand, is that the period of grace that we are currently living under will expire. The Master will return. How will He find you living when He comes?

MATTHEW 24:44-51 (NKJV):

"Therefore you also be ready, for the Son of Man is coming at an hour you do not expect.

Who then is a faithful and wise servant, whom his master made ruler over his household, to give them food in due season? Blessed is that servant whom his master, when he comes, will find so doing. Assuredly, I say to you that he will make him ruler over all his goods. But if that evil servant says in his heart, 'My master is delaying his coming,' and begins to beat his fellow servants, and to eat and drink with the drunkards, the master of that servant will come on a day when he is not looking for him and at an hour that he is not aware of, and will cut him in two and appoint him his portion with the hypocrites."

Grace is unmerited favor from God and our salvation was attained through unmerited grace. Grace is also a limited period in which to turn from sin in repentance and learn to live righteously by following God's commands.

ROMANS 6:1-2 (NKJV):

Shall we continue in sin that grace may abound? Certainly not! How shall we who died to sin live any longer in it?

2 THESSALONIANS 2:16 (NKJV):

Now may our Lord Yeshua Messiah (Jesus Christ) Himself, and our God and Father, who has loved us and given us everlasting consolation and good hope by grace.

HEBREWS 10:26-29 (NKJV):

For if we sin willfully after we have received the knowledge of the truth, there no longer remains a sacrifice for sins, but a certain fearful expectation of judgment, and fiery indignation which will devour the adversaries. Anyone who has rejected Moses' law dies without mercy on the testimony of two or three witnesses. Of how much worse punishment, do you suppose, will he be thought worthy who has trampled the Son of God underfoot, counted the blood of the covenant by which he was sanctified a common thing, and insulted the Spirit of grace?

JUDE 1:4 (NKJV):

For certain men have crept in unnoticed, who long ago were marked out for this condemnation, ungodly men, who turn the grace of our God into lewdness and deny the only Lord God and our Lord Yeshua Messiah (Jesus Christ).

Grace does not abolish God's commandments, nor does grace give anyone a license to sin freely continually. Grace is a period to overcome sin, not to live in it perpetually. God has given us everlasting consolation, not everlasting grace. Grace periods expire. People who rely solely on God's grace, who are sinning willfully, who are refusing to repent, are insulting the grace period afforded them in this age and are in danger of losing their salvation.

LORDSHIP SALVATION

By George Lujack

Lordship salvation is a term used to describe a doctrinal belief that one must submit to Messiah (Christ) as Lord, and not only as Savior. Lordship salvation is the doctrinal belief that receiving Messiah (Christ) involves repentance, a turning from lawlessness and sin to practicing righteousness through commandment keeping. Lordship salvation is basically the opposite of antinomianism, or easy believism, which teaches that one must merely acknowledge Yeshua (Jesus) for salvation, but not obey Him. Opponents of lordship salvation contend that commandment keeping consists of works and those who keep the commandments of God are attempting to earn their salvation. Lordship salvation teaches that we must obey His commandments; easy believism teaches that we do not need to. This article will define and defend the tenets of lordship salvation.

KEEPING THE COMMANDMENTS OF GOD IS NOT 'WORKS'

Generally speaking, keeping the commandments of God is not works, it a lifestyle change from unrighteous living in sin to righteous living through commandment keeping. The works of the law (Romans 9:32, Galatians 2:16, 3:2-10) are a reference to commandment keeping, but law keeping is not to be confused with good works.

One may have to work at being righteous, but this is a lifestyle change, not works befitting repentance (Acts 26:20). Is it really 'work' for a righteous man to stay home for the evening with his family, as opposed to an unrighteous man to going out, getting drunk, cheating on his wife in adultery, then returning home? Those who proclaim that keeping God's commandments are doing unnecessary works are deceiving themselves.

Good works befitting repentance differ from required commandment keeping. Good works befitting repentance would include charitable giving, doing good deeds, feeding the poor, ministering to prisoners through mail or personal visits, volunteering, etc.

Another often stated objection to lordship salvation is that no one can keep God's commandments perfectly. The truth is that Scripture proclaims that we can keep His commandments, but even if not perfectly we are to try to by practicing righteousness.

<u>1 JOHN 2:3-6 (NKJV)</u>:

Now by this we know that we know Him, IF WE KEEP HIS COMMANDMENTS. He who says, "I know Him," and does not keep His commandments, is a liar, and the truth is not in him. But whoever keeps His word, truly the love of God is perfected in him. By this we know that we are in Him. He who says he abides in Him ought himself also to walk just as He walked.

1 JOHN 3:10 (NKJV):

In this the children of God and the children of the devil are manifest: WHOEVER DOES NOT PRACTICE RIGHTEOUSNESS IS NOT OF GOD, nor is he who does not love his brother.

DO WE NEED TO KEEP THE COMMANDMENTS TO EARN OUR SALVATION

Many try to deceive by stating that those who keep the commandments of God are trying to earn their salvation, so therefore it is wrong to keep them. This sure is one warped view of how to justify breaking God's commandments!

ISAIAH 5:20 (NKJV):

Woe to those who call evil good, and good evil.

MATTHEW 15:6; MARK 7:9 (NKJV):

"Thus you have made the commandment of God of no effect by your tradition."

Many in these end times are rejecting the commandments of God through false doctrines. Anyone who calls God's good commandments evil, and by extension calls those who keep His commandments evil, woe to them! Those who justify wickedness and condemn righteousness are like an abomination to God (Proverbs 17:15).

SALVATION IS A FREE GIFT OF GOD THAT CANNOT BE EARNED

EPHESIANS 2:8-9 (NKJV):

For by grace you have been saved through faith, and that not of yourselves; it is the gift of God, not of works, lest anyone should boast.

Generally speaking, those who keep the commandments of God out of obedience to God are not trying to earn their salvation. True believers understand that salvation is a free gift that cannot be earned. Commandment keeping is not about earning salvation, it is about living righteously according to how God wants us to live.

WHAT MUST WE DO TO BE SAVED?

MATTHEW 19:16-17 (NKJV):

Now behold, one came and said to Him, "Good Teacher, what good thing shall I do that I may have eternal life?"

So He said to him, "Why do you call Me good? No one is good but One, that is, God. BUT IF YOU WANT TO ENTER INTO LIFE, KEEP THE COMMANDMENTS."

1 CORINTHIANS 7:19 (NKJV):

Keeping the commandments of God is what matters.

Keeping God's commandments is a necessary component for salvation. Keeping His commandments cannot earn us our salvation and there is no conflict in Scripture here. Keeping God's commandments is necessary, but salvation came through the atonement work of Messiah (Christ), not by commandment keeping.

Now that salvation for mankind has been paid for, by Yeshua (Jesus), commandment keeping is a required component to enter into eternal life. What is the alternative? Yeshua (Jesus) didn't give us salvation so that we would never repent and live in sin perpetually.

LUKE 13:3,5 (NKJV):

"I tell you, no; BUT UNLESS YOU REPENT you will all likewise perish."

2 PETER 3:9 (NKJV):

The Lord is not slack concerning His promise, as some count slackness, but is longsuffering toward us, not willing that any should perish BUT THAT ALL SHOULD COME TO REPENTANCE.

Unrepentant sinners CANNOT enter God's kingdom and will be turned away from it.

Do not be deceived! We must repent and keep His commandments.

1 CORINTHIANS 6:9-10 (NKJV) (HSV†):

Do you not know that the unrighteous will not inherit the reign of Elohim (kingdom of God)? Do not be deceived. Neither fornicators, nor idolaters, nor adulterers, nor effeminate, nor homosexuals, nor thieves, nor covetous (†greedy of gain), nor drunkards, nor revilers, nor swindlers will inherit the kingdom of God (†reign of Elohim).

GALATIANS 5:19-21 (NKJV) (HSV†):

Now the works of the flesh are evident, which are: adultery, fornication, uncleanness, lewdness, idolatry, drug sorcery, hatred, quarrels, jealousies, fits of rage, selfish ambitions, dissensions, heresies, envy, murders, drunkenness, revelries, and the like; of which I tell you beforehand, just as I also told you in time past, that those who practice such things will not inherit the kingdom of God (†reign of Elohim).

EPHESIANS 5:5-6 (NKJV):

For this you know, that no fornicator, unclean person, nor covetous man, who is an idolater, has any inheritance in the kingdom of Messiah (Christ) and God. Let no one deceive you with empty words, for because of these things the wrath of God comes upon the sons of disobedience.

REVELATION 21:7-8 (NKJV):

He who overcomes shall inherit all things, and I will be his God and he shall be My son. The cowardly, untrustworthy, abominable, murderers, sexually immoral, drug sorcerers, idolaters, and all liars shall have their part in the lake which burns with fire and brimstone, which is the second death.

JUST CALL ON THE LORD AND YOU WILL BE SAVED DECEPTION

ACTS 16:31 (NKJV):

"Believe on the Lord Yeshua Messiah (Jesus Christ), and you will be saved, you and your household."

ROMANS 10:9 (NKJV):

If you confess with your mouth the Lord Yeshua (Jesus) and believe in your heart that God has raised Him from the dead, you will be saved.

According to antinomianism (easy believism), merely acknowledging Him and calling upon the Lord is all that is necessary for salvation. Taking a few verses out of context to sustain a doctrine is completely deceptive and misleading. If one believes on the Lord, then he or she must obey His commandments.

ROMANS 10:10 (NKJV):

For with the heart one BELIEVES UNTO RIGHTEOUSNESS, and with the mouth confession is made unto salvation.

Romans 10:10 follows 10:9 and proclaims we must *believe unto righteousness*, and that means we must obey God's commands to practice righteousness.

MANY UNREPENTANT SINNERS WILL BE KEPT OUTSIDE OF HIS KINGDOM

MATTHEW 7:21-23 (NKJV):

"Not everyone who says to Me, 'Lord, Lord,' shall enter the kingdom of heaven, but he who does the will of My Father in heaven. Many will say to Me in that day, 'Lord, Lord, have we not prophesied in Your name, cast out demons in Your name, and done many wonders in Your name?' And then I will declare to them, 'I never knew you; depart from Me, you who practice lawlessness!'

REVELATION 22:14-15 (NKJV):

BLESSED ARE THOSE WHO DO HIS COMMANDMENTS, that they may have the right to the tree of life, and may enter through the gates into the city. But outside are dogs and sorcerers and sexually immoral and murderers and idolaters, and whoever loves and practices a lie.

Lawless believers, many who do things in His name, will be turned away from His kingdom, because they did not repent of their sins and continued practicing lawlessness. Salvation cannot be earned, but it can be lost through unrepentant, lawless sin.

DISPENSATIONALISM: DISPENSING GOD'S ETERNAL COMMANDMENTS

Dispensationalists often 'dispense' with God's eternal commandments, as if they were commands for a certain age. Tenets of dispensationalism are correct, teaching a historical progression of man's reunification with God, consisting of a series of periods of God's revelation and plan of salvation. But Scripture is clear that God's laws and His words will never pass away (Matthew 5:18, 24:35; Mark 13:31; Luke 16:17, 21:33).

PSALM 119:115 (NKJV):

Depart from me, you evildoers, for I will keep the commandments of my God!

JOHN 14:21 (NKJV):

"He who has My commandments and keeps them, it is he who loves Me. And he who loves Me will be loved by My Father, and I will love him and manifest Myself to him."

YESHUA MESSIAH (JESUS CHRIST) IS LORD AND SAVIOR

MATTHEW 28:18 (NKJV):

And Yeshua (Jesus) came and spoke to them, saying, "All authority has been given to Me in heaven and on earth."

2 PETER 3:17-18 (NKJV):

You therefore, beloved, since you know this beforehand, beware lest you also fall from your own steadfastness, being led away with the error of the wicked; but grow in the grace and knowledge of our Lord AND Savior Yeshua Messiah (Jesus Christ).

To Him be the glory both now and forever.

Do not be led away from the tenets of lordship salvation with the error of easy believism. Yeshua Messiah (Jesus Christ) is Lord *and* Savior, not just the Savior.

ANTINOMIANISM - EASY BELIEVISM;
THE GOSPEL OF LAWLESSNESS

By George Lujack

Antinomianism (Greek *anti*, "against"; *nomos*, "law") is a Christian doctrine that asserts salvation is by faith and divine grace to the point of proclaiming that the saved are not bound to obey the laws of Moses, including the Ten Commandments. This article will refute the doctrine of antinomianism, also known as easy believism, which is a resurgent, widely held end time belief.

Antinomianism has been around in some form since the early Christian churches formed. The doctrine of antinomianism sprang forth from the Protestant Reformation and controversies concerning the law and the gospel. The doctrine was first attributed to Johann Agricola, an assistant of Martin Luther.[28]

Antinomianism is soundly refuted throughout Scripture. Many who hold to the doctrine will proclaim that God's laws are too difficult and / or impossible to follow. This false premise asserts that God has intentionally given mankind impossible laws to obey, so man was destined to fail at keeping them.

ARE GOD'S COMMANDMENTS TOO DIFFICULT TO DO?

DEUTERONOMY 30:9-16 (NKJV):

For this commandment which I command you today IS NOT TOO MYSTERIOUS FOR YOU, nor is it far off. It is not in heaven, that you should say, 'Who will ascend into heaven for us and bring it to us, that we may hear it and do it?' Nor is it beyond the sea, that you should say, 'Who will go over the sea for us and bring it to us, that we may hear it and do it?' But the word is very near you, in your mouth and in your heart, THAT YOU MAY DO IT. See, I have set before you today life and good, death and evil, in that I command you today to love YHWH (the Lord) your God, to walk in His ways, and to keep His commandments, His statutes, and His judgments, that you may live and multiply; and YHWH (the Lord) your God will bless you...

ARE BELIEVERS REQUIRED TO KEEP HIS COMMANDMENTS TODAY?

1 JOHN 2:3-4 (NKJV):

Now by this we know that we know Him, IF WE KEEP HIS COMMANDMENTS. He who says, "I know Him," and does not keep His commandments, is a liar, and the truth is not in him.

1 JOHN 2:5-6 (NKJV):

But whoever keeps His word, truly the love of God is perfected in him. By this we know that we are in Him. He who says he abides in Him ought himself also to walk just as He walked.

MATTHEW 7:21-23 (NKJV):

"Not everyone who says to Me, 'Lord, Lord,' shall enter the kingdom of heaven, BUT HE WHO DOES THE WILL OF MY FATHER IN HEAVEN. Many will say to Me in that day, 'Lord, Lord, have we not prophesied in Your name, cast out demons in Your name, and done many wonders in Your name?' And then I will declare to them, 'I never knew you; depart from Me, you who practice lawlessness!'

MATTHEW 24:35; MARK 13:31; LUKE 21:33 (NKJV):

"Heaven and earth will pass away, but My words will by no means pass away."

ARE GOD'S COMMANDMENTS REALLY IMPOSSIBLE TO FOLLOW?

MATTHEW 17:20 (NKJV):

So Yeshua (Jesus) said to them, "Because of your unbelief; for assuredly, I say to you, if you have faith as a mustard seed, you will say to this mountain, 'Move from here to there,' and it will move; and NOTHING WILL BE IMPOSSIBLE for you."

MATTHEW 19:26; MARK 10:27 (NKJV):

"With God ALL THINGS are possible."

With God ALL THINGS are possible, not all things *except* obeying His commandments. It is an indictment against God, proclaiming Him to be a liar and an unfair taskmaster, if anyone proclaims that His commandments are impossible to follow. Yeshua (Jesus) has given believers a light yoke, which is to obey His commandments (Matthew 11:30). The easy yoke is not mere belief in Him, for even the demons believe (James 2:19).

REPENT AND BELIEVE OR REFUSE TO REPENT AND PERISH

HOSEA 4:6 (NKJV):

My people are destroyed for lack of knowledge ... forgotten the law of your God.

MARK 1:15 (NKJV):

"Repent, and believe in the gospel."

LUKE 13:3,5 (NKJV):

"Unless you repent you will all likewise perish."

Antinomianism or easy believism, mere belief in Him for salvation through faith and grace only, while rejecting the necessity of repentance and obeying His commandments, is a doctrine of lawlessness and a phony license to sin freely.

CALVINISM PREDESTINATION DOCTRINE; ARE SALVATION AND DAMNATION PREDESTINED?

By George Lujack

John Calvin (1509-1564) was a French pastor and theologian who became known for the theology known as Calvinism, which includes the doctrine of predestination: the predestined fate of a human being concerning his or her salvation or damnation. This article will review the doctrine of predestination, expose its flawed logic, and declare it to be false.

John Calvin held a view on predestination, or double predestination, that God has pre-chosen some people for salvation and others for damnation. This view is based on Calvin's view of the sovereignty of God, which is that God can do what He pleases, but Calvin's view ignores the free will of man.

PREDESTINATION IN SCRIPTURE

ROMANS 8:29-30 (NKJV):

For whom He foreknew, He also predestined to be conformed to the image of His Son, that He might be the firstborn among many brethren. Moreover whom He predestined, these He also called; whom He called, these He also justified; and whom He justified, these He also glorified.

EPHESIANS 1:3-10 (NKJV):

Blessed be the God and Father of our Lord Yeshua Messiah (Jesus Christ), who has blessed us with every spiritual blessing in the heavenly places in Messiah (Christ), just as He chose us in Him before the foundation of the world, that we should be holy and without blame before Him in love, having predestined us to adoption as sons by Yeshua Messiah (Jesus Christ) to Himself, according to the good pleasure of His will, to the praise of the glory of His grace, by which He made us accepted in the Beloved.

In Him we have redemption through His blood, the forgiveness of sins, according to the riches of His grace which He made to abound toward us in all wisdom and prudence, having made known to us the mystery of His will, according to His good pleasure which He purposed in Himself, that in the dispensation of the fullness of the times He might gather together in one all things in Messiah (Christ), both which are in heaven and which are on earth - in Him.

EPHESIANS 1:11-12 (NKJV):

In Him also we have obtained an inheritance, being predestined according to the purpose of Him who works all things according to the counsel of His will, that we who first trusted in Messiah (Christ) should be to the praise of His glory.

In the epistles to the Romans and the Ephesians written by the Apostle Paul, Scripture does speak of the predestination of believers, before the foundation of the world, to be holy and without blame by God's will and be adopted by God. When God created man, He had a *preordained plan* of salvation for man if man chose to sin: His Son Yeshua (Jesus) to atone for man's sin.

1 PETER 1:20-21 (NKJV):

He [YESHUA (JESUS)] indeed was foreordained before the foundation of the world, but was manifest in these last times for you who through Him believe in God, who raised Him from the dead and gave Him glory, so that your faith and hope are in God.

ROMANS 5:18-19 (NKJV):

Therefore, as through one man's offense judgment came to all men, resulting in condemnation, even so through one Man's righteous act the free gift came to ALL men, resulting in justification of life. For as by one man's disobedience many were made sinners, so also by one Man's obedience many will be made righteous.

Salvation is indeed offered to all, but many - not all, will accept God's free gift, be justified and made righteous, and will receive salvation.

2 PETER 3:9 (NKJV):

The Lord is not slack concerning His promise, as some count slackness, but is longsuffering toward us, NOT WILLING THAT ANY SHOULD PERISH but that ALL should come to repentance.

Calvin's belief system incorrectly teaches the absolute predestination of man. Calvinism's predestination doctrine greatly errs in assuming that predestination for salvation is for some people, but not all people. A predestination-minded Calvinist would say that only the elect, (themselves of course), are predestined to be saved, and if a person is predestined to be eternally damned there is nothing that he or she can do about it. Calvin's predestination doctrine erroneously teaches that some persons cannot accept Yeshua (Jesus), repent, or live righteously in hopes of receiving salvation.

ROMANS 10:9-10,13 (NKJV):

If you confess with your mouth the Lord Yeshua (Jesus) and believe in your heart that God has raised Him from the dead, you will be saved. For with the heart one believes unto righteousness, and with the mouth confession is made unto salvation. ...
For *"WHOEVER calls on the name of the Lord shall be saved."*

God's ability to peer into the future is different than man's ability to understand it. God, through the prophets in Scripture, has accurately prophesied events before they have occurred.

God lives outside of the confines of space and time, so He can see into the future and know who will be saved and who will not be saved. When Scripture speaks of those 'predestined to salvation,' all who are to be saved are predestined as such. All who were ever born are predestined to be either be saved or damned, because those are the only two ultimate destinies man has!

PROVERBS 11:30 (NKJV):

The fruit of the righteous is a tree of life, and he who wins souls is wise.

If a person's fate was determined and sealed by predestination, then there could be no way to win a soul over to salvation or truth. Believers are to fulfill the great commission (Matthew 28:18-20), preach the truth, and win souls. Our work for the kingdom, to win souls, is not in vain. We will find out who is written in the book of life when it is the appointed time for us to know (Philippians 4:3; Revelation 3:5, 13:8, 17:8, 20:12-15, 21:27, 22:19).

No one will be turned away from God's kingdom due to a 'predestination to damnation' if he or she, in this age, accepts Yeshua Messiah (Jesus Christ), repents, and lives righteously according to His commandments. Likewise, no one should be so assured of his or her 'predestined salvation' (or believe in a guaranteed 'once saved always saved' salvation) that he or she feels no necessity to repent and live righteously.

PRETERISM: WERE ALL SCRIPTURE PROPHECIES FULFILLED BY 70 A.D.?

By George Lujack

Preterism is a doctrinal belief proclaiming that all of Scripture prophecy was fulfilled by 70 A.D. While most Messianic and Christian believers do not accept the doctrine of Preterism, and rightly consider it absurd, Preterists do twist some Scripture verses to uphold their doctrine, confusing believers, and many are not sure how to adequately refute Preterists' alleged Scripture-based claims. This article will analyze Preterism, declare it a false doctrine, and equip believers with a proper understanding of the verses used by Preterists in order to aid them in responding to this false theology.

The origin of Preterism began with Luis de Alcazar (1554-1613), a Jesuit priest, whose purpose in proclaiming the doctrine was to defend the Catholic Church from Christian reformers who rightly began to identify the Roman Catholic Church as Mystery Babylon of Romans 17. The term 'Preterist' is Latin for 'past.' Preterists proclaim Scripture prophecy all occurred in the past, having all been fulfilled by 70 A.D.

THE BASIC TENETS OF PRETERISM AND REBUTTALS TO THEM:

1. ANTIMESSIAH (ANTICHRIST):

There will be no future Antimessiah (Antichrist). Nero fulfilled that role.

Nero was the 5th Roman emperor whose reign was from 54 to 68 A.D. Many tyrannical acts have been attributed to Nero, including starting the Great Fire of Rome and setting Christians on fire, which would make him an antimessiah (antichrist), but not the Antimessiah (Antichrist). The Antimessiah (Antichrist) will cause all to receive a 666 computerized mark on their right hand or on their forehead, and no one will be able to buy or sell unless they receive the mark (Revelation 13:16-18).

2. THE GREAT TRIBULATION, THE FALL OF BABYLON, AND ARMAGEDDON:

Preterists say these events occurred when the Roman army destroyed Jerusalem between 66-70 A.D.

The destruction of Jerusalem did occur in 70 A.D, but there was no great tribulation period preceding its destruction, Jerusalem is not Babylon, and Rome did not represent the king(s) of the Earth and world's armies that are prophesied to one day gather at Armageddon (Revelation 16:14-16). The 70 A.D. destruction of Jerusalem did not fulfill Yeshua's (Jesus') prophecy of the destruction of the Temple in Jerusalem.

The Western Wall of the second Temple still remained standing after 70 A.D. Yeshua (Jesus) said, regarding the Temple, "Not one stone shall be left upon another, that shall not be thrown down" (Matthew 24:2; Mark 13:2; Luke 19:44; Luke 21:6).

3. THE RETURN OF MESSIAH (CHRIST):

Preterists say that Messiah (Christ) 'returned' to witness the destruction of Jerusalem by the Roman army in 70 A.D.

Preterists claim that Messiah (Christ) returned and appeared before some of His followers who He spoke to. They cite Matthew, Mark, and Luke:

MATTHEW 16:28; MARK 9:1; LUKE 9:27 (NKJV):

"Assuredly, I say to you, there are some standing here who shall not taste death till they see the Son of Man coming in His kingdom."

Matthew 16:28, Mark 9:1, and Luke 9:27 are similarly worded verses, but they are not verses concerning the return of Messiah (Christ). The verses should be understood in the following manner:

MATTHEW 16:28; MARK 9:1; LUKE 9:27 (NKJV) [WITH INTERPRETATION]:

"Assuredly, I say to you, there are some standing here who shall not taste death till they see the Son of Man coming in [TO] His kingdom."

Matthew 16:28, Mark 9:1, and Luke 9:27 are verses that Yeshua (Jesus) spoke of regarding Him coming into His kingdom at His Ascension, not His return to Earth. Some of those standing there with Him when He spoke those words were prophesied to be witnesses to His Ascension, if they had not yet died when His Ascension was soon after to take place (Acts 2:32-33).

MARK 16:19 (NKJV):

So then, after the Lord had spoken to them, He was received up into heaven, and sat down at the right hand of God.

LUKE 24:51 (NKJV):

Now it came to pass, while He blessed them, that He was parted from them and carried up into heaven.

4. REPLACEMENT THEOLOGY:

God replaced Israel as God's chosen people with the [Catholic] Church, and this is a subsequent adopted belief by the Protestant churches.

God does not break or 'replace' His covenant promises. God has not cast away His people Israel, whom He foreknew. Israel is God's chosen people by His word (Exodus 6:7,19:5). The Gentile peoples are to be grafted into Israel; they are not to be a replacement for them (Romans 11).

5. THE MILLENNIUM KINGDOM:

Preterists proclaim that the [Catholic] Church age is the literal Millennium Kingdom and that the 1,000-year period is figurative, not literal.

Yeshua Messiah (Jesus Christ) must be ruling Earth during the millennium kingdom. The Catholic Church is not His millennium reign and the Catholic pope is certainly not the Vicar of Christ, or God's representative on Earth. Yeshua's (Jesus') millennium reign will be for a literal 1,000-years of which there will be world peace and no deceptions from Satan, among the nations, as Satan will be bound during the millennium (Revelation 20).

6. SATAN BOUND:

Preterists declare that Satan has already been bound to his hell prison and cannot hinder the spread of the Gospel.

When Messiah's (Christ's) millennium reign begins, Satan will be bound. The purpose of binding Satan is not so the Gospel can go forth; Satan could never prevent that. Satan will be bound during Messiah's (Christ's) millennium reign so that he cannot influence the nations (Revelation 20:3). After the 1,000-year millennium reign period comes to its conclusion, Satan will be released and lead the defiant hostile nations in one final rebellion against God's kingdom and His saints (Revelation 20:7-8). Satan will be defeated again and then will be forever imprisoned (Revelation 20:10).

Preterism is a false doctrine conjured up by a Catholic Jesuit priest. Sin and death are still ongoing in this world and when Yeshua (Jesus) returns, they will be no more (1 Corinthians 15:54-55; Revelation 21:4). Many Preterists apparently take comfort in Preterism due to personal security reasons, as they are unwilling to face the truth of the horrors that are prophesied to occur in the end times and would rather cling to the idea that there is nothing to worry about as all Scripture prophecy was fulfilled all by 70 A.D.

THE PROSPERITY GOSPEL

By George Lujack

This article will expose some of the fallacious assertions of the Prosperity Gospel and advise believers to reject this deceptive theological covetousness through giving for financial blessings works-based faith that proposes donating money for the sole purpose of getting a prosperous return on one's charitable 'investments.'

The Prosperity Gospel is a religious belief held by some Christians that financial blessing is the will of God for them as a result of having faith, living positively, and by giving generous donations primarily to Christian ministries. The prosperity theology proposes that one cannot out-give God and that God will repay faithful givers exponentially for their faithful donations with health, security, and financial prosperity. While it is certainly within God's power to bless whomever He chooses and bless those who give generously, the danger of the Prosperity Gospel is that the message of the true gospel gets lost. The focus of the Prosperity Gospel is to receive financial blessings, but not to be a blessing; to give with the expectation and sole intent of receiving greater prosperity in return.

GOD'S PROMISE OF OUR BEST LIFE IS NOT NOW; IT IS YET TO COME

1 CORINTHIANS 2:9 (NKJV):

But as it is written: "Eye has not seen, nor ear heard, nor have entered into the heart of man the things which God has prepared for those who love Him."

The Prosperity Gospel emphasizes working for and living "Your Best Life Now." Ironically, people believing in the Prosperity Gospel and living their best life now may actually be doing just that, for if they are denied entrance into God's kingdom, this life may wind up being their best life. Scripture advises that we should live righteously now with the promise that God will reward us with our best life in the age that is yet to come.

THE GOSPEL PROMISES BELIEVERS PERSECUTION, REVILING, AND SUFFERING;
THE PROSPERITY GOSPEL DOES NOT

MATTHEW 5:11 (NKJV):

"Blessed are you when they revile and persecute you, and say all kinds of evil against you falsely for My sake."

LUKE 6:22 (NKJV):

"Blessed are you when men hate you, and when they exclude you, and revile you, and cast your name as evil, for the Son of Man's sake."

ROMANS 8:18 (NKJV):

For I consider that the sufferings of this present time are not worthy to be compared with the glory, which shall be revealed in us.

1 TIMOTHY 4:10 (NKJV):

For to this end we both labor and suffer reproach, because we trust in the living God, who is the Savior of all men, especially of those who believe.

The Prosperity Gospel omits the persecution, reviling, and suffering that we, as Messianic or Christian believers, will endure if we live as examples of Messiah (Christ) in this age. The Prosperity Gospel only emphasizes that God's desire for us is to be blessed, happy, and financially prosperous.

GIVE TO BE REPAID IN GOD'S KINGDOM

LUKE 14:12-14 (NKJV):

Then He [Yeshua (Jesus)] also said to him who invited Him, "When you give a dinner or a supper, do not ask your friends, your brothers, your relatives, nor rich neighbors, lest they also invite you back, and you be repaid. But when you give a feast, invite the poor, the maimed, the lame, the blind. And you will be blessed, because they cannot repay you; for you shall be repaid at the resurrection of the just."

The Prosperity Gospel says that when we give to God (through wealthy Prosperity Gospel preachers), we should expect to be repaid with interest, in this life, through God's abundant financial blessings. Yeshua (Jesus) said that we should give to the poor, who cannot repay us, and that we will be repaid at the resurrection in God's kingdom.

DO NOT LAY UP EARTHLY TREASURES, BUT HEAVENLY ONES

MATTHEW 6:19 (NKJV):

"Do not lay up for yourselves treasures on earth, where moth and rust destroy and where thieves break in and steal; but lay up for yourselves treasures in heaven, where neither moth nor rust destroys and where thieves do not break in and steal. For where your treasure is, there your heart will be also."

LUKE 12:15-18 (NKJV):

And He [Yeshua (Jesus)] said to them, "Take heed and beware of covetousness, for one's life does not consist in the abundance of the things he possesses."

Then He spoke a parable to them, saying: "The ground of a certain rich man yielded plentifully. And he thought within himself, saying, 'What shall I do, since I have no room to store my crops?' So he said, 'I will do this: I will pull down my barns and build greater, and there I will store all my crops and my goods.

LUKE 12:19-21 (NKJV):

And I will say to my soul, 'Soul, you have many goods laid up for many years; take your ease; eat, drink, and be merry.' But God said to him, 'Fool! This night your soul will be required of you; then whose will those things be which you have provided?'

So is he who lays up treasure for himself, and is not rich toward God."

LUKE 12:33-34 (NKJV):

"Sell what you have and give alms; provide yourselves money bags which do not grow old, a treasure in the heavens that does not fail, where no thief approaches nor moth destroys. For where your treasure is, there your heart will be also."

The Prosperity Gospel focuses on material blessings and abundance for this life *now*, whereas the gospel of Yeshua (Jesus) warns us against coveting things in this age, against storing up treasures for this life. If your treasures are on Earth, in this life, then your heart is also on Earth and focused on this earthly life, and is not looking forward to the spiritual life and on heavenly treasures in God's eternal kingdom.

BE CONTENT WITH NECESSARY THINGS AND YOUR WAGES

LUKE 3:14 (NKJV):

Likewise the soldiers asked him [John the Baptist], saying, "And what shall we do?"

So he said to them, "Do not intimidate anyone or accuse falsely, and be content with your wages."

LUKE 12:29-31 (NKJV):

"And do not seek what you should eat or what you should drink, nor have an anxious mind. For all these things the nations of the world seek after, and your Father knows that you need these things. But seek the kingdom of God, and all these things shall be added to you."

1 TIMOTHY 6:6-11 (NKJV):

Now godliness with contentment is great gain. For we brought nothing into this world, and it is certain we can carry nothing out. And having food and clothing, with these we shall be content. But those who desire to be rich fall into temptation and a snare, and into many foolish and harmful lusts, which drown men in destruction and perdition. For the love of money is a root of all kinds of evil, for which some have strayed from the faith in their greediness, and pierced themselves through with many sorrows. But you, O man of God, flee these things and pursue righteousness, godliness, faith, love, patience, gentleness.

HEBREWS 13:5 (NKJV):

Let your conduct be without covetousness; be content with such things as you have.

We come into the Earth with nothing and leave it with nothing. Any earthly treasure that anyone acquires may be passed on to a spouse or children, or given to charity upon one's death, but cannot be taken into God's kingdom in the next life. The love of money, and material things that can be bought with money, is the root of all kinds of evil. The love of God, and being content with what we have, is the way of righteousness.

IT IS HARD FOR THE RICH TO ENTER HEAVEN

MATTHEW 19:24; MARK 10:25; LUKE 18:25 (NKJV):

"It is easier for a camel to go through the eye of a needle than for a rich man to enter the kingdom of God."

Yeshua (Jesus) explained to His disciples that it is hard for the rich, those who trust in their riches, to enter the kingdom of God.

The Prosperity Gospel would have people believe that it is God's desire that everyone should be rich. Being blessed by God with wealth is not a sin, but the means by which many of the world's rich acquire their wealth is sinful. Compromising righteousness to attain wealth is what can keep the rich from entering God's kingdom.

WE ARE GOD'S SERVANTS; GOD IS NOT OUR SERVANT

MALACHI 3:17-18 (NKJV):

"They shall be Mine," says YHWH (the Lord) of hosts, "on the day that I make them My jewels. And I will spare them as a man who spares his own son who serves him." Then you shall again discern between the righteous and the wicked, BETWEEN THE ONE WHO SERVES GOD AND THE ONE WHO DOES NOT SERVE HIM.

The Prosperity Gospel has the relationship between God and man wrong, as it proposes that God becomes our servant *if* we give generously to Him.

GOD IS NOT A GENIE, GIVING US WHATEVER WE ASK OF HIM

MATTHEW 21:22 (NKJV):

"And whatever things you ask in prayer, believing, you will receive."

MARK 11:24 (NKJV):

"Therefore I say to you, whatever things you ask when you pray, believe that you receive them, and you will have them."

JOHN 14:13-14 (NKJV):

"And whatever you ask in My name, that I will do, that the Father may be glorified in the Son. If you ask anything in My name, I will do it."

Many people have read the verses about asking for *anything* in prayer, in Yeshua's (Jesus') name, and that He would give them *anything* that they asked for. So... naturally, people often pray for material blessings and wealth. Why not pray to win the lottery, if Yeshua (Jesus) said that we can ask for anything in His name, and we will receive it?

Prosperity Gospel preachers have taken advantage of the covetousness of man and have deceptively *added* to these verses, saying that if you give to God (through their ministry), *and then ask anything in His name*, He will return financial blessings to you.

MATTHEW 6:31-33 (NKJV):

"Therefore do not worry, saying, 'What shall we eat?' or 'What shall we drink?' or 'What shall we wear?' For after all these things the Gentiles seek. For your heavenly Father knows that you need all these things. But seek first the kingdom of God and His righteousness, and all these things shall be added to you."

If we first truly seek the kingdom of God, and we seek to truly serve God in righteousness, then He will bless us with the material things that we need.

PHILIPPIANS 4:19 (NKJV):

And my God shall supply all your need according to His riches in glory by Messiah Yeshua (Christ Jesus).

JAMES 4:1-3 (NKJV):

Where do wars and fights come from among you? Do they not come from your desires for pleasure that war in your members? You lust and do not have. You murder and covet and cannot obtain. You fight and war. Yet you do not have because you do not ask. YOU ASK AND DO NOT RECEIVE, BECAUSE YOU ASK AMISS, THAT YOU MAY SPEND IT ON YOUR PLEASURES.

Covetousness has caused many believers to stumble. Verses that proclaim that Yeshua (Jesus) will give us anything that we ask for, are read out-of-context and are not understood. We may ask for anything in His name *that will glorify God*, and He will do it for us. God will give us *anything we ask for that we need*, to serve Him. When Prosperity Gospel believers ask God for financial windfalls, and do not receive them, it is because they are asking Him for money to spend on their own materialistic pleasures, and not to serve Him. Prosperity Gospel believers give offerings, not out of love for God and their fellow man, but in hopes of receiving an exponential miraculous financial return to spend on their own pleasures.

BLESSINGS COME FROM KEEPING GOD'S COMMANDMENTS; CURSES COME FROM DISOBEYING OR NOT HEARING THEM

DEUTERONOMY 30:15-19 (NKJV):

"See, I have set before you today life and good, death and evil, in that I command you today to love YHWH (the Lord) your God, to walk in His ways, and to keep His commandments, His statutes, and His judgments, that you may live and multiply; and YHWH (the Lord) your God will bless you in the land which you go to possess. But if your heart turns away so that you do not hear, and are drawn away, and worship other gods and serve them, I announce to you today that you shall surely perish; you shall not prolong your days in the land which you cross over the Jordan to go in and possess. I call heaven and earth as witnesses today against you, that I have set before you life and death, blessing and cursing; therefore choose life, that both you and your descendants may live; …"

GOD LOVES A CHEERFUL GIVER

2 CORINTHIANS 9:7 (NKJV):

So let each one give as he purposes in his heart, not grudgingly or of necessity; for God loves a cheerful giver.

GIVING TO GOD OR TO PROSPERITY GOSPEL PREACHERS?

Prosperity Gospel televangelist preachers are the greatest financial beneficiaries of the Prosperity Gospel. Prosperity Gospel preachers *steal* from God, as they use most, if not all, of the donated offering monies sent to them for their own materialistic pleasures and wealth accumulation. The top Prosperity Gospel preachers have their own private jet planes, numerous multi-million dollar homes, own every materialistic luxury item that they desire, and hoard stockpiles of unreported cash in various accounts, which are held domestically and abroad.

PROSPERITY GOSPEL PREACHERS ARE FALSE TEACHERS

2 PETER 2:1-3 (NKJV):

But there were also false prophets among the people, EVEN AS THERE WILL BE FALSE TEACHERS AMONG YOU, who will secretly bring in destructive heresies, even denying the Lord who bought them, and bring on themselves swift destruction. And many will follow their destructive ways, because of whom the way of truth will be blasphemed. BY COVETOUSNESS THEY WILL EXPLOIT YOU WITH DECEPTIVE WORDS.

Prosperity Gospel televangelist preachers proclaim that they receive financial blessings from God, in order to deceive their congregants into believing that they too can receive similar financial blessings. Prosperity Gospel preachers, in reality, receive their vast wealth through the financial offering donations of their deceived television congregation audience of whom they exploit with the Prosperity Gospel.[29]

MATTHEW 16:26; MARK 8:36; LUKE 9:25 (NKJV):

For what profit is it to a man if he gains the whole world, and loses his own soul?

Many false teaching, lawless Prosperity Gospel preachers have gained the whole world and are in grave danger of hearing the following message from Yeshua (Jesus) in the age that is to come:

MATTHEW 7:21-23 (NKJV):

"Not everyone who says to Me, 'Lord, Lord,' shall enter the kingdom of heaven, but he who does the will of My Father in heaven. Many will say to Me in that day, 'Lord, Lord, have we not prophesied in Your name, cast out demons in Your name, and done many wonders in Your name?' And then I will declare to them, 'I never knew you; depart from Me, you who practice lawlessness!'"

THE SERPENT SEED DOCTRINE

By George Lujack

The Serpent Seed doctrine is a controversial religious belief that attempts to explain the Scriptural account of the fall of man by saying that the serpent in the Garden of Eden mated with Eve, impregnated her, and that the offspring of their union was Cain. Much of Scripture was written allegorically, figuratively, prophetically, and symbolically. Proponents of the Serpent Seed doctrine decipher the Genesis account of the fall of man with the understanding that it was written symbolically. The problem is that the Serpent Seed doctrine follows a preconceived storyline and refuses to look at the Scripture and scientific exculpatory evidence that proves that the serpent in the garden could not have impregnated Eve, but instead makes leaps in assumptions and logic, liberally using Scripture to support the doctrine. This article will review excerpts of the Serpent Seed doctrine, in *italics*, and will show that man's original sin was an act of disobedience to God in the Garden of Eden, but was not an act of sex between Eve and the serpent. This article will also show that the serpent did not impregnate Eve, resulting in Cain being born as the spawn of the serpent.

The origin of the Serpent Seed doctrine goes back thousands of years, appearing in Gnostic writings and early Jewish texts. Mainstream Christian theologians and the early Christian church rightly rejected the Serpent Seed doctrine as unscriptural.

THE DOCTRINE OF THE SERPENT SEED[30]

SERPENT SEED DOCTRINE:

"And the Lord God said unto the Serpent, Because thou hast done this, thou art cursed above all cattle, and every beast of the field; upon thy belly thou shalt go, and dust shalt thou eat all the days of thy life and I will put enmity between thee and the woman, and between thy seed and her seed; it shall bruise thy head, and thou shall bruise his heel."
- **Genesis 3:14-15 (KJV)**

GENESIS 3:1 (NKJV):
Now the serpent was more cunning than any beast of the field, which YHWH (the Lord) God had made.

The serpent was *more cunning than any beast of the field*. Scripture does not declare that the serpent *was* a beast of the field.

The Serpent Seed doctrine promotes the idea that Genesis 3:14-15 is to be understood in the following way:

SERPENT SEED DOCTRINE:

"And the Lord God said unto the Serpent, Because thou hast done this, thou art cursed above all cattle, and every beast of the field; upon thy belly thou shalt go, and dust shalt thou eat all the days of thy life and I will put enmity between thee and the woman, and between thy [SERPENT'S] seed and her [ADAM'S] seed; it [CAIN] shall bruise thy [ABEL'S] head, and thou shall bruise his heel."

- **Genesis 3:14-15** (KJV)

The Serpent Seed doctrine is rebuked in the NKJV with the following [INTERPRETATIONS]:

GENESIS 3:14-15 (NKJV) [WITH INTERPRETATION]:

So YHWH (the Lord) God said to the serpent:

"Because you have done this, you are cursed more than all cattle, and more than every beast of the field; on your belly you shall go, and you shall eat dust all the days of your life. And I will put enmity between you [SATAN] and the woman [EVE'S OFFSPRING - MANKIND], and between your [SATAN'S] seed [OF REBELLION SIN] and her [RIGHTEOUS] Seed [YESHUA (JESUS)]. He [YESHUA (JESUS)] shall bruise your [SATAN'S] head, and you [SATAN] shall bruise His [YESHUA'S (JESUS')] heel."

A problem of omission in the Serpent Seed doctrine is that Genesis 3:15 proclaims, "He shall bruise your head, *and* you shall bruise His heel." Cain did bruise Abel's head...

GENESIS 4:8 (NKJV):

Cain talked with Abel his brother; and it came to pass, when they were in the field, that Cain rose up against Abel his brother and killed him.

Cain bruised Abel's head and killed him by taking a rock and striking him in the head with it. "He shall bruise your head, and you shall bruise His heel" reveals that IF Genesis 3:15 was a reference to Cain who bruised Abel's head, THEN Abel died without ever bruising Cain's heel. The bruising of the head and heel is a reference the spiritual conflict between Yeshua (Jesus) and Satan.

ROMANS 16:20 (NKJV):

And the God of peace will crush Satan under your feet shortly.

REVELATION 20:2-3,10 (NKJV):

He laid hold of the dragon, that serpent of old, who is the Devil and Satan, and bound him for a thousand years; and he cast him into the bottomless pit.

The devil... was cast into the lake of fire and brimstone where the beast and the false prophet are. And they will be tormented day and night forever and ever.

Yeshua (Jesus) will crush Satan under His feet and bruise his head, but He will not kill him. Satan will be cast alive and confined in hell forever.

PSALM 22:16 (NKJV):

They pierced My hands and My feet.

Satan bruised Yeshua's (Jesus') heel, at least one of them, when Yeshua (Jesus) was nailed through His hands and feet to the cross and crucified.

LAW OF REPRODUCTION

SERPENT SEED DOCTRINE:

Now, it is stated in Genesis 1:11,12 and 24 that God commanded every species of life, whether plant or animal life, to bring forth seed after its own kind. Therefore to hybridize two different species of animals is to go against God's commandment and law of reproduction. (Keep this law in mind so that you may understand later how, and why, the hybridizing of Mankind with the Serpent-kind had brought forth the sin that could be passed down to all men today.)

The hybridizing of man and serpent as being the reason sin is passed down to all men today is not recorded in Scripture and is rebuked by Scripture.

ROMANS 5:12 (NKJV):

Therefore, just as THROUGH ONE MAN SIN ENTERED THE WORLD, and death through sin, and thus death spread to all men, because all sinned.

1 CORINTHIANS 15:22 (NKJV):

In Adam all die, even so in Messiah (Christ) all shall be made alive.

Sin entered the world through Adam, not by a hybrid offspring of Adam. All men inherit sin and die through Adam's sin of disobedience.

CERTAIN BREEDS COULD CROSSBREED

SERPENT SEED DOCTRINE:

The seed of the Serpent could fuse with the egg of the woman. This seems very far-fetched to most people. But just look at what some men have done with some of the animals. They have produced a liger, a cross between a lion and a tigress; a zedonk, a hybrid between a zebra and a she-ass. The most common hybrid that we know is the mule, which is a mixture of the donkey and the mare. Scientists have tried to commingle beast and man without success. Beast and man cannot intermingle and reproduce. But the chemical affinity between them proves their close relationship. However, the intermingling between an animal (Serpent) and a woman (Eve) did take place in the garden of Eden. But God had completely destroyed that pattern of the Serpent, and no other beast can commingle with man again.

JOHN 3:6 (NKJV):

"That which is born of the flesh is flesh, and that which is born of the Spirit is spirit."

Eve could not have been cross-kind impregnated by the serpent, whether the serpent was a beast of the field or a spirit being, Satan himself.

Many unscientific assumptions are made to uphold the Serpent Seed doctrine.

The foremost unscientific assumption is that the seed of the serpent could, and did, fuse with the egg of the woman, Eve. Kinds can crossbreed with similar kinds, but kinds cannot cross-kind. Ligers, mules, and zedonks are all hybrid offspring from the same kind of animals. Humans can reproduce interracially, but not with any other kind of animal, beast, or spirit being (Satan).

God created all creatures, including man, to be able to reproduce according to their own kind and prevented creatures from breeding outside their kind (Genesis 1:24-25). A dog cannot cross-kind reproduce with a pig.

GENESIS 1:26 (NKJV):

Then God said, "Let Us make man in Our image, according to Our likeness; LET THEM HAVE DOMINION over the fish of the sea, over the birds of the air, and over the cattle, over all the earth and over every creeping thing that creeps on the earth."

GENESIS 2:18-20 (NKJV):

And YHWH (the Lord) God said, "It is not good that man should be alone; I will make him a helper comparable to him." Out of the ground YHWH (the Lord) God formed every beast of the field and every bird of the air, and brought them to Adam to see what he would call them. And whatever Adam called each living creature, that was its name. So Adam gave names to all cattle, to the birds of the air, and to every beast of the field. But for Adam THERE WAS NOT FOUND A HELPER COMPARABLE TO HIM.

GENESIS 3:1 (NKJV):

Now the serpent was more cunning than any beast of the field, which YHWH (the Lord) God had made.

The Serpent Seed doctrine acknowledges that modern man has not been able to breed with any animal, but assumes in the garden that this was not the case. The Serpent Seed doctrine claims the serpent to be an upright, bipedal, talking, and walking beast of the field, *comparable* to Adam and Eve, capable of mating with Eve. Scripture proclaims that Adam and Eve had dominion over every living thing that moved on the Earth (Genesis 1:28). Scripture further proclaims that Adam did not have a helper comparable to him (Genesis 2:20). The serpent therefore could not be comparable to Eve, nor could the serpent impregnate Eve, since it was a being, either a beast of the field, or a spirit being, that was not comparable, not the same kind of being, that Adam was.

SPIRITUAL SEED, NOT FLESH AND BLOOD SEED

JOHN 8:44 (NKJV):

"You are OF YOUR FATHER THE DEVIL, and the desires of your father you want to do."

A Serpent Seed doctrine adherent believes that a person is the literal descendant of Satan, instead of one who is *spiritually of Satan* by doing evil.

1 JOHN 3:9-12 (NKJV):

Whoever has been born of God does not sin, for HIS SEED remains in him; and he cannot sin, because he has been born of God. In this the children of God and the children of the devil are manifest: Whoever DOES NOT PRACTICE RIGHTEOUSNESS is not of God, nor is he who does not love his brother. For this is the message that you heard from the beginning, that we should love one another, not as Cain who was of the wicked one and murdered his brother. And why did he murder him? BECAUSE HIS WORKS WERE EVIL and his brother's righteous.

EPHESIANS 6:12 (NKJV):

For we do not wrestle against flesh and blood, but against principalities, against powers, against the rulers of the darkness of this age, against spiritual hosts of wickedness in the heavenly places.

Whoever repents and is spiritually born of God, and remains faithful to God, His *spiritual seed* remains in that person. The children of God are those who practice righteousness and the children of the devil are those who do evil works. We are not God's children or Satan's children through biological seed genealogy, but through our deeds, whether they are righteous or evil. Our battle is not a flesh battle, over biological seed, but is spiritual warfare against the wickedness of Satan.

FROM SERPENT TO SNAKE

SERPENT SEED DOCTRINE:

In passing His judgment, God did not destroy the Serpent, whose head was the Devil. Instead he cursed him above all the creatures of the field. The Serpent was cursed and transformed from an upright animal to a belly crawling reptile - a snake! Without his limbs, dust would become a part of his diet every time he feeds himself - "dust shalt thou eat all the days of thy life." Remember, he went on his belly after the curse, and not before.

To suggest that the serpent, a beast of the field, was an upright, bipedal, human-like creature, made in the image of man, is a great assumption and takes a leap of faith and reason to believe. The serpent was Satan who spoke directly to Adam and Eve. Satan is an upright, bipedal, human-like angelic being who was made in the image of God.

LEVITICUS 20:15-16 (NKJV):

If a man mates with an animal, he shall surely be put to death, and you shall kill the animal. If a woman approaches any animal and mates with it, you shall kill the woman and the animal. They shall surely be put to death. Their blood is upon them.

When beasts are abused and misused they are subject to being cursed or killed, even though the beast itself is not responsible for its actions, as a superior being, man or Satan, forces or guides the animal in sin.

ONE FLESH - TWO PEOPLE

SERPENT SEED DOCTRINE:

The crossing of the two lines of people, generation after generation, from Enoch to Noah, naturally caused the bloodstream of the sons of God to be perverted with the evil nature of the Serpent seed. The spiritual quality of

199

divine revelation within them gradually became watered down. Evil attributes were bred (increased) while the righteous traits diminished (decreased) throughout those generations until the two peoples became one flesh. The intermingling of the seeds was so complete in the generation prior to the Flood that all the people of the earth were involved. Noah, who was the last of the pure righteous firstborn of the Sethic line (Gen.5:28-29), also took to wife a Cainite, or a woman of mixed seed.

ACTS 17:26 (NKJV):

And He has made FROM ONE BLOOD EVERY NATION OF MEN to dwell on all the face of the earth.

Scripture rejects the Serpent Seed doctrine's notion that man had two bloodlines. There is no serpent-man hybrid bloodline of people, past or present. God created all men of one blood. Men of one blood dwell in every nation on the Earth. Righteousness is not a matter of bloodline, but of obedience to God.

SIN OF DISOBEDIENCE

SERPENT SEED DOCTRINE:

THE FORNICATION of the woman with the Serpent had brought forth DEATH to the world. It was actually Eve's disobedience to God's commandment not to eat of that Tree of Knowledge of Good and Evil.

It was through Adam's sin of disobedience, not Eve's sin of fornication, that sin entered the world.

ROMANS 5:12 (NKJV):

Therefore, just as THROUGH ONE MAN SIN ENTERED THE WORLD, and DEATH THROUGH SIN, and thus death spread to all men, because all sinned.

If Adam had not sinned, after Eve had, it has been theologically argued that sin could have been dealt with in the garden, and would not have been spread to the world. That scenario is a matter for theological debate, as Adam did sin, and Adam was blamed for causing sin to enter the world.

PLEASANT - WISE - SEXUAL UNION?

SERPENT SEED DOCTRINE:

Genesis 3:6 says that the tree was "pleasant to the eyes, and a tree to be desired to make one wise..." How could the eating of the fruit of the forbidden tree make one wise? Because Eve harkened to the whispers of the Serpent and was enchanted with the Tree of the Knowledge of Good and Evil (Perverted Knowledge), and "saw that the tree was good for food, and that it was pleasant to the eyes, and a tree desired to make one wise, she took of the tree thereof, and did eat" She lusted for that knowledge by what she saw (understood) of it, and not knowing that she was being deceived, she fornicated with the Serpent.

The Serpent Seed doctrine makes a valid point in asking, "How could the eating of the fruit of the forbidden tree make one wise?"

GENESIS 3:2-7 (NKJV):

And the woman said to the serpent, "We may eat the fruit of the trees of the garden; but of the fruit of the tree which is in the midst of the garden, God has said, 'You shall not eat it, nor shall you touch it, lest you die.'" Then the serpent said to the woman, "You will not surely die. For God knows that in the day you eat of it your eyes will be opened, and you will be like God, knowing good and evil."

So when the woman saw that the tree was good for food, that it was pleasant to the eyes, and a tree desirable to make one wise, she took of its fruit and ate. She also gave to her husband with her, and he ate. Then the eyes of both of them were opened, and they knew that they were naked; and they sewed fig leaves together and made themselves coverings.

To say that Eve merely looked at a physical tree and deduced that its fruit was not only edible, but that by consuming it she would become wise, does not seem like a good, literal explanation. The Serpent Seed doctrine leads adherents to believe that Eve thought that by having sex with the serpent, this would make her wise. The only 'wisdom' Eve could have possibly gained by fornication with the serpent was unlawful carnal knowledge.

To suggest that the serpent was the fruit and Eve had sex with the serpent, and that Adam afterward had sex with Eve, and that Eve conceived twin sons, Cain from the serpent and Abel from Adam, takes great leaps in assumption to believe. The storyline of the Serpent Seed doctrine has many gaps in the Genesis account and in science, which the doctrine fills by liberally applying Scripture with loose scientific facts to adhere to the tale.

HOW WAS EVE TEMPTED BY A PIECE OF FRUIT PLEASING TO THE EYES, WHICH COULD SUPPOSEDLY MAKE HER WISE?

GENESIS 3:6 (NKJV):

So when the woman saw that the tree was good for food, that it was pleasant to the eyes, and a tree desirable to make one wise, she took of its fruit and ate. She also gave to her husband with her, and he ate.

Scripture does not specifically say how or why Eve was tempted by a piece of fruit, but using a little conjecture and imagination it may have been a temptation like the following scenario...

The serpent (Satan) struck up a conversation with Eve. He was friendly and seemed wise. He lured Eve over to the midst of the garden, where the tree of the knowledge of good and evil was. Satan then took from the tree's fruit and ate of it himself, showing her by example, then ...

GENESIS 3:4-5 (NKJV):

Then the serpent said to the woman, "You will not surely die. For God knows that in the day you eat of it your eyes will be opened, and you will be like God, knowing good and evil."

So, Eve saw that the serpent (Satan) was enjoying this fruit, and he seemed to be wise, so...

GENESIS 3:6 (NKJV):

So when the woman saw that the tree was good for food, that it was pleasant to the eyes, and a tree desirable to make one wise, she took of its fruit and ate. She also gave to her husband with her, and he ate.

As human beings, we all can recall sometime during our life when someone first approached us, then tempted us with some unlawful fruit. There was a time when someone was smoking a cigarette before us and said, "Try one, it's enjoyable and it won't kill you." Then we observed that person smoking, seemingly enjoying it and it not killing the person, so we took a cigarette and smoked.

The fruit could be a cigarette, cigar, narcotic drug, alcohol (as a minor), or something else that we knew we shouldn't have been doing.

This is the most plausible, most likely explanation of how Eve was tempted by a piece of fruit.

1 TIMOTHY 2:14 (NKJV):

And Adam was not deceived, but the woman being deceived, fell into transgression.

While Eve was deceived into believing the fruit could make her wise, it should be noted that Adam was not deceived as Eve was, but ate anyway. Adam most likely sinned and ate of the fruit, as he did not want to be parted in knowledge or culpability from his helper, Eve.

WHO WAS THE SERPENT?

GENESIS 3:1 (NKJV):

Now the serpent was MORE CUNNING than ANY BEAST of the field.

The fruit of the tree of the knowledge of good and evil that Eve ate from was not sex with the serpent. The serpent was not a beast of the field, but was more cunning than any beast of the field. Beasts of the field do not speak.

GENESIS 3:2-3 (NKJV):

And the woman said to the serpent, "We may eat the fruit of the trees of the garden; but of THE FRUIT OF THE TREE WHICH IS IN THE MIDST OF THE GARDEN, God has said, 'You shall not eat it, nor shall you touch it, lest you die.'"

The serpent approached Eve *somewhere* in the garden (not in the midst), and Eve said to the serpent that the tree and the fruit from the tree IN THE MIDST OF THE GARDEN was what she was commanded not to eat or touch. The serpent lured Eve to the midst of the garden and she ate fruit from the tree, not the serpent's fruit (or sexual organ). Therefore, the serpent's fruit was not the fruit from the tree in the midst of the garden that the Serpent Seed doctrine maintains Eve fornicated with. The serpent in the garden was Satan himself and the tree Eve ate fruit of was from a stationary tree in the midst of the garden that the serpent (Satan) lured her to.

REVELATION 12:9 (NKJV):

So the great dragon was cast out, THAT SERPENT OF OLD, called the Devil and Satan, who deceives the whole world.

REVELATION 20:2 (NKJV):

He laid hold of the dragon, THAT SERPENT OF OLD, who is the Devil and Satan, and bound him for a thousand years.

The fruit of the tree was not Satan's sexual organ that he used to impregnate Eve with. Satan is a spiritual being, not a flesh and blood human being. Yeshua Messiah (Jesus Christ) is the only spiritual being to have ever crossed over from the spirit realm to take on human flesh (Romans 8:3).

THE SERPENT CURSED

GENESIS 3:14-15 (NKJV):

So YHWH (the Lord) God said to the serpent:

"Because you have done this, you are cursed more than all cattle, and more than every beast of the field; on your belly you shall go, and you shall eat dust all the days of your life. And I will put enmity between you and the woman, and between your seed and her Seed; He shall bruise your head, and you shall bruise His heel."

A strictly literal explanation of the serpent's curse was that the serpent was a beast of the field that Satan spoke through and God cursed this animal, transforming it into a snake that goes on its belly. This image has been engrained in many people's minds.

The serpent of the garden is Satan, so a more figurative interpretation of the serpent's curse is necessary. God devalued the serpent (Satan) beneath all of His creatures and crippled him.

GENESIS 3:14-15 (NKJV) [WITH INTERPRETATION]:

So YHWH (the Lord) God said to [SATAN] the serpent:

"Because you have done this, you are cursed more than all cattle, and more than every beast of the field; on your belly you shall go, and you shall eat dust all the days of your life [YOU ARE CURSED TO HUNGER AND WILL 'EAT DUST,' NOT BE SATISFIED OR RECEIVE BLESSINGS ANY LONGER]. And I will put enmity [SPIRITUAL WARFARE] between you [SATAN] and the woman [EVE], and between your seed [OF SPIRITUAL UNRIGHTEOUSNESS] and her Seed [YESHUA (JESUS), THE WAY THE TRUTH AND THE LIFE - JOHN 14:16]; He shall bruise your head [BIND YOU - REVELATION 20:2], and you shall bruise His [YESHUA'S (JESUS')] heel [BY SEEING THAT HE IS NAILED TO THE CROSS - PSALM 22:16]."

ADAM AND EVE WERE WARNED THAT THEY WOULD BE CURSED

GENESIS 2:15-17 (NKJV):

Then YHWH (the Lord) God took the man and put him in the garden of Eden to tend and keep it. And YHWH (the Lord) God commanded the man, saying, "Of every tree of the garden you may freely eat; but of the tree of the knowledge of good and evil you shall not eat, for in the day that you eat of it you shall surely die."

The Serpent Seed doctrine proclaims that God would not have cursed Adam and Eve to death if they merely disobeyed Him by eating fruit from a tree. God commanded Adam not to eat of the tree of the knowledge of good and evil, and promised him that if he did eat of it, he would die. God is holy and keeps His covenant promises and His word, lest He would not be holy. An act of disobedience against God was sufficient enough to curse Adam and to cause all of mankind to inherit original sin.

CHRISTMAS AND EASTER;
CHRISTMAS AND EASTER ARE PAGAN FESTIVALS NOT ACCEPTABLE TO GOD

By George Lujack

Christmas and Easter are the two most celebrated Christian holidays. Many people do not know the evils associated with these adopted pagan-based festivals and naively enjoy these holidays believing that they are of God.

What do Christmas trees, exchanging gifts, Santa Claus, Easter bunnies, and painted chicken eggs have to do with celebrating the birth, death, and resurrection of the Messiah (Christ)? This article will examine the pagan origins of Christmas and Easter and will show why true believers, who worship God in spirit and truth, should not partake in these false holidays.

CHRISTMAS: YESHUA (JESUS) WAS NOT BORN ON DECEMBER 25TH

LUKE 2:4-8 (NKJV):
Joseph also went up from Galilee, out of the city of Nazareth, into Judea, to the city of David, which is called Bethlehem, because he was of the house and lineage of David, to be registered with Mary, his betrothed wife, who was with child. So it was, that while they were there, the days were completed for her to be delivered.
And she brought forth her firstborn Son, and wrapped Him in swaddling cloths, and laid Him in a manger, because there was no room for them in the inn.
Now there were in the same country SHEPHERDS LIVING OUT IN THE FIELDS, KEEPING WATCH OVER THEIR FLOCK BY NIGHT.

In the Bethlehem region, south of Jerusalem, December 25th is the coldest part of the year. First century shepherds would not have been living out in the field, day and night, watching their flocks in winter. The time of Messiah's (Christ's) birth was not in the winter on December 25th. Shepherds in the Bethlehem region do not live out in the fields, and their herds are not out in the pasture, in wintertime to this day.

Christmas was first celebrated on December 25th by decree of Roman Emperor Constantine in 336 AD. Catholic Pope Julius I officially declared that the birth of Yeshua (Jesus) was on December 25th in 350 AD. Catholic Pope Julius I did not choose December 25th as Yeshua's (Jesus') birthday by any direction or indication from the Scriptures, but instead incorporated the pagan festivals of Saturnalia and the winter solstice into Christianity and called it Christmas, and declared December 25th as Christ's birthday to replace other pagan gods' birthdays celebrated on that date.

The dominant Gentile pagan culture rampant in Rome, Greece, and Egypt worshiped various gods, and Catholicism accommodated them through Christmas. Nimrod was acknowledged as being born on December 25th and was replaced by Christ. Christianity was perverted and the pagans were satisfied. Christians who celebrate Christmas as Yeshua Messiah's (Jesus Christ's) birthday are unwittingly following the 4th century dictates of Roman Emperor Constantine and Catholic Pope Julius I. Christmas is not a festival of God.

WHEN WAS YESHUA (JESUS) BORN?

The exact date of Messiah's (Christ's) birth is unknown, but most true Scripture scholars believe it was during the Feast of Tabernacles (Sukkot) in the fall, typically near the end of September on the Gregorian calendar.

CHRISTMAS TREES ARE IDOLS

JEREMIAH 10:2-5 (NKJV):
Thus says YHWH (the Lord):

"Do not learn the way of the Gentiles. Do not be dismayed at the signs of heaven, for the Gentiles are dismayed at them. For the customs of the peoples are worthless. For one cuts a tree from the forest, the work of the hands of the workman, with an ax. They decorate it with silver and gold; they fasten it with nails and hammers so that it will not topple. They are upright like a palm tree, and they cannot speak. They must be carried, because they cannot go by themselves."

YHWH (the Lord) says DO NOT do this: take a tree from the forest, decorate it with silver and gold, fasten it at its base so it does not topple, stand it up as a palm tree and carry it in and out, for these dead trees cannot move by themselves. Yet every Christmas season, Christians do this: erect a Christmas tree in spite of what YHWH (the Lord) has told them not to do.

As the saying goes, "If it looks like a duck, walks like a duck, and quacks like a duck, then it's a duck." Christmas trees are carried like idols, because they cannot move by themselves. They cannot speak, just as idols cannot speak. They are set up in a prominent place in the home to be displayed, just as an idol would be. They are adorned, just as an idol is adorned. They are bowed before and worshiped, just as an idol is.

When people buy gifts to exchange with others on Christmas, they sacrifice their labor, money, and time to buy and wrap those gifts, then bow before the Christmas tree idol in the home and place their sacrifices under the tree. This is idolatry, sacrifice, and worship, whether acknowledged by believers or not.

Songs have been written and praises sung to Christmas tree idols in worship.

"O Christmas Tree, O Christmas Tree, How steadfast are your branches!
Your boughs are green in summer's clime, And through the snows of wintertime.
O Christmas Tree, O Christmas Tree, How steadfast are your branches!

O Christmas Tree, O Christmas Tree, What happiness befalls me,

When oft at joyous Christmas-time, Your form inspires my song and rhyme.

O Christmas Tree, O Christmas Tree, What happiness befalls me.

O Christmas Tree, O Christmas Tree, Your boughs can teach a lesson,

That constant faith and hope sublime, Lend strength and comfort through all time.

O Christmas Tree, O Christmas Tree, Your boughs can teach a lesson."

WHEN YESHUA (JESUS) RETURNS HE WILL END CHRISTMAS

ISAIAH 14:8 (NKJV) [WITH INTERPRETATION]:

Indeed the cypress trees rejoice over you, and the cedars of Lebanon, saying, 'Since You have come down [FROM HEAVEN, HAVE RETURNED], no woodsman has come up against us.'

When Yeshua (Jesus) returns, He will end the annual practice of axmen going to the forest to chop down trees for the pagan festival of Christmas.

SANTA CLAUS UNSCRAMBLED IS SATAN LUCAS

What does Satan Lucas (Lucifer), disguised as Santa Claus, have to do with celebrating the birth of Yeshua (Jesus)? Santa Claus takes children's focus off of Yeshua (Jesus), instills in them the values of coveting, makes them believe that Santa knows when they have been bad or good (replacing Almighty, all-knowing, omnipresent God in this role), and tells them to be good for goodness' sake (not for righteousness' sake).

Often when children come of age, they learn to distrust their parents who lied to them, telling them Santa Claus was real. Doubts are placed in their hearts as to whether they should believe in God or if God should just be considered another fairy tale.

EASTER ETYMOLOGY: EASTER NAMED AFTER PAGAN GODDESS ISHTAR

The early Christian churches did all they could to accommodate the religions of the world and incorporate them into what would become Christianity. Slickly renaming the Passover 'Easter' was one of these deceptions. Ishtar was the pagan goddess of fertility, love, sexuality, and war and it was the early Christian churches that renamed the Passover 'Easter,' in honor of this pagan goddess.

Christians, who may deny that the word 'Easter' has anything to do with Ishtar, should ask, "Where then is the word Easter derived from?"

The origin of the word Easter, as officially declared by Christianity, is 'unknown' at best and is possibly linked to a pagan goddess at worst.

1 CORINTHIANS 5:7 (NKJV):

For indeed Messiah (Christ), our Passover, was sacrificed for us.

Passover means that God's wrath passes over us. Yeshua (Jesus) said, "Do this in remembrance of Me" (Luke 22:19). Do what? Remember Him as our Passover Lamb (Luke 22:15; 1 Corinthians 5:7). His blood covers our sins so that God's wrath 'passes over' us, just as lambs' blood had covered the doorposts of the enslaved Hebrews in Egypt, so that the angel of death would 'pass over' their dwellings.

THE KING JAMES BIBLE REPLACES PASSOVER WITH EASTER

ACTS 12:4 (KJV):

And when he had apprehended him, he put him in prison, and delivered him to four quaternions of soldiers to keep him; intending after EASTER to bring him forth to the people.

The word 'Easter' appears in one verse within the imperfect King James Bible, obviously inserted there in place of 'Passover' in the 17th century by a biased King James translator who made the word switch. Easter was properly corrected to Passover in the New King James Bible.

ACTS 12:4 (NKJV):

So when he had arrested him, he put him in prison, and delivered him to four squads of soldiers to keep him, intending to bring him before the people after PASSOVER.

The disciples in the book of Acts never celebrated Easter. They celebrated the Passover in remembrance of Yeshua (Jesus). All true believers should likewise do so. Easter *became* a separate holiday apart from Passover, on an independent date from the Jewish calendar, based on rulings from early Christian bishops at the First Council of Nicea in 325 AD.

YESHUA (JESUS) WAS NOT CRUCIFIED ON GOOD FRIDAY, NOR DID HE RISE ON EASTER SUNDAY

The Good Friday to Easter Sunday holiday observed by most Christians is a corrupted representation of the Passover sacrifice of Yeshua the Messiah (Jesus the Christ), His time in the grave, and His resurrection. Yeshua (Jesus) did not die on Friday evening and rise on Sunday morning.

THREE DAYS AND THREE NIGHTS DOES NOT EQUATE TO GOOD FRIDAY TO EASTER SUNDAY

MATTHEW 12:40 (NKJV):

For as Jonah was three days AND three nights in the belly of the great fish, so will the Son of Man be three days AND three nights in the heart of the earth.

Counting the days of a Good Friday crucifixion through Sunday morning resurrection does not equal three days and three nights. Being in the grave from only Good Friday (evening) to Easter Sunday (at sunrise) would have meant He was in the grave on Friday evening, Saturday day, and Saturday evening, which is only one day and two nights.

JOHN 20:1-2 (NKJV):

Now the first day of the week Mary Magdalene went to the tomb early, WHILE IT WAS STILL DARK, and saw that the stone had been taken away from the tomb. Then she ran and came to Simon Peter, and to the other disciple, whom Yeshua (Jesus) loved, and said to them, "They have taken away the Lord out of the tomb, and we do not know where they have laid Him."

There was a special high Sabbath during the Passover week that Yeshua (Jesus) was crucified on (Mark 16:1). When Mary Magdalene went to the tomb of Yeshua (Jesus) Sunday morning, *before* sunrise, she found it empty. Yeshua (Jesus) did not therefore rise Sunday morning. He had obviously risen beforehand on Saturday evening. Yeshua (Jesus) was crucified Wednesday afternoon and was placed in His tomb on Wednesday before sunset. Yeshua (Jesus) was in the grave Wednesday night, Thursday day, Thursday night, Friday day, Friday night, Saturday day, and rose Saturday night. He was in the grave three days and three nights just as He said He would be.

Christians who claim that they want to continue to observe Easter to celebrate the resurrection should do it right and celebrate the Passover in remembrance of Him (Luke 22:15-19). Messiah (Christ) is not our Easter; He is our Passover (1 Corinthians 5:7).

BUT GOD KNOWS MY HEART

JEREMIAH 7:8-10 (NKJV):

Behold, you trust in lying words that cannot profit. Will you steal, murder, commit adultery, swear falsely, burn incense to Baal, AND WALK AFTER OTHER GODS WHOM YOU DO NOT KNOW, AND THEN COME AND STAND BEFORE ME IN THIS HOUSE WHICH IS CALLED BY MY NAME, AND SAY, 'WE ARE DELIVERED TO DO ALL THESE ABOMINATIONS'?

JEREMIAH 17:9 (NKJV):

The heart is deceitful above all things, and desperately wicked; who can know it?

MATTHEW 7:14 (NKJV):

"Because narrow is the gate and difficult is the way which leads to life, and there are few who find it."

Many deceive themselves into believing that celebrating Christmas and Easter are OK, because God knows their heart. Are Christians really being honest when they say that they are celebrating Christmas and Easter for God or are they really celebrating these holidays for themselves?

The road is harder to not follow the ways of the world than it is to partake in them.

LIPSTICK ON A PIG - SPIRITUAL FORNICATION

Celebrating Christmas and Easter, to honor our holy God, is like putting lipstick on a pig and calling it a woman. It is still a pig. Christmas and Easter are pagan festivals honoring a pagan god and goddess. To transfer these festivals and honor the God of Scripture through them is spiritual fornication.

Celebrating Christmas and Easter to honor God is like a rich man who loves his good faithful wife, but has decided to end his marriage as he has found a younger, more exciting woman who he wants to make into his new wife. So, the man tells his wife that he is leaving her for another woman. The wife is devastated at the news and the man feels bad that he has hurt his faithful wife's feelings. So the man decides to try to cheer up his wife by having a surprise party for her. He organizes a surprise party for his wife on his mistress's birthday. His wife comes home and the husband introduces his wife to his mistress, who he is committing adultery with, and then a bunch of strippers pop out from the cake, which is in the center of the home, and the strippers all say "Happy Birthday!" to the man's wife and everyone joins in the hedonistic festivities of this chaotic party. The wife, in shock and horror, turns her back and leaves her residence unable to look upon her husband, who is dishonoring her with this sleaze-filled party.

The analogy here is that the husband is like the believer who thinks he can worship God in any manner he chooses. The mistress is like the goddess Ishtar. The birthday cake, set up in a prominent place in the home, is like the Christmas tree idol. The strippers, who pop out from the cake, are like the falsehoods and evils that are part of paganism (Santa Claus, elves, Easter bunnies, painted eggs). The faithful wife, who comes home to the horror of this celebration in honor of her, is like God.

Spiritual fornication is how Yeshua (Jesus) views Christmas and Easter, the honoring of Him through festivals of falsehoods, idolatry, and paganism.

ISAIAH 45:9 (NKJV):
Woe to Him who strives with his Maker! ... Shall the clay say to him who forms it, 'What are you making?'

JOHN 4:23-24 (NKJV):
"True worshipers will worship the Father in spirit and truth; for the Father is seeking such to worship Him. God is Spirit, and those who worship Him must worship in spirit and truth."

It is not for the creation to tell the Creator how he or she will honor and worship God, but that is what many people do when they refuse to worship God in spirit and truth and instead honor and worship Him in a manner of their own choosing. If Christmas and Easter were festivals that God wanted man to worship Him through, He would have declared so in Scripture. We MUST worship Him in spirit and truth, not through worldliness and untruth.

GOD'S FESTIVALS ARE NOT 'JEWISH' HOLIDAYS

LEVITICUS 23:1-2 (NKJV):
And YHWH (the Lord) spoke to Moses, saying, "Speak to the children of Israel, and say to them: 'The feasts of YHWH (the Lord), which you shall proclaim to be holy convocations, THESE ARE *MY* FEASTS.

Due to the fact that there is much confusion coming forth from organized Christianity and Judaism, and because of the historic separation of Christianity from the Jews, God's festivals have been classified as 'Jewish' holidays.

THE SEVEN FEASTS OF YHWH (THE LORD)

- **Passover (Pesach)**
- **Unleavened Bread**
- **First Fruits**
- **Shavuot (Weeks) (Pentecost)**
- **Trumpets**
- **Atonement (Yom Kippur)**
- **Sukkoth (Booths) (Tabernacles) (Wedding)**

In addition to Christmas and Easter, other Christian or secular holidays, which to some greater or lesser degree are evil, man-made, pagan, or secular in origin would include: Ash Wednesday, Corpus Christi, Halloween, Thanksgiving, St. Patrick's Day, St. Valentine's Day, and many others. These holidays of man take people away from the holy festivals of God.

The feasts of YHWH (the Lord) are not Jewish holidays; they are God's holy day convocation festivals. Christians who see and understand this truth, and who wish to come out of Christian-Babylonian pagan worship of God, and who wish to worship Him in spirit and truth, should study God's festivals and find out more about them by attending a Messianic Hebrew Roots congregation, where the festivals of YHWH (the Lord) are known, observed, and practiced.

WHAT'S A BELIEVER TO DO DURING CHRISTMAS AND EASTER?

1 CORINTHIANS 5:9-10 (NKJV):

I wrote to you in my epistle not to keep company with sexually immoral people. Yet I certainly did not mean with the sexually immoral people of this world, or with the covetous, or extortioners, or idolaters, SINCE THEN YOU WOULD NEED TO GO OUT OF THE WORLD.

A believer can still attend a Christmas or Easter gathering and not partake in the pagan festivities.

Believers are permitted to meet with family, friends, or relatives during pagan events, but should not partake in the rituals involved in these events. It is permissible to meet with family and friends, eat and greet with them as usual, but a believer should not participate in decorating the Christmas tree, exchanging gifts, singing Christmas carols, forsaking the dietary commands by eating Christmas or Easter ham, practice paganism by coloring Easter eggs, or playing Easter games.

A true believer should use the opportunity of pagan holidays, such as Christmas and Easter, to reveal the truth of what God's word says about these false holidays and expose them.

ACTS 17:30 (NKJV):

Truly, these times of ignorance God overlooked, but now commands all men everywhere to repent.

Christmas and Easter are holidays not truly dedicated to God, but to the things of this world. Christmas is a celebration of mystical things in celebration of material covetousness. Christmas trees are idols; Santa represents Satan who miraculously knows all things; his elves represent his co-working demons; and Santa provides gifts for children by delivering them on Christmas Eve on reindeer that fly. Easter is a counterfeit Passover that celebrates the resurrection of Yeshua the Messiah (Jesus the Christ), but does so in a corrupted way by declaring the actual time the Messiah (Christ) spent in the grave was a day and two nights, rather than three days and three nights; renames Passover 'Easter' in honor of the pagan goddess Ishtar; uses rabbits to extol fertility (and sexual promiscuity); and painted eggs to represent offspring (and sacrifice of offspring). Easter subtly glorifies fertility as the way of new life, in place of the resurrection of Yeshua (Jesus) as the resurrection to new life.

Some people say "Keep Christ in Christmas." Christ never was in Christmas in the first place, so it is appropriate to keep the X in Xmas. Likewise, Easter the name of a pagan goddess Ishtar, has nothing to do with the resurrection of Messiah (Christ). We are to do this: Passover, in remembrance of Him (Luke 22:14-19).

Worshiping God through the false pagan holidays of the world, which are not His holy festivals (Leviticus 23), is not worshiping Him in truth. Believers are told that we MUST worship God in spirit and truth (John 4:23-24). Worshiping God the way the world incorrectly honors Him is NOT an option and we should not partake in the evil things of this world, which are disguised as good (1 John 2:15-17, 4:4-6; 2 Corinthians 11:13-15).

WHO IS SANTA CLAUS?

By George Lujack

Santa Claus is not a historical figure, but is actually a conjured up character who has been brought into existence through deceptive evil spirits.

The Second Vatican Council formally stated that no Roman Catholic bishop by the name of Nicholas ever existed and Vatican II further admitted that the legends attributed to this 'saint' had no Christian origin and *probably* came from pagan origins. The Vatican, in the 1970's, demoted Saint Nicholas as a major saint and characterized him as a mythological figure.[31]

The name 'Santa Claus,' in English, is an anagram that when unscrambled reveals the true identity behind the obese man with white beard in a red suit.

Santa = Satan; Claus = Lucas.

Satan is the name of God's adversary: the devil - the evil one.
The meaning of the name 'Santa' in Latin is 'Saint,' and 'holy.'
Lucas is an abbreviated form of Lucifer.
Lucas in Latin means 'bringer of light' and in Greek, 'light giving.'
Lucifer is a Latin derived name meaning 'bringing light.'
Santa Claus unscrambled means 'Satan Lucifer - holy saint, bringer of light.'

JOHN 8:12 (NKJV):
Then Yeshua (Jesus) spoke to them again, saying, "I am the light of the world. He who follows Me shall not walk in darkness, but have the light of life."

Santa Claus (Satan Lucifer) is an imposter of Yeshua Messiah (Jesus Christ). Santa Claus (Satan Lucifer) is NOT the light of the world. Santa (Satan) also goes by the name Saint Nick and Kris Kringle. Old Nick (saint Nick) is a name for the devil, Satan. Kris Kringle is a name that refers to Christkind, the Austrian and German Christmas gift-bringer, the Christ Child.

Santa (Satan), according to a folk song, is coming to town.

"You better watch out, you better not cry, you better not pout, I'm telling you why, Santa Claus is comin' to town…"

Yeshua Messiah (Jesus Christ) is coming, and you better watch out for Him:

REVELATION 22:12 (NKJV):

Behold, I am coming quickly... and My reward is with Me, to give to every one according to his work.

Santa (Satan) rides his sleigh in the clouds to every household, to all people around the world and comes like a thief in the night, leaving presents.

Yeshua (Jesus) will come in the clouds so that every eye shall see Him and will come as a thief to those who are not watching for Him.

REVELATION 1:7 (NKJV):

Behold, He is coming with clouds, and every eye will see Him.

REVELATION 3:3 (NKJV):

Therefore if you will not watch, I will come upon you as a thief, and you will not know what hour I will come upon you.

Santa (Satan), according to a folk song, keeps a list, judges, and rewards according to who is naughty and nice:

"He's making a list and checking it twice, gonna find out who's naughty and nice..."

Yeshua (Jesus) is keeping a list of the saints in a book. He will award and judge the righteous according to their works.

REVELATION 3:5 (NKJV):

He who overcomes shall be clothed in white garments, and I will not blot out his name from the Book of Life; but I will confess his name before My Father and before His angels.

DEUTERONOMY 32:36; HEBREWS 10:30 (NKJV):

YHWH (the Lord) will judge His people.

REVELATION 22:12 (NKJV):

My reward is with Me, to give to every one according to his work.

Santa (Satan), according to a folk song, knows all things.

"He sees you when you're sleeping, He knows when you're awake, He knows if you've been bad or good, So be good for goodness sake..."

Santa (Satan) does not know all things; only God knows all things:

1 JOHN 3:20 (NKJV):

God is greater than our heart, and knows all things.

Children are encouraged to leave 'offerings' of cookies (cake) and milk (drink) for Santa (Satan) when he visits each year, coming down the chimney to pass through the fire (wood kindled fireplace). These offerings to other 'gods' are an offense to God that can provoke Him to anger.

DEUTERONOMY 18:10 (NKJV):

There shall not be found among you anyone who makes his son or his daughter pass through the fire... (Leviticus 18:21; Deuteronomy 18:10; 2 Kings 16:3, 17:17, 21:6, 23:10; 2 Chronicles 33:6; Ezekiel 20:26,31).

JEREMIAH 7:18 (NKJV):

The children gather wood, the fathers kindle the fire, and the women knead dough, to make cakes for the queen of heaven; and they pour out drink offerings to other gods, that they may provoke Me to anger.

Posing as Santa Claus, Satan Lucifer appears as an angel of light - a 'bringer of light,' gifts and joy to the world, but is an imposter keeping many distracted from knowing the true light of the world, Yeshua Messiah (Jesus Christ).

2 CORINTHIANS 11:14 (NKJV):

Satan himself transforms himself into an angel of light.

Santa Claus (Satan Lucifer) is a liar who deceives the whole world.[32]

REVELATION 12:9 (NKJV):

So the great dragon was cast out, that serpent of old, called the Devil and Satan, who deceives the whole world; he was cast to the earth, and his angels were cast out with him.

Believers, consider that Santa Claus is not just some harmless fairy tale of a jolly fat man with a white beard and a red suit, but Satan Lucifer himself deceiving the whole world through a pagan festival known as Christmas.

Parents, who participate in the Santa Claus deception, lie to their children in telling them that Santa is real. They encourage their children to believe in Santa, to write and ask (pray) to Santa for material things that they desire (covet). This starts a child's life out with a lie, encourages covetousness, and misplaces a child's faith in a false deity being. Later on in life, it should be no surprise that children who were once lied to - have learned how to lie, who were once encouraged to want things - become materialistic, and who once believed in Santa Claus and found out that he didn't exist - have a difficult time believing in a God who they also believe may not exist. Praise and worship are to be given to God and His Son Yeshua (Jesus) only; not to (or through) some mythical character known as Santa Claus, who usurps glory from Messiah (Christ), and whose real identity is Satan Lucifer.

EXODUS 34:14 (NKJV):

You shall worship no other god, for YHWH (the Lord), whose name is Jealous, is a jealous God.

SPEAKING IN TONGUES, HANDLING SERPENTS, AND DRINKING DEADLY THINGS

By George Lujack

This article is primarily directed at the various Pentecostal Christian denominations who believe in demonstrating their faith through displays of speaking in tongues, snake handling, and drinking strychnine poison.

SPEAKING IN TONGUES

There is nothing glorious or edifying in speaking in gibberish and rolling on the ground. The Scripture-declared purpose of speaking in tongues is to enable believers to speak the gospel to unbelievers and other people in their native language, so that they will have faith that those proclaiming the gospel message are truly sent from God (1 Corinthians 14:22). If someone claims to be speaking in a tongue (another language) and no one can interpret his or her words, it is better for them to keep quiet (1 Corinthians 14:27-28).

Paul cautions the modern-day tongue speakers, who attempt to manifest speaking in tongues, but are speaking in undecipherable gibberish, that others will perceive them as being "out of their mind."

1 CORINTHIANS 14:16-23 (NKJV):

If you bless with the spirit, how will he who occupies the place of the uninformed say "Amen" at your giving of thanks, since he does not understand what you say? For you indeed give thanks well, but the other is not edified. I thank my God I speak with tongues more than you all; YET IN THE CHURCH I WOULD RATHER SPEAK FIVE WORDS WITH MY UNDERSTANDING, THAT I MAY TEACH OTHERS ALSO, THAN TEN THOUSAND WORDS IN A TONGUE. Brethren, do not be children in understanding; however, in malice be babes, but in understanding be mature. In the law it is written: "With men of other tongues and other lips, I will speak to this people; And yet, for all that, they will not hear Me," says the Lord. Therefore tongues are for a sign, not to those who believe but to unbelievers; but prophesying is not for unbelievers but for those who believe.

THEREFORE IF THE WHOLE CHURCH COMES TOGETHER IN ONE PLACE, AND ALL SPEAK WITH TONGUES, AND THERE COME IN THOSE WHO ARE UNINFORMED OR UNBELIEVERS, WILL THEY NOT SAY THAT YOU ARE OUT OF YOUR MIND?

HANDLING SERPENTS AND DRINKING DEADLY THINGS

MARK 16:17-18 (NKJV):

"And these signs will follow those who believe: In My name they will cast out demons; they will speak with new tongues; they will take up serpents; and if they drink anything deadly, it will by no means hurt them; they will lay hands on the sick, and they will recover."

God is not a circus act (handling serpents / drinking poison). Believers are not required to handle poisonous snakes or drink strychnine poison to demonstrate their faith. Believers do not need to display their faith, but rather proclaim it. Believers are not to put God to the test with dangerous stunts to demonstrate their faith. Believers shouldn't likewise jump off a roof of a building and say that God will protect them from falling to the ground and injuring themselves. Should believers, in like manner, put their necks inside lions' mouths or swim in shark-infested waters? OF COURSE NOT! God does not need us to perform dangerous stunts to prove to Him that we have faith. God will test us, or allow us to be tested, if He deems it appropriate. Sadly, many people have needlessly died handling poisonous snakes and drinking poison in the Pentecostal churches throughout the recent centuries.

Yeshua (Jesus) says believers shall "take up serpents," and "drink deadly things," and will not be hurt (Mark 16:18). What did Yeshua (Jesus) mean by this? God promises to equip us to handle SPIRITUAL SERPENTS AND WORKERS OF EVIL and to DRINK DEADLY DOCTRINES (LIES AND PROPAGANDA) that defy Scripture that spew from the false teachers and the workers of iniquity of this age (Luke 13:27). We will not be harmed by spiritual serpents and their servant workers of iniquity or be deceived by false doctrines, lies, and propaganda.

Yeshua (Jesus) often spoke in figurative language (John 16:25). Handling serpents and drinking deadly things is an example of figurative language. Satan is referred to as a serpent of old in Scripture (Revelation 12:9, 20:2). Yeshua (Jesus) referred to the false teachers of His day as serpents and a brood of vipers (Matthew 3:7, 12:34, 23:33; Luke 3:7).

LUKE 10:19 (NKJV):

"Behold, I give you the authority to trample on serpents and scorpions, and over all the power of the enemy, and nothing shall by any means hurt you."

God empowers us to handle SPIRITUAL SERPENTS, SPIRITUAL SCORPIONS, and HAVE POWER OVER THE ENEMY. What enemy? Enemies of God! We are to beware of evil workers (Philippians 3:2). We are to put on the whole armor of God and withstand Satan and the spiritual hosts of wickedness in heavenly places (Ephesians 6:12-13) and the workers of iniquity here on Earth (Luke 13:27). It is these wicked spiritual serpents and serpent workers of iniquity that God has equipped us to take up and handle, not slithering poisonous snakes.

REBUKING VS. JUDGING

By George Lujack

Scripture is not in conflict with itself when it calls on believers to rebuke while instructing us not to judge. The meaning of the words 'rebuke' and 'judge' have become synonymous in modern times. 'Rebuke' and 'judge' are two different words with two very different meanings.

Confusion over the definitions of 'rebuke' and 'judge' has made it difficult for some believers to rebuke their fellow brethren or neighbors. Some believers may feel intimidated into not rebuking people whom they know are engaged in sin or inappropriate behavior for fear of being branded 'judgmental.' Some believers may feel that they should speak out against sin, but get frozen, intimidated into silence and acceptance of sin while failing to rebuke it.

rebuke:
Express sharp disapproval or criticism of (someone) because of their behavior or actions.[33]

Rebuking concerns the reproof, correction, and proper instruction of a matter.

judge:
Form an opinion or conclusion about. Synonyms: try, sit in judgment on, decide, give a ruling on, give a verdict on, pass judgment on.[34]

Judging entails prosecuting, extracting justice, or imposing some kind of punishment.

Typically, when a well-meaning believer rebukes someone engaged in sin, the response often received is, "Don't judge me!" What the sinner is actually telling the believer is that he or she wishes to be left alone in that sin.

As parents rebuke their children for bad behavior, so too should believers rebuke their brethren and neighbors for sinful behavior. Good parents who rebuke their child would outright dismiss the child's protest if that disobedient child, for the purpose of continuing in misbehavior said, "Don't judge me." Likewise, good believers who rebuke sinners should outright dismiss the protest of sinners who, for the purpose of continuing in sin say, "Don't judge me."

As righteous believers we are called to be watchmen for the wicked (Ezekiel 33).

Does this mean that as believers we should go around rebuking everybody?

Answer: No.

Do not throw your pearls (of wisdom) before swine (Matthew 7:6). Rebuke those who have ears to listen so that you can guide them to a proper understanding and instruct those who are open-minded to the truth of the Scriptures.

Yeshua (Jesus) is our ultimate judge. Yeshua (Jesus) said, "Do not judge, for the measure you dole out is the measure you will reap" (Matthew 7:1-2). Judging, according to Yeshua (Jesus), includes "doling out measures," so judging certainly encompasses more than mere verbal rebuke. The judging that Yeshua (Jesus) spoke of imposes some kind of punishment. He does not want people to stone sinners any longer, as was done when living under the law, but wants people to repent of their sinful behavior in this age of grace. Without instruction and rebuke, sinners will often go right on ignorantly sinning without any correction from the wise.

LEVITICUS 19:17 (NKJV):

You shall surely REBUKE your neighbor, and not bear sin because of him.

PROVERBS 24:25 (NKJV):

But those who REBUKE the wicked will have delight and a good blessing will come upon them.

ECCLESIASTES 7:5 (NKJV):

It is better to hear the REBUKE of the wise than for a man to hear the song of fools.

LUKE 17:3 (NKJV):

"Take heed to yourselves. If your brother sins against you, REBUKE him; and if he repents, forgive him."

1 TIMOTHY 5:20 (NKJV):

Those who are sinning REBUKE in the presence of all, that the rest also may fear.

2 TIMOTHY 4:2 (NKJV):

Preach the word! Be ready in season and out of season. Convince, REBUKE, exhort, with all longsuffering and teaching.

TITUS 1:13 (NKJV):

This testimony is true. Therefore REBUKE them sharply, that they may be sound in the faith.

TITUS 2:15 (NKJV):

Speak these things, exhort, and REBUKE with all authority. Let no one despise you.

How quickly do the unrighteous of this world point out that Yeshua (Jesus) said, "Do not judge," while omitting the fact that Yeshua (Jesus) also instructed believers to rebuke sin (Luke 17:3)! Scripture instructs believers to rebuke sin.

RAINBOW: A PROMISE OF GOD, NOT A SYMBOL OF PRIDE

By George Lujack

GENESIS 9:12-16 (NKJV):

And God said: "This is the sign of the covenant which I make between Me and you, and every living creature that is with you, for perpetual generations: I set My rainbow in the cloud, and it shall be for the sign of the covenant between Me and the earth. It shall be, when I bring a cloud over the earth, that the rainbow shall be seen in the cloud; and I will remember My covenant which is between Me and you and every living creature of all flesh; the waters shall never again become a flood to destroy all flesh. The rainbow shall be in the cloud, and I will look on it to remember the everlasting covenant between God and every living creature of all flesh that is on the earth."

The rainbow is a creation of Almighty God proclaiming a covenant promise that He would never again flood the Earth in judgment as He did in the Genesis flood of Noah's time. Scripture records that God has judged the Earth and its inhabitants numerous times after the Genesis flood. God did not say or make a promise that He would never again judge the Earth, but *only* that He wouldn't do so through a worldwide flood.

The rainbow flag, commonly called the gay pride flag or LGBT pride flag, is a 6-striped rainbow colored flag that is a self-proclaimed symbol of lesbian, gay, bisexual, and transgender (LGBT) pride. A variation of the LGBT pride flag is a similar striped flag with an added blue field of fifty stars adopted from the current U.S. flag, now fittingly so, after the U.S. Supreme Court ruled gay marriage constitutional in all fifty states on June 26, 2015.[35]

San Francisco, California artist and gay rights activist Gilbert Baker designed the gay pride flag in 1978.[36] It can be argued, from a spiritual perspective, that Satan inspired the gay pride flag. The rainbow is officially comprised of 7-colors, not 6. A rainbow's colors can be remembered through the acronym ROY G BIV, which are red, orange, yellow, green, blue, indigo, and violet. An observation about the gay pride flag is that it contains six colored stripes, not seven. Six is the spiritual number of Satan while seven is the number of completion, a number of God. The gay pride flag's colors are ROY G BV, which are red, orange, yellow, green, blue, and violet. Missing from the gay pride flag is the color indigo.

There are six colored stripes on the gay pride flag. The U.S. Supreme Court's ruling in favor of gay marriage came on a Friday - the 6th day of the week, in June - the 6th month of the year, and on the twenty-6th day of June.

Satan is thumbing his nose at God, using one of God's own creations - the rainbow, as a symbol to provoke Him to anger. God will never flood the entire Earth again, as He will keep His rainbow covenant promise, but God will judge the Earth.

After male homosexuality became rampant in Sodom, as messengers merely walking through the city streets and then entering into Lot's home were accosted by homosexual predators, God had seen enough and judged Sodom with fire from heaven (Genesis 19).

Homosexuals in America and other Western 'Christian' nations will not rest on their laurels with their gay marriage political victories. They will behave more evilly, just as they always have, whenever and wherever homosexuality was tolerated, celebrated, and institutionalized. Homosexuals will become more sexually aggressive and predatory, more intolerant, and more hostile towards Messianic and Christian believers in the times ahead.

The gay pride flag is not a flag of diversity, love, and tolerance. It is a battle flag that proudly flaunts sexual depravity, in all its LGBT forms, and is a flag of intolerance to those opposed to the sinful homosexual lifestyle that mocks the God of Scripture.

God will not be mocked indefinitely (Galatians 6:7). Judgment will come to the unrepentant LGBT community and their ignorant heterosexual supporters who wrap themselves around their gay pride flag.

ARE THE JEWISH PEOPLE CHOSEN, HOLY, AND SPECIAL TO GOD?

By George Lujack

Jewish people take pride in being called God's chosen people. But, as the proverb goes, "Pride goes before destruction and a haughty spirit before a fall" (Proverbs 16:18). This article will discuss Jewish pride, the 'chosen' status of the Jews of Israel, whether being Jewish makes someone more special to God than non-Jews, and if the Jews of Israel are still chosen today.

DEUTERONOMY 7:6-11 (NKJV):

For you are a HOLY PEOPLE to YHWH (the Lord) your God; YHWH (the Lord) your God has CHOSEN YOU to be a people for Himself, a SPECIAL TREASURE above all the peoples on the face of the earth. YHWH (the Lord) did not set His love on you nor CHOOSE YOU because you were more in number than any other people, for you were the least of all peoples; but because YHWH (the Lord) loves you, and because He would keep the oath which He swore to your fathers, YHWH (the Lord) has brought you out with a mighty hand, and redeemed you from the house of bondage, from the hand of Pharaoh king of Egypt.

Therefore know that YHWH (the Lord) your God, He is God, the faithful God who keeps covenant and mercy for a thousand generations with those who love Him and keep His commandments; and He repays those who hate Him to their face, to destroy them. He will not be slack with him who hates Him; He will repay him to his face. Therefore you shall keep the commandment, the statutes, and the judgments which I command you today, to observe them.

DEUTERONOMY 14:2 (NKJV):

For you are a HOLY PEOPLE to YHWH (the Lord) your God, and YHWH (the Lord) has CHOSEN YOU to be a people for Himself, a SPECIAL TREASURE above all the peoples who are on the face of the earth.

God chose the Jewish people to be a treasured people on the Earth, to be His example nation to the other nations of the world. God did not choose the Jews *because* they were holy and special; He chose them *to be* a holy and special people.

The Jews failed in their covenant with God, to keep His commandments and statutes. As a man divorces his wife for repeated unrepentant acts of marital adultery, YHWH (the Lord) divorced the twin kingdoms of Israel and Judah for their continued acts of spiritual adultery in worshiping other gods.

ISAIAH 50:1 (NKJV):

Thus says YHWH (the Lord):

"Where is the certificate of your mother's divorce, whom I have put away? Or which of My creditors is it to whom I have sold you? For your iniquities you have sold yourselves, and for your transgressions your mother has been put away."

JEREMIAH 3:6-10 (NKJV):

YHWH (the Lord) said also to me in the days of Josiah the king: "Have you seen what backsliding Israel has done? She has gone up on every high mountain and under every green tree, and there played the harlot. And I said, after she had done all these things, 'Return to Me.' But she did not return. And her treacherous sister Judah saw it. Then I saw that for all the causes for which backsliding Israel had committed adultery, I had put her away and given her a certificate of divorce; yet her treacherous sister Judah did not fear, but went and played the harlot also. So it came to pass, through her casual harlotry, that she defiled the land and committed adultery with stones and trees. And yet for all this her treacherous sister Judah has not turned to Me with her whole heart, but in pretense," says YHWH (the Lord).

ISRAEL CEASED BEARING SPIRITUAL FRUIT TO THE WORLD

MATTHEW 21:18-19; MARK 11:12-14 (NKJV):

Now in the morning, as Yeshua (Jesus) returned to the city, He was hungry. And seeing a fig tree by the road, He came to it and found nothing on it but leaves, and said to it, "Let no fruit grow on you ever again."

LUKE 13:6-9 (NKJV):

Yeshua (Jesus) also spoke this parable: "A certain man had a fig tree planted in his vineyard, and he came seeking fruit on it and found none. Then he said to the keeper of his vineyard, 'Look, for three years I have come seeking fruit on this fig tree and find none. Cut it down; why does it use up the ground?' But he answered and said to him, 'Sir, let it alone this year also, until I dig around it and fertilize it. And if it bears fruit, well. But if not, after that you can cut it down.'"

The fig tree, symbolically throughout Scripture, represents the nation of Israel. Although Israel was chosen to be a holy special nation, they failed at their calling and were cursed by God to not be the nation any longer that would bear spiritual fruit to the world.

WHO IS A JEW AND WHO IS CHOSEN NOW?

ROMANS 2:25-27 (NKJV):

For circumcision is indeed profitable if you keep the law; but if you are a breaker of the law, your circumcision has become uncircumcision. Therefore, if an uncircumcised man keeps the righteous requirements of the law, will not his uncircumcision be counted as circumcision? And will not the physically uncircumcised, IF HE FULFILLS THE LAW, JUDGE YOU who, even with your written code and circumcision, are a transgressor of the law?

ROMANS 2:28-29 (NKJV):

FOR HE IS NOT A JEW WHO IS ONE OUTWARDLY, nor is circumcision that which is outward in the flesh; BUT HE IS A JEW WHO IS ONE INWARDLY; and circumcision is that of the heart, in the Spirit, not in the letter; whose praise is not from men but from God.

A Jew or a Hebrew to God is one by faith, meaning one who has crossed over from all false religions and has accepted God in truth. Romans 2:27 proclaims that the uncircumcised Gentile will judge the unrighteous circumcised Jew.

LIVING STONES OF YESHUA MESSIAH (JESUS CHRIST) ARE NOW CHOSEN

1 PETER 2:4-10 (NKJV):

Coming to Him as to A LIVING STONE, rejected indeed by men, BUT CHOSEN BY GOD AND PRECIOUS, you also, AS LIVING STONES, are being built up a spiritual house, a holy priesthood, to offer up spiritual sacrifices acceptable to God through Yeshua Messiah (Jesus Christ).

Therefore it is also contained in the Scripture,

"Behold, I lay in Zion a chief cornerstone, elect, precious, and he who believes on Him will by no means be put to shame."

Therefore, to you who believe, He is precious; but to those who are disobedient,

"The stone which the builders rejected has become the chief cornerstone," **and** ***"A stone of stumbling and a rock of offense."***

They stumble, being disobedient to the word, to which they also were appointed.

BUT YOU ARE A CHOSEN GENERATION, A ROYAL PRIESTHOOD, A HOLY NATION, HIS OWN SPECIAL PEOPLE, that you may proclaim the praises of Him who called you out of darkness into His marvelous light; WHO WERE ONCE NOT A PEOPLE BUT ARE NOW THE PEOPLE OF GOD, who had not obtained mercy but now have obtained mercy.

Yeshua (Jesus), the chief cornerstone, was rejected by the builders (the religious architects and elders of Israel), as their Messiah. This rejection has caused the Jews of Israel to stumble in blindness.

ARE THE JEWS STILL CHOSEN?

The Jewish people are not currently chosen to lead the world to God, but God has not forgotten them either. They have been returned to the land of Israel as foretold (Ezekiel 11:17). God has a special purpose for the Jewish people of Israel in His end time plans. They are His lost sheep. One day the world's righteous will be taken to Israel and Jerusalem will be the beloved capital city of the world (Revelation 20:9).

MATTHEW 15:24 (NKJV):

Yeshua (Jesus) answered and said, "I was not sent except to the lost sheep of the house of Israel."

ROMANS 11:1-2 (NKJV):

I say then, has God cast away His people? Certainly not! For I also am an Israelite, of the seed of Abraham, of the tribe of Benjamin. God has not cast away His people whom He foreknew.

ROMANS 11:11-12,25 (NKJV):

What then? Israel has not obtained what it seeks; but the elect have obtained it, and the rest were blinded. Just as it is written:

"God has given them a spirit of stupor, eyes that they should not see and ears that they should not hear, to this very day."

And David says:

Let their table become a snare and a trap, a stumbling block and a recompense to them.

Let their eyes be darkened, so that they do not see, and bow down their back always."

I say then, have they stumbled that they should fall? Certainly not! But through their fall, to provoke them to jealousy, salvation has come to the Gentiles. Now if their fall is riches for the world, and their failure riches for the Gentiles, how much more their fullness!...

For I do not desire, brethren, that you should be ignorant of this mystery, lest you should be wise in your own opinion, that blindness in part has happened to Israel until the fullness of the Gentiles has come in.

The Jews' "fall" from being the chosen people and source of spiritual fruit for the world is explained in Romans 11. Believers should understand that God Himself claims credit for giving the Jews "a spirit of stupor with eyes that cannot see and ears that cannot hear." And why did God do this and allow His chosen people to stumble? This was done so that the Gentiles and all believers of Yeshua (Jesus) could be grafted into Israel, not through election or ethnic nationality, but by grace through faith (Romans 11:5-6).

ARE THE ETHNIC JEWS CURSED?

MATTHEW 27:22-25 (NKJV):

Pilate said to them, "What then shall I do with Yeshua (Jesus) who is called Messiah (Christ)?"

They all said to him, "Let Him be crucified!"

Then the governor said, "Why, what evil has He done?"

But they cried out all the more, saying, "Let Him be crucified!"

When Pilate saw that he could not prevail at all, but rather that a tumult was rising, he took water and washed his hands before the multitude, saying, "I am innocent of the blood of this just Person. You see to it." AND ALL THE PEOPLE ANSWERED AND SAID, "HIS BLOOD BE ON US AND ON OUR CHILDREN."

MATTHEW 23:31-33,37-39 (NKJV) [WITH INTERPRETATION]:

"Therefore you are witnesses against yourselves that you are sons of those who murdered the prophets. Fill up, then, the measure of your fathers' guilt. Serpents, brood of vipers! How can you escape the condemnation of hell?...

O Jerusalem, Jerusalem, the one who kills the prophets and stones those who are sent to her! How often I wanted to gather your children together, as a hen gathers her chicks under her wings, but you were not willing! See! Your house is left to you desolate; for I say to you, you shall see Me no more till you say, *'Blessed is He [YESHUA / JESUS] who comes in the name of [YHWH] (the Lord)!'"*

The Jews of the house of Israel, ethnic national Jews, are under a certain curse. God does punish disobedience and sin. When Joseph's brothers sold him into slavery in Egypt, even though Joseph forgave his brothers, this evil deed did not go unpunished by God. Joseph's brother's children became slaves of Egypt. Joseph's brother's children were cursed with slavery for the slavery they imposed upon Joseph. God saw to it that Joseph's brothers were tormented throughout much of their lives with guilt and their children, and their children's children, were punished with slavery in Egypt for four hundred years (Genesis 15:13; Exodus 12:40).

JEWS ARE AMONG THE MOST BLESSED PEOPLE IN THE WORLD

GENESIS 12:1-3 (NKJV):

Now YHWH (the Lord) had said to Abram:

"Get out of your country, from your family, and from your father's house, to a land that I will show you. I will make you a great nation; I will bless you and make your name great; and you shall be a blessing. I will bless those who bless you, and I will curse him who curses you; and in you all the families of the earth shall be blessed."

The ethnic national Jews of Israel are in a peculiar position with God. They are simultaneously both under a covenant blessing and a national curse. Should believers unconditionally bless Israel or have nothing to do with the Jews at all? God will bless Jews if they keep the commandments and statutes of God (Deuteronomy 7:10-11), just as He will bless all other people of all other nations for doing so. God does not love the Jews unconditionally and neither should believers. Believers wishing to support ethnic Jews should do so by supporting righteous Jews, even if they currently deny their Messiah. Supporting everything ethnic Jews do is not what God would want. Supporting the nation of Israel in general is good, as God has given the land of Israel to the Jews by covenant. Tel Aviv, Israel hosts one of the largest gay pride parades of the world every June. Many Israelis and tourists flock to the city during this time to participate in this national disgrace, flaunting sin, and mocking God. Should believers support the Jews in this? Of course not! God's definition of a Jew is not one outwardly, but inwardly (Romans 2:28-29).

GOD SHOWS NO PARTIALITY FOR THE JEW OVER THE GENTILE

JOB 37:24 (NKJV):

He shows no partiality TO ANY who are wise of heart.

MATTHEW 8:11-12 (NKJV) [WITH INTERPRETATION]:

"And I say to you that many [GENTILES] will come from east and west, and sit down with Abraham, Isaac, and Jacob in the kingdom of heaven. But the sons of the kingdom [UNRIGHTEOUS ETHNIC JEWS] will be cast out into outer darkness. There will be weeping and gnashing of teeth."

ACTS 10:34-35 (NKJV):

Then Peter opened his mouth and said: "In truth I perceive that GOD SHOWS NO PARTIALITY. But in every nation whoever fears Him and works righteousness is accepted by Him.

ACTS 15:8-9 (NKJV) [WITH INTERPRETATION]:

So God, who knows the heart, acknowledged them [GENTILES] by giving them the Holy Spirit, just as He did to us [JEWS], and made no distinction between us [JEWS] and them [GENTILES], purifying their hearts by faith.

ROMANS 2:8-11 (NKJV):

To those who are self-seeking and do not obey the truth, but obey unrighteousness - indignation and wrath, tribulation and anguish, on every soul of man who does evil, of the Jew first and also of the Greek; but glory, honor, and peace to everyone who works what is good, to the Jew first and also to the Greek. FOR THERE IS NO PARTIALITY WITH GOD.

JEWISH PRIDE, ETHNIC SUPERIORITY, AND SEPARATION MENTALITY

Many Christians proclaim the law was given to the Jews and was for the Jews only. Likewise, many Jews believe that they are an eternal special set apart people, ethnically superior, and as such the Torah (law) was for them only. Even in some Messianic Judaism congregations, which are heavily influenced by Jews coming out from Pharisaic Talmudic Judaism - and bringing their false religious doctrinal baggage with them, they try to make a distinction between Jews and Gentiles, saying that the Gentiles do not need to obey the 'ceremonial,' 'dietary,' and 'Mosaic' laws as the Jews were commanded to. Messianic Judaism has cited Acts 15, using the chapter to proclaim that Gentiles do not need to obey the Torah (law) as the Jews do.

ACTS 15:1 (NKJV):

And certain men came down from Judea and taught the brethren, "Unless you are circumcised according to the custom of Moses, you cannot be saved."

ACTS 15:10 (NKJV):

Now therefore, why do you test God by putting a yoke on the neck of the disciples which neither our fathers nor we were able to bear?

The yoke spoken of in Acts 15:10 is adult circumcision, NOT the Torah (law). Circumcision was for the eighth day and ONLY the eighth day (Leviticus 12:3). Yeshua (Jesus) died and removed the ordinance penalty, which was to be cut off from God's people, from male converts who were uncircumcised. Adult circumcision is optional. Gentile believers should circumcise their male children on their eighth day.

ACTS 15:19-20 (NKJV):

Therefore I judge that we should not trouble those from among the Gentiles who are turning to God, but that we write to them to abstain from things polluted by idols, from sexual immorality, from things strangled, and from blood.

Some Messianic Jews are attempting to say that the only laws Gentiles were required to keep were sexual morality laws, to abstain from foods offered to idols, and from animals that were strangled and thereby not properly slaughtered and drained of blood. The advice to Gentiles was due to widespread Gentile issues of the time, practiced by Roman, Greek, Babylonian, and other surrounding cultures. To suggest that these were the ONLY commands Gentiles were ever required to follow is sheer lawlessness absurdity.

Ethnic Jewish Messianics, who teach that Gentiles are not required to obey many of God's laws, are likely motivated by an ethnocentric superiority mentality and a desire to separate and elevate themselves above Gentile Messianic believers who they worship together with. There is no distinction between Jew and Gentile (Acts 15:8-9).

MATTHEW 28:18-20 (NKJV) [WITH INTERPRETATION]:

And Yeshua (Jesus) came and spoke to them, saying, "All authority has been given to Me in heaven and on earth. Go therefore and make disciples of ALL THE NATIONS, baptizing them in the name of the Father and of the Son and of the Holy Spirit, TEACHING THEM [GENTILES] TO OBSERVE ALL THINGS THAT I HAVE COMMANDED YOU [JEWS]; and lo, I am with you always, even to the end of the age."

There is one law for Jews and Gentiles. Yeshua (Jesus) commanded His Jewish apostles to teach the Gentiles all things, including all the law, which He had taught them. The Gentiles were given the law, along with the Gospel; it is fully contained in the complete set of the books of Scripture. When Jews and Gentiles enter God's kingdom, there will not be a kosher Jewish kitchen and a Gentile all-creatures-you-can-eat kitchen. There will not be Jew circumcised bathrooms and Gentile uncircumcised bathrooms.

JOHN 10:16 (NKJV):

And other sheep I have which are not of this fold; them also I must bring, and they will hear My voice; and there will be ONE FLOCK and one shepherd.

All ethnic Jews and Gentiles who will enter into God's kingdom will all be as Jews, those who are Hebrew having 'crossed over' and will worship God as one, in spirit and truth (John 4:23-24). We will be one flock.

MATTHEW 12:30; LUKE 11:23 (NKJV):

"He who is not with Me is against Me, and he who does not gather with Me scatters abroad."

ROMANS 11:28 (NKJV):

Concerning the gospel they are enemies for your sake, but concerning the election they are beloved for the sake of the fathers.

The ethnic national Judaic Jews, as far as spreading the gospel of Messiah (Christ) is concerned are against Yeshua (Jesus), but are under His covenant protection as His elect people who will one day call on Him to save themselves (Matthew 23:39).

ARE BELIEVERS PERMITTED TO CRITICIZE JEWS OR ISRAEL?

GENESIS 12:3 (NKJV) [WITH INTERPRETATION]:

I will bless those who bless you [ISRAEL], and I will curse him who curses you [ISRAEL]; and in you [ISRAEL] all the families of the earth shall be blessed.

Many Christians and other believers have been conditioned to never speak evil against the nation of Israel, or ethnic Jewish people, even if they are doing evil. If a nation or an individual is engaged in sin, then a believer is to rebuke sin, whether the evil is coming from an ethnic Jew or a Gentile.

There are certainly many ethnic Pharisaic Talmudic Jews who cite Scripture and promote the idea to Christians and other believers that they should unconditionally bless Jews and Israel to receive God's blessings, but warn to never speak evil of Jews or Israel, so as to not be cursed by God. Rebuking sin, whether committed by Jews or commenting on the national sins of Israel, is not cursing Israel.

AMOS 7:14-17 (NKJV) [WITH INTERPRETATION]:

Then Amos answered, and said to Amaziah:

"I was no prophet, nor was I a son of a prophet, but I was a sheepbreeder and a tender of sycamore fruit. Then YHWH (the Lord) took me as I followed the flock, and YHWH (the Lord) said to me, 'Go, prophesy to my people Israel.' Now therefore hear the word of YHWH (the Lord): You [ISRAEL] say, 'Do not prophesy against Israel, and do not spout against the house of Isaac.'

Therefore, thus says YHWH (the Lord):

'Your wife shall be a harlot in the city; your sons and daughters will fall by the sword; your land will be divided by survey line; you shall die in a defiled land; and Israel shall surely be led away captive from his own land.'"

God rose up Amos (and others) to prophesy against Israel. Israel's reaction to Amos was the same reaction that many Jews have today if you speak out against the sins of a Jew, the false practices within Pharisaic Talmudic Judaism, or say anything critical about the national sins of Israel.

WILL ALL JEWS BE SAVED, EVEN EVIL JEWS?

ROMANS 11:26 (NKJV):

And so all Israel will be saved, ...

The word 'Israel' is interchangeably used throughout Scripture as national Israel, ethnic Israel (Jacob and the offspring of Jacob - Genesis 35:10), and spiritual Israel.

ROMANS 2:28-29 (NKJV):

For he is not a Jew who is one outwardly, nor is circumcision that which is outward in the flesh; but he is a Jew who is one inwardly.

A Jew or Hebrew to God is one who has overcome the wicked ways of the world and has crossed over to worship Him in spirit and truth (John 4:23-24, 14:17; 2 Thessalonians 2:13; 1 John 2:13-14, 4:6, 5:4).

MATTHEW 8:10-12 (NKJV) [WITH INTERPRETATION]:

"Assuredly, I say to you, I have not found such great faith, not even in [THE NATION OF] Israel! And I say to you that many [GENTILES] will come from east and west, and sit down with Abraham, Isaac, and Jacob in the kingdom of heaven. But the sons of the kingdom [EVIL ETHNIC JEWS] will be cast out into outer darkness. There will be weeping and gnashing of teeth."

LUKE 13:24-29 (NKJV) [WITH INTERPRETATION]:

"Strive to enter through the narrow gate [OF RIGHTEOUSNESS], for many, I say to you, will seek to enter and will not be able. When once the Master of the house has risen up and shut the door, and you begin to stand outside and knock at the door, saying, 'Lord, Lord, open for us,' and He will answer and say to you, 'I do not know you, where you are from,' then you will begin to say, 'We [ETHNIC JEWS] ate and drank in Your presence, and You taught in our streets [OF ISRAEL].'

But He will say, 'I tell you I do not know you, where you are from. Depart from Me, all you workers of iniquity.' There will be weeping and gnashing of teeth, when you [ETHNIC JEWS] see Abraham and Isaac and Jacob and all the prophets in the kingdom of God, and yourselves thrust out. They [GENTILES] will come from the east and the west, from the north and the south, and sit down in the kingdom of God."

Evil ethnic Jews of Israel will not be saved, nor will they be spared the judgment of God, as they will be cast out from His kingdom.

Romans 11:26 should be understood in the following contextual manner:

ROMANS 11:25-26 (NKJV) [WITH INTERPRETATION]:

For I do not desire, brethren, that you should be ignorant of this mystery, lest you should be wise in your own opinion, that blindness [OF THE GOSPEL MESSAGE] in part has happened to [NATIONAL] Israel until the fullness of the Gentiles has come in. And so all [SPIRITUAL] Israel [JEWS AND GENTILES] will be saved, …

WILL GENTILES NEED TO BE LED INTO GOD'S KINGDOM BY THE JEWS?

ZECHARIAH 8:23 (NKJV) [WITH INTERPRETATION]:

Thus says YHWH (the Lord) of hosts: "In those days ten men from every language of the nations shall grasp the sleeve [CORNER OF THE GARMENT] of a Jewish man, saying, 'Let us go with you, for we have heard that God is with you.'"

A 'Jewish man' in Zechariah 8:23 can be a reference to a righteous ethnic Jew or Gentile, a crossed-over Jew (Romans 2:28-29). Some superior-minded ethnic Jews believe Zechariah 8:23 can only be a reference to ethnic Jews, as Gentile Christians do not wear tassels (tzittzits) on the corners of their garments (Numbers 15:37-40; Deuteronomy 22:12). Messianic Gentiles do wear tzittzits though, and many Jews often do not wear them. The clothing we are now wearing will not be the same attire we are clothed with in God's kingdom.

REVELATION 6:11 (NKJV):

Then a WHITE ROBE was given to each of them; and it was said to them that they should rest a little while longer, until both the number of their fellow servants and their brethren, who would be killed as they were, was completed.

REVELATION 7:9 (NKJV):

After these things I looked, and behold, a great multitude which no one could number, OF ALL NATIONS, TRIBES, PEOPLES, AND TONGUES, standing before the throne and before the Lamb, CLOTHED WITH WHITE ROBES...

REVELATION 7:13-14 (NKJV):

Then one of the elders answered, saying to me, "Who are these arrayed in WHITE ROBES, and where did they come from?"

And I said to him, "Sir, you know."

So he said to me, "These are the ones who come out of the great tribulation, and washed their robes and made them white in the blood of the Lamb.

Gentile believers will come out of the great tribulation, either through the rapture or immediately after being beheaded. The Jews, who have not accepted Yeshua (Jesus), as their Messiah, will live through the great tribulation.

God will clothe the raptured and resurrected righteous Gentiles in white robes and those robes will have tassels (tzittzits) on them, if God so desires it.

GOD'S CHOSEN PEOPLE ARE THOSE WHO ARE WITH YESHUA (JESUS)

REVELATION 17:14 (NKJV):

These will make war with the Lamb, and the Lamb will overcome them, for He is Lord of lords and King of kings; AND THOSE WHO ARE WITH HIM ARE CALLED, CHOSEN, AND FAITHFUL.

Believers in Yeshua Messiah (Jesus Christ) are God's chosen people. As chosen people, we are not to support and 'worship' the Jews in everything that they do. Believers should not be afraid to speak out against Jewish practices that are sinful. Yeshua (Jesus) spoke out against the Jewish religious authorities and their wickedness; His faithful servants can also.

God's called, chosen, and faithful people will join Yeshua (Jesus) when He returns to Earth to save His lost people, the Jews of Israel, from annihilation.

Believers should have a certain respect for the Jews, who have imperfectly brought forth the salvation message to the world (John 4:22). The Jews are prophesied to one day come to understand the full truth of their Messiah Yeshua (Christ Jesus) and many of them will be grafted back into the family of God (Ezekiel 37; Matthew 24:30, 26:64; Mark 13:26, 14:62; Luke 21:27; Romans 11:23-24).

JEWISH IDOLATRY

By George Lujack

Are Jews who pray through the Western Wall in Israel engaged in idolatry? Is this really any different than Catholics who bow before carved images of stone or wood and use prayer beads when they pray?

EZEKIEL 13:3-16 (NKJV):

Thus says YHWH (the Lord) GOD: "Woe to the foolish prophets, who follow their own spirit and have seen nothing! O Israel, your prophets are like foxes in the deserts. You have not gone up into the gaps to build A WALL for the house of Israel to stand in battle on the day of YHWH (the Lord). They have envisioned futility and false divination, saying, 'Thus says YHWH (the Lord)!' But YHWH (the Lord) has not sent them; yet they hope that the word may be confirmed. Have you not seen a futile vision, and have you not spoken false divination? You say, 'YHWH (The Lord) says,' but I have not spoken."

Therefore thus says YHWH (the Lord) God: "Because you have spoken nonsense and envisioned lies, therefore I am indeed against you," says YHWH (the Lord) GOD. "My hand will be against the prophets who envision futility and who divine lies; they shall not be in the assembly of My people, nor be written in the record of the house of Israel, nor shall they enter into the land of Israel. Then you shall know that I am YHWH (the Lord) God.

Because, indeed, because they have seduced My people, saying, 'Peace!' when there is no peace - and one builds A WALL, and they plaster it with untempered mortar - say to those who plaster it with untempered mortar, that it will fall. There will be flooding rain, and you, O great hailstones, shall fall; and a stormy wind shall tear it down. Surely, when THE WALL has fallen, will it not be said to you, 'Where is the mortar with which you plastered it?'"

Therefore thus says YHWH (the Lord) God: "I will cause a stormy wind to break forth in My fury; and there shall be a flooding rain in My anger, and great hailstones in fury to consume it. So I will break down THE WALL you have plastered with untempered mortar, and bring it down to the ground, so that its foundation will be uncovered; it will fall, and you shall be consumed in the midst of it. Then you shall know that I am YHWH (the Lord).

Thus will I accomplish My wrath on THE WALL and on those who have plastered it with untempered mortar; and I will say to you, 'THE WALL is no more, nor those who plastered it, that is, the prophets of Israel who prophesy concerning Jerusalem, and who see visions of peace for her when there is no peace,'" says YHWH (the Lord) God.

LUKE 21:5-6 (NKJV):

Then, as some spoke of the temple, how it was adorned with beautiful stones and donations, He said, "These things which you see - the days will come in which not one stone shall be left upon another that shall not be thrown down."

The prophesy of the destruction (throwing down) of the temple wall is yet to be fulfilled.

2 KINGS 18:4 (NKJV):

He (Hezekiah) removed the high places and broke the sacred pillars, cut down the wooden image and broke in pieces the BRONZE SERPENT that Moses had made; for until those days the children of Israel burned incense to it, and called it Nehushtan.

Praying through a wall is not the first instance in which the Jewish people engaged in praying through objects that once served a legitimate purpose. The Hebrews, after the Exodus from Egypt, began to worship the bronze serpent that was set up in the desert that was used for healing snakebites (Numbers 21:9).

Jews who pray through a man-made wall of their former temple are engaged in idolatry. Elohim (God) hates all forms of idolatry and the use of objects to engage Him in prayer. We are to worship and pray in SPIRIT and in TRUTH, not through the use of man-made walls or objects with supposed 'points of contact' to Elohim (God).

STAR OF DAVID OR STAR OF REMPHAN?

By George Lujack

The Jewish star, commonly referred to as the 'Star of David,' 'Shield of David,' or the 'Seal of Solomon' is a six-pointed hexagram star comprised of two overlaid equilateral triangles. This star is most closely identified with Jewish identity and it appears on many things Jewish, including the flag of the State of Israel, clothing, jewelry, synagogues, tombstones, and many other Jewish items. This article will discus the origins of what is commonly called the Star of David and whether this star should be avoided by Messianic believers as pertaining to a false god with pagan origins.

There is no Scripture reference to a 'Star of David,' 'Shield of David,' or a 'Seal of Solomon.' Mainstream Judaism acknowledges that they do not know where the Star of David symbol originated. Scripture does condemn a Jewish star.

AMOS 5:26 (NKJV):

You also carried Sikkuth your king and Chiun, your idols, THE STAR of your gods, which you made for yourselves.

ACTS 7:43 (NKJV):

You also took up the tabernacle of Moloch, and THE STAR of your god Remphan, images which you made to worship.

The Star of David is not exclusively a Jewish symbol. This star appears in other cultures and religious practices dating back hundreds of years before the birth of Messiah (Christ). The six-pointed hexagram star is used in Buddhism, Free Masonry, Hinduism, Kabala, the occult, Saturn worship, and witchcraft. The six-pointed hexagram star has been used as a talisman and for conjuring up spirits in Satanic occult magic.[37]

It is quite evident that the Jews are still carrying a star of their god Remphan, which they still make for themselves today. While they may not acknowledge a 'god' associated with this star, this does not make it non-offensive to God who is holy, who does not allow His people to possess charms, idols, or talismans. Catholics have idols, mainstream Christians have Christmas trees (Jeremiah 10:1-5), and the Jews have talisman star charms, all in violation of God's laws against idolatry.

ROMANS 10:19 (NKJV):

"I will provoke you to jealousy by those who are not a nation."

During the 19th century a significant motivating factor for adopting the hexagram star as a symbol of Israel and of the Jewish people was the desire to imitate the influence of the Christian cross.[38] The Jews were provoked to jealously by Christianity, by a faith that was not a nation and knew no borders.

JEREMIAH 3:12-13 (NKJV):

'Return, backsliding Israel,' says the Lord; I will not cause My anger to fall on you. For I am merciful,' says YHWH (the Lord); 'I will not remain angry forever. Only acknowledge your iniquity, that you have transgressed against the Lord your God, and have scattered your charms to alien deities under every green tree, and you have not obeyed My voice,' says YHWH (the Lord).

Mainstream Judaism is not going to acknowledge its iniquity in making the hexagram charm in honor of Remphan and in defiance of God until Yeshua (Jesus) returns. The Star of David is used in Messianic Judaism to pander to Jews who loathe and fear the cross. Christians have historically persecuted the Jews and the symbol of the cross is anathema to many Jews. To attract Judaic Jews into converting to Messianic Jews, Messianic Judaism has forsaken the cross in favor of the 'Star of David.'

While evil-minded Catholics and Christians have historically persecuted the Jews, the cross of Messiah (Christ) and the message of salvation cannot be compromised with a forbidden talisman hexagram six-pointed star symbol of pagan origin. Messianic and other faithful believers should not have anything to do with the six-pointed hexagram symbol, by either displaying it or wearing it, not even to support the Jewish people.

CENTRAL MESSAGE OF THE SCRIPTURES

By George Lujack

The center and shortest chapter in the Scriptures is Psalm 117 (2 verses).

PSALM 117:1-2 (NKJV):

Praise YHWH (the Lord), all you nations: praise Him, all you people. For His merciful kindness is great towards us: and the truth of YHWH (the Lord) endures forever. Praise YHWH (the Lord).

The longest chapter in the Scriptures is Psalm 119 (176 verses).

There are 594 chapters before Psalm 117 and 594 chapters after Psalm 117.

594 + 594 = 1188

Psalm 118:8 is located between the shortest chapter of the Scriptures, (Psalm 117), and the longest chapter of the Scriptures (Psalm 119).

PSALM 118:8 (NKJV):

It is better to trust in YHWH (the Lord) than to put confidence in man.

ARE YOU REALLY BORN AGAIN?

By George Lujack

Many evangelical and fundamentalist Christians refer to themselves as 'born again' believers. The meaning of the phrase 'born again,' as spoken by Yeshua (Jesus), has been misunderstood by many resulting in some confusion. This article will analyze the verses, clear up the confusion, and reveal the mystery of what Yeshua (Jesus) really meant when He said that we must be 'born again' in order to enter the kingdom of God.

Many Christians believe that to be born again means undergoing a spiritual rebirth or a regeneration of the human spirit by the Holy Spirit. While experiencing a spiritual rebirth is a component of being 'born again,' Yeshua (Jesus) was speaking of something much greater.

JOHN 3:3-13 (NKJV):

Yeshua (Jesus) answered and said to him, "Most assuredly, I say to you, unless one is born again, he cannot see the kingdom of God."

Nicodemus said to Him, "How can a man be born when he is old? Can he enter a second time into his mother's womb and be born?"

Yeshua (Jesus) answered, "Most assuredly, I say to you, unless one is born of water and the Spirit, he cannot enter the kingdom of God.

That which is born of the flesh is flesh, and that which is born of the Spirit is spirit. Do not marvel that I said to you, 'You must be born again.' The wind blows where it wishes, and you hear the sound of it, but cannot tell where it comes from and where it goes. So is everyone who is born of the Spirit."

Nicodemus answered and said to Him, "How can these things be?"

Yeshua (Jesus) answered and said to him, "Are you the teacher of Israel, and do not know these things? Most assuredly, I say to you, We speak what We know and testify what We have seen, and you do not receive Our witness.

If I have told you earthly things and you do not believe, how will you believe if I tell you heavenly things? No one has ascended to heaven but He who came down from heaven, that is, the Son of Man who is in heaven."

When Yeshua (Jesus) explained to Nicodemus that a man must be born again, He was not speaking of being born again into a flesh and blood existence. He was talking of being born again in a spirit existence.

To be born flesh of water is to be born of amniotic fluid, which is nutrient-enhanced water, through the womb. When one is baptized in water, in the name of the Father, Son, and Holy Spirit, and accepts Yeshua (Jesus) as Lord and Savior, he or she makes a declaration of faith (Matthew 28:19).

To be born of Spirit, many believe, is to have the Holy Spirit indwell within and renew our human spirit. While having our spirit 'renewed' is good, when Yeshua (Jesus) said that we must be "born of the Spirit," He meant something more than just having the Holy Spirit indwelling within us.

JOHN 3:5-6 (NKJV) (HSV†):

Yeshua (Jesus) answered, "Most assuredly, I say to you, unless one is born of water *AND the Spirit*, he cannot enter the kingdom of God (†reign of Elohim). That which is born of the flesh is flesh, and that which is born of the Spirit is spirit."

1 CORINTHIANS 15:50 (NKJV) (HSV†):

Now this I say, brethren, that flesh and blood cannot inherit the kingdom of God (†reign of Elohim); neither doth corruption inherit incorruption.

All human beings are flesh and blood beings who have sinned and have fallen short of the glory of God (Romans 3:23). All flesh is stained with the corruption of sin and therefore cannot enter the kingdom of God.

Having the Holy Spirit indwelling in us is necessary, but it does not actually mean that we have been 'born' of the Spirit. The most righteous Spirit-filled believers still possess flesh and blood bodies and flesh and blood cannot inherit the kingdom of God, even if they are filled with the Holy Spirit.

JOHN 3:7 (NKJV):

"Do not marvel that I said to you, 'You must be born again.'"

Yeshua (Jesus) told Nicodemus not to marvel about what it meant to be born again, as Nicodemus pondered how this could be. Many to this day have wondered what it means to be born again and have come up a little bit short.

JOHN 3:12-13 (NKJV):

"If I have told you earthly things and you do not believe, how will you believe if I tell you heavenly things? No one has ascended to heaven but He who came down from heaven, that is, the Son of Man who is in heaven."

Yeshua (Jesus), when speaking of being "born again" of Spirit, was not speaking of an earthly thing, that is, He was not speaking of a believer who had the Holy Spirit indwelling within him or her on Earth. He was speaking of a heavenly thing, a heavenly rebirth. He explained to Nicodemus that all throughout history, no one had ascended to heaven, for all men are flesh and blood and flesh and blood cannot enter the kingdom of God.

REPENTANCE, BAPTISM, OBEYING TRUTH AS BORN AGAIN SEED

JOHN 3:5 (NKJV) (HSV†):

Yeshua (Jesus) answered, "Most assuredly, I say to you, unless one is born of WATER *and* the SPIRIT, he cannot enter the kingdom of God (†reign of Elohim)."

There are two components of being born 'again': to be born again of WATER (through baptism and faith) *and* to be born again into a spirit body.

1 PETER 1:22-23 (NKJV):

Since you have purified your souls in obeying the truth through the Spirit in sincere love of the brethren, love one another fervently with a pure heart, having been BORN AGAIN, not of corruptible SEED but incorruptible, through the word of God which lives and abides forever.

To be born of water also means to come to repentance, be baptized *in water*, to purify your soul through righteous living, and to obey the truth through the word of God contained in the Scriptures and be led by the Holy Spirit. Once born again of water through baptism, a believer has become a righteous SEED of God, awaiting the fullness of being born again of the Spirit.

1 JOHN 3:9 (NKJV):

Whoever has been born of God does not sin, for His seed remains in him; and he cannot sin, because he has been born of God.

THE MYSTERY OF BEING BORN AGAIN INTO A SPIRIT BODY

Being "born of God" does not mean being "born again." When a person is *initially* born of God, he or she accepts Yeshua (Jesus) as Lord and Savior and obeys His commands. Believers who claim that they have been 'born again' are still flesh and blood beings and do not understand that they haven't really been born again yet *in a new spirit body*.

MATTHEW 19:28 (NKJV):

So Yeshua (Jesus) said to them, "Assuredly I say to you, that in THE REGENERATION, when the Son of Man sits on the throne of His glory, you who have followed Me will also sit on twelve thrones, judging the twelve tribes of Israel."

ROMANS 8:21-23 (NKJV):

Because the creation itself also will be delivered from the bondage of corruption into the glorious liberty of the children of God. For we know that the whole creation groans and labors with BIRTH PANGS together until now. Not only that, but we also who have the first-fruits of the Spirit, even we ourselves groan within ourselves, EAGERLY WAITING FOR THE ADOPTION, THE REDEMPTION OF OUR BODY.

1 CORINTHIANS 15:42-44 (NKJV) [WITH INTERPRETATION]:

The body is sown in corruption, it is raised in incorruption. It is sown in dishonor, it is raised in glory. It is sown in weakness, it is raised in power. It is sown a natural body, it is raised A SPIRITUAL BODY. There is a natural body, AND THERE IS A SPIRITUAL BODY.

1 CORINTHIANS 15:51-53 (NKJV) [WITH INTERPRETATION]:

BEHOLD, I TELL YOU A MYSTERY: We shall not all sleep, but we shall all be changed [BORN AGAIN] - in a moment, in the twinkling of an eye, at the last trumpet. For the trumpet will sound, and the dead will be raised [BORN AGAIN] incorruptible, and we shall be changed [BORN AGAIN]. For this corruptible [FLESH AND BLOOD BODY] must put on incorruption [A NEW SPIRIT BODY], and this mortal [FLESH AND BLOOD BODY] must put on immortality.

REVELATION 21:5 (NKJV):

Then He who sat on the throne said, "BEHOLD, I MAKE ALL THINGS NEW."

Flesh and blood believers must be 'born again' into new bodies. Our corrupted, sin-stained flesh and blood bodies will be 'redeemed,' 'regenerated,' and 'restored' in a twinkling of an eye into new, incorruptible, sin-free spirit bodies and then we will be 'adopted' by God. It is when we are changed from flesh and blood persons to new, incorruptible, sin-free spirit beings that we will truly be born again.

JOHN 4:24 (NKJV):

"God is Spirit, and those who worship Him must worship in spirit and truth."

God is comprised of spirit, not flesh and blood. As believers we should look forward to the redemption and transformation of our corrupted flesh and blood bodies, as children ready to be born again into new spirit-composed bodies and to be adopted sons and daughters of God (2 Corinthians 6:18).

ONCE SAVED, ALWAYS SAVED?

By George Lujack

Should believers proclaim that they are once saved, always saved (OSAS) or state that they are *already saved*? Can a believer lose his or her salvation? This article will examine the once saved, always saved doctrinal belief.

ONCE SAVED, ALWAYS SAVED IS NOT IN SCRIPTURE

The phrase, 'Once saved, always saved,' is not found anywhere in Scripture. To the contrary, there are numerous plainspoken Tanakh (Old Testament) and B'rit Hadashah (New Testament) verses that attest to the fact that righteous living persons can lose their salvation if they turn from living righteously to living sinfully.

EZEKIEL 18:24 (NKJV):
But when a righteous man turns away from his righteousness and commits iniquity, and does according to all the abominations that the wicked man does, shall he live? All the righteousness, which he has done, shall not be remembered; because of the unfaithfulness of which he is guilty and the sin, which he has committed, because of them he shall die.

HEBREWS 10:26-29 (NKJV):
For if we sin willfully after we have received the knowledge of the truth, there no longer remains a sacrifice for sins, but a certain fearful expectation of judgment, and fiery indignation which will devour the adversaries. Anyone who has rejected Moses' law dies without mercy on the testimony of two or three witnesses. Of how much worse punishment, do you suppose, will he be thought worthy who has trampled the Son of God underfoot, counted the blood of the covenant by which he was sanctified a common thing, and insulted the Spirit of grace?

2 PETER 2:20-22 (NKJV):
For if, after they have escaped the pollutions of the world through the knowledge of the Lord and Savior Yeshua Messiah (Jesus Christ), they are again entangled in them and overcome, the latter end is worse for them than the beginning. For it would have been better for them not to have known the way of righteousness, than having known it, to turn from the holy commandment delivered to them. But it has happened to them according to the true proverb: *"A dog returns to his own vomit,"* and, *"a sow, having washed, to her wallowing in the mire."*

WE WILL OFFICIALLY BE SAVED AT THE LAST TRUMPET

No one is 'saved' yet. We are all still living in corrupted flesh and blood bodies, capable of sin, and all are subject to death and the grave. Believers who die before Yeshua (Jesus) returns are not going straight to heaven (John 3:13); they are going to the grave to await the resurrection. As faithful believers in Yeshua (Jesus), obeying His commandments and worshiping Him in spirit and truth, we can have the assurance that we *will be* saved (in the future), if we endure in righteousness till the end, but to say we are *already saved* is inaccurate, presumptuous, and is borderline arrogant.

1 CORINTHIANS 15:51-54 (NKJV):

Behold, I tell you a mystery: We shall not all sleep, but we shall all be changed - in a moment, in the twinkling of an eye, at the last trumpet. For the trumpet will sound, and the dead will be raised incorruptible, and we shall be changed. For this corruptible must put on incorruption, and this mortal must put on immortality. So when this corruptible has put on incorruption, and this mortal has put on immortality, then shall be brought to pass the saying that is written: *"Death is swallowed up in victory."*

1 THESSALONIANS 4:15-17 (NKJV):

For this we say to you by the word of the Lord, that we who are alive and remain until the coming of the Lord will by no means precede those who are asleep. For the Lord Himself will descend from heaven with a shout, with the voice of an archangel, and with the trumpet of God. And the dead in Messiah (Christ) will rise first. Then we who are alive and remain shall be caught up together with them in the clouds to meet the Lord in the air. And thus we shall always be with the Lord.

After we believing saints are transformed into spirit beings, then we can officially proclaim that we are saved. We will be made into immortal incorruptible beings (1 Corinthians 15:53-54). Hypothetically, can a saved person who has been transformed into an immortal, incorruptible spirit being lose his or her salvation?

2 PETER 2:4 (NKJV):

God did not spare the angels who sinned, but cast them down to hell and delivered them into chains of darkness, to be reserved for judgment.

Scripture proclaims that we will be made incorruptible. Presumably, no one would want to lose his or her salvation. However, if it were possible to rebel against God after being transformed into an incorruptible, immortal spirit being, then the fate of such a person would be the same as Satan and the angels who rebelled against God in heaven, who were assumably 'saved.'

THE DANGERS OF ONCE SAVED, ALWAYS SAVED PHILOSOPHY

Christians who believe and proclaim to be once saved, always saved, can use their belief to destroy their righteousness within themselves. When Christians believe they became OSAS on a certain date, and there is no possibility of their salvation being lost, they risk opening the door to sin and unrighteousness. Once saved, always saved is used by many as a false sense of security, a license to sin freely, with no consequences and no chance of possibly losing salvation.

THE PREMISE THAT WE ARE *ALREADY SAVED* IS FALSE

MATTHEW 24:13; MARK 13:13 (NKJV):

"But he who endures to the end *shall be saved*."

HEBREWS 10:39 (NKJV):

But we are not of those who draw back to perdition, but of those who believe *to the saving of the soul*.

HEBREWS 10:39 (TLV):

But we are not among the timid ones on the path to destruction, but among the faithful ones *on the path to the preservation of the soul*.

He or she who endures [IN RIGHTEOUSNESS] to the end shall be [FUTURE TENSE] saved. Some believers' end is the end of their life, others will endure until they are raptured, and others will endure until the end of the age and the return of Messiah (Christ).

A person can draw back to living unrighteously and lose salvation. Those who are to be saved are those who live righteously by faith and are ON THE PATH to being saved.

EPHESIANS 4:30 (NKJV):

And do not grieve the Holy Spirit of God, by whom you were sealed for the day of redemption.

As Messiah (Christ) believers, God does 'seal' us through His Spirit, by having His Spirit indwell in us, but warns us not to grieve the Spirit within us, through willfully sinning, as we can unseal the Holy Spirit from dwelling within us by rejecting God and willfully sinning.

We are NOT yet redeemed or 'saved' when we accept Yeshua (Jesus); His Spirit seals us *for the day of redemption*, which is in the future, when we are transformed from flesh and blood beings into spirit beings.

Ephesians 4:30 does not say, "And do not grieve the Holy Spirit of God, by whom you are once saved and always saved."

LUKE 19:9 (NKJV):

And Yeshua (Jesus) said to him, "Today salvation has come to this house…"

1 JOHN 3:9 (NKJV):

Whoever has been born of God does not sin, for His seed remains in him; and he cannot sin, because he has been born of God.

"Today salvation" and being "born of God" does not mean once saved always saved. These are promises of assured future salvation.

1 CORINTHIANS 6:9-10 (NKJV) (HSV†):

Do you not know that the unrighteous will not inherit the reign of Elohim (kingdom of God)? Do not be deceived. Neither fornicators, nor idolaters, nor adulterers, nor effeminate, nor homosexuals, nor thieves, nor covetous (†greedy of gain), nor drunkards, nor revilers, nor swindlers will inherit the kingdom of God (†reign of Elohim).

GALATIANS 5:19-21 (NKJV) (HSV†):

Now the works of the flesh are evident, which are: adultery, fornication, uncleanness, lewdness, idolatry, drug sorcery, hatred, quarrels, jealousies, fits of rage, selfish ambitions, dissensions, heresies, envy, murders, drunkenness, revelries, and the like; of which I tell you beforehand, just as I also told you in time past, that those who practice such things will not inherit the kingdom of God (†reign of Elohim).

EPHESIANS 5:5-6 (NKJV) (HSV†):

For this you know, that no fornicator, unclean person, nor covetous man, who is an idolater, has any inheritance in the kingdom (†reign) of Messiah (Christ) and God. Let no one deceive you with empty words, for because of these things the wrath of God comes upon the sons of disobedience.

REVELATION 21:7-8 (NKJV):

He who overcomes shall inherit all things, and I will be his God and he shall be My son. The cowardly, untrustworthy, abominable, murderers, sexually immoral, drug sorcerers, idolaters, and all liars shall have their part in the lake which burns with fire and brimstone, which is the second death.

Do not be deceived with the empty promise of 'once saved, always saved' guaranteed salvation. A believer can turn back to sin and lose his or her salvation (Hebrews 10:26). Righteousness in not imputed onto a believer through the blood of Yeshua (Jesus), so that a believer can live lawlessly, sinning freely. Living righteously is what God calls us as believers to do and it is a prerequisite for any man or woman who wishes to inherit the kingdom of God (Leviticus 11:44-45, 20:7; 2 Peter 3:11; 1 John 2:3-6). True worshipers, those who worship God in spirit and truth, *can live with the assurance today* that they will be saved (Luke 19:9; John 4:23-24), but actual salvation will not occur until we are transformed into incorruptible spirit beings at the last trumpet (1 Corinthians 15:51-54).

DOES GOD HATE THE SIN, BUT LOVE THE SINNER?

By George Lujack

A well-known slogan amongst evangelical Christians is "Love the sinner, hate the sin." This article will examine the origin of this slogan, reveal whether there is any Scriptural basis for this claim, and answer the question, "Does God hate the sin, but love the sinner?"

The origin of the phrase, "Love the sinner, hate the sin," comes from Augustine, a Catholic bishop who wrote in his letter numbered 211, "*Cum dilectione hominum et odio vitiorum*," which translates roughly to "With love for mankind and hatred of sins." Mohandas Gandhi, in his 1929 autobiography wrote, "Hate the sin and not the sinner," which is a more recent version of the phrase. "Love the sinner, hate the sin" does not appear in Scripture, but other verses have been used in support of the philosophical phrase.

JOHN 3:16 (NKJV):

"For God so loved the world that He gave His only begotten Son, that whoever believes in Him should not perish but have everlasting life."

ROMANS 5:8 (NKJV):

But God demonstrates His own love toward us, in that while we were still sinners, Messiah (Christ) died for us.

Neither John 3:16 nor Romans 5:8 directly say, "God loves sinners." God so loved *the world*… and the world does have sinners in it, but the world also has God-seeking, righteous-living people in it. God loves the righteous. Yeshua (Jesus) came to save sinners from unrighteousness, to show them the way of righteousness, and then die to atone for our *past* sins. He died for us while we were still sinners, but with a conditional message that we should repent and stop sinning. God knew our potential to transform from sinners into becoming righteous beings, and His plan was to save us from His righteous judgment through His Son.

GOD HATES THE SIN AND THE SINNER, BUT LOVES RIGHTEOUSNESS

PSALM 5:4-6 (NKJV):

For You are not a God who takes pleasure in wickedness, nor shall evil dwell with You. The boastful shall not stand in Your sight. YOU HATE ALL WORKERS OF INIQUITY. You shall destroy those who speak falsehood. YHWH (the Lord) abhors the bloodthirsty and deceitful man.

PSALM 11:5,7 (NKJV):

YHWH (the Lord) tests the righteous, BUT THE WICKED AND THE ONE WHO LOVES VIOLENCE HIS SOUL HATES. For YHWH (the Lord) is righteous, He loves righteousness.

GOD'S WRATH IS AGAINST THE SIN AND UPON THE SINNER

JOHN 3:36 (NKJV):

He who believes in the Son has everlasting life; and he who does not believe the Son shall not see life, but the wrath of God abides on him.

ROMANS 1:18-19 (NKJV):

For the wrath of God is revealed from heaven against all ungodliness and unrighteousness of men, who suppress the truth in unrighteousness, because what may be known of God is manifest in them, for God has shown it to them.

ROMANS 2:5 (NKJV):

But in accordance with your hardness and your impenitent heart you are treasuring up for yourself wrath in the day of wrath and revelation of the righteous judgment of God, who *"will render to each one according to his deeds."*

Righteous saints have repented of their sins and live righteously according to God's laws, while habitual or unrepentant sinners are people who continually sin. We are what we do and we will be judged according to our deeds. God will not throw sin into hell and spare the sinners from hell out of love for the sinners. He is going to throw unrepentant sinners into hell together with their sins.

THE GOOD NEWS

1 PETER 2:21-24 (NKJV):

For to this you were called, because Messiah (Christ) also suffered for us, leaving us an example, that you should follow His steps:

"Who committed no sin, nor was deceit found in His mouth;"

who, when He was reviled, did not revile in return; when He suffered, He did not threaten, but committed Himself to Him who judges righteously; who Himself bore our sins in His own body on the tree, that we, having died to sins, might live for righteousness - by whose stripes you were healed.

The Good News is that God has taken His righteous wrath against sinners out on His Son, so that we do not need to be judged by our deeds. However, avoiding the judgment of our deeds is conditional. The condition is that we must accept Yeshua (Jesus), repent of sin, stop sinning, and live righteously.

The problem with the philosophy that "God hates the sin, but loves the sinner," is that it divides and separates the sin from the sinner. Lukewarm believers can get very comfortable and confused with their sins and might not understand the need to repent and stop sinning.

It's fine for people to say that they love people, but to say that they love sinners is a verbal condoning of sin. Homosexual advocates have successfully used the 'love the sinner' philosophy to push acceptance of their LGBT lifestyle upon society by implementing programs for parents who do not approve of their child's choice to engage in homosexuality. Gay propaganda family counseling sessions urge parents to publicly state, "I love my *gay* son," which is a verbal acceptance, consenting, and proclamation of a child's sin, in place of "I love my son," which is a normal thing for loving parents to say of their child.

MATTHEW 4:17 (NKJV):

From that time Yeshua (Jesus) began to preach and to say, "Repent, for the kingdom of heaven is at hand."

MATTHEW 9:12-13; LUKE 5:32 (NKJV):

Yeshua (Jesus) answered and said to them, "Those who are well have no need of a physician, but those who are sick. I have not come to call the righteous, but sinners, to repentance."

The kingdom of heaven is soon going to be at hand again, when Yeshua (Jesus) returns to rule the world with a rod of iron (Revelation 19:15). People who are comfortable living with their sins are spiritually sick and need to repent, stop sinning, get spiritually well, and start living righteously. Comforting sinners with the empty slogan, "God hates the sin, but loves the sinner," does nothing to encourage them to repent and get right with God.

FAITH AND WORKS

By George Lujack

'Faith and Works' has been debated among Christianity for millennia. Scripture even appears to have some seemingly contradictory verses on the subject. Are we saved by faith alone? Are works necessary for salvation? What are the works of the law? Is faith without works dead? What are the different kinds of works? This article will address the contentious topic of faith and works.

WE ARE JUSTIFIED AND SAVED BY GOD'S GRACE THROUGH FAITH, NOT BY WORKS OR THE WORKS OF THE LAW

ACTS 26:17-18 (NKJV):

"I now send you, to open their eyes, in order to turn them from darkness to light, and from the power of Satan to God, that they may receive forgiveness of sins and an inheritance among those who are sanctified BY FAITH IN ME."

ROMANS 3:27-28, 5:1 (NKJV):

Where is boasting then? It is excluded. By what law? Of works? No, but by the law of faith. Therefore we conclude that a man is JUSTIFIED BY FAITH apart from the deeds of the law. ...

Therefore, having been JUSTIFIED BY FAITH, we have peace with God through our Lord Yeshua Messiah (Jesus Christ).

GALATIANS 2:16,21, 3:11 (NKJV):

A man is NOT JUSTIFIED BY THE WORKS OF THE LAW BUT BY FAITH in Yeshua Messiah (Jesus Christ), even we have believed in Messiah Yeshua (Christ Jesus), that we might be JUSTIFIED BY FAITH in Messiah (Christ) and NOT BY WORKS OF THE LAW; FOR BY THE WORKS OF THE LAW NO FLESH SHALL BE JUSTIFIED.

...

I do not set aside the grace of God; for if righteousness comes through the law, then Messiah (Christ) died in vain.

...

But that NO ONE IS JUSTIFIED BY THE LAW in the sight of God is evident, for "*THE JUST SHALL LIVE BY FAITH.*"

EPHESIANS 2:8-9 (NKJV):

FOR BY GRACE YOU HAVE BEEN SAVED THROUGH FAITH, and that not of yourselves; it is the gift of God, NOT OF WORKS, lest anyone should boast.

ATTAINING SALVATION CANNOT BE ACHIEVED THROUGH OBEDIENTLY DOING THE WORKS OF THE TORAH (LAW)

ROMANS 9:30-32 (NKJV):

Gentiles, who did not pursue righteousness, have attained to righteousness, even the righteousness of belief; but Israel, pursuing the law (Torah) of righteousness, has not attained to the law (Torah) of righteousness. Why? Because they did not seek it by faith, but as it were, by the works of the law (Torah).

GALATIANS 3:10-13 (NKJV):

For as many as are of the works of the law are under the curse; for it is written, *"Cursed is everyone who does not continue in all things which are written in the book of the law, to do them."* But that no one is justified by the law in the sight of God *is* evident, for *"the just shall live by faith."* Yet the law is not of faith, but *"the man who does them shall live by them."*

Messiah (Christ) has redeemed us from the curse of the law, having become a curse for us...

We have attained salvation through faith in the sacrifice of Yeshua Messiah (Jesus Christ) to atone for our sins, and could not have attained salvation in any other way. Works or works of the law cannot save us, for if they could, Yeshua (Jesus) died in vain. Yeshua (Jesus) prayed to the Father, before His crucifixion, asking that if it was possible [TO SAVE MANKIND WITHOUT HIS SUFFERING AND DEATH] to let the cup pass from Him (Matthew 26:39). It was NOT possible, and Yeshua (Jesus) suffered, shed His blood, and died to atone for the sins of man (Matthew 26:42).

ARE WE SAVED BY FAITH ALONE?

Scripture has seemingly contradictory statements of faith and works. Romans 3:28 says, "We conclude that a man is justified by faith apart from the deeds of the law." James 2:24 states, "a man is justified by works, and not by faith only." Romans 3:28 and James 2:24 are speaking of two different types of works. Romans 3:28 explains that a man is only justified by faith; his obedience to the Torah (law) cannot save him. James 2:24 is commentary of the actions of Abraham and Rahab, who were driven to do works because of their faith. Their faith was working together with their works and by these works, faith was made perfect (James 2:22). So THIS FAITH, *working together* with their works, justified them.

FAITH WITHOUT WORKS IS DEAD

JAMES 2:14-17 (NKJV):

What does it profit, my brethren, if someone says he has faith but does not have works? Can faith save him? If a brother or sister is naked and destitute of daily food, and one of you says to them, "Depart in peace, be warmed and filled," but you do not give them the things which are needed for the body, what does it profit? Thus also FAITH BY ITSELF, IF IT DOES NOT HAVE WORKS, IS DEAD.

JAMES 2:18-20 (NKJV):

But someone will say, "You have faith, and I have works." Show me your faith without your works, and I will show you my faith by my works. You believe that there is one God. You do well. Even the demons believe - and tremble! But do you want to know, O foolish man, that FAITH WITHOUT WORKS IS DEAD?

JAMES 2:24 (NKJV):

You see then that A MAN IS JUSTIFIED BY WORKS, *AND NOT BY FAITH ONLY.*

JAMES 2:26 (NKJV):

For as the body without the spirit is dead, so FAITH WITHOUT WORKS IS DEAD also.

Works of the law demonstrate faith. Faith without works would equate to someone who believes in Yeshua (Jesus), but refuses to obey His commandments or help his or her neighbor. Someone who has faith without works is an unworthy, unprofitable servant as illustrated in the parable of the talents in Matthew 25:14-30. In that parable, the king cast the lazy and wicked servant into the outer darkness, or hell (Matthew 25:30).

The parable of the talents is a reflection of how Yeshua (Jesus) views lazy, unprofitable, "lukewarm" believers. According to Revelation 3:15-16, He will say to many in the various churches that He knows their works (or more accurately their evil works or lack of good works), and that these believers are neither hot nor cold, but lukewarm, and because they are lukewarm, He will figuratively vomit them out of His mouth.

God did not spare the angels who sinned, but cast them out of His kingdom (2 Peter 2:4). Demons believe (have faith), yet are not saved (James 2:19). Mere faith that Yeshua (Jesus) exists is insufficient for salvation. Many Christian theologians have needlessly argued over 'Faith vs. Works,' and/or 'Faith or Works?' for salvation. The proper approach is to understand that faith and works compliment each other. Faith saves us, but if you do not do the works of the law (obey the commandments), then your faith is dead.

1 JOHN 2:3-6 (NKJV):

Now by this we know that we know Him, if we keep His commandments. He who says, "I know Him," and does not keep His commandments, is a liar, and the truth is not in him. But whoever keeps His word, truly the love of God is perfected in him. By this we know that we are in Him. He who says he abides in Him ought himself also to walk just as He walked.

Who can claim to have faith, yet not do the works of the law (obey His commandments) and live lawlessly? Anyone can merely profess to believe, but if a person lives lawlessly and just merely states belief, there is no demonstration of faith exhibited at all. This type of 'faith' IS DEAD.

ROMANS 3:31 (NKJV):

Do we then make void the law through faith? Certainly not! On the contrary, we establish the law.

And even if someone does have faith, but *believes* he or she can live lawlessly, this faith is dead also. There will be many believers, who lawlessly lived '*by faith alone*,' who will be turned away from the kingdom of heaven...

MATTHEW 7:21-23 (NKJV):

"Not everyone who says to Me, 'Lord, Lord,' shall enter the kingdom of heaven, but he who does the will of My Father in heaven. Many will say to Me in that day, 'Lord, Lord, have we not prophesied in Your name, cast out demons in Your name, and done many wonders in Your name?' And then I will declare to them, 'I never knew you; depart from Me, you who practice lawlessness!'"

CHARITABLE WORKS

Apart from the works of the law (obeying the commandments), charitable deeds are another type of works. As with works of the law (obeying the commandments), no amount of charitable works can save a person; only faith in Yeshua (Jesus) saves. Doing charitable work is not done for attaining salvation, but is fitting for the saints to demonstrate faith.

MATTHEW 6:1-4 (NKJV):

"Take heed that you do not do your charitable deeds before men, to be seen by them. Otherwise you have no reward from your Father in heaven. Therefore, when you do a charitable deed, do not sound a trumpet before you as the hypocrites do in the synagogues and in the streets, that they may have glory from men. Assuredly, I say to you, they have their reward. But when you do a charitable deed, do not let your left hand know what your right hand is doing, that your charitable deed may be in secret; and your Father who sees in secret will Himself reward you openly."

LUKE 12:32-34 (NKJV):

"Do not fear, little flock, for it is your Father's good pleasure to give you the kingdom. Sell what you have and give alms; provide yourselves money bags which do not grow old, a treasure in the heavens that does not fail, where no thief approaches nor moth destroys. For where your treasure is, there your heart will be also."

OCCUPATIONAL WORKS OF THE HANDS

Scripture commands and encourages believers to do occupational work. We are commanded to work six-days of the week (Exodus 16:26, 20:9, 23:12, 34:21, 35:2; Leviticus 23:3; Deuteronomy 5:13). The Apostle Paul was a tentmaker by occupation, who continued making tents during his ministry.

ACTS 18:1-4 (NKJV):

After these things Paul departed from Athens and went to Corinth. And he found a certain Jew named Aquila, born in Pontus, who had recently come from Italy with his wife Priscilla (because Claudius had commanded all the Jews to depart from Rome); and he came to them. So, because he was of the same trade, he stayed with them and worked; *for by occupation they were tentmakers*. And he reasoned in the synagogue every Sabbath, and persuaded both Jews and Greeks.

EPHESIANS 4:28 (NKJV):

Let him who stole steal no longer, *but rather let him labor, working with his hands* what is good, that he may have something to give him who has need.

1 THESSALONIANS 4:10-12 (NKJV):

But we urge you, brethren, that you increase more and more; that you also aspire to lead a quiet life, to mind your own business, *and to work with your own hands*, as we commanded you, that you may walk properly toward those who are outside, and that you may lack nothing.

WE WILL BE GRADED AND JUDGED BY OUR WORKS

MATTHEW 5:18-19 (NKJV):

"For assuredly, I say to you, till heaven and earth pass away, one jot or one tittle will by no means pass from the law till all is fulfilled. Whoever therefore breaks one of the least of these commandments, and teaches men so, SHALL BE CALLED LEAST in the kingdom of heaven; but whoever does and teaches them, HE SHALL BE CALLED GREAT in the kingdom of heaven."

REVELATION 20:12-13 (NKJV):

And I saw the dead, small and great, standing before God, and books were opened. And another book was opened, which is the Book of Life. And the dead were JUDGED ACCORDING TO THEIR WORKS, by the things which were written in the books. The sea gave up the dead who were in it, and Death and Hades delivered up the dead who were in them. And they were JUDGED, EACH ONE ACCORDING TO HIS WORKS.

GOOD WORKS WILL FOLLOW THE RIGHTEOUS INTO GOD'S KINGDOM

REVELATION 14:12-13 (NKJV):

Here is the patience of the saints; here are those WHO KEEP THE COMMANDMENTS OF GOD *AND* THE FAITH of Yeshua (Jesus).

Then I heard a voice from heaven saying to me, "Write: 'Blessed are the dead who die in the Lord from now on.'"

"Yes," says the Spirit, "that they may rest from their labors, AND THEIR WORKS FOLLOW THEM."

SALVATION

Salvation is attained through faith in Messiah (Christ) who was sacrificed in our place as atonement for the sins of mankind, so that we may receive eternal life. Without Messiah's (Christ's) sacrifice and had He not risen, then neither faith, nor good works, nor faith and good works could save us (1 Corinthians 15:14). Salvation is attained through an unmerited gift of grace from God and no one can earn it through works.

Faith in Yeshua (Jesus) brings forth fruit, which brings forth repentance, obedience, and good works. Faith without works is dead. Works, as a sole means to attain salvation while rejecting Messiah (Christ), are in vain. Faith and works go hand and hand together.

THE NEW COVENANT, WHAT IS IT?

By George Lujack

Mainstream Christianity often erroneously teaches that we are living under the New Covenant now and the Old Covenant (meaning the law) is abolished. This article will address what the New Covenant is, correct the misconception that the law itself is the Old Covenant replaced by the New Covenant, will identify what the Old Covenant is that was replaced by the New Covenant, and will declare that God's laws are eternal.

HEBREWS 8:6-13 (NKJV):

He is also Mediator of a better covenant, which was established on better promises. For if that first covenant had been faultless, then no place would have been sought for a second. Because finding fault with them, He says: "Behold, the days are coming, says YHWH (the Lord), when I will make a new covenant with the house of Israel and with the house of Judah - not according to the covenant that I made with their fathers in the day when I took them by the hand to lead them out of the land of Egypt; because they did not continue in My covenant, and I disregarded them, says YHWH (the Lord). For this is the covenant that I will make with the house of Israel after those days, says YHWH (the Lord): I will put My laws in their mind and write them on their hearts; and I will be their God, and they shall be My people. None of them shall teach his neighbor, and none his brother, saying, 'Know YHWH (the Lord),' for all shall know Me, from the least of them to the greatest of them. For I will be merciful to their unrighteousness, and their sins and their lawless deeds I will remember no more." In that He says, "A new covenant," He has made the first obsolete. Now what is becoming obsolete and growing old is ready to vanish away.

Yeshua Messiah (Jesus Christ), whose life was holy, perfect, and without sin met the qualifications to permanently take away the sins of the world. Yeshua (Jesus) fully paid for the remission of sin, therefore there are to be no more animal sacrifices or offerings for sin, as required annually under the Old Covenant, as these sacrificial measures to atone for sin have been made obsolete in the New Covenant. Yeshua (Jesus) has sacrificed Himself once and forever to atone for sin (Hebrews 10:1-18).

THE NEW COVENANT WAS FORETOLD IN JEREMIAH

JEREMIAH 31:31-32 (NKJV):

"Behold, the days are coming, says YHWH (the Lord), when I will make a new covenant with the house of Israel and with the house of Judah - not according to the covenant that I made with their fathers in the day that I took them by the hand to lead them out of the land of Egypt, My covenant which they broke, though I was a husband to them, says YHWH (the Lord).

JEREMIAH 31:33-34 (NKJV):

But this is the covenant that I will make with the house of Israel after those days, says YHWH (the Lord): I will put My law in their minds, and write it on their hearts; and I will be their God, and they shall be My people. No more shall every man teach his neighbor, and every man his brother, saying, 'Know YHWH (the Lord),' for they all shall know Me, from the least of them to the greatest of them, says YHWH (the Lord). For I will forgive their iniquity, and their sin I will remember no more."

THE OLD COVENANT

EXODUS 19:3-8 (NKJV):

And Moses went up to God, and YHWH (the Lord) called to him from the mountain, saying, "Thus you shall say to the house of Jacob, and tell the children of Israel: 'You have seen what I did to the Egyptians, and how I bore you on eagles' wings and brought you to Myself. Now therefore, if you will indeed obey My voice and keep My covenant, then you shall be a special treasure to Me above all people; for all the earth is Mine. And you shall be to Me a kingdom of priests and a holy nation.' These are the words which you shall speak to the children of Israel."

So Moses came and called for the elders of the people, and laid before them all these words that YHWH (the Lord) commanded him. Then all the people answered together and said, "All that YHWH (the Lord) has spoken WE WILL DO."

The Hebrews failed to live up to their word when they declared, *"All that YHWH (the Lord) has spoken, we will do,"* (Exodus 19:8). The Hebrews would soon make a golden calf graven image idol as well as break God's laws in many other ways after their declaration of loyalty in Exodus 19:8. When the Hebrews eventually settled in their promised homeland of Israel, they once again sinned, breaking their exclusive covenant with God that they had made. Therefore, God divorced Israel (yet remained faithful to them) as a husband who divorces his unfaithful wife for committing unrepentant adultery and breaking their marriage covenant (Jeremiah 3:8). Israel's national sin was not only in breaking their covenant with God, for disobeying His laws, but also for worshiping other gods of their neighboring nations - committing spiritual adultery.

The Old Covenant, given at Sinai to the Hebrews, was an EXCLUSIVE COVENANT. God had declared that He was choosing a people, the Hebrews, of whom He would lead to the promised land of Israel and He would exclusively be their God. God was not going out to the people of the world at this time to teach His laws and offer salvation through repentance. God was dealing exclusively with the Hebrews, to show them as a shining example to the world as a nation that knew the one true God.

The Hebrews, due to their national sins, didn't live up to the promise offered to them under the Old Covenant and YHWH (the Lord) divorced them. Yet, even though YHWH (the Lord) divorced Israel, He remained faithful to Israel due to His EXCLUSIVE COVENANT that He had made with them. It was not possible for God, under the exclusive Old Covenant that He had made with Israel, to go out among the other nations and proclaim His word, yet it was possible for someone outside of Israel to be grafted into the house of Israel through faith and learn of God's word. We see this in the Scripture examples of Ruth and the woman of Canaan.

RUTH 1:16 (NKJV):

… For wherever you go, I will go and wherever you lodge, I will lodge. Your people shall be my people, and your God, my God.

MATTHEW 15:21-28 (NKJV):

Then Yeshua (Jesus) went out from there and departed to the region of Tyre and Sidon. And behold, a woman of Canaan came from that region and cried out to Him, saying, "Have mercy on me, O Lord, Son of David! My daughter is severely demon-possessed."

But He answered her not a word. And His disciples came and urged Him, saying, "Send her away, for she cries out after us." But He answered and said, "I was not sent EXCEPT TO THE LOST SHEEP OF THE HOUSE OF ISRAEL."

Then she came and worshiped Him, saying, "Lord, help me!"

But He answered and said, "It is not good to take the children's bread and throw it to the little dogs."

And she said, "Yes, Lord, yet even the little dogs eat the crumbs which fall from their masters' table."

Then Yeshua (Jesus) answered and said to her, "O woman, GREAT IS YOUR FAITH! Let it be to you as you desire." And her daughter was healed from that very hour.

YESHUA (JESUS) REMAINED FAITHFUL TO THE EXCLUSIVE COVENANT HE HAD MADE WITH THE JEWS UNTO HIS DEATH

Why did YHWH (the Lord) remain faithful to faithless Israel? Why didn't God make another covenant with another nation or nations? It was because He was under an exclusive covenant with Israel, and ONLY DEATH ends a covenant.

MATTHEW 10:5-6 (NKJV):

These twelve Yeshua (Jesus) sent out and commanded them, saying: "Do not go into the way of the Gentiles, and do not enter a city of the Samaritans. But go rather to the lost sheep of the house of Israel …"

When Yeshua (Jesus) said not to go the way of the Gentiles, to preach to them, it was because He was under an EXCLUSIVE COVENANT with the Jews of territorial Israel. Death ended His exclusive covenant with the Jews.

MATTHEW 28:18-20 (NKJV):

And Yeshua (Jesus) came and spoke to them, saying, "All authority has been given to Me in heaven and on earth. Go therefore and make disciples of ALL THE NATIONS, baptizing them in the name of the Father and of the Son and of the Holy Spirit, teaching them to observe all things that I have commanded you; and lo, I am with you always, even to the end of the age."

The exclusive covenant between Yeshua (Jesus) and the Jews was broken upon the death of Yeshua (Jesus). His new command to preach the Good News and God's laws to all the nations, in Matthew 28:18-20, superseded His previous command in Matthew 10:5-6 to preach exclusively to the Jews and to not preach to the non-Israelite Gentile nations.

After the death of Yeshua Messiah (Jesus Christ), His exclusive covenant pact with the Jews of Israel ended, and He was allowed to make a New Covenant with all the nations of the world. The command to not preach to the Gentiles given in Matthew 10:5-6 was rescinded by Yeshua (Jesus) in Matthew 28:18-20. In Acts 10, Peter refused to meet with Cornelius - a Gentile, for he believed it was wrong for Jews to interact with Gentiles due to tradition and also because of the command Yeshua (Jesus) gave in Matthew 10:5-6. Peter was instructed through the Spirit that what God had made clean (the Gentiles) he should not call unclean. Peter then realized the meaning of the vision and met with Cornelius and his men.

THE EVERLASTING COVENANT PROVIDES ATONEMENT AND RE-ESTABLISHES THE COVENANT (LAW)

EZEKIEL 16:60-63 (NKJV):

"Nevertheless I will remember My covenant with you in the days of your youth, and I will establish an everlasting covenant with you. Then you will remember your ways and be ashamed, when you receive your older and your younger sisters; for I will give them to you for daughters, but not because of My covenant with you. And I will establish My covenant with you. Then you shall know that I am YHWH (the Lord), that you may remember and be ashamed, and never open your mouth anymore because of your shame, when I provide you an atonement for all you have done," says YHWH (the Lord) GOD.

THE NEW COVENANT HAS MADE THE FIRST COVENANT OBSOLETE

The everlasting New Covenant is Yeshua's (Jesus') atonement sacrifice on the cross that has made God's word available to all the nations that come to Him through faith and repentance, obeying His laws and doing His will. The New Covenant is yet to be completely fulfilled, as in this age many live in ignorance or disobedience, not living righteously according to God's laws. The law did not pass away, nor will it ever pass away (Matthew 5:17-19, 24:35; Mark 13:31; Luke 16:7, 21:33). The law (Torah) is good and rewards those, in this life and in the life to come, who obey it.

WHAT IS THE FIRST COVENANT?

GENESIS 2:16 (NKJV):

And YHWH (the Lord) God commanded the man, saying, "Of every tree of the garden you may freely eat; but of the tree of the knowledge of good and evil you shall not eat, for in the day that you eat of it you shall surely die."

The actual first covenant God made with man was with Adam in the Garden of Eden. YHWH (the Lord) God made a covenant promise to Adam that if he were to disobey Him and sin, he would die. Adam disobeyed God, sinned, and died. All men have thus inherited sin from Adam and have fallen short of the glory of God (Romans 3:23).

The first covenant that YHWH (the Lord) God made with Adam was the covenant of sin and death. Messiah Yeshua (Christ Jesus) has freed mankind from the first covenant, the law of sin and death (Romans 8:2). Death remained under the Old Covenant, but eternal life is given to us under the New Covenant (Matthew 26:28; Mark 14:24; Luke 22:20; 1 Corinthians 11:25).

Yeshua's (Jesus') sacrifice is the New Covenant; His blood has been shed for many, once and forever, for the remission of sins (Hebrews 7:27, 10:10). The New Covenant has canceled out the animal sacrifices of the Old Covenant that were required to temporarily atone for sin, rendering them obsolete (Hebrews 9:11-28, 10:1-10). The New Covenant has made the first covenant (Genesis 2:16), the law of sin and death (Romans 8:2), obsolete and the first covenant ordinances, requiring death, are soon to pass away (1 Corinthians 15:54-57; Revelation 21:4).

God also made a first covenant with the Hebrews at Mt. Sinai…

HEBREWS 8:7-9 (NKJV):

For if that first covenant had been faultless, then no place would have been sought for a second. Because finding fault with them, He says: *"Behold, the days are coming, says the Lord, when I will make a new covenant with the house of Israel and with the house of Judah - not according to the covenant that I made with their fathers in the day when I took them by the hand to lead them out of the land of Egypt; BECAUSE THEY DID NOT CONTINUE IN MY COVENANT, and I disregarded them, says the Lord.*

What was the 'fault' of the first covenant given to Adam in the Garden of Eden, and what was the fault of the covenant given to the Hebrews at Mt. Sinai? Was the law itself, a law that was allegedly impossible to follow, at fault? NO! In both cases the fault was not the law itself, it was that neither Adam nor the Hebrews continued in God's covenant.

JEREMIAH 31:33 (NKJV):

This is the covenant that I will make with the house of Israel after those days, says YHWH (the Lord): I WILL PUT MY LAW IN THEIR MINDS, AND WRITE IT IN THEIR HEARTS; and I will be their God, and they shall be My people.

EZEKIEL 36:26-27 (NKJV):

I will give you a new heart and put a new spirit within you; I will take the heart of stone out of your flesh and give you a heart of flesh. I will put My Spirit within you and CAUSE YOU TO WALK IN MY STATUTES, and you will keep My judgments and do them.

HEBREWS 8:10-11,13 (NKJV):

I will put MY LAWS IN THEIR MIND AND WRITE THEM ON THEIR HEARTS; and I will be their God, and they shall be My people. None of them shall teach his neighbor, and none his brother, saying, 'Know the Lord,' for all shall know Me, from the least of them to the greatest of them….

In that He says, "A new covenant," He has made THE FIRST obsolete. Now what is becoming obsolete and growing old is ready to vanish away.

Scripture states that the New Covenant has made the first covenant obsolete. Does this mean that the New Covenant, Yeshua's (Jesus') atonement sacrifice on the cross, makes the law (Torah) obsolete and that law (Torah) is ready to pass away? NO!

LUKE 21:33 (NKJV):

"Heaven and earth will pass away, but My words will by no means pass away."

Yeshua's (Jesus') words, which include His commandments, will never pass away. God will write His eternal laws and statutes on our minds and hearts. There is no fault in His laws, the fault is with us. The New Covenant does not make obsolete His laws, it makes obsolete the faulty way by which they were upheld by mankind.

It is a commonly held belief that the New Covenant has replaced law (Torah); that the New Covenant of accepting Yeshua Messiah (Jesus Christ) as an atonement sacrifice for our sins has replaced the law, freeing us from having to obey the commandments and laws (Torah) of God. The New Covenant did not replace the law (Torah), but rather it supplemented it with grace and truth.

JOHN 1:17 (NKJV):

For the law was given through Moses, but grace and truth came through Yeshua Messiah (Jesus Christ).

Scripture declares that the first covenant has been rendered obsolete by the New Covenant (Hebrews 8:13). The ordinance penalty of the first covenant, death, has been removed. The New Covenant does not abolish the law. The law is to be strongly established on our minds and on our hearts, so that we will walk according to His laws and statutes for all time, throughout eternity.

1 CORINTHIANS 7:19 (NKJV):

Keeping the commandments of God is what matters.

REVELATION 14:12 (NKJV):

Here is the patience of the saints; here are those who keep the commandments of God and the faith of Yeshua (Jesus).

Blessed are those who now willingly walk according to His commandments and obey His statutes.

Yeshua's (Jesus') sacrifice is the new covenant, which is to redeem mankind and also is to establish His laws and statutes on our minds and hearts for all eternity.

THE GREAT COMMISSION;
WHAT HAPPENS TO PEOPLE WHO HAVE NEVER HEARD THE GOSPEL?

By George Lujack

Many people throughout the centuries have wondered, "What happens to people who have never heard the gospel message? If they never knew Yeshua (Jesus), does this mean that they will automatically go to hell when they die?" This article will discuss the Great Commission and address the salvation concern over persons who have never heard the Good News.

THE GREAT COMMISSION

MATTHEW 28:18-20 (NKJV):

And Yeshua (Jesus) came and spoke to them, saying, "All authority has been given to Me in heaven and on earth. *Go therefore and make disciples of all the nations,* baptizing them in the name of the Father and of the Son and of the Holy Spirit, teaching them to observe all things that I have commanded you; and lo, I am with you always, even to the end of the age."

MARK 16:15-16 (NKJV):

And He [Yeshua (Jesus)] said to them, "Go into all the world and preach the gospel to every creature. He who believes and is baptized will be saved; but he who does not believe will be condemned…"

Yeshua Messiah (Jesus Christ), upon His resurrection - on a mountain in Galilee, in what was later termed, 'The Great Commission,' instructed His disciples to spread His teachings to all the nations.

There have been many preachers throughout millennia who have proclaimed, "Without Jesus, thou cannot be saved." Then they go a step further and erroneously go on to explain the 'Bad News' concerning persons who have unfortunately never heard the gospel message, that they are hell bound.

Yeshua (Jesus) didn't come to condemn, but to save. He didn't come to condemn righteous-living people who never heard the gospel salvation message. He will condemn those who have heard the gospel message and reject it *and* the unrighteous who haven't heard His name.

WE ARE JUDGED BY OUR DEEDS

ROMANS 2:6-11 (NKJV):

The righteous judgment of God, who "WILL RENDER EACH ONE ACCORDING TO HIS DEEDS," eternal life to those who by patient continuance in doing good seek for glory, honor, and immortality; but to those who are self-seeking and do not obey the truth, but obey unrighteousness indignation and wrath, tribulation and anguish, on every soul of man who does evil, of the Jew first and also of the Greek; but glory, honor, and peace to everyone who works what is good, to the Jew first and also to the Greek. For there is no partiality with God.

THE DOERS OF THE LAW WILL BE JUSTIFIED

ROMANS 2:12-29 (NKJV):

For as many as have sinned without law will also perish without law, and as many as have sinned in the law will be judged by the law (FOR NOT THE HEARERS OF THE LAW ARE JUST IN THE SIGHT OF GOD, BUT THE DOERS OF THE LAW WILL BE JUSTIFIED; for when Gentiles, who do not have the law, by nature do the things in the law, these, although not having the law, are a law to themselves, who show the work of the law written in their hearts, their conscience also bearing witness, and between themselves their thoughts accusing or else excusing them) in the day when God will judge the secrets of men by Yeshua Messiah (Jesus Christ), according to my gospel.

Indeed you are called a Jew, and rest on the law, and make your boast in God, and know His will, and approve the things that are excellent, being instructed out of the law, and are confident that you yourself are a guide to the blind, a light to those who are in darkness, an instructor of the foolish, a teacher of babes, having the form of knowledge and truth in the law. You, therefore, who teach another, do you not teach yourself? You who preach that a man should not steal, do you steal? You who say, "Do not commit adultery," do you commit adultery? You who abhor idols, do you rob temples? You who make your boast in the law, do you dishonor God through breaking the law? For *"the name of God is blasphemed among the Gentiles because of you,"* as it is written.

For circumcision is indeed profitable if you keep the law; but if you are a breaker of the law, your circumcision has become uncircumcision. Therefore, if an uncircumcised man keeps the righteous requirements of the law, will not his uncircumcision be counted as circumcision? And will not the physically uncircumcised, if he fulfills the law, judge you who, even with your written code and circumcision, are a transgressor of the law? For he is not a Jew who is one outwardly, nor is circumcision that which is outward in the flesh; but he is a Jew who is one inwardly; and circumcision is that of the heart, in the Spirit, not in the letter; whose praise is not from men but from God.

Concerning circumcision, if a circumcised man is an unrepentant adulterer or fornicator, what righteousness is there in circumcision? If an uncircumcised man who is celibate or only engages in sexual intimacy with his wife, what unrighteousness is there in an uncircumcision? It is not circumcision or uncircumcision that justifies a man, but how a man conducts himself in matters of sexual morality, whether he is circumcised or not.

JOHN 3:16 (NKJV):

"For God so loved the world that He gave His only begotten Son, *that whoever believes in Him* should not perish but have everlasting life."

ACTS 4:12 (NKJV):

Nor is there salvation in any other, for there is no other name under heaven given among men by which we must be saved.

1 TIMOTHY 1:15-16 (NKJV):

This is a faithful saying and worthy of all acceptance, that Messiah Yeshua (Christ Jesus) came into the world to save sinners, of whom I am chief. However, for this reason I obtained mercy, that in me first Yeshua Messiah (Jesus Christ) might show all longsuffering, as a pattern to those who are going to believe on Him for everlasting life.

How can people throughout the world be saved if they have never heard the name of Yeshua Messiah (Jesus Christ)? Upon their resurrection, they will be judged by their deeds and will then hear the name of Yeshua Messiah (Jesus Christ) then, when they meet Him.

If what some preachers have said were true, that if a person in some region of the world who has never heard the name of Yeshua Messiah (Jesus Christ), and therefore could not accept Him or the gospel message, that such persons were automatically doomed to hell, then it would also mean that all children who died in early childhood or infancy, including aborted babies, would also be doomed to hell. Infants cannot accept Yeshua (Jesus).

The Catholic Church attempted to address the concern of salvation of babies through infant baptism, but infants cannot be saved by baptism. Baptism can only be rightly done on those who willingly accept and submit to Yeshua Messiah (Jesus Christ), who are making a public declaration of their faith, and are symbolically having their sins cleansed through submersion in water.

ALL PEOPLE INSTINCTIVELY BELIEVE IN A RIGHTEOUS GOD

ROMANS 1:20 (NKJV):

For since the creation of the world His invisible attributes are clearly seen, being understood by the things that are made, even His eternal power and Godhead, so that they are without excuse...

There are people who have heard the Scriptures and the Good News and deny there is a God and live lawlessly. There are people who have not known the Scriptures or heard the gospel message and believe in a God and live righteously. Instinctively, all people everywhere know that there is a righteous God and are without excuse.

EZEKIEL 18:32 (NKJV):

"For I have no pleasure in the death of one who dies," says YHWH (the Lord) GOD. "Therefore turn and live!"

EZEKIEL 33:11 (NKJV):

"As I live," says YHWH (the Lord) GOD, "I have no pleasure in the death of the wicked, but that the wicked turn from his way and live. Turn, turn from your evil ways!"

2 PETER 3:9 (NKJV):

The Lord is not slack concerning His promise, as some count slackness, but is longsuffering toward us, not willing that any should perish but that all should come to repentance.

Yeshua (Jesus) didn't issue the Great Commission to His disciples, so that they should hurry up and spread the salvation message of Yeshua Messiah (Jesus Christ), lest the people of the nations didn't hear it before they died, then they would all perish in hell. All righteous-living people who have never heard the salvation message through Yeshua Messiah (Jesus Christ), from all the nations, will have an opportunity to be saved after they are resurrected. Unrighteous-living people will be condemned for rejecting Yeshua (Jesus) if they have heard of Him, or if they never heard of Him, for their unrighteous deeds. Righteous-living people will not be condemned if they have never heard the name of Yeshua (Jesus); they will be judged by their righteousness and have an opportunity to accept Him upon their resurrection.

People will be condemned for REJECTING Yeshua Messiah (Jesus Christ), and for unrighteousness, NOT for never having heard His name or the gospel's salvation message.

THE TRUE GOSPEL MESSAGE INCLUDES OBEYING HIS COMMANDMENTS

Mainstream Christianity has accepted Yeshua Messiah (Jesus Christ) as Savior, but has rejected many of His commandments.

MATTHEW 28:18-20 (NKJV):

And Yeshua (Jesus) came and spoke to them, saying, "All authority has been given to Me in heaven and on earth. Go therefore and make disciples of ALL THE NATIONS, baptizing them in the name of the Father and of the Son and of the Holy Spirit, TEACHING THEM TO OBSERVE ALL THINGS THAT I HAVE COMMANDED YOU; and lo, I am with you always, even to the end of the age."

Yeshua (Jesus) taught His disciples to obey His commandments, from the greatest to the least of His commands (Matthew 5:17-19). He instructed His Jewish disciples to make disciples of all the people of all the nations, which included instructing them on observing His commandments, the law. All of His commandments are commandments, not suggestions, and they are for all the people, of all the nations.

WHY DOES GOD ALLOW EVIL, PAIN, AND SUFFERING TO EXIST IN THE WORLD?

By George Lujack

Many agnostics and atheists have asked the question, "If God exists, then why does He allow evil, pain, and suffering to continue in the world?" God does exist and He does allow evil, pain, and suffering to occur in this world. This article will explain why God allows the evil, pain, and sufferings of this world to continue.

A better way to view the question is not to lay the blame on God, asking why *He* allows evil, pain, and suffering to occur in the world, but instead ask why man is evil and causes so much evil, pain, and suffering in the world. Agnostic and atheist skeptics use the argument that since there is evil, pain, and suffering in the world, then God surely does not exist. That there is evil in the world, which results in pain, suffering, and death, does not disprove the existence of God, but merely shows that God is currently permitting evil, pain, suffering, and death to occur in the world at this current time.

GOD KEEPS HIS WORD

GENESIS 2:15-17 (NKJV):

Then YHWH (the Lord) God took the man and put him in the garden of Eden to tend and keep it. And the Lord God commanded the man, saying, "Of every tree of the garden you may freely eat; but of the tree of the knowledge of good and evil you shall not eat, for in the day that you eat of it you shall surely die."

It was Adam who decided to disobey God and ate from the forbidden tree of the knowledge of good and evil. We are all descendants of Adam and Eve, and as such, we are all descendants of the fateful decision Adam made to disobey God, resulting in the evil, pain, suffering, and death that this world experiences to this day.

Adam, in his decision to eat of the tree of the knowledge of good and evil, declared to God that he would decide, apart from the wisdom of God, what is good and what is evil. He didn't heed God's warning that if he did eat from the tree of the knowledge of good and evil, he would die.

GENESIS 3:22-24 (NKJV):

Then YHWH (the Lord) God said, "Behold, the man has become like one of Us, to know good and evil. And now, lest he put out his hand and take also of the tree of life, and eat, and live forever" - therefore YHWH (the Lord) God sent him out of the garden of Eden to till the ground from which he was taken. So He drove out the man.

After Adam had 'become like God' in that he was able to discern between good and evil, God had to keep His word that Adam and his descendants, all of mankind, would die. Adam could not be permitted to eat from the knowledge of the tree of life and live forever. Although Adam now knew good and evil, he chose not to put his faith in God for His wisdom to show him to properly discern between good and evil. Adam had declared to God, in sum and substance, that he would be the one to decide what is good and evil in his life, and God, in sum and substance, declared to Adam, OK, go ahead, see how that works out for you, but now you will die and you cannot eat from the tree of life and live forever.

EVIL, PAIN, SUFFERING, AND DEATH ARE THE RESULT OF SIN

ROMANS 5:12 (NKJV):

Therefore, just as through one man sin entered the world, and death through sin, and thus death spread to all men, because all sinned.

WHY DO PEOPLE, EVEN CHRISTIANS, DIE PREMATURELY?

Some people are murdered in the prime of their lives, others are aborted in the womb, others have died in wars, and many die as a result of the sin of murder being in the world. After Adam sinned in disobedience, it didn't take long for the world's first murder to occur, as Adam's son Cain killed his brother Abel (Genesis 4:8).

Many people acquire diseases, because of sin, and die prematurely.

ROMANS 1:27 (NKJV):

Likewise also the men, leaving the natural use of the woman, burned in their lust for one another, men with men committing what is shameful, and receiving in themselves the penalty of their error which was due.

1 CORINTHIANS 6:18 (NKJV):

Flee fornication. Every sin that a man does is outside the body, but he who commits fornication sins against his own body.

Homosexuality has been declared by God to be an abomination and an unnatural lust (Leviticus 18:22, 20:13). Men who engage in the sin of homosexuality, and others who engage in other forms of sexual immorality, can acquire sexually transmitted diseases and die prematurely.

ISAIAH 66:17 (NKJV) [WITH INTERPRETATION]:

"Those who sanctify and purify themselves ... eating swine's flesh and the abomination [SEA CREATURES WITHOUT FINS AND SHEDDING, OVERLAPPING SCALES] and the mouse, shall be consumed [BY DISEASE] together," says YHWH (the Lord).

People acquire cancer and a whole host of other bodily diseases, due to the fact that either through ignorance, a lack of knowledge, or willful disobedience to God's dietary laws, they eat unclean creatures that were never sanctioned by God to be food. Many people also smoke cigarettes and use narcotic and pharmaceutical drugs to damage their health and shorten their life spans.

ISAIAH 55:9 (NKJV):

For as the heavens are higher than the earth, so are My ways higher than your ways, and My thoughts than your thoughts.

JOHN 14:6 (NKJV):

Yeshua (Jesus) said to him, "I am THE WAY, the truth, and the life. No one comes to the Father except through Me."

REVELATION 22:14 (NKJV):

Blessed are those who do His commandments, that they may have the right to the tree of life, and may enter through the gates into the city.

God is allowing mankind to continue in evil, pain, suffering, and death, so that man can learn an eternal lesson from the experience and foolish thinking that we know anything better than God does. His ways are higher than our ways. He is the way and His commandments are life.

GOD WANTS AS MANY WHO CAN BE SAVED TO BE SAVED

2 PETER 3:9 (NKJV) [WITH INTERPRETATION]:

The Lord (Yeshua / Jesus) is not slack concerning His promise [TO RETURN], as some count slackness, but is longsuffering toward us, not willing that any should perish but that all should come to repentance.

1 CORINTHIANS 15:54-58 (NKJV):

Then shall be brought to pass the saying that is written:

"Death is swallowed up in victory. O Death, where is your sting? O Hades, where is your victory?" The sting of death *is* sin, and the strength of sin *is* the law. But thanks *be* to God, who gives us the victory through our Lord Yeshua Messiah (Jesus Christ).

Therefore, my beloved brethren, be steadfast, immovable, always abounding in the work of the Lord, knowing that your labor is not in vain in the Lord.

REVELATION 7:16-17 (NKJV):

They shall neither hunger anymore nor thirst anymore; the sun shall not strike them, nor any heat; for the Lamb who is in the midst of the throne will shepherd them and lead them to living fountains of waters. And God will wipe away every tear from their eyes.

REVELATION 19:15 (NKJV):

Now out of His mouth goes a sharp sword, that with it He should strike the nations. And He Himself will rule them with a rod of iron.

REVELATION 21:4 (NKJV):

And God will wipe away every tear from their eyes; there shall be no more death, nor sorrow, nor crying. There shall be no more pain, for the former things have passed away.

We are living in an age of grace, where sin abounds, resulting in evil, pain, suffering, and death for all. The age of grace will expire and Yeshua (Jesus) will come to judge the inhabitants of the Earth. He will rule with a rod of iron - putting an end to evil, pain, suffering, and death, but before He returns He is being patient and wants as many who can be saved to be saved.

REVELATION 6:10-11 (NKJV) [WITH INTERPRETATION]:

And they cried with a loud voice, saying, "How long, O Lord, holy and true, until You judge and avenge our blood [OF THE BEHEADED SAINTS] on those who dwell on the earth?" Then a white robe was given to each of them; and it was said to them that they should rest a little while longer, until both the number of their fellow servants and their brethren, who would be killed as they were, was completed.

The saints who miss the rapture, due to living in some sin that prevents them from making the rapture and are left behind, will have an opportunity to repent, but they will need to refuse to receive the mark of the beast, and will be beheaded. Many will come to repentance and refuse the mark. Even the beheaded saints, resurrected and in the presence of Yeshua (Jesus), are prophesied to grow impatient for His return to the Earth, but Yeshua (Jesus) will tell them to be patient while their fellow brethren demonstrate their repentance and get killed through the guillotine, just as they were.

JAMES 4:14 (NKJV):

For what is your life? It is even a vapor that appears for a little time and then vanishes away.

ROMANS 8:18 (NKJV):

For I consider that the sufferings of this present time are not worthy to be compared with the glory, which shall be revealed in us.

1 CORINTHIANS 2:9 (NKJV):

But as it is written:

"Eye has not seen, nor ear heard, nor have entered into the heart of man the things which God has prepared for those who love Him."

2 CORINTHIANS 4:17-18 (NKJV):

For our light affliction, which is but for a moment, is working for us a far more exceeding and eternal weight of glory, while we do not look at the things which are seen, but at the things which are not seen. For the things which are seen are temporary, but the things which are not seen are eternal.

Whoever has ever lived, whether rich, poor, free, slave, ruler, or servant, his or her life on Earth is but a vapor, a speck in time compared to the vast ocean of time that awaits in eternity. The evil, pain, suffering, and death of this present age are a result of man's rebellion against God and are not worthy to be compared to the eternal love and glory that God will bestow upon those who love Him.

WHY DID YESHUA (JESUS) SPEAK TO PEOPLE IN FIGURATIVE LANGUAGE AND IN PARABLES?

By George Lujack

Scripture is a book of confusion and mystery for many, because of the fact that much of it has been written in allegoric, figurative, metaphoric, parabolic, and prophetic language. Many cannot understand the mysteries of Scripture and don't even try to, but instead look to their religious institutions as a place through which they merely express their faith, on their own terms, without being concerned about learning the deeper mysteries (the truths) of the kingdom of heaven. The organized religious institutions further confound people's knowledge of Scripture with their doctrinally incorrect teachings. This article will explain why the mysteries of the kingdom of heaven are known to some, but why they remain a mystery to many.

MATTHEW 13:10-15 (NKJV):

And the disciples came and said to Him, "Why do You speak to them in parables?"

Yeshua (Jesus) answered and said to them, "Because it has been given to YOU to know the mysteries of the kingdom of heaven, but to THEM it has not been given. For whoever has, to him more will be given, and he will have abundance; but whoever does not have, even what he has will be taken away from him. Therefore I speak to THEM in parables, because seeing THEY do not see, and hearing THEY do not hear, nor do THEY understand. And in THEM the prophecy of Isaiah is fulfilled, which says:

'Hearing you will hear and shall not understand, and seeing you will see and not perceive; For the hearts of this people have grown dull. Their ears are hard of hearing, and their eyes they have closed, lest they should see with their eyes and hear with their ears, LEST THEY SHOULD UNDERSTAND WITH THEIR HEARTS AND TURN [REPENT], so that I should heal them.'"

Yeshua (Jesus) said that the mysteries of the kingdom of heaven have been given to His disciples, but not to 'them.' Who are 'them?'

'Them' are the multitudes who are NOT obeying His commandments, sinners who have NOT repented, including people of faith who do NOT believe His laws are applicable to them today. Their hearts are dull, their ears are hard of hearing, and their eyes are closed TO THE LAW, lest they should understand with their hearts and repent!

PROVERBS 28:9 (NKJV):

One who turns away his ear from hearing THE LAW, even his prayer is an abomination.

ISAIAH 30:9-10 (NKJV):

Lying children, WHO WILL NOT HEAR THE LAW OF YHWH (the Lord); Who say to the seers, "Do not see," and to the prophets, "Do not prophesy to us right things; speak to us smooth things, prophesy deceits."

The multitudes, then and today, instead of turning and repenting, turn their ears away from hearing the law and declare the law done away with. When they hear the law, rather than turning from their sin in repentance, they turn to false prophets, teachers of lawlessness who approve of their sin and speak smooth words to comfort them in their sins. They fail to acknowledge God as the Supreme Lawmaker, fail to realize that His laws are eternal (Psalm 102:27, 119:160; Isaiah 40:8; Malachi 3:6; Matthew 5:17-19, 24:35; Mark 13:31; Luke 16:17, 21:33; Hebrews 1:12; James 1:17), fail to realize that He is the same yesterday, today, and forever (Hebrews 13:8), and thus they do not turn and repent from their sins. Therefore, since they do not have faith in Him as the Supreme Lawmaker, and do not obey His commandments, He speaks to the multitudes in parables, so that the mysteries of the kingdom of heaven are not revealed to them.

JOHN 4:23-24 (NKJV):

"But the hour is coming, and now is, when the TRUE WORSHIPERS will worship the Father in spirit and truth; for the Father is seeking such to worship Him. God is Spirit, and those who worship Him must worship in spirit and truth."

JOHN 16:25 (NKJV):

"These things I have spoken to you in figurative language; but the time is coming when I will no longer speak to you in figurative language, but I will tell you plainly about the Father."

The true worshipers, the righteous, those who seek to serve God in spirit and truth, and who obey His commandments are the ONLY ones who can understand the allegoric, figurative, metaphoric, parabolic, and prophetic language of Scripture.

The multitudes, whether they are lawless-minded false prophets, their congregations, or the people of society in general, cannot understand the mysterious language of Scripture, because they are not worshiping God in spirit and truth, are not obeying His commandments, and thus the kingdom of heaven, the very words of Scripture, are not revealed to them.

Yeshua (Jesus) said He spoke in parables because they see and do not see and hear and do not hear THE LAW, and He doesn't want them to know the mysteries of the kingdom, *or they would repent*. Why would Yeshua (Jesus) NOT want to explain things literally, so people would repent?

LUKE 16:31 (NKJV):

"If they do not hear Moses and the prophets, neither will they be persuaded though one rise from the dead."

Faith. Yeshua (Jesus) has offered all the proof that He is going to offer that God exists, through Himself, Moses (representing the law), and the prophets. He is the Lawmaker whose commandments we must keep.

ISAIAH 6:9; ACTS 28:26 (NKJV):

Hearing you will hear, and shall not understand; and seeing you will see, and not perceive.

There are many modern examples of those who hear, but do not understand, and see, but do not perceive.

THE EUCHARIST TRANSUBSTANTIATION DOCTRINE

LUKE 22:19-20 (NKJV):

And He took bread, gave thanks and broke it, and gave it to them, saying, "This is My body which is given for you; DO THIS IN REMEMBRANCE OF ME."

Likewise He also took the cup after supper, saying, "This cup is the new covenant in My blood, which is shed for you."

JOHN 6:53-67 (NKJV):

Then Yeshua (Jesus) said to them, "Most assuredly, I say to you, UNLESS YOU EAT THE FLESH OF THE SON OF MAN AND DRINK HIS BLOOD, you have no life in you. Whoever EATS MY FLESH AND DRINKS MY BLOOD has eternal life, and I will raise him up at the last day.

For MY FLESH IS FOOD INDEED, AND MY BLOOD IS DRINK INDEED. HE WHO EATS MY FLESH AND DRINKS MY BLOOD abides in Me, and I in him. As the living Father sent Me, and I live because of the Father, so he who feeds on Me will live because of Me. This is the bread which came down from heaven - not as your fathers ate the manna, and are dead. He who eats this bread will live forever."

These things He said in the synagogue as He taught in Capernaum.

Therefore many of His disciples, when they heard this, said, "THIS IS A HARD SAYING; WHO CAN UNDERSTAND IT?"

When Yeshua (Jesus) knew in Himself that His disciples complained about this, He said to them, "Does this offend you? What then if you should see the Son of Man ascend where He was before? It is the Spirit who gives life; the flesh profits nothing. The words that I speak to you are spirit, and they are life. But there are some of you who do not believe." For Yeshua (Jesus) knew from the beginning who they were who did not believe, and who would betray Him. And He said, "Therefore I have said to you that no one can come to Me unless it has been granted to him by My Father."

From that time many of His disciples went back and walked with Him no more. Then Yeshua (Jesus) said to the twelve, "Do you also want to go away?"

Catholics do not understand what Yeshua (Jesus) meant when He said, "Do this in remembrance of Me" (Luke 22:19). Catholics believe they must LITERALLY eat His flesh and LITERALLY drink His blood in remembrance of Him. He said do this (PASSOVER - Luke 22:15), to remember Him, as Yeshua (Jesus) is our New Passover Lamb, who covers our sins with His blood, so that God's wrath passes over us.

Ah, but Catholics respond with John 6:55, that His flesh is LITERAL FOOD INDEED, AND HIS BLOOD IS DRINK INDEED. Indeed His flesh and blood are food for the soul, but not LITERAL flesh, like bread (or a communion wafer), for His flesh is spiritual flesh and His blood is spiritual blood that we must cover ourselves with for the atonement of our sins, which if we eat and drink of these figuratively in honor of Him, we shall live forever (John 6:58).

Many of Yeshua's (Jesus') disciples heard these sayings and walked away. Catholics frequently respond with the questions, "Why did they walk away then?" and "Why didn't Yeshua (Jesus) stop them and declare He was speaking figuratively?" To declare beforehand that one is speaking figuratively defeats the purpose of speaking figuratively. Yeshua (Jesus) didn't stop the unbelievers and explain to them (John 6:64) lest He should prove Himself so they would understand with their hearts and turn (repent) (Matthew 10:15).

JOHN 6:64 (NKJV):

"But there are some of you who do not believe." For Yeshua (Jesus) knew from the beginning who they were who did not believe, and who would betray Him.

Judas Iscariot was not the only one who did not believe and was not the only one who betrayed Yeshua (Jesus).

Catholics hear these explanations but do not understand, and see these same verses but do not perceive.

WHY? It is because they do not hear the law of YHWH (the Lord) or honor the Lawmaker's perpetual laws. If they did, they would know that Yeshua (Jesus) could not possibly be speaking literally, commanding His followers to violate His own dietary laws to eat human flesh as a cannibal would, and drink human blood as a vampire would.

LEVITICUS 3:17 (NKJV):

This shall be a PERPETUAL STATUTE throughout your generations in all your dwellings: you shall EAT NEITHER FAT NOR BLOOD.

Almighty God is the Sovereign Supreme Lawmaker, but Catholics idolatrize their Catholic Church and err in believing that their church is the infallible lawmaker. If Catholics would first hear and obey the law of YHWH (the Lord), THEN they could hear, understand, see, perceive, and know when Yeshua (Jesus) was speaking figuratively and know when He was speaking literally.

RISE PETER, KILL AND EAT?

ACTS 10:9-13 (NKJV):

Peter went up on the housetop to pray, about the sixth hour. Then he became very hungry and wanted to eat; but while they made ready, he fell into a trance and saw heaven opened and an object like a great sheet bound at the four corners, descending to him and let down to the earth. In it were all kinds of four-footed animals of the earth, wild beasts, creeping things, and birds of the air. And a voice came to him, "Rise, Peter; kill and eat."

Why do many, after reading Acts 10, come to the determination that humans can now eat unclean creatures? It is because they use this verse (and many others) to turn their ears away from hearing the law (Proverbs 28:9). Peter did NOT eat anything unclean as a result of receiving the vision in Acts 10, as he did not turn his ear, his mind, or his heart away from hearing and keeping the law.

ACTS 10:14 (NKJV):
But Peter said, "Not so, Lord! For I have never eaten anything common or unclean."

Peter didn't eat any unclean creature as a result of receiving his vision and knew the command to "kill and eat" could not be a literal command, because God's dietary laws were written on his heart (Romans 2:15). Peter thought on the vision and later came to realize that Yeshua (Jesus), the Lord, was speaking to him in metaphoric language.

ACTS 10:28 (NKJV):
God has shown me that I should not call any MAN common or unclean.

Unclean creatures were used as a metaphor for the Gentile races. Peter came to understand that He was not to call any man common or unclean, since God cleansed the Gentiles and offered salvation to all people (Acts 11:18).

WAS THE TORAH (LAW) FOR THE JEWS ONLY?

A mainstream Christian false message is that the Tanakh (Old Testament) containing the Torah (law) within the first five books of the Scriptures is applicable to the Jews only; the Jews were given the law through Moses at Mount Sinai, but the Gentiles were never given the law and are therefore not bound to keep any of the 'Jewish' laws or festivals.

LEVITICUS 23:1-2 (NKJV):
And YHWH (the Lord) spoke to Moses, saying, "Speak to the children of Israel, and say to them: 'The feasts of YHWH (the Lord), which you shall proclaim to be holy convocations, THESE ARE *MY* FEASTS."

LEVITICUS 24:22 (NKJV):
You shall have the SAME LAW for the stranger and for one from your own country; for I am YHWH (the Lord) your God.

MATTHEW 28:18-20 (NKJV) [WITH INTERPRETATION]:
And Yeshua (Jesus) came and spoke to them, saying, "All authority has been given to Me in heaven and on earth. Go therefore and make disciples of all the nations, baptizing them in the name of the Father and of the Son and of the Holy Spirit, TEACHING THEM [THE GENTILES] TO OBSERVE ALL THINGS [COMMANDMENTS] THAT I HAVE COMMANDED YOU; and lo, I am with you always, even to the end of the age."

The truth is that the Gentiles were given the Torah (law) at the same time they received the B'rit Hadashah (New Testament) containing the Good News Gospel of Yeshua Messiah (Jesus Christ). The Gentiles were given the same law as the Jews were, as it was handed to them with the Gospel. The Jewish festivals are not 'Jewish' feasts; they are God's feasts.

To know the mysteries of the kingdom of heaven, first fear God as sovereign ruler and lawmaker, then learn and keep His commandments, and then you will be able to hear, understand, see, and perceive the allegoric, figurative, metaphoric, parabolic, and prophetic language of the Scriptures.

DEUTERONOMY 30:9-14 (NKJV):

For YHWH (the Lord) will again rejoice over you for good as He rejoiced over your fathers, IF YOU OBEY the voice of YHWH (the Lord) your God, to keep His commandments and His statutes which are written in this Book of the Law, and if you turn to YHWH (the Lord) your God with all your heart and with all your soul. For this commandment, which I command you today is NOT TOO MYSTERIOUS FOR YOU, nor is it far off. It is not in heaven, that you should say, 'Who will ascend into heaven for us and bring it to us, that we may hear it and do it?' Nor is it beyond the sea, that you should say, 'Who will go over the sea for us and bring it to us, that we may hear it and do it?' But the word is very near you, in your mouth and in your heart, THAT YOU MAY DO IT.

SHOULD WE BELIEVE IN 'LAW IS DONE AWAY WITH' LAWLESSNESS OR PRACTICE RIGHTEOUSNESS? SHOULD WE DO ALL HIS COMMANDMENTS?

MATTHEW 7:13-14 (NKJV):

"Enter by the narrow gate; for wide is the gate and broad is the way that leads to destruction, and there are many who go in by it. Because narrow is the gate and difficult is the way which leads to life, and there are few who find it."

MATTHEW 7:21-23 (NKJV):

"Not everyone who says to Me, 'Lord, Lord,' shall enter the kingdom of heaven, but he who does the will of My Father in heaven. Many will say to Me in that day, 'Lord, Lord, have we not prophesied in Your name, cast out demons in Your name, and done many wonders in Your name?' And then I will declare to them, 'I never knew you; depart from Me, YOU WHO PRACTICE LAWLESSNESS!'"

There are many end times false prophets who promote lawlessness by proclaiming that keeping His commandments are burdensome and unnecessary. Others say that the Torah (law) was for the Jews and was given to the Jews only.

It is not the law-doers who will be prohibited from entering the kingdom of heaven, but the ones who practice lawlessness. Gentiles who turn their ear from hearing the law are without excuse.

Many end times prophets proclaim that the law is impossible to keep. Did God give us laws that are impossible to keep? Which one(s)? If God gave us impossible commandments, then He would be an unfair God.

DANIEL 12:10 (NKJV):

Many shall be purified, made white, and refined, but the wicked shall do wickedly; and none of the wicked shall understand, but the wise shall understand.

1 JOHN 3:10 (NKJV):

In this the children of God and the children of the devil are manifest: Whoever does not practice righteousness is not of God.

True worshipers must strive to practice righteousness, not practice lawlessness, believing the law is done away with, for such beliefs and such persons who advocate such beliefs are not of God.

ROMANS 2:13 (NKJV):

For not the hearers of the law are just in the sight of God, but the doers of the law will be justified.

JAMES 1:22-25 (NKJV):

But be doers of the word, and not hearers only, deceiving yourselves. For if anyone is a hearer of the word and not a doer, he is like a man observing his natural face in a mirror; for he observes himself, goes away, and immediately forgets what kind of man he was. But he who looks into the perfect law of liberty and continues in it, and is not a forgetful hearer but a doer of the work, this one will be blessed in what he does.

Blessed are those who do His commandments. How will they be blessed?

REVELATION 20:6 (NKJV):

Blessed and holy is he who has part in the first resurrection. Over such the second death has no power, but they shall be priests of God and of Messiah (Christ), and shall reign with Him a thousand years.

REVELATION 22:14 (NKJV):

Blessed are THOSE WHO DO HIS COMMANDMENTS, that they may have the right to the tree of life, and may enter through the gates into the city.

The mysteries of the kingdom of heaven are revealed to those who keep God's commandments, those who acknowledge Him as the Almighty Supreme God and Lawgiver. Those who keep God's commandments are of the first resurrection (and rapture) and will enter into the kingdom of heaven and reign with Messiah (Christ) for a thousand years in His Millennium Kingdom.

ROMANS 14 *EXPLAINED*

By George Lujack

ROMANS 14:1-4 (NKJV):

Receive one who is weak in the faith, but not to disputes over doubtful things. For one believes he may eat all things, but he who is weak eats only vegetables. Let not him who eats despise him who does not eat, and let not him who does not eat judge him who eats; for God has received him. Who are you to judge another's servant? To his own master he stands or falls. Indeed, he will be made to stand, for God is able to make him stand.

Mainstream Christianity often teaches that the Apostle Paul is addressing food issues in verses 1-4. Many Christians misunderstand these verses to mean that the one who is not weak can eat all things, clean *and* unclean creatures alike, proclaiming that God's dietary laws are no longer in effect. God's dietary laws are eternal, so they remain in effect. Paul is addressing fellowship issues among believers with differing knowledge of God's dietary commands.

The one who is "weak" eats only vegetables, indicating that such persons are non-meat eating vegetarians, being weak in the knowledge of the faith that God permits man to eat certain sanctified animals (Leviticus 11; Deuteronomy 14). The one who believes he may eat "all things" also applies to Christians who believe the dietary laws have been done away with and they can now eat all things. The one who eats all proper things, according to the law, should not despise and be judgmental towards the vegetarian, nor towards the one who believes he can eat all things, the clean and unclean creatures.

ROMANS 14:5-10 (NKJV):

One person esteems one day above another; another esteems every day alike. Let each be fully convinced in his own mind. He who observes the day, observes it to the Lord; and he who does not observe the day, to the Lord he does not observe it. He who eats, eats to the Lord, for he gives God thanks; and he who does not eat, to the Lord he does not eat, and gives God thanks. For none of us lives to himself, and no one dies to himself. For if we live, we live to the Lord; and if we die, we die to the Lord. Therefore, whether we live or die, we are the Lord's. For to this end Messiah (Christ) died and rose and lived again, that He might be Lord of both the dead and the living. But why do you judge your brother?

Or why do you show contempt for your brother? For we shall all stand before the judgment seat of Messiah (Christ).

ROMANS 14:11-13 (NKJV):

For it is written:

"As I live, says YHWH (the Lord), every knee shall bow to Me, a every tongue shall confess to God."

So then each of us shall give account of himself to God. Therefore let us not judge one another anymore, but rather resolve this, not to put a stumbling block or a cause to fall in our brother's way.

Paul continues to address brethren over being overly judgmental towards fellow believers. It seems that Paul was anticipating what would be the coming confusion over the proper Sabbath day, God's festival days, and His dietary commands. These issues are worth discussing, but believers will disagree on these issues and they shouldn't get into judgmental disputes over them. Yeshua (Jesus) said that He did not come to bring peace and unity, but rather strife and division (Matthew 10:34-36). Arguments and disputes will arise among brethren. Believers who know and obey the truth (the seventh-day Sabbath, the Leviticus 23 festivals, and the dietary commands of Genesis 1:29, Leviticus 11, and Deuteronomy 14), should not be overly judgmental towards their fellow less spiritually knowledgeable brethren over these non-salvation issues (1 Corinthians 6:9-10; Galatians 5:19-21; 1 John 3:15; Revelation 21:7-8) concerning the lesser parts of the law, but teach these laws to them diligently and with love if they will listen.

ROMANS 14:14-23 (NKJV):

I know and am convinced by the Lord Yeshua (Jesus) that there is nothing unclean of itself; but to him who considers anything to be unclean, to him it is unclean. Yet if your brother is grieved because of your *food*, you are no longer walking in love. Do not destroy with your *food* the one for whom Messiah (Christ) died. Therefore do not let your good be spoken of as evil; for the kingdom of God is not eating and drinking, but righteousness and peace and joy in the Holy Spirit. For he who serves Messiah (Christ) in these things is acceptable to God and approved by men. Therefore let us pursue the things that make for peace and the things by which one may edify another. Do not destroy the work of God for the sake of *food*. All things indeed are pure, but it is evil for the man who eats with offense. It is good neither to eat meat nor drink wine nor do anything by which your brother stumbles or is offended or is made weak. Do you have faith? Have it to yourself before God. Happy is he who does not condemn himself in what he approves. But he who doubts is condemned if he eats, because he does not eat from faith; for whatever is not from faith is sin.

If someone today were somewhere and there was nothing but halal meat prepared under Islamic Shariah law to eat, a believer should not be concerned if the animal may have been slaughtered in the name of Allah, but only whether the meat is from a clean animal that is acceptable for food.

Romans 14:14-23 declares that there is no *food* that is unclean of itself. Unclean creatures *are not food*. Unclean creatures *are unclean*, which is why they are called 'unclean' creatures. Clean creatures that are food are not unclean of themselves. These verses speak of food that was first offered to idols or pagan gods that some believers may regard as having become unclean. The Apostle Paul wrote that he was convinced by Yeshua (Jesus) that food does not become unclean by itself, even if it were first offered to pagan gods or idols. Pagan gods and idols have no effect on food, so if someone were to bless or sacrifice food to a pagan god or idol, that food does not miraculously become unclean by itself or as a result of a pagan blessing, ritual, or sacrifice.

COLOSSIANS 2:16-17 *EXPLAINED*

By George Lujack

COLOSSIANS 2:16-17 (NKJV):

So let no one judge you in food or in drink, or regarding a festival or a new moon or sabbaths, which are a shadow of things to come, but the substance is of Messiah (Christ).

Mainstream Christians often cite Colossians 2:16-17 in proclaiming that they should not be judged (rebuked) for consuming unclean creatures and for not observing the seventh-day Sabbath. Many Christians also state that it is legalistic for anyone to try to use God's 'abolished' dietary laws to restrain them from eating whatever 'food' they desire and that they can choose to observe the Sabbath on any day of the week of their choosing, or not at all. Modern-day mainstream Christians lack a fundamental understanding of who Paul was addressing in his Colossian epistles, the era in which he wrote them, and they believe that Paul's writings were addressed to non-law-abiding Christians. Colossians 2:16-17, when understood from its proper historical context and perspective, has a completely different meaning than what many modern-day mainstream Christians understand it to be.

Paul was addressing new Messianic (Christian) Colossian converts who lived among the heavy influence of Babylonian, Greek, and Roman culture (Colossians 1:1-2). The Babylonian, Greek, and Roman culture of the time, which the new Colossian converts came out of, consumed all manner of unclean creatures, celebrated pagan festivals, and observed the first-day as the Sabbath day. Paul was instructing the Colossian converts to not be concerned with those who judged (mocked / ridiculed) them in eating food and drink according to God's dietary laws (Leviticus 11; Deuteronomy 14), or regarding God's festivals (Leviticus 23), or new moon celebrations (Numbers 29:6), or the seventh-day Sabbath (Exodus 31:16).

Christianity later adopted Babylonian, Greek, and Roman culture (including their diet and first-day Sabbath) unto itself. The Colossian believers whom Paul wrote to observed new moon celebrations in accordance with Scripture. Christians do not observe new moons, so Paul was NOT addressing modern-day mainstream Christianity in Colossians 2:16-17.

Colossians 2:16-17 are applicable verses to Messianic and Christian believers who often receive judgment (mocking / ridicule) from their non-law-abiding Christian brethren for observing God's dietary commandments found in Leviticus 11 and Deuteronomy 14, and for observing God's seventh-day Sabbath.

THE SHADOW OF THINGS TO COME...

Many Christians misunderstand Colossians 2:16-17 to mean that God's Sabbath and dietary laws were merely a shadow of things to come and now that Christ has come we no longer need to observe the Sabbath day or obey His dietary commands. Many people twist Paul's words to do away with God's perpetual laws (2 Peter 3:16).

Yeshua (Jesus) *had already come and gone* when the Apostle Paul wrote Colossians. Colossians was not a Tanakh (Old Testament) prophecy concerning the Messiah (Christ) who was still yet to come. Consuming proper food and drink, and observing God's festivals, new moons, and Sabbaths *are still things that are yet to come* for the majority of people living in the world. Yeshua (Jesus) plainly said He did not come to abolish the law (Matthew 5:17-19), and the law is proclaimed to be perpetual throughout Scripture, so Colossians 2:16-17 should be understood with the precept understanding that God's laws are eternal.

REVELATION 19:15 (NKJV):

Now out of His mouth goes a sharp sword, that with it He should strike the nations. And He Himself will rule them with a rod of iron.

Believers who obey God's seventh-day Sabbath and dietary commands, which are not commonly followed in this world, are like a shadow of things to come... a shadow of how things *will be done* when Messiah (Christ) returns. When Yeshua (Jesus) returns, He is going to rule the world with a rod of iron. Then *everyone* will be obeying the seventh-day Sabbath and His dietary laws. Right now, those who observe the seventh-day Sabbath and eat according to His dietary commands do so like a shadow of things that are yet to come. When His kingdom comes, believers who observe the seventh-day Sabbath and obey His food and drink laws will no longer be the shadow; they will be the substance of Messiah (Christ), they will be the norm.

LUKE 11:2-4 (NKJV):

Yeshua (Jesus) said to them, "When you pray, say: Our Father who is in heaven, Hallowed be Your name. Your kingdom come. YOUR WILL BE DONE ON EARTH as it is in heaven. Give us day by day our daily bread. And forgive us our sins, For we also forgive everyone who is indebted to us. And do not lead us into temptation, But deliver us from the evil one."

IT IS GOD'S WILL that we observe the Sabbath and rest from our labors on the seventh-day, which He sanctified at creation when He rested on the seventh-day after forming the Earth during the 6-days of creation week (Genesis 2:3).

IT IS GOD'S WILL that we consume sanctified creatures for food and abstain from eating unclean creatures according to His dietary commands (Leviticus 11; Deuteronomy 14), to keep ourselves fit and healthy, and to prevent us from acquiring various bodily cancers, diseases, and plagues, so as to not be consumed by them (Isaiah 66:17).

God's will is not currently being done on Earth, even by most professing Christians. God's will *will be* done when Yeshua (Jesus) returns. When Yeshua (Jesus) returns to Earth, He will impose His laws and rule over man with a rod of iron. Those who willingly obey Him now, in matters of diet, festivals, and Sabbaths, are a shadow of things to come, the obedient first-fruits of His coming kingdom (James 1:18).

DID THE JEWS KILL YESHUA (JESUS)?

By George Lujack

Many historically within Christianity have blamed the Jews for killing Yeshua (Jesus). Blaming the Jews for the death of Messiah (Christ) has been a cause of anti-Semitism and persecution of the Jews as a people throughout millennia. This article will declare that it wasn't *only* the Jews who killed Yeshua (Jesus), but it was *all* of humanity that played a role in His death, a death that was necessary for the salvation of *all* mankind.

THE BETRAYAL AND THE CONSPIRACY

<u>**MATTHEW 26:14-16, LUKE 22:3-6 (NKJV):**</u>

Then one of the twelve, called Judas Iscariot, went to the chief priests and said, "What are you willing to give me if I deliver Him to you?" And they counted out to him thirty pieces of silver. So from that time he sought opportunity to betray Him.

<u>**LUKE 22:48 (NKJV):**</u>

Yeshua (Jesus) said to him, "Judas, are you betraying the Son of Man with a kiss?"

The chief priests, who conspired to arrest Yeshua (Jesus), and Judas who betrayed Him, were all Jewish. Shortly after Yeshua's (Jesus') betrayal and arrest, He would be brought before the chief priests, elders, Roman Governor Pontius Pilate, and the Jewish multitudes. But the Jews who wanted to kill Yeshua (Jesus) had a problem...

THE JEWS' PROBLEM IN EXECUTING YESHUA (JESUS)

<u>**JOHN 18:29-31 (NKJV):**</u>

Pilate then went out to them and said, "What accusation do you bring against this Man?"

They answered and said to him, "If He were not an evildoer, we would not have delivered Him up to you."

Then Pilate said to them, "You take Him and judge Him according to your law."

Therefore the Jews said to him, "IT IS NOT LAWFUL FOR US TO PUT ANYONE TO DEATH."

The Jews, living under Roman occupation, were not permitted to execute anyone. If the Jewish authorities wished to bring a capital offense charge upon someone, seeking to execute that person, they would have to present evidence to the Roman authorities and the Romans would then carry out the death sentence via crucifixion.

JOHN 18:38-40 (NKJV):

Pilate went out again to the Jews, and said to them, "I find no fault in Him at all. But you have a custom that I should release someone to you at the Passover. Do you therefore want me to release to you the King of the Jews?"

Then they all cried again, saying, "Not this Man, but Barabbas!"

Now Barabbas was a robber.

JOHN 19:1-4 (NKJV):

So then Pilate took Yeshua (Jesus) and scourged Him. And the soldiers twisted a crown of thorns and put it on His head, and they put on Him a purple robe. Then they said, "Hail, King of the Jews!" And they struck Him with their hands.

Pilate then went out again, and said to them, "Behold, I am bringing Him out to you, that you may know that I find no fault in Him."

Roman Governor Pontius Pilate found no fault in Yeshua (Jesus) at all, yet he was so weak-willed that he catered to the whims of his conquered Jewish subjects and had Yeshua (Jesus) tortured at the hands of Roman soldiers.

JOHN 19:5-7 (NKJV):

Then Yeshua (Jesus) came out, wearing the crown of thorns and the purple robe. And Pilate said to them, "Behold the Man!"

Therefore, when the chief priests and officers saw Him, they cried out, saying, "Crucify Him, crucify Him!"

Pilate said to them, "You take Him and crucify Him, for I find no fault in Him."

The Jews answered him, "We have a law, and according to our law He ought to die, because He made Himself the Son of God."

Pilate, thinking he could satisfy the Jewish mob by scourging Yeshua (Jesus), only made the mob more bloodthirsty to see to it that He died.

JOHN 19:10-11 (NKJV):

Then Pilate said to Him, "Are You not speaking to me? Do You not know that I have power to crucify You, and power to release You?" Yeshua (Jesus) answered, "You could have no power at all against Me unless it had been given you from above. Therefore THE ONE WHO DELIVERED ME TO YOU HAS THE GREATER SIN."

MATTHEW 27:24 (NKJV):

When Pilate saw that he could not prevail at all, but rather that a tumult was rising, he took water and washed his hands before the multitude, saying, "I am innocent of the blood of this just Person. You see to it."

The last words Yeshua (Jesus) spoke to Pilate were that the one who delivered Him to be crucified had the greater sin, *than Pilate*. Pilate symbolically washed his hands to signify to the Jewish multitude that he was innocent of the blood of Yeshua (Jesus), but washing his hands with water could not absolve Pilate's sin role in the torture and death of Yeshua (Jesus). Yeshua (Jesus) declared that Pilate's hands were guilty of sin.

MATTHEW 27:27-31,35 (NKJV):

Then THE SOLDIERS OF THE GOVERNOR took Yeshua (Jesus) into the Praetorium and gathered the whole garrison around Him.

And THEY stripped Him and put a scarlet robe on Him.

When THEY had twisted a crown of thorns, THEY put it on His head, and a reed in His right hand. And THEY bowed the knee before Him and mocked Him, saying, "Hail, King of the Jews!" Then THEY spat on Him, and took the reed and struck Him on the head. And when THEY had mocked Him, THEY took the robe off Him, put His own clothes on Him, and led Him away to be crucified. Then THEY crucified Him...

It was the Jews who conspired to have Yeshua (Jesus) killed, and saw to it that He was, but it was the Romans soldiers who carried out the deed and killed Yeshua (Jesus).

MARK 8:31-33 (NKJV):

And He began to teach them that the Son of Man must suffer many things, and be rejected by the elders and chief priests and scribes, and be killed, and after three days rise again. He spoke this word openly. Then Peter took Him aside and began to rebuke Him. But when He had turned around and looked at His disciples, He rebuked Peter, saying, "Get behind Me, Satan! For you are not mindful of the things of God, but the things of men."

God sent His Son into the world to be killed, so anyone assigning blame to any particular group of people, specifically the Jews, is misguided. It wasn't all the Jews who wanted to see Yeshua (Jesus) die and certainly Jewish people centuries later had nothing to do with killing Him. God chose the perfect time to send His Son, Yeshua (Jesus) into the world to die on behalf of all humanity. The Jews played a part in His death, as did the Romans, who represented the Gentiles. Jews and Gentiles, all humanity, were symbolically responsible for killing Yeshua (Jesus), who died as an atonement sacrifice for all mankind.

MATTHEW 10:5-6 (NKJV):

These twelve Yeshua (Jesus) sent out and commanded them, saying: "Do not go into the way of the Gentiles, and do not enter a city of the Samaritans. But go rather to the lost sheep of the house of Israel."

MATTHEW 15:24 (NKJV):

Yeshua (Jesus) answered and said, "I was not sent except to the lost sheep of the house of Israel."

MATTHEW 28:18-19 (NKJV):

And Yeshua (Jesus) came and spoke to them, saying, "All authority has been given to Me in heaven and on earth. Go therefore and make disciples of ALL THE NATIONS..."

GOD THE FATHER GAVE US HIS SON, TO DIE FOR ALL OF US

Yeshua (Jesus) came for the Jews of Israel, but died to atone for the sins of ALL the nations.

JOHN 3:16 (NKJV):

"For God so loved the world that He gave His only begotten Son, that whoever believes in Him should not perish but have everlasting life."

JOHN 18:11 (NKJV):

So Yeshua (Jesus) said to Peter, "Put your sword into the sheath. Shall I not drink the cup which My Father has given Me?"

ISAIAH 53:10,12 (NKJV) [WITH INTERPRETATION]:

It pleased YHWH (the Lord) to bruise Him; He [the Father] has put Him [the Son] to grief. …
And He bore the sin of many, and made intercession for the transgressors.

COLOSSIANS 1:19-20 (NKJV):

For it pleased the Father that in Him all the fullness should dwell, and by Him to reconcile all things to Himself, by Him, whether things on earth or things in heaven, having made peace through the blood of His cross.

NO ONE TOOK YESHUA'S (JESUS') LIFE; HE LAID IT DOWN HIMSELF

JOHN 10:17-18 (NKJV):

"Therefore My Father loves Me, because I lay down My life that I may take it again. No one takes it from Me, but I lay it down of Myself."

THE JEWS KILLED YESHUA (JESUS) AND THE GENTILES DID TOO

1 THESSALONIANS 2:14-15 (NKJV):

For you, brethren, became imitators of the churches of God, which are in Judea in Messiah Yeshua (Christ Jesus). For you also suffered the same things from your own countrymen, just as they did from the Judeans, who killed both the Lord Yeshua (Jesus) and their own prophets, and have persecuted us; and they do not please God and are contrary to all men…

The Jews did kill Yeshua (Jesus), but so did the Romans representing the Gentiles. All humanity participated in the sacrifice of the Lamb of God, Yeshua the Messiah (Jesus the Christ). If an anti-Semitic, ethnic-minded, self-righteous believer proclaims that the Jews alone killed Yeshua (Jesus), by taking verses out-of-context from the entirety of Scripture, and absolves the Gentiles from their role in His death, then the blood of Yeshua (Jesus) cannot cover that person's sins. Blood cannot cover the sins of one who is not a participant of the sacrifice.

DOES GOD APPROVE OF RAPE AND SLAVERY?

By George Lujack

Some scoffers mock the God of the Holy Scriptures, declaring that He approves of rape and slavery by citing verses that address these criminal sins. This article will explain the verses in question that may seem to some to suggest that God condones and approves of rape and slavery.

RAPE?

DEUTERONOMY 22:23-24 (NKJV):

If a young woman who is a virgin is betrothed to a husband, and a man finds her in the city and lies with her, then you shall bring them both out to the gate of that city, and you shall stone them to death with stones, the young woman because she did not cry out in the city, and the man because he humbled his neighbor's wife; so you shall put away the evil from among you.

Deuteronomy 22:23-24 concerns the sin of adultery, which for Hebrews living in Israel 'under the law' was a death penalty offense. If a betrothed virgin, who was the betrothed wife of a man, but had not yet consecrated her marriage through sexual intercourse with him, does carnally lie with another man, her betrothed husband could have her stoned to death (Deuteronomy 22:13-21), or write her a certificate of divorce (Deuteronomy 24:1-4). This was the option that Joseph had when he discovered Mary pregnant and he believed Mary had committed adultery. Joseph, being a just man, had decided to put Mary away (divorce) secretly and not stone her (Matthew 1:18-19).

DEUTERONOMY 22:28-29 (NKJV):

If a man finds a young woman who is a virgin, who is not betrothed, and he seizes her and lies with her, and they are found out, then the man who lay with her shall give to the young woman's father fifty shekels of silver, and she shall be his wife because he has humbled her; he shall not be permitted to divorce her all his days.

Deuteronomy 22:28-29 does not describe rape; it describes fornication (premarital sex). A man "seizes" his girlfriend, and lies with her carnally, and they both do so secretly, attempting to not be "found out." If these verses described rape, the woman would most certainly cry out, and report the man who forcibly raped her. What God's law does in this case is to try to make lemonade out of a couple of lemons, to make the best of a sinful deed and correct it. The man and woman committed the sin of fornication (premarital sex) and the virgin woman lost her virginity. A virgin woman was to keep and protect her virginity until her wedding, but when a young woman engages in fornication (premarital sex) this cannot be done. The law stated that if a virgin woman was "found out" to have lost her virginity to her boyfriend through voluntarily fornication (premarital sex), she must marry him. The law commanded the man, who took the woman's virginity, to pay a sum of shekels (in humility) to the young woman's father and marry her.

EXODUS 21:2-6 (NKJV):

If you buy a Hebrew servant, he shall serve six years; and in the seventh he shall go out free and pay nothing. If he comes in by himself, he shall go out by himself; if he comes in married, then his wife shall go out with him. If his master has given him a wife, and she has borne him sons or daughters, the wife and her children shall be her master's, and he shall go out by himself. But if the servant plainly says, 'I love my master, my wife, and my children; I will not go out free,' then his master shall bring him to the judges. He shall also bring him to the door, or to the doorpost, and his master shall pierce his ear with an awl; and he shall serve him forever.

God's law concerning indentured servitude dealt with the harsh reality of the economics of the times. People were willing to sell themselves into servitude. A Hebrew male who sold his services would agree to a contract of six years and be freed on the seventh, in reflection of the Sabbath week of working six days and resting on the seventh. If the man gave his daughter to be the wife for his Hebrew slave, then the man could retain his daughter, or free her to go with her Hebrew servant husband. If the man refused to let his daughter go, then the Hebrew slave could volunteer to stay on as a servant. It was not uncommon for a good young male servant, if he loved his master, to voluntarily serve a wealthy older master until the master died, take the master's daughter as his wife, and the master's household as an inheritance. Volunteer Hebrew servants were also free to negotiate the contract terms of their servitude in variation of the Exodus 21:2-6 guidelines. Jacob agreed to be a servant to Laban for seven years for Laban's daughter Rachel, so he could marry her, and he wound up serving Laban for fourteen years after Laban deceived him into marrying his older daughter Leah. So, Jacob wound up serving his master Laban for fourteen years and received from him two wives for his service (Genesis 29:18-27).

SEX SLAVES?

EXODUS 21:7-11 (NKJV):

If a man sells his daughter to be a female slave, she shall not go out as the male slaves do. If she does not please her master, who has betrothed her to himself, then he shall let her be redeemed. He shall have no right to sell her to a foreign people, since he has dealt deceitfully with her. And if he has betrothed her to his son, he shall deal with her according to the custom of daughters. If he takes another wife, he shall not diminish her food, her clothing, and her marriage rights. And if he does not do these three for her, then she shall go out free, without paying money.

It is very easy for people of modern times to mock the customs and ways of the times of thousands of years ago. Some have suggested that God condoned sex slavery, but this is not the case at all. The Exodus 21:7-11 verses deal with arranged marriages and / or indentured servitude. Very often a father would try to find a good husband for his daughter(s), or a good household for them to live under if he was poor. The payment to the father was a dowry for his daughter. Women didn't have the options back then of going to college, starting a career, or relying on a social welfare state for their sustainability. Young women typically lived under the care and protection of their father or of the man of the household who they were sold to. A concubine was typically a female household servant, not a sex slave. Concubines could eventually marry the man who purchased her, or his son, and then they would become the married wife of the father or son.

SLAVERY? THE RIGHT TO BEAT SERVANTS THROUGH CORPORAL PUNISHMENT?

EXODUS 21:20-21 (TLV):

If a male strikes his male or female servant with a staff, who dies by his hand, he must surely be punished. Notwithstanding, if the servant gets up in a day or two he will not be punished, for he is his property.

At first glance, Exodus 21:20-21 seems to permit a master the right to strike his male or female servant and to not be held liable, unless he kills his male or female servant. The verses must be read in the context of all the verses of Exodus 21 specifically verses 12 through 26. Many people have a preconceived notion of slavery, and use the Exodus 21:20-21 verses to show that God approved not only of slavery, but beating slaves. Exodus 21:12-26 must be read in totality. These verses deal with when men quarrel. So, if it should come to pass that a servant was quarreling with his master, and this quarrel led to a physical fight, then the master would be held responsible by judges if the servant was severely injured or died (Exodus 21:18-19,23-25). Likewise, if the servant struck his master so that the master died, the servant would surely be held liable for his master's death (Exodus 21:12). God's law protected indentured servants, as Exodus 21:26 shows.

A master could not abuse his servant, and if he did the servant was to go free.

EXODUS 21:26 (NKJV):

If a man strikes the eye of his male or female servant, and destroys it, he shall let him go free for the sake of his eye. And if he knocks out the tooth of his male or female servant, he shall let him go free for the sake of his tooth.

FORCEABLE SLAVERY?

LEVITICUS 25:39-46 (NKJV):

And if one of your brethren who dwells by you becomes poor, and sells himself to you, you shall not compel him to serve as a slave. As a hired servant and a sojourner he shall be with you, and shall serve you until the Year of Jubilee. And then he shall depart from you - he and his children with him - and shall return to his own family. He shall return to the possession of his fathers. For they are My servants, whom I brought out of the land of Egypt; they shall not be sold as slaves. You shall not rule over him with rigor, but you shall fear your God. And as for your male and female slaves whom you may have - from the nations that are around you, from them you may buy male and female slaves. Moreover you may buy the children of the strangers who dwell among you, and their families who are with you, which they beget in your land; and they shall become your property. And you may take them as an inheritance for your children after you, to inherit them as a possession; they shall be your permanent slaves. But regarding your brethren, the children of Israel, you shall not rule over one another with rigor.

They declare that brethren (fellow Hebrews) could become hired servants for a period of time, but not slaves, and then go free. Non-Hebrews from the surrounding nations and strangers could be purchased as slaves, become permanent slaves, property, and passed down as an inheritance. These passages do not say that slaves were herded like cattle in chains to the Israeli marketplace and sold against their will. The non-Hebrews were voluntary slaves who agreed to be servants to their Hebrew masters for food, shelter, and security. These verses need to be understood in the context and time in which they were written. God had made a covenant with Israel to be their God and they would serve Him as His chosen people. The servitude of non-chosen people to the chosen people was the way things were, and still are, to this day. Non-Hebrew servants often served the Hebrew chosen people, as the middle class and poor of today serve the rich.

DEUTERONOMY 23:15-16 (NKJV):

You shall not give back to his master the slave who has escaped from his master to you. He may dwell with you in your midst, in the place which he chooses within one of your gates, where it seems best to him; you shall not oppress him.

Harsh treatment of slaves was not permissible. If a foreign slave wished to ultimately leave his master to be free, a slave owner was not permitted to oppress him, prevent him from departing, and was not allowed to retrieve his slave if his slave had departed.

EXODUS 21:16 (NKJV):

He who kidnaps a man and sells him, or if he is found in his hand, shall surely be put to death.

It is clear that forced bondage slavery was not permitted under God's laws. God never allowed for the capture, kidnapping, or stealing of a man's life, to forcibly hold a man against his will, to be sold or retained as a slave.

JOSEPH'S STORY

GENESIS 37:23-28 (NKJV):

So it came to pass, when Joseph had come to his brothers, that they stripped Joseph of his tunic, the tunic of many colors that was on him. Then they took him and cast him into a pit. And the pit was empty; there was no water in it. And they sat down to eat a meal.

Then they lifted their eyes and looked, and there was a company of Ishmaelites, coming from Gilead with their camels, bearing spices, balm, and myrrh, on their way to carry them down to Egypt. So Judah said to his brothers, "What profit is there if we kill our brother and conceal his blood? Come and let us sell him to the Ishmaelites, and let not our hand be upon him, for he is our brother and our flesh." And his brothers listened. Then Midianite traders passed by; so the brothers pulled Joseph up and lifted him out of the pit, and sold him to the Ishmaelites for twenty shekels of silver. And they took Joseph to Egypt.

Joseph's brothers did an evil thing in capturing their brother Joseph and selling him to Ishmaelite traders. Joseph's brothers lived on in shame, not being able to comfort their grieving father Jacob, who mourned the loss of Joseph in believing he was dead, as this was the story Joseph's brothers told their father (Genesis 37:31-35). Joseph went on to be a good and valued slave in Egypt, was falsely accused of attempted rape, and imprisoned (Genesis 39).

Then it came to pass that Joseph was summoned before the Pharaoh of Egypt and was able to rightly decipher the disturbing dreams Pharaoh was having and was able to warn him concerning a coming famine. Joseph was appointed governor of Egypt and he prospered in all that he did (Genesis 41). As fate and the plans of God would have it, Joseph's family would reunite with Joseph, as the famine of the region caused Joseph's brothers to seek food in Egypt, where Joseph had become governor (Genesis 42:1-6). It may seem to many that the reunion of Joseph with his father and brothers, and his forgiveness to his brothers for what they did to him, was a happy end to the story. That is not quite so. Joseph died, and Joseph's brothers' descendants were afflicted by rigorous slavery in the land of Egypt.

EXODUS 1:8-14 (NKJV):

Now there arose a new king over Egypt, who did not know Joseph. And he said to his people, "Look, the people of the children of Israel are more and mightier than we; come, let us deal shrewdly with them, lest they multiply, and it happen, in the event of war, that they also join our enemies and fight against us, and so go up out of the land." Therefore they set taskmasters over them to afflict them with their burdens. And they built for Pharaoh supply cities, Pithom and Raamses. But the more they afflicted them, the more they multiplied and grew. And they were in dread of the children of Israel. So the Egyptians made the children of Israel serve with rigor. And they made their lives bitter with hard bondage - in mortar, in brick, and in all manner of service in the field. All their service in which they made them serve was with rigor.

It was not by mere unfortunate circumstance that God's chosen people, the Hebrews, fell into harsh slavery. Joseph's brothers' descendants were punished in slavery for what Joseph's brothers had done to Joseph, which was selling Joseph into forced slavery.

GENESIS 15:13 (NKJV):

Then YHWH (the Lord) said to Abram: "Know certainly that your descendants will be strangers in a land that is not theirs, and will serve them, and they will afflict them four hundred years."

EXODUS 12:40 (NKJV):

Now the sojourn of the children of Israel who lived in Egypt was four hundred and thirty years.

EXODUS 20:5; DEUTERONOMY 5:9 (NKJV):

For I, YHWH (the Lord) your God, am a jealous God, visiting the iniquity of the fathers upon the children to the third and fourth generations of those who hate Me.

God does not approve of rape or slavery and His laws were written to protect women and impoverished indentured servants in less opportunistic civil and economic times. Scripture contains laws that deal with fornication and indentured servitude, which are sometimes twisted to be confused with rape and slavery by ill-informed ridiculers of God and Scripture.

IS THE KING JAMES BIBLE THE PURE - PERFECT - PRESERVED WORD OF GOD FOR THE ENGLISH-SPEAKING PEOPLE?

By George Lujack

Some Christians believe in the inerrancy and infallibility of the King James Bible as the pure - perfect - preserved word of God for the English-speaking people. This article will discuss the origins of the King James Bible Only doctrine, present irrefutable proofs that the King James Bible is not perfectly translated into English, and will declare the King James Bible Only doctrine to be false.

ORIGIN OF THE 'KING JAMES VERSION BIBLE ONLY' DOCTRINE

Many persons since the early 1600's have proclaimed that the English people must read the King James Version Bible ONLY, being that it is the inspired, perfect, preserved, pure word of God for the English-speaking people, and all other English translations are inaccurate and / or inferior. This doctrinal belief originated from King James himself. Bishops of the Church of England, under orders of King James, exercising 'ecclesiastical authority and jurisdiction' wrote many articles and promoted the distribution and placement of the Authorized Version of the King James Bible in the English churches and elsewhere. It was King James, through the Church of England, who first introduced the concept that the King James Bible translators were inspired by God and that *only* the Authorized Version King James Bible was inerrant and infallible.[39]

KING JAMES BIBLE TRANSLATORS WERE COMMISSIONED BY KING JAMES, THEY WERE NOT INSPIRED TRANSLATORS OF GOD

2 TIMOTHY 3:16 (NKJV):
All Scripture is *given* by *inspiration* of God...

The Scriptures, given to us in their original Hebrew and Greek languages, are the inspired word of God. The King James Bible is not the original written Scriptures and was not given to us by the inspiration of God, but is a translation of His given inspired word to the English language. God directly *inspired* the prophets and apostles to write the Scriptures. King James *commissioned* translators to translate the Scriptures into English.

THE KING JAMES BIBLE IS WRITTEN IN OLD ARCHAIC ENGLISH

There are many Christian ministers who believe that archaic old English is a more godly language than modern English. They like to appear more holy when preaching in the pulpits in old English, saying King James phrases such as, "Thus saith the Lord," instead of "Thus says the Lord," or "Our Father which art in heaven, Hallowed be thy name," instead of "Our Father who is in heaven, Holy is Your name." Old English is not a holy language, nor is it any holier than modern English. To believe that old English is the language of God, one is basically worshiping the old English language as being of God. God first communicated to Adam in the Garden of Eden, in the language He gave Adam at that time, then later on to Moses in Hebraic. The Scriptures do not record God ever communicating with man in any form of English. King James Bible Only ministers communicate to their congregations in the confusing old English language in a similar manner that Catholic priests do when conducting their Catholic mass while speaking in Latin. The Catholic congregations are confused, and have no idea of what their priest is saying, because their priest is speaking in a language that they cannot understand. Many Catholics are deceived into believing that Latin is a holy mysterious language that their priest is using to communicate with God. Likewise, King James Bible Only preachers use an old form of English that modern English-speaking persons have difficulty understanding, confusing and deceiving them into believing that old English is the holy language of God.

WORSHIPING THE KING OF KINGS OR THE KING JAMES BIBLE?

PSALM 12:6-7 (KJV):
The words of the LORD are pure words: as silver tried in a furnace of earth, purified seven times. Thou shalt keep them, O LORD, thou shalt preserve them *from this generation* for ever.

King James Version Only advocates often cite and misapply Psalm 12:6-7 to uphold their doctrine that God preserved His word perfectly in the King James Bible for the English-speaking people. The words of YHWH (the Lord) were preserved in their original Hebrew [40] and Greek[41] language, from the generation in which they were written, and they will be preserved forever.

The Scriptures have been kept, copied exactly word-for-word throughout the generations, in the Hebrew and Greek languages that they were written in, have been preserved to this day, and they will be preserved forever. These verses do not in any way indicate that the words of YHWH (the Lord) were to be preserved in English, in the King James Bible only.

The King James Version English Bible was completed in 1611. The KJV is a translation of God's pure words. God's actual pure words were preserved from the generation in which they were written, not since 1611. Scripture does not declare that God commanded King James of England to translate His Scriptures or that His word was to be preserved perfectly in English by God-inspired translators commissioned by King James. The King James Version is not a perfect English translation of the Scriptures, nor is there any perfect English translation. Many terms or words used in the original Scriptures are currently unknown, yet they are part of the original Scriptures. Translators therefore cannot translate words that they do not know, and have often best guessed at translating them in times past. Many modern English speaking people who use a King James Version Bible also need to use an early modern English dictionary to understand their KJV Bible when casually reading it.

The King James Version Bible is hardly a perfect English translation for modern day English speaking persons. Although there are numerous minor errors in the King James Version Bible, there are no substantial errors that are so major as to throw believers off course from God, or cause people to lose their salvation, but to proclaim that the King James Version Bible is a 100% pure perfect word-for-word inerrant English translation is a misguided belief and false doctrine. The King James Version Bible is a good translation, but not a perfect one.

NO FOUNDATIONAL BASIS FOR CLAIMING THE KING JAMES VERSION PERFECT

The King James Bible was not the first bible published in English. The Geneva Bible was first published in 1560. The King James was later released in 1611. The Geneva Bible was the first bible taken to America and was used by the Pilgrims and Puritans. Where in Scripture is it written that the King James Bible is the official God-preserved bible for the English-speaking people? On what basis, other than the authority of King James, do King James Bible Only advocates proclaim that only the Authorized King James Version Bible is the pure, perfect, and preserved word of God for the English-speaking people? Why the King James and not the Geneva or some other English version bible translation?

THE KING JAMES BIBLE HAS FOUR-FOOTED CREEPING FOWLS, LEAPING BEETLES, AND UNICORNS

LEVITICUS 11:20-22 (KJV):
All FOWLS that creep, *going on all four,* **shall be an abomination to you. Yet these may ye eat of every flying creeping thing that goeth upon all four, which have legs above their feet, to leap withal upon the earth; Even these of them ye may eat; the locust after his kind, and the bald locust after his kind, and the BEETLE** *after his kind,* **and the grasshopper after his kind.**

Fowls or birds do not go on four legs or feet. Flying insects have six legs, four of which are used EXCLUSIVELY for walking (or creeping) with two legs that are also used either as hands or for hind leaping legs. The 'beetle' is a translation error in the King James Bible. Beetles do not have special jointed hind legs for leaping upon the Earth. Beetles are not the same kind of insects that locusts, bald locusts, and grasshoppers are. King James Bible Only defenders sometimes cite the click beetle to explain the beetle error translation. It is estimated that there are about 450,000 different types of beetles in the world. Out of all of those beetles, there are a few that can leap. The click beetle, if inverted on its back, can propel itself without using its legs to return to its feet. The click beetle uses elastic energy in its body and releases it abruptly to launch itself in the air.[42] The insect, mistranslated 'beetle' in the King James Bible, and all the related insects after its kind, are described as having special jointed hind jumping legs to leap upon the Earth. Click beetles do not have these type of jumping legs. No species of beetle has special jointed hind jumping legs with which to leap upon the Earth with.

The King James insect mistranslated 'beetle' *and ALL beetles after their kind'* do not correctly fit the description of the leaping insects of Leviticus 11:21-22. The four-footed fowls and beetle(s) translation errors in the King James Bible were properly corrected to 'flying insects' and 'cricket(s)' in the New King James Bible and are listed as flying insects and cricket(s) in most other English translated versions of Scripture.

<u>NUMBERS 23:22 (KJV):</u>

God brought them out of Egypt; he hath as it were the strength of an unicorn.*

*Also: Numbers 24:8; Deuteronomy 33:17; Job 39:9-10; Psalm 22:21, 29:6, 92:10; Isaiah 34:7.

King James Bible Only defenders claim that 'unicorn' is not a mistranslation. They defend the use of the term unicorn by saying that it is not the mythical horned horse-like creature, but it is instead a rhinoceros. The problem with that explanation is that it defies the very thing King James Bible Only defenders proclaim, namely that the King James Bible is the perfect translated word of God for the English-speaking people. Ask any English-speaking person what a unicorn is, even back in 1611, and the response would be that it is a mythical horned horse-like creature, not a rhinoceros. King James Bible Only defenders must *translate* unicorn to rhino to uphold their doctrine of the inerrancy of the King James Bible, because unicorn is not a proper English term for a rhino.

The unicorn translation error in the King James Bible is properly translated to an ox or wild ox in the New King James Bible and most other English translations.

There are many other, mostly minor, translation errors in the King James Bible that are far too numerous to list in this article that have been discovered and listed.[43]

KING JAMES BIBLE ONLYISM, A CULT-LIKE FANATICAL BELIEF

King James Bible Only advocates share a cult-like misguided faith with the Roman Catholic Church. King James Bible Only advocates proclaim that the King James Bible commissioned translators were infallible and produced a perfectly translated English version of the Scriptures. The Catholic Church proclaims that its popes throughout the ages have been, and are, infallible. Infallibility and perfection are attributes of God. The original Scriptures, inspired by God, are infallible, as only God is infallible. No translation of man, or any pope or clergyman, is infallible or perfect - as all men err.

King James Only advocates sometimes rhetorically ask, "If the King James Version Bible is NOT the perfect translated word of God into English, then what version is?" This is a presumptive question, like asking, "When was the last time you beat your wife?" to a man who has never harmed his wife. Catholics, when faced with the errors of Catholic teachings, defend their church by asking the same presumptive type question, "If the Catholic Church is not the one true church, then what church is?"

There is no true, pure, perfect, preserved English translation of the Holy Scriptures, just as there is no one true apostolic Christian church that the Roman Catholic Church claims to be.

The Jews are God's chosen people who were given His perfect word. The Tanakh (Old Testament) Scriptures were written in Hebrew and the B'rit Hadashah (New Testament) Scriptures books were written in either Greek or Hebrew, have been copied word-for-word, and have been preserved. Imperfect translators have translated His perfect preserved word into the English language and other languages.

King James translators were neither infallible nor perfect. God did preserve His perfect word, but His perfect word was not perfectly translated to English for the English-speaking people by King James translators. God's perfect word was also not perfectly translated to the Arabic, Bulgarian, Chinese, Croatian, Dutch, French, German, Hungarian, Indian, Japanese, Korean, Latin, Moldavian, Norwegian, Polish, Russian, Serbian, Spanish, Swedish, Swiss, Turkish, Ukrainian, Vietnamese, Welch, Yemeni, Zulu, or to any other written language of the world.

WHAT ENGLISH VERSION BIBLE SHOULD BELIEVERS USE?

The King James Bible is a good, but not perfect translation of the Holy Scriptures. The King James Bible (KJV) should be used in conjunction and cross-referenced with the New King James Bible (NKJV), the Halleluyah Scriptures (HSV), the Tree of Life Scriptures (TLV) and other good versions of Scripture when searching for the truth of God's word.

IS THE MESSIANIC HEBREW ROOTS MOVEMENT A CULT?

By George Lujack

This article will discuss the Messianic Hebrew Roots movement, the growing hostility towards it from various Christian sects, and answer the charge as to whether or not the Messianic Hebrew Roots movement is a cult.

The Messianic Hebrew Roots is a movement that advocates the return and adherence to the first century walk of faith and obedience to the Torah (law).[44] The Hebrew Roots movement seeks a better understanding of the culture, history, and the religious-political background of the time period which led to the core differences with both the Jewish and Christian communities.[45]

The Messianic Hebrew Roots movement is not so much a denomination, but rather the mindset held by non-denominational believers who emphasize the Hebrew roots of the Messianic-Christian faith and who seek to emulate Yeshua Messiah (Jesus Christ) as much as humanly possible (1 John 2:6).[46] Messianic Hebrew Roots believers consist of Jews and Gentiles who together worship Yeshua the Messiah (Jesus the Christ).

JEREMIAH 18:15 (NKJV):

Because My people have forgotten Me, they have burned incense to worthless idols and they have caused themselves to stumble in their ways, from the ancient paths.

JOHN 4:23-24 (NKJV):

"But the hour is coming, and now is, when the true worshipers will worship the Father in spirit and truth; for the Father is seeking such to worship Him. God is Spirit, and those who worship Him must worship in spirit and truth."

Mainstream Christians who continue in lawlessness, observing pagan-based holidays and worthless traditions rather than returning to the ancient paths to worship God in spirit and truth, often become defensive concerning their faith and are resistant to change and correction. Some have lashed out at the Messianic Hebrew Roots movement, branding it a cult.

cult:

- A system of religious veneration and devotion directed toward a particular figure or object.

- A relatively small group of people having religious beliefs or practices regarded by others as strange or sinister.

- A misplaced or excessive admiration for a particular person or thing.[47]

By the standard definitions of a religious cult, the Messianic Hebrew Roots movement does not fit the description. It could be said that Messianic believers have "religious beliefs or practices regarded by others as strange," but by that broad definition everyone could be accused of belonging to a cult. By that standard, everyone who was not a Catholic in the Dark Middle Ages was therefore a cultist heretic.

Messianic believers do not have any excessive admiration towards a particular figure, object, person, or thing, other that Yeshua (Jesus). Catholics who excessively admire their pope and other figures, and Christians who replace Christ by putting their messenger first in proclaiming their declared faith (Calvinists, Lutherans, etc.), do demonstrate an excessive admiration for a particular person. Mainstream Judaism rejects the Messiah, but keeps the law; mainstream Christianity accepts the Messiah, but rejects the law; the Messianic faith rightly accepts the Messiah and keeps the law.

MATTHEW 5:17 (NKJV):

"Do not think that I came to destroy the Law or the Prophets. I did not come to destroy but to fulfill."

A major difference that the Messianic Hebrew Roots faith has with mainstream Christianity is that mainstream Christians believe that Jesus Christ came to do away with the law and start a new religion; whereas Messianic Hebrew Roots followers believe that Yeshua Messiah did not come to do away with the law or start a new religion, He came to further clarify the law and fulfill the role of the Messiah foretold by the prophets of the already established faith.

1 JOHN 2:6 (NKJV):

He who says he abides in Him ought himself also to walk just as He walked.

To walk just as Yeshua (Jesus) walked means to strive to live as He lived, to obey the Torah (the law), all of it - just as Yeshua (Jesus) did, as best as one can. Mainstream Christianity advocates, to various degrees, that the law is done away with. Mainstream Christianity teaches that the 'Mosaic' laws, the dietary laws (which they classify as ceremonial laws), the Sabbath, and God's Leviticus 23 feasts (often referred to as Jewish holidays), do not need to be obeyed or observed. Christianity has replaced God's feasts with pagan-based holidays, adopting paganism into their faith.

A mainstream Christian, when confronted with the non-Scriptural, pagan-based origins of much of his or her faith, will often defend them by saying, "God knows what's in my heart." God does not ask that we worship Him based on what's in our heart (Proverbs 28:26; Jeremiah 17:9); He requires of us that we worship Him in spirit and truth (John 4:23-24).

JEW HATRED

There are various Christian individuals who continually say vile things against the Messianic faith; against Jews who have accepted Yeshua Messiah (Jesus Christ) as Lord, Messiah, and Savior and against Gentiles who keep the law (Torah), calling them Judaizers. Historically there were Jews killed for refusing to convert to Christianity, while today there are some Christians who hate the Jews even *after* they have accepted Yeshua (Jesus) as their Messiah. It seems there are some people who will always irrationally hate the Jews no matter what they believe or do.

If Yeshua (Jesus) were to speak to common, typical mainstream Christians today, some of whom criticize the Messianic Hebraic Roots faith as a cult, He might say something like this:

JOHN 4:22 (NKJV) [WITH INTERPRETATION]:

"You [CHRISTIANS] worship what you do not know [FALSEHOODS THROUGH PAGANISM]; we [MESSIANICS] know what we worship, for salvation is of the Jews."

Many Christians, who do not want to change their law abolishing, pagan-based ways, label the Messianic Hebraic Roots movement a cult. They believe that the Scripture-based foundation of the Hebrew Roots Messianic faith is erroneous, while blindly proclaiming that the pagan-based roots of the mainstream Christian faith are right!

denomination:
A recognized autonomous branch of the Christian Church.[48]

denomination synonyms:
Sect, church, CULT, faith community, body, persuasion, religious persuasion.

By definition, ALL CHRISTIAN DENOMINATIONS ARE CULTS, to a greater or lesser extent. Denominational Christian church organizations will not be corrected by Scripture, so in practice these churches behave as cults. Christians adhering to the denominational teachings of their particular branch of Christianity are following the cult teachings of the denomination that they belong to, and not necessarily Scripture.

The Messianic Hebrew Roots movement is not a cult. For Jews, it is the acceptance of Yeshua (Jesus) as their Messiah. For Gentiles, it is a shedding of Christian falsehoods and pagan practices; a return to the ancient paths (Jeremiah 18:15) of the roots of the faith to worship God in truth; and an acknowledgement that God is the same yesterday, today, and forever (Hebrews 13:8).

PAUL: FALSE PROPHET OR TRUE APOSTLE?

By George Lujack

There are some Torah-abiding Messianic and law-following Christian believers who have rejected Paul as a false apostle and prophet. This article will affirm that Paul was a true apostle and prophet of God and declare that those who reject Paul are misguided and misinformed by mainstream Christianity's teachings and do not understand the true meanings of Paul's Scripture writings.

At the heart of the matter as to why some have decided to reject Paul is the following Romans verse:

ROMANS 6:14 (NKJV):

For sin shall not have dominion over you, *for you are not under law but grace.*

Romans 6:14 is perhaps the single greatest twisted verse in all of Scripture. The mainstream Christian gospel of grace rejects the need for believers to repent, live righteously, and obey God's laws. Lawless-minded believers use Romans 6:14 to reject God's Tanakh (Old Testament) laws, live lawlessly, teach others to live lawlessly, and to live solely under God's grace. The mainstream Christian gospel of grace rejects the need for believers to repent and to live righteously by obeying God's laws.

Lawful-minded Messianic and Christian believers have rightfully rejected the gospel of grace that negates the need for repentance and righteous living. In doing so, some have incorrectly accepted mainstream Christianity's twisted teaching and understanding of Paul's words, recorded in Romans 6:14, and have therefore rejected Paul as a false apostle and prophet who advocated lawlessness and infinite grace.

MATTHEW 5:17-19 (NKJV):

Do not think that I came to destroy the Law or the Prophets. I did not come to destroy but to fulfill. For assuredly, I say to you, till heaven and earth pass away, one jot or one tittle will by no means pass from the law till all is fulfilled. Whoever therefore breaks one of the least of these commandments, and teaches men so, shall be called least in the kingdom of heaven; but whoever does and teaches them, he shall be called great in the kingdom of heaven.

Yeshua (Jesus) plainly stated that He did not come to destroy the law and that the law would not pass away. Believers who reject Paul claim that Paul's words contradict Yeshua's (Jesus') words in the B'rit Hadashah (New Testament), so therefore Paul should be rejected as a false apostle and prophet.

PAUL'S WORDS IN ROMANS 6:14 ARE TAKEN OUT OF CONTEXT, TWISTED, AND ARE DIFFICULT FOR SOME TO UNDERSTAND

2 PETER 3:15-16 (NKJV):

Our beloved brother Paul, according to the wisdom given to him, has written to you, as also in all his epistles, speaking in them of these things, IN WHICH ARE SOME THINGS *HARD TO UNDERSTAND*, WHICH UNTAUGHT AND UNSTABLE PEOPLE *TWIST* to their own destruction, as they do also THE REST OF THE SCRIPTURES.

The Apostle Peter confirms the Apostle Paul as having wisdom that was recorded in his written epistles, of which some things contained within them are hard to understand, which improperly taught people twist to their own destruction. Peter also confirms that Paul's written epistles are Scripture. Peter mentions Paul's writings as being part of *the rest of the Scriptures*, thereby confirming Paul's writings as Scripture. Paul wrote in Romans that we should not sin freely and live under grace alone, but we should establish, not make void, the law:

ROMANS 3:31 (NKJV):

Do we then make void the law through faith? Certainly not! On the contrary, we establish the law.

ROMANS 6:1-2 (NKJV):

What shall we say then? Shall we continue in sin that grace may abound? Certainly not! How shall we who died to sin live any longer in it?

ROMANS 6:6 (NKJV):

Our old man was crucified with Him, that the body of sin might be done away with, that we should no longer be slaves of sin.

ROMANS 6:11-13 (NKJV):

Likewise you also, reckon yourselves to be dead indeed to sin, but alive to God in Messiah Yeshua (Christ Jesus) our Lord. Therefore do not let sin reign in your mortal body, that you should obey it in its lusts. And do not present your members as instruments of unrighteousness to sin, but present yourselves to God as being alive from the dead, and your members as instruments of righteousness to God.

ROMANS 6:15 (NKJV):

What then? Shall we sin because we are not under law but under grace? Certainly not!

Does Paul contradict his own writings, and the rest of the Scriptures, with his most often quoted (and twisted) verse, Romans 6:14?

ROMANS 6:14 (NKJV):

For sin shall not have dominion over you, for you are *not under law but under grace*.

Scripture does not contradict Scripture. Paul's writings are Scripture and he did not contradict himself, nor did he contradict the rest of the Scriptures. Romans 6:14, when taken out-of-context and read alone, has been twisted by many in mainstream Christianity for the deceitful intent purpose to live lawlessly, and to teach others to likewise live lawlessly, under grace alone.

Romans 6:14 should be understood by believers in the following manner:

ROMANS 6:14 (NKJV) [WITH INTERPRETATION]:

For sin shall not have dominion over you, for you are not under [THE ORDINANCES FOR BREAKING THE] law but under [GOD'S FAVOR AND SANCTIFYING] grace.

Yeshua (Jesus) paid the ordinance penalty for us, for our breaking of the law, which was death. Yeshua (Jesus) did not die so that we could sin freely and live under infinite, unending, unlimited grace.

MATTHEW 7:15 (NKJV):

Beware of false prophets, who come to you in sheep's clothing, but inwardly they are ravenous wolves.

MATTHEW 7:21-23 (NKJV):

Not everyone who says to Me, 'Lord, Lord,' shall enter the kingdom of heaven, but he who does the will of My Father in heaven. Many will say to Me in that day, 'Lord, Lord, have we not prophesied in Your name, cast out demons in Your name, and done many wonders in Your name?' And then I will declare to them, 'I never knew you; depart from Me, you who practice lawlessness!'

MATTHEW 24:11-12 (NKJV):

Then many false prophets will rise up and deceive many. And because LAWLESSNESS WILL ABOUND, the love of many will grow cold.

Many false prophets in mainstream Christianity have taken a few difficult things Paul has written out-of-context, twisted the meanings of his words, and have deceived many into believing that they are permitted to live lawlessly under perpetual grace.

It is not the law-abiding who will be turned away from entering the kingdom of heaven by Yeshua (Jesus), but the lawless (Matthew 7:23).

Paul is a true apostle and prophet of God who did not advocate living lawlessly. Paul wrote that sin shall not have dominion over us, that we should not be slaves of sin, thereby negating the idea that we can keep sinning freely. Paul wrote that we should establish the law and live righteously; that we should certainly not continue in sin so that grace should abound, but we should establish the law (Romans 3:31). The objections to Paul's writings come from some law-abiding Messianic believers, who would like to dismiss Paul's epistles as being unscriptural. Yet, the Apostle Peter confirms Paul's writings as being part of the Scriptures (2 Peter 3:15-16).

The Apostle Paul's objectors do not understand God's purpose in using Paul writings to serve His kingdom's purpose. God inspired all of the apostles' writings, and Paul's epistles were also inspired (2 Timothy 3:16).

What then was the purpose of God's inspired words to Paul?

Certainly, the Tanakh (Old Testament) is clear. God's commandments are eternal, perpetual, and they shall not pass away. Numerous verses confirm this.

The writings of Paul are not essential to the Scriptures. So, what was God's purpose in some of the apparent ambiguous Scripture language of the writings of the Apostle Paul?

MARK 4:2-9 (NKJV):

Then He [YESHUA (JESUS)] taught them many things by parables, and said to them in His teaching: "Listen! Behold, a sower went out to sow. And it happened, as he sowed, that some seed fell by the wayside; and the birds of the air came and devoured it. Some fell on stony ground, where it did not have much earth; and immediately it sprang up because it had no depth of earth. But when the sun was up it was scorched, and because it had no root it withered away. And some seed fell among thorns; and the thorns grew up and choked it, and it yielded no crop. But other seed fell on good ground and yielded a crop that sprang up, increased and produced: some thirtyfold, some sixty, and some a hundred." And He said to them, "He who has ears to hear, let him hear!"

Paul is a sower, as are all of the apostles. Some of his words have been used by false prophets to abolish the commandments of God, to make many fall by the wayside, to fall by the stony ground, to choke and wither away, yielding no fruit.

God has used Paul's words to separate the good crop from the bad crop, the good seed from the tares (Matthew 13:24-43); those who will obey all His commandments from those who will obey some of His commandments (Matthew 5:18-19).

Paul is a true apostle and prophet of God who did not advocate living lawlessly. Paul wrote that sin shall not have dominion over us, that we should not be slaves of sin, thereby negating the idea that we can keep sinning freely. Paul wrote that we should establish the law and live righteously; that we should certainly not continue in sin that grace should abound.

MUST EVERYONE ALWAYS SUBMIT TO THE GOVERNING OR RELIGIOUS AUTHORITIES?

By George Lujack

There are many sheepish persons in the world who often criticize the bold, critical-thinking, and discerning who question authority, saying to them that they must always obey the government authorities and their church leaders, and cite Romans 13:1 as the basis for this worldview. This article will examine the whole of Romans 13 and will declare that the notion to always obey authority is not of God or of Scripture.

ROMANS 13:1-2 (NKJV):

Everyone is to obey the governing authorities, because there is no authority except from God and so whatever authorities exist have been appointed by God. Therefore whoever resists the authority resists the ordinance of God, and those who resist will bring judgment on themselves.

Romans 13:1, if read alone and out of the context of the rest of Romans 13, would seem to indicate that whoever is in government power is appointed and ordained by God and must be obeyed without question. As with all Scripture, verses read alone and out of context - without supporting verses, should not be used to create a doctrine or a worldview.

ROMANS 13:3-4 (NKJV):

For rulers are not a terror to good works, but to evil. Do you want to be unafraid of the authority? Do what is good, and you will have praise from the same. For he is God's minister to you for good. But if you do evil, be afraid; for he does not bear the sword in vain; for he is God's minister, an avenger to execute wrath on him who practices evil.

The Apostle Paul is speaking of good, righteous rulers. Evil rulers *are* a terror to good citizens and to the good works of good citizens. Good, righteous rulers are God's ministers who will punish evil citizens.

ROMANS 13:5-7 (NKJV):

Therefore you must be subject, not only because of wrath but also for conscience' sake. For because of this you also pay taxes, for they are God's ministers attending continually to this very thing. Render therefore to all their due: taxes to whom taxes are due, customs to whom customs, fear to whom fear, honor to whom honor.

Citizens are subject to good and evil rulers and must pay taxes to both.

1 PETER 2:13-17 (NKJV):

Therefore submit yourselves to every ordinance of man for the Lord's sake, whether to the king as supreme, or to governors, as to those who are sent by him for the punishment of evildoers and for the praise of those who do good. For this is the will of God, that by doing good you may put to silence the ignorance of foolish men - as free, yet not using liberty as a cloak for vice, but as bondservants of God. Honor all people. Love the brotherhood. Fear God. Honor the king.

The Apostle Peter wrote that we should obey every ordinance of man, kings, and governors. But the ordinances he spoke of were NOT ordinances of evil, they were ordinances issued by righteous rulers who punish evildoers and praise those who do good deeds.

ACTS 5:27-32 (NKJV):

And the high priest asked them, saying, "DID WE NOT STRICTLY COMMAND YOU NOT TO TEACH IN THIS NAME? And look, you have filled Jerusalem with your doctrine, and intend to bring this Man's blood on us!"

But Peter and the other apostles answered and said: "WE OUGHT TO OBEY GOD RATHER THAN MEN. The God of our fathers raised up Yeshua (Jesus) whom you murdered by hanging on a tree. Him God has exalted to His right hand to be Prince and Savior, to give repentance to Israel and forgiveness of sins. And we are His witnesses to these things, and so also is the Holy Spirit whom God has given to those who obey Him."

Peter and the other apostles with him were sent to the common prison by the religious governing authorities of Jerusalem (Acts 5:17). They were commanded by these rulers NOT to teach in the name of Yeshua (Jesus). Peter ignored an ordinance of men that was in direct conflict with the ordinance given to Him by God, and boldly declared to the high priest who had them arrested, "We ought to obey God rather than men."

ACTS 5:40-42 (NKJV):

And when they had called for the apostles and beaten them, they commanded that they should not speak in the name of Yeshua (Jesus), and let them go. So they departed from the presence of the council, rejoicing that they were counted worthy to suffer shame for His name. And daily in the temple, and in every house, they did not cease teaching and preaching Yeshua as the Messiah (Jesus as the Christ).

Once again the apostles were taken, beaten, and commanded that they should not speak in the name of Yeshua (Jesus), and again the apostles ignored the ordinance of the religious rulers and continually declared Yeshua the Messiah (Jesus the Christ).

2 SAMUEL 23:3 (NKJV):

The God of Israel said, the Rock of Israel spoke to me: "He who rules over men must be just, ruling in the fear of God."

PSALM 2:10-11 (NKJV):

Now therefore be wise, O kings; be instructed, you judges of the earth. Serve YHWH (the Lord) with fear, and rejoice with trembling.

If the governing authorities are lawfully compliant with God's laws, are just, wise, ruling in the fear of God, we are to obey them, but if not, then we are to rebel against them and obey God rather than men.

EVIL LEADERS - WHAT TO DO ABOUT THEM?

Historically, people have tried to assassinate evil world leaders. Estimates vary, but there were a reported thirty-five failed assassination attempts of Adolph Hitler. Should the righteous attempt to kill the evil rulers of the world?

JEREMIAH 51:19-20 (NKJV):

YHWH (the Lord) of hosts is His name.

"You are My battle-ax and weapons of war: for with you I will break the nation in pieces; with you I will destroy kingdoms."

PROVERBS 21:1 (NKJV):

The king's heart is in the hand of YHWH (the Lord), like the rivers of water; He turns it wherever He wishes.

It is not for the individual to take down a king. Kingdoms rise and kingdoms fall by the decree of God. God raises other kingdoms to take down evil kings. Sometimes God raises the people of a nation to take down its own leader. The fate of the lone assassin is usually not a good one. Even if an assassination of an evil ruler is successful, often the evil ruler will be glorified as a martyr and the assassin will be killed and vilified.

DAVID FLEES KING SAUL

David fled the presence of God's appointed king of Israel, Saul. Saul sought to kill David, as he grew jealous of David's popularity with the people of Israel. Rather than confront Saul, David fled Israel and honored God's appointed king of Israel, rather than seeking to kill him and take over his throne, or to prevent Saul from first killing him.

RELIGIOUS AUTHORITIES - TEST THE CHURCH FATHERS

GALATIANS 1:6-9 (NKJV):

I marvel that you are turning away so soon from Him who called you in the grace of MESSIAH (Christ), to a different gospel, which is not another; but there are some who trouble you and want to pervert the gospel of Messiah (Christ). BUT EVEN IF WE, OR AN ANGEL FROM HEAVEN, PREACH ANY OTHER GOSPEL TO YOU THAN WHAT WE HAVE PREACHED TO YOU, LET HIM BE ACCURSED. AS WE HAVE SAID BEFORE, SO NOW I SAY AGAIN, IF ANYONE PREACHES ANY OTHER GOSPEL TO YOU THAN WHAT YOU HAVE RECEIVED, LET HIM BE ACCURSED.

ACTS 17:11 (NKJV):

They received the word with all readiness, AND SEARCHED THE SCRIPTURES DAILY TO FIND OUT WHETHER THESE THINGS WERE SO.

1 THESSALONIANS 5:21 (NKJV):

Test all things; hold fast what is good.

Many Catholics and other denominational-minded believers rely on the teachings of their church 'fathers,' their traditional doctrinal teachings, or the understandings of their local congregational minister. False shepherds unfortunately mislead many people. Far too few lions are bold enough to just search the Scriptures daily to verify whether or not what they hear, or have heard, in their teachings is true or not.

The ultimate religious authority on Earth is not any figure, not any man, not any church, but the authority of the word of God as written in the Holy Scriptures. Wise men have historically searched the Scriptures to verify the religious preaching of men, to find out whether the things they say are true. Wise men still do.

THE COMING ANTIMESSIAH (ANTICHRIST) SATANIC GOVERNING AUTHORITY

REVELATION 13:16-17 (NKJV):

He causes all, both small and great, rich and poor, free and slave, to receive a mark on their right hand or on their foreheads, and that no one may buy or sell except one who has the mark or the name of the beast, or the number of his name.

As the end of the age is soon approaching, the Antimessiah (Antichrist) will arise out of the world economic collapse and great tribulation, and his satanic government will be the governing authority. He will command everyone in the world to take his mark.

REVELATION 14:9-11 (NKJV):

"If anyone worships the beast and his image, and receives his mark on his forehead or on his hand, he himself shall also drink of the wine of the wrath of God, which is poured out full strength into the cup of His indignation. He shall be tormented with fire and brimstone in the presence of the holy angels and in the presence of the Lamb. And the smoke of their torment ascends forever and ever; and they have no rest day or night, who worship the beast and his image, and whoever receives the mark of his name."

REVELATION 20:4 (NKJV):

Then I saw the souls of those who had been beheaded for their witness to Yeshua (Jesus) and for the word of God, who had not worshiped the beast or his image, and had not received his mark on their foreheads or on their hands. And they lived and reigned with Messiah (Christ) for a thousand years.

Left behind repentant believers in the Sovereign of sovereigns, the King of kings, Yeshua the Messiah (Jesus the Christ) are commanded from the highest governing authority - the kingdom of God, to not accept the Antimessiah's (Antichrist's) implant mark, even to the point of being beheaded, rather than submitting to the Antimessiah (Antichrist) satanic governing authority.

TITHING;
DOES IT MEAN GIVING GOD THE FIRST TENTH OF YOUR INCOME?

By George Lujack

Tithing the first tenth of one's income to God (via a congregational worship ministry) has been a longstanding traditional teaching. Does God command believers to give ten percent of their income to their chosen congregation? This article will address tithes, offerings, and God's laws concerning them.

TITHES ARE PRODUCE OF THE FIELD (LAND): ANISE, CUMMIN, FRUIT, GRAIN, HERBS, HONEY, MINT, OIL, RUE, SEED, AND WINE

LEVITICUS 27:30 (NKJV):

And all the tithe of the land, whether of the seed of the land or of the fruit of the tree, is YHWH's (the Lord's). It is holy to YHWH (the Lord).

DEUTERONOMY 12:17 (NKJV):

You may not eat within your gates the tithe of your grain or your new wine or your oil, of the firstborn of your herd or your flock, of any of your offerings which you vow, of your freewill offerings, or of the heave offering of your hand.

DEUTERONOMY 14:22,28 (NKJV):

You shall truly tithe all the increase of your grain that the field produces year by year. ...

At the end of every third year you shall bring out the tithe of your produce of that year and store it up within your gates.

DEUTERONOMY 26:12-13 (NKJV):

When you have finished laying aside all the tithe of your increase in the third year - the year of tithing - and have given it to the Levite, the stranger, the fatherless, and the widow, so that they may eat within your gates and be filled, then you shall say before YHWH (the Lord) your God: 'I have removed the holy tithe from my house, and also have given them to the Levite, the stranger, the fatherless, and the widow, according to all Your commandments which You have commanded me.'

2 CHRONICLES 31:5 (NKJV):

As soon as the commandment was circulated, the children of Israel brought in abundance the first-fruits of grain and wine, oil, and honey, and of all the produce of the field; and they brought in abundantly the tithe of everything.

NEHEMIAH 13:12 (NKJV):

Then all Judah brought the tithe of the grain and the new wine and the oil to the storehouse.

MATTHEW 23:23 (NKJV):

"Woe to you, scribes and Pharisees, hypocrites! For you pay tithe of mint and anise and cummin, and have neglected the weightier matters of the law: justice and mercy and faith."

LUKE 11:42 (NKJV):

"But woe to you Pharisees! For you tithe mint and rue and all manner of herbs, and pass by justice and the love of God."

The law of tithing was to give to the Levites who were taken from among the people of Israel to serve as tabernacle priests over the land of Israel. The Levites did not own any of the land of Israel, so the tithes were collected for them as their inheritance for the work they did as priests of Israel.

NUMBERS 18:6-7 (NKJV):

Behold, I Myself have taken your brethren the Levites from among the children of Israel; they are a gift to you, given by YHWH (the Lord), to do the work of the tabernacle of meeting. Therefore you and your sons with you shall attend to your priesthood for everything at the altar and behind the veil; and you shall serve. I give your priesthood to you as a gift for service...

NUMBERS 18:20-21 (NKJV):

Then YHWH (the Lord) said to Aaron: "You shall have no inheritance in their land, nor shall you have any portion among them; I am your portion and your inheritance among the children of Israel.

Behold, I have given the children of Levi all the tithes in Israel as an inheritance in return for the work which they perform, the work of the tabernacle of meeting."

The law of tithing specifically applied to the people of Israel, to the eleven tribes of Israel who were apportioned land as an inheritance, to support the Levite tribe of Israel, who did not receive a land inheritance, but served God daily as tabernacle priests. Tithes given to the Levites were of the produce of the land, including cattle and all manner of crops and products derived from vegetation. Income tithing of ten percent to be taken from the people of Israel was not a part of the law of tithing. Tithes were specifically set aside to be used to supply the needs of the Levites, the poor, foreigners, widows, and orphans (Deuteronomy 26:12-13). They were to be a blessing for the poor and needy.

FREEWILL OFFERINGS ARE DIFFERENT THAN TITHES

Mainstream Christianity has traditionally proclaimed a doctrine of tithing, which maintains that believers should donate ten percent of their income to their congregational assembly.

The tithing doctrine is a guilt-causing, income-generating, self-serving falsehood. God never commanded believers to tithe ten percent of their income or salary. As the term suggests, freewill offerings of cash, gold, silver, and all other items that were given to the treasury of YHWH (the Lord) were voluntarily given out of one's own free will. Freewill offerings were not tithes, which were commanded by God's law to be taken from the Israelites and given to the Levites (Exodus 35:29, 36:3; Leviticus 22:18,21,23, 23:38; Numbers 15:3, 29:39; Deuteronomy 12:6,17, 16:10; 2 Chronicles 31:14; Ezra 3:5, 7:16, 8:28; Psalm 119:108; Amos 4:5).

Malachi 3:8-10 has often been used by mainstream denominations to proclaim that believers who do not tithe ten percent of their income as an offering are stealing from God.

MALACHI 3:8-10 (NKJV):

"Will a man rob God? Yet you have robbed Me! But you say, 'In what way have we robbed You?' In tithes and offerings. You are cursed with a curse, for you have robbed Me, even this whole nation. Bring all the tithes into the storehouse, that there may be food in My house, and try Me now in this," says YHWH (the Lord) of hosts, "If I will not open for you the windows of heaven and pour out for you such a blessing that there will not be room enough to receive it."

Is Malachi 3:8-10 really saying that believers who do not tithe ten percent of their income are stealing from God? NO! God was not addressing the general population of Israel in Malachi 3:8-10. God was addressing the Levite priests in the tabernacle of meeting where He would meet with them (Numbers 18:21). God told the Levite priests that THEY were the ones who robbed God. And how did the Levite priests rob God? They stole from God by taking offerings from the treasuries and tithes from the storehouses, by enriching themselves and not providing for the aliens, widows, and orphans (Malachi 3:5).

JOHN 12:4-6 (NKJV):

But one of His disciples, Judas Iscariot, Simon's son, who would betray Him, said, "Why was this fragrant oil not sold for three hundred denarii and given to the poor?" This he said, not that he cared for the poor, but because he was a thief, and had the money box; and he used to take what was put in it.

It is those who are in charge of a ministry's treasury who steal from God if they use the offerings on themselves instead of primarily doing God's work with the ministry funds. Prosperity gospel preachers likewise steal from God today. Very often they receive huge cash offerings from their congregation and television audience members and use the money to spend it lavishly on themselves. THEY are the ones stealing from God, as they are not using their offerings received, in the name of God, for any other purpose other than to make themselves rich.

In these end times, many false prophets have arisen, proclaiming God's laws are abolished. The one law they will never claim is abolished is the law of tithing ten percent of one's income, which is not even in His law. The love of money is the root of all evil, including the evil of profit-motivated ministers (1 Timothy 6:10).

Believers who cannot afford a freewill offering of ten percent of their income are not stealing from God. If a person hasn't given an offering to God, they cannot steal something they haven't given from God. It is the people who are in charge of God's treasury, ministry leaders, who are stealing from God, not the people who haven't contributed to the treasury. People who have not given are not stealing from God.

THE POOR WIDOW'S MITES

<u>MARK 12:41-44 (NKJV)</u>:

Now Yeshua (Jesus) sat opposite the treasury and saw how the people put money into the treasury. And many who were rich put in much. Then one poor widow came and threw in two mites, which make a quadrans. So He called His disciples to Himself and said to them, "Assuredly, I say to you that this poor widow has put in more than all those who have given to the treasury; for they all put in out of their abundance, but she out of her poverty put in all that she had, her whole livelihood."

Yeshua (Jesus) wasn't calculating who was or was not contributing ten percent of their income to the temple treasury, nor did He have great regard for the rich who put in much out of their abundance. Yeshua (Jesus) recognized the poor widow, who gave one hundred percent of her income, which was two mites, two small copper coins worth less than a penny.

GOD LOVES A CHEERFUL GIVER

<u>2 CORINTHIANS 9:7 (NKJV)</u>:

So let each one give as he purposes in his heart, not grudgingly or of necessity; for God loves a cheerful giver.

There is no ten percent requirement for the cheerful giver.

Assemblies, churches, congregations, prayer centers, synagogues, and other houses of worship do have expenses and need to meet those expenses through freewill offerings of their congregants. After those expenses are met, ministry treasuries should be used to do God's work, and should not be spent on ministers who live lavishly and store up treasures for themselves (Matthew 6:19-21).

Freewill cash offerings are voluntary contributions one makes in any percentage amount according to the purposes of his or her heart. Freewill offerings of cash are not tithes and are not required to be a minimum ten percent of one's income.

THE KEY TO POWERFUL AND EFFECTIVE PRAYERS

By George Lujack

This article will discuss how not to pray and will reveal the key to powerful and effective prayers, which is praying through belief, faith, living righteously, and trusting in God.

PROVERBS 15:8 (NKJV):
The prayer of the upright is His delight.

JAMES 5:16 (NKJV):
The effective, fervent prayer of a righteous man avails much.

The prayers of *the upright* and of *the righteous* are His delight and avail (produce) much. If this is the case, it stands to reason that the opposite of these verses should also be true. That is, the prayers of the crooked and unrighteous avail (produce) little. Indeed Scripture confirms that this is so.

PROVERBS 28:9 (NKJV):
One who turns his ear from hearing the law (Torah), even his prayer is an abomination.

The first and foremost thing a person must realize, if he or she wants God to answer his or her prayers, is that God will listen to the one who is practicing righteousness and He will not have regard for the prayer of the sinner, who actively sins while he or she prays.

People who are engaged in sin often pray to God and God will not regard such prayers. Such prayers are an abomination to Him. So, before praying to God, believers should make sure they are praying in righteousness, not in sin.

HOW TO IMPROPERLY PRAY TO GOD

IDOLATROUS PRAYERS

While actively engaging in idolatry, many people - often Catholics, use objects as a means to pray to God through. Bowing before an artistic or carved image of Yeshua (Jesus) and praying is praying while committing idolatry. God is a jealous God who will not share His glory with carved images (Isaiah 42:8), so how is He going to respect the prayer of a person committing idolatry as he or she prays?

Using prayer beads, images, paintings, statues, or any object to pray to God through is an offense to Him. Idolatrous prayers show a lack of faith in Him being able to hear prayers and faith in the object's special ability and power to transmit messages to God, so that prayers will have a better chance of being heard by Him.

Remember the Roman centurion, how great his faith was, in that he knew the mere spoken word of Yeshua (Jesus) was sufficient to heal his servant; he knew Yeshua (Jesus) didn't need to physically touch his servant to heal him (Matthew 8:5-13; Luke 7:1-10).

MATTHEW 8:5-13; LUKE 7:1-10 (NKJV):

Now when Yeshua (Jesus) had entered Capernaum, a centurion came to Him, pleading with Him, saying, "Lord, my servant is lying at home paralyzed, dreadfully tormented (ready to die)."

And Yeshua (Jesus) said to him, "I will come and heal him."

The centurion answered and said, "Lord, I am not worthy that You should come under my roof. But only speak a word, and my servant will be healed. For I also am a man under authority, having soldiers under me. And I say to this one, 'Go,' and he goes; and to another, 'Come,' and he comes; and to my servant, 'Do this,' and he does it."

When Yeshua (Jesus) heard it, He marveled, and said to those who followed, "Assuredly, I say to you, I have not found such great faith, not even in Israel! And I say to you that many will come from east and west, and sit down with Abraham, Isaac, and Jacob in the kingdom of heaven. But the sons of the kingdom will be cast out into outer darkness.

There will be weeping and gnashing of teeth." Then Yeshua (Jesus) said to the centurion, "Go your way; and as you have believed, so let it be done for you." And his servant was healed that same hour.

God likewise does not need an object for us to use so He can hear our prayers. The use of an object to pray through to God demonstrates a lack of faith that He cannot otherwise hear our prayers, or shows faith in the object itself, believing that God can hear our prayers *better* if we use it as a medium. The use of any and all objects to pray to God through is idolatry.

SEXUAL IMMORALITY PRAYERS

Sexual intercourse is a blessing to be shared between lawfully married heterosexual couples and *only* between lawfully married heterosexual couples. Many people disregard God's laws against sexual immorality and are unmarried, yet live sexually active lives. Some who are married cheat on their spouses. Many get hurt after being sexually used in such relationships and pray to God for a good relationship, then reenter another unlawful affair, are dissatisfied, get hurt again, and keep repeating this cycle of sin.

JAMES 4:4 (NKJV):

Adulterers and adulteresses! Do you not know that friendship with the world is enmity with God? Whoever therefore wants to be a friend of the world makes himself an enemy of God.

One may find love through the world, but God will not listen to the prayers of the unlawful sexually active who pray for a good spouse (or relationship).

COVETEOUSNESS PRAYERS

The Prosperity Gospel has deceived many to pray for material blessings, so that they can spend it on pleasures for themselves, to live their best life now.

JAMES 4:3 (NKJV):
You ask and do not receive, because you ask amiss, that you may spend it on your pleasures.

God is one who can materially bless those who serve Him, but He will not answer the prayers of those who have no desire to serve Him at all, and are merely praying to God so that they themselves can receive wealth to satisfy their covetousness and desires for material things.

PRAYERS OVER UNCLEAN CREATURES BEFORE EATING THEM

Scripture does address the prayers of those who believe that they can cleanse unclean creatures through prayer and then consume them.

ISAIAH 66:17 (NKJV) [WITH INTERPRETATION]:
"Those who sanctify and purify themselves [THROUGH PRAYER] … eating swine's flesh and the abomination [SEA CREATURES WITHOUT FINS AND OVERLAPPING SCALES] and the mouse, shall be consumed [BY DISEASE] together," says YHWH (the Lord).

Mainstream Christians often cite Timothy in deceiving themselves into believing that they can miraculously transform unclean creatures into clean creatures through the power of prayer.

1 TIMOTHY 4:4-5 (NKJV):
For every creature of God is good, and nothing is to be refused if it is received with thanksgiving; for it is sanctified by the word of God and prayer.

JOB 14:4 (NKJV):
Who can bring a clean thing out of an unclean? No one!

Creatures to be consumed cannot be sanctified by prayer alone; prayer *and* THE WORD OF GOD must sanctify them. Scripture, the word of God, distinguishes between which creatures are sanctified as clean that may be eaten and which creatures are prohibited as unclean that may not be eaten (Leviticus 11; Deuteronomy 14).

Prayers over unclean creatures, asking God to bless what He has already commanded man not to eat, are prayers of disobedience, futility, and/or ignorance. God will not answer prayers of disobedience, foolishness, and lawlessness. One might as well pray to God to bless his or her sexual promiscuity, so that he or she can commit sexual sin and be protected by God from receiving a sexually transmitted disease.

GRANDSTANDING PRAYERS

MATTHEW 6:5 (NKJV):

"And when you pray, you shall not be like the hypocrites. For they love to pray standing in the synagogues and on the corners of the streets, that they may be seen by men. Assuredly, I say to you, they have their reward."

REPETITIVE PRAYERS

The Catholic Church has traditionally taught its flock to pray repetitive prayers of 'Hail Mary,' which are improper because Mary is not a goddess who can hear or answer prayers, Mary is dead in her grave awaiting her resurrection, and these prayers are vain and repetitive.

MATTHEW 6:7 (NKJV):

"And when you pray, do not use vain repetitions as the heathen do. For they think that they will be heard for their many words."

HOW TO PROPERLY PRAY TO GOD

PRAY PRIVATELY TO GOD

MATTHEW 6:6 (NKJV):

But you, when you pray, go into your room, and when you have shut your door, pray to your Father who is in the secret place; and your Father who sees in secret will reward you openly.

To have a personal relationship with God, one needs to pray privately to Him about life's struggles and to be thankful for blessings received.

THE LORD'S PRAYER

MATTHEW 6:9-13; LUKE 11:2-4 (NKJV):

"In this manner therefore pray:

Our Father in heaven. Hallowed be Your name. Your kingdom come, Your will be done on earth as it is in heaven. Give us this day our daily bread. And forgive us our debts, as we forgive our debtors. And do not lead us into temptation, but deliver us from the evil one. For Yours is the power and the glory forever."

PRAY IN BELIEF AND FAITH

MATTHEW 17:20 (NKJV):

Yeshua (Jesus) said to them, "Because of your unbelief; for assuredly, I say to you, if you have faith as a mustard seed, you will say to this mountain, 'Move from here to there,' and it will move; and nothing will be impossible for you."

MARK 11:22-24 (NKJV):

So Yeshua (Jesus) answered and said to them, "Have faith in God. For assuredly, I say to you, whoever says to this mountain, 'Be removed and be cast into the sea,' and does not doubt in his heart, but believes that those things he says will be done, he will have whatever he says. Therefore I say to you, whatever things you ask when you pray, believe that you receive them, and you will have them."

When Yeshua (Jesus) spoke of 'moving mountains,' He was speaking figuratively of moving mountains, not literally of moving Earth's mountains and casting them into the seas. He was speaking of mountainous obstacles that faithful believers have in their lives that prevent them from serving God, and other things that disrupt the lives of His faithful servants. Pray to remove mountainous obstacles, and believe, and He will remove them.

PRAY DILIGENTLY

1 THESSALONIANS 5:17 (NKJV):

Pray without ceasing.

PRAY TO BE RELIEVED OF SUFFERING

JAMES 5:13 (NKJV):

Is anyone among you suffering? Let him pray.

PRAY IN HUMBLENESS

LUKE 18:9-14 (NKJV):

Also Yeshua (Jesus) spoke this parable to some who trusted in themselves that they were righteous, and despised others:

"Two men went up to the temple to pray, one a Pharisee and the other a tax collector.

The Pharisee stood and prayed thus with himself, 'God, I thank You that I am not like other men - swindlers, unjust, adulterers, or even as this tax collector. I fast twice a week; I give tithes of all that I possess.' And the tax collector, standing afar off, would not so much as raise his eyes to heaven, but beat his breast, saying, 'God, be merciful to me a sinner!'

I tell you, this man went down to his house justified rather than the other; for everyone who exalts himself will be humbled, and he who humbles himself will be exalted."

LUKE 23:39-43 (NKJV):

Then one of the criminals who were hanged blasphemed Him, saying, "If You are the Messiah (Christ), save Yourself and us."

But the other, answering, rebuked him, saying, "Do you not even fear God, seeing you are under the same condemnation? And we indeed justly, for we receive the due reward of our deeds; but this Man has done nothing wrong." Then he said to Yeshua (Jesus), "Lord, remember me when You come into Your kingdom." And Yeshua (Jesus) said to him, "Assuredly, I say to you today, you will be with Me in Paradise."

God hears the prayers of the penitent man, and has no regard for the petitions or prayers of the proud or unrighteous.

PRAY FOR WISDOM AND SPIRITUAL UNDERSTANDING

2 CHRONICLES 1:8-12 (NKJV):

Solomon said to God: "You have shown great mercy to David my father, and have made me king in his place. Now, O YHWH (Lord) God, let Your promise to David my father be established, for You have made me king over a people like the dust of the earth in multitude. Now give me wisdom and knowledge, that I may go out and come in before this people; for who can judge this great people of Yours?"

Then God said to Solomon: "Because this was in your heart, and you have not asked riches or wealth or honor or the life of your enemies, nor have you asked long life - but have asked wisdom and knowledge for yourself, that you may judge My people over whom I have made you king - wisdom and knowledge are granted to you; and I will give you riches and wealth and honor, such as none of the kings have had who were before you, nor shall any after you have the like."

COLOSSIANS 1:9 (NKJV):

For this reason we also, since the day we heard it, do not cease to pray for you, and to ask that you may be filled with the knowledge of His will in all wisdom and spiritual understanding.

INTERCESSORY PRAYERS (PRAYERS ON BEHALF OF OTHERS)

1 THESSALONIANS 5:25 (NKJV):
Brethren, pray for us.

JAMES 5:14 (NKJV):

Is anyone among you sick? Let him call for the elders of the church, and let them pray over him, anointing him with oil in the name of the Lord.

3 JOHN 1:2 (NKJV):

Beloved, I pray that you may prosper in all things and be in health, just as your soul prospers.

PRAY FOR YOUR ENEMIES AND THOSE WHO ABUSE YOU

LUKE 6:27-28 (NKJV):

"Love your enemies, do good to those who hate you, bless those who curse you, and pray for those who spitefully use you."

THE KEY TO POWERFUL AND EFFECTIVE PRAYERS

MATTHEW 6:33 (NKJV):

"Seek first the kingdom of God and His righteousness, and all these things shall be added to you."

In all things we should pray to God.

The key to powerful and effective prayers is to be God's righteous servant first, and in all things seek to glorify and serve Him, *then* as a righteous servant of His, pray to Him in righteousness (Proverbs 15:8; James 5:16).

A good employer listens to and rewards his or her good employees. How much more so will our righteous God listen to, protect, and reward His servants who pray to, serve, and worship Him in righteousness, spirit, and truth than that of a good earthly employer? (Deuteronomy 7:9; Daniel 9:4; Matthew 16:27; Luke 6:35, 18:6-7; John 4:24; 1 Corinthians 2:9; Ephesians 5:9; Colossians 3:23-24; James 2:5; Revelation 22:12).

THE LAST WILL BE FIRST AND THE FIRST LAST

By George Lujack

Yeshua (Jesus) made numerous statements indicating that the last will be first and the first will be last. This article will examine those statements, and the context in which they were said, showing the different applications of who the first and the last are.

MATTHEW 19:30 (NKJV):

"But many who are first will be last and the last first."

The context of the first being last and the last being first in Matthew 19:30 concerns earthly possessions, wealth, and sacrifice for Yeshua's (Jesus') name's sake.

MATTHEW 19:23-29 (NKJV):

Then Yeshua (Jesus) said to His disciples, "Assuredly, I say to you that it is hard for a rich man to enter the kingdom of heaven. And again I say to you, it is easier for a camel to go through the eye of a needle than for a rich man to enter the kingdom of God."

When His disciples heard it, they were greatly astonished, saying, "Who then can be saved?"

But Yeshua (Jesus) looked at them and said to them, "With men this is impossible, but with God all things are possible."

Then Peter answered and said to Him, "See, we have left all and followed You. Therefore what shall we have?"

So Yeshua (Jesus) said to them, "… And everyone who has left houses or brothers or sisters or father or mother or wife or children or lands, for My name's sake, shall receive a hundredfold, and inherit eternal life."

The first of this world, the rich, and those who haven't sacrificed anything, or who have sacrificed minimally for Yeshua's (Jesus') name, will be last in the kingdom of heaven. Those who have given up family, worldly pursuits, wealth, and possessions will be rewarded as the first in His kingdom.

MATTHEW 20:16 (NKJV):

"So the last will be first, and the first last."

The context of the last being first and the first being last in Matthew 20:16 concerns entrance into and rewards within the kingdom of heaven.

MATTHEW 20:1-15 (NKJV):

"FOR THE KINGDOM OF HEAVEN IS LIKE A LANDOWNER WHO WENT OUT EARLY IN THE MORNING TO HIRE LABORERS FOR HIS VINEYARD.

Now when he had agreed with the laborers for a denarius a day, he sent them into his vineyard. And he went out about the third hour and saw others standing idle in the marketplace, and said to them, 'You also go into the vineyard, and whatever is right I will give you.' So they went. Again he went out about the sixth and the ninth hour, and did likewise. And about the eleventh hour he went out and found others standing idle, and said to them, 'Why have you been standing here idle all day?' They said to him, 'Because no one hired us.' He said to them, 'You also go into the vineyard, and whatever is right you will receive.'

So when evening had come, the owner of the vineyard said to his steward, 'Call the laborers and give them their wages, beginning with the last to the first.' And when those came who were hired about the eleventh hour, they each received a denarius. But when the first came, they supposed that they would receive more; and they likewise received each a denarius. And when they had received it, they complained against the landowner, saying, 'These last men have worked only one hour, and you made them equal to us who have borne the burden and the heat of the day.' But he answered one of them and said, 'Friend, I am doing you no wrong. Did you not agree with me for a denarius? Take what is yours and go your way. I wish to give to this last man the same as to you. Is it not lawful for me to do what I wish with my own things? Or is your eye evil because I am good?'

The Jews were God's first chosen people, the first branches 'appointed' by God to tend to the things of the vineyard (the kingdom of heaven) and bring forth His word to the world. The Gentile world didn't receive the Scriptures until after Yeshua (Jesus) came as the Messiah (Christ) into the world.

MATTHEW 8:11-12 (NKJV) [WITH INTERPRETATION]:

"And I say to you that many [GENTILES] will come from east and west, and sit down with Abraham, Isaac, and Jacob in the kingdom of heaven. But the sons of the kingdom [EVIL JEWS] will be cast out into outer darkness."

Righteous Gentiles, who were last to receive the Scriptures, didn't labor for the kingdom of heaven as long as righteous Jews did, but many of them will be first into the kingdom of heaven. Evil Jews will be cast out.

LUKE 13:30 (NKJV):

"And indeed there are last who will be first, and there are first who will be last."

The context of the last being first and the first being last in Luke 13:30 concerns the entrance of the Jews and Gentiles into the kingdom of heaven. The dead in Messiah (Christ) will be resurrected first (1 Corinthians 15:51-53; 1 Thessalonians 4:15-17), and the righteous Jews who do not know Messiah (Christ) will be resurrected last, upon His return to Earth, and then they will know He is the Lord (Ezekiel 37).

LUKE 13:20-29 (NKJV) [WITH INTERPRETATION]:

And again Yeshua (Jesus) said, "To what shall I liken the kingdom of God? It is like leaven, which a woman took and hid in three measures of meal till it was all leavened."

And He went through the cities and villages, teaching, and journeying toward Jerusalem. Then one said to Him, "Lord, are there few who are saved?"

And He said to them, "Strive to enter through the narrow gate, for many, I say to you, will seek to enter and will not be able. When once the Master of the house has risen up and shut the door, and you begin to stand outside and knock at the door, saying, 'Lord, Lord, open for us,' and He will answer and say to you, 'I do not know you, where you are from,' then you will begin to say, 'We [JEWS] ate and drank in Your presence, and You taught in our streets.' But He will say, 'I tell you I do not know you, where you are from. Depart from Me, all you workers of iniquity.' There will be weeping and gnashing of teeth, when you see Abraham and Isaac and Jacob and all the prophets in the kingdom of God, and yourselves [EVIL JEWS] thrust out. They [GENTILES] will come from the east and the west, from the north and the south, and sit down in the kingdom of God."

There will be Jews who were first to see Yeshua (Jesus), who ate and drank in His presence, and listened to Him as He taught in the streets of Jerusalem and the surrounding cities and villages of Israel, who will be thrust out of His kingdom. Gentiles, who were last to hear His words, will be first into the kingdom of heaven. It is not the hearers of His words, but the doers of His words who are justified as righteous (Romans 2:13; James 1:22-25). The last being first and the first last also applies in a positive way towards righteous living Jews who have not yet accepted Yeshua (Jesus) as their Messiah, Lord, and Savior. Jews practicing righteousness through Judaism are the lost sheep of the house of Israel and Yeshua (Jesus) came for His lost sheep (Matthew 10:7, 15:24). The parables of the lost sheep and prodigal son (Luke 15) are metaphors for sinners who turn back and repent, but are also reflective of the sometimes jealous relations that Jews and Gentiles have towards each other over God.

LUKE 15:4-6 (NKJV) [WITH INTERPRETATION]:

Yeshua (Jesus) spoke this parable to them, saying:

"What man of you, having a hundred sheep [THE DIFFERENT ETHNICITIES OF THE WORLD], if he loses one of them [THE JEWS], does not leave the ninety-nine in the wilderness, and go after the one which is lost until he finds it? And when he has found it, he lays it on his shoulders, rejoicing. And when he comes home, he calls together his friends and neighbors, saying to them, 'Rejoice with me, for I have found my sheep which was lost!'"

LUKE 15:11-13 (NKJV) [WITH INTERPRETATION]:

Then He said: "A certain man had two sons [A JEW AND GENTILE]. And the younger of them [THE JEW] said to his father, 'Father, give me the portion of goods that falls to me.' So he divided to them his livelihood. And not many days after, the younger [JEWISH] son gathered all together, journeyed to a far country, and there wasted his possessions with prodigal living."

In this interpretation, the Jewish prodigal son is driven from his homeland to foreign lands, then returns to his homeland, comes to His senses and accepts Yeshua (Jesus) as his Messiah, Lord, and Savior. Afterward, there will be celebrations and rejoicing in God's kingdom.

LUKE 15:20-24 (NKJV) [WITH INTERPRETATION]:

"And he [THE JEWISH SON] arose and came to his father. But when he was still a great way off, his father saw him and had compassion, and ran and fell on his neck and kissed him. And the [JEWISH] son said to him, 'Father, I have sinned against heaven and in your sight, and am no longer worthy to be called your son.'"

"But the father [GOD] said to his servants, 'Bring out the best robe and put it on him, and put a ring on his hand and sandals on his feet. And bring the fatted calf here and kill it, and let us eat and be merry; for this my [JEWISH] son was dead and is alive again; he was lost and is found.' And they began to be merry."

Now the Gentile son, who had believed in Yeshua (Jesus) all along, got angry and jealous, and would not celebrate the return of his Jewish brother.

LUKE 15:25-32 (NKJV) [WITH INTERPRETATION]:

"Now his older [GENTILE] son was in the field. And as he came and drew near to the house, he heard music and dancing. So he called one of the servants and asked what these things meant. And he said to him, 'Your [JEWISH] brother has come, and because he has received him safe and sound, your father has killed the fatted calf.'

But he was angry and would not go in. Therefore his father [GOD] came out and pleaded with him. So he answered and said to his father, 'Lo, these many years I have been serving you; I never transgressed your commandment at any time; and yet you never gave me a young goat, that I might make merry with my friends. But as soon as this [JEWISH] son of yours came, who has devoured your livelihood with harlots, you killed the fatted calf for him.'

And he said to him, 'Son, you are always with me, and all that I have is yours. It was right that we should make merry and be glad, for your [JEWISH] brother was dead and is alive again, and was lost and is found.'"

The following interpretation will most certainly play out among some Gentile believers when they see the celebrations in God's kingdom over the return of the Jews. When the Jews of the house of Israel as a nation return to the fold, accept Yeshua (Jesus) as their Messiah, Lord, and Savior, and are regrafted into the kingdom of heaven, there will be rejoicing. Many Gentiles who were first to accept Yeshua (Jesus) will be resentful over the rejoicing over the Jews, who will be the last people to accept Yeshua (Jesus).

MARK 9:35 (NKJV):

"If anyone desires to be first, he shall be last of all and servant of all."

The context of the desire to be first, and the call to be last in Mark 9:35 concerns servitude in this age, to achieve greatness in the age to come.

MATTHEW 20:25-26; MARK 10:42-43 (NKJV):

Yeshua (Jesus) called them to Himself and said, "You know that the rulers of the Gentiles lord it over them, and those who are great exercise authority over them. Yet it shall not be so among you; but whoever desires to become great among you, let him be your servant.

MATTHEW 20:27-28; MARK 10:44-45 (NKJV):

And whoever desires to be first among you, let him be your slave - just as the Son of Man did not come to be served, but to serve, and to give His life a ransom for many."

To be first in the kingdom of heaven, one must first be a servant for His kingdom, and be last to be served of the things of this age, just as Yeshua (Jesus) came to serve and not be served.

WHY DID LOT OFFER HIS DAUGHTERS TO AN ANGRY MOB OF HOMOSEXUAL MEN?

By George Lujack

GENESIS 19:4-8 (NKJV):

Now before they lay down, the men of the city, the men of Sodom, both old and young, all the people from every quarter, surrounded the house. And they called to Lot and said to him, "Where are the men who came to you tonight? Bring them out to us that we may know them *carnally*."

So Lot went out to them through the doorway, shut the door behind him, and said, "Please, my brethren, do not do so wickedly! See now, I have two daughters who have not known a man; please, let me bring them out to you, and you may do to them as you wish; only do nothing to these men, since this is the reason they have come under the shadow of my roof."

Many believers are appalled that Lot offered his virgin daughters to the angry mob of homosexual men of Sodom. Many say that they would never offer their daughters to rapist men. So then, why did Lot do this?

Lot has been judged a righteous man (2 Peter 2:7-8). Was it a righteous action to offer one's own daughters to a mob of homosexual rapists? The gesture of Lot, offering his daughters instead of his angelic guests to the mob of Sodom that surrounded his house, is neither condoned nor condemned by God. It was merely recorded as an incident in Scripture history as to what had occurred.

Lot met the two angelic messengers of God at the gate of Sodom and persuaded them to not spend the night in the open square, but instead in his home (Genesis 19:1-3). Shortly after the angelic messengers entered his home, before they went to lie down, the men of the city of Sodom, old and young, *all the people* from every quarter surrounded Lot's house (Genesis 19:4). Lot was an elderly gentleman at the time, not a mighty Samson who could take on a city of men. These men of Sodom wanted to know Lot's visitors carnally, through abominable homosexual acts (Genesis 19:5).

There are a few reasons as to why Lot offered his daughters to the men of Sodom, negotiating with them to take his daughters instead of his guests.

1. Lot knew these visitors were angels or messengers of God. He could not live with the fact that he offered these visitors sanctuary in his home, only to see them abducted from his house to be raped by a mob of homosexual Sodomite men (Genesis 19:1-2,7-8). It was Lot's duty to protect these men, even at the cost of his daughters' chastity, their lives, or even his own.

2. Lot was surrounded by all of Sodom's perverted men. He was not mighty enough to fight them off and he had no weapon to do so. They were going to break down his door to take what they wanted - the two angelic messengers sent by God (Genesis 19:9).

3. Lot lived in Sodom and knew the wickedness of the city (2 Peter 2:7-8). He rationalized that it was the lesser of two evils to sacrifice his daughters' virginity, and possibly their lives, rather than for his guests to be sodomized.

Lot was a righteous man of God caught up in a moment of wickedness in Scripture history. He was defending the angelic messengers sent by God, through negotiating with an overpowering mob of homosexual abducting rapists. Lot did not know that the angelic messengers were capable of defending themselves using the supernatural power of God. God's angelic messengers delivered Lot from this incident, striking the homosexual men at the doorway of his house with blindness (Genesis 19:11).

2 PETER 2:7-8 (NKJV):

RIGHTEOUS LOT, who was oppressed by the filthy conduct of the wicked (for that RIGHTEOUS MAN, dwelling among them, tormented his RIGHTEOUS SOUL from day to day by seeing and hearing their lawless deeds)...

Believers should not be hypercritical of Lot for his actions in offering his daughters to an angry mob of perverted men in an extreme circumstance. God, as recorded in Scripture, has judged Lot as being a righteous man.

THE TRANSFIGURATION;
HOW DID MOSES AND ELIJAH SPEAK WITH YESHUA (JESUS) THROUGH THE VISION AT THE TRANSFIGURATION?

By George Lujack

Moses and Elijah miraculously appeared before Yeshua (Jesus) in a vision known as the Transfiguration. This article will explain that Moses and Elijah were transfigured into spirit beings *and* transported through space and time to meet with Yeshua (Jesus).

transfigure:

Transform into something more beautiful or elevated.[49]

The word 'transfigure,' the root word of 'Transfiguration,' indicates that Moses and Elijah were transformed into something that they were not. Moses and Elijah were flesh and blood human beings who were temporarily transformed into spirit beings to meet with Yeshua (Jesus) at the Transfiguration.

Moses was communing with God in the tabernacle tent of meeting near Mount Sinai when he was shown the glory of Messiah (Christ):

EXODUS 33:17-23 (NKJV):
So YHWH (the Lord) said to Moses, "I will also do this thing that you have spoken; for you have found grace in My sight, and I know you by name." And he said, "PLEASE SHOW ME YOUR GLORY." Then He said, "I will make all My goodness pass before you, and I will proclaim the name of YHWH (the Lord) before you. I will be gracious to whom I will be gracious, and I will have compassion on whom I will have compassion." But He said, "You cannot see My face; for no man shall see Me, and live." And YHWH (the Lord) said, "Here is a place by Me, and you shall stand on the rock. So it shall be, while My glory passes by, that I will put you in the cleft of the rock, and will cover you with My hand while I pass by. Then I will take away My hand, AND YOU SHALL SEE MY HINDER PARTS; but My face shall not be seen."

God the Father and Yeshua the Messiah (Jesus the Christ) are separately present in the verses of Exodus 33:19 and 20…

EXODUS 33:19 (NKJV) [WITH INTERPRETATION]:

Then He [GOD THE FATHER] said, "I will make all My goodness pass before you, and I will proclaim the name of YHWH (the Lord, Yeshua / Jesus) before you..."

EXODUS 33:20 (NKJV) [WITH INTERPRETATION]:

But He [GOD THE FATHER] said, "You cannot see My face; for no man shall see Me, and live."

No man can see God the Father's face and live, but Moses and Jacob did see Yeshua (Jesus), God the Son's face, as this is clear in Scripture.

GENESIS 32:30 (NKJV) [WITH INTERPRETATION]:

So Jacob called the name of the place Peniel: "For I have seen God [YESHUA / JESUS] FACE TO FACE, and my life is preserved."

EXODUS 33:11 (NKJV):

So YHWH (the Lord) spoke to Moses FACE TO FACE, as a man speaks to his friend.

Moses' spirit was TRANSPORTED IN TIME to the Transfiguration site when Moses went up God's mountain to receive the 10-Commandments. Moses was shown the hinder parts of the Messiah (Christ); what would happen to Yeshua (Jesus) in the His latter days on Earth as the Messiah (Christ) and His glory (Exodus 33:23). This passage does not mean that Moses saw Yeshua's (Jesus') backside. Moses' spirit being transported through space and time while he was in deep spiritual meditation is how Yeshua (Jesus) spoke with the VISION (not brought down from heaven appearance) of Moses on the mountain in the Transfiguration.

Elijah is transported somewhere, not to paradise, but to the transfiguration:

2 KINGS 2:1 (NKJV):

And it came to pass, when YHWH (the Lord) was about to take up Elijah into heaven by a whirlwind, that Elijah went with Elisha from Gilgal.

2 KINGS 2:11 (NKJV):

Then it happened, as they continued on and talked, that suddenly a chariot of fire appeared with horses of fire, and separated the two of them; and Elijah went up by a whirlwind into heaven.

2 KINGS 2:16 (NKJV):

Then they said to him, "Look now, there are fifty strong men with your servants. Please let them go and search for your master, lest perhaps the Spirit of YHWH (the Lord) has taken him up and cast him upon some mountain or into some valley."

The story of Elijah being taken up by a whirlwind, into heaven, should be understood in a different way than believing Elijah entered paradise. 2 Kings 2:1 and 11 must be understood to mean that Elijah was taken up, into the heavens, or clouds, which is often used in Scripture to describe the extended sky beyond Earth (Genesis 1:8).

2 Kings 2:16 further makes this evident, as it is written that it was believed that the Spirit of YHWH (the Lord) took Elijah up and cast him upon some mountain or into some valley. Elijah did not go to heaven, the dwelling place of God, as Yeshua (Jesus) declared that no man had yet done so.

JOHN 3:13 (NKJV):

"NO ONE has ascended to heaven but He who came down from heaven, that is, the Son of Man who is in heaven."

Yeshua the Messiah (Jesus the Christ), during His 3-year Messianic mission, declared that no one had yet ascended to heaven. Therefore, Moses and Elijah did not come down from heaven to speak with Him at the Transfiguration. The transfiguration was a vision, a spirit-transport communication exchange. Moses and Elijah did not descend from heaven to personally appear before Yeshua (Jesus), but were transported through time to converse with Him.

MATTHEW 17:9 (NKJV):

Now as they came down from the mountain, Yeshua (Jesus) commanded them, saying, "Tell THE VISION to no one until the Son of Man is risen from the dead."

Moses was alive at the time, on the mountain with God receiving the 10-Commandments, as he was transported in time and shown the glory of Yeshua (Jesus). Elijah was taken up by a chariot of fire into the sky and was transported at this time to the Transfiguration. God the Father transported Moses and Elijah through time, in the spirit, and they spoke in the spirit to Yeshua (Jesus) outside of the restraints of time and space.

ABSENT FROM THE BODY AND PRESENT WITH THE LORD

2 CORINTHIANS 5:8 (NKJV):

We are confident, yes, well pleased rather to be ABSENT FROM THE BODY and to be present with the Lord.

The Apostle Paul experienced being absent from his body to be present with the Lord. Moses and Elijah were absent from their bodies and were supernaturally transported by God through space and time to be present with Yeshua (Jesus) at the Transfiguration.

WHAT WAS THE PURPOSE AND MEANING OF THE TRANSFIGURATION?

There are some who proclaim that the appearance of Moses and Elijah symbolically represented the Law and the Prophets. They say, "God the Father's voice was heard from heaven saying, 'Listen to Him!' clearly showing that the Law and the Prophets must give way to Jesus."[50]

Lawless-minded Christians never seem to miss an opportunity to take a Scripture incident and use it to promote the idea of the law being done away with! Yeshua (Jesus) never said that the Law and the Prophets must give way to Him. He didn't come to destroy the Law or the Prophets (or make the Law and the Prophets 'give way' to Him). He didn't come to destroy the Law, but did come to fulfill the Scripture prophecies about Him written by the Prophets (Matthew 5:17-19).

The purpose of the Transfiguration was to support Yeshua (Jesus) in the task that He was about to undergo: His suffering and crucifixion at the hands of evil men for the salvation of mankind. Moses and Elijah were two of His most beloved prophets who visited Him in His time of grief to encourage Him for what He was suffering and dying for.

DID ANGELS MARRY AND CROSSBREED WITH HUMAN WOMEN (GEN. 6:1-4) ?

By George Lujack

Many have assumed by a passive reading of Genesis 6:1-4, that the sons of God were angels who came down from heaven, married human women, and had crossbred hybrid children with them known as the Nephilim. This article will examine the verses pertaining to the Nephilim (giants) and conclude that the sons of God were not literally angels who married and had children with human women.

GENESIS 6:1-4 (NKJV) (HSV†):

Now it came to pass, when men began to multiply on the face of the earth, and daughters were born to them, that the sons of God saw the daughters of men, that they were beautiful; and they took wives for themselves of all whom they chose.

And YHWH (the Lord) said, "My Spirit shall not strive with man forever, for he is indeed flesh; yet his days shall be one hundred and twenty years." The giants (†Nephilim) were on the earth in those days, and also afterward, when the sons of God came in to the daughters of men and they bore children to them. Those were the mighty men who were of old, men of renown.

Men of giant physical stature lived both before and after the global flood (Genesis 6:4; Deuteronomy 2:10-12, 20-23). After the flood, giants appear as descendants of Canaan, one of Ham's sons, who were living in Canaan when Moses sent agents to spy out the land (Numbers 13:1-2, 32-33).

Og, King of Bashan, was the last recorded giant east of the Jordan River (Joshua 12:4; 13:12). After Joshua's conquest of Canaan (Joshua 11:21-22), a few giants continued living in the Philistine cities of Gaza, Gath, and Ashdod. These giants terrorized Israel from the time they entered into Canaan until late in the reign of King David. One of those giants was Goliath, who was killed by David. King David and his 'mighty men' encountered three other giants (2 Samuel 21:16-22; 1 Chronicles 20:4-8).

Some claim that these giants were the offspring of angels mating with human women, based on a misunderstanding of Genesis.

Although God sometimes refers to angels as His sons (Job 38:7), the term "sons of God" in Genesis 6 is not exclusively used for angelic beings. God also refers to man as gods and sons of God.

PSALM 82:6 (NKJV):

I said, "You are gods, and all of you are children of the Most High."

JOHN 10:34 (NKJV):

Yeshua (Jesus) answered them, "Is it not written in your law, *'I said, "You are gods'*?"

ROMANS 8:14 (NKJV):

For as many as are led by the Spirit of God, these are sons of God.

GALATIANS 3:26 (NKJV):

For you are all sons of God through faith in Messiah Yeshua (Christ Jesus).

God can refer to either an angel or a human being as a "son of God."

Angels were created as spirit beings. As spirit beings, they cannot mate with humans. Humans exist in the physical realm and angels exist in the spiritual realm, which may also be another dimension.

MATTHEW 22:30; MARK 12:25; LUKE 20:34-36 (NKJV):

And Yeshua (Jesus) answered and said to them, "The sons of this age marry and are given in marriage. But those who are counted worthy to attain that age, and the resurrection from the dead, neither marry nor are given in marriage; nor can they die anymore, for they are equal to the angels AND ARE SONS OF GOD, being sons of the resurrection."

JOHN 3:6 (NKJV):

"That which is born of the flesh is flesh, and that which is born of the Spirit is spirit."

GENESIS 6:4 (NKJV) (HSV†):

There were giants (†Nephilim) on the earth IN THOSE DAYS, *and also afterward, when the sons of God came in to the daughters of men and they bore children to them. Those were the mighty men who were of old, men of renown.*

Note carefully that Genesis 6:4 does not say that the Nephilim (giants) came forth from the unions of the sons of God and women, as they were already in existence on the Earth "*in those days.*" Then after… "*and also afterward,*" they continued to be on the Earth "*when the sons of God came in to the daughters of men and they bore children to them.*" Those children were not classified as hybrids, but "*mighty 'men,' 'men' of renown.*" The Nephilim (giants) existed *before* the sons of God took women for wives *and also afterward*, when the sons of God had children with women. Therefore the Nephilim (giants) were not the hybrid offspring between angels and women as they existed before and after the sons of God appeared in Genesis.

Only the Son of God, who has all creative power, has ever crossed the gap between spirit and flesh, resulting in His birth as Yeshua Messiah (Jesus Christ) (Philippians 2:7). To claim that angels could cross the boundary between spirit beings and flesh and blood beings and mate with human women with the resulting offspring being Nephilim (giants) is not logical.

Kinds reproduce after their own kinds. The spirit-kind cannot mate and impregnate mankind. Only God has crossed that boundary through Yeshua (Jesus) taking on human flesh.

WHERE DID THE NEPHILIM (GIANTS) COME FROM?

Being that the Nephilim (giants) spoken of in Genesis 6:1-4 were men, and were not the hybrid offspring between angels and women, a question arises as to where they came from. The Nephilim (giants) were the offspring of man who sprang forth from the original gene pool variation that God created within man. All men were created from one blood (Acts 17:26), and Adam and Eve were capable of producing all the different varieties of mankind: tall (giants), short, muscular, fat, thin, dark-skinned, light-skinned, hairy, smooth-skinned, and all of the varieties in between.

Just as there are a wide variety of dogs that originated from the original dog kind, God created mankind with the same type of variation possibilities. Today, we still see diversity among human beings in various regions of the world, within the same regions, and even within the same families.[51]

Another factor that allowed for gigantism amongst human beings was the higher oxygen levels of the pre-flooded Earth. Scientists know from air encased within fossilized life forms that the Earth once had a 35% oxygen level, compared to the modern day level of about 20%. A richer oxygen content allowed for the greater growth of animals, the dinosaurs, and insects on Earth. Man, known as the Nephilim (giants), also grew to much larger proportions as a result of the higher oxygen levels that existed on the pre-flood Earth.[52]

WHO WERE THE "SONS OF GOD" OF GENESIS 6:2,4 ?

Although it is true that spirit beings cannot mate with human beings, spirit beings *can possess* human beings. When Scripture states that the "sons of God" saw the daughters of men, and they took wives for themselves, it is a figurative reference to demons possessing men, and then acting through men, taking wives, mating, and then bearing children to them. The people, before the flood, had rejected God and were under heavy demonic influence. All of mankind, including the Nephilim (giants), were wicked in the sight of God and man's thoughts were always evil. The "sons of God" of Genesis 6:2,4 represent the fallen angels who partook of a great earthly demonic possession of men. Fallen angels were possessing human beings and through these demonic-possessed men they were taking wives and bearing children.

GENESIS 6:5-8 (NKJV):
Then YHWH (the Lord) saw that the WICKEDNESS OF MAN was great in the earth, and that every intent of the thoughts of his heart was only evil continually. And YHWH (the Lord) was sorry that He had made MAN on the earth, and He was grieved in His heart. So YHWH (the Lord) said, "I will destroy MAN whom I have created from the face of the earth, both MAN and beast, creeping thing and birds of the air, for I am sorry that I have made them." But Noah found grace in the eyes of YHWH (the Lord).

God destroyed man from the face of the Earth, not hybrid angel-men. During the demonic possessions of men, men's thoughts and deeds were evil continually, and no one but righteous-living Noah found grace in God's eyes. God then decided to flood the Earth and rid it of all evil.

MATTHEW 24:37-39; LUKE 17:26-27 (NKJV):

"But as the days of Noah were, so also will the coming of the Son of Man be. For as in the days before the flood, they were eating and drinking, marrying and giving in marriage, until the day that Noah entered the ark, and did not know until the flood came and took them all away, so also will the coming of the Son of Man be."

As mankind enters the end times, many people's thoughts and deeds are continually evil, just as they were before the flood in the days of Noah. Surely there are people who are possessed by demons today, or who are under heavy demonic influence, and are bearing children and raising them in evil ways, just as evil men were possessed by demons in Genesis 6:1-4, who took women and had children with them. God destroyed the whole world and all the people in it, save the eight on Noah's ark (1 Peter 3:20). Mankind will be on the brink of annihilation just before Yeshua (Jesus) returns (Matthew 24:22).

MATTHEW 24:12-13 (NKJV):

"And because lawlessness will abound, the love of many will grow cold. But he who endures to the end shall be saved."

In these end times, lawless sin abounds and the love of many has grown cold as people have forsaken God and have rejected His commandments. To those who seek God, but are held captive by sin, being tormented and possessed by demons today: repent, fully submit to God, and resist the demons and then they will flee (Ephesians 6:10-13; 2 Timothy 2:24-26; James 4:7-8; 1 Peter 5:8-9).

He (or she) who endures in righteousness to the end, like Noah did, will be saved, as Noah and his family were saved from the flood.

THE LAW OF CLEAN AND UNCLEAN CREATURES

By George Lujack

God has declared certain creatures as clean and other creatures as unclean for human consumption. Man is an omnivorous being. God allows us to eat herbivore animals for meat and has prohibited us from eating carnivores and omnivores. Herbivores are creatures that eat only vegetables; carnivores eat only meat; and omnivores eat both plants and meat.

God's dietary laws forbid the eating of two types of creatures:

PREDATORS:

carnivorous animals that prey upon and kill other animals for food.*

SCAVENGERS:

carrion eaters that feed off carcasses of already dead creatures, fecal matter, and other refuse.

*Fish can be noted as somewhat of an exception. Most fish feed on smaller fish, which classifies them as a type of predatory carnivore in the strictest sense. All clean fish swim in schools however, and are not ambush or solitary predators.

LEVITICUS 11:46-47 (NKJV):

This is the law of the animals and the birds and every living creature that moves in the waters, and of every creature that creeps on the earth, to distinguish between the unclean and the clean, and between the animal that may be eaten and the animal that may not be eaten.

God's Dietary Commandments, after exhaustive and thorough meticulous Scripture and scientific research, are compiled and presented in the following comprehensive listing with artistic images, to make a distinction between the clean creatures that may be eaten and the unclean creatures that may not be eaten (Leviticus 11:46-47, 20:25, Ezekiel 44:23).

CLEAN CREATURES

VEGETABLES   RIPE FRUITS   NUTS   HONEY

MILK BUTTER EGGS CHEESE   GRAIN   BEEF

MUTTON   FISHES WITH FINS   VENISON   GAME, CHICKEN & TURKEY
          & SCALES
          GOAT

UNCLEAN CREATURES

BIRDS OF PREY

PORK, BACON   RABBITS, HARES   WEB-FOOTED BIRDS
& HAM   & RODENTS   & THEIR EGGS

ALL SHELL FISH

AND FISH WITHOUT BOTH SCALES & FINS   EELS, SNAILS AND ALL CREEPING THINGS
                                        THAT CRAWL, FLY OR SWIM.

Illustration image used by permission: The Ensign Message,
< http://www.ensignmessage.com/archives/pig.html >.

DIETARY COMMANDMENTS

PLANTS:

*You may eat plants that produce seed and the fruit of trees that contain tree-yielding seed.

*You shall not eat defiled plants, poisonous plants, or the toxic parts of edible plants.

*You shall not eat fungi, aquatic plants, seedless plants, or fruitless trees.

FLESH, MEAT, FAT, BLOOD, & ORGANS:

*You may eat the flesh of clean animals for meat.

*You shall not eat the flesh of unclean animals.

*You shall not eat the fat, blood, or organs of any animal.

MAMMALS:

*You may eat mammals that have cloven hooves parted in two and chew the cud.

*You shall not eat mammals that have cloven hooves parted in two, but do not chew the cud.

*You shall not eat mammals that chew the cud, but do not have cloven hooves parted in two.

*You shall not eat mammals that go on their paws, predator, or scavenger mammals.

*You shall not eat burrowing, flying, marine, marsupial, monotreme, or rodent mammals.

*You shall not eat young calves that are nursing on their mother's milk.

FISH & AQUATIC CREATURES:

*You may eat fish in the waters, seas, and rivers that have fins and overlapping, shedding scales.

*You shall not eat fish in the waters that do not have fins and overlapping, shedding scales.

*You shall not eat non-fish aquatic creatures in the waters, seas, and rivers.

BIRDS:

*You may eat birds with all of these characteristics:

    -They have craws or crops;
    -They have a gizzard with a double lining that can be easily separated;
    -They have three front toes with an elongated middle front toe and a hind toe;
    -They spread three front toes on one side of a perch and their hind toe on the other side;
    -They bring food to the ground and divide it with their bills, if possible, before eating it.

*You shall not eat aquatic, predator, raptor, ratite, or scavenger birds.

*You shall not eat eggs or young chicks together with their mother.

INSECTS:

*You may eat insects that have wings, four legs, and legs for leaping upon the earth.

*You shall not eat insects that do not have wings, four legs, and legs for leaping upon the earth.

REPTILES, AMPHIBIANS, & OTHER CREATURES:

*You shall not eat creatures that crawl, creep, slither, or are multi-legged.

DEAD & DISEASED:

*You shall not eat anything that dies of itself, is infected with disease, or is torn by beasts.

CONTAMINATED:

*You shall not eat anything that has been contaminated with anything unclean.

LIQUIDS:

*You may drink fruit and vegetable juice, milk, honey, and alcohol.

*You shall not drink alcohol to get drunk, when operating machinery, or during pregnancy.

*You shall not drink the blood of any creature.

*You shall not drink liquids that have been contaminated with anything unclean.

DIETARY COMMANDMENTS (WITH REFERENCES)

PLANTS:

*You may eat plants that produce seed and the fruit of trees that contain tree-yielding seed.

    GENESIS 1:29, 3:18, 9:3; LEVITICUS 19:25; DEUTERONOMY 14:23;
    PROVERBS 24:13, 25:16,27; ISAIAH 7:15,22, 30:23, 55:10; EZEKIEL 14:23.

*You shall not eat defiled plants, poisonous plants, or the toxic parts of edible plants.

    GENESIS 3:17-18; LEVITICUS 19:19, DEUTERONOMY 22:9.

*You shall not eat fungi, aquatic plants, seedless plants, or fruitless trees.

    GENESIS 1:29; AMOS 4:9; HAGGAI 2:17.

FLESH, MEAT, FAT, BLOOD, & ORGANS:

*You may eat the flesh of clean animals for meat.

    FLESH: EXODUS 12:8,46, 29:31-33; LEVITICUS 7:15, 8:31; NUMBERS 18:15-18,
    1 KINGS 19:21.
    MEAT: EXODUS 16:8,12; NUMBERS 11:4,13,18,21,33; DEUTERONOMY 12:15,20,23,27;
    1 SAMUEL 2:13-15, 25:11; 2 SAMUEL 6:19; 1 KINGS 17:6, 19:21; 1 CHRONICLES 16:3;
    JOB 31:31; PSALM 78:20,27; PROVERBS 9:2, 23:20; ISAIAH 22:13, 44:16,19; JEREMIAH 7:21;
    DANIEL 10:3; ROMANS 14:21; 1 CORINTHIANS 8:13.

*You shall not eat the flesh of unclean animals.

    LEVITICUS 11:8,11; DEUTERONOMY 14:8.

*You shall not eat the fat, blood, or organs of any animal.

    GENESIS 9:4; LEVITICUS 3:17, 7:22-27, 17:10-14, 19:26; DEUTERONOMY 12:16,23-25;
    15:23; 1 SAMUEL 14:32-34; EZEKIEL 33:25; ACTS 15:20,29; 21:25.
    *The following references indicate that fat, blood, and organs were not to used for food, but were to
    be used for offerings and sacrifices, then afterward discarded:
    GENESIS 4:4, EXODUS 23:18, 29:13-25;
    LEVITICUS 1- 4, 6:8-30, 7, 8:14-30, 9, 10:12-20, 16:14-27, 17:6-11; NUMBERS 18:17; 19:1-5;
    DEUTERONOMY 12:27; 1 SAMUEL 2:15-16; 1 KINGS 8:64; 2 KINGS 16:13-15;
    2 CHRONICLES 7:7, 29:21-35, 30:16, 35:11-14.

MAMMALS:

*You may eat mammals that have cloven hooves parted in two and chew the cud.

LEVITICUS 11:3; DEUTERONOMY 14:6.

*You shall not eat mammals that have cloven hooves parted in two, but do not chew the cud.

LEVITICUS 11:7, 26; DEUTERONOMY 14:8; ISAIAH 65:4, 66:17.

*You shall not eat mammals that chew the cud, but do not have cloven hooves parted in two.

LEVITICUS 11:4-6; DEUTERONOMY 14:7.

*You shall not eat mammals that go on their paws, predator, or scavenger mammals.

LEVITICUS 11:27.

*You shall not eat burrowing, flying, marine, marsupial, monotreme, or rodent mammals.

LEVITICUS 11:19, 29-30.

*You shall not eat young calves that are nursing on their mother's milk.

EXODUS 23:19, 34:26; DEUTERONOMY 14:21.

FISH & AQUATIC CREATURES:

*You may eat fish in the waters, seas, and rivers that have fins and overlapping, shedding scales.

LEVITICUS 11:9; DEUTERONOMY 14:9.

*You shall not eat fish in the waters that do not have fins and overlapping, shedding scales.

LEVITICUS 11:10-12; DEUTERONOMY 14:10; ISAIAH 65:4, 66:17.

*You shall not eat non-fish aquatic creatures in the waters, seas, and rivers.

LEVITICUS 11:10-12; DEUTERONOMY 14:10; ISAIAH 65:4, 66:17.

BIRDS:

*You may eat birds with all of these characteristics:

-They have craws or crops;

-They have a gizzard with a double lining that can be easily separated;

-They have three front toes with an elongated middle front toe and a hind toe;

-They spread three front toes on one side of a perch and their hind toe on the other side;

-They bring food to the ground and divide it with their bills, if possible, before eating it.

*DEUTERONOMY 14:11.

*(Based on characteristics of Scripture's known clean birds: chicken, dove (turtledove), pigeon, and quail: LEVITICUS 1:14-17, 12:8, 14:22, 15:14-15; PSALM 105:40; MATTHEW 3:16, 21:12, 23:37; MARK 1:10, 11:15; LUKE 2:24, 3:22, 13:34; JOHN 1:32, 2:14-16).

*You shall not eat aquatic, predator, raptor, ratite, or scavenger birds.

LEVITICUS 11:13-17,20; DEUTERONOMY 14:12-16,19; JOB 39:13-17;
LAMENTATIONS 4:3; REVELATION 18:2.

*You shall not eat eggs or young chicks together with their mother.

DEUTERONOMY 22:6-7.

INSECTS:

*You may eat insects that have wings, four legs, and legs for leaping upon the earth.

    LEVITICUS 11:21-22.

*You shall not eat insects that do not have wings, four legs, and legs for leaping upon the earth.

    LEVITICUS 11:23.

REPTILES, AMPHIBIANS, & OTHER CREATURES:

*You shall not eat creatures that crawl, creep, slither, or are multi-legged.

    LEVITICUS 11:29-31, 41- 44; MATTHEW 7:10; LUKE 11:11-12.

DEAD & DISEASED:

*You shall not eat anything that dies of itself, is infected with disease, or is torn by beasts.

    EXODUS 22:31; LEVITICUS 7:24, 11:39-40, 17:15-16, 22:4,8; DEUTERONOMY 14:21; EZEKIEL 4:14, 44:31; AMOS 4:9.

CONTAMINATED:

*You shall not eat anything that has been contaminated with anything unclean.

    LEVITICUS 6:28, 7:19, 11:31-38.

LIQUIDS:

*You may drink fruit and vegetable juice, milk, honey, and alcohol.

    GENESIS 1:29, 3:18, 9:3; DEUTERONOMY 14:23,26; PROVERBS 24:13, 25:16,27, 27:27; ECCLESIASTES 9:7, 10:19; SONG OF SOLOMON 5:1; ISAIAH 7:15,22, 28:9, 55:1; 1 TIMOTHY 5:23.

*You shall not drink alcohol to get drunk, when operating machinery, or during pregnancy.

    DEUTERONOMY 21:20; JOB 12:25; PSALM 107:27; PROVERBS 20:1, 23:20-21,29-35; ECCLESIASTES 10:17; ISAIAH 19:14, 28:1-3, 7-8; JEREMIAH 23:9; NAHUM 1:10; HABAKKUK 2:15; LUKE 21:34; ROMANS 13:13; 1 CORINTHIANS 5:11, 6:10; GALATIANS 5:21; EPHESIANS 5:18; 1 THESSALONIANS 5:6-7; 1 TIMOTHY 3:3,8; TITUS 1:7, 2:3; 1 PETER 4:3.

*You shall not drink the blood of any creature.

    LEVITICUS 7:26-27, 17:10-14, 19:26; DEUTERONOMY 12:16, 23-25.

*You shall not drink liquids that have been contaminated with anything unclean.

    EXODUS 7:18-24, 15:23; LEVITICUS 11:33-34; DEUTERONOMY 23:12-13.

"DIETARY COMMANDMENTS," Inspired by Scripture, composed and presented by George Lujack.

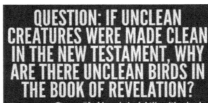

QUESTION: IF UNCLEAN CREATURES WERE MADE CLEAN IN THE NEW TESTAMENT, WHY ARE THERE UNCLEAN BIRDS IN THE BOOK OF REVELATION?

"And he cried mightily with a loud voice, saying, 'Babylon the great is fallen, is fallen, and has become a dwelling place of demons, a prison for every foul spirit, and a cage for every UNCLEAN AND HATED BIRD!'"
-Revelation 18:2

GOD'S DIETARY COMMANDS: CEREMONIAL OR PERPETUAL?

By George Lujack

Many Christians proclaim that God's dietary laws were temporary, as were God's offering and sacrificial laws. The doctrinal belief is that God's Dietary Commandments were ceremonial laws that were rescinded after Yeshua (Jesus) died on the cross. When God's dietary commands are read in context, they have nothing to do with ceremonies; they deal strictly with cleanliness and health. God's dietary commands were not issued as temporary restrictions, but as perpetual commands. Our bodies were created for optimal operation through following the Master Designer's dietary laws outlined primarily in Genesis 1:29, Leviticus 11, and Deuteronomy 14.

The word 'ceremonial' and the phrase 'ceremonially clean and unclean animals' do not appear anywhere in Scripture, yet many bibles have headnotes preceding Leviticus 11 and Deuteronomy 14 that read, "Ceremonially Clean and Unclean Animals." These added headnotes are not Scripture, but instead are an inserted false doctrinal teaching of man.

If God's dietary laws concerning clean and unclean animals were temporary in nature, as were God's animal sacrifice and offering measures, the Scriptures would clearly state so. God's dietary laws have always been in effect and have never been rescinded. The traditional dietary teachings of Catholicism and Protestantism have proclaimed that unclean animals were merely ceremonially unclean. There is nothing 'ceremonial' about clean and unclean creatures. These types of misleading statements render the word of God of no effect through tradition and false teaching (Matthew 15:6).

Many Christians proclaim that these dietary laws are of the 'old Mosaic law' of restrictions and were not meant to be permanent. The truth is that God's Dietary Commandments are perpetual and are no more ceremonial or restrictive than are His Ten Commandments.

The distinction between clean and unclean animals is first recorded in Genesis 7:2-3 and lastly in Revelation 18:2; from the first book to the last book of the Scriptures.

LEVITICUS 3:17 (NKJV):

It shall be a PERPETUAL STATUTE for your generations throughout all your dwellings, that you shall eat neither fat nor blood.

<u>LEVITICUS 11:10-11 (NKJV)</u>:

Anything in the seas or the rivers that do not have fins and scales, of the swarming creatures in the waters and of the living creatures that are in the waters, is an abomination to you. They SHALL BE an abomination to you; of their flesh you shall not eat and their carcasses you shall have in abomination.

Scripture does not support the false doctrinal belief that God's Dietary Commandments are ceremonial or that they were temporary restrictions. Leviticus 3:17 and 11:10-11 confirm that God's Dietary Commandments are not temporary, but *PERPETUAL* and they *SHALL BE* (remain, stay) in effect.

CAN WE EAT ALL MOVING THINGS? (GENESIS 9:3)

By George Lujack

Noah, when he disembarked from the ark after the great flood, was told that he could eat all moving things. Many have used this verse to justify eating all creatures, clean and unclean, and to disregard God's dietary commands concerning clean and unclean creatures listed in Leviticus 11 and Deuteronomy 14. This article will address and clarify Genesis 9:3.

GENESIS 9:3 (NKJV):

Every moving thing that lives shall be food for you. I have given you all things, even as the green herbs.

Genesis 9:3 cannot be taken literally to mean that man can eat all moving creatures. There are some creatures that can kill us if consumed and some creatures are lethal even just by touching them. Every moving creature that God has ever created is not food for man.

The true meaning and proper interpretation of what Moses wrote here, as directed by God, is that God has given mankind every *kind* of *clean* moving thing to eat. Among the moving things of the Earth, God has given us clean mammals, clean fowl, clean fish, and clean insects, just *as* He has given us green herbs for food. How has God given us green herbs to eat? God allows us to eat certain green herbs, but not all of them.

GENESIS 1:29 (NKJV):

And God said, "See, I have given you every herb *that yields seed* which is on the face of all the earth…"

Every type of moving thing is not meant for food, just as every type of green herb is not meant for food. Man is not permitted to eat non-seed bearing herbs.

LOST IN TRANSLATION

The phrase, 'moving thing' is translated from the Hebrew word 'reh'mes,' which refers to only specific types of animals that are preyed upon, or clean animals. Therefore, Genesis 9:3 should more correctly be interpreted to read, "Every clean moving thing that lives shall be food for you…"[53]

A question arises… If God's laws were already in place and are eternal, including His dietary laws, then why did Noah suddenly need permission to eat clean animals?

The answer is that Noah and his family were temporarily restricted from eating clean animals while on the ark, for the purpose of animal preservation, so that the clean animals would not become extinct.

GENESIS 6:21 (NKJV):

And you shall take FOR YOURSELF of all food that is eaten, and you shall gather it to yourself; and IT SHALL BE FOOD FOR YOU and for them.

Grain and other vegetation were gathered, stored on the ark, and used for food. When read in proper context, God restricted Noah and his family, and the animals on the ark, from eating other animals. God's declaration in Genesis 9:3 lifted the temporary restriction from eating living creatures that He placed upon Noah and his family while they were on the ark during the worldwide flood. When Noah and his family got off the ark, God removed the restriction that He issued in Genesis 6:21 and once again gave Noah and his family permission to eat every moving thing that they had eaten before.

There are those who wish to use this one Scripture verse as a license to eat whatever they desire. To understand Scripture correctly, we must compare verse upon verse, precept upon precept, and read Scripture in context to get a complete understanding (Isaiah 28:9-14). One verse should not be used to overturn and nullify numerous other verses in Scripture that clearly command what man can and cannot eat.

SEVENTH DAY ADVENTIST VEGETARIAN BELIEF

Seventh Day Adventists have argued that man was originally only permitted to eat vegetation and that *after* the flood God gave man animals to eat, thus Seventh Day Adventists promote vegetarianism, as they have concluded man's lifespan began to decline after meat was introduced into his diet. There are a few things wrong with this weak SDA doctrinal belief (Romans 14:2).

God originally gave man, as well as all living creatures, plants and fruits to eat that were *as nutritionally beneficial* as eating meat (Genesis 1:29-30). God was compelled to punish man for sin, for our sake, and cursed the ground (Genesis 3:17-19). Before the curse, plants likely had other nutritional benefits, such as higher protein levels, than they did after the curse was implemented. After the implementation of the curse, God gave man every type of living creature to eat as He had originally given us the green seed-bearing herbs and seed-bearing fruit from trees (Genesis 9:3). Cain raised sheep indicating that sheep were used for food before the great flood of Noah (Genesis 4:2).

EATERS OF "ALL" THINGS

Many Christians argue that Genesis 9:3 meant that God created all things to be eaten and that God's Dietary Commandments, given in Leviticus 11 and Deuteronomy 14, were a type of temporary restrictive law. Thus, they further perpetuate the false teaching that God's dietary laws were temporary and possibly some type of punishment imposed *only* upon the people of Israel, and erroneously believe all moving creatures were originally blessed and created by God to be consumed as food.

To those who insist on the interpretation of Genesis 9:3 to mean that God allows man to eat *all* moving things, including unclean creatures, this viewpoint can easily be dismissed. No person actually really believes that he or she can eat *all* moving things.

The faith in 'eating all moving things' can easily be put to the test by asking anyone who proclaims to believe this to eat some of the many moving things, of "all moving things," that they claim God allows man to eat such as mice, rats, roaches, skunks, slugs, toads, and worms. "Oh," they will protest, "God didn't mean for us to eat *those* moving things, but pork and shellfish are OK." Thus these "eaters of 'all' moving things" nullify God's dietary commands found in Leviticus 11 and Deuteronomy 14 while determining for themselves what moving things they will or will not eat, but they will not actually eat *all* moving things. The incorrect Genesis 9:3 interpretation of "*every moving thing* shall be food," in application and practice, then actually becomes "every moving thing *that I decide to eat* shall be food."

All moving things are not food for man.

CAN WE EAT ALL THINGS?
(1 TIMOTHY 4:1-5)

By George Lujack

We may eat the meat of every clean sanctified creature of God. God never sanctified the flesh of unclean creatures as 'food' or 'meat.' We therefore cannot sanctify through prayer that which is not sanctified as food or meat by the word of God. This article will discuss 1 Timothy 4 and the practice of prayer over food.

1 TIMOTHY 4:1-5 (NKJV):

Now the Spirit speaks expressly, that in the latter times some shall depart from the faith, giving heed to seducing spirits, and doctrines of devils. Speaking lies in hypocrisy; having their conscience seared with a hot iron; Forbidding to marry, and commanding to abstain from meats, which God created to be received with thanksgiving of them which believe and know the truth. For every creature of God is good and nothing to be refused if it be received with thanksgiving. For it is sanctified by the word of God and prayer.

Many cite the 1 Timothy 4:1-5 verses as proof that the Scriptures have no restrictions on eating unclean meats and twist these verses to say that they refer to Messianics and Christians who teach against eating unclean creatures. The misguided desire of some people to eat unclean creatures is so strong, that they actually accuse people who refer to God's Dietary Commandments, *as recorded in Scripture*, as "doctrines of devils" and those who adhere to them as persons who have "departed from the faith!"

1 Timothy 4:1-5 is a prophetic verse that was written concerning the "latter times." The Catholic Church and many of her sister churches that follow her lead have fulfilled this prophecy. They have departed from true Messianic Christian faith and have instituted their own doctrines including, but not limited to, imposing celibacy on their priests and nuns (forbidding to marry) and commanding to abstain from eating meat on Fridays and throughout their traditional Lent season (commanding to abstain from meats).[54] "Speaking lies in hypocrisy and having their conscience seared with a hot iron," is a reference to pedophile priests and those who have lied and covered up for their crimes within the Catholic Church system.

Those who "believe and know the truth" know that God does not impose celibacy upon those who preach His message (1 Corinthians 9:5; Timothy 3:1-5, 8-13) and also know that God does not require abstaining from meats on certain days, holidays, or any other traditional Christian period. The imposition of celibacy and commandments to abstain from meats are not doctrines of God, but are in fact the doctrines of devils.

"Every creature of God is good and not to be refused *if* it be received with thanksgiving." Since God did not sanctify unclean creatures to be eaten *with thanksgiving,* this verse refers to every clean creature. Unclean creatures are not considered food. The creatures that are to be received, having been "sanctified by the word of God," can be found in Leviticus 11 and Deuteronomy 14. YHWH (the Lord) instructs us to sanctify ourselves and to not defile ourselves by eating that which is unclean (Leviticus 11:44).

Here is a clearer (interpretation / translation) of 1 TIMOTHY 4:1-5:

1 TIMOTHY 4:1-5 (NKJV) [WITH INTERPRETATION]:

Now the Spirit spoke expressly [THE SPIRIT OF GOD WHO SPOKE CLEARLY TO THE APOSTLE PAUL], that in the latter times [THE END TIMES] some shall depart from the faith [CATHOLICS, HER DAUGHTER PROTESTANT CHURCHES AND OTHER FORMER FAITH-BASED CHRISTIANS], giving heed to seducing spirits [OBEYING / WORSHIPING APPARITIONS OF MARY – WHICH ARE DEMONIC SPIRITS IN DISGUISE], and doctrines of devils [MAN-MADE CATHOLIC / PROTESTANT DOCTRINES]; Speaking lies in hypocrisy [COVERING UP SEX SCANDALS WITHIN THE CATHOLIC CHURCHES WHILE HYPOCRITICALLY PREACHING AGAINST SEXUAL SINS]; having their conscience seared with a hot iron [COMMITTING ABOMINABLE SEXUAL ABUSE ACTS OF HOMOSEXUAL PEDOPHILIA WITHOUT ANY GUILTY CONSCIENCE AT ALL]; Forbidding to marry [CATHOLIC PRIESTS AND NUNS ARE FORBIDDEN TO MARRY], and commanding to abstain from meats [MEATLESS FRIDAYS AND LENT DOCTRINES], which God has created to be received with thanksgiving of them which believe and know the truth [TRUE KNOWLEDGEABLE MESSIANICS, CHRISTIANS, AND OTHERS WHO DON'T PRACTICE FALSE PIETY BY ONLY EATING FISH ON FRIDAYS AND ABSTAINING FROM MEAT DURING LENT. CATHOLICS AND CHRISTIANS WHO ENGAGE IN SUCH PRACTICES AS 'MEATLESS FRIDAYS' AND 'FASTING OF MEATS' AS SELF-IMPOSED SACRIFICES FOR MESSIAH, ARE AN INSULT TO MESSIAH. MESSIAH PAID THE PENALTY FOR ALL SINS FOR ALL TIME. ALL SELF-IMPOSED SACRIFICES ARE IN VAIN]. For every creature of God is good, and nothing to be refused, if it be received with thanksgiving: For it is sanctified by the word of God and prayer [THE WORD OF GOD, LEVITICUS 11 AND DEUTERONOMY 14, SANCTIFIES CERTAIN CREATURES AS CLEAN FOR FOOD AND DISTINGUISHES OTHERS AS BEING UNCLEAN FOR HUMAN CONSUMPTION].

Some people believe they can miraculously transform (or sanctify) unclean creatures and make them clean by praying over them. Can prayer sanctify unclean creatures? Can we pray over unclean meats, miraculously sanctify them, and then eat them? Scripture specifically warns against practicing such foolish behavior.

PROVERBS 28:9 (NKJV):

One who turns away his ear from hearing the law, even his prayer is an abomination.

Those who turn their ears from hearing God's dietary laws, their prayers to sanctify unclean creatures (before consuming them) are an abomination. This is similarly true of many Christians who have abolished God's dietary laws in their hearts and minds, and then pray to God for healing *after* acquiring diseases due to consuming unclean creatures.

God often does answer the prayers of sick Christians and blesses them with miraculous healings. Many other Christians are not always so fortunate as they acquire illnesses, suffer, and die prematurely.

ISAIAH 66:17 (NKJV):

They that sanctify themselves and purify themselves, eating swine's flesh and the abomination and the mouse, shall be consumed together, says (YHWH) the Lord.

Isaiah 66:17's warning is directed at those who think they can sanctify, purify, and then consume swine's flesh, the abomination (scale-less fish, shellfish, and other unclean sea creatures), and mice. There are misguided Christians who believe they have the power to pray, purify, and sanctify unclean creatures before eating them.

In Isaiah 66:17, the word 'mouse' is translated from the original Hebrew text meaning the 'dormouse' or the 'glis' - a small field mouse. Wealthy Romans, before the plagues of Europe, did eat mice as a delicacy. These mice were bred in captivity and kept in large jars, like goldfish, where they were fattened up on walnuts, figs, chestnuts, etc. When the mice were ready to be eaten, they were roasted and glazed with honey and sometimes poppy-seed.

People still eat mice today in some impoverished nations in Africa and Europe. Mouse meat can be found in several dishes in China and Korea, where mice are put on skewers along with lizards, scorpions, and snakes.

During these modern times it may be hard to imagine that people once consumed mice, and still do, in light of the history of the Black Death plague that devastated Europe in the 1300's. Wealthy Romans were once accustomed to eating mice, and people in parts of Africa, Europe, China, and Korea still do. In the future, some may look back on our time period and wonder how people could have regularly consumed pork and shellfish also. Eating pork, shellfish, and other unclean creatures is the primary cause of acquiring consuming diseases and plagues of our modern era.

Isaiah 66:17 specifically says that people who eat swine's flesh, abominable things (scale-less fish, shellfish, and other unclean sea creatures) and mice will be *consumed*. This verse does not mean that people eating unclean creatures will be 'consumed by the Lord' when He returns. When people acquire diseases and plagues, they are literally consumed by them. To be consumed means to be eaten as food or destroyed, ravaged or wasted away. For example, cancer consumes a person's body. Cancer cells multiply and consume healthy cells. Many of the world's consuming diseases can be avoided by following God's dietary commandments. YHWH (the Lord) commands us to not eat unclean creatures and warns that those who do consume unclean creatures will themselves be consumed (by disease) as a result of eating them.

WHAT IS FOOD?

By George Lujack

In Leviticus 11 and Deuteronomy 14, God declares which creatures are clean and unclean, making a distinction as to which creatures may be eaten for food and which creatures may not be eaten. God does not classify any unclean creature as *unclean food* or *unclean meat*, for such a classification would inappropriately allow people to consider unclean creatures as a type of food, albeit a less healthy or unclean food. It is the very definition of 'food' that confuses and causes many to stumble over God's dietary commands. Whenever the word 'food' is used in Scripture, it is a reference to clean creatures or vegetation. Unclean creatures *are not food*.

With a contextual precept knowledge and understanding that unclean creatures are never to be considered food, the following verses should not be twisted and used to justify the eating of unclean creatures:

ROMANS 14:14-23 (NKJV):

I know and am convinced by the Lord Yeshua (Jesus) that there is nothing unclean of itself; but to him who considers anything to be unclean, to him it is unclean. Yet if your brother is grieved because of your *food*, you are no longer walking in love. Do not destroy with your *food* the one for whom Messiah (Christ) died. Therefore do not let your good be spoken of as evil; for the kingdom of God is not eating and drinking, but righteousness and peace and joy in the Holy Spirit. For he who serves Messiah (Christ) in these things is acceptable to God and approved by men. Therefore let us pursue the things that make for peace and the things by which one may edify another. Do not destroy the work of God for the sake of *food*. All things indeed are pure, but it is evil for the man who eats with offense. It is good neither to eat meat nor drink wine nor do anything by which your brother stumbles or is offended or is made weak. Do you have faith? Have it to yourself before God. Happy is he who does not condemn himself in what he approves. But he who doubts is condemned if he eats, because he does not eat from faith; for whatever is not from faith is sin.

Romans 14:14-23 states that there is no *food* unclean of itself. Unclean creatures *are not food*. Unclean creatures *are unclean*, which is why they are called 'unclean' creatures. Clean creatures that are food are not unclean of themselves. These verses speak of food that was first offered to idols or pagan gods that some believers may consider to have become unclean. The Apostle Paul proclaimed that he was convinced by Yeshua (Jesus) that food does not become unclean of itself. Idols and pagan gods have no effect on food, so if someone were to bless or sacrifice food to a pagan god or idol, that food does not miraculously become cursed and unclean of itself, as a result of a pagan blessing or sacrifice.

1 CORINTHIANS 10:25-30 (NKJV):

Eat whatever is sold in the meat market, asking no questions for conscience' sake; for "the earth is the Lord's, and all its fullness." If any of those who do not believe invites you to dinner, and you desire to go, eat whatever is set before you, asking no question for conscience' sake. But if anyone says to you, "This was offered to idols," do not eat it for the sake of the one who told you, and for conscience' sake; for "the earth is the Lord's, and all its fullness." "Conscience," I say, not your own, but that of the other. For why is my liberty judged by another man's conscience? But if I partake with thanks, why am I evil spoken of for the *food* over which I give thanks?

'Meat' sold in the market does not include pork (swine) in these passages. The context of this statement refers to whatever *food* is sold in the meat market (1 Corinthians 10:30). Pork meat and other unclean creature meats *are not food*. These verses address *food* sold in the meat market that may have first been offered to idols. Idols have no effect on food, so it should not bother a believer's conscience to consume food that may have first been offered or sacrificed to an idol or a pagan god. However, some believers may think it is wrong to eat food that was first offered to idols and for their sake believers should not consume such food in the presence of their brethren if it offends them.

Should a modern-day believer eat *whatever* is sold in the meat market? If a believer is offered pork, lobster, or shrimp for dinner, the believer should politely decline to eat these creatures. Pork, lobster, shrimp, and other unclean creatures *are not food*. If someone were to say to a believer, "Eat *whatever* is in the refrigerator," logically the believer would not eat the egg cartons, ice cube trays, and milk containers. Egg cartons, ice cube trays, and milk containers *are not food*.

COLOSSIANS 2:16 (NKJV):

So let no one judge you in food or in drink, or regarding a festival or a new moon or Sabbaths...

Mainstream Christians often cite Colossians 2:16 in proclaiming that they should not be judged (rebuked) for consuming unclean creatures and state that it is wrong for anyone to use God's 'abolished' dietary laws to try to restrain them from eating whatever they desire. Modern-day mainstream Christians lack a fundamental understanding of whom Paul addressed in his Colossian epistles and the context and era in which he wrote them. Colossians 2:16, when viewed from its proper historical context and perspective, has a completely different meaning than what many modern-day mainstream Christians understand it to be.

Paul was addressing new Messianic Colossian converts who lived among the heavy influence of Babylonian, Greek, and Roman cultures (Colossians 1:1-2). The Babylonian, Greek, and Roman culture of the time, which the new Colossian converts came out of, consumed all manner of unclean creatures, celebrated pagan festivals, and observed the first-day Sunday as the Sabbath day. Paul was instructing the Colossian converts to not be concerned with those who judged (mocked / ridiculed) them in eating food and drink according to God's dietary laws (Leviticus 11; Deuteronomy 14), or regarding God's festivals (Leviticus 23), or new moon celebrations (Numbers 29:6), or the seventh-day Saturday Sabbath (Exodus 31:16).

Christianity adopted Babylonian, Greek, and Roman culture (and diet) unto itself. Colossian believers observed new moon celebrations in accordance with Scripture. Christianity does not observe new moons, so Paul was NOT addressing modern-day mainstream Christians in Colossians 2:16.

Colossians 2:16 is an applicable verse to Messianic believers who often receive judgment (mocking / ridicule) from their Christian brethren for observing God's dietary commandments found in Leviticus 11 and Deuteronomy 14.

DID PETER'S VISION HAVE ANYTHING TO DO WITH FOOD? (ACTS 10-11)

By George Lujack

ACTS 10:10-16 (NKJV):

And he became very hungry and would have eaten: but while they made ready, he fell into a trance, and saw heaven opened, and a certain vessel descending unto him, as it had been a great sheet knit at the four corners and let down to the earth. Wherein were in all manner of four-footed beasts of the earth, and wild beasts, and creeping things, and fowls of the air. And there came a voice to him, "Rise, Peter; kill and eat." But Peter said, "Not so Lord; for I have never eaten any thing that is common or unclean." And the voice spoke to him again a second time, "What God has cleansed do not call common." This was done thrice: and the vessel was received up again into heaven.

When taken and read out of context, many proclaim these verses instruct Peter to eat all things because God cleansed them through Messiah (Christ). The meaning of these verses is not so simplistic. Reading these verses alone and out of context are what many people like to do to justify eating anything they want, but to understand the true meaning of these verses, the whole of Acts chapter 10 through Acts chapter 11:18 needs to be read in its entirety.

Peter, having lived with Yeshua (Jesus), surely knew of God's dietary laws. Peter actually told the voice of the Lord in this vision that he would not eat and that he had never eaten anything common or unclean. After having this vision, Peter doubted the meaning of the vision and thought upon it, but did not eat any unclean creature (Acts 10:17-19, 11:8).

Although Peter was initially confused and doubted, a further reading of Acts reveals that Peter did come to understand the true meaning of the vision that God had given him. So what was it that God was instructing Peter through this vision? What did God cleanse that should no longer be called common?

Answer: the Gentile peoples.

ACTS 10:28 (NKJV):

Then he said to them, "You know how unlawful it is for a Jewish man to keep company with or associate with one of another nation. But God has shown me that I should not call *any man* common or unclean…"

ACTS 10:34-35 (NKJV):

Then Peter opened his mouth and said, "In truth I perceive that God is no respecter of persons. But in every nation *whoever* fears Him and works righteousness is accepted by Him…"

ACTS 10:43 (NKJV):

"…To him give all the prophets witness that, through His name, *whoever* believes in Him shall receive remission of sins."

ACTS 11:4-18 (NKJV):

But Peter explained it to them in order from the beginning, saying: "I was in the city of Joppa praying: and in a trance I saw a vision, A certain vessel descend, as it had been a great sheet, let down from heaven by four corners; and it came even to me: Upon which when I had fastened mine eyes, I considered, and saw four-footed beasts of the earth, and wild beasts, and creeping things, and fowls of the air. And I heard a voice saying unto me, "Rise, Peter; kill and eat." But I said, "Not so, Lord! For nothing common or unclean has at any time entered into my mouth." But the voice answered me again from heaven, "What God has cleansed, you must not call common." Now this was done three times and all were drawn up again into heaven. At that very moment, three men stood before the house where I was, having been sent to me from Caesarea. Then the Spirit told me go with them, doubting nothing. Moreover these six brethren accompanied me, and we entered into the man's house. And he showed us how he had seen an angel in his house, which stood and said unto him, 'Send men to Joppa, and call for Simon, whose surname is Peter, who shall tell you words by which you and all your household will be saved.' And as I began to speak, the Holy Spirit fell on them, as on us at the beginning.

Then I remembered the word of the Lord, how that he said, "John indeed baptized with water; but you shall be baptized with the Holy Spirit." If then God gave them the same gift as He gave us, when we believed on the Lord Yeshua Messiah (Jesus Christ), who was I that I could withstand God? When they heard these things, they became silent; and they glorified God, saying, "THEN GOD HAS ALSO GRANTED TO THE GENTILES REPENTANCE TO LIFE."

Peter's fellow apostles and brethren, circumcised Jews who had become Messianic believers, confronted him for meeting with Cornelius and the two other uncircumcised men with him:

ACTS 11:2-3 (NKJV):

And when Peter came up to Jerusalem, those of the circumcision contended with him, saying, "You went into the houses of uncircumcised men and ate with them!"

The Lord's vision to Peter used unclean creatures as a metaphor for the Gentile peoples of the world. Peter understood that the meaning of the vision was to meet with Cornelius, a Roman centurion and a God-fearing righteous man, and two other men. Peter was not to treat Gentiles as common or unclean persons anymore, as was the Jewish custom. This Jewish tradition was based on Scripture, as non-Jews or non-believers of the Hebrew God were referred to as unclean persons.

God separated the Israelites from the Gentile peoples through the circumcision covenant (Genesis 17:10-14).

Deuteronomy 12:15 and 22 further illustrate that God, in the Tanakh (Old Testament), referenced Israelite people as 'clean,' and non-Israelite Gentile people as 'unclean.'

DEUTERONOMY 12:15,22 (NKJV) [WITH INTERPRETATION]:

Just as the gazelle or the hart is eaten, so you [ISRAEL] may eat of it; *the unclean* **[GENTILE]** *and the clean* **[HEBREW] may eat of it.**

Yeshua Messiah (Jesus Christ), through His perfect unblemished sacrifice, cleansed all of the uncircumcised Gentile races, as well as the Jews, to be forgiven of their sins through repentance and belief in Him (Acts 11:18).

God used unclean creatures as a metaphor to illustrate that the uncircumcised Gentile races, who were once considered unclean, were no longer unclean. There is no longer any ethnicity or race of people that should be considered unclean.

When read in its complete and proper context, it is clear to see that the vision given to Peter in Acts 10 has nothing to do with eating unclean creatures. Peter never ate anything unclean during his life and did not eat anything unclean as a result of receiving this vision, even though he was very hungry (Acts 10:10). Peter spent years with Yeshua (Jesus) and knew God's dietary laws and wasn't about to start breaking them.

The Lord's vision to Peter did not mean that He died on the cross to sanctify unclean animals. The vision meant that Peter could now meet with Gentiles to preach and teach the gospel. Peter had been previously commanded by Yeshua (Jesus) not to meet with the Gentiles…

MATTHEW 10:5-7 (NKJV):

These twelve Yeshua (Jesus) sent out and commanded them, saying: "DO NOT GO INTO THE WAY OF THE GENTILES, AND DO NOT ENTER A CITY OF THE SAMARITANS. But go rather to the lost sheep of the house of Israel. And as you go, preach, saying, 'The kingdom of heaven is at hand.'"

Upon His resurrection, Yeshua (Jesus) lifted His restriction against preaching to the Gentiles, but apparently Peter wasn't paying close attention, thus He had to remind Peter with the vision of Acts 10-11.

MATTHEW 28:18-20 (NKJV):

And Yeshua (Jesus) came and spoke to them, saying, "All authority has been given to Me in heaven and on earth. Go therefore and make disciples of ALL THE NATIONS, baptizing them in the name of the Father and of the Son and of the Holy Spirit, teaching them to observe all things that I have commanded you; and lo, I am with you always, even to the end of the age."

If a believer today was to receive a vision believed to be from God, and that vision instructed him/her to go and kill someone, well… the believer should surely not obey such a vision.

Visions do not overturn God's laws.

Peter, after having received his vision in Acts chapter 10 and his subsequent refusal to obey the vision to eat unclean creatures - choosing instead to adhere to God's dietary commands, actually confirms that God's dietary laws remain in effect.

TUNAS AND FLATFISHES: UNCLEAN

By George Lujack

Most Jewish rabbinical authorities have determined that tunas, other scombrid fish (bonito, mackerel, wahoo), and flatfishes (brill, flounder, fluke, halibut, megrim, plaice, skate, sole, and turbot) are clean kosher fish. This article will challenge that determination, arguing the case against tunas and flatfishes being classified as clean kosher fish, and will declare them UNCLEAN.

Most Jewish kosher certification authorities state that in order for a fish to be Scripturally clean and kosher, it must have fins and scales. They have ALSO determined that the types of scales that clean kosher fish must have are clenoid or cycloid scales that can be easily removed with fingers OR A KNIFE without causing damage to the skin (kaskeses) of the fish. They have ALSO determined that a fish with ANY AMOUNT of scales, even just a few minute or microscopic scales, is considered a scaled fish.

Jewish rabbinical authorities have classified tunas, other scombrid fish (bonito, mackerel, wahoo), and flatfishes (flounder, fluke, halibut, plaice, sole and turbot) as clean fish, based on the fact that these fish have some type of clenoid or cycloid scales on their bodies.

DEUTERONOMY 14:9-10 & LEVITICUS 11:9-12 (NKJV):

These you may eat of all that are in the waters: you may eat all that have fins AND SCALES. And whatever does not have fins AND SCALES you shall not eat; it is unclean for you.

LOST IN TRANSLATION

The English word 'scales' is translated from the Hebrew word 'qasqeseth' in Leviticus and Deuteronomy. Qasqeseth refers to specific types of fish scales in Hebrew. Qasqeseth means the imbricated (overlapping) scales of fish.[55]

With a Hebrew knowledge of qasqeseth-specific type fish scales, the dietary commands for clean fish translated to English should be understood as:

DEUTERONOMY 14:9-10 & LEVITICUS 11:9-12 (NKJV) [WITH INTERPRETATION]:

These you may eat of all that are in the waters: you may eat all that have fins AND [OVERLAPPING, SHEDDING] SCALES. And whatever does not have fins AND [OVERLAPPING, SHEDDING] SCALES you shall not eat; it is unclean for you.

Scripture describes scales (or something like scales), as scales that fall off by themselves.

ACTS 9:18 (NKJV):

Immediately there FELL FROM HIS EYES SOMETHING LIKE SCALES, and he received his sight at once; and he arose and was baptized.

Clean fish must have overlapping scales *that fall off by themselves*. Scales that shed and re-grow remove parasites from fish that might temporarily latch onto them. Tunas and other scombrid fish have rudimentary (undeveloped) non-overlapping scales imbedded under the surface of their skin. Flatfishes have scales imbedded in their rough skin that can only be removed with a knife and deeply imbedded non-overlapping scales underneath the surface of their skin on their bottom-side smooth bodies.

What does Scripture mean by "and scales?" Did it mean "and ANY scales," or "and scales COVERING THE BODY OF THE FISH?"

scale:
Any of the numerous plates, made of various substances resembling enamel or dentine, COVERING THE BODIES of fishes.[56]

The definition of 'scale(s),' in regards to fish, indicates that scaled fish are fish whose bodies are covered with overlapping scales. Rudimentary (undeveloped) scaled tuna (scombrid) fish and half-scaled flatfish should not be considered scaled fish. The words of Scripture "and scales," (Leviticus 11:9-12; Deuteronomy 14:9-10), should be understood to mean "and overlapping scales COVERING THE FISH," not "and ANY scales."

Many will insist that if a fish has any scales it is to be considered a clean kosher fish. Most fish have what are called 'scales' or something that resembles scales. Catfish (some) have scales in childhood, but lose them in adulthood. Catfish (some) have scutes, which are scale-like bony plates covering most of their body that are imbedded deep within their skin. Sharks have placoid scales that are made of bone and are imbedded in their skin. To say that if a fish has *any scales* or *any type of scales*, it is then a clean kosher fish is a simple statement. Catfish and sharks have scale-like structures in their skin and are rightly regarded as unclean fish. A liberal interpretation could view the bony armor plating of catfish and sharks as 'scales,' but these are not the specific, free-falling, overlapping scales that Scripture refers to in regards to clean fish.

The dietary commands were given to the Hebrews at Sinai. They were issued to them in a language and terminology that they understood at the time. Tunas and flatfishes would not be fish that these Hebrews would have considered as clean, scaled fish. These Hebrews would not have inspected fish with magnifying glasses or microscopes, which didn't exist at the time, to check for scales. They would have observed tuna as a fish without visible overlapping scales, or if they spotted the very few visible scales that a tuna possesses, they then would have viewed tuna as a fish that is primarily a scale-less, smooth-bodied skin fish. These Hebrews would have inspected flatfishes and regarded them as unclean, due to their scales not being easily removable on their rough top-side skin and being scale-less on their smooth bottom-side skin.

A bald man usually has some hair on his head. Yet, a man who is primarily bald is not considered a 'man with hair.' Likewise, a rudimentary (undeveloped) scaled tuna fish, or a half-scaled flatfish, should not be considered a 'fish with scales' by description of the Scriptural terminology.[57]

Scales help prevent fish from becoming infested with parasitic worms. Rudimentary scaled tuna fish that are primarily scale-less, smooth-bodied skin fish, or half-scaled flatfishes, are not protected from parasitic infections throughout the flesh of their bodies. Primarily scale-less fish or half-scaled fish are typically infested with parasitic worms throughout their flesh.

Clean, fully scaled fish, such as salmon, can also become prone to acquiring parasitic worm infections. However, parasitic infections in clean fish are typically restricted to their exposed areas: their gills. Parasites enter and infect the gill slit areas of clean fish, but do not penetrate their scales infecting their flesh, and generally the parasites do not work their way from the gills into the body and flesh of clean fish. The flesh of clean fish typically remains parasite-free and safe to eat. In recent times, clean fish have been raised in tight quarters to be harvested for food in commercial fish farms. Clean fish live unhealthier lives in such farms, are more prone to illness and increased parasitic worm infections, and are generally less healthy than wild caught fish. Therefore, it is preferable to purchase wild caught clean fish as the healthier choice, when possible, rather than fish harvested from commercial fish farms.

TUNA FISH

Tunas have a few small visible scales on the sides of their head and have rudimentary (undeveloped) scales imbedded under the surface of their skin throughout their body. Rudimentary scales are extremely small, almost microscopic, non-overlapping scales. Tunas are PRIMARILY a scale-less, smooth-bodied skin fish, which is why they are UNCLEAN. Tunas, as a fish that is primarily a scale-less, smooth-bodied skin fish, are often infested with parasites. Tunas do not have overlapping scales covering the vast majority of their large bodies to shield them from parasitic worms and toxins that can easily penetrate their unprotected skin.

Tunas have varying unsafe levels of mercury content, something they shouldn't have if they were a clean fish and safe for human consumption. Atlantic bluefin tuna (tuna sushi) has the highest levels of mercury of any type of tuna. Several studies have determined that mercury can cause health problems for adults, including an increased risk of cardiovascular disease and neurological disorders. Pregnant women, women who might become pregnant, and children have been advised to not consume tuna as the mercury in tuna can damage the developing nervous system of infants and children.[58] The dangerous mercury content in tuna is a red flag that indicates that there is something not quite kosher about this fish.

UNCLEAN CHARACTERISTICS OF TUNAS (SCOMBRID FISH)

Tunas and other scombrid fish (bonitos, mackerels, wahoos) are unclean because they have rudimentary (undeveloped) scales and are primarily scale-less, smooth-bodied skin fish. The unclean characteristics and features of tunas and other scombrid fish are presented as further evidence to support the viewpoint that tunas and other scombrid fish are unclean.

ENDOTHERMIC (WARM-BLOODED)

Tunas are endothermic, meaning they are warm-blooded or partially warm-blooded. Tunas can maintain a body temperature higher than that of the surrounding water. Tunas are closely related to other large endothermic, unclean billfish. Endothermic warm bloodedness is a characteristic trait that tunas share with billfish, marlins, sailfish, sharks, spearfish, swordfish, and marine mammals (dolphins, porpoises, seals, whales).

FINLETS

Tunas and other scombrid fish have finlets located on the dorsal and ventral (rear top and bottom) of their body between their dorsal and anal fins and the caudal fin. These finlets are rigid, non-retractable appendages that are somewhat crustacean-like in appearance and texture. Any fish with any kind of non-retractable fins, like sharks and whales have, should be considered unclean.

TOXICITY

Fish without scales have a higher level of toxicity in their flesh than fish with scales. Tuna and mackerel fish have varying high levels of mercury content that can cause long-term health problems for adults, pregnant women, infants and children. Pacific bluefin tunas are top predators and as such they are superb swimmers. They swim across the Pacific Ocean during their life cycles before being caught, packaged, and sold for human consumption. Pacific bluefin tunas have been contaminated with trace amounts of radioactivity acquired from the Japanese Fukushima nuclear reactor accident of March 2011 that continues to leak radiation into the Pacific Ocean to this day.[59]

FLATFISH

Flatfish (brill, flounder, fluke, halibut, megrim, plaice, skate, sole, and turbot) are similar looking, bottom dwelling, bottom feeding, half-scaled fish. The scales of flatfish are imbedded in their skin and cannot be easily removed. The top dark sides of these fish have 'rough' leathery-type scales that can only be removed with a knife. The bottom white side of the fish is typically very smooth and has very few scales, if any, or they are imbedded under their skin and cannot be removed.

All flatfishes are compressed laterally and spend most of their life lying and swimming along the bottom of the waters on their side. Lying on the seafloor makes flatfish susceptible to parasitic infection, but not all worms in the flesh of flatfish originate on the outside, through their un-scaled bottom side. As bottom feeders, flatfish eat parasites that contain worms that often will work their way through the intestines and into the flesh of these fish.

UNCLEAN CHARACTERISTICS OF FLATFISH

Flatfishes share many of the characteristics and features of other unclean creatures. The primary reason flatfish are unclean is because they do not have free-falling, overlapping fish scales covering their bodies, but have imbedded scales that can only be removed with a knife on the top side of their bodies and are smooth-bodied and scale-less on their bottom side. The unclean characteristics and features of flatfish are presented as further evidence to support the viewpoint that flatfish are unclean.

AMBUSH PREDATORS

Flatfish are ambush, lie-and-wait predators. They position themselves on the sea floor, often camouflaged, then lie, wait, and ambush their prey as they crawl or swim by. All ambush, lie-and-wait predator birds, insects, and mammals are unclean. Flatfish are ambush, lie-and-wait, predator fish that are unclean.

CAMOUFLAGE

Flatfish have the ability to camouflage their skin color to match their surroundings. Camouflage is a trait that flatfish share with unclean chameleons, cuttlefish, and octopuses.

HORIZONTAL SWIMMERS (NOT VERTICAL)

Flatfish swim in a horizontal plane, rather than in a vertical, back-up/belly-down, orientation as most other fish do. When they swim, flatfish tend to glide about an inch (2.54 cm) above the contour of the sea floor. Flatfish swim horizontally, as do unclean manta ray sharks.

SAND DWELLERS

Flatfish relax and cover themselves in sand on the sea floor to camouflage and lie in wait as ambush predators. Flatfish that 'wallow in the sand' share a similar characteristic of the unclean female swine that 'wallow in the mire.'

2 PETER 2:22 (NKJV):

"A dog returns to his own vomit," and, "a sow, having washed, to her wallowing in the mire."

SCAVENGERS

Flatfish are bottom feeders and scavengers. They eat the dead carcass remains of fish and other sea creatures that fall to or die on the sea floor. All carrion-eating scavenger birds, insects, and mammals are unclean.

STEREOSCOPIC VISION

Flatfishes have two eyes on the same side of their head that are capable of independently rotating almost 360 degrees, giving these fish depth perception and an excellent field of vision. This enables them, as a predatory fish, to more easily spot and capture prey. Most other fish have eyes located on opposite sides of their head, each eye generating an independent image. Whenever flatfish are being sold in a fish market, they are always presented belly up with their eyed-side down, because people instinctively are somewhat repulsed and will not purchase fish that have two-stereoscopic predatory eyes on the same side of their body.

All clean birds, insects, and mammals have eyes on the opposite sides of their heads. Unclean predator birds, insects, and mammals have stereoscopic binocular vision, or independently rotating eyes, enabling them to more easily spot and capture prey. Independently rotating eyes, eyes that enable flatfish to see in more than one direction at the same time, is a feature that flatfish share with unclean chameleons.

SWIMMERS (SOLITARY) THAT DO NOT GROUP IN SHOALS OR SWIM IN SCHOOLS

Flatfishes are independent solitary swimmers that do not group together and swim in schools.[60] All clean birds group together in flocks when foraging or in flight, all clean insects group together in colonies and can swarm, and all clean mammals group together in herds and can stampede. Clean fish group together in shoals and swim in schools.

YESHUA (JESUS) COMMANDS SCHOOLS OF FISH INTO NETS

LUKE 5:4-6 (NKJV):

When He had stopped speaking, He said to Simon, "Launch out into the deep and let down your nets for a catch." But Simon answered and said to Him, "Master, we have toiled all night and caught nothing; nevertheless at Your word I will let down the net." And when they had done this, they caught a great number of fish, and their net was breaking.

Bottom dwelling flatfish are not caught in fishnets, but with hooks or spears. Flatfish were not the kind of fish that Peter the fisherman, a man who never ate anything unclean, caught in his nets (Acts 10:14).

OTHER UNCLEAN OR QUESTIONABLE FISH

Groupers and orange roughy (slimehead) are bottom-dwelling, bottom-feeding fish. Groupers have non-overlapping, snake-like, diamond-patterned imbedded scales that are not easily removable. Groupers are ambush predators and solitary swimmers that do not swim in schools. Groupers are typically infested with numerous parasites, including cestodes, copepods, digeneans, isopods, monogeneans, and nematodes.[61] Grouper and orange roughy fish have high levels of mercury and should not be consumed for these reasons. Codfish have smooth, non-overlapping, scarcely visible, oily scales and a well-developed chin barbell on their lower jaw. Barbells are a characteristic feature of unclean catfish. The Atlantic cod can change color between gray-green and reddish brown. Color changing and camouflage ability are traits of unclean creatures. Haddock fish have scales that are scarcely visible through the mucus with which their skin is coated. Codfish and haddock are bottom-feeders plagued with parasitic cod worm infestations throughout their flesh. Similar related bottom-feeding, reef-dwelling fish are bass, pollack, snapper, and whiting.

Though rare, there have been reported cases of ciguatera poisoning in humans after consuming groupers, snappers, and other large predatory reef species. Ciguatera poison is accumulated in large bottom-feeding, reef-dwelling fish through their diet of feeding on small herbivorous fish, which feed on dinoflagellates (microalgae), which is the source of the poison. Symptoms reported in poisoned people include gastrointestinal problems for up to several days and a general weakness in their arms and legs.[62]

All fish that have non-shedding, non-overlapping, diamond-patterned, or imbedded scales should be considered unclean.

CLEAN FISH

Bass, bluefish, herring, mahi mahi, mullet, salmon, snapper, and trout are among the healthiest and safest fish to eat, which are offered on many American restaurant menus. When selecting fish from a fish market, make sure they have visible, easily removable, overlapping scales.

Many believers may think that they are keeping kosher by avoiding pork and shellfish, while not realizing that many fish meals sold in fast food restaurants are some kind of unclean flatfish (in fish and chips) or tuna. Kosher-conscious believers need to put flatfish and tuna on their list of unclean creatures not to be eaten. Caution should be taken when buying fish from a fish market and inquiries made about fish type when ordering fish in restaurants.

Jewish rabbinical authority is NOT the final authority on determining clean and unclean fish. Rabbinical authorities rejected Messiah. They should not be considered infallible on the topic of kosher certification or determining clean and unclean creatures.

Rabbinical kosher-certifying authorities err in classifying tunas and flatfish as scaled clean fish in these two ways:

1. They classify tunas and other rudimentary-scaled, smooth-skinned scombrid fish as clean and kosher. Rudimentary (undeveloped) scales are tiny, non-overlapping scales of scombrid fish.

2. They classify flatfishes that are scaled on their topside and scale-less on their bottom side as clean and kosher. Flatfish have scales imbedded on their topside rough skin that are only removable with a knife.

The following recommended guidelines should be adhered to when selecting scientifically and Scripturally clean healthy fish:

CLEAN FISH HAVE FINS AND OVERLAPPING SCALES THAT ARE VISIBLE TO THE HUMAN EYE, OVERLAPPING SCALES THAT COVER THE ENTIRE BODY OF THE FISH, AND OVERLAPPING SCALES THAT FALL OFF EASILY BY THEMSELVES.*

*(WITHOUT THE USE OF A KNIFE).

DUCKS, GEESE, AND SWANS: UNCLEAN

By George Lujack

Most Jewish rabbinical authorities have determined that ducks, geese, and swans are clean kosher birds. This article will challenge that determination, arguing the case against ducks, geese, and swans being classified as clean kosher birds, and will declare them UNCLEAN.

Most Jewish kosher certification authorities state that in order for a bird to be Scripturally clean and kosher, it must not be a bird of prey (predator) or a carrion eater (scavenger). They have *also determined* that any bird not listed specifically as an unclean bird in Scripture is to be considered clean.

Jewish rabbinical authorities have classified ducks, geese, and swans as clean birds, based on the fact that these birds are not birds of prey (predators) and that they are not carrion eaters (scavengers).

LEVITICUS 11:13-19; DEUTERONOMY 14:12-18 (HSV):

These you shall not eat: the eagle and the vulture, and the black vulture, and the red kite, and the falcon, and the buzzard after their kinds, and every raven after its kind, and the ostrich, and the nighthawk, and the seagull, and the hawk after their kinds, the little owl, and the great owl, and the white owl, and the pelican, and the carrion vulture, and the fisher owl, and the stork, and the heron after its kind, and the hoopoe, and the bat.

Other translations have a somewhat different listing of unclean birds than the Halleluyah Scriptures version.

The New King James lists the eagle, vulture, buzzard, red kite, falcon, kite, raven, ostrich, short-eared owl, sea gull, hawk, little owl, screech owl, white owl, jackdaw, carrion vulture, fisher owl, stork, heron, hoopoe, and the bat as unclean birds.

The King James lists the eagle, ossifrage, ospray, glede, kite, vulture, raven, owl, night hawk, cuckoo, hawk, little owl, great owl, swan,* pelican, gier eagle, cormorant, stork, heron, lapwing, and the bat as unclean birds.

*The 'swan' is widely considered to be a mistranslation in the King James.

DEUTERONOMY 14:20 (NKJV):

You may eat all clean birds.

Scripture does not specify what clean birds may be eaten; so many Jewish rabbinical authorities have determined that any bird that is not a predatory bird of prey or a carrion-eating scavenger, and is not listed specifically as unclean, is to be considered a clean kosher bird. The conclusion that all birds not listed among the unclean fowl are assumed to be clean and kosher is erroneous.

Since Scripture merely states that we may eat all clean birds, but does not mention what those clean birds are, a little Scripture investigative study is necessary in determining the identity of clean birds.

Scripture states we are not to eat unclean birds and those *after their kind*. After their kind, in this case, would include after their kind of characteristics and features.

The characteristics and features of clean birds can be determined from the Scripturally known clean birds; namely the dove (turtledove), pigeon, and quail (Leviticus 1:14-17, 12:8, 14:22, 15:14-15; Psalm 105:40; Matthew 3:16, 21:12; Mark 1:10, 11:15; Luke 2:24, 3:22; John 1:32, 2:14-16).

The turtledove and pigeon are clean birds as they were used in sacrifices and only clean birds could be used for sacrifices (Leviticus 1:14-17, 12:8, 14:22, 15:14-15). A dove (the Holy Spirit) descended upon Yeshua (Jesus), illustrating that doves are clean birds (Matthew 3:16; Mark 1:10; Luke 3:22; John 1:32). Doves were sold along with oxen and sheep in the Israeli marketplace, further indicating that doves are clean birds (Matthew 21:12; Mark 11:15; John 2:14-16). Quails are clean birds as the Lord provided them to the Hebrews for food after the Hebrew exodus from Egypt (Psalm 105:40).

Clean birds have all of the following characteristics:
- they are foragers and are not birds of prey or scavengers
- they have craws or crops
- they have a gizzard with a double lining which can easily be separated
- they have three front toes with an elongated middle front toe and a hind toe
- they spread three front toes on one side of a perch and their hind toe on the other side
- they bring food to the ground and divide it with their bills, if possible, before eating it (whereas some unclean birds devour food in the air or press down on food with one foot to the ground and tear it with their bills)

Unclean birds lack one or more of the characteristics of clean birds. The characteristics and features of unclean birds can be determined from the list of unclean birds named in Scripture.

Unclean birds include those that are:
- birds of prey
- carrion-eating scavenger birds
- ratite birds
- web-footed or zygodactyl-footed birds
- waterfowl
- flying mammals (bats)*

*Scripture lists the bat, a winged mammal, with other unclean birds due to its ability to fly.

UNCLEAN CHARACTERISTICS OF DUCKS, GEESE, AND SWANS

The reason why ducks, geese, and swans are unclean is because they lack some of the characteristics and features of clean birds – they do not have crops, they have different body structures than clean birds do, their body fat is intertwined with their flesh, and they have webbed feet.

BILLS

Ducks, geese, and swans have round-tipped bills. Their bills are used for efficient foraging. As waterfowl their diet includes algae, crawfish, frogs, sea plants, and small fish.

Clean birds have beaks that are primarily used for eating grains, insects, and seeds.

CROPS - DO NOT HAVE

In a bird's digestive system, the crop is an expanded, muscular pouch near the gullet or throat. It is a part of the digestive tract, essentially an enlarged part of the esophagus. The crop is used to temporarily store and pre-digest food.[63] Ducks, geese, and swans do not possess a crop, do not chew their food, and swallow their food whole.

Clean birds possess a crop that aids them in slowly breaking down and digesting their food, which also produces crop milk that is used by them to feed new hatchlings. Ducks, geese, and swans do not chew their food and swallow their food whole.

FAT CONTENT

Ducks, geese, and swans have a high concentration of body fat intertwined throughout their flesh that helps keep them afloat in water and warm in cold weather climates.

LEVITICUS 3:17 (NKJV):

This shall be a perpetual statute throughout your generations in all your dwellings: you shall eat neither fat nor blood.

Due to the dispersion of fat contained within the flesh of ducks, geese, and swans, it is not possible to eat their flesh without consuming their fat.

Clean birds do not have body fat intertwined in their flesh. The fat of clean birds is confined primarily to their skin. To avoid eating the fat of clean birds, one only needs to remove the skin and discard it.

WATERFOWL CHARACTERISTICS

Ducks, geese, and swans float and glide upon water and they 'waddle' when they walk on land, as their legs are set on the sides and toward the rear of their body. They submerge themselves in water to search for and eat food.

Clean birds are land-based birds, not waterfowl.

WEBBED FEET

Ducks, geese, and swans use their webbed feet as paddles for swimming and for diving when submerging in water to search for food.

Clean birds do not have webbed feet.

THE PELICAN AND SEAGULL - TYPES OF UNCLEAN WATERFOWL

The pelican and the seagull are listed in Scripture among the unclean birds. The pelican and seagull possess webbed feet, as do ducks, geese, and swans. The pelican is a bird that glides upon the water and has a high percentage of body fat intertwined within its flesh to keep it buoyant in water, as do ducks, geese, and swans. The pelican is a similar kind of unclean bird that ducks, geese, and swans are.

Jewish rabbinical authority is NOT the final authority on determining clean and unclean birds. Rabbinical authorities rejected Messiah. They should not be considered infallible on the topic of kosher certification or determining clean and unclean creatures.

Rabbinical kosher-certifying authorities err on classifying clean birds in the following ways:

They classify ducks, geese, and swans as clean and kosher, because they are not specifically listed as unclean birds in Scripture. Ducks, geese, and swans do not have crops as clean birds do. Ducks, geese, and swans, as waterfowl, spend much of their time afloat, gliding upon the waters, having been designed to do so with a high concentration of body fat intertwined in their flesh that keeps them buoyant and insulates them from frigid waters in cold temperatures. Ducks, geese, and swans have fat that is intertwined within their flesh, making it impossible to eat these birds without consuming their greasy body fat, and that they have webbed-feet like the unclean pelican and seagull.

Kosher-conscious believers should avoid eating duck, geese, swans, and their eggs. Duck and goose pate is a spread that is commonly sold in tin cans. Foie gras is a luxury food product of duck or goose in which their liver has been fattened by force-feeding them corn through a feeding tube.

CLEAN BIRDS HAVE BEAKS AND DO NOT HAVE BILLS.

CLEAN BIRDS HAVE CROPS THAT HELP THEM TO DIGEST FOOD.

CLEAN BIRDS' FAT CONTENT IS CONCENTRATED AND CONFINED PRIMARILY IN THEIR SKIN, NOT INTERTWINED IN THEIR FLESH.

CLEAN BIRDS DO NOT GLIDE UPON WATERS.

CLEAN BIRDS DO NOT WADDLE WHEN THEY WALK.

CLEAN BIRDS DO NOT SUBMERGE THEMSELVES IN WATER TO SEARCH FOR AND EAT FOOD.

CLEAN BIRDS DO NOT HAVE WEBBED FEET.

MUSHROOMS: UNCLEAN

By George Lujack

Most Jewish rabbinical authorities have determined that mushrooms and other fungi (truffles) that are non-poisonous, non-toxic, and considered 'edible' are clean and kosher fungi. This article will challenge that determination, arguing the case against mushrooms as being classified as edible clean kosher fungi, and will declare them UNCLEAN.

Most Jewish kosher certification authorities classify mushrooms as clean and kosher, even though they acknowledge that mushrooms are not green-pigmented chlorophyll herbs, they do not use sunlight to synthesize nutrition from carbon dioxide and water (generating oxygen as a byproduct), and they do not produce plant-like seeds (they reproduce with spores). Jewish rabbinical authorities have classified 'edible' mushrooms and other fungi (truffles) as clean creatures, based on the fact that Scripture does not specifically list fungi as unclean.

GENESIS 1:29-30 (NKJV):

And God said, "See, I have given you every herb that yields seed, which is on the face of all the earth, and every tree whose fruit yields seed; to you it shall be for food. Also, to every beast of the earth, to every bird of the air, and to everything that creeps on the earth, in which there is life, I have given every green herb for food;" and it was so.

God's original command to man as to what he should eat for food is stated in Genesis 1:29-30. Adhering to a strict application of Genesis 1:29-30, it is not reasonable to conclude that God permits mushrooms to be consumed, as well as green herbs, simply because Scripture does not specifically forbid them to be eaten. There are no subsequent Scripture verses that grant permission for man to consume mushrooms or any other form of fungi.

'Clean fungi' is a contradiction-sounding oxymoronic phrase.

God, through the Scriptures, didn't specifically forbid every possible human activity that is harmful to human health. Smoking tobacco plants (cigarettes) is something that God did not specifically prohibit in Scripture, yet smoking is known to be harmful to human health, weakens the body, causes bodily diseases, and shortens people's life spans. Since smoking cigarettes is harmful to human health, it does not need to be specifically named as a prohibited activity in order to know that God does not approve of smoking.

UNCLEAN CHARACTERISTICS OF MUSHROOMS

CHLOROPHYLL-FREE

Mushrooms are growing fungi organisms with no chlorophyll, flowers, or leaves. Fungi get their nourishment from dead or living organic matter. Mushrooms are not chlorophyll-pigmented green vegetation herbs. Green herbs receive their life-sustaining energy by photosynthesizing energy from carbon dioxide, sunlight, and water. Mushrooms do not use sunlight for energy and thrive better in dark shaded areas. Mushrooms get their nutrition by feeding off dead or living plants and trees, rather than getting their nutrients from the soil. There are some varieties of mushrooms that are green in color, but any mushroom variety that is green is due to random coloration; their color is not derived from chlorophyll, as green vegetation herbs are.

INEDIBLE, POISONOUS, AND TOXIC VARIETIES ARE NUMEROUS

There are many inedible and poisonous species of mushrooms. People often get sick by having a negative digestive reaction after eating 'edible' mushrooms. Some people are highly allergic to all types of 'edible' mushrooms as well as all other types of fungi. Mushrooms can spoil easily and become poisonous or toxic if not stored and preserved properly. Based on the known mushroom varieties, a rough estimate is that 50% are inedible – that is, they can't be eaten because they are too tough to chew, 29% are considered edible, 20% are toxic and will make you sick if eaten, and 1% can kill you if consumed.[64]

Mushroom poisoning (also known as mycetism or mycetismus) refers to the harmful effects from the ingesting of toxic substances present in mushrooms. Symptoms can vary from slight stomach discomfort to death. Symptoms of mushroom poisoning can include nausea, stomach cramps, vomiting, and diarrhea (which can be bloody). Symptoms may show up right after eating mushrooms or may occur several hours later. Typically, mushroom poisonings that produce symptoms within 2-hours are less dangerous than mushroom poisonings that produce symptoms later on, after 6-hours.[65]

Picking mushrooms in a field at random and eating them is dangerous, as many varieties are poisonous or toxic. Only mushroom experts can tell which mushrooms are safe or not, and even the experts are fooled sometimes and have been known to get sick or die after having consumed the wrong type of mushrooms.[66]

PARASITES AND SCAVENGERS

Mushrooms are parasitic saprophyte scavengers. Mushrooms obtain their nutrition from metabolizing energy from dead or living plants and trees. As parasites, mushrooms feed off living plants and trees, behaving like vampire organisms, by deriving nutrients at the host plant or tree's expense. As scavengers, mushrooms feed off dead rotting plants and trees, which is their staple diet in woodland areas. Mushrooms play an important role in the breakdown, cleaning, and renewal of the forests.

SEEDLESS

Mushrooms, unlike plants that produce visible seeds, reproduce through budding and scattering microscopic spores. It can be argued that spores are the mushroom's seeds, just as man's sperm is his seed, but microscopic spores are not plant-like visible seeds. God allows man to eat every green herb that yields [VISIBLE] seed and every tree whose fruit yields [VISIBLE] seed (Genesis 1:29). When that command was given to Adam and Eve, they didn't have microscopes to judge as to whether or not spores should be considered seeds.

Adam and Eve could not have considered mushrooms as seed-bearing plants. Mushrooms are neither seed-bearing green herbs, nor fruit-bearing trees; they are spore-budding fungi.

AMOS 4:9; HAGGAI 2:17 (NKJV):

I blasted you with BLIGHT and MILDEW...

Blight and mildew, like mushrooms, are fungi. When the nation of Israel rebelled against God, He cursed their crops with blight and mildew fungi. Blight and mildew are fungi plant diseases. Fungi are referred to as a curse in Scripture, not a blessing.

Some Scripture scholars believe that the manna provided by God to the Hebrews, when they were dwelling in the desert after having fled Egypt, was a form of edible fungi. What exact type of food manna was is uncertain. Believers should not conclude that manna was edible fungi. Manna is described to be a food, like coriander seed, so it is more likely God fed the Hebrews a type of seed while they were wandering in the desert for 40-years (Exodus 16:31; Numbers 11:7). Mushrooms are not mentioned as food, nor are they mentioned at all, throughout Scripture.

MUSHROOMS ARE NOT VEGETABLES!

When dining out, and following a mushroom-free diet, it is important to note that if you order vegetable meals you may be served with mushrooms included with your vegetables. Restaurants will often include mushrooms in dishes such as vegetable omelets, vegetable fried rice, vegetable salads, etc. To ensure you are not served with a mushroom fungi-tainted meal, be sure to make it clear when ordering from a restaurant menu that you do not want mushrooms served with your veggies.

WHY ARE 'EDIBLE' MUSHROOMS UNCLEAN?

'Edible' mushrooms may not be initially as harmful as poisonous toxic mushrooms are, but their long term health effects on the human body are unknown. One can eat pork products, or shellfish, and not suffer immediate health consequences, but government and scientific studies have shown that eating these Scripturally unclean organisms is harmful to a person's long term health.

OTHER FUNGI EATEN:

Inuit and Japanese people are known to eat various forms of 'rock tripe,' which are ferns, lichens, molds, and mosses. These fungi have very little nutritional value and can be very dangerous to eat.

YEAST

Can yeast be lawfully consumed?

Consuming live active yeast would be unlawful, as this would be consuming fungi directly. It is lawful to consume products that are derived from yeast, as this is not consuming the yeast fungi, but the byproduct of yeast: bread, a baked good, or a fermented alcohol product.

Yeast is an interesting microscopic fungi organism. Yeast is an essential component in the making of bread, vinegar, and fermented alcohol drinks: beer and wine. Active yeast, when used in the baking process to leaven bread and baked goods, becomes inactive, dies, *and* dissolves.

Beer and wine are yeast-fermented alcohol products. Stronger spirits such as vodka are distilled alcohol products that do not use the yeast fermenting process to become alcohol. Brewer's yeast is used to ferment alcohol. Brewer's yeast, after fermenting alcohol for beer and wine, is strained from the finished alcohol product, discarded, and is not consumed. Yeast shares a function that honeybees do; both yeast and honeybees are unclean creatures that produce clean edible products for man to consume. Yeast leavens bread, other baked goods, and brews alcohol for beer and wine; bees make honey.

Consuming residual inactive yeast is not unlawful. People often inhale airborne yeast spores. Inhaled yeast can sometimes lead to a fungal infection if a person has a weakened immune system.[67] Bacteria are naturally present and consumed in many of the foods that we eat. Nutritionists have been studying good and bad bacteria for the human body for the past few decades. As it pertains to the human diet, the Scriptures do not command us to examine microscopic organisms. Mushrooms are visible growing fungi, not undetectable microscopic fungi, like yeast.

Consuming yeast-leavened bread, a yeast-leavened baked good, or a yeast-fermented alcohol product is the same as consuming honeybee-made honey. Yeast-leavened bread, baked goods, and fermented alcoholic beer and wine products are good to consume, as honey is good to eat (Proverbs 24:13).

Jewish rabbinical authority is NOT the final authority on determining whether or not mushrooms and other fungi (truffles) may be eaten. Rabbinical authorities rejected Messiah. They should not be considered infallible on the topic of kosher certification or determining clean and unclean creatures.

Rabbinical kosher-certifying authorities err in classifying 'edible' mushrooms and other fungi (truffles) in the following two ways:

1. They classify 'edible' mushrooms (and truffles) as clean fungi. God, through the Scriptures, did not give man permission to consume fungi.

2. They disregard the fact that 'edible' mushrooms (and truffles) are not green vegetation herbs. Mushrooms are growing, scavenger, seedless, spore-budding fungi organisms that feed off dead or living plants and trees.

NURSING CALVES (VEAL): UNCLEAN

By George Lujack

Most Jewish rabbinical authorities have an erroneous understanding of the Exodus and Deuteronomy Scripture verses concerning cooking a calf in its mother's milk, which prohibit the cooking and eating of veal meat. These verses are closely related to the mercy commands regarding the humane slaughter of animals. This article will argue the case against veal being classified as clean kosher meat and will declare veal to be UNCLEAN.

Cattle (bulls and cows) are clean animals. Veal is the meat from cattle calves that haven't yet been weaned off from nursing on milk. Veal meat products are often certified, marketed, and sold as kosher. Calves that haven't been weaned off from nursing on their mother's milk, that are being nourished by their mother's milk, and have their mother's milk 'in' them should not be cooked, nor eaten, and should be considered unclean.

EXODUS 23:19, 34:26; DEUTERONOMY 14:21 (NKJV):

Do not cook a calf in its mother's milk.

The Scripture verses regarding not cooking a calf in its mother's milk should be interpreted in the following way:

EXODUS 23:19, 34:26; DEUTERONOMY 14:21 (NKJV) [WITH INTERPRETATION]:

Do not cook [OR EAT] a calf in [THAT IS STILL FEEDING ON] its mother's milk.

NURSING CALVES

The command not to cook a calf in its mother's milk literally means not to cook a calf in (THAT HAS MILK INSIDE IT) from its mother. Milk is 'in' a calf that is nursing milk from its mother. While young mammals are still feeding on their mother's milk, we are commanded not to cook and thereby not consume them. The command equates to: Do not cook, or eat, young calves while their mother's milk is in them, or: Do not cook, or eat, young calves when they are still nursing on their mother's milk. Cattle nurse their calves during their first 6 to 8 months. It is prohibited to cook or eat a calf while it is in (nursing on) its mother's milk. Milk is inside the calf, and is being digested and used as nourishment. This would prohibit the eating of veal, as young cattle would have to be slaughtered while they are still nursing on their mother's milk. If a person cooks and consumes veal, he or she is cooking and eating a calf that literally still has its mother's milk digesting and providing nourishment inside it.

Calves should first be weaned off their mother's milk before they are slaughtered for meat and eaten. Veal meat, meat from a calf still nursing on milk, has a distinctively different texture and taste than matured beef.

SIMILAR MERCY COMMANDS

LEVITICUS 22:28 (NKJV):

Do not slaughter a cow or a sheep and its young on the same day.

DEUTERONOMY 22:6-7 (NKJV):

When you come upon a bird's nest along the way, in any tree or on the ground, with young ones or eggs, with the mother sitting on the young or on the eggs, do not take the mother with the young - let the mother go without fail and take the young for yourself, so that it might be well with you and that you have prolonged days.

The command against cooking young calves while they are nursing on their mother's milk is a command demonstrating God's mercy towards animals, similar to Leviticus 22:28 and Deuteronomy 22:6-7.

God commands us to not slaughter (and therefore eat) mammals and their offspring on the same day (Leviticus 22:28). Additionally, God prohibits us from capturing (slaughtering) a bird with her chicks or eggs, commanding us to let the mother go free (and live). This command of mercy, to let the mother bird go free (and live) and keep the chicks or eggs, comes with a promise of wellness and longevity.

VEAL: BAD

If a promise of wellness and prolonged days comes to those who obey God's mercy commands concerning animals, the alternative could be the case if those commands are ignored and violated. If a person slaughters and consumes a hen together with its eggs, or cooks and then eats a calf that is still feeding on its mother's milk (veal), and continually does this throughout his or her life, then a curse of sickness and a shortened lifespan could ensue. If sickness and shortened days could result from continually eating veal, then veal should be considered unclean.

GENESIS 18:7-8 (NKJV):

And Abraham ran to the herd, took a tender and good calf, gave it to a young man, and he hurried to prepare it. And he took curds and milk AND THE CALF, which he had prepared, and put it before them and he stood by them under the tree AS THEY ATE.

Genesis 18:7-8 shows that it is permissible to eat young calves, but it should be concluded that the calf served by Abraham was a mature young calf and had been weaned off from feeding on its mother's milk.

Messianic and others believers obeying God's dietary commands should avoid eating veal, the most common calves that are slaughtered while still nursing on milk. Cooking and eating veal is a violation of Exodus 23:19, 34:26, and Deuteronomy 14:21.

MEAT AND DAIRY PRODUCTS;
SHOULD THEY BE CONSUMED TOGETHER?

By George Lujack

A misunderstanding of Scripture verses has resulted in different dietary doctrines among Messianics, Jews, and Christians concerning meat and dairy consumption. This article will properly analyze and interpret the associated Scripture verses involved and will discuss the differing beliefs.

EXODUS 23:19, 34:26; DEUTERONOMY 14:21 (NKJV):

Do not cook a calf in its mother's milk.

GENESIS 18:7-8 (NKJV):

And Abraham ran to the herd, took a tender and good calf, gave it to a young man, and he hurried to prepare it. AND HE TOOK CURDS AND MILK AND THE CALF, which he had prepared, and put it before them and he stood by them under the tree AS THEY ATE.

MEAT AND DAIRY PRODUCT KASHRUT KOSHER RULES

Mainstream Judaism teaches that consuming meat and dairy products together is prohibited based on God's command, repeated 3-times in Scripture, to not cook a calf in its mother's milk. Rabbinical Judaism does not allow the mixing or the eating of meat and dairy products together. During the human digestive process, consumed food literally seethes or boils inside the stomach where food is saturated in digestive acid and is chemically broken down. Therefore, Rabbinical Judaism concludes that eating meat and milk-derived dairy products together is prohibited. Meat is not to be eaten or cooked with milk, butter, cheese, or any other dairy product. Meat and dairy products are not to be consumed together within a time period spanning two to four hours (the time it normally takes food to pass from the stomach).

Jewish Talmud kashrut kosher law requires households to make provisions that meat does not come into contact with dairy. A Jewish kashrut kosher household will have at least two sets of refrigerators, dishes, pots, pans, and utensils: one set for meat and one set for dairy products.

This is Jewish traditional law that far exceeds what Scripture requires. These misguided sets of rules are reminiscent of the 'washing of hands before eating' traditional law of the elders spoken of by the Pharisees and scribes. Yeshua (Jesus) explained that the doctrine requiring the washing of hands before eating was a false doctrine and commandment of men (Matthew 15:1-9; Mark 7:1-13).

MARK 7:7-8 (NKJV):

"And in vain they worship Me, teaching as doctrines the commandments of men. For laying aside the commandment of God, you hold the tradition of men, AS THE WASHING OF POTS AND CUPS, AND MANY OTHER SUCH THINGS YOU DO."

Rabbinical Judaism's doctrine of prohibiting the cooking and eating of meat and milk-derived dairy products together is an incorrect interpretation of God's command against "cooking a calf in its mother's milk," failing to cross-reference and acknowledge the Scripture verse (Genesis 18:7-8) that shows that meat and dairy may be served and consumed together. Due to this misinterpretation and basic lack of a precept upon precept comparison of Scripture, an erroneous belief prohibiting the consumption of meat and dairy products together has become a false doctrine and tradition. Jewish kashrut kosher rules forbidding the eating of meat and milk-derived dairy products together is incorrect.

MEAT WITH MILK

Scripture confirms that meat and dairy products may be consumed together as Abraham served YHWH (the Lord) and his other guests meat and dairy for a meal. Abraham served a calf together with milk and curds to YHWH (the Lord) and the two men who were with Him and they did eat (Genesis 18:7-8).

YHWH (the Lord) did not admonish Abraham for serving meat and dairy together. It is not possible that YHWH (the Lord) would eat meat and dairy together if this was a violation of God's dietary laws. If it were unlawful to eat meat and dairy together, Abraham, as well as YHWH (the Lord) and the men with Him, would be guilty of sin by violating a dietary law. Since YHWH (the Lord) did eat what Abraham served and did not rebuke Abraham for serving meat and dairy together, we can conclude that meat and dairy consumed together is permissible.

Genesis 18:7-8 is scriptural proof that meat and milk-based dairy products may be consumed together.

What then is the meaning or interpretation of what God commanded when He said to not boil (seethe) a young goat (kid) it its mother's milk (Exodus 23:19, 34:26; Deuteronomy 14:21)?

Cattle are not mothers of lambs. If one was to eat lamb and drink a glass of milk from a cow, the milk consumed did not come from the lamb's mother. Therefore, the rabbinical command and doctrine of not eating ALL meat and ALL dairy products together, from ALL mammal species, far exceeds the specific command to not eat a young mammal with its OWN MOTHER'S MILK.

PROPER INTERPRETATION

The Scripture verses regarding not cooking a calf in its mother's milk should be interpreted in the following way:

EXODUS 23:19, 34:26; DEUTERONOMY 14:21 (NKJV) [WITH INTERPRETATION]:

Do not cook a calf in [THAT IS STILL FEEDING ON] its mother's milk.

NURSING MAMMALS

The command not to boil/seethe a young goat/kid in its mother's milk literally means not to boil/seethe (COOK) a young goat/kid (CALF) in (THAT IS STILL FEEDING ON) its mother's milk. Milk is 'in' a calf that is nursing milk from its mother. All mammals nurse their newborn young, and while young mammals are still feeding on their mother's milk, we are commanded not to cook or consume them. The command equates to: Do not cook young calves while their mother's milk is in them, or: Do not cook young calves when they are still nursing on their mother's milk. Cattle nurse their calves during their first 6 to 8 months. It is prohibited to cook a calf while it is in (nursing on) its mother's milk. This would prohibit the eating of veal, where young cattle are slaughtered while they are still nursing on their mother's milk. If you cook and consume veal, you are cooking and eating a calf that literally still has its mother's milk digesting and providing nutrition inside it. Mammals should first be weaned off their mother's milk before they are slaughtered for meat and consumed.

SIMILAR MERCY COMMANDS

LEVITICUS 22:28 (NKJV):

Do not slaughter a cow or a sheep and its young on the same day.

DEUTERONOMY 22:6-7 (NKJV):

When you come upon a bird's nest along the way, in any tree or on the ground, with young ones or eggs, with the mother sitting on the young or on the eggs, do not take the mother with the young - let the mother go without fail and take the young for yourself, so that it might be well with you and that you have prolonged days.

The command against cooking young mammals while they are nursing on their mother's milk is a command demonstrating God's mercy towards animals, similar to Leviticus 22:28 and Deuteronomy 22:6-7. God commands us to not slaughter (and therefore eat) mammals and their offspring on the same day (Leviticus 22:28). Additionally, God prohibits us from capturing (slaughtering) a bird with her chicks or eggs, commanding us to let the mother go free (and live). This command of mercy, to let the mother bird go free (and live) and keep the chicks or eggs, comes with a promise of wellness and longevity.

STRANGLED ANIMALS

It is a command to abstain from eating mammals or birds with blood that have been strangled (Leviticus 19:26; 1 Samuel 14:33-34; Acts 15:20,29, 21:25). The command to avoid strangled creatures is also a mercy command. The most humane way to properly slaughter animals for their meat is to make a quick deep stroke across their neck with a clean sharp blade to drain their body of blood.

Messianic and other believers who wish to properly obey the command not to cook a calf in its mother's milk should simply avoid eating veal, the most common mammal calf that is slaughtered while still nursing on its mother's milk. Cooking and consuming veal is a violation of Exodus 23:19, 34:26 and Deuteronomy 14:21. Meat and dairy products can otherwise be consumed together. So go ahead and enjoy your cheeseburger, as long as it is grass-fed, hormone-free, lean, and low fat!

SEAWEED AND BLUE-GREEN ALGAE: UNCLEAN

By George Lujack

Many Jewish rabbinical authorities have determined that seaweed and blue-green algae are clean kosher products. This article will challenge that determination, arguing the case against seaweed and blue-green algae being classified as clean and kosher, and will declare them UNCLEAN.

Various seaweed and blue-green algae products are certified, marketed, and sold as kosher. Sea plants can be categorized into two general types: those having roots that are attached to the ocean bottom and those not having roots that simply drift about with the water. Sea plants or organisms, drifting or rooted, are unclean. Commonly eaten drifting sea plants and organisms are seaweed and blue-green algae.

Many Jewish rabbinical authorities have classified seaweed, blue-green algae, and other sea plants (kelp) as clean and kosher, based on the misnomer that these sea plants or organisms are vegetation.

GENESIS 1:29 (NKJV):
Every herb that yields SEED which is on the face of all the earth, and every tree whose fruit yields SEED; to you it shall be for food.

DEUTERONOMY 14:9-10; LEVITICUS 11:9-12 (NKJV):
These you may eat of all that are in the waters: you may eat all that have FINS AND SCALES. And WHATEVER does not have FINS AND SCALES you shall not eat; it is unclean for you.

Sea plants, sometimes referred to as sea 'vegetation,' do not yield seed and are therefore unclean (Genesis 1:29). To call algae, kelp, nori, spirulina (spiralina), carrageenan, or any 'sea-weed' a 'vegetable' is biologically incorrect or simple ignorance of marine life.

Despite their plant-like appearance, scientists do not group algae with terrestrial plants, but instead group them in differing microscopic classifications of the animal kingdom. Algae lack true roots, stems, seeds, leaves, and flowers. Algae differ from flowering plants in that they have a holdfast instead of roots, a stipe instead of a stem, and a blade or thallus instead of leaves. Without roots or internal tissues to conduct water, algae absorb minerals and gases directly from seawater through the surface of their blades. Algae (all seaweeds) are nature's water filters.

SEAWEED

Seaweeds are saltwater-dwelling marine algae. Seaweed is a name applied to almost any plantlike marine organism that is large enough to be seen with the unaided eye. Seaweeds can be found growing in underwater beds, floating on the sea surface, attached to rocks and piers, and washed up on shore.

ORIENTAL CUISINE

Seaweed is commonly used in Chinese, Japanese, and Korean salads, soups, and other dishes. Nori seaweed is used to wrap raw fish and rice for sushi. For dietary law-minded believers who eat sushi, the fish consumed should be of a clean fish, such as salmon, and it should be ordered à la carte or sashimi, without a seaweed roll or wrap.

BLUE-GREEN ALGAE

Blue-green algae, commonly known as pond scum, are microscopic plant organisms that form in warm, shallow, slow moving, or still water including ponds and lakes. Blue-green algae are scientifically known as cyanobacteria.

SNAKE OIL

Beware of snake oil salesmen who promise you health in a bottle. They peddle blue-green algae, fish liver oil, shark liver oil, and other such 'miracle' products as remedies or preventive medicine foods. Phony dietary 'health' supplements, medicines, and tonics proclaiming to treat or cure various ailments have always been promoted and sold to a scripturally uninformed and gullible public. Miraculous claims associated with any such dietary supplement product should be thoroughly researched by the consumer. Often these phony medicines contain creatures that are scripturally unclean for human consumption, thereby offsetting any dubious medicinal benefits.

Blue-green algae has been promoted to treat or cure a host of ailments, including asthma, allergies, anxiety, depression, fatigue, hypoglycemia, digestive problems, and attention deficit disorder, and even help with weight loss, improve memory and mental ability, 'detoxify' the body, and boost the immune system.

Blue-green algae can be easily contaminated with toxic substances, notably microcystins and heavy metals. The presence of blue-green algae toxins in surface waters used for drinking water sources and recreation is a public health concern. Algae blooms can be toxic to humans and sometimes kill dogs that lap up the slime. Of the more than 1500 known species, some have been reported to cause feelings of general malaise, gastroenteritis, gastrointestinal discomfort, hepatitis, and jaundice.[68]

Some blue-green algae advocates have proposed a spiritually disturbing sales pitch that humanity evolved from the sea and we all once ate blue-green algae as part of our natural diet in our primordial past. If a person believes that we were once algae-consuming fish that evolved eons ago to become oxygen-breathing humans, then perhaps blue-green algae may be a product for him or her! As for Messianics, Christians, and others who believe that God created man, and has instructed man what to eat for food via His Dietary Commandments, then blue-green algae is something to be avoided as unclean. Blue-green algae are basically pond scum peddled as a health supplement bottled in the form of capsules, pills, and powders.

Persons who have consumed blue-green algae supplements to detoxify their body have often experienced the pain and discomfort of adding toxins to it.

Seaweed and blue-green algae do not produce seed, nor do they have fins and scales, which renders them unclean (Genesis 1:29; Leviticus 11:9-12; Deuteronomy 14:9-10).

BEETLES: UNCLEAN

By George Lujack

God's Dietary Commandments make a provision for man to consume insects. This article will discuss the dietary command concerning insects, will argue that 'beetle' is an English translation error in the King James Bible, and will declare beetles UNCLEAN.

Beetles are the most widely consumed insects in the world. Insects are eaten as human food in 80% of the world's nations.[69] About 344 different species of beetles are known to be consumed as food and are usually eaten in the larvae stage.[70] The mealworm is the most commonly eaten beetle species. The larvae of the darkling beetle and the rhinoceros beetle are also commonly eaten.

The original King James Bible of 1611, which is still in print to this day, has numerous translation errors contained within its pages and one of those errors is in regard to a dietary command concerning the classification of clean and unclean insects.

LEVITICUS 11:21-22 (KJV):

Yet these may ye eat of every flying creeping thing that goeth upon all four, which have legs above their feet, to leap withal upon the earth; Even these of them ye may eat; the locust after his kind, and the bald locust after his kind, AND THE BEETLE AFTER HIS KIND, and the grasshopper after his kind.

King James Bible Only believers fail to acknowledge or understand that the King James Bible is not the infallible English version written Scriptures given to us by the inspiration of God, but is a King James commissioned translation of His inspired word into the English language.

The 'beetle' is a translation error in the King James Bible. The King James Bible insect, mistranslated 'beetle,' and all the beetles after its kind, are described as having special hind jumping legs to leap upon the earth. No species of beetle has these rear jumping legs to leap upon the earth. Beetles are not the same kind of insects that locusts, bald locusts, and grasshoppers are. Locusts, bald locusts, destroying locusts, grasshoppers, *and crickets* all have jointed legs above their feet that they use for leaping upon the earth.

The beetle error in the King James Bible was properly corrected to 'cricket' in the New King James Bible and is currently listed as cricket in most other modern English translated versions of Scripture.

LEVITICUS 11:21-22 (NKJV):

Yet these you may eat of every flying insect that creeps on all fours: those which have jointed legs above their feet with which to leap on the earth. These you may eat: the locust after its kind, the destroying locust after its kind, THE CRICKET AFTER ITS KIND, and the grasshopper after its kind.

CLEAN INSECTS MUST HAVE WINGS, FOUR LEGS, AND TWO ABOVE-BODY JOINTED SPECIALIZED HIND LEAPING LEGS.

King James Bible authorization is not the final infallible authority in classifying beetles as clean insects. The Tanakh (Old Testament) Scriptures are the inspired word of God, written in Hebrew, and were given to His chosen people - the Jews. The English-speaking people of the world are not God's chosen people. God did not inspire King James Bible translators; King James of England commissioned them. King James translators were not infallible in translating God's inspired word to the English language. With a little study using proper discernment, it is evident that 'beetle' is a mistranslation of the King James Bible and beetles are unclean insects.

ALCOHOL, COFFEE, AND TEA:
SCRIPTURALLY FORBIDDEN INTOXICANT AND STIMULANT BEVERAGES OR SCRIPTURALLY PERMITTED HEALTH DRINKS?

By George Lujack

This article will discuss the blessings and dangers of alcohol, coffee, and tea consumption and answer the question as to whether or not Scripture allows believers to consume these beverages.

WHAT ARE ALCOHOL, COFFEE, AND TEA?

alcohol:

A liquid produced through the distilling or fermentation of grains or fruit juice that is the intoxicating constituent of wine, beer, spirits, and other drinks.[71]

coffee:

A drink made from the roasted and ground beanlike seeds of a tropical shrub, served hot or iced.[72]

tea:

A drink made by infusing the dried, crushed leaves of the tea plant in boiling water.[73]

Alcohol and coffee are both derived from clean edible plant products: fruits, grains, and seeds.

GENESIS 1:29 (NKJV):
And God said, "See, I have given you every herb that yields seed which is on the face of all the earth, and every tree whose fruit yields seed; to you it shall be for food."

ALCOHOL

It is written in God's law that man is permitted to drink alcohol, but with the restriction to not drink to excess in drunkenness.

DEUTERONOMY 14:26 (NKJV):

And you shall spend that money for whatever your heart desires: for oxen or sheep, *for wine or strong drink*, for whatever your heart desires; and you shall eat there before YHWH (the Lord) your God, and you shall rejoice, you and your household.

EPHESIANS 5:18 (NKJV):

And *be not drunk* with wine, *in which there is excess*, but be filled with the Spirit.

1 TIMOTHY 5:23 (NKJV):

No longer drink only water, *but use a little wine* for your stomach's sake and your frequent infirmities.

Alcohol has been both a blessing and a curse to humanity throughout the generations. Moderate alcohol drinkers reap many benefits including a cheerful disposition and improved health. There are numerous medical studies that show moderate alcohol drinkers and even heavy drinkers outlive people who abstain from alcohol altogether.[74]

ALCOHOL MAKES THE HEART GLAD AND MERRY

There are many positive aspects of consuming alcohol. Various Scripture references refer to alcoholic wine as a drink that makes one merry, glad, and is something to drink when rejoicing (Deuteronomy 14:26; Judges 9:13; Ruth 3:7; Esther 1:10; Psalm 104:15; Ecclesiastes 9:7, 10:19).

WINE AND ALCOHOLIC DRINKS: A BLESSING FROM GOD

God provided wine and alcohol as a blessing for His people (Genesis 27:28; Deuteronomy 7:13, 11:14, 14:26, 33:28; 2 Kings 18:32; Isaiah 62:8-9, 65:8; Joel 2:19,24, 3:18; Amos 9:13-14). God likewise withheld wine from His people when He cursed their lands (Deuteronomy 28:39; Hosea 2:8-9; Joel 1:10-12; Micah 6:15; Haggai 1:11).

YESHUA (JESUS) DRANK ALCOHOLIC WINE

LUKE 7:33-34 (NKJV):

For John the Baptist came neither eating bread *nor drinking wine*, and you say, 'He has a demon.' The Son of Man has come eating *and drinking*, and you say, 'Look, a glutton *and a winebibber*, a friend of tax collectors and sinners!'

Yeshua (Jesus) stated that He ate bread and drank alcoholic wine while simultaneously pointing out the hypocrisy of His adversaries who made accusations against both Him (who drank alcohol) and John the Baptist (who did not drink alcohol) (Matthew 3:4; Mark 1:6).

The accusatory Pharisees and lawyers rejected God through Yeshua (Jesus), accusing Him of *drinking*, and they also rejected John the Baptist who *did not drink* (Luke 7:30).

Yeshua (Jesus) served wine at His last supper (Matthew 26:26-29) and He created wine at the wedding feast at Cana (John 2:1-11). Yeshua (Jesus) never got drunk.

BAPTIST TEMPERANCE DOCTRINE

During the Colonial America period, Puritans expected Christians to drink alcohol. Many Southern ministers operated stills and sold alcohol during the 1800's. Parishioners who owned stills would often tithe their alcohol and preachers would receive whiskey as part of their salary for their services.[75]

The doctrine of temperance is the belief that to serve or consume alcohol is a sin, thus requiring the believer to totally abstain from consuming alcoholic drinks altogether. As Christian theology, the doctrine prescribing a total prohibition of alcohol consumption is a relatively new American phenomenon. The American Temperance movement began to change the culture of Christianity's view of alcohol in the South. John Wesley introduced the teaching that consuming any and all alcohol is sinful in the late 1700's.

The temperance movement organized church leaders into having their congregations completely abstain from alcohol. Southern Baptists did not adopt the idea of alcohol as sin until the early 1800's. In 1896, the Southern Baptist Convention officially denounced alcohol and asked that churches excommunicate anyone who drank or sold alcohol. Up until that time, alcohol was a normal part of Southern Baptist Christian life. For the first time in Southern Baptist history, drinking alcohol was considered immoral. Baptists had decided, for societal reasons, that alcohol itself was wrong and sinful. Afterward they turned to the Scriptures to find support for their Temperance Doctrine.[76]

As Southern Baptists began to abstain from alcohol, they attempted to support their abstinence view by twisting Scripture and intentionally misreading verses. Specifically, the Baptists proclaimed that whenever Scripture spoke of the blessing of wine, it was speaking of unfermented grape juice. Thus, Southern Baptists created a new product out of thin air, 'unfermented wine,' of which there is no such product.

FERMENTED WINE OR GRAPE JUICE?

Southern Baptist teachings attempt to make the case that all wine spoken of in Scripture that Yeshua (Jesus) and the prophets drank was unfermented, non-alcoholic grape juice and that any use of fermented alcoholic wine is always condemned in Scripture. This argument does not hold up to any reasonable Scripture scrutiny.

NOAH AND LOT GOT DRUNK - Noah drank wine, got drunk, and passed out naked in his tent (Genesis 9:21). Lot became drunk on consecutive nights when his daughters served him wine to excess. Lot's daughters, after weakening their father's perception with wine, proceeded to conceive children with their father through acts of incestuous sex while Lot was drunk (Genesis 19:30-38). Noah and Lot were righteous men of Scripture in whom YHWH (the Lord) found grace (Genesis 6:8-9, 19:19). Both Noah and Lot drank wine, to the point of intoxication, indicating that it was *alcoholic* wine that they consumed. If drinking alcoholic wine was a sin, Noah and Lot would never have drank alcoholic wine at all. It is not a sin to drink alcohol, but getting drunk can be problematic - even for the righteous.

There may have been a scientific reason that Noah and Lot got drunk. They both got drunk *after* the great flood. It has been scientifically verified that the oxygen content of the pre-flood Earth was around 35% and was reduced to 20% after the flood. Noah and Lot may not have been adjusted to Earth's new oxygen-depleted atmosphere, which could have caused them to not be able to handle the alcohol amount that they had previously consumed before the flood, and they were therefore not able to remain sober and got drunk.

ALCOHOLIC WINE REQUIRES NEW WINESKINS - **Yeshua (Jesus) said, "Nor do they put new wine into old wineskins, or else the wineskins break, the wine is spilled and the wineskins are ruined. But they put new wine into new wineskins and both are preserved" (Matthew 9:17; Mark 2:22; Luke 5:37-38 - NKJV).** It is clear that (Yeshua) Jesus is speaking of alcoholic *fermenting* wine. During fermentation, to make wine alcoholic, new wine expands. If new wine were filled into old wineskins, wineskins that have already been stretched out from a previous wine fermentation procedure, the new fermentation process would stretch out the old wineskins even further and burst them. Therefore it is necessary to put new fermenting wine into new wine skins. If Yeshua (Jesus) were referring to grape juice, the fact is that it would be possible to put non-fermenting grape juice into old wineskins, since grape juice does not expand. New grape juice poured into old wineskins will not cause the old wineskins to burst. Therefore, it can only be fermenting alcoholic wine that Yeshua (Jesus) refers to when speaking of 'new wine.'

INDEED MY BELLY IS LIKE WINE THAT HAS NO VENT; IT IS READY TO BURST LIKE NEW WINESKINS (Job 32:19 - NKJV). Job is comparing his belly to new wineskins containing fermenting wine. New wineskins become 'ready to burst' after they have been expanded by wine that is fermenting inside of them.

ALCOHOL USE IN THE EARLY CHRISTIAN CHURCH - The Apostle Paul admonished the Corinthians in a letter to them, explaining that it was not proper for the church to congregate for the purpose of eating the Lord's Supper or to *drink and get drunk* inside the church of God. Paul further explains that the congregation should not eat *or drink* in the church of God, *but should do so in their own houses* (1 Corinthians 11:22). This clearly indicates that the early church used alcoholic wine.

THE ENDS: RIDDING SOCIETY OF ALCOHOL ABUSE, DON'T JUSTIFY THE MEANS: A FALSE ALCOHOL ABSTINENCE DOCTRINE

The Baptist Temperance Doctrine is a false doctrine that was perhaps started with good intentions - to eradicate alcohol abuse, but also involves issues of church control, criminalizing drinkers, and the spreading of falsehoods. The Temperance Doctrine is an evil doctrine of men, because it falsely accuses anyone who chooses to drink alcohol in moderation as being a sinner for doing so. Believers have the choice as to whether to drink responsibly or to not drink. Alcohol, when consumed in moderation, is a blessing and when consumed in excess becomes a curse. The same can be said of food, yet no Christian denomination is calling for Christians to abstain from food! Scripture does not demand alcohol abstinence, but permits alcohol consumption while giving many warnings about not drinking to excess.

VOLUNTARILY ABSTAINING FROM ALCOHOL

THE NAZIRITE VOW (NUMBERS 6:1-21). The vow of the Nazirite was a *voluntary* vow that an Israelite man or woman made to separate him or herself to YHWH (the Lord) (Numbers 6:2). It required abstaining from alcoholic drinks, as well as all grape products (Numbers 6:3-4). It was also required to let the locks of hair grow and that no razor would touch his or her head. When taking the Nazirite vow, the Nazirite was permitted to drink wine after an offering was made to YHWH (the Lord) and before beginning to abstain from alcohol (Numbers 6:20). God also decreed certain Scripture figures to be Nazirites even before they were born. Scripture's most notable figures who lived by the Nazirite vow and abstained from alcohol throughout their lives were Samson (Judges 13, 16:17) and John the Baptist (Luke 1:11-15).

NUMBERS 6:1-3 (NKJV):

Then YHWH (the Lord) spoke to Moses, saying, "Speak to the children of Israel, and say to them: 'When either a man or woman consecrates an offering to take the vow of a Nazirite, to separate himself to YHWH (the Lord), he shall separate himself from wine and similar strong drink; he shall drink neither vinegar made from wine nor vinegar made from similar drink; neither shall he drink any grape juice, nor eat fresh grapes or raisins.'"

When an Israeli man or woman made the vow of the Nazirite, he or she separated themselves to YHWH (the Lord) and it was required that they not consume wine OR grape juice. Wine and grape juice are TWO DIFFERENT DISTINCT DRINKS as Scripture verifies in Numbers 6:1-3. Wine is fermented alcoholic grape juice. Grape juice is fresh squeezed juice from grapes. There is NO SUCH THING AS UNFERMENTED WINE! That's why Scripture calls wine, 'wine' and grape juice, 'grape juice.'

Yeshua (Jesus) was born in Bethlehem and afterward moved to Nazareth, but the Scriptures do not record Him taking the vow of the Nazirite. Yeshua (Jesus) drank alcoholic wine on numerous occasions. It would be unnecessary and illogical for Yeshua (Jesus) to take the vow of the Nazirite. Yeshua Messiah (Jesus Christ) *is* the Lord, so He could not take a vow that would separate Himself unto Himself.

If God's law forbade alcohol, the Nazirite vow would be meaningless and pointless. If consuming alcohol were a sin, it would be pointless to make a vow not to drink alcohol, since one would be required already by the law of God to abstain from alcohol. Making a vow to do what is already in the law is meaningless and proves that Southern Baptist and Seventh Day Adventist alcohol prohibition teachings are wrong.

DANGERS OF ALCOHOL ABUSE

Excessive alcohol consumption has caused the ruin of many lives. Alcohol abusers negatively affect those around them and society in general. Excessive alcohol use is detrimental to health and shortens the lifespan and quality of life of the abuser.

Today there are dangers associated with consuming alcohol that did not exist for persons in the times that the Scriptures were written. Alcohol intoxicated persons pose a potential serious threat not only to themselves, but also to people all around them. Dangers involved with the consumption of alcohol in the post-Industrial Age involve the use of machinery, particularly, but not limited to the operation of motor vehicles. Approximately 37% of all automobile fatalities in the United States were alcohol-related in 2008.[77]

Alcohol abuse has many negative effects on societies. Alcohol is a contributor in birth defects, homicides, and a significant factor in most other types of crime. Heavy alcohol drinking, primarily vodka, causes an extraordinary number of deaths in Russia, where male life expectancy is about 60 years.[78]

The Alcohol Beverage Labeling Act (ABLA) is a United States federal law enacted in 1988. The act requires that labels of alcoholic beverages carry a government warning that reads:

GOVERNMENT WARNING:

(1) ACCORDING TO THE SURGEON GENERAL, WOMEN SHOULD NOT DRINK ALCOHOLIC BEVERAGES DURING PREGNACY BECAUSE OF THE RISK OF BIRTH DEFECTS.

(2) CONSUMPTION OF ALCOHOLIC BEVERAGES IMPAIRS YOUR ABILITY TO DRIVE A CAR OR OPERATE MACHINERY, AND MAY CAUSE HEALTH PROBLEMS.

Scripture warns alcohol drinkers to not linger long with wine and to stop drinking when wine begins *to move*, i.e. when a drinker begins to become intoxicated (Proverbs 23:29-35).

Alcohol drinkers who come to realize that they are alcoholics or problem drinkers, who cannot limit or control their drinking once they get started, make a wise decision in choosing to abstain from alcohol altogether.

SCRIPTURE WARNINGS AGAINST DRUNKENNESS

There are many verses in Scripture that speak of the dire consequences of excessive alcohol consumption and drunkenness. Scripture warns that consuming excess wine and strong drink causes a man to stumble (Job 12:25; Psalm 107:27; Isaiah 19:14). Wine and strong drink make a person unwise (Proverbs 20:1, 23:29-35, 26:9, 31:4-7; Isaiah 5:11,22, 28:1,7). Wine *and* harlotry can enslave a man's heart (Hosea 4:11). A lover of wine will become poor financially, physically, and spiritually (Proverbs 21:17). Believers should not have close associations with drunkards (Proverbs 23:20; 1 Corinthians 5:11-13). Drunkards will not inherit the kingdom of God (1 Corinthians 6:10, Galatians 5:21). Ultimately, drunkards pay a terrible price for alcohol abuse.

drunkard:
A person who is habitually drunk.[79]

PROVERBS 23:29-35 (NKJV):

Who has woe? Who has contentions? Who has complaints? Who has wounds without cause? Who has redness of eyes? Those who linger long at the wine. Those who go in search of mixed wine. Do not look on the wine when it is red, when it sparkles in the cup, when it swirls around smoothly; at the last it bites like a serpent, and it stings like a viper. Your eyes will see strange things, and your heart will utter perverse things. Yes, you will be like one who lies down in the midst of the sea, or like one who lies at the top of the mast, saying: "They have struck me, but I did not feel it.
When shall I wake that I may seek another drink?"

A drunkard is not someone who drinks responsibly, but is an alcoholic who is habitually drunk, has contentions, problems, wounds from falling down in drunkenness, and seeks alcohol continually.

COFFEE AND TEA

Coffee and tea are derived from plants. Coffee and tea contain a mild stimulant, caffeine, which helps keep coffee and tea drinkers alert and awake. It is the very thing that makes coffee and tea desired drinks, their caffeine content, which has given them a bad rap among some people.

Numerous studies have shown that moderate coffee and tea consumption reaps numerous health benefits, but drinking decaffeinated coffee is actually not healthy.

Seventh Day Adventist Ellen G. White and Mormon Joseph Smith both condemned the drinking of coffee and tea. There is no Scripture basis for condemning naturally caffeinated beverages such as coffee or tea, derived from seeds and leaves.

ALCOHOL AND COFFEE TOGETHER

As it turns out, new studies have shown that while drinking alcohol and coffee in moderation individually is beneficial to health, consuming them together is even more beneficial. Alcohol drinkers who drink coffee regularly reduce the incidence of Alzheimer's and liver disease that can be caused by heavy drinking.[80][81]

God has blessed man with alcohol, coffee, and tea. These beverages can be abused, as can most blessings that God has bestowed upon man. Moderation, responsibility, and self-control with consuming alcohol, coffee, and tea is the key to reaping their benefits.

GOVERNMENT WARNINGS AND SCIENTIFIC RESEARCH ON THE EFFECTS OF EATING UNCLEAN CREATURES

By George Lujack

There is ample data from numerous comprehensive studies conducted by government and scientific agencies that confirm that the dietary laws of Scripture are accurate, applicable today, and true. Consuming Scripturally unclean creatures has been shown to be harmful to human health.

HOG, PIG, PORK, SWINE

A World Health Organization press release reported that consuming processed pork products such as bacon, pork hot dogs, and sausage causes cancer.[82]

Consumption of pork causes stress and internal toxicity. Eating freshly killed pork products causes acute responses, such as inflammations of the appendix and gallbladder, biliary colics, acute intestinal catarrh, gastroenteritis with typhoid and paratyphoid symptoms, acute eczema, carbuncles, sudoriparous abscesses, and other responses. These symptoms can be observed after consuming pork products.[83]

Pork meat is infested with the microscopically small trichinae worm. Once ingested, the worm can lodge itself in the human brain, intestines, muscles, or spinal cord causing trichinosis and other health issues.[84] Consumers are advised to thoroughly cook pork before eating it, to kill all parasitic worms in the meat.[85] Even if pork is thoroughly cooked, people who consume swine are still eating dead trichinae worms.

SHELLFISH

The California Department of Public Health (CDPH) has warned consumers not to eat recreationally harvested bivalve shellfish (such as clams, mussels, or scallops) from Monterey or Santa Cruz Counties due to dangerous levels of naturally occurring domoic acid toxin that can cause illness or death. The domoic acid toxin, also known as Amnesic Shellfish Poisoning (ASP), can cause illness or death in humans. Symptoms of domoic acid poisoning can occur within 30 minutes to 24 hours after consuming toxic shellfish. In mild cases, symptoms can include abdominal cramps, diarrhea, dizziness, headache, and vomiting. Mild case symptoms are temporary and typically go away after several days. In severe cases, a person can experience troubled breathing problems, excessive bronchial secretions, cardiovascular instability, confusion, disorientation, permanent loss of short term memory, coma, or death.[86]

The Food and Drug Administration has warned people not to eat raw or partially cooked shellfish harvested from New York's Oyster Bay Harbor as they have been linked to cases of foodborne illnesses in several states. The FDA says that oysters and clams from the Long Island Harbor may be contaminated with the Vibrio parahaemolyticus bacteria that causes cramping, diarrhea, nausea, vomiting, and other symptoms.[87]

Vibrio vulnificus is a bacterium found naturally on raw oysters. While it poses no immediate threat to most healthy people and can be killed by fully cooking oysters, the bacterium can be deadly in rare cases for people with the following health conditions:

- Liver diseases (such as hepatitis and cirrhosis)
- Diabetes
- Chronic kidney disease
- Cancer (especially during active treatment)
- AIDS or HIV-positive status
- Steroid dependency (such as treatments for asthma or arthritis)
- Inflammatory bowel disease
- Stomach problems (including previous stomach surgery)
- Hemochromatosis (an iron disorder)

Source: Centers for Disease Control and Prevention

After the death of a 51-year-old man who had eaten raw oysters, the Cincinnati Health Department considered recommending that all city restaurants serving raw oysters carry a warning on their menus about the potential health risks. Vibrio vulnificus, a bacteria linked to oysters, was the suspected cause of death of the 51-year-old man. Washington Platform, the restaurant where the man ate the oysters, already had warnings against consuming shellfish on its menu.[88]

FISH WITHOUT SCALES

Tuna fish is a popular scale-less fish that has been improperly classified as a clean, kosher fish with scales. Most people eat tuna straight out of a can. As the fish has already had its skin removed, consumers are not able to inspect tuna fish for scales and are unaware that tunas do not possess overlapping, shedding scales and assume it is a Scripturally clean fish, because it has been ruled so by rabbinical authorities.

Tunas have rudimentary (undeveloped) scale-like structures beneath the surface of their skin that are not clearly visible by the human eye and a relatively few minute scales near its head. Upon inspection of a full tuna fish, most people would say that tunas are a scale-less fish. The scientific research on tunas attest to the fact that there are health risks associated with tuna consumption. Tuna fish have been misclassified as a clean fish with scales, but should be considered an unclean fish without overlapping, shedding fish scales.

Tuna fish naturally contain varying levels of mercury content that is unsafe for human consumption. Atlantic bluefin tuna (tuna sushi) has the highest levels of mercury of any type of tuna.

Several studies have determined that mercury from tuna can cause severe health problems for adults, including an increased risk of cardiovascular disease and neurological disorders.[89]

Pacific bluefin tunas have been contaminated with trace amounts of radioactivity acquired from the Japanese Fukushima nuclear reactor accident of March 2011 that continues to leak radiation into the Pacific Ocean to this day.[90]

MOSES VS. JOHN PAUL II;
THE HEALTH, LONGEVITY, AND VITALITY OF TWO SPIRITUAL TEACHERS

By George Lujack

This article will discuss the two different worldviews of two spiritual teachers and the beliefs of their respective flocks concerning God's Dietary Commandments found primarily in Leviticus 11 and Deuteronomy 14.

MOSES

Moses was one of the greatest figures and spiritual teachers in all of Scripture. His life was a testimony of obedience to God and of being the deliverer of his Hebrew people from Egyptian bondage.

GENESIS 6:3 (NKJV):
And YHWH (the Lord) said, "My Spirit shall not strive with man forever, for he is indeed flesh; yet his days shall be one hundred and twenty years."

After the great flood of Noah's time, YHWH (the Lord) shortened man's lifespan to 120-years. 120-years is the apportioned lifespan of modern man.

DEUTERONOMY 34:7 (NKJV):
Moses was one hundred and twenty years old when he died. His eyes were not dim nor his natural vigor diminished.

NUMBERS 33:39 (NKJV):
Aaron was one hundred and twenty-three years old when he died on Mount Hor.

Moses was a healthy, long-lived man of 120-years. Moses' brother Aaron lived to be 123-years-old. Moses lived and obeyed God's commandments, including God's Dietary Commandments. Moses and his followers never ate pork, shellfish, or any other unclean creature.

PSALM 105:37 (NKJV):
He also brought them out with silver and gold, and there was NONE FEEBLE among His tribes.

As the spiritual teacher and deliverer of the Hebrew nation tribes, God, via Moses, instructed the Hebrews concerning God's Dietary Commandments. As a result of obedience to His dietary commands, there was not one feeble person, NOT ONE, among the twelve Hebrew tribes who departed Egypt in the Exodus. Imagine a whole nation, the elderly included, and not one person was feeble!

JOHN PAUL II

Catholic Pope John Paul II was born Karol Jozef Wojtyla on 18 May 1920 and died on 2 April 2005. John Paul II served as the Roman Catholic Pontiff from 16 October 1978 until his death in 2005 at 84-years-old. He was the second longest serving Catholic pope in history.

Continuing on with the early traditions of the Roman Catholic Church, John Paul II lived (in his personal diet) and taught that God's Dietary Commandments were done away with.

The Roman Catholic Pope John Paul II suffered from Parkinson's disease and perhaps various other acquired diseases before he died a helpless, feeble man. John Paul II must have believed that he could violate God's Dietary Commands with impunity. John Paul II frequently ate tripe (pork intestines) for breakfast, lunch, and dinner. The once avid skier and hiker was halting in speech, barely able to walk, and in constant pain from effects of what medical experts believed was an advanced case of Parkinson's. Leading up to his death, John Paul II was attended around the clock by private male nurses who helped wash and dress him and gave him an occasional massage. Pope John Paul II died following a urinary tract infection that progressed into a bloodstream infection[91]. He was 84-years-old.

John Paul II, dead at 84, could hardly walk or speak and was in constant pain in his last years on Earth. Why?

God's Dietary Commands apply to kings and peasants, to the rich and poor, to clergymen and their flock, to the Jew and to the Gentile. Those who apply God's dietary laws, whether through knowledge of them or not, reap health blessings from doing so, while those who do not apply God's dietary laws, whether they know them or not, are cursed with disease, feebleness, and premature death from not doing so. Catholic popes have no right or special privilege to discard God's Dietary Commands, nor teach others to do so. Catholic priests, and other false teachers, are the same as the priests in Ezekiel 22:26. The dietary teachings of the Catholic and mainstream Protestant churches are in opposition to what Scripture instructs us concerning the human diet.

Doctors are fully aware (or most are) of the blood-destroying, disease-causing effects that consuming unclean creatures have on the human body over time. John Paul II was NOT above God's Dietary Commandments and suffered a horribly painful and premature death as a result of disobeying them. John Paul II often ate pork and other animal organs, for breakfast! Near the end of his life, on doctor's orders, John Paul II stuck to a mostly vegetarian diet, avoiding breakfasts that once included prosciutto (pork) or roast beef, and meals of Polish favorites like tripe (pork and other animal organs and intestines).

Catholic Pope John Paul II was the leader of over a billion Catholics, most of whom have been taught and believe that God's Dietary Commands have been done away with. There is much cancer, disease, illness, old-age feebleness, and premature death among Catholics and Protestants, who are fond of eating unclean creatures in violation of God's Dietary Commands listed in Leviticus 11 and Deuteronomy 14.

Many Catholics and Protestants, like John Paul II, do not obey God's Dietary Commands, but will follow their doctor's orders only *after* they get sick.

There are two dietary paths one can follow. Believe in God's word, eat according to His dietary laws, and reap long-term health blessings as Moses and Aaron did, or believe that God's Dietary Commands do not apply to you, eat all manner of unclean and unhealthy creatures, and reap bodily curses, disease, feebleness, and premature death as John Paul II did.

PREVENTION: THE BEST MEDICINE AND THE ONLY WAY TO STOP CANCER

By George Lujack

"What did you take? You took away my breath sometimes. You took away my running. What did you take? You took my hair. You took my husband, my grandmother, my dad. You tried to take me. You try to take everyone, but I won't let you. We will stop you with therapies, with immune cells, with genetic testing, clinical trials, and cutting edge research. With team science and a team approach to actually bring discoveries to patients. We will stop you by treating every single patient just like family, with dignity and compassion, in ways that we would want to be treated ourselves. We're not scared of you anymore. We're not scared of you anymore. We know you better than you know yourself. My dad will survive you; I want everyone to survive you. See this is a fight, it's a battle and we're an army, thousands strong, and cancer you're going to lose and we are going to win."[92]

- MD Anderson Cancer Center (TV Commercial)

October is Breast Cancer Awareness Month and the above anti-cancer commercial has been airing frequently on many broadcast stations nationally. The MD Anderson Cancer Center may very well be one of the finest cancer research and treatment centers in the world, but their approach to fighting cancer will not stop cancer; it will guarantee that cancer remains a widespread disease for them, and others, to treat. There is one method that the MD Anderson Cancer Center failed to mention in their commercial that is the *only known way* to stop cancer: PREVENTION.

Speaking to cancer in silly, feel-good, meaningless commercials will not stop cancer. Cancer is a disease that cannot and does not hear what people say to it. Likewise, wearing pink ribbons and articles of clothing, coming up with slogans such as "You're history, cancer," and all other forms of wishful thinking will not make cancer go away, nor will it stop cancer; only prevention will.

What the MD Anderson Cancer Center, and others like them, count on is for people to first acquire cancer, then seek their medical treatment. Medical cancer treatment centers will fight cancer only *after* the disease is acquired in patients. That is not stopping cancer, but is more like being in a business partnership with cancer.

This is not to say that cancer treatment centers do not do good work in helping cancer patients get well, but their good work only happens after people acquire cancer, get sick, and then receive treatment. People who acquire cancer suffer diminished quality of life, pain from the disease itself and the treatments for it, shortened life spans, and very often premature death.

"Despite the insights of some eminent doctors, medicine still focuses on disease, giving it a failure orientation. Its practitioners still act as though disease catches people, rather than understanding that people catch disease by becoming susceptible to the seeds of illness to which we are all constantly exposed. Although the best physicians have always known better, medicine as a whole has rarely studied the people who don't get sick. Most doctors seldom consider how a patient's attitude towards life shapes that life's quantity and quality."

-Bernie S. Siegel, M.D.

The entire approach of Western medicine in fighting cancer is profit-motivated, treatment-based, and unwise. Prevention is not part of the equation, for if cancer ceased to exit, all the medical centers treating this disease would have to close down, pharmaceutical companies would stop manufacturing cancer drugs, and many doctors and nurses who treat cancer patients would be seeking new employment in other fields. Not many in the medical industry are sincerely trying to cure cancer; they are mainly only interested in treating it for profit.

What preventive measures can be taken to prevent the onset of cancer? In most cases, a common sense approach is all that is needed. To prevent lung cancer, don't smoke. To prevent skin cancer, don't frequently burn your skin through sun exposure and wear non-toxic sunscreen protection. To prevent internal organ cancers and blood-borne diseases such as leukemia, consume a healthy diet. Many Christians of the Western nations do not follow the dietary commands in their own bibles, found in Leviticus 11 and Deuteronomy 14, having been taught to believe that they are no longer in effect or were written for the Jews only. Specifically, mainstream Christians of the Westernized nations consume a diet that often includes swine (pork), shellfish (clam, crab, lobster, shrimp) and fish without scales (catfish, tuna). This disregard for God's dietary laws is the primary reason why Christians are plagued with the disease known today as cancer.

The North American Plains Indians did not have knowledge of God's dietary commands found in the Scriptures, yet they unknowingly obeyed them and reaped tremendous health benefits for doing so. Before the arrival of the Europeans in America, the Plains Indians consumed a diet consisting of bison (a clean mammal) and vegetation. The Plains Indians typically lived to be 85 to 90-years-old and **never** acquired cancer, heart disease, or even suffered a heart attack. It is believed that the Plains Indians, as a people, would have lived well beyond 100 years with adequate dental care.[93]

ISAIAH 66:17 (NKJV) [WITH INTERPRETATION]:

"Those who sanctify themselves and purify themselves, ... eating swine's flesh and the abomination [SEA CREATURES WITHOUT FINS AND OVERLAPPING, SHEDDING SCALES] and the mouse, shall be consumed [WITH DISEASE] together," says YHWH (the Lord).

When people acquire cancer, they are literally consumed by the disease. Cancer cells multiply *and consume* healthy cells. YHWH (the Lord) commands us to not eat unclean creatures and warns that those who do consume unclean creatures will themselves be consumed (by disease) as a result of eating them. YHWH's (the Lord's) dietary warning has gone unheeded by many of His own people (mainstream Christians) and as a result various cancers that consume the body have plagued the Christian populations. Cancer centers will not stop cancer; they will only medically treat cancer once it is acquired. Mainstream Christians who continue to eat unclean creatures will continue to acquire cancer and seek treatment only *after* the onset of the disease. Prevention (following a proper diet and lifestyle) is the ONLY way to truly stop cancer.

TATTOOS AND SKIN PIERCINGS

By George Lujack

This article will affirm that tattoos and skin piercings are 'desecration of the flesh' practices, which are forbidden by God in Scripture.

LEVITICUS 19:28 (NKJV):

You shall not make any *cuttings in your flesh* for the dead, *nor print any marks upon you*: I am YHWH (the Lord).

DEUTERONOMY 14:1 (NKJV):

You are the children of YHWH (the Lord) your God: *you shall not cut yourselves*, nor make any baldness between your eyes for the dead.

A tattoo is a series of puncture wounds that carry dye into the different levels of the skin.

Most people who have a tattoo do not develop any problems. However, problems with tattoos do occur including:

- Infection at the tattoo site
- Minor or serious skin allergic reactions to the tattooing method or dye
- Scarring, which can include raised scar tissue
- Spread of infectious disease, such as hepatitis B, C, tetanus, tuberculosis, or HIV if a dirty needle or equipment is used

In general, the reason a person gets a tattoo varies from individual to individual. The reasons people generally say that they get a tattoo are to:

- Feel more rebellious
- Feel more sexy, macho
- Feel more spiritual

Often, individuals who have gotten tattooed experience tattoo regret afterward, wishing that they had never gone under the tattoo needle and permanently marked their skin.

DESECRATION OF THE FLESH

Scripture declares that man is created in God's image (Genesis 1:26-27; 1 Corinthians 11:7). To desecrate the human body with a tattoo(s) is to disrespect 'God's image' and to disrespect God's image is to disrespect God.

A tattoo is a desecration of the flesh, forbidden by YHWH (the Lord). Our bodies are not canvasses for tattoo artists. There should be no graffiti found on the human body. Our bodies are temples of the Holy Spirit.

Tattoos are images upon the flesh. Yeshua (Jesus) commands us to not print any image representing Him, in remembrance of Him, in remembrance of a deceased loved one, or any other tattoo image to mark the human body.

Tattooing the body rejects the human image to reflect 'art.' In some rare cases, people have taken tattooing to the extreme. Some mentally disturbed tattooed persons have completely rejected their image as being the image of God to become the image of God's creation (animals). There are people who have donned tattoos from head to toe in an attempt to reflect the image of an animal and in some extreme cases they even live out their lives emulating animals. This is certainly a form of rejecting the Creator and worshiping the creature (Romans 1:24-25).

Believers should be examples of clean proper living and a light of wisdom to the world. It is difficult, if not impossible, to project an image of righteousness and wholesomeness as a tattooed believer. When someone desecrates his or her flesh with a tattoo, it is practically an advertisement of promiscuity, rebelliousness, unclean, and unhealthy living. In many cases, having a tattoo in a visible area will reduce a person's employability. Employers often won't hire a tattooed person because they want their employees to project a clean-cut professional image that reflects their company or organization.

If a person received a tattoo before turning to YHWH (the Lord) in repentance and obedience, a question arises as to what should be done with regard to already tattooed skin. Scripture does not address removing tattoos specifically, so a remedial path, if any, must be given some thought.

Tattooed skin is imaged skin. Scripture does command God's followers to destroy all types of images (Exodus 23:24, 34:13, Deuteronomy 7:5,25, 12:3; 2 Samuel 5:21; 2 Kings 10:26, 11:18, 18:4, 23:14,24, 2 Chronicles 14:3-5, 23:17, 31:1, 34:3-7).

Tattooing, while permanent, is not an unforgivable sin. So the first step any tattooed sinner should take is to pray for forgiveness. It is clear that God does not want any image marks printed on our skin, so it is a worthwhile endeavor to remove all ink marks from our skin. As an act of repentance, it is advisable to consult with a certified tattoo removal specialist who can use laser technology to permanently remove tattoos. There are also some tattoo removal creams that have recently become commercially available.

Ear lobe and other body piercing could be considered 'cuttings' of the flesh (Leviticus 19:28; Deuteronomy 14:1). Many believers might balk at the notion that having pierced ear lobes adorned with jewelry is sinful in nature, but to pierce the ear lobes you must cut into flesh.

Scripture does mention instances of ear piercing when a servant wished to become a permanent bondservant to his master (Exodus 21:6; Deuteronomy 15:17). The adorning of jewelry for the ears is noted in the Scripture (Genesis 35:4; Exodus 32:2-3, 35:22; Numbers 31:50; Judges 8:24-26; Ezekiel 16:12; Hosea 2:13). Nose jewelry is also noted in Scripture (Exodus 35:22; Ezekiel 16:12). Earrings were said to be 'in the ears' (Genesis 35:4; Exodus 32:2-3) which indicates that flesh piercing was common in Tanakh (Old Testament) times.

Piercing of the flesh, like tattooing, has been taken to further lengths with some people. What began as fashionably acceptable ear and nose piercing has led to many other forms of piercing. It is not that uncommon to see pierced belly button navels, eyebrows, lips, tongues, nipples, and genitalia. More extreme people have had horns implanted into their foreheads or scalps, have braided and branded their skin, and have mutilated many other parts of their flesh. The risk of getting an infection with a body piercing is high. When pierced skin is fresh and exposed, it is susceptible to the invasion of microorganisms such as bacteria and fungi.

Believers are commanded to refrain from tattooing, skin piercing, cutting, branding, and all other desecrations and mutilations of their flesh.

JEHOVAH'S WITNESSES' NO BLOOD TRANSFUSION DOCTRINE; DOES GOD ALLOW BLOOD TRANSFUSIONS?

By George Lujack

According to official Jehovah's Witnesses' doctrine, Scripture prohibits the human-to-human transfusion of blood, even in the case of a medical emergency where the patient faces certain death. This article will reveal that blood transfusions are permissible with God and will expose the Jehovah's Witnesses' No Blood Transfusion doctrine as erroneous and misguided.

The (8) basic tenet beliefs of Jehovah's Witnesses' blood doctrine are discussed and refuted here to reveal the truth and expose the falseness of these doctrines.

THE 8 - BASIC TENETS OF JEHOVAH'S WITNESSES' NO BLOOD TRANSFUSION DOCTRINE:

1. Blood is sacred to God.[94]

REBUTTAL:
Scripture does not say that blood, in and of itself, is sacred. Only Yeshua Messiah's (Jesus Christ's) blood was sacred. Yeshua (Jesus) is the Son of God and everything about Yeshua (Jesus) is and was sacred, including Yeshua's (Jesus') blood that was shed on the cross.

2. Blood means life in God's eyes[95]

REBUTTAL:
Blood does not mean life in God's eyes. The life OF THE FLESH is in the blood (Leviticus 17:11), meaning that the life of flesh is impossible without blood. Life is of the flesh and blood *is a fluid* that SUSTAINS life (Leviticus 17:14).

3. Blood must not be eaten *or* transfused.[96]

REBUTTAL:

While it is true that blood should never be eaten, Scripture does not address human-to-human transfusion of blood for the purpose of sustaining life. Scripture directly forbids the EATING OF BLOOD FROM BIRDS AND BEASTS (Leviticus 7:26, 17:13). Scripture does not forbid human-to-human transfusions of blood.

4. Blood leaving the body of a human or animal must be disposed of, except for autologous blood transfusions considered part of a 'current therapy.'[97][98][99]

REBUTTAL:

Blood leaving the body of animals, AFTER BEING KILLED either for food or sacrifice, is to be drained and that blood should normally be properly disposed of (Leviticus 17:13; Deuteronomy 12:16, 15:23). However, Scripture also records that animal blood obtained from sacrifices was gathered and handled by priests and used in various rituals as commanded by God (Exodus 24:6-8, 29:12-21; Leviticus 1:5-11, 3:2-13, 4:5-34, 5:9, 6:27-30, 7:2-14, 8:15-30, 9:9-18, 14:14-28,51-52, 16:14-19, 17:6; Numbers 18:17, 19:4-5, 2 Chronicles 30:16, 35:1). Additionally, during the Exodus from Egypt, Hebrews placed blood above and around their doors to avoid God's final plague of the death of the firstborns of Egypt (Exodus 12:13-23). Autologous blood transfusions (blood donations made by the donor to be used by the donor - typically for a scheduled surgery) are not forbidden. Furthermore, human-to-human blood transfusions are not prohibited in Scripture.

5. Blood was reserved for only one special use, the atonement for sins, which led up to Jesus' shed blood.

REBUTTAL:

Shed ANIMAL BLOOD was typically reserved for one use in Scripture, which was for the temporary atonement of sins, until Yeshua's (Jesus') shed blood became a permanent atonement for sin that rendered animal blood sacrifice rituals obsolete (Hebrews 10:1-18). In the times that Scripture was written, there was no other use for animal blood, as there is no other use for *animal blood* today. With the advancements in science in the fields of medicine, human-to-human blood transfusion became possible, for the purpose of life preservation. Human blood can and is used to save lives.

6. When Christians abstain from blood, they are in effect expressing faith that only the shed blood of Jesus Christ can truly redeem them and save their life.[100]

REBUTTAL:

God commands us to abstain from *EATING* THE BLOOD from animals as part of the human diet. Yeshua's (Jesus') shed blood on the cross was meant to redeem our SPIRITUAL LIFE, and was not meant to spare our earthly bodily life from death. Human-to-human blood transfusions can save a person's earthly life, whereas Yeshua's (Jesus') shed blood on the cross was not meant for that purpose.

7. Even in the case of an emergency, it is not permissible to sustain life with transfused blood.[101]

REBUTTAL:

The Good Samaritan, who saw a dying man along the roadside, came to help and preserve the life of the dying man. A priest and a Levite had passed by the dying man earlier, but avoided the dying man and did not do anything to help him. Yeshua (Jesus) posed a question as to who had done right to the dying man.

A lawyer answered identifying the Samaritan. Yeshua (Jesus) said to go and do likewise (Luke 10:30-37). Is it really conceivable that Yeshua (Jesus) would not permit people to sustain and preserve the life of our neighbor(s), whom we are commanded to love as ourselves, through human-to-human blood transfusions?

8. Conscientious violation of this doctrine is considered a serious offense, after which a member is subject to organized shunning.[102][103][104][105]

REBUTTAL:

Organized shunning by believers against believers, especially over an issue that is not addressed specifically in Scripture, goes against what Scripture tells us to do. Believers are not supposed to fight and shun one another over disputes about food, days, or circumcision (Acts 15:1-21; Romans 14). If Jehovah's Witnesses truly feel that blood transfusions are related to the prohibition against man consuming blood, they should follow the advice of the Apostle Paul and not get into disputes, or promote shunning of their members or other believers who do not believe in their blood transfusion doctrines.

Jehovah's Witnesses' doctrines on blood are man-made doctrines. These false doctrines are no different than other doctrines of men, such as the washing of hands before eating doctrine (Matthew 15:1-9) or the many man-made doctrines imposed by the Catholic Church.[106]

GENESIS 9:4 (NKJV):

But you shall not eat flesh with its life, that is, its blood.

LEVITICUS 3:17 (NKJV):

This shall be a perpetual statute throughout your generations in all your dwellings: you shall eat neither fat nor blood.

LEVITICUS 17:11-14 (NKJV):

For the life of the flesh is in the blood, and I have given it to you upon the altar to make atonement for your souls; for it is the blood that makes atonement for the soul. Therefore

I said to the children of Israel, No one among you shall eat blood, nor shall any stranger who dwells among you eat blood. Whatever man of the children of Israel, or of the strangers who dwell among you, who hunts and catches any animal or bird that may

be eaten, he shall pour out its blood and cover it with dust; for it is the life of all flesh.

Its BLOOD SUSTAINS LIFE. Therefore I said to the children of Israel, You shall not eat the blood of any flesh, for the life of all flesh is its blood. Whoever eats it shall be cut off.

DEUTERONOMY 12:23 (NKJV):

Only be sure that you do not eat the blood, *for the blood is the life*; you may not eat the life with the meat.

Jehovah's Witnesses' blood doctrine is based on the belief that HUMAN-TO-HUMAN BLOOD TRANSFUSIONS are tantamount to the *EATING* OF ANIMAL BLOOD. The belief is that after digestion, food is broken down and enters the bloodstream. Therefore if a person has TRANSFUSED HUMAN

BLOOD DIRECTLY INJECTED INTO THEIR BLOODSTREAM, according to Jehovah's Witnesses' doctrine, it is virtually the same as if a person consumes and digests human blood.

While it is forbidden to consume animal blood, the transfusion of human blood is not mentioned in Scripture at all. Where Jehovah's Witnesses' doctrine misguides is that God's Dietary Commandments concerning blood prohibit humans from *EATING THE BLOOD* of Scripture-sanctified clean animals. Scripture does not address consuming human blood. It would be wrong, of course, to consume human blood, as all blood is forbidden by God to be consumed. Cannibalism, in any form, is evil.

Scripture does not address the issue of human-to-human BLOOD TRANSFUSIONS. A human-to-human blood transfusion, in which blood is directly transferred from one person to another or stored blood is infused into a patient, is far different than blood being consumed and passing through the human digestive system where it eventually breaks down and winds up in the human bloodstream *AFTER* DIGESTION. It is unlawful to eat human blood, which serves no purpose, but blood transfusions can and do save lives.

God describes all animal blood as 'the life' of the animal. No animals or human beings can live without blood circulating throughout their body. A human-to-human blood transfusion preserves the life of the receiver of the blood and it is a gift of life preservation from the donor.

God's dietary law prohibiting the eating or drinking of animal blood is meant to preserve human life from sickness and disease. A human-to-human blood transfusion is a measure used to preserve life in the event of an emergency.

If a person allows a neighbor to die, because he or she would not donate some blood to save the neighbor's life, would this not be a form of murder by neglect?

The Good Samaritan may have technically broken the Sabbath to save a dying stranger on the roadside (Luke 10:30-35). If the Good Samaritan acted on the Sabbath day, he broke the Sabbath to uphold a greater part of God's law: to love his neighbor.

There is a time when God asks us to lay down our life. When asked to deny Messiah (Christ) or the gospel, even under the threat of death to ourselves, we are commanded to never deny Him (Matthew 10:28-33, 16:24-25; Mark 8:34-35; Luke 9:23-24). God never commanded us to lay down our life or that of our neighbor by refusing to partake in a blood transfusion.

Yeshua (Jesus) miraculously healed a woman with a blood issue (Matthew 9:20-22; Mark 5:25-34; Luke 8:43-48). Although this was not a blood transfusion, Scripture provides believers with an example that demonstrates that blood may be treated for blood-related ailments to be made free from disease.

There are dangers inherent in blood transfusions, which Jehovah's Witnesses are often eager to point out to support their doctrine. Of course, there are dangers with blood transfusions as there are dangers with any medical procedure. Believers are not forbidden to undergo medical procedures because there are dangers. There are operations meant to extend people's lives, but are risky and the patient could die on the operating table. A person diagnosed with a narrowing of an aortic valve may be informed that he or she has less than one year to survive unless open-heart surgery is undergone. To replace the valve on this patient would risk the possibility of death on the operating table. However, if the patient was to survive, the life expectancy of the patient could be extended for many more years. Therefore the patient must make a decision whether to risk his or her 'short-term' life for the chance of living a 'long-term' life.

In the case of a blood transfusion, where there is *NO OTHER VIABLE ALTERNATIVE* available to preserve life, a patient or relative of a patient may be concerned about the risk of acquiring a blood-borne disease from tainted blood. This is a valid concern of course, but if the alternative were death, it would be better to get tainted blood. If someone loses a limb, and the physicians are able to reattach the limb, most patients are unlikely to stop the medical procedure because the limb may not function as well as it did before it was severed. Most people would choose life with the possibly of receiving imperfect tainted blood, rather than death.

Blood screening and testing standards are different around the world. Blood is often screened and tested for diseases that are more prevalent in the donors' particular part of the world and blood testing costs often determine whether blood gets extensively tested or not.[107] Better blood screening and testing procedures mean a safer blood supply. The World Health Organization recommends that donated blood be minimally tested for hepatitis B & C, HIV, and syphilis. In 2006, the WHO reported that 56 out of 124 countries surveyed did not use these minimally basic tests on all blood donations.[108]

Blood-borne diseases that recipient patients have acquired through blood transfusions include HIV/AIDS, hepatitis, STD's, and many other diseases. A patient may also suffer immune system reactions from a blood transfusion. There will always be some risk in receiving a blood transfusion, therefore a blood transfusion from an unknown donor should only be accepted if there is *no other alternative* to preserve a life.

There is virtually no danger to a blood donor when giving blood. Hospital staffs are required to use new needles to safely draw a minimal amount of blood from a donor, typically one pint. The human body will quickly remanufacture the lost blood of the blood donor, who can typically resume normal activities immediately after donating his or her blood.

Believers living sexually pure and faithful lives should be encouraged to donate blood, because the blood acquired from God-fearing believers is much less likely to be contaminated with disease than blood received from the general population at large.

The eternal spiritual aspects of God often reflect the temporal earthly aspects of man. Yeshua (Jesus) shed His blood on the cross to save our eternal spiritual lives (Matthew 26:28; Mark 14:24; Luke 22:20). When believers donate blood, the purpose is to shed some of their blood to save or preserve the earthly life of a loved one or neighbor.

THE LORD OF THE SABBATH;
IS YESHUA MESSIAH (JESUS CHRIST) LORD OF THE SABBATH OR IS THE CATHOLIC CHURCH?

By George Lujack

History reveals that it was centuries after the death of the apostles that the Roman Catholic political-religious system emerged, which officially repudiated the seventh-day Sabbath of Scripture and substituted the observance of the first-day of the week in its place. Roman Emperor Constantine, working with the Roman Catholic Church altered the Sabbath commandment issued by God as recorded in Exodus 20:8, which states, "Remember the Sabbath day, to keep it holy." Catholicism reworded the fourth commandment to say, "Remember to keep holy the Sabbath day." The Catholic Church then changed the Sabbath day from Saturday to Sunday, the first-day of the week.

By their own admission, Catholic Church authorities, without any direction from Scripture, intended to change the Sabbath day from the seventh-day of the week to the first-day.

Catholic Church authorities cited a few reasons defending why they intended to change the Saturday Sabbath to Sunday:

1. They believe Christ rose on Sunday, and this somehow gave them the justification to change the perpetual Sabbath day from Saturday to Sunday.

2. They proclaim that the change was part of their 'divine mission,' an act of their ecclesiastical power and authority in religious matters.

There are other sinister reasons why the Catholic Church authorities intended to change the seventh-day Sabbath to Sunday, the first-day:

1. Sunday worship is the traditional pagan day of worship.

2. The Catholic Church authorities wanted to differentiate themselves from the Jews, refusing to worship on the same day the Jews did.

3. Catholicism is in active rebellion against God's laws.

Catholicism's stated belief that Jesus rose on Sunday morning is not a valid reason to change the Sabbath day to Sunday, the first-day of the week. No man can change God's perpetual times and laws. Catholics, Protestants (protesting Catholics), and most mainstream Christians honor Sunday as the Sabbath day incorrectly in place of God's perpetual seventh-day Saturday Sabbath.

DANIEL 7:25 (NKJV) [WITH INTERPRETATION]:

He [CATHOLIC POPES PAST AND PRESENT] shall speak pompous words against the Most High, shall persecute the saints of the Most High, and shall intend to change times and law.

Catholic popes (all of them) have fulfilled this prophecy. All Catholic popes have either intended to change God's times and laws or have upheld the intended changes of Catholic popes who preceded them.

Notice how Scripture states, "He shall *INTEND* to change times and law."

Catholic popes CANNOT change God's times and laws, though that is their intention. God's times and laws REMAIN as God originally commanded them. Therefore the seventh-day Saturday Sabbath remains, no matter how many Christian churches and people observe Sunday instead.

The Catholic Church, in statements through the centuries, freely admits that it is responsible - without any direction from Scripture, for intending to change God's Sabbath day from Saturday to Sunday.

CATHOLIC STATEMENTS ON THE SABBATH

"But you may read the Bible from Genesis to Revelation, and you will not find a single line authorizing the sanctification of Sunday. The Scriptures enforce the religious observance of Saturday, a day which we never sanctify."
-James Cardinal Gibbons, The Faith of our Fathers, 88th ed., p. 89, 1876.

"The Bible says, 'Remember the Sabbath day, to keep it holy.' The Catholic Church says, No! By my divine power I abolished the Sabbath day, and command you to keep the first day of the week. And lo, the entire civilized world bows down in reverent obedience to the command of the holy Catholic Church!"
-T. Enright, C.S.S.R. of the Redemptoral College, Kansas City, MO, "History of the Sabbath," p. 802, February 18, 1884.

"The Catholic Church, by virtue of her divine mission, changed the day from Saturday to Sunday."
-The Catholic Mirror, official publication of James Cardinal Gibbons, Sept. 23, 1893.

"The Catholic Church took the pagan Sunday and made it the Christian Sunday. And thus the pagan Sunday, dedicated to Balder (a pagan god) became the Christian Sunday, sacred to Christ."
-Catholic World, March, 1894.

"Sunday is a Catholic institution and its claim to observance can be defended only on Catholic principles. From beginning to end of Scripture there is not a single passage that warrants the transfer of weekly public worship from the last day of the week to the first."
-Catholic Press, Sydney, Australia, 1900.

QUESTION:

Have you any other way of proving that the Church has power to institute festivals of precept?

ANSWER:

"Had she not such power, she could not have done that in which all modern religionists agree with her - she could not have substituted the observance of Sunday, the first day of the week, for the observance of Saturday, the seventh day, a change for which there is no Scriptural authority."

-Stephen Keenan, A Doctrinal Catechism 3ʳᵈ ed., p. 174, 1916.

QUESTION:

Which is the Sabbath day?

ANSWER:

Saturday is the Sabbath day.

QUESTION:

Why do we observe Sunday instead of Saturday?

ANSWER:

"We observe Sunday instead of Saturday because the Catholic Church, in the Council of Laodicea (A.D. 336) transferred the solemnity from Saturday to Sunday."

-Peter Geiermann, "The Convert's Catechism of Catholic Doctrine," p. 50, 1930.

"Perhaps the boldest thing, the most revolutionary change the church ever did happened in the first century. The holy day, the Sabbath, was changed from Saturday to Sunday not from any directions noted in the Scriptures, but from the Catholic Church's sense of its own power."

-Saint Catherine Catholic Church Sentinel, May 21, 1995.

THE SABBATH WAS INSTITUTED AT CREATION

GENESIS 2:2-3 (NKJV):

And on the seventh day God ended His work, which He had done, and He rested on the seventh day from all His work which He had done. Then God blessed the seventh day and sanctified it, because in it He rested from all His work, which God had created and made.

THE SABBATH DAY IS PERPETUAL; IT CANNOT BE CHANGED

EXODUS 31:13 (NKJV):

And YHWH (the Lord) spoke to Moses, saying, "Speak also to the children of Israel, saying: 'Surely My Sabbaths you shall keep, for it is a sign between Me and you *throughout your generations*, that you may know that I am YHWH (the Lord) who sanctifies you. …

EXODUS 31:16-17 (NKJV):

Therefore the children of Israel shall keep the Sabbath, to observe the Sabbath throughout their generations as a PERPETUAL COVENANT. It is a sign between Me and the children of Israel FOREVER; for in six days YHWH (the Lord) made the heavens and the earth, and on the seventh day He rested and was refreshed.'"

LUKE 23:56 (NKJV):

And they rested on the Sabbath *according to the commandment.*

MAN HAS BROKEN THE EVERLASTING SABBATH COVENANT

ISAIAH 24:5 (NKJV):

The earth is also defiled under its inhabitants, because they have transgressed the laws, changed the ordinance, broken the everlasting covenant.

CHOOSE THIS DAY WHOM YOU SERVE

JOSHUA 24:15 (NKJV):

Choose for yourselves this day whom you will serve, ...

But as for me and my house, we will serve YHWH (the Lord).

Every Christian believer should ask him / herself the following question:

Who is it that I honor and serve, Yeshua (Jesus) or Roman Emperor Constantine and the Roman Catholic Church, as Lord of the Sabbath?

YESHUA (JESUS) IS LORD OF THE SABBATH

MATTHEW 12:8; MARK 2:28; LUKE 6:5 (NKJV):

"The Son of Man is also Lord of the Sabbath."

THE SABBATH WAS MADE FOR MAN, AND NOT MAN FOR THE SABBATH

By George Lujack

Is the Sabbath serving you or are you serving the Sabbath? Many orthodox Talmudic Jews 'serve' the Sabbath, rather than having the Sabbath serve them (even to this day). How does one 'serve the Sabbath?' This is done by following Pharisaic Talmud-based rules rather than obeying the intent of the Sabbath. The Talmudic laws are rabbinical man-made religious rules.

As it applies to the Sabbath, rabbinical Jews have made all kinds of rules that cause them to serve the Sabbath. One of these is to not use electricity on the Sabbath. This is why many orthodox Jews place tape over their telephone receivers so their phone does not ring on the Sabbath, place tape over their interior light on their refrigerators (yet make an exception and leave their refrigerators plugged in so that their food does not spoil). They unscrew their light bulbs and basically are forbidden to flip a switch, to turn anything on or off on the Sabbath, as this is considered 'work.'

Many orthodox Jews will walk miles to synagogue on the Sabbath because they are instructed not to use their cars. Their cars are getting a rest, but to walk long distances to synagogue is not resting one's own body. The Sabbath is meant as a day of rest for man, not machines.

The sun still shines on the Sabbath. The Earth still rotates on the Sabbath. Yeshua (Jesus) rode a donkey on the Sabbath and would have used a car on the Sabbath if one were available.

LUKE 6:1-5 (NKJV):

Now it happened on the second Sabbath after the first that He went through the grain fields. And His disciples plucked the heads of grain and ate them, rubbing them in their hands. And some of the Pharisees said to them, "Why are you doing what is not lawful to do on the Sabbath?" But Yeshua (Jesus) answering them said, "Have you not even read this, what David did when he was hungry, he and those who were with him: how he went into the house of God, took and ate the showbread, and also gave some to those with him, which is not lawful for any but the priests to eat?" And He said to them, "The Son of Man is also Lord of the Sabbath."

Yeshua (Jesus) and His disciples were once accused of 'working' on the Sabbath for plucking grains and eating as they were passing through a grain field on the Sabbath.

The Pharisees would have been correct in their accusation *if* the apostles were gathering grain for a WEEKLY HARVEST. This was not the case as they were just hungry and were eating for the moment, as they were passing by. It is not unlawful to eat on the Sabbath.

DEUTERONOMY 25:4; 1 CORINTHIANS 9:9; 1 TIMOTHY 5:18 (NKJV):

You shall not muzzle an ox while it treads out the grain.

The apostles were walking among the grain fields on the Sabbath and were hungry. Oxen are not prohibited from eating as they pass through a grain field. The Pharisees wanted to treat the apostles worse than field oxen!

MARK 2:27-28 (NKJV):

And He said to them, "The Sabbath was made for man, and not man for the Sabbath. Therefore the Son of Man is also Lord of the Sabbath."

The Sabbath was made to serve man, for man to rest and be refreshed, not for man to serve the Sabbath, by working harder and resting our appliances.

THE SEVENTH DAY SABBATH - HOW TO KEEP IT?

By George Lujack

The seventh-day Sabbath is sanctified by God as a blessing, for us to rest from our weekly labor and work. Many in this age do not know how to properly keep the Sabbath or even know what day it should be kept. This article will explain how and when to properly keep the Sabbath day.

GENESIS 2:1-3 (NKJV):

Thus the heavens and the earth, and all the host of them were finished. And on the seventh day God ended His work which He had done, and He rested on the seventh day from all His work which He had done. Then God blessed the seventh day and sanctified it, because in it He rested from all His work which God had created and made.

God blessed and sanctified the seventh-day as the Sabbath day after He ended His work that He had done during the first six-days of the creation week (Genesis 2:2-3). Beginning Friday at sundown through Saturday sundown is the seventh-day Sabbath, according to how God counted the days during the creation week. The purpose of the Sabbath is for a time set aside for physical and mental rest, spiritual refreshment, a time to give thanks to God, and to ponder the magnificence and wonder of His creation.

EXODUS 20:8-11 (NKJV):

Remember the Sabbath day, to keep it holy. Six days you shall labor and do all your work, but the seventh day is the Sabbath of YHWH (the Lord) your God. In it you shall do no work: you, nor your son, nor your daughter, nor your male servant, nor your female servant, nor your cattle, nor your stranger who is within your gates. For in six days the Lord made the heavens and the earth, the sea, and all that is in them, and rested the seventh day. Therefore YHWH (the Lord) blessed the Sabbath day and hallowed it.

EXODUS 31:12-15 (NKJV):

And YHWH (the Lord) spoke to Moses, saying, "Speak also to the children of Israel, saying: 'Surely My Sabbaths you shall keep, for it is a sign between Me and you throughout your generations, that you may know that I am YHWH (the Lord) who sanctifies you. You shall keep the Sabbath, therefore, for it is holy to you. Everyone who profanes it shall surely be put to death; for whoever does any work on it, that person shall be cut off from among his people.

EXODUS 31:15-18:

Work shall be done for six days, but the seventh is the Sabbath of rest, holy to YHWH (the Lord). Whoever does any work on the Sabbath day, he shall surely be put to death. Therefore the children of Israel shall keep the Sabbath, to observe the Sabbath throughout their generations as a perpetual covenant. It is a sign between Me and the children of Israel forever; for in six days YHWH (the Lord) made the heavens and the earth, and on the seventh day He rested and was refreshed.'"

And when He had made an end of speaking with him on Mount Sinai, He gave Moses two tablets of the Testimony, tablets of stone, written with the finger of God.

God included the Sabbath in the Ten Commandments with guidelines of how to observe the day that He blessed and sanctified. The seventh-day Sabbath is a perpetual covenant and an everlasting sign (Exodus 31:16-17). Church attendance and fellowship with other believers is by no means the only requirement of properly keeping the Sabbath.

1. The Sabbath is to be observed on the seventh-day, not on Sunday, a day of our choosing, any other day, or every day. God did not give man the option to observe the Sabbath as a matter of his own preference. Choosing to revere Sunday over Saturday as the Sabbath day to honor God is not in accordance with God's command to *remember* the seventh-day Sabbath (Exodus 20:8).

2. The Sabbath is a day of rest from weekly labor. No work should be done on this day (Exodus 20:10,31:14-15,35:2; Jeremiah 17:21-24). Employers should not employ workers and workers should not be employed on the Sabbath. That said, it is not a sin to do essential services such as medical care and emergency response work (fire, medical, military, police), nor is it wrong to come to the aid of a stranger. Messiah (Christ) taught that it is not wrong to do good deeds on the Sabbath (Matthew 12:12; Mark 3:4; Luke 6:9,13:14).

3. The Sabbath is a day to not buy, sell, or trade in any for profit marketplace (Nehemiah 10:28-31, 13:15-22). Purchases for food and essentials should be made in advance, before the Sabbath begins - in preparation for the Sabbath, so that they are available when the Sabbath arrives.

4. The Sabbath is a day of no household chores or cooking. Warming food with a microwave or making coffee is permissible, but most household meal preparations should be prepared beforehand, on Friday afternoon (Preparation Day) so a person does not do the labor of cooking on the Sabbath day (Exodus 16:22-30). God commands that no fire be lit in our dwellings on the Sabbath day, which would include lighting a flame to cook meals (Exodus 35:3).

5. The Sabbath is a day of reverence to YHWH (the Lord). It is a day to gather in fellowship with other believers to honor God (Luke 4:16; Acts 13:14,16:13).

6. The Sabbath is a day set apart to delight in YHWH (the Lord), to refrain from doing our own pleasure, sexual gratification, and worldly entertainment; a day set apart to be intimate with God, not with our spouses or with the things of this world (Isaiah 58:13-14).

EXODUS 20:9 (NKJV):

Six days you shall labor and do all your work...

EXODUS 31:15 (NKJV):

Work shall be done for six days…

A believer cannot observe the Sabbath every day of the week, as some say they do in denying God's seventh-day Sabbath. That would mean that they never purchase or sell anything nor do any labor or work and revere God ceaselessly. This would not be practical and God does not want us to observe the Sabbath in such a manner as we choose. God commands us to do labor and work on the first six-days of the week and to rest and observe the Sabbath on the seventh-day.

LEGALISM AND THE SABBATH

Yeshua (Jesus) and His disciples were often accused of breaking the Sabbath. In Luke chapter 6, the Pharisees accused Yeshua's (Jesus') disciples of plucking grains and eating them on the Sabbath, considering this 'work.' The disciples were hungry and were eating as they passed through a grain field. The law also states that it is unlawful to muzzle an ox while it treads out the grain (Deuteronomy 25:4; 1 Corinthians 9:9; 1 Timothy 5:18).

What the Pharisees were doing was being legalistic over the Sabbath and treating Yeshua's (Jesus') disciples worse than field oxen. If the disciples had been in the field gathering grain for a weekly harvest, the Pharisees would have been correct in accusing them of breaking the Sabbath, as this would have constituted weekly labor. The disciples did not violate the Sabbath, as it is not unlawful to eat on the Sabbath, and that is all that the disciples did.

DEATH PENALTY FOR BREAKING THE SABBATH

EXODUS 31:14 (NKJV):

You shall keep the Sabbath, therefore, for it is holy to you. Everyone who profanes it shall surely be put to death; for whoever does any work on it, that person shall be cut off from among his people.

NUMBERS 15:32-36 (NKJV):

Now while the children of Israel were in the wilderness, they found a man gathering sticks on the Sabbath day. And those who found him gathering sticks brought him to Moses and Aaron, and to all the congregation. They put him under guard, because it had not been explained what should be done to him.

Then YHWH (the Lord) said to Moses, "The man must surely be put to death; all the congregation shall stone him with stones outside the camp." So, as YHWH (the Lord) commanded Moses, all the congregation brought him outside the camp and stoned him with stones, and he died.

A man was once put to death, by YHWH (the Lord) under the law for gathering sticks on the Sabbath day.

1 CORINTHIANS 6:9-10 (NKJV):

Do you not know that the unrighteous will not inherit the reign of Elohim (kingdom of God)? Do not be deceived. Neither fornicators, nor idolaters, nor adulterers, nor effeminate, nor homosexuals, nor thieves, nor covetous (greedy of gain), nor drunkards, nor revilers, nor swindlers will inherit the reign of Elohim (kingdom of God).

GALATIANS 5:19-21 (NKJV):

Now the works of the flesh are evident, which are: adultery, fornication, uncleanness, lewdness, idolatry, drug sorcery, hatred, quarrels, jealousies, fits of rage, selfish ambitions, dissensions, heresies, envy, murders, drunkenness, revelries, and the like; of which I tell you beforehand, just as I also told you in time past, that those who practice such things will not inherit the reign of Elohim (kingdom of God).

REVELATION 21:7-8 (NKJV):

He who overcomes shall inherit all things, and I will be his God and he shall be My son. The cowardly, untrustworthy, abominable, murderers, sexually immoral, drug sorcerers, idolators, and all liars shall have their part in the lake which burns with fire and brimstone, which is the second death.

Due to the changing of the Sabbath day from Saturday to Sunday by the Roman Catholic Church, and the first-day Sabbath subsequently being adhered to by most Protestants and other denominations of Christianity throughout millennia, many believers have not observed the Sabbath correctly throughout the generations. Thankfully God, in His grace and mercy, will not turn away deceived, ignorant, improper Sunday Sabbath observers from inheriting His kingdom, according to 1 Corinthians 6:9-10, Galatians 5:19-21, and Revelation 21:7-8.

The sin of Sabbath breaking is not listed amongst the sins that can keep a believer from inheriting God's kingdom, but Sunday Sabbath observers will need to be rebuked and corrected before entering His kingdom. Violating the Sabbath is a death penalty offense for which a man was once put to death for gathering sticks, by YHWH (the Lord), so proper Sabbath day observance is something that God is going to eventually require of all His believers.

It is perfectly fine to attend church services or to gather together for Scripture studies on Sunday or any other day of the week. The disciples came together on the first-day of the week to eat and have fellowship together (Acts 20:7). The Sabbath entails more than congregational church service or fellowship. The Sabbath is a set apart day, to rest and do no labor or work, no household chores, no employing, buying, or selling, and is a day to honor God and not pursue our own pleasures.

Those who properly adhere to God's seventh-day Sabbath now, in this age, are a shadow of things to come when everyone will know and observe His true Sabbath day (Colossians 2:17).

Rejoice in God's blessed and sanctified Sabbath day!

Shabbat Shalom (Peaceful Sabbath)!

KINDLE NO FIRE ON THE SABBATH

By George Lujack

This article will discuss the historic and modern day application of the Exodus 35:3 verse, to kindle no fire on the Sabbath day.

Why does God command us to not kindle a fire on the Sabbath day?

kindle:
To light or set on fire.

EXODUS 35:1-3 (NKJV):

Then Moses gathered all the congregation of the children of Israel together, and said to them, "These are the words which the Lord has commanded you to do: Work shall be done for six days, but the seventh day shall be a holy day for you, a Sabbath of rest to the Lord. Whoever does any work on it shall be put to death. You shall kindle no fire throughout your dwellings on the Sabbath day."

When read in its full context, not lighting a fire on the Sabbath day pertains to keeping the Sabbath properly. The question is, "Why are we not to light a fire on the Sabbath day?"

God does not want us to cook on the Sabbath. Lighting a fire to cook on a stove is labor that is not to be conducted on the Sabbath day.

God wants us to set apart the Sabbath day, as holy and special, from Friday sundown through Saturday sundown. We are not to buy or sell on the Sabbath, nor do any work on the Sabbath, which would include kindling fire and cooking.

MARK 15:42 (NKJV):

Now when evening had come, because it was the Preparation Day, that is, the day before the Sabbath...

The Day of Preparation or the Preparation Day is the Friday before the Sabbath. Food is to be prepared beforehand on the Preparation Day to be served throughout the Sabbath. The labor of cooking food shall not be done on the Sabbath day.

TALMUDIC JUDAIC TRADITIONAL SABBATH OBSERVANCE

The traditional Sabbath observance has been taken to extremes and the command to not kindle a fire on the Sabbath is violated in Talmudic Judaism as well as in some Messianic circles.

Formal Talmudic observance of the Shabbat, or Sabbath, begins with the woman of the home lighting the Sabbath candles after Friday sundown as the Sabbath begins. It is customary to light one candle for each member of the household.[109]

ISAIAH 50:11 (NKJV):
Look, all you who kindle a fire, who encircle yourselves with sparks: walk in the light of your fire and in the spark you have kindled. This you shall have from My hand: you shall lie down in torment.

The Jewish people certainly have suffered torment since Isaiah was written around 740 B.C. Jewish candle lighting tradition does not trump Scripture. While it can be argued that the command to not kindle a fire on the Sabbath generally pertains to cooking, to rest from the chore of preparing heated meals, the command is not limited to cooking. The Jewish traditional practice of setting up and lighting candles on the Sabbath is not a command from God. Ritualistic candle lighting is associated with the occult and witchcraft, and believers are not to partake in such practices (Deuteronomy 18:10-11). The Sabbath candle lighting tradition is in clear violation of God's command to not kindle a fire throughout your dwellings on the Sabbath day (Exodus 35:3; Isaiah 50:11).

While strict Talmudic Judaism engages in the practice of setting up and kindling fire for candles on the Sabbath, they forbid the use of motor vehicles, electricity, and telephones on the Sabbath. In a traditional Talmudic-observant Jewish home, family members unhook telephones, unscrew light bulbs, and tape switches down so as to not accidentally turn on an electric appliance. They make an electricity exception for their refrigerators, which they leave plugged in so as to keep food from spoilage, but they place tape over the fridge's interior light switch so that the light will not go on when someone opens the refrigerator door. In Israel, building elevators are set on automatic to stop on every floor, so that those who enter the elevator do not need to push an elevator button (considered 'work').

God does not forbid the use of electricity on the Sabbath day. It is not work to flip a switch or to push an elevator button any more than it is work to pluck grain on the Sabbath and eat (Matthew 12:1-8; Mark 2:23-28).

Overusing electricity by needlessly running electricity continually throughout the Sabbath day, for the sake of refusing to flip a switch, is a waste of God-given blessings of energy, money, and resources.

The Sabbath day is a day of rest and refreshment. It is a day for man to rest, not for the automobiles and electronics that serve man to rest. It is not a command from God to refrain from using a car on the Sabbath day.

Traditional Talmudic Judaic Jews often walk long distances to synagogues for Sabbath observance. Those who have to travel far are often exhausted from their long walks to and from synagogue. The mistake they are making is that the Sabbath is a day of rest for man, not for the automobiles and machines that serve man.

The command to not kindle a fire on the Sabbath day pertains to kindling a fire *within a dwelling*. The igniting and fuel burning of an automobile is done outside a dwelling. A power plant that burns fuel to provide electricity throughout a home is done outside of a dwelling. Not burning a fire at all, anywhere - even outside of a dwelling, is adding to Scripture and we are commanded to not add to His word (Deuteronomy 4:2; Proverbs 30:6).

MARK 2:27 (NKJV):
And Yeshua (Jesus) said to them, "The Sabbath was made for man, and not man for the Sabbath."

The Sabbath was made for man, not for our motorized vehicles.

Taking extraordinary measures in observing the Sabbath, such as refusing motorized transport while instead opting to physically exert oneself in walking long distances, is an example of man serving the Sabbath and not being served by the Sabbath. Igniting an automobile's spark plug and fuel system is not kindling a fire within a dwelling, as motorized internal combustion propelled vehicles are transportation machines ignited *outside* of the home that serve and aid us in resting as we travel on the Sabbath.

WHAT IF?

God commands us to kindle no fire in our dwellings on the Sabbath, but what if...

What if you are living in a cold region and the pilot light goes out of your heating system? Would it be OK to kindle a fire to restart your heating system or light a fireplace to keep warm on the Sabbath?

Yes. God does not expect us to freeze to death or get sick due to frigid temperatures for the sake of keeping a component command of the Sabbath.

Yeshua (Jesus) demonstrated to us that we are to observe the Sabbath in deed and spirit, from our heart. We are to do good deeds on the Sabbath. If an emergency arrives on the Sabbath, we are not to neglect common sense and doing the right thing for the sake of keeping the Sabbath.

MATTHEW 12:12; LUKE 14:5 (NKJV):
Then He said to them, "What man is there among you who has one sheep, and if it falls into a pit on the Sabbath, will not lay hold of it and lift it out? Of how much more value then is a man than a sheep? Therefore it is lawful to do good on the Sabbath."

The Sun does not stop shining on the Sabbath. The Sabbath was meant to serve man and not for man to serve the Sabbath. We are not to light fires in our dwellings on the Sabbath, as we are to rest from all labor including cooking. The Jewish ritual tradition of setting up and lighting candles in the home, as the Sabbath begins, stands in violation of God's law to not kindle (light) a fire throughout your dwellings on the Sabbath day, which is a practice that should not be observed by law-keeping believers.

SEVENTH-DAY ADVENTIST DOCTRINE: SUNDAY SABBATH OBSERVANCE, IS IT THE MARK OF THE BEAST?

By George Lujack

Seventh-day Adventist doctrine proclaims that Sunday Sabbath observance equates to receiving the mark of the beast as prophesied in Revelation. This article will discuss this belief and explain it to be a false doctrine.

EXODUS 31:12-13,16-17 (NKJV):

And YHWH (the Lord) spoke to Moses, saying, "Speak also to the children of Israel, saying: 'Surely My Sabbaths you shall keep, for it is a SIGN between Me and you *throughout your generations* ...

Therefore the children of Israel shall keep the Sabbath, to observe the Sabbath throughout their generations as a PERPETUAL COVENANT. It is a SIGN between Me and the children of Israel *forever*; for in six days YHWH (the Lord) made the heavens and the earth, and on the seventh day He rested and was refreshed."

SABBATH DAY CHANGED BY THE CATHOLIC CHURCH

The Roman Catholic Church changed the Sabbath day from Saturday to Sunday and claimed the change as a "mark" of its authority.

"Of course the Catholic Church claims that the change [OF THE SABBATH DAY] *was her act...*
And the act is a MARK of her ecclesiastical power and authority in religious matters."
- Letter from C.F. Thomas, Chancellor of Cardinal Gibbons, October 28, 1895.

DANIEL 7:25 (NKJV) [WITH INTERPRETATION]:

He [CATHOLIC POPES] shall speak pompous words against the Most High, shall persecute the saints of the Most High, and shall *intend* to change times and law.

Though the Catholic Church claims responsibility for changing the Sabbath day from Saturday to Sunday, it has no authority or power to do so. God's laws and times are eternal; no one can change them. The Catholic Church *intended* to change the Sabbath day from the seventh-day of the week to the first-day, but did not. The Sabbath day is on the seventh-day as a perpetual covenant and will remain on the seventh-day forever (Exodus 31:16-17).

Ellen G. White and her fellow Seventh-day Adventist Church founders proclaimed as doctrine that the Catholic Church's intended Sabbath change, from Saturday to Sunday, was the mark of the beast spoken of in Revelation.

"Here we find the mark of the beast. The very act of changing the Sabbath into Sunday, on the part of the Catholic Church, without any authority from the Bible."
- Ellen G. White, "The Mark of the Beast," page 23.

"The Sunday Sabbath is purely a child of the Papacy. It is the mark of the beast."
- Advent Review, Vol. I, No. 2, August, 1850.

"The change of the Sabbath is the sign or mark of the authority of the Romish church."
"The keeping of the counterfeit Sabbath is the reception of the mark."
- Ellen G. White, "The Great Controversy," Vol. 4, page 281.

ISAIAH 24:5 (NKJV):

The earth is also defiled under its inhabitants, because they have transgressed the laws, *changed the ordinance, broken the everlasting covenant.*

The Catholic Church has deceived many mainstream Christians into honoring Sunday, the first-day of the week, as the Sabbath day. Not observing the proper seventh-day Sabbath day was a death penalty offense in Scripture (Exodus 31:14-15,35:2; Numbers 15:32-36). We are living under an age of grace and God knows of the deceptions that unscholarly Christians are under, being misled by Sunday Sabbath-honoring organized Christian religious institutions.

1 CORINTHIANS 6:9-10 (NKJV) (HSV†):

Do you not know that the unrighteous will not inherit the reign of Elohim (kingdom of God)? Do not be deceived. Neither fornicators, nor idolaters, nor adulterers, nor effeminate, nor homosexuals, nor thieves, nor covetous (†greedy of gain), nor drunkards, nor revilers, nor swindlers will inherit the reign of kingdom of God (†reign of Elohim).

GALATIANS 5:19-21 (NKJV) (HSV†):

Now the works of the flesh are evident, which are: adultery, fornication, uncleanness, lewdness, idolatry, drug sorcery, hatred, quarrels, jealousies, fits of rage, selfish ambitions, dissensions, heresies, envy, murders, drunkenness, revelries, and the like; of which I tell you beforehand, just as I also told you in time past, that those who practice such things will not inherit the reign of kingdom of God (†reign of Elohim).

REVELATION 21:7-8 (NKJV):

He who overcomes shall inherit all things, and I will be his God and he shall be My son. The cowardly, untrustworthy, abominable, murderers, sexually immoral, drug sorcerers, idolators, and all liars shall have their part in the lake which burns with fire and brimstone, which is the second death.

Christians, throughout millennia, have been misled by the first-day Sunday Sabbath deception. God, in His mercy, did not list Sabbath breakers among sinners to be excluded from inheriting the kingdom of God, according to 1 Corinthians 6:9-10, Galatians 5:19-21, and Revelation 21:7-8, but improper Sabbath day keepers will need to be corrected before entering His kingdom.

THE 666 MARK OF THE BEAST IN REVELATION

REVELATION 13:16-18 (NKJV):

He causes all, both small and great, rich and poor, free and slave, to receive a mark on their right hand or on their foreheads, *AND THAT NO ONE MAY BUY OR SELL* except one who has the mark or the name of the beast, or the number of his name.

Here is wisdom. Let him who has understanding calculate the number of the beast, for it is the number of a man: His number is 666.

The problem, obviously, with Seventh-day Adventists' doctrinal belief that Sunday Sabbath observance equates to receiving the mark of the beast, is that the mark of the beast of Revelation has nothing to do with the Sabbath. Saturday Sabbath observers are not prevented from buying or selling. The Antimessiah (Antichrist), after the collapse of the world's economies, will impose some type of electronic mark to be implanted on the right hand or forehead, which will allow people to buy and sell. No one, small or great, rich or poor, free or slave, will be able to buy or sell anything without receiving this mark on *any* day of the week.

Seventh-day Adventists have argued against the literal buying and selling aspect of the mark for the sake of their doctrine. They claim that the mark on the forehead figuratively represents first-day Sabbath acceptance and the mark on the right hand symbolized first-day Sabbath work.

Breaking any of God's commands is a type of a mark of disobedience. There are many antimessiahs (antichrists), but only one Antimessiah (Antichrist) (1 John 2:18). There are many types of marks (Genesis 4:15; Job 10:14; Ezekiel 9:4,6), but only one mark of the beast (Revelation 13:16-18,14:9-11,15:2,16:2,19:20,20:4).

REVELATION 16:1-2 (NKJV):

Then I heard a loud voice from the temple saying to the seven angels, "Go and pour out the bowls of the wrath of God on the earth." So the first went and poured out his bowl upon the earth, and a *foul and loathsome sore* came upon the men who had the mark of the beast and those who worshiped his image.

Sunday Sabbath observers do not get sores from their incorrect Sabbath day observance, nor are they engaged in worshiping an image of the beast (Antimessiah / Antichrist). These sores, a bowl judgment of the wrath of God, will be physical sores from receiving the physical 666 mark of the beast. Seventh-day Adventists are correct in proclaiming the seventh-day Sabbath as a perpetual covenant that will last forever, but err in proclaiming that Sunday Sabbath observers have received the mark of the beast.

STATE OF THE DEAD ...
WHAT HAPPENS WHEN WE DIE?

By George Lujack

Do the souls of the righteous go to heaven upon death, or are the dead saints awaiting the resurrection as they rest in peace unconsciously in death? Will the souls of the dead return back to the world to re-inhabit their earthly bodies? This article will address this emotionally contentious issue, arguing that no one has yet ascended to heaven, with the exception of Yeshua (Jesus).

Christian ministers, throughout millennia, have comforted many grieving believers' families by telling them that their recently deceased loved ones have gone on to a better place, heaven, and that they are with God now. Often the impulse to tell this story is to alleviate grief and comfort those who are mourning. A lie or untruth is still a lie or untruth however, and as such shouldn't be told no matter what the rationale is, even if it is to comfort the grief stricken.

WHY IS HEAVEN UPON DEATH TAUGHT AND BELIEVED?

People do not want to believe in death, but rather in the immortality of the soul.

GENESIS 3:1-5 (NKJV):

Now the serpent was more cunning than any beast of the field that YHWH (the Lord) God had made. And he said to the woman, "Has God indeed said, 'You shall not eat of every tree of the garden'?" And the woman said to the serpent, "We may eat the fruit of the trees of the garden; but of the fruit of the tree which is in the midst of the garden, God has said, 'You shall not eat it, nor shall you touch it, lest you die.'" Then the serpent said to the woman, "YOU WILL NOT SURELY DIE. For God knows that in the day you eat of it your eyes will be opened, and you will be like God, knowing good and evil."

People desire to believe in the lie the serpent told Eve in the Garden of Eden with a twist: "You will surely not die. Your soul will instantly leave your body and live in heaven, with God." People want to believe their deceased loved ones are dwelling securely in heaven with God, rather than the truth that they are dead in their graves awaiting their resurrection.

IS ABSENT FROM THE BODY, IN DEATH, TO BE PRESENT WITH THE LORD, IN HEAVEN?

Many have falsely believed that the Apostle Paul wrote to be absent in the body (in death) meant to be present with the Lord (in heaven), by imposing their belief upon Scripture.

2 CORINTHIANS 5:6-9 (NKJV):

So we are always confident, knowing that while we are at home in the body we are absent from the Lord. For we walk by faith, not by sight. We are confident, yes, well pleased rather to be ABSENT FROM THE BODY AND TO BE PRESENT WITH THE LORD. Therefore we make it our aim, whether present or absent, to be well pleasing to Him.

The true meaning of what Paul wrote was to be absent from the body (in deep prayer and meditation) was to be spiritually present with the Lord.

PHILIPPIANS 1:19-23 (NKJV):

For I know that this will turn out for my deliverance through your prayer and the supply of the Spirit of Jesus Christ, according to my earnest expectation and hope that in nothing I shall be ashamed, but with all boldness, as always, so now also Messiah (Christ) will be magnified in my body, whether by life or by death.

For to me, to live is Messiah (Christ), and to die is gain. But if I live on in the flesh, this will mean fruit from my labor; yet what I shall choose I cannot tell. For I am hard-pressed between the two, having a desire to depart and be with Messiah (Christ), which is far better.

Did Paul think that to die was gain, because he would go straight to heaven and instantaneously be with the Messiah (Christ)? No. What Paul was saying is that he was to live for Messiah (Christ), and bear fruit through his labor for God's kingdom, or die for Messiah (Christ) in martyrdom. Paul knew to die for Messiah (Christ) meant eventual gain in God's kingdom. Paul so desired not to be in this world that he thought it better to die for Messiah (Christ) and gain through receiving the martyr's reward in God's kingdom. Paul knew that when he died, his next conscious moment would be standing before Messiah (Christ).

THE DEAD KNOW NOTHING AND CANNOT PRAISE OR SERVE GOD

PSALM 115:17 (NKJV):

The dead do not praise the Lord, nor do any who go down into silence.

ECCLESIASTES 9:5 (NKJV):

For the living know that they will die, but the dead know nothing.

The dead cannot serve or please God and the dead know nothing, as they are in a state of unconsciousness in death. If the dead went directly to heaven upon death, it could not be written in Scripture that the dead know nothing. The dead know nothing, because they are dead and void of life. The dead are no longer conscious and aware. The dead are not alive, have no consciousness, and are therefore lifeless by definition.

MAN WAS CREATED A LIVING BEING / SOUL / SPIRIT

GENESIS 2:7 (NKJV):

And YHWH (the Lord) God formed man of the dust of the ground, and breathed into his nostrils the breath of life; and man became a living being* (*soul KJV).

Man was created as a living being / soul / spirit. The soul does not live apart from the body, nor does the body live apart from the soul. When a man dies, he dies body and soul. The soul is not immortal; his soul dies with him.

OUR SOULS ARE IN GOD'S HANDS WHEN WE DIE

LUKE 23:46 (NKJV):
And when Yeshua (Jesus) had cried out with a loud voice, He said, "Father, into Your hands I commit My spirit." Having said this, He breathed His last.

When Yeshua (Jesus) died, His spirit was in God's care until God resurrected Him 3-days later. Likewise, the souls of the dead are in God the Father's care until He resurrects the dead on the last day.

IS THE SOUL IMMORTAL? CAN THE SOUL DIE?

The soul is not immortal. The souls of unrepentant sinners will perish and die.

EZEKIEL 18:4,20 (NKJV):
The soul who sins shall die.

LUKE 13:3,5 (NKJV):
"I tell you, no; but unless you repent you will all likewise perish."

MATTHEW 10:28 (NKJV):
"And do not fear those who kill the body but cannot kill the soul. But rather fear Him who is able to DESTROY BOTH SOUL AND BODY in hell."

JAMES 5:20 (NKJV):
Let him know that he who turns a sinner from the error of his way will save a SOUL FROM DEATH and cover a multitude of sins.

All the souls of the dead will be resurrected from the first death. Souls who are judged to hell will die and cease to exist. They will not suffer eternal torment. The righteous will inherit eternal life and the unrighteous, those who refuse to repent, will be judged to die the second death (Revelation 2:11, 20:6,14, 21:8).

NO ONE, EXCEPT YESHUA (JESUS), HAS ASCENDED TO HEAVEN

JOHN 3:13 (NKJV):
"No one has ascended to heaven except He who came down from heaven, the Son of Man."

Yeshua's (Jesus') own testimony in Scripture affirms that there has been no human being on Earth, who has lived and died, who has ascended to heaven.

JOHN 11:11-14 (NKJV):

Yeshua (Jesus) said to them, "Our friend Lazarus sleeps, but I go that I may wake him up." Then His disciples said, "Lord, if he sleeps he will get well." However, Yeshua (Jesus) spoke of his death, but they thought that He was speaking about taking rest in sleep. Then Yeshua (Jesus) said to them plainly, "Lazarus is dead."

JOHN 11:20-24 (NKJV):

Now Martha, as soon as she heard that Yeshua (Jesus) was coming, went and met Him, but Mary was sitting in the house. Now Martha said to Yeshua (Jesus), "Lord, if You had been here, my brother would not have died. But even now I know that whatever You ask of God, God will give You."

Yeshua (Jesus) said to her, "Your brother will rise again."

Martha said to Him, "I know that he will rise again IN THE RESURRECTION AT THE LAST DAY."

Martha knew Lazarus did not go to heaven when he died. She also believed the dead, including Lazarus, would live again at the resurrection.

Yeshua (Jesus) compared Lazarus' death to sleep. Yeshua (Jesus) did not call Lazarus' soul down from heaven and back into his body, but instead He "woke" him. Yeshua (Jesus) resurrected Lazarus from the unconsciousness of death.

DID ENOCH AND ELIJAH ASCEND TO HEAVEN?

Many have assumed that Scripture declares that Enoch and Elijah were taken into God's heavenly kingdom. This belief should be rejected based on Yeshua's (Jesus') testimony that no one has ascended to heaven, but Himself (John 3:13).

GENESIS 5:24 (NKJV):

And Enoch walked with God; and he was not, for God took him.

Enoch "was not." Enoch was not found among the dead. God took Enoch *somewhere*, and buried him *someplace*. Many assume that God took Enoch to heaven, to dwell with Him, but that is not what Scripture actually says.[110]

2 KINGS 2:1,11 (NKJV):

And it came to pass, when the Lord was about to take up Elijah into heaven by a whirlwind, that Elijah went with Elisha from Gilgal. …

Then it happened, as they continued on and talked, that suddenly a chariot of fire appeared with horses of fire, and separated the two of them; and Elijah went up by a whirlwind into heaven.

The account of Elijah being taken up by a whirlwind, into 'heaven,' does not mean Elijah entered paradise. 2 Kings 2:1 and 11 should be understood to mean that Elijah was taken up into the heaven or clouds, which is often used in Scripture to describe the firmament or sky (Genesis 1:8).

2 KINGS 2:16 (NKJV):

Then they said to him, "Look now, there are fifty strong men with your servants. Please let them go and search for your master, lest perhaps the Spirit of YHWH (the Lord) has taken him up and cast him upon some mountain or into some valley."

It was believed by the men who witnessed Elijah being taken up by a chariot of fire, that the Spirit of YHWH (the Lord) took Elijah up into the sky and cast him upon some mountain or into some valley (2 Kings 2:16), and did not take Elijah to dwell with Him in paradise.

Elijah could not have gone to heaven, the paradise dwelling place of God, as Yeshua (Jesus) declared that no man had yet ascended to heaven (John 3:13).

Elijah likely spent the rest of his life on Earth dwelling with God and serving him, before dying on His mountain.

DID YESHUA (JESUS) DECLARE MOSES, ABRAHAM, ISAAC, AND JACOB TO BE AMONG THE LIVING?

MARK 12:25-27 (NKJV):

"FOR WHEN THEY RISE FROM THE DEAD, they neither marry nor are given in marriage, but are like angels in heaven. BUT CONCERNING THE DEAD, that they rise, have you not read in the book of Moses, in the burning bush passage, how God spoke to him, saying, 'I am the God of Abraham, the God of Isaac, and the God of Jacob'?
HE IS NOT THE GOD OF THE DEAD, but the God of the living.
You are therefore greatly mistaken."

Many are greatly mistaken in believing that this passage means that Abraham, Isaac, and Jacob are LIVING in heaven. That is not what Yeshua (Jesus) actually said. What He did say about Abraham, Isaac, and Jacob WHO WERE DEAD, is that God is not the God of the dead (Abraham, Isaac, and Jacob), but the living. What God meant when He spoke to Moses through the burning bush, is that He was the God of Abraham, Isaac, and Jacob, but now they are dead and He is not the God of the dead, but the living.

Abraham, Isaac, and Jacob ARE DEAD. God is not God of the dead (including Abraham, Isaac, and Jacob). That is, God does not rule over the dead in their state of sleep, but He is the God of the living. When the dead rise from their graves, (including Abraham, Isaac, and Jacob), *then* God will resume His role as being God over Abraham, Isaac, and Jacob, as they will no longer be dead, but alive again after their resurrection.

Abraham, Isaac, and Jacob all died before the birth of Messiah (Christ). Yeshua Messiah (Jesus Christ) said plainly that no one had ascended to heaven. Therefore, Abraham, Isaac, and Jacob are not living in heaven, because no one had yet ascended to heaven when Yeshua (Jesus) spoke these words:

JOHN 3:13 (NKJV):

"NO ONE has ascended to heaven but He who came down from heaven, that is, the Son of Man."

DID THE CRIMINAL (ALLEGED THIEF) ON THE CROSS GO TO PARADISE?

The English translators made a simple error in comma placement that has led many to falsely believe that the alleged thief on the cross (a criminal whose actual crime is not confirmed in Scripture - Luke 23:32-33,39) went with Yeshua (Jesus) to paradise on the day they both died.[111]

COMMON INCORRECT (comma placement):

LUKE 23:43 (NKJV):

And Yeshua (Jesus) said to him, "Assuredly, I say to you(,) today you will be with Me in Paradise."

PROPER CORRECT (comma placement):

LUKE 23:43 (NKJV):

And Yeshua (Jesus) said to him, "Assuredly, I say to you today(,) you will be with Me in Paradise."

Yeshua (Jesus) did not go to paradise the day He died. Yeshua (Jesus) was crucified, was unconscious in death for three days and three nights, and was then resurrected. Upon His resurrection, He first spoke with Miriam (Mary) Magdalene:

JOHN 20:17 (NKJV):

YESHUA (Jesus) said to her, "Do not cling to Me, for I HAVE NOT YET ASCENDED TO MY FATHER; but go to My brethren and say to them, 'I am ascending to My Father and your Father, and to My God and your God.'"

The criminal (thief on the cross) will be with Yeshua (Jesus) in paradise, in the future, after he is resurrected to everlasting life.

WAS MIRIAM (MARY) ASSUMED INTO HEAVEN?

There is no Scripture verse, at all, to support the Catholic doctrine that Mary, the mother of Yeshua (Jesus) was assumed into heaven. The Catholic faith is a deceptive faith that often plays with words and uses language confusion to deceive the Catholic flock. The Catholic Church is well aware of Yeshua's (Jesus') declaration that no one has ascended to heaven (John 3:13). So, rather than say that Mary ASCENDED to heaven, they declare that she was ASSUMED into heaven, as if that verbiage makes a difference. The Catholic Church changes terms in an attempt to twist and change Scripture to accommodate their faith. They spin falsehoods without any Scripture support. Catholics may call a Catholic divorce an annulment, but it is still a divorce.

KING DAVID DID NOT ASCEND TO HEAVEN

ACTS 2:29,34 (NKJV):

Men and brethren, let me speak freely to you of the patriarch David, that he is both dead and buried, and his tomb is with us to this day. ...
For David did not ascend into the heavens.

YESHUA (JESUS) WILL DESCEND FROM HEAVEN TO THE CLOUDS; THE DEAD WILL RISE; THEY WILL NOT DESCEND

MARK 12:25-26 (NKJV):

"For when they RISE FROM THE DEAD, they neither marry nor are given in marriage, but are like angels in heaven. BUT CONCERNING THE DEAD, THAT THEY RISE..."

1 CORINTHIANS 15:20-23 (NKJV):

But now Christ is risen from the dead, and has become the first-fruit of those who have fallen asleep [DIED]. For since by man came death, by Man also came the resurrection of the dead. For as in Adam all die, even so in Messiah (Christ) all SHALL BE MADE ALIVE. But each one in his own order: Messiah (Christ) the first-fruit, AFTERWARD those who are Messiah's (Christ's) AT HIS COMING.

1 CORINTHIANS 15:51-53 (NKJV):

Behold, I tell you a mystery: We shall not all sleep, but we shall all be changed - in a moment, in the twinkling of an eye, at the last trumpet. For the trumpet will sound, and THE DEAD WILL BE RAISED incorruptible, and we shall be changed. For this corruptible must put on incorruption, and this mortal must put on immortality.

1 THESSALONIANS 4:15-17 (NKJV):

For this we say to you by the word of the Lord, that we who are alive and remain until the coming of the Lord will by no means precede those carried up who are asleep [DEAD]. FOR THE LORD HIMSELF WILL DESCEND FROM HEAVEN with a shout, with the voice of an archangel, and with the trumpet of God. AND THE DEAD IN MESSIAH (CHRIST) WILL RISE FIRST. Then we who are alive and remain shall be caught up together with them in the clouds to meet the Lord in the air. And thus we shall always be with the Lord.

Scripture proclaims that Yeshua (Jesus) will descend from heaven and the dead will rise from death. The souls of the dead will not descend from heaven, with Yeshua (Jesus), and go back into their earthly bodies. The dead in Messiah (Christ) at His coming will rise from sleep (death) and shall be made alive, will be changed into incorruptible beings, and then ascend to the clouds to be forever with Yeshua (Jesus).

Yeshua (Jesus) will gather His risen and raptured saints and afterward, when He returns to Earth to establish His Millennium Kingdom, He will return with them (Revelation 20:4-6). Until the dead are raised in their resurrection, their souls remain in a state of death, resting in peace, unconscious, and unaware of the passage of time.

DID THE APOSTLE PAUL DECLARE THAT TO BE ABSENT FROM THE BODY, IN DEATH, IS TO BE PRESENT WITH THE LORD?

By George Lujack

Many misunderstand Paul's statements to mean that Paul desired to be dead, that Paul would 'rather' be dead than living in the present, so that he could be present with the Lord. This is not the case at all, for the dead cannot serve or please God, the dead know nothing, and God does not rule over the dead.

2 CORINTHIANS 5:6-9 (NKJV):

So we are always confident, knowing that while we are at home in the body we are absent from the Lord. For we walk by faith, not by sight. We are confident, yes, well pleased *rather* TO BE ABSENT FROM THE BODY AND TO BE PRESENT WITH THE LORD. Therefore we make it our aim, WHETHER PRESENT OR ABSENT, to be well pleasing to Him.

PSALM 115:17 (NKJV):

The dead do not praise the Lord, nor any who go down into silence.

ECCLESIASTES 9:5 (NKJV):

The dead know nothing...

All who have ever died cannot please God in death and are awaiting the resurrection in a state of death and unconsciousness. What then did Paul mean when he declared, "to be absent from the body is to be present with the Lord?" He was speaking of being absent from the body, *in prayer and meditation*.

There are two ways to interpret and understand 2 Corinthians 5:6-9:

2 CORINTHIANS 5:6-9 (NKJV) [WITH INTERPRETATION]:

So we are always confident, knowing that while we are at home in the body we are absent from the Lord. For we walk by faith, not by sight. We are confident, yes, well pleased rather to be absent from the body [IN DEATH] and to be present with the Lord. Therefore we make it our aim, whether present or absent [DEAD], to be well pleasing to Him.

2 CORINTHIANS 5:6-9 (NKJV) [WITH INTERPRETATION]:

So we are always confident, knowing that while we are at home in the body we are absent from the Lord. For we walk by faith, not by sight. We are confident, yes, well pleased rather to be absent from the body [IN PRAYER AND MEDITATION] and to be present with the Lord. Therefore we make it our aim, whether present or absent [IN PRAYER AND MEDITATION], to be well pleasing to Him.

Paul meditated in prayer through which he was in communion with Yeshua (Jesus), who directed Paul to write his epistles. Paul's letters were the word of God, and he received instruction from Yeshua (Jesus) of what to write, when he was ABSENT FROM THE CONGREGATION DURING TRAVELS -OR- ABSENT FROM THE BODY IN PRAYER AND MEDITATION. We can clearly see this from other related similar verses.

1 CORINTHIANS 5:3 (NKJV):

For I indeed, AS ABSENT IN BODY BUT PRESENT IN SPIRIT, have already judged (as though I were present) him who has so done this deed.

2 CORINTHIANS 10:1,11 (NKJV):

I, Paul, myself am pleading with you by the meekness and gentleness of Messiah (Christ) - who IN PRESENCE am lowly among you, but BEING ABSENT am bold toward you. ...

Let such a person consider this, that WHAT WE ARE BY LETTERS WHEN WE ARE ABSENT, such we will also be in deed WHEN WE ARE PRESENT.

2 CORINTHIANS 13:2,10 (NKJV):

I have told you before, and foretell as IF I WERE PRESENT the second time, AND NOW BEING ABSENT I write to those who have sinned before, and to all the rest, that if I come again I will not spare. ...

Therefore I write these things BEING ABSENT, LEST BEING PRESENT I should use sharpness, according to the authority that the Lord has given me for edification and not for destruction.

PHILIPPIANS 1:27 (NKJV):

Only let your conduct be worthy of the gospel of Messiah, so that whether I come and see you OR I AM ABSENT, I may hear of your affairs, that you stand fast in one spirit, with one mind striving together for the faith of the gospel...

PHILIPPIANS 2:12-13 (NKJV):

Therefore, my beloved, as you have always obeyed, NOT AS IN MY PRESENCE ONLY, BUT NOW MUCH MORE IN MY ABSENCE, work out your own salvation with fear and trembling; for it is God who works in you both to will and to do for His good pleasure.

COLOSSIANS 2:5 (NKJV):

FOR THOUGH I AM ABSENT IN THE FLESH, yet I am with you in spirit, rejoicing to see your good order and the steadfastness of your faith in Messiah.

It is clear through a comprehensive reading of Scripture, upon reading other verse examples, that when Paul spoke of being absent from the body and present with the Lord, he was speaking of being absent from the body in spiritual meditation and prayer, not absent from the body in death.

Believers are likewise instructed to meditate, pray, and study God's word.

PSALM 19:14 (NKJV):

Let the words of my mouth and the MEDITATION of my heart be acceptable in Your sight, O Lord, my strength and Redeemer.

PSALM 119:15-16,27,48,78,148 (NKJV):

I will MEDITATE on Your precepts, and contemplate Your ways. I will delight in Your statutes; I will not forget Your word.

I shall MEDITATE on Your wonderful works. … I will MEDITATE on Your statutes. …

I will MEDITATE on Your precepts. … That I may MEDITATE on Your word.

DID YESHUA (JESUS) DECLARE ABRAHAM, ISAAC, AND JACOB TO BE AMONG THE LIVING?

By George Lujack

Many are greatly mistaken in believing that Yeshua (Jesus) declared that Abraham, Isaac, and Jacob are living and are assumably in heaven.

MARK 12:25-27 (NKJV):

"FOR WHEN THEY RISE FROM THE DEAD, they neither marry nor are given in marriage, but are like angels in heaven. BUT CONCERNING THE DEAD, that they rise, have you not read in the book of Moses, in the burning bush passage, how God spoke to him, saying, 'I am the God of Abraham, the God of Isaac, and the God of Jacob'? HE IS NOT THE GOD OF THE DEAD, but the God of the living. You are therefore greatly mistaken."

What Yeshua (Jesus) said, about Abraham, Isaac, and Jacob WHO WERE DEAD, is that God is not the God of the dead (Abraham, Isaac, and Jacob), but of the living. What He said is that God spoke to Moses through the burning bush, saying He was the God of Abraham, Isaac, and Jacob, but now they are dead and He is not the God of the dead, but of the living.

Abraham, Isaac, and Jacob ARE DEAD. God is not God of the dead (including Abraham, Isaac, and Jacob). That is, God does not rule over the dead in their state of death, but He is the God of the living. When the dead rise from their graves, (including Abraham, Isaac, and Jacob), *then* God will resume His role as being God over Abraham, Isaac, and Jacob, as they will no longer be dead, but among the living again after their resurrection.

Abraham, Isaac, and Jacob all died before the birth of Messiah (Christ). Yeshua Messiah (Jesus Christ) said plainly that no one had ascended to heaven. Therefore, Abraham, Isaac, and Jacob are not among the living in heaven, because no one had yet ascended to heaven when Yeshua (Jesus) spoke these words:

JOHN 3:13 (NKJV):

"NO ONE has ascended to heaven but He who came down from heaven, that is, the Son of Man."

DID THE DEAD, BEFORE MESSIAH (CHRIST), GO TO SPIRIT PRISON?

By George Lujack

Yeshua (Jesus) did not go to hell and visit with souls in spirit prison. Hell is death. There is no consciousness in death nor is there a spirit prison located in a place called hell. This belief is based on some very misunderstood B'rit Hadashah (New Testament) verses:

1 PETER 3:18-20 (NKJV):

For Messiah (Christ) also suffered once for sins, the just for the unjust, that He might bring us to God, being put to death in the flesh but made alive by the Spirit, BY WHOM ALSO HE WENT AND PREACHED TO THE SPIRITS IN PRISON, who formerly were disobedient, when once the Divine longsuffering waited in the days of Noah, while the ark was being prepared, in which a few, that is, eight souls, were saved through water.

How should we interpret what 1 Peter 3:18-20 means? These verses must be read in the context of other related verses such as Acts 26:23.

ACTS 26:23 (NKJV):

The Messiah (Christ) would suffer, that He would be THE FIRST to rise from the dead, and would proclaim light to the Jewish people and to the Gentiles.

Yeshua (Jesus) was the first to rise from the grave (to eternal life). If one believes that ever since Adam, people rose from the grave and were sent to spirit prison, this is faulty thinking based on Acts 26:23, along with many other corresponding Scripture verses that declare that the dead are unconscious, in their graves, and know nothing. Yeshua Messiah (Jesus Christ) was the first to rise from the dead. Adam, Noah, and all before Him therefore could not have risen from death to be sent to spirit prison.

What then of 1 Peter 3:18-20? Who did Yeshua (Jesus) visit and how? Spirits in prison refers to *living spirits* (human beings) in actual prisons. When God made Adam, he was made a living spirit (or soul - Genesis 2:7). While we may think the word 'spirit' does not pertain to living beings, Scripture often uses the word 'spirit' in this manner.

GENESIS 2:7 (NKJV):

And YHWH (the Lord) God formed man of the dust of the ground, and breathed into his nostrils the breath of life; and man became a living soul.

Yeshua (Jesus), as the Messiah, visited those who were in spiritual prison, in bondage to sin, to declare the truth and set them free.

JOHN 8:31-36 (NKJV):

Then Yeshua (Jesus) said to those Jews who believed Him, "If you abide in My word, you are My disciples indeed. And you shall know the truth, and the truth shall make you free."

They answered Him, "We are Abraham's descendants, and have never been in bondage to anyone. How can You say, 'You will be made free'?"

Yeshua (Jesus) answered them, "Most assuredly, I say to you, whoever commits sin is a slave of sin. And a slave does not abide in the house forever, but a son abides forever. Therefore if the Son makes you free, you shall be free indeed."

MATTHEW 9:12-13; MARK 2:17; LUKE 5:31-32 (NKJV):

Yeshua (Jesus) said to them, "Those who are well have no need of a physician, but those who are sick. I have not come to call the righteous, but sinners, to repentance."

Yeshua (Jesus) may have also visited living beings (spirits), saints being held in (Roman) prisons. How could He have visited them? If He did, and it was not otherwise recorded in Scripture, it would have been through His Spirit, in the same manner that He had once appeared to the Apostle Paul.

ACTS 9:3-5 (NKJV):

As he journeyed he came near Damascus, and suddenly a light shone around him from heaven. Then he fell to the ground, and heard a voice saying to him, "Saul, Saul, why are you persecuting Me?" And he said, "Who are You, Lord?"

Then the Lord said, "I am Yeshua (Jesus), whom you are persecuting..."

1 PETER 3:18-20 should be understood in the following way:

1 PETER 3:18-20 (NKJV) [WITH INTERPRETATION]:

For Messiah also suffered once for sins [ON THE CROSS], the just for the unjust, that He might bring us to God, being put to death in the flesh but made alive by the Spirit [MADE ALIVE BY THE FATHER THROUGH THE HOLY SPIRIT], by whom [BY THE HOLY SPIRIT] also He went and preached [YESHUA (JESUS) ALSO WENT AND PREACHED FOR FORTY DAYS AFTER HE WAS RESURRECTED – ACTS 1:3] to the spirits in prison [TO PEOPLE IN BONDAGE TO SIN], who formerly were disobedient [BUT BECAME OBEDIENT AND RIGHTEOUS], when once the Divine longsuffering waited in the days of Noah while the ark was being prepared, in which a few, that is, eight souls, were saved through water [YESHUA (JESUS) WAITED, SINCE THE DAYS OF NOAH, TO BECOME THE MESSIAH AND SAVIOR OF THE WORLD, AS HE ONCE SAVED EIGHT LIVING SOULS ON NOAH'S ARK FROM THE FLOOD WATERS].

Scripture declares that when we die, we remain in a state of death until the resurrection. We don't go to spirit prison or heaven. To believe otherwise is to believe the oldest lie of Satan with a twist… that we don't really die when we die, *because our spirit lives on* (Genesis 3:1-5).

HELL: ETERNAL TORMENT OR SECOND DEATH?

By George Lujack

There are two prevailing Scripture-based beliefs concerning the everlasting destiny of condemned sinners: eternal torment in hellfire or the second death. This article will examine both possibilities and argue that condemned sinners will ultimately cease to exist and die a second death. Additionally, Satan, the beast, and the false prophet will spend eternity in hell prison.

The theological belief in hell as a fiery place of eternal torment, where unrepentant sinners will be judged to burn in a lake of fire and flames forever, comes primarily from a parable that Yeshua (Jesus) told.

PARABLE OF THE RICH MAN AND LAZARUS

<u>LUKE 16:19-31 (NKJV)</u>:
"There was a certain rich man who was clothed in purple and fine linen and fared sumptuously every day. But there was a certain beggar named Lazarus, full of sores, who was laid at his gate, desiring to be fed with the crumbs which fell from the rich man's table. Moreover the dogs came and licked his sores. So it was that the beggar died, and was carried by the angels to Abraham's bosom. The rich man also died and was buried.

And being in torments in Hades, he lifted up his eyes and saw Abraham afar off, and Lazarus in his bosom.

"Then he cried and said, 'Father Abraham, have mercy on me, and send Lazarus that he may dip the tip of his finger in water and cool my tongue; for I am tormented in this flame.' But Abraham said, 'Son, remember that in your lifetime you received your good things, and likewise Lazarus evil things; but now he is comforted and you are tormented. And besides all this, between us and you there is a great gulf fixed, so that those who want to pass from here to you cannot, nor can those from there pass to us.'

"Then he said, 'I beg you therefore, father, that you would send him to my father's house, for I have five brothers, that he may testify to them, lest they also come to this place of torment.' Abraham said to him, 'They have Moses and the prophets; let them hear them.' And he said, 'No, father Abraham; but if one goes to them from the dead, they will repent.' But he said to him, 'If they do not hear Moses and the prophets, neither will they be persuaded though one rise from the dead.'"

parable:
A simple *story* used to illustrate a moral or spiritual lesson, as told by Yeshua (Jesus) in the gospels.[112]

MATTHEW 13:10-11 (NKJV):

And the disciples came and said to Him, "Why do You speak to them in parables?"

He [Yeshua (Jesus)] answered and said to them, "Because it has been given to you to know the mysteries of the kingdom of heaven, but to them it has not been given…"

The parable of the rich man and Lazarus should not be viewed as a literal account, but as a fable told to illustrate a spiritual lesson. Yeshua (Jesus) was asked why He spoke in parables by His disciples and He replied that it was to withhold the mysteries of the kingdom of heaven from the multitudes (Matthew 13:2-11). God has revealed the mysteries of gospel to the first-fruits of His kingdom and He will later on reveal His truths to all humanity (John 16:25).

The lesson that Yeshua (Jesus) imparted from the parable of the rich man and Lazarus was that if people would not listen to Moses and the prophets, to obey the law and repent, then they would likewise not listen to one (Himself) even if He were to rise from the dead.

Yeshua (Jesus) said that He did not come to destroy the law, but came to fulfill the prophets (Matthew 5:17). Those who turn away from hearing the law, even their prayers are an abomination (Proverbs 28:9).

Yeshua (Jesus) illustrates in the parable of the rich man and Lazarus that He didn't come to Earth to persuade the world through absolute proof to believe in Him by rising from the dead. Evidence of God already exists through Moses and the prophets and we should listen to them, repent, and keep the law.

The following reasons are why the parable of the rich man and Lazarus should not be accepted as a literal account:

1. Yeshua (Jesus) stated, "No one has ascended to heaven" (John 3:13). Abraham is in the grave awaiting the resurrection, as are all men (John 11:24).

2. Abraham is not a giant kangaroo with a pouch to hold the righteous dead near his chest. When righteous people die they are not taken by angels to Abraham's bosom to dwell (Luke 16:22).

3. If the rich man were flesh and blood, constantly being burned and regenerated so as to be burned and tormented eternally, then a drop of water on the tip of Lazarus' finger brought to the rich man's tongue wouldn't do anything to relieve his torment from the flames (Luke 16:24).

4. In the very parable itself, Abraham says, "between us and you there is a great gulf fixed, so that those who want to pass from here to you cannot, nor can those from there pass to us" (Luke 16:26). There is a great gulf that exists between the living and the dead. We cannot communicate with the dead. There is also no communication between those in God's kingdom and those condemned to hell. Believers in God's kingdom will not be communicating with people condemned to hell.

MARK 9:43-44 (NKJV):

If your hand causes you to sin, cut it off. It is better for you to enter into life maimed, rather than having two hands, TO GO TO HELL, INTO THE FIRE THAT SHALL NEVER BE QUENCHED - WHERE 'THEIR WORM DOES NOT DIE AND THE FIRE IS NOT QUENCHED.'

MARK 9:45-48 (NKJV):

And if your foot causes you to sin, cut it off. It is better for you to enter life lame, rather than having two feet, TO BE CAST INTO HELL, INTO THE FIRE THAT SHALL NEVER BE QUENCHED - WHERE 'THEIR WORM DOES NOT DIE AND THE FIRE IS NOT QUENCHED.'

And if your eye causes you to sin, pluck it out. It is better for you to enter the kingdom of God with one eye, rather than having two eyes, TO BE CAST INTO HELL FIRE - WHERE 'THEIR WORM DOES NOT DIE AND THE FIRE IS NOT QUENCHED.'

Many have misunderstood Mark 9:43-48 to mean that people who are cast into hell will be kept alive; that worms will constantly feed off their flesh and they will be tortured eternally with fire that will not burn out. Yeshua (Jesus) is once again speaking in descriptive figurative parabolic language in Mark 9, referring to Scripture prophesy of Isaiah 66.

ISAIAH 66:22-24 (NKJV):

"For as the new heavens and the new earth which I will make shall remain before Me," says YHWH (the Lord). "So shall your descendants and name remain. And it shall come to pass that from one New Moon to another, all flesh shall come and worship before Me," says YHWH (the Lord). And they shall go forth and look upon the CORPSES OF THE MEN who have transgressed against Me. For their worm does not die, and their fire is not quenched. They shall be an abhorrence to all flesh."

Those cast into hell will be corpses, dead bodies, not eternally tormented sinners kept alive for worms to eat and for fire to burn in everlasting torment. The reason the worms will not die is because after the worms (maggots) consume the flesh of the decomposing corpses, they will transform into flies and fly away. The flames of hell can be kept burning by God, who has lit countless stars throughout the universe that burn without quenching.

SOULS ARE NOT ETERNAL; THEY CAN BE DESTROYED AND DIE

destroy:
Put an end to the existence of (something) by damaging or attacking it.[113]

death:
The action or fact of dying or being killed; the end of the life of a person or organism.[114]

GENESIS 2:16-17 (NKJV):

And YHWH (the Lord) God commanded the man, saying, "Of every tree of the garden you may freely eat; but of the tree of the knowledge of good and evil you shall not eat, for in the day that you eat of it you shall surely DIE."

Satan's original lie, that we really don't die when we die, continues to be believed by the multitudes to this day. People generally believe that the soul does not die, but instead goes to straight to heaven, or that the soul will be judged to hell and live in eternal torment there. Death is the cessation of life, not the instantaneous continuation of it in soul-spirit form.

PROVERBS 19:16 (NKJV):

He who keeps the commandment KEEPS HIS SOUL; but he who is careless of his ways shall DIE.

EZEKIEL 18:4,20 (NKJV):

The SOUL who sins shall DIE.

CONDEMNED UNREPENTANT SINNERS WILL BE DESTROYED, CAST INTO HELL, AND DIE; HELL IS A PLACE OF DEATH

PSALM 55:15 (NKJV):

Let DEATH seize them; let them go down alive into HELL.

PROVERBS 5:3-5 (NKJV):

For the lips of an immoral woman drip honey, and her mouth is smoother than oil, but in the end she is bitter as wormwood, sharp as a two-edged sword. Her feet go down to DEATH; her steps lay hold of HELL.

PROVERBS 7:27 (NKJV):

Her house is the way to HELL, descending to the chambers of DEATH.

PROVERBS 9:18 (NKJV):

But he does not know that the DEAD are there, that her guests are in the depths of HELL.

PROVERBS 15:9-11 (NKJV):

The way of the wicked is an abomination to YHWH (the Lord), but He loves him who follows righteousness. Harsh discipline is for him who forsakes the way, and he who hates correction will DIE. HELL and DESTRUCTION are before YHWH (the Lord).

PROVERBS 15:24 (NKJV):

The way of LIFE winds upwards for the wise, that he may turn away from HELL below.

ISAIAH 14:9 (NKJV):

HELL from beneath is excited about you, to meet you at your coming. It stirs up the DEAD for you.

MATTHEW 10:28 (NKJV):

And do not fear those who KILL the body but cannot KILL the soul. But rather fear Him who is able to DESTROY *BOTH* SOUL *AND* BODY IN HELL.

LUKE 12:5 (NKJV):

"And I say to you, My friends, do not be afraid of those who kill the body, and after that have no more that they can do. But I will show you whom you should fear: Fear Him who, AFTER HE HAS KILLED, has power to cast into HELL; yes, I say to you, fear Him!"

THOSE WHO RECEIVE THE MARK OF THE BEAST WILL BE JUDGED IN THE FLESH WITH FIRE AND BRIMSTONE

REVELATION 14:9-11 (NKJV):

Then a third angel followed them, saying with a loud voice, "If anyone worships the beast and his image, and receives his mark on his forehead or on his hand, he himself shall also drink of the wine of the wrath of God, which is poured out full strength into the cup of His indignation. He shall be TORMENTED with FIRE AND BRIMSTONE in the presence of the holy angels and in the presence of the Lamb. And the smoke of their TORMENT ascends forever and ever; and they have no rest day or night, who worship the beast and his image, and whoever receives the mark of his name."

Some have read and misunderstood Revelation 14:9-11 to mean that anyone who receives the mark of the beast will be cast into hell and be tormented forever there. This is not actually the case. Whoever receives the mark will be tormented on Earth, through the judgment of the Lamb (Yeshua / Jesus). Those who receive the mark will be judged on Earth, through various fire and sulfur plagues (nuclear annihilations carried out by the Antimessiah / Antichrist and other world armies). The smoke of the torment of the earthly flesh and blood bodies of those who have received the mark, after being incinerated, will ascend forever.

CONDEMNED UNREPENTENT SINNERS WHO ARE CAST INTO HELL WILL BE BURNED UP AND WILL DIE THE SECOND DEATH

REVELATION 2:11 (NKJV) (HSV†):

"He who has an ear, let him hear what the Spirit says to the churches (†assemblies). He who overcomes shall not be hurt by the SECOND DEATH."

REVELATION 20:6 (NKJV):

Blessed and holy is he who has part in the first resurrection. Over such the SECOND DEATH has no power, but they shall be priests of God and of Messiah (Christ), and shall reign with Him a thousand years.

REVELATION 20:14-15 (NKJV):

This is the SECOND DEATH. And anyone not found written in the Book of Life was cast into the lake of fire.

REVELATION 21:8 (NKJV):

"But the cowardly, unbelieving, untrustworthy, abominable, murderers, sexually immoral, drug sorcerers, idolaters, and all liars shall have their part in the lake which burns with fire and brimstone, which is the SECOND DEATH."

The second death awaits condemned unrepentant sinners, not eternal torment in a torture chamber known as hell. Unrepentant sinners will die the first death in their flesh and blood bodies. Upon being resurrected, the soul (spirit) of those condemned will be judged to die a second time and then be thrown into hell where they will die the second death.

SATAN, THE BEAST, AND THE FALSE PROPHET WILL NOT DIE THE SECOND DEATH, BUT WILL BE TORMENTED FOREVER

torment:

Severe physical or mental suffering.[115]

REVELATION 19:19-21 (NKJV):

And I saw the beast, the kings of the earth, and their armies, gathered together to make war against Him who sat on the horse and against His army. Then the beast was captured, and with him the false prophet who worked signs in his presence, by which he deceived those who received the mark of the beast and those who worshiped his image. These two were cast alive into the lake of fire burning with brimstone. AND THE REST WERE KILLED with the sword, which proceeded from the mouth of Him who sat on the horse. And all the birds were filled with their flesh.

REVELATION 20:10 (NKJV):

The devil, who deceived them, was cast into the lake of fire and brimstone where the beast and the false prophet are. And THEY will be TORMENTED day and night FOREVER AND EVER.

Satan, the beast (Antimessiah / Antichrist), and the false prophet (final Catholic pope) will be kept alive and tormented forever in hell. The rest (their armies, those who receive the mark) will be killed.

Why doesn't God kill Satan? This is a theological question that is not answered in Scripture. It can be theorized that God had already granted Satan and the angels eternal life. Since God is holy, once He gives His word He must keep it. Therefore, if God cannot kill Satan without going back on His promise of granting Satan eternal life before Satan sinned, He must imprison Satan forever instead of judging Satan to eternal death.

As for the beast (Antimessiah / Antichrist) and false prophet, as flesh and blood human beings, why do they not die the second death? Again, this is a theological question not answered in Scripture, but it can be surmised that they may have pledged their souls to serve Satan, and God in judgment, will grant them their wish and they will exist with Satan, alive and tormented, for all eternity.

Scripture proclaims that these three, Satan, the beast, and the false prophet will be *tormented* forever. That does not mean that they will be searing in burning torture forever. Being held in hell prison forever will be torment. These three will be tormented mentally in their spirit bodies; they will not exist in flesh and blood bodies that are capable of burning in agonizing pain, then having their flesh supernaturally renewed by God to be in a state of unthinkable continual agonizing torture.

SATAN WILL BE BOUND FOR ONE THOUSAND YEARS OF HELL PRISON *BEFORE* BEING SENTENCED TO ETERNAL HELL PRISON

REVELATION 20:1-2 (NKJV):

Then I saw an angel coming down from heaven, having the key to the bottomless pit and a great chain in his hand. He laid hold of the dragon, that serpent of old, who is the Devil and Satan, and BOUND him for a thousand years;

REVELATION 20:3,7-8 (NKJV):

and he cast him into the bottomless pit, and shut him up, and set a seal on him, so that he should deceive the nations no more till the thousand years were finished. But after these things he must be released for a little while. ...

Now when the thousand years have expired, Satan will be released from his PRISON and will go out to deceive the nations...

Satan will be bound in hell prison for a thousand years, released for a while, and then will be bound once again in hell prison with the beast and false prophet for all eternity. Being held in hell prison *will be* torment for these three evil beings for all eternity.

torture:

The action or practice of inflicting severe pain on someone as a punishment or to force them to do or say something, or for the pleasure of the person inflicting the pain.[116]

EZEKIEL 18:32, 33:11 (NKJV):

"For I have no pleasure in the death of one who dies," says YHWH (the Lord) GOD. "Therefore turn and live!" ...

'As I live,' says YHWH (the Lord) GOD, 'I have no pleasure in the death of the wicked, but that the wicked turn from his way and live. Turn, turn from your evil ways! For why should you die...?

PSALM 116:5 (NKJV):

Yes, our God is merciful.

(Exodus 34:6; Deuteronomy 4:31; 2 Chronicles 30:9; Nehemiah 9:17,31; Joel 2:13; Jonah 4:2; Hebrews 2:17).

Our God is a merciful God, not a torturer. Torture is evil and sadistic. God is not one who receives pleasure from torture. God will have mercy on condemned humanity, destroying them in the second death. God, in His mercy, will not keep condemned mankind bound alive and tortured for all eternity. God will not even inflict torture on Satan, the beast, and the false prophet, who surely deserve it, but will keep them imprisoned forever. Hell is a place of the second death for condemned sinners and will be the eternal holding prison for Satan, the beast, and the false prophet.

INHERITING THE KINGDOM OF GOD

By George Lujack

Are some Christians giving up their chance to inherit the kingdom of God for a particular sin as Esau gave up his worldly birthright inheritance for a bowl of stew?

GENESIS 25:29-33 (NKJV):

Jacob cooked a stew; and Esau came in from the field, and he was weary. And Esau said to Jacob, "Please feed me with that same red stew, for I am weary." Therefore his name was called Edom. But Jacob said, "Sell me your birthright as of this day." And Esau said, "Look, I am about to die; so what is this birthright to me?" Then Jacob said, "Swear to me as of this day." So he swore to him, and sold his birthright to Jacob. And Jacob gave Esau bread and stew of lentils; then he ate and drank, arose, and went his way. Thus Esau despised his birthright.

Is there a deeper meaning in the story of Esau giving up his worldly birthright inheritance? Could this story be a reflection of how *many persons* will give up their inheritance to the kingdom of God for a bowl of stew (some sin)?

There are many who believe in God, yet deceive themselves, believing that they can still have their bowl of stew (sin) and will be able to inherit the kingdom of God. Scripture declares that this will not be the case…

MATTHEW 7:21 (NKJV):

"Not everyone who says to Me, 'Lord, Lord,' shall enter the kingdom of heaven, but he who does the will of My Father in heaven."

LUKE 13:24 (NKJV):

Yeshua (Jesus) said, "Strive to enter through the narrow gate, for many, I say to you, will seek to enter and will not be able."

Why will many 'not be able' to enter the kingdom of heaven?

It is because many people of this world cling to some sin, some particular 'cup of stew,' and in doing so forfeit their birthright to inherit the kingdom of heaven.

1 CORINTHIANS 6:9-10 (NKJV) (HSV†):

Do you not know that the unrighteous will not inherit the reign of Elohim (kingdom of God)? Do not be deceived. Neither fornicators, nor idolaters, nor adulterers, nor effeminate, nor homosexuals, nor thieves, nor covetous (†greedy of gain), nor drunkards, nor revilers, nor swindlers will inherit the kingdom of God (†reign of Elohim).

GALATIANS 5:19-21 (NKJV) (HSV†):

Now the works of the flesh are evident, which are: adultery, fornication, uncleanness, lewdness, idolatry, drug sorcery, hatred, quarrels, jealousies, fits of rage, selfish ambitions, dissensions, heresies, envy, murders, drunkenness, revelries, and the like; of which I tell you beforehand, just as I also told you in time past, that those who practice such things will not inherit the kingdom of God (†reign of Elohim).

REVELATION 21:7-8 (NKJV):

He who overcomes shall inherit all things, and I will be his God and he shall be My son. The cowardly, untrustworthy, abominable, murderers, sexually immoral, drug sorcerers, idolators, and all liars shall have their part in the lake which burns with fire and brimstone, which is the second death.

1 Corinthians 6:9-10, Galatians 5:19-21, and Revelation 21:7-8 serve as checklists of the serious sins that can keep believers from inheriting the kingdom of God, if they are actively practicing these sins or are unrepentant after having committed them.

Many believe that lesser laws in the Tanakh (Old Testament) are no longer sins, are permissible, or obsolete, and cannot keep a believer from inheriting the kingdom of God. Many delude themselves into believing that they can disregard the Sabbath, observe pagan-inspired holidays such as Christmas and Easter, smoke cigarettes, eat unclean creatures, and still be acceptable before God to enter the kingdom of God. After all, these sins are not listed as sins in 1 Corinthians 6:9-10, Galatians 5:19-21, and Revelation 21:7-8, which can keep us out of the kingdom of heaven.

All sins are sins that cause us to fall short of the glory of God. Worship God through condemned pagan practices and you are guilty of idolatry; use narcotic drugs, smoke cigarettes, and eat forbidden unclean creatures and you are guilty of coveting something forbidden by God and murder, as you are defiling and slowly killing your own body. The first sin was, after all, disobedience to God by eating from the forbidden fruit of the tree of the knowledge of good and evil (Genesis 3:6).

MATTHEW 5:17-19 (NKJV):

"Do not think that I came to destroy the Law or the Prophets. I did not come to destroy but to fulfill. For assuredly, I say to you, till heaven and earth pass away, one jot or one tittle will by no means pass from the law till all is fulfilled. Whoever therefore breaks one of the least of these commandments, and teaches men so, SHALL BE CALLED LEAST IN THE KINGDOM OF HEAVEN; but whoever does and teaches them, he SHALL BE CALLED GREAT IN THE KINGDOM OF HEAVEN."

Sabbath breaking, celebrating Christianized pagan holidays, and eating unclean creatures may not cause ignorant believers to lose their inheritance to the kingdom of God, but they will need to receive correction before entering. There will be some who break the lesser laws of God (laws not mentioned in 1 Corinthians 6:9-10), and teach others to break them, who will be called 'least' in the kingdom of heaven, and there will be those who obey the lesser laws (laws not mentioned in 1 Corinthians 6:9-10, Galatians 5:19-21, and Revelation 21:7-8), and teach others to obey them, who will be called 'great' in the kingdom of heaven (Matthew 5:18-19).

2 CORINTHIANS 13:5 (NKJV):
Examine yourselves as to whether you are in the faith. Test yourselves.

Instead of excusing sin, even little sins, Scripture instructs us to examine ourselves.

1 JOHN 2:6 (NKJV):
He who says he abides in Him ought himself also to walk just as He walked.

We test ourselves through Scripture, to align ourselves to live as Yeshua (Jesus) lived. This is what we are instructed to do.

Scripture records that God loved Jacob and hated Esau (Malachi 1:2-3; Romans 9:12-13). God loves those who live and walk in faith, seeking Him while valuing their blessings and their eternal inheritance.

We are all sinners, yet God will forgive and forget the sins of those who repent and obey Him in all matters. The faithful, obedient, penitent person will be seen as righteous by God with all his or her sins covered by the blood of Yeshua (Jesus).

The lawless, or those who covet their stew (particular sin), will be hated by God and will lose their birthright claim to inherit the kingdom of God.

This does not necessarily mean that all who do not inherit the kingdom of God will be cast to hell, but it is preferable to be among the blessed, rather than to be among the many who will not be able to initially enter the kingdom of heaven as an inheritance. The blessed are of the first-fruits of the rapture and of the resurrection. The rest (of the second resurrection) are not blessed, but will be judged (Revelation 20:4-6).

Yeshua (Jesus) is going to say one of two things to us when we meet Him.

MATTHEW 25:21,23; LUKE 19:17 (NKJV):
"Well done good and faithful servant…"

- or -

MATTHEW 7:23 (NKJV):
"I never knew you; depart from Me, you who practice lawlessness!"

Lastly, concerning Esau and his bowl of stew…

<u>HEBREWS 12:14-17 (NKJV)</u>:

Pursue peace with all people, and holiness, without which no one will see the Lord: looking carefully lest anyone fall short of the grace of God; lest any root of bitterness springing up cause trouble, and by this many become defiled; lest there be any fornicator or profane person like Esau, who for one morsel of food sold his birthright. For you know that afterward, when he wanted to inherit the blessing, he was rejected, for he found no place for repentance, though he sought it diligently with tears.

As Esau gave up his inheritance for a bowl of stew, sadly many believers may be giving up their chance to inherit the kingdom of God for some morsel of sin, such as some form of sexual immorality, that they are unwilling to part with, sinning willfully insulting God's grace (Hebrews 10:29), and they will be rejected from inheriting the kingdom of God as a blessing through the narrow gate.

REVILERS WILL NOT INHERIT THE KINGDOM OF GOD

By George Lujack

Do you know someone who is a reviler? Is your minister or pastor a reviler? Many believers have witnessed various forms of reviling, but few recognize it as a serious sin. This article will cover the sin of reviling, a sin that some believers engage in that may cause them to lose the kingdom of God as an inheritance.

revile:
Criticize in an abusive or angrily insulting manner.[117]

Religious revilers are passionate persons, who in some manner proclaim to believe in God, but are often doctrinally incorrect on various topics, defend their incorrect doctrines, and revile people who disagree with their religious worldviews. Atheistic secular people can be revilers also, but they are typically foolish mockers of God, and mock people who believe in God, but are not revilers in the strictest sense (Psalm 14:1,53:1).

1 TIMOTHY 6:3-5 (NKJV):

If anyone teaches otherwise and does not consent to wholesome words, even the words of our Lord Yeshua Messiah (Jesus Christ), and to the doctrine which accords with godliness, he is proud, knowing nothing, but is obsessed with disputes and arguments over words, from which come envy, strife, REVILING, evil suspicions, useless wranglings of men of corrupt minds and destitute of the truth, who suppose that godliness is a means of gain.

2 TIMOTHY 2:23-25 (NKJV):

But avoid foolish and ignorant disputes, knowing that they generate strife. And a servant of the Lord must not quarrel but be gentle to all, able to teach, patient, in humility correcting those who are in opposition, if God perhaps will grant them repentance, so that they may know the truth...

Messianic and Christian believers who revile fellow believers over matters of doctrinal faith issues go well beyond rebuking them. Believers are to rebuke sinners (Leviticus 19:17; 2 Timothy 4:2), but are not to revile fellow believers over doctrinal disagreements.

CALLING OTHERS APOSTATES, BLASPHEMERS, AND HERETICS

Revilers often revile doctrinally incorrect believers, sometimes over small doctrinal differences, with harsh words that generate strife. Instead of reviling believers who hold different doctrinal viewpoints, as 'apostates,' 'blasphemers,' and 'heretics,' Scripture commands us to not be quarrelsome, and to teach others who have incorrect opposing viewpoints with gentleness and humility in leading them to truth.

Ironically, revilers are often themselves wrong on matters of doctrine when they revile a fellow believer. The reason for this is quite logical and simple: if a reviler is doctrinally correct, he can use Scripture to rebuke a doctrinally incorrect believer. But if the reviler is doctrinally incorrect, and unwilling to admit or change his or her denominational Scripturally held incorrect doctrinal position, a reviler then often attacks a messenger of truth - a fellow believer, through reviling. Reviling is a tactic often used to kill the messenger to stop the message.

REVILING OFTEN LEADS TO PERSECUTION

MATTHEW 26:63-65 (NKJV):

And the high priest answered and said to Him, "I put You under oath by the living God: Tell us if You are the Messiah (Christ), the Son of God!"

Yeshua (Jesus) said to him, "It is as you said. Nevertheless, I say to you, hereafter you will see the Son of Man sitting at the right hand of the Power, and coming on the clouds of heaven."

Then the high priest tore his clothes, saying, "HE HAS SPOKEN BLASPHEMY! What further need do we have of witnesses? Look, now YOU HAVE HEARD HIS BLASPHEMY!"

MARK 14:61-64 (NKJV):

Again the high priest asked Him, saying to Him, "Are You the Messiah (Christ), the Son of the Blessed?"

Yeshua (Jesus) said, "I am. And you will see the Son of Man sitting at the right hand of the Power, and coming with the clouds of heaven."

Then the high priest tore his clothes and said, "What further need do we have of witnesses? YOU HAVE HEARD THE BLASPHEMY!"

JOHN 10:33 (NKJV):

The Jews answered Him, saying, "For a good work we do not stone You, but for blasphemy, and because You, being a Man, make Yourself God."

Yeshua (Jesus) was arrested, persecuted, and executed, but before that happened He was falsely accused and reviled as a blasphemer by the high priests and Pharisees, because He bore witness to the truth (John 18:37) and challenged their traditions, doctrinal beliefs, and moral authority.

The Inquisition was a Catholic ecclesiastical tribunal court established in the thirteenth century for the stated purpose of suppressing heresy. Inquisitions were a means by which evil men of the Catholic Church used to revile anyone who would not be obedient to the Catholic Pope and the teachings of the Roman Catholic Church. It is estimated that the Roman Catholic Church killed between 100-150 million people during the Dark Middle Ages in their crusades, inquisition trials, and subsequent executions.

COLOSSIANS 3:8 (NKJV):

But now you yourselves are to put off all these: anger, wrath, malice, blasphemy, filthy language out of your mouth.

1 PETER 2:21-23 (NKJV):

For to this you were called, because Messiah (Christ) also suffered for us, leaving us an example, that you should follow His steps: *"Who committed no sin, nor was deceit found in His mouth,"* **who, WHEN HE WAS REVILED, DID NOT REVILE IN RETURN…**

1 JOHN 2:6 (NKJV):

He who says he abides in Him ought himself also to walk just as He walked.

Yeshua (Jesus) was a rebuker of evil men, hypocrites, and sin, but He was not a reviler. Those who claim to know Him as a Messianic or Christian believer should follow His example, follow His steps, and ought to walk just as He walked.

It is unbefitting conduct for believers to revile fellow believers as apostates, blasphemers, and heretics, as Yeshua (Jesus) did not revile people as such. It is proper to rebuke sinners and correct false doctrines by teaching fellow believers who hold incorrect opposing doctrinal viewpoints with concern and love in leading them to truth.

MESSIANICS AND CHRISTIANS SHOULD EXPECT TO BE REVILED

MATTHEW 5:11 (NKJV):

"Blessed are you when they REVILE and persecute you, and say all kinds of evil against you falsely for My sake."

LUKE 6:22 (NKJV):

"Blessed are you when men hate you, and when they exclude you, and REVILE you, and cast your name as evil, for the Son of Man's sake."

A servant is not above his Master (Matthew 10:24), and if the world reviled Messiah (Christ), the world will also revile His followers (John 15:20). Those who are reviled for His sake will be blessed.

REVILERS WILL NOT INHERIT THE KINGDOM OF GOD (REIGN OF ELOHIM)

1 CORINTHIANS 6:9-10 (NKJV) (HSV†):

Do you not know that the unrighteous will not inherit the reign of Elohim (kingdom of God)? Do not be deceived. Neither fornicators, nor idolaters, nor adulterers, nor effeminate, nor homosexuals, nor thieves, nor covetous (†greedy of gain), nor drunkards, NOR REVILERS, nor swindlers will inherit the kingdom of God (†reign of Elohim).

Believers and preachers who go around reviling fellow believers over minor doctrinal differences, such as what bible version should be used, calling law keepers 'Judaizers,' and condemning people as hell bound apostates, blasphemers, and heretics if they do not believe as they do over other similar issues, are themselves in great danger of being judged by God as revilers.

Revilers will not inherit the kingdom of God.

SCIENCE & SCRIPTURE:
SCRIPTURE REVEALS SCIENCE AND SCIENCE CONFIRMS SCRIPTURE

By George Lujack

Secular scientific-minded persons have often scoffed that Scripture is not compatible with science. Scripture is not primarily a science book, but it does reveal many scientific laws and principles that have aided man in discovery. This article will provide numerous examples that demonstrate Scripture has revealed science long before man confirmed many scientific truths and will show how man has often erred in understanding science, as Scripture-based science proclamations were later proven to be true.

AIR HAS WEIGHT, VOLUME, PRESSURE, AND MASS

<u>**JOB 28:24-25 (NKJV):**</u>
For He looks to the ends of the earth, and sees under the whole heavens, to establish a weight for the wind.

Evagelista Torricelli (1608-1647), Italian physicist and mathematician, invented the barometer and discovered that air has weight in 1640.

Robert William Boyle (1627-1691), Irish chemist, inventor, natural philosopher, and physicist, experimented with air pumps and discovered many properties of air. Boyle's law states that the volume of gases varies inversely to the pressure upon the gas. Boyle's work with air pumps was published in 1660, "New Experiments Physico-Mechanicall, Touching the Spring of the Air, and its Effects."

ANESTHESIOLOGY - ANESTHESIA - SCIENCE OF PAIN RELIEF

<u>**GENESIS 2:21 (NKJV):**</u>
And YHWH (the Lord) God caused a deep sleep to fall on Adam, and he slept; and He took one of his ribs, and closed up the flesh in its place.

Sir James Young Simpson (1811-1870), Scottish obstetrician, discovered the anesthetic properties of chloroform and successfully pioneered its use for anesthesia in 1847. Simpson, a Scripture-believing Christian, was inspired by Genesis 2:21, which led him to transform surgeries into painless procedures.

THE ANT QUEEN AND HER COLONY

PROVERBS 6:6-8 (NKJV):

Go to the ant, you sluggard! Consider her ways and be wise, which, having no captain, overseer, or ruler, provides her supplies in the summer, and gathers her food in the harvest.

Entomology, the scientific study of insects, has confirmed what was written in Scripture about the ant: the queen ant is supplied with food by the colony ants that gather for her (Proverbs 30:25).

ANTIBACTERIAL SOAP

NUMBERS 19:6,9,17,19 (NKJV) (condensed):

Take cedar wood and hyssop and scarlet, and cast them into the midst of the fire burning the heifer. Gather up the ashes of the heifer, and store them outside the camp in a clean place and they shall be kept for the water of purification. Take some of the ashes of the heifer burnt for purification, and running water shall be put on them in a vessel. Take hyssop and dip it in the water, sprinkle it on the tent, on all the vessels, on the persons who were there. He shall purify himself, wash his clothes, and bathe in water; and at evening he shall be clean.

To make antibacterial soap, cedar wood, hyssop (aromatic plant), and scarlet material (wool) are cast upon a burning heifer. Once the mix has been consumed by fire, the ashes are gathered and placed in water to remove uncleanness. When water is poured through the ashes, an antiseptic called 'thymol' is produced, which contains antibacterial and antifungal properties.

Early American pioneer settlers would make soap as Scripture instructed.

BLOOD MAINTAINS LIFE

LEVITICUS 17:11 (NKJV):

The life of the flesh is in the blood.

William Harvey (1578-1657), English physician, discovered in 1620 that the heart circulates blood throughout the body and life is maintained by blood, which brings nourishment and carries away waste. His book, "De Motu Cordis - On the Motion of the Heart and Blood," was published in 1628.

Many physicians practiced 'bleeding' their patients to alleviate them of their ailments, but inadvertently wound up killing them (ex: George Washington).

BREAD RECIPE

EZEKIEL 4:9 (NKJV):

Also take for yourself wheat, barley, beans, lentils, millet, and spelt; put them into one vessel, and make bread of them for yourself.

Bread makers follow this recipe and variations of it to bake nutritious bread.

CHICKEN OR THE EGG: WHICH CAME FIRST?

GENESIS 1:21-22 (NKJV):

So God created … every winged bird according to its kind. And God blessed them, saying, "Be fruitful and multiply, …, and let birds multiply on the earth."

The "chicken or the egg, which came first?" question has plagued evolution-minded philosophers for centuries. Evolutionists have a dilemma in trying to explain the paradox that an egg cannot form without a chicken, and a chicken could not be formed without a Creator. Scripture is clear in proclaiming that the chicken came first, and God commanded that the chicken (and all birds) were to multiply on the Earth thereafter.

CIRCUMCISION IS IDEALLY SUITED FOR THE EIGHTH DAY

GENESIS 17:12 (NKJV):

He who is eight days old among you shall be circumcised, every male child in your generations.

LEVITICUS 12:3 (NKJV):

And on the eighth day the flesh of his foreskin shall be circumcised.

Medical science has recently discovered that the blood clotting chemical prothrombin peaks in a newborn male child on the eighth day. On the eighth day, the amount of prothrombin present is actually elevated above 100% of normal and this is the only day in a male's life in which this will be the case. The eighth day is the safest day to circumcise a male child.[118]

THE LAW OF THE CONSERVATION OF MASS

NEHEMIAH 9:6 (NKJV):

You have made heaven, the heaven of heavens, with all their host, the earth and everything on it, the seas and all that is in them, and You preserve them all.

ECCLESIASTES 1:9-10, 3:14-15 (NKJV):

That which has been is what will be, that which is done is what will be done, and there is nothing new under the sun. Is there anything of which it may be said, "See, this is new"? It has already been in ancient times before us. …

I know whatever God does, it shall be forever. Nothing can be added to it, and nothing taken from it. God does it, that men should fear before Him. That which has already been, and what is to be has already been.

Antoine Lavoisier (1743-1794), French chemist, discovered that although matter may change its form or shape, its mass always remains the same.

The law of the conservation of mass: There is no new mass or matter being created within our time-space-matter universe. The total amount of mass in the universe remains constant - it is merely changing from one form to another.

CONTAGION – THE SPREAD OF COMMUNICABLE DISEASES

LEVITICUS 15:2-13 (NKJV):

When any man has a discharge from his body, his discharge is unclean. And this shall be his uncleanness in regard to his discharge - whether his body runs with his discharge, or his body is stopped up by his discharge, it is his uncleanness. Every bed is unclean on which he who has the discharge lies, and everything on which he sits shall be unclean. And whoever touches his bed shall wash his clothes and bathe in water, and be unclean until evening. He who sits on anything on which he who has the discharge sat shall wash his clothes and bathe in water, and be unclean until evening. And he who touches the body of him who has the discharge shall wash his clothes and bathe in water, and be unclean until evening. If he who has the discharge spits on him who is clean, then he shall wash his clothes and bathe in water, and be unclean until evening. Any saddle on which he who has the discharge rides shall be unclean. Whoever touches anything that was under him shall be unclean until evening. He who carries any of those things shall wash his clothes and bathe in water, and be unclean until evening. And whomever the one who has the discharge touches, and has not rinsed his hands in water, he shall wash his clothes and bathe in water, and be unclean until evening. The vessel of earth that he who has the discharge touches shall be broken, and every vessel of wood shall be rinsed in water.

And when he who has a discharge is cleansed of his discharge, then he shall count for himself seven days for his cleansing, wash his clothes, and bathe his body in running water; then he shall be clean.

NUMBERS 19:13-16 (NKJV):

Whoever touches the body of anyone who has died, and does not purify himself, defiles the tabernacle of the Lord. He shall be unclean, because the water of purification was not sprinkled on him; his uncleanness is still on him. This is the law when a man dies in a tent: All who come into the tent and all who are in the tent shall be unclean seven days; and every open vessel, which has no cover fastened on it, is unclean. Whoever in the open field touches one who is slain by a sword or who has died, or a bone of a man, or a grave, shall be unclean seven days.

Scripture spoke of contagion and the methodology to prevent it through hygiene and quarantine rules. For many centuries, doctors wore bloodstained gowns while operating on their patients until it became known that they were infecting them with contagions. Since the early 1900's, doctors and surgeons began wearing clean white long-sleeved coats, gowns, or scrubs and the spread of contagions from hospital operating tables was greatly reduced.

THE HUMAN DIET: CONSUMING UNCLEAN CREATURES CAUSES FEEBLENESS, ILLNESS, PLAGUES, AND PREMATURE DEATH

Leviticus 11 and Deuteronomy 14 list the creatures that may be eaten as food and unclean creatures that are not to be eaten. Among the unclean creatures listed are swine and all sea creatures that do not have fins and overlapping, shedding scales.

A 2015 World Health Organization press release reported that consuming processed pork products such as bacon, pork hot dogs, and sausage causes cancer.[119] Numerous government reports have periodically warned consumers of the dangers of consuming shellfish. Fish without scales are plagued with parasites and have higher levels of mercury and other toxins than fish with overlapping, shedding scales. It has been scientifically confirmed that consuming Scripture-listed unclean creatures causes a variety of health issues, diseases, feebleness, weakening of the body, and premature death.

DINOSAURS DESCRIBED IN SCRIPTURE

JOB 40:15-18 (NKJV) [WITH INTERPRETATION]:

Look now at the behemoth [BRACHIOSAURUS], which I made along with you; he eats grass like an ox. See now, his strength is in his hips, and his power is in his stomach muscles. He moves his tail like a cedar; the sinews of his thighs are tightly knit. His bones are like beams of bronze, his ribs like bars of iron.

JOB 41:1-2,13-15,25-30,33-34 (NKJV) [WITH INTERPRETATION]:

Can you draw out Leviathan [TYRANNOSAURUS REX] with a hook or snare his tongue with a line which you lower? Can you put a reed through his nose or pierce his jaw with a hook? …

Who can remove his outer coat? Who can approach him with a double bridle? Who can open the doors of his face, with his terrible teeth all around? His rows of scales are his pride, shut up tightly as with a seal…

When he raises himself up, the mighty are afraid. Because of his crashings they are bewildered. Though the sword reaches him, it cannot avail; nor does spear, dart, or javelin. He regards iron as straw and bronze as rotten wood. The arrow cannot make him flee and sling-stones become like stubble to him. Darts are regarded as straw and he laughs at the threat of javelins. His undersides are like sharp potsherds. …

On earth there is nothing like him - one that is made without fear. He beholds every high thing. He is king over all.

Sir Richard Owen (1804-1892), English biologist, comparative anatomist, and paleontologist first coined the term 'dinosaur' in 1842 after he and other geologists found many large reptilian-like fossils.

Job 40 and 41 describe dinosaurs that were created and lived with man. The narrative that dinosaurs lived millions of years ago is false.

EARTH IS A CIRCULAR SPHERE HANGING ON NOTHING IN SPACE

JOB 26:7 (NKJV):

He [GOD] hangs the earth on nothing.

JOB 26:10 (NKJV):

He drew a circular horizon on the face of the waters, at the boundary of light and darkness.

ISAIAH 40:22 (NKJV):

It is God who sits above the circle of the earth.

Sir Isaac Newton (1643-1727), English mathematician, philosopher, and physicist, wrote "Principia" in 1684, which explained that the planets are suspended in empty space, held in their orbits by an invisible force - gravity.

Ferdinand Magellan (1480-1521), Portuguese explorer, organized the first voyage to circumnavigate the globe, providing proof to the world that the Earth was round. Until then, it was widely believed that the Earth was flat.

EARTH HAS THE RIGHT AMOUNT OF WATER

JOB 28:25-26 (NKJV):
God apportioned the waters by measure when He made a law for the rain.

ISAIAH 40:12 (NKJV):
God has measured the waters in the hollow of His hand.

Science has confirmed that the Earth has the right amount of water to support life and that the Earth is located in the perfect Goldilocks Zone in its distance away from the Sun. The definition of the 'Goldilocks Zone' or 'Habitable Zone' is the region of space where conditions are favorable for life as it is found on Earth, allowing for the existence of liquid water and life. If Earth revolved around the Sun at a greater distance, the water on Earth would freeze over. If Earth were too close to the Sun, the liquid water on Earth would evaporate.

EARTH SPINS ON ITS AXIS

JOB 38:14 (KJV) [WITH INTERPRETATION]:
It [THE EARTH] is turned as clay to the seal [ON A POTTER'S WHEEL]; and they [THE CLOUDS - JOB 38:9] stand as a garment.

Heraclides Ponticus (387–312 BC), Greek astrologer and philosopher, first proposed that the Earth rotates on its axis. Many people continued to believe that the Earth did not move, based on a misunderstanding of Scripture verses that say the Earth is established and cannot be moved (Psalm 93:1, 104:5; 1 Chronicles 16:30). "The Earth cannot be moved" is a reference to the Earth's stability, and that it is established in orbit and cannot be moved out of orbit.

EARTH'S CORE IS HOT

JOB 28:5 (NKJV):
As for the earth, from it comes bread, but underneath it is turned up as by fire.

Inge Lehmann (1888-1993), Danish geophysicist and seismologist, discovered that the Earth has a solid inner core inside a molten outer core.

Seismic wave measurements show that the Earth's inner core "turns up" its outer core with immense heat. Scientists have since discovered that the Earth's inner core is hotter than the surface of the Sun.

EARTH'S CONTINENTS WERE FORMED BY WATER

GENESIS 1:2-3,9-10 (NKJV):

The earth was without form, and void; and darkness was on the face of the deep. And the Spirit of God was hovering over the face of the waters. ...

Then God said, "Let the waters under the heavens be gathered together into one place, and let the dry land appear"; and it was so. And God called the dry land Earth, and the gathering together of the waters He called Seas.

2 PETER 3:5 (NKJV) [WITH INTERPRETATION]:

By the word of God... the earth [IS] standing out of water and in the water.

During the 20th century, geologists came to understand that the Earth's continents are comprised of sediment that is less dense than the sediment at the sea floor. The waters of the seas press down on the denser oceanic crust, which gives rise to the less dense continental crust. Geologists have concluded that the Earth's continents were formed by seawater.

Cosmic evolutionists promote the theory that the Earth, billions of years ago, was a very hot, molten planet that eventually began to cool when meteors showered it with water, which later formed the seas. Scripture and verifiable science refute the theory of a hot, molten Earth.

ELECTRONIC COMMUNICATIONS

JOB 38:35 (NKJV):

Can you send out lightnings that they may go and say to you, 'Here we are!'?

James Clerk Maxwell (1831-1879), Scottish mathematical physicist, theorized that light waves could be sent out and manifested as speech.

Alexander Graham Bell (1847-1922), Scottish-born American, applied Maxwell's Electromagnetic Radiation Theory when he invented the telephone in 1876.

Electromagnetic waves composed of light and radio waves are forms of light that are the basis for all electromagnetic communications. Today, using electric signal transmissions, we send out "lightnings" to transmit communications through cell phones, the Internet, radio, and television.

FABRICS: WEARING WOOL AND LINEN TOGETHER

LEVITICUS 19:19 (NKJV):

Nor shall a garment of mixed linen and wool come upon you.

DEUTERONOMY 22:11 (NKJV):

You shall not wear a garment of different sorts, such as wool and linen mixed together.

Otto Heinrich Warburg (1883-1970), German medical doctor and physiologist, identified the atomic signature frequency number of the average healthy human being to be 70-90. Science has determined that when fabrics are worn, which emit a higher frequency than humans, they support human health and healing.

Linen and wool each have an atomic frequency of 5,000. Individually they both maintain health and heal the human body. Linen bed sheets are known to give the best restful night's sleep, better than cotton sheets, which have a much lower atomic frequency.

Scientific studies have shown that when linen and wool are mixed in a fabric, or are worn together, the energy generated by the two fabrics collapses their electrical fields. The two fabrics individually each emit 5,000 atomic signature frequencies, but when mixed or worn together their atomic fields cancel each other out and can cause pain and weakness to sensitive persons who wear linen and wool together.[120]

FLIGHT BY MANKIND

ISAIAH 60:8 (NKJV):

Who are these who fly like a cloud, and like doves to their roosts?

HOSEA 11:11 (NKJV):

They shall come trembling like a bird from Egypt, like a dove from the land of Assyria.

ISAIAH 18:1 (NKJV) (HSV†):

Woe to the land shadowed with buzzing (†whirring) wings, which is beyond the rivers of Ethiopia.

The Wright brothers, Orville (1871-1948) and Wilbur (1867-1912), American inventors and aviation pioneers, are credited with inventing, building, and flying the world's first successful airplane.

Igor Ivanovich Sikorsky (1889-1972), Russian-American, designed the first viable American helicopter in 1939, and later reconfigured the design for the first mass-produced helicopters in 1942.

Before controlled manned flight, many churches smugly uttered the axiom, "If God had meant for man to fly, He would have given him wings." If the Christian churches had known their Scriptures, they would not have uttered such phrases, for the Scriptures declared that man would fly.

LIGHT CAN BE DIVIDED

JOB 38:25 (NKJV), (KJV*), (HSV†):

By what way is light diffused (*parted), (†divided)?

Sir Isaac Newton (1643-1727), English mathematician, philosopher, and physicist, discovered in 1666 that white light could be divided into a spectrum of colors, because white light was composed of particles with different colors that traveled with different speeds through the prism.

Before Newton's Corpuscular Theory of Light, which was later confirmed, it was believed that white light was colorless and that the prism itself produced the colors.

LIGHT TRAVELS IN A WAY

JOB 38:19 (NKJV):

Where is the way to the dwelling of light?

Ole Romer (1644-1710), Danish astronomer, demonstrated in 1676 that light has a finite speed at which it travels. Before the 17th century, scientists believed that the transmission of light was instantaneous and did not travel in any "way."

LEAVES CONTAIN HEALING COMPOUNDS

EZEKIEL 47:12 (NKJV):

Their fruit will be for food, and their leaves for medicine.

REVELATION 22:2 (NKJV):

The leaves of the tree were for the healing of the nations.

Modern science has discovered what many ancient cultures have known: that there are healing compounds found in leaves. Approximately 12,000 leaf compounds have been isolated thus far. Leaf extracts are widely used to treat a variety of ailments including burns, skin treatment, wounds, and as herbal remedies for a host of other internal organ issues.

OPEN WOUND DISINFECTION AND PROTECTION

LUKE 10:34 (NKJV):

"So he went to him and bandaged his wounds, pouring on oil and wine."

Yeshua (Jesus), when telling the parable story of the Good Samaritan, gave man knowledge in how to treat and protect open wounds. Today, we know that wine contains ethyl alcohol and traces of methyl alcohol both of which are good disinfectants. Olive oil is also a good disinfectant, as well as a soothing lotion, moisturizer, and protector. Both wine and olive oil help protect and heal open wounds.

Sadly, during the Middle Ages right up until the 20th century, millions of people died due to man not knowing how to treat and protect open wounds.

ALL HUMANS ARE GENETICALLY RELATED, YET EACH PERSON IS UNIQUE

JOB 37:7 (NKJV):

He seals the hand of every man.

ACTS 17:26 (NKJV):

And He has made from one blood every nation of men to dwell on all the face of the earth.

Every man and woman who has ever been born is unique. No two persons, even identical twins, share the same fingerprint or handprint. Evolutionists have claimed that human beings evolved from apes millions of years ago, but their atheistic-driven theory is scientifically unsupported. Science has recently determined, through DNA and chromosome testing that all human beings share the same gene pool and thus all persons are uniquely different, yet all of mankind are genetically related.[121][122][123]

MAN WAS MADE FROM THE DUST OF THE EARTH

GENESIS 2:7, 3:19 (NKJV):

And YHWH (the Lord) God formed man of the dust of the ground. …

In the sweat of your face you shall eat bread till you return to the ground, for out of it you were taken; for dust you are, and to dust you shall return.

PSALM 139:15 (NKJV):

My frame was not hidden from You, when I was made in secret, and skillfully wrought in the lowest parts of the earth.

1 CORINTHIANS 15:47 (NKJV):

The first man was of the earth, made of dust.

Researchers at NASA's Ames Research Center published an article in Reader's Digest in 1982 that said, "We are just beginning to learn. The biblical scenario for the creation of life turns out to be not far off the mark." The researchers found that the human body is composed of the same elements and minerals found in the Earth's crust.[124] Scientists had previously dismissed the simplicity of Scripture's account of the creation of man, as they did not think there was any way that the complex structure of the human body was formed from dust.

METEOROLOGY: CLOUD FORMATION AND LIGHTNING

PSALM 135:7 (NKJV):

He causes the vapors to ascend from the ends of the earth; He makes lightning for the rain.

Aristotle, (384-322 BC), Greek philosopher and scientist, first theorized the formation of clouds forming from vapors of waters from the Earth and attributed heavier rain to greater lightning. Aristotle wrote in "Meteorology," "Cloud is a vaporous mass, concentrated and producing water. Rain is produced from the compression of a closely condensed cloud, varying according to the pressure exerted on the cloud; when the pressure is slight it scatters gentle drops; when it is great it produces a more violent fall, and we call this a shower, being heavier than ordinary rain, and forming continuous masses of water falling over earth."

OCEANS HAVE MOUNTAINS AND SPRINGS (FOUNTAINS)

GENESIS 7:11 (NKJV):

On that day all the fountains (springs) of the great deep were broken up.

JOB 38:16 (NKJV):

Have you entered the springs (fountains) of the sea?

PROVERBS 8:28 (NKJV):

He strengthened the fountains (springs) of the deep.

JONAH 2:3,5-6 (NKJV):

"For You cast me into the deep, into the heart of the seas. … The waters surrounded me, even to my soul; the deep closed around me; weeds were wrapped around my head. I went down to the moorings (bottoms) of the mountains."

In the 20th century, oceanographers discovered that there are mountain ranges under the sea. Some of these mountains rise more than 3,000 feet above the sea floor, but do not reach the water's surface (sea level). Until recently, scientists believed that oceans were fed water only by rain and rivers. In the 1970's, using submarines and deep diving oceanography equipment, researchers discovered springs on the ocean floors.

PETROLEUM: SCRIPTURE REVEALS MAN WOULD UTILIZE OIL

DEUTERONOMY 32:13, 33:19 (NKJV):

He made him draw honey from the rock, and oil from the flinty rock. … For they shall partake of the abundance of the seas and the treasures hidden in the sand.

Petroleum is based on Latin meaning 'petra' (rock), and 'oleum' (oil). Scripture foretold that man would draw oil from beneath the Earth's crust and that there would be treasure hidden in the sand, long before man had invented an internal combustion engine or had any use for oil.

SABBATH REST - THE HEART BEATS SLOWER ON THE SABBATH

GENESIS 2:2 (NKJV):

And on the seventh day God ended His work which He had done, and He rested on the seventh day from all His work which He had done.

EXODUS 31:16-17 (NKJV):

Therefore the children of Israel shall keep the Sabbath, to observe the Sabbath throughout their generations as a perpetual covenant. It is a sign between Me and the children of Israel forever; for in six days YHWH (the Lord) made the heavens and the earth, and on the seventh day He rested and was refreshed.

God instituted the Seventh-day Sabbath after the creation, and He rested on the Sabbath. The Sabbath is not for the Jews only, but for all mankind.

Scientific tests have determined that for everybody, regardless of race or religious belief, the heart beats more slowly on Saturday than on any other day of the week. Even if a person has a day off on any other day of the week, the heart still beats more slowly on Saturdays.[125]

STARS CANNOT BE COUNTED, BUT GOD KNOWS THEIR NUMBER

GENESIS 15:5 (NKJV):

Then YHWH (the Lord) brought Abram outside and said, "Look now toward heaven, and count the stars if you are able to number them."

JEREMIAH 33:22 (NKJV) [WITH INTERPRETATION]:

As the host of heaven [STARS OF THE UNIVERSE] cannot be numbered, nor the sand of the sea measured.

PSALM 147:4 (NKJV):

YHWH (the Lord) counts the number of the stars; He calls them all by name.

Modern high-powered and space-based telescopes have enabled astronomers to peer far out into the known universe and view trillions of stars. Scripture was accurate in proclaiming that man would not be able to count the number the stars, but declares God knows their number and calls them by name.

STARS MAKE SOUND

JOB 38:7 (NKJV):

When the morning stars sang together.

PSALM 148:3 (NKJV):

Praise Him, all you stars of light!

1 CORINTHIANS 15:41 (NKJV):

There is one glory of the sun, another glory of the moon, and another glory of the stars; for one star differs from another star in glory.

Astronomers have discovered that stars emit light and radio waves, which produce sounds that can be received on Earth. The insides of stars pulsate, which create sound waves that move through a star. Every star has its own unique sound that is different from other stars.

STARS MOVE

JOB 38:32 (NKJV) [WITH INTERPRETATION]:

Can you bring out constellations [STARS] in their season?

MATTHEW 2:9 (NKJV):

And behold, the star that they had seen in the East went before them, till it came and stood over where the young Child was.

JUDE 1:12-13 (NKJV):

They are... wandering stars for whom is reserved the blackness of darkness forever.

Aryabhata (476-550), Indian astronomer and mathematician, correctly advocated that the Earth turns on its own axis, which accounted for the apparent movement of the stars, contrary to the then prevailing view that the sky rotated around the Earth. Aryabhata incorrectly presumed that the stars did not move at all.

Edmond Halley (1656-1742), English astronomer, geophysicist, mathematician, meteorologist, and physicist, best known for computing the orbit of Halley's Comet named after him, in 1718 discovered the motion of stars through astrometric measurements.

Doppler spectroscopy detects the 'wobble' of stars as planets cause their parent star to wobble slightly as the planet revolves around the mass of the star, tugging at it and causing it to wobble.

Today, astronomers have observed stars moving in orbit in galaxies that revolve around black holes believed to be located at the galaxy's center.

TIME HAD A BEGINNING

GENESIS 1:1 (NKJV):

In the beginning God created the heavens and the earth.

2 TIMOTHY 1:9 (NKJV):

His own purpose and grace, which was given to us in Messiah Yeshua (Christ Jesus) before time began.

TITUS 1:2 (NKJV):

In hope of eternal life, which God who cannot lie, promised before time began.

Albert Einstein (1879-1955), German-born Jewish American theoretical physicist, developed the General Theory of Relativity. Einstein's theory proposed that time was intricately connected to matter and space. His theory helped the world understand that time was finite and had a beginning.

Before Einstein's theory, many believed that time, space, and matter always existed.

God exists outside of the confines of time, space, and matter, which He created.[126]

WIND CIRCUITS AND OCEAN CURRENTS

PSALM 8:8 (NKJV) [WITH INTERPRETATION]:

The birds of the air, and the fish of the sea pass through the paths [WIND CIRCUITS AND OCEAN CURRENTS] of the seas.

ECCLESIASTES 1:6-7 (NKJV):

The wind goes toward the south, and turns around towards the north; the wind whirls around continually, and comes again in its circuit. All the rivers run into the sea, yet the sea is not full; to the place from which the rivers come, there they return again.

Matthew Fontain Maury (1806-1873), American astronomer, author, cartographer, educator, geologist, historian, oceanographer, and meteorologist, was nicknamed "Pathfinder of the Seas," and "Father of Modern Oceanography and Naval Meteorology," and "Scientist of the Seas," due to his extensive work and publications including "The Physical Geography of the Seas" (1855). Maury, a Christian inspired by Psalm 8:8, dedicated his life to discovering the paths of the seas. Maury's discoveries aided sailing vessels to take advantage of sea and air currents, reducing by many days the time required for ships to transverse the seas. His work also aided whaling ships to understand that whales followed predictable migrating sea patters.

Modern day meteorologists use wind currents to predict weather patterns, and to chart the courses of storms and hurricanes.

DOES SCIENCE PROVE OR DISPROVE THE EXISTENCE OF GOD?
SCIENTIFIC AND THEOLOGICAL EXPLANATIONS OFFERED BY THEISTS AND ATHEISTS ARGUING FOR AND AGAINST THE EXISTENCE OF A DIVINE CREATOR - GOD

By George Lujack

The belief or disbelief in God is a hotly debated topic between atheists, those who do not believe in a God as the Creator of the universe and all life within it, and theists who do. This article will present the dominant prevailing arguments of both sides of the debate and conclude that both the scientific and theological evidences support the existence of a Divine Creator - God.

THE EVIDENCE:
THE UNIVERSE (TIME, SPACE, AND MATTER), THE ORDERLY UNIVERSE, THE EXISTENCE OF LIFE ON EARTH, THE VARIATION OF LIFE FORMS, WHERE IS GOD?, SCRIPTURE EYEWITNESS ACCOUNTS, AND FAKE SCIENCE

THE BEGINNING OF THE UNIVERSE; TIME, SPACE, AND MATTER

ATHEISTS ARGUE that the origin of the universe coming into existence occurred as a result of a big bang explosion in space. The Big Bang Theory posits that the universe originated billions of years ago in an explosion from a single point of nearly infinite energy .[128] Confronted with the realization that the Big Bang Theory requires 'infinite energy' as a starting point, which would also require a beginning to the origin of the infinite energy itself, atheistic scientists have tried to explain that the original big bang was an event where absolute nothing exploded, which then expanded into the entire universe.

The Big Bang Theory is scientifically refutable, as the theory violates the first law of thermodynamics.

Antoine Lavoisier (1743-1794), French chemist, discovered that although matter may change its form or shape, its mass always remains the same.

THE FIRST LAW OF THERMODYNAMICS: THE CONSERVATION OF ENERGY

The first law of thermodynamics states that no new energy or matter is being created within our time-space-matter universe. The total amount of mass in the universe remains constant - it is merely changing from one form to another.

In order for the universe to have come into existence, something from nothing, there would need to be a supernatural, unscientifically explainable phenomenon event to occur. Absolute nothing simply cannot explode, as there is, by definition, nothing to explode from nothing. The Big Bang Theory violates the first law of thermodynamics.

The Big Bang Theory also ignores the theoretical density and inescapable gravity of black holes. If the universe began as an incredibly dense energy and matter singularity, as a single solitary black hole, then theoretically the universe in such a state would not be able to explode, as observable black holes do not explode due to their extreme gravity, although they do churn and jettison energy and matter out at their poles.

THEISTS EXPLAIN that God created the heavens and the Earth from nothing.

GENESIS 1:1 (NKJV):

In the beginning God created the heavens and the earth.

HEBREWS 11:3 (NKJV) [WITH INTERPRETATION]:

By faith we understand that the worlds were framed by the word of God, SO THAT THE THINGS WHICH ARE SEEN [THE UNIVERSE] WERE NOT MADE OF THINGS WHICH ARE VISIBLE.

God exists outside of His creation and was in existence before time, space, and matter. God created the universe and is not bound to the laws of it.[129]

THE ORDERLY UNIVERSE

ATHEISTS ARGUE that after the big bang explosion, the matter in the universe coalesced over time to form billions of galaxies that contain all the stars and planets in the universe. From a disorderly big bang explosion emerged an orderly universe through cosmic evolution.

An orderly universe emerging as a result of a disorderly big bang explosion is scientifically refutable, as this theory violates the second law of thermodynamics.

THE SECOND LAW OF THERMODYNAMICS: THINGS NATURALLY PROGRESS FROM ORDER TO DISORDER (NOT FROM DISORDER TO ORDER)

The second law of thermodynamics is that in any closed system where something proceeds where unavailable energy is, entropy increases. Disorder increases with time, as things progress from order to disorder or from available energy to unavailable.

THEISTS EXPLAIN that God directs and brings order to the universe. He created the Earth *and* afterward formed it to be habitable. He measures His creation and He hangs the Earth in orbit and stretches out the heavens (thus directs their orderly assembly).

GENESIS 1:2 (NKJV):

The earth was without form, and void; and darkness was on the face of the deep.

GENESIS 1:14 (NKJV):

Then God said, "Let there be lights in the firmament of the heavens to divide the day from the night; and let them be for signs and seasons, and for days and years."

ISAIAH 45:18 (NKJV) [WITH INTERPRETATION]:

For thus says YHWH (the Lord), Who created the heavens [UNIVERSE], Who is God, Who formed the earth AND made it [HABITABLE], Who has established it, Who did not create it in vain, Who formed it to be inhabited.

GENESIS 15:5 (NKJV):

Then YHWH (the Lord) brought Abram outside and said, "Look now toward heaven, and count the stars if you are able to number them."

JEREMIAH 33:22 (NKJV) [WITH INTERPRETATION]:

As the host of heaven [STARS OF THE UNIVERSE] cannot be numbered, nor the sand of the sea measured.

JOB 26:7 (NKJV):

He hangs the earth on nothing.

JOB 38:4-5 (NKJV):

Where were you when I laid the foundations of the earth? Tell me if you have understanding. Who determined its measurements?

JOB 38:32 (NKJV) [WITH INTERPRETATION]:

Can you bring out constellations [STARS] in their season?

PSALM 147:4 (NKJV):

YHWH (the Lord) counts the number of the stars; He calls them all by name.

ISAIAH 40:22 (NKJV):

It is He who sits above the circle of the earth, and its inhabitants are like grasshoppers, who stretches out the heavens like a curtain, and spreads them out like a tent to dwell in.

ISAIAH 44:24 (NKJV):

"I am YHWH (the Lord), who makes all things, who stretches out the heavens all alone, who spreads abroad the earth by Myself."

ZECHARIAH 12:1 (NKJV):

YHWH (the Lord) stretches out the heavens, lays the foundation of the earth, and forms the spirit of man within him.

The fact that the universe is stable and orbital bodies within it are so precise that they can be used to measure seasons, days, and years (Genesis 1:14), indicates the handiwork of a Supreme Being - God. The theory that after the big bang explosion, the matter coalesced into a colossal, orderly, and precisely timed galactic universe violates the second law of thermodynamics.

THE EXISTENCE OF ALL THE VARIOUS KINDS OF LIFE ON PLANET EARTH

ATHEISTS ARGUE that after the big bang, and after the matter of the universe coalesced into galaxies, molecules arranged themselves into the first self-sustaining, self-replicating life forms on planet Earth. Then, after molecules formed into simple life, over time this simple life then evolved into all the more complex and higher forms of life.

There are two major scientific evidences against molecules arranging themselves into simple life forms and then evolving into higher, more complex life thereafter:

1. Life has never been observed to come from non-life.
2. There is no known observable process by which new genetic information can be added to the genetic code of an organism.[130]

Molecules transforming to life and then life randomly generating new advanced genetic information within itself and then, over time, eventually producing all the various forms of life, including human life, is a supernatural occurrence that is not scientifically observable. The theory of molecules to life evolution (abiogenesis) and simple life acquiring new genetic information to become higher, more complex forms of life goes against the second law of thermodynamics: things go from order to disorder, not from order to greater complexity, so molecules cannot arrange themselves to life, and life cannot advance into more complex life.

The simplest scientifically observable life forms are incredibly complex, more so than a space shuttle.[131] Science demonstrates that all life forms have the ability to microevolve, but not macroevolve. If a man lifts weights, his muscles will grow (microevolve) to adapt to the added stress placed on his body. If a man jogs regularly, his endurance will increase. If a man lies in the sun frequently his skin's pigment will tan. There are limitations to microevolution. No man will ever be able to bench press 10,000 pounds (4,500 kg) or run a mile in 30 seconds, no matter how long and hard he trains. As for macroevolution, this does not occur in nature. A man can spend his entire life submerged in water and he will not develop gills, or he could flap his arms his entire life and his arms will not transform into feathered wings, giving him the ability to fly. If the genetic code information is not within an organism, it cannot acquire it. This is why dinosaurs could not have acquired feathered wings to become birds.

THEISTS EXPLAIN that God created life fully developed and functional from the onset, capable of reproducing after their kinds, but without the capability of reproducing or transforming into other kinds of life.

GENESIS 1:20-21 (NKJV):

Then God said, "Let the waters abound with an abundance of living creatures, and let birds fly above the earth across the face of the firmament of the heavens."

So God created great sea creatures and every living thing that moves, with which the waters abounded, ACCORDING TO THEIR KIND, and every winged bird ACCORDING TO ITS KIND.

GENESIS 1:24-25 (NKJV):

Then God said, "Let the earth bring forth the living creature ACCORDING TO ITS KIND: cattle and creeping thing and beast of the earth, each ACCORDING TO ITS KIND"; and it was so. And God made the beast of the earth ACCORDING TO ITS KIND, cattle ACCORDING TO ITS KIND, and everything that creeps on the earth ACCORDING TO ITS KIND.

GENESIS 1:26 (NKJV):

Then God said, "Let Us make man in Our image, ACCORDING TO OUR LIKENESS."

In nature we see that animals reproduce after their kinds. There are variations within kinds, but kinds are only capable of reproducing after their own kind. Experiments have been conducted to try to crossbreed kinds, even using chimp sperm in an attempt to fertilize human eggs, without success.[132] Kinds are limited to reproducing after their kind and cannot evolve or reproduce into another kind of animal.

The fact that we observe fully developed life forms, limited to reproducing after their kinds, and the fossil record has not produced transitional fossils, indicates that the molecules to life theory of evolution opposes observable science.

WHERE IS GOD IF HE EXISTS?

ATHEISTS ARGUE that if there is a God, then why does He not reveal himself? If God exists, then He should show Himself. Since God does not show Himself, He therefore does not exist.

THEISTS EXPLAIN that man has separated himself from God through sin.

ISAIAH 54:8 (NKJV):

With a little wrath I hid my face from you for a moment; but with everlasting kindness I will have mercy on you," says YHWH (the Lord), your Redeemer.

The notion that God must show Himself to prove His existence, and if He doesn't He therefore does not exist, is flawed. An orphan abandoned by his biological parents would be incorrect in declaring that he has no father or mother. The orphan does have a father and mother, but due to unknown circumstances he may not know his father or mother, but they do exist.

SCRIPTURE EYEWITNESS ACCOUNTS OF GOD

ATHEISTS ARGUE that they do not believe the written Scriptures and declare that these were made up stories from over 2,000 years ago.

THEISTS EXPLAIN that eyewitness oral and written testimony is admissible in a court of law and can be used to prove or disprove cases beyond a reasonable doubt. Numerous accounts of man's interaction with God by various witness accounts in Scripture are evidence of a God, whether atheists acknowledge this evidence or not. Yeshua Messiah (Jesus Christ) came to Earth as the Son of God and performed miracles that cannot be accounted for by science. Witness accounts testify that they saw Yeshua (Jesus) resurrected from the grave and ascend into heaven.

FAKE SCIENCE IS THE RESULT OF ANGER AND REBELLION TOWARDS GOD

ATHEISTS ARGUE that their disbelief in God is based purely on science and nothing else, but their own testimonies often reveal that is not the case at all.

"I have a slight problem with the celestial dictatorship premise."
- Stephen Hawking[133]

Stephen Hawking's mind and scientific worldview are handicapped by an angry, rebellious premise: a refusal to believe in God, because he has a problem with the authority of God who makes laws and is the ruler over His creation. It is this anti-God biased mindset that drives Hawking's theories, not the scientific evidence contained within his theories. Hawking, who is widely regarded as a great scientific mind by the secular world, has spent his entire life trying to disprove the existence of God in futility.

JAMES 4:4 (NKJV):
Do you not know that friendship with the world is enmity with God? Whoever therefore wants to be a friend of the world makes himself an enemy of God.

The secular world is also at enmity, in rebellion, against God, which is why the secular scientific community embraces atheistic fake science while excluding any logical scientific explanation that would include a Supreme Being as a Creator.

SCIENTIFIC AND THEOLOGICAL CONCLUSIONS

The universe was created by a supernatural event. Atheists do not have a valid scientific explanation for how such an event could possibly occur. All they can offer is to say "nothing exploded." Theists explain that a Supernatural God, who is not bound by space and time or the laws of His creation, created the universe.

The universe is orderly, not chaotic. Atheists explain that the universe started chaotically and then became orderly; order from disorder. Theists explain that God created the universe and directed it, to make it orderly.

Life exists, but how did life originate and why are there so many different variations of kinds of life upon the Earth? Atheists argue that molecules somehow arranged themselves, over time, forming into the earliest simple life forms, then somehow gained new genetic code information and gradually, over time, evolved into all the various life forms on Earth. Theists explain that God created life after their kinds, capable of reproducing after their kinds, with limited variations within those kinds to account for the variations within kinds of life on Earth.

If there is a God, then why does He not reveal Himself? Atheists argue that there is no God, because if there was a God He would surely reveal Himself. Theists explain that sin has separated man from God, but God has revealed Himself to His creation during human history and God desires people to believe in Him through reasoned faith in truth.

The Scriptures testify of man interacting with God. Atheists argue that the Scriptures should not be believed, often finding minuscule alleged imperfections in the Scriptures to try to raise doubt about the authenticity of truth and the eyewitness accounts within them. Theists argue that the evidence of a God is fully supported by established scientific law principles, logic, reason, and the Scriptures.

The big bang explosion, an orderly universe emerging from the disorder of the chaotic explosion of the big bang, life spontaneously arising from non-life, then simple life acquiring new genetic code information to become higher, more advanced life forms, is atheistic secular science's attempt to explain how everything came to be. Theists rightly view the Big Bang Theory and molecules to man Evolution Theory as fake science, comparable to a fairy tale story of a frog becoming a prince.

ROMANS 1:20-23 (NKJV) [WITH INTERPRETATION]:

For since the creation of the world His invisible attributes are clearly seen, being understood by the things that are made [HIS CREATION], even His eternal power and Godhead, so that they [ATHEISTS] are without excuse, because, although they knew God, they did not glorify Him as God, nor were thankful, but became futile in their thoughts [CAME UP WITH 'SCIENTIFIC' THEORIES ATTEMPTING TO DISPROVE THE EXISTENCE OF GOD], and their foolish hearts were darkened. Professing to be wise [PH.D COLLEGE PROFESSORS, ETC.], they became [ATHEISTIC] fools, and changed the glory of the incorruptible God [HIS CREATION: MAN, MADE IN HIS IMAGE] into an image made like corruptible man [EVOLUTION SCIENTISTS ARTISTIC DRAWINGS OF MAN EVOLVING FROM APES] - and birds and four-footed animals and creeping things [DEPICTED ALSO EVOLVING].

Real observable and testable science, the physical universe, the Earth, life, theological explanations, and eyewitness Scripture accounts are evidences that logically PROVE the existence of God who created the universe, the Earth, and all life within it.

HOW OLD IS THE EARTH?

By George Lujack

Scripture and recent scientific discoveries show that there are many components of the Earth, components that make the Earth both young (around 6,000-years-old) AND much older. This article will discuss the various age of the Earth theories while presenting an in-depth comprehensive study that supports old Earth creationism.

Young Earth Creationists and Evolution Theory Scientists disagree passionately over their beliefs on the age of the Earth. Young Earth Creationists generally believe that the universe, the Earth, and the first creatures upon the Earth were created approximately 6,000-years ago. Evolution Theory Scientists currently believe that the universe is approximately 14-billion-years-old, the Earth is 4.5-billion-years-old, and the first self-replicating life forms evolved upon the Earth about 2.5-billion-years ago. Young Earth Creationists make errors in Scripture interpretation while evolution theorists hold unproven, unscientific, unsubstantiated, and faith-based beliefs to support their worldview.

The words "IN THE BEGINNING" and "THE EARTH WAS" are key phrases in understanding the timeframe of God's creation and will be emphasized throughout this article, along with some other key words.

GENESIS 1:1-2 (NKJV):

IN THE BEGINNING God created the heavens and the earth. THE EARTH WAS without form, and void; and darkness was on the face of the deep.

BERESHITH (GENESIS) 1:1-2 (HSV):

IN THE BEGINNING Elohim created the shamayim and the earth. And THE EARTH CAME TO BE formless and empty, and darkness was on the face of the deep.

The phrases "THE EARTH WAS," or "CAME TO BE," are past tense indicating a significant passage of time. Therefore there was a significant passage of time between IN THE BEGINNING (Genesis 1:1) and day-1 of creation week, when God created light for the Earth (Genesis 1:2-3). Genesis 1:2 states that THE EARTH WAS without form or CAME TO BE formless (for life) and void (of life). If IN THE BEGINNING were day-1 of the creation week, it would be pointless for God to declare the obvious, that THE EARTH WAS without form and void. Of course the Earth would have been without form (to sustain life) and void (of life) if God, hypothetically, had just made it! The fact that Scripture declares that THE EARTH WAS without form and void indicates a passage of time.

God purposely declared that IN THE BEGINNING THE EARTH WAS without form (to sustain life) and void (of life) to negate the idea of Evolution Theory. Life did not arise from non-life, nor did God use evolution as a means, over time, to produce life upon the planet.

THE EARTH WAS without form (to sustain life) and void (of life) throughout its ancient past. God formed the Earth and created all life upon it during the 6-day creation week (Genesis 1:21-25).

THE EARTH WAS there, created IN THE BEGINNING, before creation week began in Genesis 1:3.

THE EARTH WAS without form (water covered the planet and it did not have a life-sustaining, breathable atmosphere) and THE EARTH WAS void (of life) (Genesis 1:2). Creation week served to form the Earth, to make it suitable to support life, and to inhabit it with life.

IN THE BEGINNING… when was that? Was it 6,000-years ago, 4.5-billion years ago, or 14-billion years ago? No one can know for sure (at this time) when THE BEGINNING of time and creation occurred. Scripture does not declare when the beginning of God's creation was. We can reasonably conclude that IN THE BEGINNING represents a significant period of time and signifies an interval of time before God acted in creating light for the Earth in Genesis 1:3. The beginning was therefore ages longer than 6,000-years ago.

GENESIS 2:4 (KJV):
These are THE GENERATIONS of the heavens and of the earth when they were created, in the day that the LORD God made the earth and the heavens.

GENESIS 2:4 (NKJV):
This is THE HISTORY of the heavens and the earth when they were created, in the day that the Lord God made the earth and the heavens.

The heavens and the Earth experienced generations of time, a significant history, after they were created IN THE BEGINNING, and before God revisited the Earth during the 6-day creation week. During the creation week account in Genesis, there is no mention of God making the Earth itself; that is, God did not create THE FOUNDATION of the Earth: the core, crust, dirt, mantle, mountains, rocks, soil, or water of the Earth during creation week. The land and water of THE EARTH WAS already in place before creation week began. The land and water of THE EARTH WAS created IN THE BEGINNING and was not made during the creation week of Genesis 1:3-22.

THE GENESIS ACCOUNT OF CREATION:

IN THE BEGINNING:

GENESIS 1:1-2 (NKJV):
IN THE BEGINNING God created the heavens and the earth. THE EARTH WAS without form, and void; …
The heavens (universe) and THE FOUNDATION of the Earth were created.

CREATION WEEK (*After* THE BEGINNING):

CREATION WEEK DAY-1:

GENESIS 1:3-5 (NKJV):

Then God said, "Let there be light," and there was light. And God saw the light, that it was good; and God divided the light from the darkness. God called the light Day, and the darkness He called Night. So the evening and the morning were the first day.

Light was created for the Earth on day-1 (Genesis 1:3-5). The light created on the first day was not the Sun, nor the beginning of creation, nor the 'Big Bang,' but temporary light created to illuminate the Earth before the illumination of the Sun on day-4 of creation week.

CREATION WEEK DAY-2:

GENESIS 1:6-8 (NKJV):

Then God said, "Let there be a firmament in the midst of the waters, and let it divide the waters from the waters." Thus God made the firmament, and divided the waters that were under the firmament from the waters that were above the firmament; and it was so. And God called the firmament Heaven. So the evening and the morning were the second day.

A life-sustaining breathable atmosphere was made for the Earth, referred to as 'firmament' and 'heaven' on day-2 (Genesis 1:6-8).

CREATION WEEK DAY-3:

GENESIS 1:9-13 (NKJV):

Then God said, "Let the waters under the heavens be gathered together into one place, and let the dry land appear"; and it was so. And God called the dry land Earth, and the gathering together of the waters He called Seas. And God saw that it was good.

Then God said, "Let the earth bring forth grass, the herb that yields seed, and the fruit tree that yields fruit according to its kind, whose seed is in itself, on the earth"; and it was so. And God saw that it was good. So the evening and the morning were the third day.

Water (on Earth) was gathered together and separated from the land. The water gathered together was called seas and the dry land was called Earth. God also brought forth grass and vegetation upon the dry land on day-3.

NOTE: On day-3 the waters and the dry land were not made or created. The waters and land were already in existence, as they were of the Earth that was created IN THE BEGINNING (Genesis 1:1). The waters were GATHERED away from the land causing dry land to APPEAR. God did not make the Earth, the seas, and the dry land on day-3; He merely gathered the already existing waters together and formed the seas and He raised the already existing land, that became dry land after the water was gathered away from it, causing the dry land to appear to form the continents (Genesis 1:9).

CREATION WEEK DAY-4:

GENESIS 1:14-19 (NKJV):

Then God said, "Let there be lights in the firmament of the heavens to divide the day from the night; and let them be for signs and seasons, and for days and years; and let them be for lights in the firmament of the heavens to give light on the earth"; and it was so. Then God made two great lights: the greater light to rule the day, and the lesser light to rule the night. He made the stars also. God set them in the firmament of the heavens to give light on the earth, and to rule over the day and over the night, and to divide the light from the darkness. And God saw that it was good. So the evening and the morning were the fourth day.

The Sun was illuminated and light was made to shine upon the Earth - the sunlight for the day and the moonlight for the night on day-4. The Sun and Moon were also to be used for signs, seasons, days, and years (dating and calendars) (Genesis 1:14-19).

NOTE: God made the two great 'lights' (Genesis 1:16). Many creationists proclaim that the Sun and Moon were created on day-4, but Scripture says God made "two great lights," not the Sun and Moon. It is likely that He did not create the Sun and Moon on day-4, but instead ignited and illuminated the Sun, creating the two great light sources for the Earth; the Sun for the day and the Moon for the night.

NOTE: "He made the stars also," (Genesis 1:16) is a confirmation of what God had *already done* IN THE BEGINNING (Genesis 1:1), rather than a proclamation that He made the stars on day-4 of creation week.

The sentence context within the paragraph structure of Genesis 1:16 is like saying, "General Motors employees made this new model car on day-4 (Wednesday). They made the GM factory also." One would not logically conclude that the General Motors workers made the factory on the same day-4 that they made its new model car. We likewise shouldn't believe that God made all of the countless trillions of stars of the universe on the same day that He ignited the Sun to illuminate the Earth.

God created the heavens (cosmos / stars) IN THE BEGINNING, not on day-1 of creation week when God created light to illuminate the Earth, nor on day-4 of creation week when God reaffirmed "He made the stars also."

All throughout the creation week account, when God created, Scripture records God's actions in a consistent sequential manner indicating an action having taken place or completed as God spoke the creation into existence. If God created the stars, all of them, on day-4 of creation week, Scripture would be more concise to say something like, "Then God said, 'Let there be many stars throughout the heavens.' And it was so." Scripture does not say this as Genesis 1:16 fleetingly proclaims, "He made the stars also."

CREATION WEEK DAY-5:

GENESIS 1:20 (NKJV):

Then God said, "Let the waters abound with an abundance of living creatures, and let birds fly above the earth across the face of the firmament of the heavens."

GENESIS 1:21-23 (NKJV):

So God created great sea creatures and every living thing that moves, with which the waters abounded, according to their kind, and every winged bird according to its kind. And God saw that it was good. And God blessed them, saying, "Be fruitful and multiply, and fill the waters in the seas, and let birds multiply on the earth." So the evening and the morning were the fifth day.

All the sea creatures and the birds were created on day-5.

CREATION WEEK DAY-6:

GENESIS 1:24-27,31 (NKJV):

Then God said, "Let the earth bring forth the living creature according to its kind: cattle and creeping thing and beast of the earth, each according to its kind"; and it was so. And God made the beast of the earth according to its kind, cattle according to its kind, and everything that creeps on the earth according to its kind. And God saw that it was good.

Then God said, "Let Us make man in Our image, according to Our likeness; let them have dominion over the fish of the sea, over the birds of the air, and over the cattle, over all the earth and over every creeping thing that creeps on the earth." So God created man in His own image; in the image of God He created him; male and female He created them. …

So the evening and the morning were the sixth day.

All the land creatures and mankind were created on day-6.

CREATION WEEK DAY-7:

GENESIS 2:2-3 (NKJV):

And on the seventh day God ended His work that He had done, and He rested on the seventh day from all His work that He had done. Then God blessed the seventh day and sanctified it, because in it He rested from all His work that God had created and made.

God rested from all His work that He had done on day-7.

THE CREATION, IN SUMMATION:

IN THE BEGINNING:

God created the heavens (the universe) and THE FOUNDATION of the Earth (Genesis 1:1).

CREATION WEEK DAY-1:

God created temporary light for the Earth by saying, "Let there be light" (Genesis 1:3).

CREATION WEEK DAY-2:

God made Earth's atmosphere (firmament / heaven) (Genesis 1:6).

CREATION WEEK DAY-3:

God gathered the existing water that was on Earth to form seas and let the dry land appear (Genesis 1:9). God then created the grass, herbs, fruit trees, and all vegetation on the dry land (Genesis 1:11).

CREATION WEEK DAY-4:

God made the two great light sources for the Earth (Genesis 1:16). He ignited and illuminated the Sun to light the Earth for the day and for the Moon to reflect the Sun's light at night. The Sun and Moon were also to be used for signs, seasons, days and calendar years.

CREATION WEEK DAY-5:

God created all the sea creatures and all the birds (Genesis 1:20).

CREATION WEEK DAY-6:

God created all the land creatures and mankind (Genesis 1:24-27).

CREATION WEEK DAY-7:

God rested from all His work that He had done (Genesis 2:2).

The creation week consisted of six 24-hour periods, NOT ages or periods of time. Upon completion of each day of creation week, it was recorded, "And the evening and the morning were the first day," … through the sixth day, indicating six 24-hour night and day periods.

HOW LONG DID IT TAKE GOD TO CREATE THE HEAVENS AND THE EARTH?

GENESIS 2:4 (NKJV):
… IN THE DAY that the LORD God made the earth and the heavens.

God made the heavens and the Earth IN THE BEGINNING, in a SINGLE DAY. Afterward God formed the Earth to sustain life and created life upon the Earth during the 6-day creation week. IN THE DAY God made the Earth and the heavens was IN THE BEGINNING, before the 6-day creation week. IN THE BEGINNING (Genesis 1:1) was a time period before God measured Earth's days in 24-hour intervals, counting the evening and the morning for each day (Genesis 1:5,8,13,19,23,31).

God made the Earth and heavens in a single day according to Genesis 2:4. What is a day to an eternal God? Scripture reveals that one day to God is as a thousand years and a thousand years is as one day (2 Peter 3:8). God most likely took about 1,000 Earth years (one day to Him) to create the vast cosmos and the Earth (Genesis 1:1-2, 2:4; 2 Peter 3:8). After those thousand years, or one God-day, God ruled over His creation in glory before THE EARTH WAS formed to sustain life (John 17:5). Then God formed the Earth for life and created life upon the Earth during the 6-day creation week (Genesis 1:3-31).

YOUNG EARTH CREATIONISTS

Young Earth Creationists believe that the Earth and the entire universe were created approximately 6,000-years ago. They base their calculations on the generations of Scripture going back chronologically to about 4,000

B.C. Young Earth Creationists have incorrectly linked the age of the Earth with the time that life first appeared upon the Earth. Scripture declares that THE EARTH WAS in existence IN THE BEGINNING *prior* to the creation week. Young Earth Creationists err in not understanding that the Earth is old, believing and proclaiming the physical Earth to be young, coming into existence about 6,000-years ago.

Many Young Earth Creationists believe that proclaiming the Earth to be old "opens the door" for evolution. This is not so. No amount of time, be it hundreds, thousands, billions, trillions, or even an eternity of years could cause life to come from non-life.

God created the heavens and the Earth IN THE BEGINNING, then revisited the Earth some time afterward, approximately 6,000-years ago, and THE EARTH WAS *still* void (of life) and without form (to sustain life). Life did not arise from non-life, nor could it, nor did God use evolution as a means of creating all the various kinds of life on Earth.

Scripture declares that THE EARTH WAS of old, created IN THE BEGINNING existing in a state that was without form and void of life. When God revisited the Earth it was still without form (to sustain life) and void (of life) (Genesis 1:2). Then God acted upon the Earth that was without form and void, to form the Earth to sustain life and then created all the kinds of life upon it, approximately 6,000-years ago.

The heavens and the Earth, God's declared "works of old," refute the idea that the Earth and universe are relatively young.

PSALM 102:25 (NKJV):

OF OLD You laid THE FOUNDATION of the earth, and the heavens are the work of Your hands.

NOTE:
THE FOUNDATION of the Earth is OF OLD. The Earth's foundation was created IN THE BEGINNING, long ago, and then God FINISHED the Earth approximately 6,000-years ago during the 6-day creation week (Genesis 2:1).

PROVERBS 8:22-23 (NKJV):

YHWH (the Lord) possessed Me at the beginning of His way, before His works OF OLD. I have been established from everlasting, from the beginning, before there ever was an earth.

2 TIMOTHY 1:9 (NKJV):

His own purpose and grace that was given to us in Messiah Yeshua (Christ Jesus) BEFORE TIME BEGAN...

TITUS 1:2 (NKJV):

In hope of eternal life that God, who cannot lie, promised BEFORE TIME BEGAN...

God existed before time itself began. God created time, which did have a beginning.

2 PETER 3:5 (NKJV):

For this they willfully forget: that by the word of God the heavens were OF OLD.

The heavens are OF OLD, created IN THE BEGINNING.

JOHN 17:5 (NKJV):

"And now, O Father, glorify Me together with Yourself, with the glory that I had with You BEFORE THE WORLD WAS."

The world was created IN THE BEGINNING, yet Yeshua (Jesus) speaks of a time that He was glorified with the Father BEFORE THE WORLD WAS. Yeshua (Jesus) was reigning throughout the cosmos with the Father in glory, BEFORE THE WORLD WAS *formed for life* during the 6-day creation week.

To believe that the entire universe, the Earth, and all matter came into existence 6,000-years ago is a quandary itself and places God in a box. It would mean that God existed in a vacuum of space and time. It limits God as a Creator to a 6-day period, 6,000-years ago. No artist or creator works for 6-days, having never created before, or after, his or her one-week of work. Young Earth Creationists basically believe God did just that.

IN THE BEGINNING signals the creation of time, the time the physical universe, as we know it, began. IN THE BEGINNING God created matter, space, and time. Time was created *before* creation week. Yeshua (Jesus) reigned with the Father in glory, *before* THE WORLD WAS, which indicates a time period before the world was formed 6,000-years ago.

There are several hundred billion stars that form our Milky Way Galaxy and there are an estimated one hundred billion known galaxies. The universe is so vast; there are more stars in the universe than all the grains of sand on all the Earth's beaches. The Earth, in comparison to the vast cosmos, is infinitesimally small. All things are possible with God, but to believe that God spent six 24-hour days creating the Earth and one 24-hour day creating the entire universe is overwhelmingly disproportional and a very Earth-centric view of the creation that is not supported through a careful examination of Scripture.

2 PETER 3:8 (NKJV):

With YHWH (the Lord) one day is as a thousand years, and a thousand years as one day.

Understanding that time is relative - according to science (Einstein's Theory of Relativity), and God lives outside-of-time, what is a thousand years to us is as one day to God.

Young Earth Creationists often cite Exodus 20:11 and 31:17 to support their belief that the Earth and universe were created 6,000-years ago.

EXODUS 20:11 (NKJV):

For in six days the Lord made the heaven and the earth, the sea, and all that is in them, and rested the seventh day.

EXODUS 31:17 (NKJV):

For in six days the Lord made heaven and earth, and on the seventh day he rested, and was refreshed.

These two verses are the strongest argument Young Earth Creationists use as Scriptural proof that God created the entire universe and the Earth in six literal days, approximately 6,000-years ago. Upon careful examination of these verses, using a precept upon precept comparison with other verses, this is not the case at all.

The Hebrew word for heaven(s) is shamayim. Shamayim, or heaven, is used interchangeably throughout Scripture as meaning God's dwelling place, the universe, the cosmos, the sky, or atmosphere.[134] Scripture itself, in the Genesis account, reveals that the word 'heaven' is used to refer to Earth's firmament (atmosphere / sky). A key verse in understanding mystery of God's creation is Genesis 1:8.

GENESIS 1:8 (NKJV):

And God called the firmament Heaven.

In Exodus 20:11 and 31:17, the word 'heaven' (singular) is used, not 'heavens' (plural) indicating that 'heaven' is referring to Earth's firmament (atmosphere) and not the heavenly cosmos.

Another Scripture example:

GENESIS 7:19 (NKJV):

And the waters prevailed exceedingly on the earth, and all the high hills under the whole heaven were covered.

The 'global' flood did not flood the whole heavenly universe. During the global flood, all the high hills under the whole heaven (Earth's atmosphere) were covered. 'Heaven,' when used in Genesis 7:19, Exodus 20:11, and 31:17, refers to the Earth's atmosphere / firmament / sky (Genesis 1:8).

A correct interpretation of Exodus 20:11 and 31:17 should be understood to mean:

EXODUS 20:11 (NKJV) [WITH INTERPRETATION]:

For in six days YHWH (the Lord) made the heaven [SKY] and the earth [SUITABLE FOR LIFE], the sea, and all [LIFE] that is in them, and rested the seventh day.

EXODUS 31:17 (NKJV) [WITH INTERPRETATION]:

For in six days YHWH (the Lord) made heaven [EARTH'S SKY] and earth [SUITABLE FOR LIFE], and on the seventh day he rested, and was refreshed.

Young Earth Creationists have a paradox dilemma: When were the stars created? They believe IN THE BEGINNING (Genesis 1:1) represents day-1 of creation week, but most Young Earth Creationists believe the stars were created on day-4 of creation week (Genesis 1:16).

GENESIS 1:1 (NKJV) [WITH INTERPRETATION]:

IN THE BEGINNING God created the heavens [INCLUDING THE STARS] and the earth.

GENESIS 1:16,19 (NKJV):

He made the stars also. … So the evening and the morning were the forth day.

The stars were created IN THE BEGINNING, which was long before day-1 of creation week. Genesis 1:16 is a confirmation that God made the stars also - IN THE BEGINNING. The two great lights - the Sun and Moon, were illuminated on day-4 of creation week.

TWO SCIENTIFIC EVIDENCES THAT SUPPORT AN OLD EARTH

There are two well-established, hard to refute, observable evidences that the Earth and the universe are old and did not come into existence 6,000-years ago.

1. DISTANT STARLIGHT

Distant starlight from galaxies far, far away, which takes far longer than 6,000-years to reach Earth at light speed, is visible on Earth. The oldest known detected starlight to reach Earth has been calculated to be over 13-billion-years old.

Distant starlight, starlight that takes billions years to reach Earth, is observable scientific evidence that stars are much older than 6,000-years. Young Earth Creationists negate the science that measures and estimates the time distant starlight reaches Earth, by citing the following verse:

ISAIAH 42:5 (NKJV):

Thus says God YHWH (the Lord), who created the heavens and stretched them out.

God did create the heavens, and He did stretch them out. The universe is still expanding to this day and its expansion is believed to be accelerating, not decelerating. Young Earth Creationists generally believe that God created the stars on day-4 of creation week, and then He stretched the stars outward while stretching their starlight back toward Earth so that distant, otherwise unobservable, starlight would be visible on Earth.

Young Earth Creationists' theory is that God stretched back the light emitted from stars to Earth, while simultaneously stretching forth the stars outward faster than the speed of light throughout the universe, to account for distant starlight. Young Earth Creationists also theorize that the speed of light traveling through space may not have been constant in ages past. What Young Earth Creationists are proclaiming is that God supernaturally stretched forth the stars to make it appear that distant starlight takes billions of years to reach Earth or that somehow light speeding through space was somehow much faster thousands of years ago, allowing us to see stars billions of light years away.

God doesn't trick us with the evidences and timeframes of His creation. Young Earth Creationists' theory accounting for distant starlight that takes billions of years to reach Earth is completely unscientific and should be outright dismissed.

2. CRATER IMPACTS

Asteroids, comets, and meteors colliding with the ancient Earth left many detectable and observable crater impacts. Many of Earth's crater impact areas, while still detectable, have been worn away over thousands, millions, or billions of years through erosion on an active Earth. The most preserved crater impact site, Meteor Crater in Arizona, USA, is the result of a collision between an asteroid and planet Earth that occurred approximately 50,000-years ago.

HOW CAN WE KNOW THAT THE UNIVERSE AND THE UNFORMED EARTH WERE ORIGINALLY CREATED "IN THE BEGINNING" AND NOT DURING THE 6-DAY CREATION WEEK?

1. IN THE BEGINNING does not indicate the start of day-1 of God's 6-day creation week. IN THE BEGINNING represents a significant span of time before day-1. After the original creation IN THE BEGINNING and after the end of each day of the creation week, the start of each new creation day begins with the phrase, "Then God said..."

"IN THE BEGINNING (not day-1) God created the heavens and the Earth" (Genesis 1:1).

Day-1 STARTS: "Then God said..." (Gen. 1:3), Day-1 ENDS (Gen. 1:5).

Day-2 STARTS: "Then God said..." (Gen. 1:6), Day-2 ENDS (Gen. 1:8).

Day-3 STARTS: "Then God said..." (Gen. 1:9), Day-3 ENDS (Gen. 1:13).

Day-4 STARTS: "Then God said..." (Gen. 1:14), Day-4 ENDS (Gen. 1:19).

Day-5 STARTS: "Then God said..." (Gen. 1:20), Day-5 ENDS (Gen. 1:23).

Day-6 STARTS: "Then God said..." (Gen. 1:24), Day-6 ENDS (Gen. 1:31).

It would be inconsistent for God to start day-1 of creation week with the phrase, "IN THE BEGINNING," and start all the other days of the week with the phrase, "Then God said..."

2. Genesis 1:1-2 proclaims that THE EARTH "WAS" in existence before the creation week.

3. Genesis 1:3-31 covers the creation week, but does NOT record the Earth itself as being created on this week. On creation days 1 through 6, there is no verse that says God created THE FOUNDATION of the Earth on any of those days, but Scripture declares THE EARTH WAS created IN THE BEGINNING (Genesis 1:1). Planet Earth's foundation existed of old, from IN THE BEGINNING, before creation week began (Psalm 102:25). God acted upon an already existing Earth on creation days 1-6, when He made the Earth suitable for life and inhabited it with life.

4. Yeshua (Jesus) was reigning in the cosmos / universe with God the Father BEFORE THE WORLD WAS formed for life (John 17:5). THE EARTH WAS made IN THE BEGINNING, so Yeshua (Jesus) was reigning throughout the cosmos with the Father IN THE BEGINNING, but *before* THE WORLD WAS (formed for life) during the 6-day creation week.

5. The heavens and Earth experienced a history or generations of time (Genesis 2:4). A history or generations of the heavens and the Earth do not represent a 1-week period. THE DAY (Genesis 2:4), the God-day that God made the heavens and the Earth lasted about 1,000-years (2 Peter 3:8).

6. Scripture proclaims THE FOUNDATION of the Earth to be OF OLD (Psalm 102:25).

7. Numerous crater impacts upon the Earth are much older than 6,000-years.

THE GAP THEORY

There are some theologians who understand the gap between IN THE BEGINNING and creation week day-1. However, many who proclaim the Gap Theory add to Scripture with their own personal opinions and theories that are unsubstantiated by Scripture.

The traditional Gap Theory proposes that the phrase "without form and void," of Genesis 1:2 should actually be translated "ruined and desolate." It proposes that Satan and his demons once inhabited the Earth, with the dinosaurs, and God brought forth a divine cataclysmic judgment upon the Earth, similar to the flood of Noah's time.

Gap theorists further rationalize and state that God would have never created the Earth in a ruined state and that the Earth must have been destroyed as a result of Satan's sin. Gap Theory proponents cite Isaiah 45:18 as basis for their belief that God didn't create an Earth that was without form and void.

ISAIAH 45:18 (NKJV):

For thus says YHWH (the Lord), who created the heavens; who formed the earth and made it; who has established it, who did not create it in vain, who formed it to be inhabited: ...

Isaiah 45:18 actually says God formed the Earth (Genesis 1:3-31) *AND* made it (Genesis 1:1-2), indicating two separate acts of creation. God formed the Earth during the 6-day creation week *and* made the Earth IN THE BEGINNING.

A correct interpretation of Isaiah 45:18 should be understood to mean:

ISAIAH 45:18 (NKJV) [WITH INTERPRETATION]:

For thus says YHWH (the Lord), who created the heavens; who formed the earth [DURING THE 6-DAY CREATION WEEK] and made it [IN THE BEGINNING]; who has established it [TO SUSTAIN LIFE], who did not create it in vain [TO REMAIN VOID], who formed it to be inhabited [DURING THE 6-DAY CREATION WEEK]: ...

Gap theorists believe that there was an age of life, ruled by Satan, that God wiped out through judgment in Genesis 1:2. Scripture records that it was through man's sin, not Satan's, that sin and death entered the physical world. Satan is a spiritual being who exists in the spiritual realm, not a physical being who once inhabited the physical realm on Earth. There was no death of any creatures, including dinosaurs, in the world before Adam's sin.

ROMANS 5:12 (NKJV):

Therefore, just as through one man sin entered the world, and death through sin...

1 CORINTHIANS 15:21-22 (NKJV):

For since by man came death, by Man also came the resurrection of the dead. For as in Adam all die, even so in Messiah (Christ) all shall be made alive.

God has created many things that are without form and void. Man doesn't always know all the purposes of God's creations. Some of His creation has a more significant purpose, some less. God has created many planetary bodies in our Solar System and throughout the universe that we are only now beginning to discover. These planets (such as Mars) may, at the moment, be unformed, but perhaps God will form them (for life) in the future. All this is speculation, of course. The Gap Theory errs in assuming that God could not have originally made an unformed Earth and then formed it afterward to be suitable for life.

Genesis 1:28 is a verse often cited to support the theory that the Earth was flooded twice in judgment.

GENESIS 1:28 (KJV):
And God blessed them, and God said unto them, Be fruitful, and multiply, and REPLENISH the earth and subdue it…

It is believed by Gap theorists that man, Adam and Eve, were commanded by God to replenish life upon the Earth, after it was flooded from Satan's rebellion and all life was wiped out on Earth.

The New King James and the Halleluyah Scriptures versions translate Genesis 1:28 somewhat differently than the King James, using "fill the earth" instead of "replenish the earth." Adam and Eve didn't replenish the Earth; they filled it.

GENESIS 1:28 (NKJV):
Then God blessed them, and God said to them, "Be fruitful and multiply; FILL the earth and subdue it…"

BERESHITH (GENESIS) 1:28 (HSV):
And Elohim barak them, and Elohim said to them, "Bear fruit and increase, and FILL the earth and subdue it…"

EVOLUTION THEORY SCIENTISTS

YHWH (the Lord) questioned Job … and this question is relevant to modern Evolution Theory scientists, who act and think like they know all the answers.

JOB 38:4 (NKJV):
Where were you when I laid the foundations of the earth?
Tell Me if you have understanding.

Evolution Theory scientists estimate that the Earth is 4.5-billion-years-old and that the universe is 13.8-billion-years-old. In coming to these assumed dates, Earth's rocks are tested using highly unreliable radiometric dating methods and the expanse of the universe is measured in reverse to try to come to a zero starting point of when the universe began according to the Big Bang Theory. The oldest known starlight is estimated to be about 13.6-billion-years-old. The Earth is as old as the universe. IN THE BEGINNING God created the heavens (universe) and the Earth (Genesis 1:2). There is no age difference between the Earth and the universe as many secular astronomists proclaim.

ARE DINOSAURS AND OTHER FOSSILIZED CREATURES MILLIONS OF YEARS OLD?

No. Dinosaurs, as land creatures, were created on day-6 of creation week. The first dinosaurs that lived were created approximately 6,000-years ago.

Radiometric dating methods have been shown to be highly unreliable, and are completely unreliable when dating objects older than four thousand years old.[135][136][137]

The rate of decay of carbon and other isotope elements are used to date fossils and Earth's rocks to determine their age. Since fossils and rocks cannot be measured beyond a few thousand years, because we cannot assume the rate of decay beyond those unknown years was constant (due to various environmental factors), radiocarbon and radiometric dating are based on faith, not verifiable science.

Scientists have often made a proclamation that a certain creature has been extinct for millions of years and then afterward the so-called extinct creature has been discovered to be alive and well, unchanged by evolution, and living somewhere on Earth. Such was the case with the coelacanth fish. Coelacanths were thought to be extinct for over 50-million-years, but were rediscovered off the coast of South Africa in 1938.[138]

Recent Tyrannosaurus rex dinosaur bone exams have revealed intact soft tissue and blood fragments.[139] These discoveries strongly refute the Evolution Theory scientists' view that dinosaurs lived millions of years ago.[140] Yet in spite of this new scientific evidence, Evolution Theory scientists proclaim that it is amazing that blood and soft tissue from a 70-million-year-old dinosaur could have remained intact.

It would be difficult for any creature's blood and soft tissue to remain intact for 7-years, 70-years, 700-years, or 7,000-years. It would be impossible for dinosaur blood and soft tissue to remain intact for 70,000,000-years! 70-million-years are a LOT of years for blood and soft tissue to survive intact on an active Earth!

Evolution Theory scientists are in scientific denial about recent findings of dinosaur blood and soft tissue; scientific evidence refutes their theory that dinosaurs lived millions of years ago. Evolution Theory scientists are so sure that dinosaurs lived millions of years ago that they cannot even grasp the concept that most of the dinosaurs died thousands of years ago in the great flood of Noah's time. Even when presented with compelling blood and soft tissue evidence, they cling to their theory that dinosaurs died out 65-70-million-years-ago.[141]

HOW OLD IS THE UNIVERSE?

How long ago was IN THE BEGINNING, when the heavens and the Earth first came into existence? No one can say for sure. To compare Scripture with distant starlight, a certain theoretical formula can be attained.

God created the heavens and the Earth in the beginning (Genesis 1:1), in a day (Genesis 2:4).

A God day = 1,000-years (2 Peter 3:8).

The heavens and the Earth experienced a history, a passage of generations of time (Genesis 2:4).

If a God day = 1,000-years, then a God year = 365,000-years.

A generation at 40-years would mean a generation of the heavens and the Earth would be 365,000-years x 40 = 14,600,000-years.

If a generation of the heavens and the Earth was 14.6-million-years, then 1,000 generations of the heavens and the Earth would = 14.6-billion-years.

Based on distant starlight, scientists estimate the universe to be at least 13-billion-years-old. It is unknown how many generations of the heavens and the Earth passed before God formed the Earth and created life upon it approximately 6,000-years-ago during the 6-day creation week.

If it were 1,000-generations of the heavens and the Earth that passed, since the beginning, that would make the universe approximately 14.6-billion-years-old. Man cannot know the exact age of the universe at this time.

HOW OLD IS THE EARTH?

The age of the Earth is a complex question with no single answer. The Earth's foundation was created along with the universe in a single day (a God-day or thousand year period - 2 Peter 3:8) IN THE BEGINNING (Genesis 1:1, 2:4). The Earth was formed to be habitable for life and life was created upon the Earth about 6,000-years ago during the 6-day creation week (Genesis 1:3-2:2; Exodus 20:11, 31:17). The Earth is composed of different elements that have different ages.

The Earth itself, (the foundation of the Earth), and the universe, are old (Psalm 102:25; Proverbs 8:22-23, 2 Peter 3:5). All life upon Earth is young, going back 6,000-years (Genesis 1:11-13, 20-31).

The Earth's foundation (the core, crust, dirt, mantle, mountains, rocks, soil, and water of the Earth) was created IN THE BEGINNING. The foundation of the Earth is as old as the universe itself, as the heavens and the Earth were created together IN THE BEGINNING (Genesis 1:1). The Earth was in existence before God acted upon it during the 6-day creation week, to make it suitable for sustaining life and filling it with life. The age of the Earth is unknown, as Scripture does not reveal the Earth's age, but it is likely billions of years old based on scientific observations of distant starlight.

The Earth's atmosphere, the majority of it, is approximately 6,000-years-old. God made the atmosphere (sky / firmament / heaven) for the Earth on day-2 of creation week (Genesis 1:6-8). The Earth, as a planetary body large enough to retain an atmosphere, would most likely have had some type of atmosphere from when it was originally created IN THE BEGINNING. Therefore, the Earth's atmosphere is likely a mix of gaseous elements created by God on day-2 of creation week and the atmospheric gases that were retained by the Earth IN THE BEGINNING, from billions of years ago.

All life upon Earth began approximately 6,000-years-ago. God created the grass, herbs, fruit trees, and all vegetation on day-3 of creation week (Genesis 1:11-13). God created all the sea creatures and birds on day-5 of creation week (Genesis 1:20-23). God created all the land creatures and mankind on day-6 of creation week (Genesis 1:24-31).

These are currently the best-known age(s) of the Earth, the sky, and life upon the Earth.

GEOCENTRISM:
DOES THE EARTH MOVE?
IS THE EARTH LOCATED AT THE CENTER OF THE UNIVERSE?

By George Lujack

The geocentric Earth-centered universe belief has been experiencing a revival recently among some within Christianity. This article will examine the geocentric model of the universe, the heliocentric model, the helical model, and Scripture-related verses used in justifying the geocentric model to determine if Scripture actually supports the theory that the Earth does not move and is located at the center of the universe.

geocentrism:

The belief that the Earth is the center of the universe, does not move, and that the Sun, the planets, and all the stars revolve around the Earth.[142][143]

The geocentric model of the universe is a description of the cosmos in which Earth is at the orbital center of all the universe's celestial bodies. The geocentric model was developed in earlier civilizations from ancient Greece and throughout Rome, and, in spite of scientific evidences against the geocentric model it has been experiencing a revival of sorts among some in Christian circles.

There are two main foundational reasons for the belief in geocentrism:

1. From the perspective of an Earth-bound observer, the Earth does not appear to move. The stars, the Sun, and planets appear to revolve around the Earth each day, making the Earth appear to be the center of the universe.

2. There are Scripture verses that proclaim that the Earth does not move.

A problem with determining Earth's place in the universe is that we are trying to do so while being bound upon Earth, with the limited understanding of the universe that we have. Geocentrists fail to understand, or ignore the fact, that from the perception of being on Earth, we are like fish in a fishbowl. If a fish inside of a fishbowl had a mind, it would view its fishbowl as the center of the universe. Everything else it observed, its outer surroundings beyond its glass bowl, people coming and going, etc., would be viewed as revolving around its fishbowl. The fish would observe that its fishbowl does not move. Even if you placed the fishbowl in a commercial airplane, traveling smoothly at 500 mph (800 kph), the fish would observe that its fishbowl is stable and does not move, even though it is in a plane traveling at high rate of speed.

From the fish's relative perspective, its fishbowl appears to be the center of the universe, it apparently is not moving, and everything in its observable universe seems to be revolving around it.

There is no verse in all of Scripture that proclaims that the Earth is the center of the universe. Geocentrism is deduced based on the following Scripture verses. (NOTE: The KJV, NKJV, and HSV translations are shown when there are some slight English word translation differences):

1 CHRONICLES 16:30 (KJV):
The world also shall be stable, that it be not moved.

1 CHRONICLES 16:30 (NKJV):
The world also is firmly established; it shall not be moved.

PSALM 93:1 (NKJV):
Surely the world is established, so that it cannot be moved.

PSALM 96:10 (NKJV):
The world also is firmly established; it shall not be moved.

PSALM 104:5 (KJV):
Who laid the foundations of the earth, that it should not be removed for ever.

PSALM 104:5 (NKJV):
You who laid the foundations of the earth, so that it should not be moved forever.

A literal translation is understood by geocentrists to mean that the Earth does not move and *therefore* the entire universe revolves around the Earth. Applying this literal interpretation and scientific application of it to the Earth, the Sun, the Solar System, and the universe is erroneous. The context of what is the spoken of in these verses pertains to the Earth's stability. The oceans move, the wind blows, the Earth moves via tectonic plates, and the Earth moves during earthquakes. Scripture also declares that the Earth moves and turns:

JOB 38:14 (KJV) [WITH INTERPRETATION]:
It [EARTH] is turned as clay to the seal [ON A POTTER'S WHEEL]; and they [THE CLOUDS - JOB 38:9] stand as a garment.

JOB 38:14 (HS) [WITH INTERPRETATION]:
It [EARTH] is changed like clay under a seal [OF A POTTER'S WHEEL]; and they [THE CLOUDS - JOB 38:9] stand out like a garment.

PSALM 99:1 (NKJV):
Let the earth be moved!

The Earth moves, but is stable and does not move on its surface; is stable in orbit and does not move out of orbit. A proper way to scientifically apply, interpret, and understand Scripture's declaration that the Earth "does not move" in regards to the universe is thus:

1 CHRONICLES 16:30 (KJV) [WITH INTERPRETATION]:

The world also shall be stable [IN ORBIT], that it be not moved [OUT OF ORBIT].

1 CHRONICLES 16:30 (NKJV) [WITH INTERPRETATION]:

The world also is firmly established [IN ORBIT]; it shall not be moved [OUT OF ORBIT].

PSALM 93:1 (NKJV) [WITH INTERPRETATION]:

Surely the world is established [IN ORBIT], so that it cannot be moved [OUT OF ORBIT].

PSALM 96:10 (NKJV) [WITH INTERPRETATION]:

The world also is firmly established [IN ORBIT]; it shall not be moved [OUT OF ORBIT].

PSALM 104:5 (KJV) [WITH INTERPRETATION]:

Who laid the foundations of the earth [IN ORBIT], that it should not be removed [FROM ITS ORBIT] for ever.

PSALM 104:5 (NKJV) [WITH INTERPRETATION]:

You who laid the foundations of the earth [IN ORBIT], so that it should not be moved [FROM ITS ORBIT] forever.

Geocentrists believe that the Earth is fixed in space, not orbiting the Sun, not rotating, and not moving at all. Scripture disputes this claim.

JOB 26:7 (NKJV):

He hangs the earth ON NOTHING.

The Earth, while hurling through space, is not fixed in space or locked into position at the center of the universe; it hangs on nothing. God hangs the Earth *on nothing*. 'Nothing' cannot prevent the Earth from moving; only *something* can prevent the Earth from moving through space.

The Earth does not rest on *physical* pillars and is hanging in the vacuum of empty space (nothing). Even if geocentrists claim that God supernaturally keeps the Earth from moving, that would not be 'nothing,' that would be God, through the power of His Holy Spirit, using something to hold the Earth motionless in space. Scripture does not make the claim that the Earth is fixed in space, but simply states that it hangs on nothing. Gravity holds the Earth in place, in orbit around the Sun. Gravity consists of 'nothing' and God hangs the Earth on nothing, *but gravity*. A scientific interpretation of Job 26:7 should be understood as:

JOB 26:7 (NKJV) [WITH INTERPRETATION]:

He hangs the earth [IN ORBIT] on nothing [BUT GRAVITY].

heliocentrism:

The astronomical model in which the Earth and planets revolve around the Sun at the center of the Solar System.[144]

Galileo, the Italian astronomer, engineer, mathematician, and philosopher championed heliocentrism, and for doing so got himself into trouble by a Roman Catholic Inquisition in 1615, was forced to recant, and spent the rest of his life under house arrest. Galileo understood that smaller objects would be 'moved' by the gravity fields of larger objects.

The heliocentric model of the universe is in line with observable science and the geocentric model is not. We know and observe that smaller objects are gravitationally attracted to larger objects and are 'moved' by them. In our own Solar System, we observe moons orbiting their larger planets. The smaller Earth revolves around the much larger Sun.

In 1971, on an Apollo 15 Moon walk, astronaut David Scott demonstrated that a hammer and feather, with no atmosphere resistance to slow down the descent of the feather, were equally caught under the gravity of the Moon and they dropped to its surface at the same rate of speed.[145]

The heliocentric model of the universe applies scientific principles and known observable science to its model of the Sun-centered Solar System, while the geocentric model completely ignores science and applies misinterpreted Scripture verses as a basis for its view of the Earth-centered Solar System.

In 2012, DjSadhu, a self-described music producer, video artist, developer, and researcher produced a video of the Sun and the Solar System that he called the helical model, claiming that the Solar System operated like a vortex. In the video, he claims that the Sun is like a comet, dragging the planets in its wake, creating a spiraling vortex.[146]

While this recent helical model properly indicates the movement of the Sun, as it does move in a spiral orbit around the center of the Milky Way Galaxy, it ignores the observable science that our Solar System and other galaxies are disc-shaped. Another scientific problem with the helical model is that in spiraling vortexes, the rotation continually spirals down. If the planets were rotating in a spiraling vortex trailing the Sun, they would eventually spiral down and fall in line directly behind the Sun, in its wake.

The helical model would be a more scientifically accurate model if it showed the Sun in motion and the planets revolving around the Sun on the same plane, rotating around a moving Sun, towards the center and then away from the center of the Milky Way Galaxy.

THE PRINCIPLE (MOVIE)

The Principle is a 2014 film questioning the Copernican principle and advances the philosophy of geocentrism. The Copernican principle, named after Nicolaus Copernicus, states that the Earth is not in any special favored or central location in the universe.

The Principle movie makes a lot of bold unsubstantiated claims, such as, "Science has found evidence that Earth is the center of the universe."

Science has found no such evidence. The Earth may very well be somewhere near the center of the observable universe. Stars can be observed in the night sky in every direction that we point our telescopes. This may indicate that the Milky Way Galaxy is near the center of the universe, but there is absolutely no direct scientific evidence to claim that the Earth is an unmoving planet located at the center of the universe or that the universe revolves around the Earth.

Modern-day geocentrists make the claim that the Earth is at the center of the universe and held in an unmoving dead-center position by all the universe's celestial bodies that pull on it equally in all directions. The Moon's gravity pulls on the Earth's waters, shifting their position on the planet, causing tidal movement. Geocentrists claim that while the Earth's waters move, the Earth itself does not. That claim is not scientifically plausible. The reason we see the Earth's waters move, and not the Earth itself, is because liquid water is more flexible than the Earth's landmasses and shifts accordingly due to the Moon's gravitational pull exerted over them. If the Earth were at the center of the universe, in a perfect dead-center locked position and not affected by the gravitational pull of any celestial body, then the Earth's waters would likewise not be affected by the Moon's gravitational pull on them.

The entire premise of *The Principle* is that either the geocentric (alleged biblical) model of the Earth and universe is correct, or the Big Bang Theory is correct. Either the Earth is at the center of the universe and we are significant, or the Earth is not at the center of the universe and we are insignificant.

If the Earth were hypothetically located at the edge or the outer portion of the observable universe, would mankind - made in God's image, be insignificant? If being centrally located in the universe indicates significance, shouldn't heaven, God's dwelling place, be at the center of the universe and thus the universe should therefore revolve around Him in heaven? Is not God more significant than His creation?

Evolution-minded Big Bang theorists propose that the universe is one large cosmic accident and we are all insignificant beings created from leftover stardust. Geocentrists claim that Earth is God's creation located at the center of the universe and we are significant. It is not an either / or proposition choice between these two theories; there are other possibilities. The Copernican model of the Solar System does not negate God, nor does it declare the Big Bang Theory to be true.

There are three classifications of galaxies: elliptical, spiral, and irregular. In all the known galaxies, stars are observed revolving around their galaxy core centers - presumably with planets revolving around those stars, and moons revolving around those planets. Geocentrists would have us believe that of all the billions of galaxies in the universe (current estimate 100-200 billion), the laws of physics work differently in the Milky Way. Planet Earth, according to geocentrists, bound by nothing (Job 26:7), is not only the center of the Milky Way Galaxy, where the Sun and the planets of the Solar System revolve around it, but Earth is also the center of the entire universe which also revolves around it.

PSALM 19:1 (NKJV):

The heavens declare the glory of God.

We do not need to close our eyes to observable science and believe in geocentrism in order to believe that we are significant. We are created in the image of God and that is what makes us significant (Genesis 1:26). The universe is God's creation and declares the glory of God; the universe does not declare the significance of man.

FLAT EARTH THEORY:
IS THE EARTH FLAT?
DOES THE EARTH REST ON PILLARS?
IS THE EARTH SHAPED LIKE A CIRCULAR DISC?

By George Lujack

It is the twenty-first century and there are still modern flat Earth societies proclaiming that the Earth is a flat disc-shaped planet. A renewed interest in the discussion of whether or not the Earth is flat has cropped up among some conspiracy theorists who believe, or claim to believe, that NASA and / or other organizations have been perpetuating the lie that the Earth is a sphere and have been covering up evidence that the Earth is a flat disc. This article will address the flat-earthers' claims and examine the Scripture verses that flat-earthers use to justify their belief in declaring the Earth to be flat. This article will reveal that the Scripture verses used by flat-earthers are misinterpreted and then misapplied, and will declare the Flat Earth Theory to be false.

IS THE EARTH FLAT?

There is no Scripture verse that plainly states that the Earth is flat. There are verses that allegorically proclaim that the Earth has corners, edges, and that the Earth rests on pillars.

ISAIAH 11:12; REVELATION 7:1; REVELATION 20:8 (NKJV):
From the four corners of the earth; at the four corners of the earth; in the four corners of the earth...

WHAT ARE THE FOUR CORNERS OF THE EARTH?

The Earth is not a flat rectangle or square, so Scripture's reference to the four corners of the Earth does not refer to literal corners. The central starting map location of Scripture is the nation of Israel. The four corners of the Earth, spoken of in Scripture, are the compass points north, south, east, and west of Israel.

DOES THE EARTH REST ON PILLARS?

1 SAMUEL 2:8 (NKJV):
For the pillars of the earth belong to YHWH (the Lord) and He has set the world upon them.

JOB 9:6 (NKJV):

He shakes the earth out of its place, and the pillars tremble.

'Pillars' has more than one definition.

pillar:

1. A tall vertical structure of stone, wood, or metal, used as support for a building, or as an ornament or monument.

2. Something shaped like a pillar: "a pillar of smoke."

3. A person or thing regarded as reliably providing essential support for something: "he was a pillar of his local community."[147]

When all the various definitions of 'pillar' are applied to the Scripture verses that declare that the Earth rests on pillars, it should not be concluded that Scripture proclaims that a flat Earth rests on external physical pillar structures.

Scripture also refers to pillars as "pillars of smoke."

JOEL 2:30 (NKJV):

And I will show wonders in the heavens and in the earth: Blood and fire and pillars of smoke.

There are two applications of what Scripture refers to when saying that the Earth rests on pillars.

The pillars belong to YHWH (the Lord), according to 1 Samuel 2:8, so the pillars are a reference to God providing essential support for the Earth.

GENESIS 1:9 (NKJV):

Then God said, "Let the waters under the heavens be gathered together into one place, and let the dry land appear"; and it was so.

The continents (and oceans) rest atop giant slab pillars called tectonic plates that make up the Earth's outer crust. These plates float like rafts on the hot, semi-liquid mantle below the crust. Slow-moving currents deep inside Earth send the plates (and the land or ocean that rests on them) slowly moving across the surface of the planet.[148]

Pillars the Earth rests on that are mentioned in Scripture are a reference to internal pillars within the Earth. When God formed the Earth during the 6-day creation week, He raised the land from the waters to let the dry land (continents) appear. Scripture is referring to pillars within the Earth (tectonic plates) that God used as a means to raise the continents from the waters. The Earth does rest on pillars; they are internal pillars called tectonic plates. They could have easily been called tectonic pillars.

JOB 26:7 (NKJV):

He hangs the earth on nothing.

Scripture declares that the Earth is free floating in space, not a stationary object resting on pillars. The Earth hangs in orbit, on nothing, by means of gravity.

IS THE EARTH SHAPED LIKE A CIRCULAR DISC?

ISAIAH 40:22 (NKJV):

It is He who sits above the circle of the earth...

When viewed from a high altitude, one can see the arc circle of the sphere of the Earth. The Earth is not declared to be a circular disc, according to Isaiah 40:22.

SATELLITE IMAGES OF THE EARTH

NASA and other space agencies have provided mankind with countless satellite images of a spherical rotating Earth.[149][150] NASA is not a conspiracy agency supplying doctored Earth images and suppressing knowledge of a flat Earth, as flat-earthers maintain. Astronomy hobbyists have sent their iPhones into the edge of space using weather balloons and have provided further video evidence that the Earth is spherical.[151][152]

Scripture does not proclaim the Earth to be a flat circular disc. Flat Earth believers are either ignorant in understanding the true meanings of the Scripture verses used to proclaim a flat Earth or they intentionally twist the figurative language of Scripture to maintain their false Flat Earth Theory.

WHAT CAUSED THE EXTINCTION OF THE DINOSAURS?

By George Lujack

Dinosaurs once populated the planet in great numbers and were suddenly wiped out by a cataclysmic mass extinction event. Most evolution and creation scientists can agree upon that much. This article will discuss the two contrasting dominant theories of how the dinosaurs became extinct: a large asteroid, comet, or meteor impact and the great worldwide flood recorded in Genesis.

"Millions of years ago dinosaurs ruled the world, then suddenly - about 65-million-years ago, became extinct." Many people have heard this presumptive statement, in sum and substance, and have accepted it as scientific fact without realizing that there are four scientifically unobservable and unproven assumptions in that one sentence.

ASSUMPTION 1:

"Millions of years ago dinosaurs…"

Scripture, as well as recent scientific discoveries, refute the narrative that dinosaurs lived millions of years ago.

Scripture declares that all land animals were created on day-6 of creation week, approximately 6,000-years ago (Genesis 1:24-25).

Scientists have been discovering, for many years now, dinosaur bones with flesh and blood vessels still intact within them. Many dinosaur bones discovered are not fossilized rock, but are still bones; something that would be impossible if these bones were 65-million-years-old or older.[153][154][155]

ASSUMPTION 2:

"… dinosaurs ruled the world …"

Did dinosaurs actually rule the world or were they simply great beasts of their age that lived in or near their own water source habitat?[156] Would a tyrannosaurus rex have ventured far inland to terrorize and attack man, assuming they lived during the same time period, or would a t-rex keep to its own territory and prey upon herbivore dinosaurs, other animals, and scavenge for food within its own terrain as predators do today?

There are many beasts that could kill man. Animals instinctively know to stay away from man and for the most part they do. God gave EVERY animal, including the dinosaurs, an instinctive sense to be terrified of man.

GENESIS 9:2 (NKJV):

The fear of you and the dread of you shall be upon EVERY beast of the earth, on every bird of the air, on all that move on the earth, and on all the fish of the sea. They are given into your hand.

One thing man can do, and animals cannot, is forge tools to be used as weapons. The mightiest African lion in the wild is no match against a team of able-bodied men with guns or spears. Dinosaurs, likewise, would have been no match against a group of able-bodied men, with arrows, clubs, spears, or swords. Dinosaur brains were also extremely small, so they were unintelligent instinctive creatures, unlikely to venture outside of their familiar habitat. Man would have easily outsmarted them.

ASSUMPTIONS 3 & 4:

Dinosaurs… "then suddenly, about 65-million-years ago, became extinct."

This statement assumes that all dinosaurs are in fact extinct and that their mass extinction occurred about 65-million-years ago. Many scientists proclaim that all the dinosaurs that have ever lived are extinct. Such a declaration is incorrectly made under the presumption that all of the Earth's landmasses have been fully explored. They haven't been. As inconceivable as this may sound to some, actual dinosaurs may yet still be discovered alive and well, living in heavily forested swampy regions deep within the unpopulated, unexplored central regions of the African continent. The actual size of Africa is quite vast, much larger than it is typically portrayed in globes or maps. The landmass of the continent of Africa is slightly larger than the continental United States, United Kingdom, Eastern Europe, China, Japan, India, Germany, France, Italy, Spain, Portugal, Belgium, Netherlands, and Switzerland COMBINED.[157]

There have been, and are, expeditions planned to search for living dinosaurs in Africa by dedicated creationists hoping to prove that dinosaurs still exist and to utterly rebuke the theory of evolution. One such dinosaur that the creationists are searching for is a sauropod-type brachiosaur dinosaur. This dinosaur, known by the native Baka pygmy people as Mokele-mbembe, is said to live in the swamps and rivers deep within Central Africa.[158]

Whether dinosaurs will eventually be found living in Africa, or not, is yet to be determined. It is possible that intercontinental Africa may have provided a safe haven and a suitable climate for some types of dinosaurs to survive.

DINOSAUR DEFINED:

A dinosaur is a bipedal or quadruped egg-laying reptilian animal. Dinosaurs walk upright with their feet below their hips; unlike reptiles that have feet and legs angled away from their bodies and lie on and drag their undersides when they move. Dinosaurs have neither flippers nor wings.

Two dinosaur-type creatures are the plesiosaur, which is considered a marine reptile, and the pterodactyl, that is classified as a flying reptile.

'Dinosaur' is a word that derives from two Greek words 'deinos' (terrible, powerful, wondrous) and 'sauros' (lizard). The word 'dinosaur' became popular after biologist and paleontologist, Sir Richard Owen coined the term 'dinosauria' in 1842.

DINOSAURS IN SCRIPTURE

The word 'dinosaur,' a term that was coined in 1842, will not be found in the Scriptures that date back millennia before the word 'dinosaur' originated. Dinosaurs are mentioned within the pages of Scripture under the names 'behemoth,' 'leviathan,' and 'dragon.'

JOB 40:15-24 (NKJV):

"Behold now behemoth, which I made along with you. He eats grass like an ox. See now, his strength is in his hips and his power is in his stomach muscles. HE MOVES HIS TAIL LIKE A CEDAR. The sinews of his thighs are tightly knit. His bones are like beams of bronze. His ribs like bars of iron. He is the first of the ways of God. Only He who made him can bring near His sword. Surely the mountains yield food for him and all the beasts of the field play there. He lies under the lotus trees in a covert of reeds and marsh. The lotus trees cover him with their shade. The willows by the brook surround him. Indeed the river may rage, yet he is not disturbed; he feels safe even if the Jordan gushes into his mouth. Before his eyes, shall he be caught with snares or if one pierces his nose?"

Behemoth is a creature that moves his tail like a cedar tree and has bones like beams of bronze (Job 40:17-18). This is an apt description of a brachiosaur dinosaur. Large mammals, such as elephants, hippos, and rhinos have short thin tails. A brachiosaur is the only known land animal with a tail like that of a cedar tree and large limbs that are literally like large beams of bronze. The brachiosaur is the only known creature that fits the description of behemoth.

Scripture records that behemoth, the largest of the dinosaurs, was created along with man on the sixth day of the creation week, around 6,000-years ago (Genesis 1:24-31; Job 40:15).

JOB 41:1-18 (NKJV):

"Can you draw out Leviathan with a hook or snare his tongue with a line which you lower? Can you put a reed through his nose or pierce his jaw with a hook? Will he make many supplications to you? Will he speak softly to you? Will he make a covenant with you? Will you take him as a servant forever? Will you play with him as with a bird or will you leash him for your maidens? Will your companions make a banquet of him? Will they apportion him among the merchants? Can you fill his skin with harpoons or his head with fishing spears? Lay your hand on him and remember the battle to never do it again! Indeed, any hope of overcoming him is false; Shall one not be overwhelmed at the sight of him?

No one is so fierce that he would dare stir him up. Who then is able to stand against Me?

Who has preceded Me, that I should pay him? Everything under heaven is Mine. I will not conceal his limbs, his mighty power or his graceful proportions. Who can remove his outer coat? Who can approach him with a double bridle? Who can open the doors of his face, with his terrible teeth all around? His rows of scales are his pride, shut up tightly as with a seal. One is so near another that no air can come between them. They are joined one to another. They stick together and cannot be parted. His snorting flashes forth light and his eyes are like the eyelids of the morning.

JOB 41:19-34 (NKJV):

Out of his mouth go burning lights; sparks of fire shoot out. Smoke goes out of his nostrils as from a boiling pot or caldron. His breath kindles coals and a flame goes out of his mouth. Strength dwells in his neck and sorrow dances before him. The folds of his flesh are joined together; they are firm on him and cannot be moved. His heart is as hard as stone, even as hard as the lower millstone. When he raises himself up, the mighty are afraid. Because of his crashings they are bewildered. Though the sword reaches him, it cannot avail; nor does spear, dart, or javelin. He regards iron as straw and bronze as rotten wood. The arrow cannot make him flee and sling-stones become like stubble to him. Darts are regarded as straw and he laughs at the threat of javelins. His undersides are like sharp potsherds.

He spreads pointed marks in the mud. He makes the deep boil like a pot. He makes the sea like a pot of ointment. He leaves a shining wake behind him. One would think the deep had white hair. On earth there is nothing like him - one that is made without fear.

He beholds every high thing. He is king over all the children of pride."

Leviathan was a fire-breathing land and sea dinosaur. Leviathan had terrible teeth all around (Job 41:14). Tyrannosaurus rex, appropriately named, is a combination Greek / Latin term meaning "tyrant lizard king." Scripture describes leviathan as a creature that was the mightiest king of all creatures, a tyrannosaurus rex (Job 41:34).

The leviathan KIND of dinosaurs includes all of the variations of the similar-featured, bipedal, carnivorous, theropod dinosaurs, including the allosaurus, carcharodontosaurus, giganotosaurus, spinosaurus, and tyrannosaurus rex. The description of leviathan in Job 41 tells us things about these kinds of dinosaurs that current conventional paleontologists have not yet discovered or declared about them. Leviathans, or t-rexes, breathed flames and snorted smoke from their nostrils (Job 41:18-21). Stories of fire-breathing dinosaurs, known as fire-breathing dragons, have been documented in the early histories of many cultures spanning the world. Bombardier beetles produce near-boiling water through chemical compounds within their bodies that they eject from their abdomen. Creation scientists theorize that t-rexes could also have produced boiling steam that flared out of their nostrils that are produced from chemical reactions in their bodies and elaborate skulls.

The leviathan / t-rex dwelled in both the land and sea. The leviathan / t-rex cooled himself off in the sea, leaving a shining wake behind him, and used his feet to make marks in the mud, possibly digging burrows, near his water supply (Job 41:30-32). The t-rex lived near a water source and regulated its body temperature by going in and out of water. As with all large animals, living near a water source was ideal and essential for t-rex's survival. A t-rex would certainly need to drink a lot of water daily for sustenance. Living near water ensured that a t-rex had an ample supply of water to drink from and had herbivore dinosaurs nearby, also dependent on water, to prey upon for food. The leviathan-type spinosaurus had a long crocodile-like snout and a large sail on it's back, indicating that it spent much of its time in the water.

Popular Hollywood movies often like to depict the t-rex and other leviathan type dinosaurs as roaming, land-based, man-eating, wild beasts that terrorized man's villages. Scripture infers that predator dinosaurs were territorial, living in or near their water supply, much like an alligator does today. The leviathan / t-rex, being dependent on and living near its water source, meant that it would not have been a wandering lethal menace to man.

Leviathans / t-rexes could be 'stirred up' by man (Job 41:10). When contemplating this verse, along with Job 41:30-32, t-rexes apparently spent much of their time either sleeping, lurking in water, or sunbathing in mud or on land. Lions sleep 20-hours a day and alligators spend much of their time being idle in water while sunbathing. T-rexes could be stirred up or agitated by man, if man entered the t-rex's habitat and purposely provoked it, but the t-rex, as a territorial beast, didn't venture far from his habitat to stir up or attack man. Leviathan could be stirred up, but man didn't dare do so. Man left the t-rex alone in his habitat and was wise to not to stir it up, and the t-rex left man alone in his villages. Dragon, a reference to a dinosaur, is mentioned in Revelation chapters 12, 13, 16, and 20.

THE MASS EXTINCTION OF THE DINOSAURS

The two prevailing theories that account for the mass extinction of the dinosaurs are that a large asteroid impacted in the Yucatan Peninsula or that the worldwide flood recorded in Genesis caused the demise of the dinosaurs.

THE ASTEROID IMPACT THEORY

The prevailing secular scientific hypothesis is that a large asteroid, roughly the size of the Martian moon Deimos – about 6-9 mi / 10-15 km radius, fell into the Yucatan Peninsula at the Chicxulub crater, Mexico about 65-million-years ago. The Chicxulub crater is considered to be the likely impact site of a meteor that struck the Earth and caused the extinction of the dinosaurs. The impact is believed to have released the same amount of energy as over a billion times the energy of the atom bombs that were dropped on Japan at the end of World War II.

The volcanic theory was once embraced before the asteroid impact theory had become widely adopted by the secular scientific community. The volcanic theory suggests massive volcanoes erupted spewing large amounts dust and debris into the atmosphere. Some secular scientists believe that the dinosaur extinction involved a combination of an asteroid impact simultaneously occurring along with massive volcanic activity. Asteroids, comets, and meteors have impacted the Earth during its ancient past and there are numerous crater sites around the planet that attest to this.

THE TEN GREATEST ASTEROID-EARTH IMPACTS AND THE SCIENTIFIC ESTIMATES OF THE DATE, LOCATION, AND SCOPE OF THEIR IMPACT

1. Vredefort Crater
Asteroid impact date: Estimated 2 billion years ago
Location: Free State, South Africa
Estimated Radius: 118 miles / 190 kilometers

2. Sudbury Basin
Asteroid impact date: Estimated 1.8 billion years ago
Location: Ontario, Canada
Estimated Diameter: 81 miles / 130 kilometers

3. Acraman Crater

Asteroid impact date: Estimated 580 million years ago

Location: South Australia, Australia

Estimated Diameter: 56 miles / 90 kilometers

4. Woodleigh Crater

Asteroid impact date: Estimated 364 million years ago

Location: Western Australia, Australia

Estimated Diameter: 25-75 miles / 40-120 kilometers

5. Manicouagan Crater

Asteroid impact date: Estimated 215 million years ago

Location: Quebec, Canada

Estimated Diameter: 62 miles / 100 kilometers

6. Morokweng Crater

Asteroid impact date: Estimated 145 million years ago

Location: North West, South Africa

Estimated Diameter: 43 miles / 70 kilometers

7. Kara Crater

Asteroid impact date: Estimated 70.3 million years ago

Location: Nenetsia, Russia

Estimated Diameter: 40 miles / 65 kilometers

8. Chicxulub Crater

Asteroid impact date: Estimated 65 million years ago

Location: Yucatán, Mexico

Estimated Diameter: 106-186 miles / 170-300 kilometers

9. Popigai Crater

Asteroid impact date: Estimated 35.7 million years ago

Location: Siberia, Russia

Estimated Diameter: 62 miles / 100 kilometers

10. Chesapeake Bay Crater

Asteroid impact date: Estimated 35 million years ago

Estimated Diameter: 53 miles / 85 kilometers[159]

Assuming these crater impacts are reasonably scientifically accurately dated, give or take a few million of years, and the devastation that they caused was substantial, none of them, including the Chicxulub crater, could have caused the extinction of the dinosaurs. These asteroid / comet / meteor impacts all occurred long before there was life on planet Earth, including the dinosaurs. Asteroid impacts upon the old Earth that existed before life was created upon it, upon the old Earth that was created IN THE BEGINNING, did not cause the extinction of the dinosaurs (Genesis 1:1). THE EARTH WAS, (the old Earth), void (of life) and without form (to sustain life) (Genesis 1:2). Dinosaurs were created, along with man, approximately 6,000-years ago, during the 6-day creation week, when God reformed the Earth and created life upon it (Genesis 1:24-31; Job 40:15).

THE WORLDWIDE FLOOD

GENESIS 6:13 (NKJV):

And God said to Noah, "The end of all flesh has come before Me, for the earth is filled with violence through them; and behold, I will destroy them with the earth…"

Scripture declares that God flooded the Earth to destroy all living flesh AND the Earth. God not only destroyed all life, but also the pristine state of the Earth itself. The pre-flood Earth was and is different from the post-flood Earth. The Earth, after the flood, was never fully restored to its pre-flood condition state, even though the waters receded and the Earth was repopulated.

GENESIS 7:7 (NKJV):

So Noah, with his sons, his wife, and his sons' wives, went into the ark because of the waters of the flood.

GENESIS 7:11-12 (NKJV):

And it came to pass after seven days that the waters of the flood were on the earth. … on that day all the fountains of the great deep were broken up, and the windows of heaven were opened. And the rain was on the earth forty days and forty nights.

GENESIS 7:17-24 (NKJV):

Now the flood was on the earth forty days. The waters increased and lifted up the ark, and it rose high above the earth. The waters prevailed and greatly increased on the earth, and the ark moved about on the surface of the waters. And the waters prevailed exceedingly on the earth, and all the high hills under the whole heaven were covered. The waters prevailed fifteen cubits upward, and the mountains were covered. And ALL FLESH DIED THAT MOVED ON THE EARTH: birds and cattle and beasts and every creeping thing that creeps on the earth, and every man. All in whose nostrils was the breath of the spirit of life, all that was on the dry land, died. So HE DESTROYED ALL LIVING THINGS that were on the face of the ground: both man and cattle, creeping thing and bird of the air. They were destroyed from the earth. Only Noah and those who were with him in the ark remained alive. And the waters prevailed on the earth one hundred and fifty days.

The story of the global flood of Genesis has been recorded in nearly every culture in the world. While details of the worldwide deluge vary, the same basic account is told in all versions.[160]

A recently deciphered 4,000-year-old clay tablet, discovered in modern day Iraq (ancient Mesopotamia) confirms the Scripture account of a global flood and an ark that preserved the animals aboard.[161]

GENESIS 9:8-11 (NKJV):

Then God spoke to Noah and to his sons with him, saying: "And as for Me, behold, I establish My covenant with you and with your descendants after you, and with every living creature that is with you: the birds, the cattle, and every beast of the earth with you, of all that go out of the ark, every beast of the earth. Thus I establish My covenant with you: Never again shall all flesh be cut off by the waters of the flood; never again shall there be a flood to destroy the earth."

The great flood was a worldwide deluge, not a local flood. There are many secular scientists who acknowledge the evidences of a global flood, but dismiss the evidence and the Scripture account of a worldwide flood as being various local floods in different regions.

God said that He would never again flood the Earth to destroy ALL flesh and the WHOLE Earth (Genesis 9:11). Local floods still occur frequently on Earth and they destroy some flesh and some areas of the Earth, but not all flesh and the whole Earth. Those who proclaim the great flood recorded in Genesis was that of a local flood are calling the Scripture account a lie and God a liar.

FOUR SCIENTIFIC EVIDENCES OF A WORLDWIDE FLOOD

1. Fossils of sea creatures are found high above sea level, atop every mountain range in the world, due to the ocean waters flooding over all the high mountains of the world (Genesis 7:19).

2. Rapid burials of plants and animals. Fossil graveyards attest to a catastrophic destruction and burial of many kinds of fossilized creatures.

3. Rapidly deposited sediment layers spread across vast areas and long distances. The Tapeats Sandstone and Redwall limestone of the Grand Canyon can be traced across the entire United States, to Canada and even across the Atlantic Ocean to England.

4. Strata rock layers were laid down in rapid succession with no evidence of erosion. Flat, knife-edge boundaries between rock layers indicate continuous deposits of one layer after another, with no time for erosion. Had the rock layers been laid down over lengthy periods of time, erosion would be found throughout the laid down strata layers.[162]

Waterfalls, such as Niagara Falls, and canyons, such as the Grand Canyon, are themselves evidences of a relatively recent global deluge, just over 4,500-years ago. Waterfalls should not exist, unless there was a global flood that caused them to be. If waterfalls were continuously flowing for millions of years, the bedrock that they flow over would have long ago eroded, ending the life of the waterfall. The Grand Canyon could not have been carved out by a mere river stream. The Grand Canyon was carved out by a deluge of water, carrying with it glaciers that carved out the canyon, while depositing boulders throughout the mainland where boulders should not be.

SCRIPTURE DECLARES THAT GOD DESTROYED THE LEVIATHAN / T-REX

PSALM 74:13-17 (NKJV) [WITH INTERPRETATION]:

For God is my King from of old, working deliverance in the midst of the earth. You divided the sea by your might; You broke the heads of the sea serpents [DINOSAURS] in the waters [DURING THE GREAT FLOOD]. You broke the heads of Leviathan [TYRANNOSAURUS REX KIND DINOSAURS] in pieces, and gave him as food for the creatures of the wilderness. You broke open the fountain and the flood [DURING THE GREAT FLOOD – GENESIS 7:11]. You dried up mighty rivers [GENESIS 8:1-3]. The day is Yours, the night is Yours also. You have established the light and the sun. You have appointed all the borders of the earth. You have made summer and winter [SUMMERS AND WINTERS BEGAN AFTER THE GREAT FLOOD - GENESIS 8:22].

WHY DIDN'T THE DINOSAURS REPOPULATE THE EARTH AFTER THE FLOOD?

Assuming the dinosaurs were taken aboard Noah's ark, there are several reasons and various factors as to why the dinosaurs didn't repopulate and inhabit the Earth as they had before the flood.

A canopy of water and ice surrounded the planet before the flood, which served as a greenhouse shield against the sun's harmful radiation while regulating the Earth's temperature (Genesis 1:6-7).

GENESIS 1:6-7 (NKJV):

Then God said, "Let there be a firmament in the midst of the waters, and let it divide the waters from the waters." Thus God made the firmament, and divided the waters which were under the firmament from the waters which were above the firmament; and it was so.

The firmament, or sky, divided the water under the sky (the seas) from the water above the sky (the canopy of water / ice above the atmosphere).

GENESIS 7:10-12 (NKJV):

And it came to pass after seven days that the waters of the flood were on the earth. In the six hundredth year of Noah's life, in the second month, the seventeenth day of the month, on that day all the fountains of the great deep were broken up, and the windows of heaven were opened. And the rain was on the earth forty days and forty nights.

God caused it to rain upon the Earth for 40-days and 40-nights. He opened 'windows' in the upper atmosphere (heaven) and the protective canopy of water covering the Earth rained through those windows. After the flood, the canopy of water was not restored above the firmament (sky) and living conditions on Earth drastically changed.

The canopy of water not being restored above the atmosphere caused at least three major negative changes to living conditions in the post-flood Earth compared to the pre-flood Earth.

In the post-flood Earth there was no regulation of planetary temperature (greenhouse effect), the Sun's harmful rays were no longer shielded, and oxygen levels were drastically reduced. These changes to Earth's atmosphere were extremely detrimental to the dinosaurs, but also to every living creature - including man. In the pre-flood Earth, man was recorded to have lived as long as 969-years (Genesis 5:27). In the post-flood Earth, God reduced man's lifespan to 120-years (Genesis 6:3). 120-years is about the maximum number of years that post-flood, modern man can live.

GENESIS 8:22 (NKJV):

As long as the earth remains, seedtime and harvest, COLD AND HEAT, WINTER AND SUMMER, and day and night shall not cease.

In Genesis 8:22, it is apparent that God declared that "cold and heat, winter and summer," were being instituted on Earth, and would not cease. Seasons of hot and cold would have been devastating to dinosaurs disembarking from the ark. As reptiles, they would only be able to survive as other reptiles do today, in warm tropical climates, not worldwide as they had once populated the Earth before the flood. Dinosaur fossils have been discovered in great numbers in Antarctica, indicating that Antarctica had a tropical climate before the worldwide flood of Genesis.[163][164][165]

Secular evolution-minded scientists and creation scientists agree that the fossil records indicate that oxygen levels on the Earth were higher in the past. An oxygen rich atmosphere fueled insect gigantism in the pre-flood Earth. Giant seagull-sized dragonflies, as well as other super-sized insects, are presumed to have grown to their larger than modern-day sizes due to a higher concentration of oxygen in the atmosphere.

Earth's current atmospheric oxygen content, at just over 20%, was once around 35% in the pre-flood Earth. Oxygen-rich environments cause animals to grow larger. Dinosaurs, as large animals, were dependent upon higher oxygen levels to fuel their growth and sustain their larger sizes. The post-flood Earth's 20% oxygen level was not conducive for dinosaur life to thrive as they once had during the pre-flood Earth's oxygen-rich past.

GENESIS 7:1-2 (NKJV):

Then YHWH (the Lord) said to Noah, "Come into the ark, you and all your household, because I have seen that you are righteous before Me in this generation. You shall take with you SEVEN OF EACH CLEAN ANIMAL, a male and his female; TWO EACH OF ANIMALS THAT ARE UNCLEAN, a male and his female.

Dinosaurs faced an immediate numerical problem in order for them to survive and repopulate the Earth after disembarking from the ark. Of the clean beasts upon the Earth, there are mammals, fish, birds, and insects (Leviticus 11; Deuteronomy 14). There are no clean dinosaurs or reptiles. All dinosaurs, as unclean reptile animals, were taken on the ark by twos and none of them, including herbivore dinosaurs, were taken on the ark by sevens.

Clean mammals were taken on the ark by sevens. Unclean predator mammals, taken on the ark by twos, could immediately prey upon clean mammals after disembarking from the ark without causing the extinction of a particular clean mammal species. Herbivore dinosaurs, dinosaurs that were preyed upon by predator dinosaurs, were taken on the ark by twos. Predator dinosaurs may have preyed upon many of the herbivore dinosaurs, and their eggs / hatchlings, before the herbivores were able to reproduce and repopulate.

If a predator dinosaur upon disembarking from the ark attacked and killed one or both, the male or female, of a particular kind of herbivore dinosaur, it would have meant the immediate extinction of the species. This imbalance of numbers in the dinosaur food chain likely caused the quick extinction of many of the herbivore dinosaurs, and then sometime after many of the predator dinosaurs, who relied on the herbivores for food.

Predator dinosaurs also faced extinction at the hands of man after the flood. Man hunted the remaining struggling predator dinosaurs to extinction. As man began to repopulate the Earth, he likely saw the remaining predator dinosaurs as potentially dangerous beasts and hunted them for sport to extinction. Predator dinosaurs, due to reduced oxygen levels in a post-flood Earth, were likely somewhat smaller and easier for man to kill than before the flood.

Stories, accurate paintings, and carved depictions of dragons or dinosaurs are a part of many cultures worldwide including Africa, Asia, Australia, Central, North and South America, Eastern and Western Europe, the Far East, the Middle East, the United Kingdom, and many of the island nations scattered across the globe. There are numerous tales and early-recorded historical accounts of men slaying dragons. The most famous of these accounts is the story of Saint George, a third century Roman soldier, slaying a dragon that lived in a pond in Libya.

Dragons of old folklore, as recorded by many cultures, were dinosaurs. While prehistoric accounts of man slaying dragons are anecdotal evidence that dinosaurs were survivors of the global flood, those stories are evidence nonetheless. Legends are based on truth.

SUMMATION

Dinosaurs once populated the Earth in great numbers and their remains have been found on every continent, including Antarctica, in the world. The worldwide flood, recorded in Genesis, wiped out the dinosaurs along with all life on the planet, Noah, his family and the animals on the ark, including the dinosaurs, survived the great flood. Dinosaurs were not ideally suited for survival and repopulation after disembarking from the ark, due to Earth's new post-flood world conditions. The Earth's climate was no longer regulated by the greenhouse effect, as the canopy of water that previously surrounded the Earth above the atmosphere was not restored after the worldwide deluge. Earth's oxygen levels were reduced from around 35% to 20%, thus not enabling dinosaurs to grow to the large proportion sizes they had known before the global flood. The post-flood Earth began having seasons and extreme temperature variations: winter and summer, hot and cold. Dinosaurs, as either warm or cold-blooded egg-laying reptilian beasts, could only survive near tropical regions and could not repopulate throughout the entire planet as they had previously done before the flood. All of the dinosaurs were taken aboard the ark by twos. Carnivorous dinosaurs likely preyed upon herbivores dinosaurs immediately after disembarking from the ark and thus may have inadvertently caused many of the herbivores to become quickly extinct. Predator dinosaurs, that survived in smaller sizes and in smaller numbers, were likely considered to be dangerous and were later hunted to extinction by man. Some sauropod-type dinosaurs may have survived extinction. Native peoples living in central Africa say that they have encountered this kind of dinosaur and claim that they still exist to this day.

EVOLUTION = THE LIE

By George Lujack

GENESIS 1:1 (NKJV):

In the beginning God created the heavens and the earth.

THE LIE is that there is no God, the universe created itself from nothing, and then billions of years later life arose from non-life into the first self-sustaining, self-replicating life forms that later evolved into all the various kinds of life on planet Earth. This article will present the theory of evolution as scientifically impossible and as THE LIE that is spoken of in Scripture.

"The greatest trick the Devil ever pulled was convincing the world he didn't exist."
- Charles Baudelaire, 1864

Not quite so. The greatest trick the Devil ever pulled was convincing many in the world that God doesn't exist. Therefore, God did not create the heavens and the Earth and all life on Earth. Also, if God does not exist then neither does Satan or good and evil. Thus man can live without absolute moral laws.

There are 6-forms of 'evolution,' and of the six forms only one is scientifically observable and proven. The other 5-forms have never been observed to occur and are theoretical.

1. Cosmic Evolution (The Big Bang) – the origin of time, space, and matter
2. Stellar and Planetary Evolution – the origin of stars and planets
3. Chemical Evolution – the origin of higher elements from hydrogen
4. Organic Evolution – the origin of life
5. Macroevolution – the changing of one kind (species) into another kind
6. Microevolution – the variations within kinds (species)

Of all 6-forms of evolution only number 6, microevolution, has been scientifically observed to occur. Microevolution defined is the evolutionary change (adaptation) within a species (kind) over a short period of time.[166]

COSMIC EVOLUTION

Cosmic Evolution Theory proposes that absolutely nothing created the big bang. Updated variations of the Big Bang Theory have given the universe a head start, namely, that matter always existed.

The Big Bang Theory proposes that a great cosmic explosion and the rapid expansion of matter, from a state of extremely high density and temperature, marked the origin of the universe.

"Of course it's counterintuitive that you can get something from nothing. Of course common sense doesn't allow you to get something from nothing. That's why it's interesting. It's got to be interesting in order to give rise to the universe at all. SOMETHING pretty mysterious had to give rise to the origin of the universe." … *"Something can come from nothing."*
- Richard Dawkins, 2013[167]

"Some intelligence may have created the universe, and all life upon it, but that something could not be God,"
- Richard Dawkins[168]

Richard Dawkins, atheist and evolutionary biologist, in his own words, attempts to redefine 'nothing' as 'something.' To usurp the creation from the Creator, evolution 'scientists' have theorized that absolutely nothing created the universe, as absurd as that sounds. Furthermore, they assert that there may exist some intelligence responsible for the creation of the universe, and life within it, but that intelligence could not be God.

STELLAR AND PLANETARY EVOLUTION

Stellar and planetary evolution means that all the stars, planets, moons, and other cosmic bodies and matter had to have evolved from absolutely nothing. Stellar evolution is the process by which a star undergoes a sequence of radical changes during its lifetime. Stellar evolution is not studied by observing the life of a single star, as most stellar changes occur too slowly to be detected, even over millennia. Astrophysicists theorize how stars evolve by observing numerous stars at various points in their lifetime, and by simulating stellar structure using computer models[169]

CHEMICAL EVOLUTION

Chemical Evolution Theory defined is the formation of complex organic molecules from simpler organic molecules through chemical reactions. Chemical evolution proposes that all of the elements on the periodic table must have evolved from hydrogen.[170]

ORGANIC EVOLUTION

Organic evolution is the sequence of events involved in the evolutionary development of a species. Organic evolution, or abiogenesis, is the explanation of how life got started from inorganic molecules. Organic evolution is theorized to have occurred during Earth's early history, in the oceans, as the first steps of the formation of life on the planet.

Evolution scientists, professing to be wise, often write long-winded, scientifically authoritative sounding columns in scientific journals about how chemical reactions cause elements to react that may have caused the first self-sustaining and self-replicating life forms to appear.[171] It is scientifically observable that elements react to other elements, causing a chemical reaction, but to believe that chemical reactions can produce even the simplest of self-sustaining, self-replicating life forms requires belief and faith in the scientifically unobservable and inconceivably improbable.

MACROEVOLUTION

Macroevolution means major evolutionary changes and transitions from one kind of organism to another kind of organism over long periods of time.

There are no legitimate transitional fossils in the fossil record that show one kind (species) changing into another kind (species) of animal. Even Charles Darwin acknowledged this scientific truth.

"Not one change of species into another is on record … we cannot prove that a single species has been changed."
- Charles Darwin, 'My Life & Letters,' 1887.

"Lastly, looking not to any one time, but to all time, if my theory be true, numberless intermediate varieties, linking closely together all the species of the same group, must assuredly have existed."
- Charles Darwin, 'Origin of Species,' 1859.

What Charles Darwin said and believed about evolution and the origin of species is irrelevant. Darwin was just a man with a theory who has been propped up in prominence as a great scientific mind by evolution advocates. Any person who understands and believes the Scriptural account of the creation has a better understanding of the origin of species than did Charles Darwin.

MICROEVOLUTION

Microevolution is defined as evolutionary change within a species over a short period of time. Microevolution is more aptly termed adaptation. Microevolution, or adaptation within a species, is observable and scientific.

Species adapt to environmental and physical changes. Environment and climate variations account for the 5-different types of bears that exist in the world. Bears that migrated north to the Arctic developed thicker coats of fur, whereas bears that migrated south into warmer climates developed thinner coats. A difference in coat thickness or coat color is not evidence of mutation or evolution, but of adaptation. Genes for thicker and thinner coats were already in the DNA encoding of the bears. No new information can enter the gene code of any species, allowing a bear to change into another kind of animal (macroevolution). All types of bears have a common ancestor: a bear.

Human beings adapt over the course of their lifetime. If a light-skinned man works or lies out in the sun, his exposed skin will pigment and darken. If a man lifts weights, his body will grow muscles to adapt. These changes are made possible by the DNA variations within the genes of human beings.

2 MAJOR SCIENTIFIC EVIDENCES AGAINST EVOLUTION

1. Life has never been observed to come from non-life.
2. There is no known observable process by which new genetic information can be added to the genetic code of an organism.

Evolution in the sense that life came from non-life and then that life began to randomly generate new genetic information and over time it eventually produced humans is something that doesn't hold up against science. Molecules to man evolution (abiogenesis) is not scientifically possible and therefore should not be viewed as scientific fact. It is in great opposition to science, that is, observational science, the kind of science we can test and repeat and use our 5-senses to understand. Science demonstrates that over time living organisms lose genetic information, they don't gain it. Science also demonstrates that life doesn't arise from non-life.[172] 'Simple life' is a misnomer. Even the simplest of forms of life, bacteria, are incredibly complex[173]

PUNCTUATED EQUILIBRIUM

In order to account for the lack of evidence in the fossil record of kinds changing into other kinds of life forms, evolutionists have come up with a new conjectured theory: punctuated equilibrium. Punctuated equilibrium is an Evolution Theory component belief that proposes that instead of evolving very gradually over a long period of time, evolution happens in short bursts interspersed with much longer periods where virtually no evolutionary change occurs. Punctuated equilibrium would allow fish to acquire lungs and walk on land. Punctuated equilibrium solves the problem that evolutionists have with the lack of evidence from the fossil record, but violates a law of science in that there is no known observable process by which new genetic information can be added to the genetic code of an organism. No new species of pig has ever been born with wings.

NATURA NON FACIT SALTUM … Latin for: NATURE DOES NOT MAKE JUMPS

In his book, *The Origin of Species*, Charles Darwin defended the principle of 'natura non facit saltum,' and acknowledged that species made gradual and minute changes over time, rather than sudden changes resulting in the rapid emergence of new kinds of life forms.

There is no scientific evidence at all to support punctuated equilibrium. The fossil record and laws of science do not support punctuated equilibrium. Nature does not make jumps.

SUSPENSION OF DISBELIEF

Suspension of disbelief or willing suspension of disbelief is a term coined in 1817 by the poet and aesthetic philosopher Samuel Taylor Coleridge, who suggested that if a writer could infuse a "human interest and a semblance of truth" into a fantastic tale, the reader would suspend judgment concerning the implausibility of the narrative. Suspension of disbelief often applies to fictional works of the action, comedy, fantasy, and horror genres.[174]

People suspend disbelief when watching a science fiction movie, such as the *Teenage Mutant Ninja Turtles*, the *X-Men* movie series, or the movie *Waterworld*. In these particular cinematic stories, beneficial mutations are added to turtles or man, and a major species change occurs. Turtles take on human qualities in *Teenage Mutant Ninja Turtles*, human mutants take on new genetic material and become super-humans in *X-Men*, and Kevin Costner acquires gills in *Waterworld*.

The narrative theme of the *X-Men* series movies is beneficial mutation: "Mutation: it is the key to our evolution. It has enabled us to evolve from a single-celled organism into the dominant species on the planet. Its process is slow, and normally taking thousands and thousands of years. But every few hundred millennia, evolution leaps forward."

An evolutionary deception to try to account for the lack of evidence of transitional fossils, in the fossil record, is to suggest that macroevolution change may have occurred suddenly in species without leaving transition fossils showing one species changing into another. This sudden evolutionary change theory breaks the laws of science by suddenly allowing an organism to drastically change without any means of attaining new DNA genetic code information to account for the change.

In the movie *Waterworld*, the character played by Kevin Costner is a mutant who developed gill slits behind his ears and is capable of breathing underwater. This kind of beneficial mutation is impossible because gills are not genetically coded into the DNA of human beings. These kinds of mutations cannot gradually occur over time. Whales and dolphins breathe using lungs, which is how they were created. Whales and dolphins have not acquired gills, despite the fact that they spend all of their lives submerged in water, except when they surface to breathe.

People suspend disbelief when watching a science fiction movie, so that they can enjoy the show, yet evolution scientists have ever increasingly demanded that the public accept evolution science fiction (theory) as truth when presented in textbooks. They have banned opposing viewpoints and beliefs from being presented in education institutions, most notably the creation account of Genesis or the theory of intelligent design.

A frog transforms into a prince in storybooks and everyone knows this is a fairytale; a frog evolves into a human being in science biology textbooks and many willfully present this as a scientific fact or a plausible theory. Those who ardently believe, defend, and proclaim the theory of molecules to man evolution as a fact, when faced with the hard scientific truths that render evolution theory impossible, literally suspend disbelief and are under a strong delusion (2 Thessalonians 2:11).

FAITH IN EVOLUTION VS. FAITH IN GOD

Molecules to man evolution theory is a theory that requires faith above reason or blind faith. It is not plausible on the surface, so evolutionists add billions of years to account for evolutionary changes that are unobservable in science. Thus evolutionists have faith in time, that time can do the miraculous acts required of evolution that are unobservable in science.

A belief that God created the heavens, the Earth, and life requires faith also, but this is reasoned informed faith. Science itself disproves evolution, so to believe in cosmic evolution, and in molecules to man evolution, is illogical by observable, testable, scientific standards.

An argument often presented by evolution-believing atheists is that scientific progress and breakthroughs will cease if people continue to believe in God. This claim is utterly absurd as many of the world's great inventors and scientists were believers in a Divine Being and Creator. These same inventors and scientists often proclaimed that the more they discovered, the deeper their faith in God became. Whether one believes in creationism or evolution is irrelevant. Scientific breakthroughs and discoveries do not depend on belief or disbelief in God, or belief or disbelief in evolution.

GOD CREATED CREATURES ACCORDING TO THEIR KINDS

<u>GENESIS 1:24-25 (NKJV):</u>

Then God said, "Let the earth bring forth the living creature ACCORDING TO ITS KIND: cattle and creeping thing and beast of the earth, each ACCORDING TO ITS KIND"; and it was so. And God made the beast of the earth ACCORDING TO ITS KIND, cattle ACCORDING TO ITS KIND, and everything that creeps on the earth ACCORDING TO ITS KIND. And God saw that it was good.

There are many believers who attempt to mix parts of the evolution account with their faith in God. Many compromise their faith, proclaiming that evolution was a means that God used to create life, and accept that the Genesis account of the creation of life was a mythical tale.

God, in retelling the Genesis account of the creation of life, seems to have taken into account that Satan would try to use evolution as a means to deceive people. Scripture is very clear and specific in proclaiming that God made life according to its kind, that life reproduces according to its kind, and that life did not evolve over time from one kind to another kind. In nature and in observable science we witness that kinds always reproduce after their kinds, just as Scripture states.

THE LIE OF EVOLUTION

THE LIE of evolution, in summation, is basically the theory of how the universe and everything in it came to be in existence, without God the Creator, and that the creation itself is the creator. Evolution is THE LIE that evolved from the original lie told to Eve in the Garden of Eden.

<u>GENESIS 3:1-5 (NKJV):</u>

Now the serpent was more cunning than any beast of the field that the Lord God had made. And he said to the woman, "Has God indeed said, 'You shall not eat of every tree of the garden'?"

And the woman said to the serpent, "We may eat the fruit of the trees of the garden; but of the fruit of the tree which is in the midst of the garden, God has said, 'You shall not eat it, nor shall you touch it, lest you die.'"

Then the serpent said to the woman, "You will not surely die. For God knows that in the day you eat of it your eyes will be opened, and YOU WILL BE LIKE GOD, knowing good and evil."

The root of THE LIE of evolution is that you will evolve and transition into God; you will become like God; YOU WILL BE LIKE GOD.

<u>ROMANS 1:22-25 (NKJV):</u>

Professing to be wise, they became fools, and changed the glory of the incorruptible God into an image made like corruptible man - and birds and four-footed animals and creeping things.

Therefore God also gave them up to uncleanness, in the lusts of their hearts, to dishonor their bodies among themselves, who exchanged the truth of God for THE LIE, and worshiped and served the creature rather than the Creator, who is blessed forever.

2 THESSALONIANS 2:11-12 (NKJV):

And for this reason God will send them strong delusion, that they should believe THE LIE, that they all may be condemned who did not believe the truth but had pleasure in unrighteousness.

Evolution science scholars "professing to be wise," often cite their worldly education credentials and enlightenment, while belittling believers of the Genesis account of creation as 'uneducated' and 'unsophisticated.' Scripture proclaims that they "became fools," because they have said in their heart that there is no God in favor of their evolution theory (Psalm 14:1). Under "strong delusion" evolution theorists "changed the glory" of God's creation using illustrative drawings "like corruptible man," drawings of man and images of man-like creatures transitioning from monkeys to man, that are fictional artist renderings.

Evolutionists 'worship' the creature rather than the Creator. They believe that life rose up from the elements and became the creature and that the creature, over time, evolved into all the various kinds of life on Earth, including man. They usurp glory away from God as the Creator and bestow it upon the creature. Evolutionists worship the creature, and not the Creator, in the sense that they believe that the creature created itself and that God did not create the creature.

Evolution Theory is atheistic secular science's attempt to explain the creation of the universe and the formation of life upon the Earth without a Creator.

Don't believe THE LIE of evolution.

THE TREASURY OF SNOW AND HAIL

By George Lujack

This article will discuss the mystery of the treasury of snow and hail as well as the configuration of water and ice, both of which reveal God the Creator's artistic handiwork and well-thought-out scientific design in nature.

JOB 38:22 (NKJV):

Have you entered the treasury of snow, or have you seen the treasury of hail?

Before the advent of microscopes, man could not truly appreciate the majestic splendor of the treasury of snow and hail.

Snowflakes and ice crystals are formed when snow or hail falls to the Earth. Snowflakes are characterized by having a crystalline-structured six-fold radial symmetry with each snowflake having six arms. No two snowflakes are the same as each one is formed differently with various environmental factors shaping the formation of each snowflake crystal.

Wilson Bentley is accredited as being among the first known photographers to capture images of snowflakes. Bentley discovered a way to catch snowflakes on black velvet and capture their image before they melted. Using a camera attached to a compound microscope, Bentley photographed his first snowflake on January 15, 1885.[175]

JOB 38:28-30 (NKJV):

Has the rain a father? Or who has begotten the drops of dew? From whose womb comes the ice? And the frost of heaven, who gives it birth? The waters harden like stone, and the surface of the deep is frozen.

Ice is 9% less dense than liquid water. God designed water with a molecular structure such that when configured into solid ice, it is less dense than when it is in its liquid state. This allows water to *harden like stone* (ice), upon *the surface of the deep* (waters).

Lakes and rivers freeze from the top down and the frozen ice remains afloat at the surface of the water. This allows fish to survive even when the surface of a lake or river has frozen over. If ice were to sink to the bottom of lakes and rivers, the water in them would be forced to the surface and be exposed to the colder atmospheric temperature, which would cause the lakes and rivers to freeze solid and all aquatic life within them to die.

PSALM 19:1 (NKJV) [WITH INTERPRETATION]:

The heavens declare the glory of God; and the firmament [INCLUDING WATER IN THE SKY] shows His handiwork.

ROMANS 1:20 (NKJV):

For since the creation of the world His invisible attributes are clearly seen, being understood by the things that are made.

God's attributes can be clearly seen in hail, snow, water, and ice. The treasure-like structures of hail and snow, and the molecular formation that allows ice to float above the waters, reveal the handiwork of Almighty God.

SEXUAL INTERCOURSE;
BECOMING ONE FLESH AT THE GENETIC LEVEL

By George Lujack

Recent scientific studies have shown that through sexual intercourse, women can carry the DNA of all their male sexual partners for life. This article will show the connection that modern science has made with the Scripture verses that declare men and women become one flesh; that is, men and women do not only become one flesh during the union of sexual intercourse, but also literally remain one flesh genetically through DNA transfer for life.

Microchimerism is defined as the presence of two genetically distinct cells in the same individual. Male michrochimerism appears in women who have given birth to sons, and also in many women who have *not* given birth to sons.

Scientists have recently discovered that sizable minorities of women who have never given birth to sons possess male Y-chromosome gene sequences in their blood. How did male DNA get in these women's bloodstreams?

Immunologists at the Fred Hutchinson Cancer Center conducted a study in 2004, which concluded that the possible sources of male DNA present in women's blood included pregnancies, miscarriages, a vanished male twin, or sexual intercourse.[176] The findings concluded that through sexual intercourse alone, women could hold onto the male genes and DNA of all their sexual partners within their bloodstreams and organs for life.[177]

GENESIS 2:24 (NKJV):
Therefore a man shall leave his father and mother and be joined to his wife, and they shall become one flesh.

God did not intend, nor does He permit, men and women to have sex outside of marriage. Premarital sex is fornication and sex outside of a lawful marriage is adultery. A marriage union of husband and wife is till death.

1 CORINTHIANS 6:13-14 (NKJV) (KJV*):
The body IS NOT FOR SEXUAL IMMORALITY (*FORNICATION) but for the Lord, and the Lord for the body. And God both raised up the Lord and will also raise us up by His power.

1 CORINTHIANS 6:15-20 (NKJV) (KJV*):

Do you not know that your bodies are members of Messiah (Christ)? Shall I then take the members of Messiah (Christ) and make them members of a harlot? Certainly not! Or do you not know that he who is joined to a harlot is one body with her? For *"the two,"* **He says,** *"shall become one flesh."* **But he who is joined to the Lord is one spirit with Him. FLEE SEXUAL IMMORALITY (*FORNICATION). Every sin that a man does is outside the body, BUT HE WHO COMMITS SEXUAL IMMORALITY (*FORNICATION) SINS AGAINST HIS OWN BODY. Or do you not know that your body is the temple of the Holy Spirit who is in you, whom you have from God, and you are not your own? For you were bought at a price; therefore glorify God in your body and in your spirit, which are God's.**

God did not create the human body for fornication. Science has now revealed that there are lifetime consequences for having numerous sexual partners. Men transfer their DNA, becoming and remaining one flesh with their female sex partners for life, and women carry the DNA and male genes of their male sexual partners within them for life.

LEVITICUS 19:19 (NKJV):

You shall not sow your field with mixed seed.

Leviticus 19:19 may seem like an unrelated verse to the topic of sexual promiscuity and the consequences of it, but the verse is basic to the discussion. God, the Creator of heaven and Earth and all life within, patterned His creation after His character and will. God does not want man to sow his field (plant in his garden) with mixed seed. How much more would God not want women to sow their fields (their bodies) with mixed seeds of different men (sexual partners), and men to not sow their seeds (through sexual intercourse) in different fields (not their own wives)?

MATTHEW 19:4-6; MARK 10:5-8 (NKJV):

And Yeshua (Jesus) answered and said to them, "Have you not read that He who made *them* **at the beginning** *'made them male and female,'* **and said,** *'For this reason a man shall leave his father and mother and be joined to his wife, and the two shall become one flesh'*?**
So then, they are no longer two but one flesh. Therefore what God has joined together, let not man separate."

EPHESIANS 5:28-33 (NKJV):

Husbands ought to love their own wives as their own bodies; he who loves his wife loves himself. For no one ever hated his own flesh, but nourishes and cherishes it, just as the Lord does the church. For we are members of His body, of His flesh and of His bones. *"For this reason a man shall leave his father and mother and be joined to his wife, and the two shall become one flesh."* **This is a great mystery, but I speak concerning Messiah (Christ) and the church. Nevertheless let each one of you in particular so love his own wife as himself, and let the wife see that she respects her husband.**

When a man and woman become one flesh through sexual intercourse, the man also transfers his DNA genes and Y-chromosomes into the woman and literally shares his flesh with her for life.

1 CORINTHIANS 6:9-11 (NKJV):

Do you not know that the unrighteous will not inherit the kingdom of God? Do not be deceived. Neither FORNICATORS, nor idolaters, nor ADULTERERS, nor homosexuals, nor sodomites, nor thieves, nor covetous, nor drunkards, nor revilers, nor extortioners will inherit the kingdom of God. AND SUCH WERE SOME OF YOU. BUT YOU WERE WASHED, BUT YOU WERE SANCTIFIED, BUT YOU WERE JUSTIFIED IN THE NAME OF THE LORD YESHUA (JESUS) AND BY THE SPIRIT OF OUR GOD.

Many men and women, former fornicators and adulterers, carry with them the emotional scars of past sexual encounters. Women may now be realizing that they also are carrying around more than they bargained for: the physical DNA and genes of their past sexual partners. Men likewise, may now be aware that they have passed their DNA and genes around to every woman who they ever had sex with.

It may be quite disconcerting recognizing the full consequences of sin and the impact it has on one's own and other people's lives, but the good news is that fornication and adultery are not unforgivable sins. Believers however must repent of these sins if they wish to be washed, sanctified, and justified in the name of Yeshua Messiah (Jesus Christ) and through God's Spirit.

Anyone who is engaged in sex outside of a lawful marriage should consider what they are doing, repent, and ask God for forgiveness. All who have ever engaged in sexual intercourse outside of marriage have stained their bodies with the mark of sexual immorality at the genetic level.

There are consequences of sin, even after forgiveness has taken place.

ISAIAH 1:18 (NKJV):

Says YHWH (the Lord),

"Though your sins are like scarlet, they shall be as white as snow; though they are red like crimson, they shall be as wool."

ISAIAH 64:6 (NKJV):

But we are all like an unclean thing, and all our righteousnesses are like filthy rags.

Many, who were once sexually immoral, remain crimson-stained like an unclean thing, but for those who repent and live sexually pure lives going forward, these physical stains of sexual immorality will all one day be fully removed by God. It is not only the transmission of sexually transmitted diseases that taints our bodies as being impure, but also becoming one flesh at the DNA genetic level with Scripturally unlawful sex partners.

MATTHEW 19:28 (NKJV):

Yeshua (Jesus) said to them, "Assuredly I say to you, that IN THE REGENERATION, when the Son of Man sits on the throne of His glory, you who have followed Me will also sit…"

1 CORINTHIANS 15:51-53 (NKJV):

Behold, I tell you a mystery: We shall not all sleep, but WE SHALL ALL BE CHANGED - in a moment, in the twinkling of an eye, at the last trumpet. For the trumpet will sound, and the dead will be raised incorruptible, and WE SHALL BE CHANGED. For this corruptible must put on incorruption, and this mortal must put on immortality.

God will cleanse, regenerate, and renew the corrupted, sin-stained bodies of repentant, former fornicators and adulterers, into incorruptible, pure, stain-free spirit beings.

God only permits a man, through sanctified lawful marriage to become one flesh through sexual intercourse with his wife and consequently to become one flesh at the DNA micro-chromosome genetic level with his wife.

THE ZOMBIE APOCALYPSE THAT WILL NEVER HAPPEN ... MONSTERS AND SUPERHEROES WHO WILL NEVER EXIST

By George Lujack

Popular culture through books, comics, and movies, has created an altered human existence of which many people are fascinated with and idolize. This alternate universe is void of reality and scientific truth. These genres are not entertainment for critical-thinking persons. This article will expose some evils that are at the root of some of the zombie / monster / superhero pop culture character phenomenon and the subtle brainwashing propaganda dangers inherent in these stories that cause many to reject God.

ZOMBIES

Zombies are fictional, resurrected, undead creatures regularly encountered in horror and fantasy-themed works. They are typically depicted as mindless, reanimated corpses with a hunger for human flesh, and particularly for human brains in some depictions.

The 1968 film, *Night of the Living Dead*, by George A. Romero, is where the zombie genre got started. Today there are many spin-off movies and a television series, *The Walking Dead,* in which 'walkers' live to attack the living.

The main theme of zombies is that they have come back to life through some type of man-made radiation or virus strain. When they return to life as the undead, they are typically stronger than non-affected living humans with an instinct to attack, infect, and eat human flesh.

The idea of dead corpses coming back to life, in many cases stronger than their unaffected living human counterparts, with a mindless desire to bite human flesh is beyond absurd. It is just a cheap entertainment form of cannibalism. When humans, dead or alive, are exposed to dangerous nuclear radioactive material or viruses, they are weakened and can die. Nuclear waste does not reanimate life. The dead have no functioning organs, so eating human flesh, or eating anything, wouldn't provide anything nourishing to them at all and wouldn't even be possible.

Chemistry cannot bring the dead back to life. Once dead, corpses remain dead.

ECCLESIASTES 9:5-6 (NKJV):

... the dead know nothing, and they have no more reward. Also their love, their hatred, and their envy have now perished. Nevermore will they have a share in anything done under the sun.

MONSTERS

VAMPIRES

Dracula is the original nocturnal 'undead' vampire. In order to maintain life, vampires must feed every evening on human blood. Vampires are capable of metamorphosing into a bat or a wolf. Vampires cannot be exposed to the light of the sun, or they will be burned to ashes by it, thus they operate in the darkness, rising from their tomb every evening after sunset and returning to it before sunrise.

Vampires have been glorified and glamorized in the recent *Twilight* film series. Sadly, there are many people today who desire to become actual vampires, having forsaken God for the desire to become an evil mythical creature that does not exist.

VAMPIRES AND SCRIPTURE

VAMPIRES MUST FEED ON BLOOD TO SUSTAIN THEIR 'UNDEAD' LIFE

LEVITICUS 3:17 (NKJV):

This shall be a perpetual statute throughout your generations in all your dwellings: you shall eat neither fat nor blood.

LEVITICUS 17:11,14 (NKJV):

For the life of the flesh is in the blood. ...

You shall not eat the blood of any flesh, for the life of all flesh is its blood.

DEUTERONOMY 12:23 (NKJV):

... do not eat the blood, for the blood is the life; you may not eat the life ...

VAMPIRES WALK IN DARKNESS AND CANNOT BE EXPOSED TO THE LIGHT.

LAMENTATIONS 3:2 (NKJV):

He has led and made me walk in darkness and not in light.

JOHN 3:20 (NKJV):

"For everyone practicing evil hates the light and does not come to the light, lest his deeds should be exposed."

THE WOLF MAN

The Wolf Man, aka a werewolf, is a mythical human who is under a curse, having been bitten or scratched by a werewolf and after having survived the attack, has become a werewolf. As a werewolf is exposed to the light of a full moon in human form, he morphs into a human/wolf hybrid creature, roaming the night hunting flesh.

Humans do not have the ability to morph into any other mammal, either as a result of infection or by intention. Nature's greatest morph is the mimic octopus, which has the ability to shape-shift and mimic at least 15-different forms of life.

THE WOLF MAN (WEREWOLF) AND SCRIPTURE

THE WOLF MAN IS UNDER A CURSE AND MORPHS INTO A WEREWOLF WHEN EXPOSED TO THE LIGHT OF A FULL MOON

PSALM 81:3 (NKJV):

Blow the trumpet at the time of the New Moon, at the full moon, on our solemn feast day.

ISAIAH 66:23 (NKJV):

And it shall come to pass that from one New Moon to another, …, all flesh shall come and worship before Me, says YHWH (the Lord).

HOSEA 5:7 (NKJV):

They have dealt treacherously with YHWH (the Lord), for they have begotten pagan children. Now a New Moon shall devour them and their heritage.

FRANKENSTEIN

Frankenstein has become synonymous with the monster creation of Dr. Victor Frankenstein, the creator of the monster. Dr. Frankenstein constructs his 'creation' from an assortment of human beings and by using a mix of chemistry and electricity, he animates his 'creation' to life, in essence creating life from human parts.

Chemistry and electricity cannot bring the dead back to life.

FRANKENSTEIN AND SCRIPTURE

FRANKENSTEIN IS GIVEN LIFE

GENESIS 2:7 (NKJV):

And YHWH (the Lord) God formed man of the dust of the ground, and breathed into his nostrils the breath of life; and man became a living being.

SUPERHEROES

SPIDERMAN

Peter Parker gets bitten by a radioactive spider at a science exhibit and, through genetic fusion, acquires the agility and proportional strength of a spider. Along with his newfound strength, Parker gains the ability to adhere to walls and ceilings, like a spider, with tensile-strong fibers that protrude from his hands and feet. Parker also has the ability to shoot webbing from his wrists that allows him to travel like Tarzan among New York City's skyscrapers as well as use his webbing as an weapon against criminals and spin webs.

When spiders bite humans, they typically release neurotoxic venom, which attacks the nervous system. The bite of a spider does not release spider DNA into the bite victim. Adding radioactivity to such a bite will not cause human and arachnid cells to fuse into a hybrid. In nature hybrids can and do occur, but the offspring of such unions are not stronger or superior to the original mating species. For example, a mule is the offspring of a male donkey and a female horse. Mules have 63 chromosomes, a mixture of the horse's 64 and the donkey's 62. The different structure and number typically prevents the chromosomes from pairing up properly rendering most mules infertile. Superior life through hybridization is a false premise of the theory of evolution that gets propagandized in sci-fi movies.

THE INCREDIBLE HULK

Bruce Banner absorbs a massive lethal dose of gamma radiation in a laboratory accident. Instead of dying, he seems unscathed, but later learns that when triggered by anger, he becomes a raging, Incredible Hulk with limitless superhuman strength. In the real world, over-exposure to gamma radiation and other forms of radioactive material totally destroys the cells of the body. Thousands of people have been killed, acquired cancers, and have become disabled as a result of accidents in Chernobyl, Fukushima, and many other smaller scale nuclear accidents throughout the world.

X-MEN

The X-Men are a team of mutant superheroes. They have all been born with beneficial mutations that they have to learn to socially accept and live with. These mutants have incredible abilities, either mental, physical, or both.

NARRATIVE THEME OF THE X-MEN MOVIE SERIES

"Mutation. It is the key to our evolution. It has enabled us to evolve from a single-celled organism to the dominant species on the planet. This process is slow, normally taking thousands and thousands of years. But every few hundred millennia evolution leaps forward."

X-Men are a characterization of, and represent, modern evolution theory. To say that the human race evolved from single-celled organisms (amoeba to man theory) is completely unsubstantiated by science, without scientific proof, and is a wild baseless speculation. Spontaneous beneficial mutation has NEVER occurred, nor can it ever occur. It is IMPOSSIBLE. Two human beings CANNOT give birth to a mutant human who has wings. Wings are not in the genetic code of the parents, so such an offspring is NOT POSSIBLE.

People go to the movies often for escapism and they suspend disbelief. That is perfectly fine to do, to enjoy works of fiction from time to time. Certain works of fiction, the resurrection, glorification, and fear of the living dead are cinematic stories that should be avoided. Remembering that these stories are works of fiction that can never occur is the point of this article.

<u>DEUTERONOMY 18:10-11 (NKJV):</u>

There shall not be found among you anyone who makes his son or his daughter pass through the fire, or one who practices witchcraft, or a soothsayer, or one who interprets omens, or a sorcerer, or one who conjures spells, or a medium, or a consulter with familiar spirits, or a wizard, or a necromancer: one who calls up the dead.

2 TIMOTHY 1:7 (NKJV):

For God has not given us a spirit of fear, but of power and of love and of a sound mind.

When watching movies that depict the dead coming back to life, one isn't literally calling up the dead, but the imagery of watching the dead being called up from the grave is engrained in the brain and is mentally harmful. The pagan festival of Halloween is the festival of the dead, which has now been extended through movies and television series, which depict the dead returning to life, to instill a spirit in fear in people. Believers should have nothing to do with unfruitful works of darkness (Romans 13:12; Ephesians 5:11).

IS THE ROMAN CATHOLIC CHURCH THE ONE TRUE HOLY APOSTOLIC CHURCH?

By George Lujack

The Roman Catholic Church, from its establishment, has proclaimed to be the one true holy apostolic church founded by Jesus Christ. This article will examine this self-serving claim and expose it as false.

The sketch-drawing image above the title of this article is idolatrous. Its not-so-subtle message is to worship the Catholic Church in place of God. Much of what the Catholic Church does is to usurp glory away from Messiah (Christ) to bestow glory upon itself. The Catholic Church claims to be the one true holy apostolic church, founded by Jesus Christ. The claim itself is an assumptive one, in that it *assumes* that Yeshua Messiah (Jesus Christ) did found one true holy apostolic denominational church. He didn't.

IS THE ROMAN CATHOLIC CHURCH 'ONE?'

Answer: No.

There are numerous divisions within Catholicism known as 'rites,' each one with its own set of differing doctrines. The Catholic Church is not united as one denomination in body or in truth.

IS THE ROMAN CATHOLIC CHURCH 'TRUE?'

Answer: No.

Throughout its history and to this day, the Roman Catholic Church has NOT been true to the Scriptures and claims apostolic tradition-based authority over the Scriptures. The Catholic Church has claimed that salvation comes through its denominational church. To say that the Catholic Church is the way of salvation, or is truth, is usurping glory away from Yeshua (Jesus).

JOHN 14:6 (NKJV):
Yeshua (Jesus) said to him, "I am THE WAY, THE TRUTH, and the life. No one comes to the Father EXCEPT THROUGH ME."

Yeshua (Jesus) is the WAY, the TRUTH, and the life. Neither the Roman Catholic Church, nor any other denominational church, can claim to be the way or the truth.

IS THE ROMAN CATHOLIC CHURCH 'HOLY?'

Answer: No.

Scripture does not declare any denominational church 'holy.' Churches, including the Roman Catholic Church, are institutions of men, and all men running all Catholic Churches and all other denominational churches have sinned and have fallen short of the glory of God (Romans 3:23).

1 SAMUEL 2:2 (NKJV):
No one is holy like YHWH (the Lord), for there is NONE besides You, nor is there any rock like our God.

IS THE ROMAN CATHOLIC CHURCH 'APOSTOLIC?'

Answer: No.

There is no apostolic succession from Simon Peter. Peter never served as bishop or pope of a Roman Catholic Church and no amount of Catholic lies, propaganda, and revisionist history will change that fact. Scripture records the travels of Peter. Peter was the apostle to the circumcised Jews, not a leader of the apostles or afterward of a Catholic Church. Peter, as apostle to the Jews, NEVER traveled to Rome (Galatians 2:7-8; 1 Peter 1:1).

Yeshua (Jesus) never founded the Roman Catholic denominational church organization no matter how Catholics twist Matthew 16:16-18 to proclaim that He did.

The word 'church' in Scripture is a mistranslation The proper translation for 'church' throughout Scripture is either 'assembly,' 'congregation,' 'group,' or 'called out ones.'

Can a false church, one that is filled with corruption, man-made false doctrines, lies, and unscriptural practices really be the one true church? Of course not!

DID THE ROMAN CATHOLIC CHURCH GIVE US THE SCRIPTURES?

Answer: No.

The Scriptures were not given to us by Catholics, are not Catholic writings, and the Catholic Church is not a church that adheres to the Scriptures.

God has given us the Scriptures!

2 TIMOTHY 3:16 (NKJV):
All Scripture is given by inspiration of God.

"*Do you know who taught the eagles to find their prey? That same God teaches his hungry children to find their Father in his Word. Far from having given us the Scriptures, it is you [CATHOLICS] who have hidden them from us; it is you who burn those who teach them; and if you could, you would burn the Scriptures themselves.*"

"*I defy the Catholic pope and all his laws. If God spare my life for many years, I would cause the boy that drives the plough to know more of the Scriptures than you.*"

- William Tyndale

CATHOLICS, COME OUT AND STAY AWAY!

By George Lujack

During the two major pagan-adopted holiday celebration seasons, Christmas and Easter, the Catholic Church typically runs ad campaigns appealing to ex-Catholics' sense of nostalgia and tradition in an attempt to persuade ex-Catholics to "come home" to the Catholic Church. This article will urge Catholics to come out of the Catholic Church, and ex-Catholics considering returning to stay away from Catholicism and find a new home.

COME OUT FROM AMONG THEM AND BE SEPARATE

ISAIAH 42:8 (NKJV):

I am YHWH (the Lord), that is My name, and My glory I will not give to another, nor My praise to carved images.

2 CORINTHIANS 6:16-17 (NKJV):

And what agreement has the temple of God with idols? For you are the temple of the living God. As God has said:

"I will dwell in them and walk among them. I will be their God, and they shall be My people. Therefore COME OUT FROM AMONG THEM AND BE SEPARATE, says YHWH (the Lord)."

The Catholic Church is a house of idols. The Catholic faithful deny this obvious truth. Utilizing carved, molten, painted, and stone images of Jesus, Mary, the saints, and others, to use them in any manner is in violation of the first and second commandments and is a condemned practice throughout all of Scripture.

The Catholic Church is not a true church, nor is it the church that Jesus Christ or Peter started. Ex-Catholics, you came out of the Catholic Church for a reason, because it is a church of deception. There are good, well-intentioned people in the Catholic Church, but that is not a reason to either remain in the Catholic Church or to return to it.[178]

WE MUST WORSHIP GOD IN SPIRIT AND TRUTH

JOHN 4:23-24 (NKJV):

"True worshipers will worship the Father in spirit and truth; for the Father is seeking such to worship Him. God is Spirit, and those who worship Him must worship in spirit and truth."

SCRIPTURE MAKES ONE WISE FOR SALVATION THROUGH FAITH; SALVATION DOES NOT COME THROUGH THE CATHOLIC CHURCH

2 TIMOTHY 3:15-17 (NKJV):

From childhood *you have known* the Holy Scriptures, which are able to make you wise for salvation through faith which is in Messiah Yeshua (Christ Jesus). All Scripture is given by inspiration of God, and is profitable for doctrine, for reproof, for correction, for instruction in righteousness, that the man of God may be complete, thoroughly equipped for every good work.

Contrary to what the Catholic Church has told its flock throughout millennia, God does want His believers to study *and know* the Scriptures.

EX-CATHOLICS, DON'T LOOK BACK

GENESIS 19:24-26 (NKJV):

Then the Lord rained brimstone and fire on Sodom and Gomorrah, from the Lord out of the heavens. So He overthrew those cities, all the plain, all the inhabitants of the cities, and what grew on the ground. But his wife looked back behind him, and she became a pillar of salt.

Ex-Catholics, remember the story of Lot and his wife. God commanded Lot and his family to leave Sodom AND NOT LOOK BACK. Sodom was a high standard of living city, but it was a city full of corruption and wickedness. God decided to judge Sodom to destruction, but Lot, a righteous man, was spared the judgment of God and was ordered to leave Sodom with his family AND NOT LOOK BACK. But, as it came to pass, Lot's wife looked back at Sodom and she became a pillar of salt.

Ex-Catholics, who have left the comforts, falsehoods, grand cathedrals, idolatrous imagery, and other enticements of the Catholic Church, don't be like Lot's wife. DON'T LOOK BACK!

EX-CATHOLICS, DO NOT RETURN TO SPIRITUAL BONDAGE

NUMBERS 14:2-4 (NKJV):

And all the children of Israel complained against Moses and Aaron, and the whole congregation said to them, "If only we had died in the land of Egypt! Or if only we had died in this wilderness! Why has the Lord brought us to this land to fall by the sword, that our wives and children should become victims? Would it not be better for us to return to Egypt?" So they said to one another, "Let us select a leader and return to Egypt."

Ex-Catholics, remember the Hebrews' Exodus from Egypt. The Hebrews dwelt in Egypt and became slaves (Exodus 1:8-14). The Hebrews were in bondage to the Egyptians for 400-years (Genesis 15:13; Exodus 12:40-41). God raised up Moses from within Egypt to be His deliverer to free the Hebrews from their Egyptian slave masters (Exodus 3:10; Acts 7:35). God performed many miracles to release the Hebrew people from the bondage of Egypt, but while they were traveling in the desert, many of the Hebrews began to grumble and complain. They wanted to return to Egypt!

Egypt was a magnificent city, for sure, and many of the Hebrews preferred to be slaves in the security of Egypt, rather than free people traveling through a desert to a land of promise and uncertainty.

Ex-Catholics, who miss the grand cathedrals and comforts of the Catholic Church, remember that these are just material things that keep you in bondage from the freedom and truth you have in Yeshua Messiah (Jesus Christ) and the Scriptures.

STAY AWAY AND DO NOT RETURN

2 PETER 2:20-22 (NKJV):
For if, after they have escaped the pollutions of the world through the knowledge of the Lord and Savior Yeshua Messiah (Jesus Christ), they are again entangled in them and overcome, the latter end is worse for them than the beginning. For it would have been better for them not to have known the way of righteousness, than having known it, to turn from the holy commandment delivered to them. But it has happened to them according to the true proverb: "A dog returns to his own vomit," and, "a sow, having washed, to her wallowing in the mire."

Ex-Catholics, you who have escaped the pollutions of the Catholic Church and have gained knowledge of the truth of the Scriptures, do not be like a dog that returns to his vomit, or a pig that returns to her mud. Ex-Catholics, you who know the Catholic Church to be a false church, why would you consider returning to your former bondage? Stay away and do not return to the Catholic Church.

PROTESTANTS, PROTESTING CATHOLICS, COME OUT AND STAY AWAY

The Protestant churches are daughter churches of the Catholic Church. As their name suggests, Protestants are protesting Catholics, protesting some, but not all of Catholicism. The Catholic Church is the mother church of all the Protestant churches, which still cling to many of the falsehoods of Catholicism, such as the Sunday Sabbath, the eating of unclean creatures, numerous unscriptural man-made laws, and the replacement of God's holy feast days (Leviticus 23) with pagan holidays.

God's love for His children is greater than any comfort or sense of security that the Catholic Church can seemingly provide. It may be initially difficult to come out from the Catholic Church, or her daughter Protestant churches, and stay away and navigate through the desert to find a new home - a good Scripture-studying church, but it will be well worth it.

MESSIAH (CHRIST) IS THE ROCK, NOT PETER

By George Lujack

The Roman Catholic Church is founded upon the false claim that it is the one true apostolic church of God that Jesus Christ founded through Peter. This article will chronicle the 28-Scripture verses that proclaim Yeshua Messiah (Jesus Christ) is the only Rock of Scripture and will explain the deception of the Catholic Church in using Matthew 16:16-18 to proclaim Peter as the rock upon which Jesus Christ built His church.

DEUTERONOMY 32:4 (NKJV):

He is the ROCK, His work is perfect; For all His ways are justice, A God of truth and without injustice; Righteous and upright is He.

DEUTERONOMY 32:15 (NKJV):

Then he forsook God who made him, and scornfully esteemed the ROCK of his salvation.

DEUTERONOMY 32:18 (NKJV):

Of the ROCK who begot you, you are unmindful and have forgotten the God who fathered you.

DEUTERONOMY 32:31 (NKJV):

For their rock is not as our ROCK.

1 SAMUEL 2:2 (NKJV):

There is none holy like YHWH (the Lord), for there is none besides You, nor is there any ROCK like our God.

2 SAMUEL 22:2 (NKJV):

YHWH (the Lord) is my ROCK, and my fortress, and my deliverer.

2 SAMUEL 22:32 (NKJV):

For who is God, except YHWH (the Lord)? And who is a ROCK, except our God?

2 SAMUEL 22:47 (NKJV):

YHWH (the Lord) lives! Blessed be my ROCK! Let God be exalted, the ROCK of my salvation!

2 SAMUEL 23:3 (NKJV):

The God of Israel said, the ROCK of Israel spoke to me: 'He who rules over men must be just, ruling in the fear of God.'

PSALM 18:2 (NKJV):

YHWH (the Lord) is my ROCK and my fortress and my deliverer; My God, my strength, in whom I will trust; My shield and the horn of my salvation, my stronghold.

PSALM 28:1 (NKJV):

To You I will cry, O YHWH (Lord) my ROCK: Do not be silent to me, lest, if You are silent to me, I become like those who go down to the pit.

PSALM 31:2-3 (NKJV):

Be my ROCK of refuge, a fortress of defense to save me. For you are my ROCK and my fortress.

PSALM 42:9 (NKJV):

I will say to God my ROCK, "Why have You forgotten me? Why do I go mourning because of the oppression of the enemy?"

PSALM 61:2 (NKJV):

Lead me to the ROCK that is higher than I.

PSALM 62:2 (NKJV):

He only is my ROCK and my salvation; He is my defense; I shall not be greatly moved.

PSALM 62:,6-7 (NKJV):

He only is my ROCK and my salvation; He is my defense; I shall not be moved.
In God is my salvation and my glory; the ROCK of my strength, and my refuge is in God.

PSALM 71:3 (NKJV):

Be my strong refuge, to which I may resort continually; You have given the commandment to save me, for you are my ROCK and my fortress.

PSALM 78:35 (NKJV):

Then they remembered that God was their ROCK, and the Most High God their Redeemer.

PSALM 89:26 (NKJV):

He shall cry to Me, 'You are my Father, my God, and the ROCK of my salvation.

PSALM 92:15 (NKJV):

To declare that YHWH (the Lord) is upright; He is my ROCK, and there is no unrighteousness in Him.

PSALM 92:22 (NKJV):

But YHWH (the Lord) has been my defense, and my God the ROCK of my refuge.

PSALM 95:1 (NKJV):

Let us shout joyfully to the ROCK of our salvation.

ISAIAH 17:10 (NKJV):

Because you have forgotten the God of your salvation, and have not been mindful of the ROCK of your stronghold.

MATTHEW 16:18 (NKJV) (HSV†):

"And I also say to you that you are Peter, and on this ROCK I will build My church (†assembly), and the gates of hell shall not prevail against it."

1 CORINTHIANS 10:4 (NKJV):

And all drank the same spiritual drink. For they drank of that spiritual ROCK that followed them, and that ROCK was Messiah (Christ).

In the preceding aforementioned 26-verses, YHWH (the Lord) God or Messiah (Christ) were referred to as being the Rock a total of 28-times. Roman Catholics misappropriated the title of 'Rock,' which belongs to Messiah (Christ), and bestowed it upon the Apostle Peter to establish Peter as Catholicism's first pope. The Catholic Church was founded on a lie, upon a self-serving intentional twisting of one single solitary verse of Scripture to establish itself as the one true church that Jesus Christ founded through Peter 'the rock.'

PROPER CONTEXTUAL INTERPRETATION OF MATTHEW 16:16-18

MATTHEW 16:16-18 (NKJV) (HSV†):

Simon Peter answered and said, "You are the Messiah (Christ), the Son of the living God."

Yeshua (Jesus) answered and said to him, "Blessed are you, Simon Bar-Jonah, for flesh and blood has not revealed this to you, but My Father who is in heaven. And I also say to you that you are Peter, and on this rock I will build My church (†assembly), and the gates of hell shall not prevail against it."

Peter identified Yeshua (Jesus) as the Messiah (Christ). Yeshua (Jesus) said that Peter was blessed by a revelation from His Father in heaven, who revealed that He was the Messiah (Christ) to Peter.

After Peter answered who Yeshua (Jesus) was, He replied in kind saying. "You are Peter…" then said, "and upon this rock I will build *My* church."

1. Yeshua (Jesus) never calls Peter a rock. He said, "You are Peter…"

2. Yeshua (Jesus) then said, "and upon *this rock,*" in reference to the statement that Peter just made about Himself in which Peter said, "You are the Messiah (Christ), the Son of the living God."

3. Yeshua (Jesus) said, "I will build *My* church," NOT the church of Peter.

4. Yeshua (Jesus) was NOT building a denominational church. The word 'church' itself is a mistranslated word in English bibles; a pagan-based word meaning 'circle,' having to do with a Greek goddess of mythology. The proper interpretation for 'church' in Matthew 16:18 is 'assembly,' and elsewhere in Scripture 'church' should be properly translated as 'assembly,' 'called out ones,' 'congregation,' or 'group.'

5. Yeshua's (Jesus') assembly is when two or three are gathered in His name, worshiping Him in spirit and in truth (Matthew 18:20; John 4:24).

A proper interpretation and the totality of Scripture identifies the Messiah (Christ) as the Rock of Matthew 16:18.

Catholics worship a different rock: Peter, as their first history-revised pope, and worship all men who have subsequently held the title of pope of the Roman Catholic Church.

Peter never served as a bishop or pope of Rome. There is no Scriptural evidence that Peter was ever in Rome at all. Scripture records Peter's travels and Rome was not on the list (1 Peter 1:1). Peter was an apostle to the Jews (Galatians 2:7-8).

Scripture nowhere indicates that Peter was the leader of the disciples. The apostles asked among themselves who would be the greatest (Mark 9:34) and this occasion would have been a perfect time for Messiah (Christ) to declare the supremacy of Peter. Yeshua (Jesus) replied that he who would be first would be last and servant of all (Mark 9:35). Yeshua (Jesus) declared that there are rulers and those who are great exercise authority over men, yet it shall not be so among you (Matthew 20:25-26).

Peter never went on to build or establish the Roman Catholic Church.

Shortly after Matthew 16:16-18, Peter would go on to deny Messiah (Christ) three times (Matthew 26:69-75; Mark 14:66-72; Luke 22:55-62). Initially, Peter went fishing for fish, and not for men, after the death of Messiah (Christ) (John 21:3). Peter, in denying Messiah (Christ) three times and by going fishing after the resurrection of Yeshua (Jesus), was not the personification of a rock.

QUESTION:

2 SAMUEL 22:32 (NKJV):
Who is a ROCK, except our God?

CATHOLIC ANSWER:

Peter is the rock!

CORRECT ANSWER:

1 SAMUEL 2:2 (NKJV):

There is none besides You, nor is there any ROCK like our God.

1 CORINTHIANS 10:4 (NKJV):

And all drank the same spiritual drink. For they drank of that spiritual ROCK that followed them, and that ROCK was Messiah (Christ).

CATHOLICISM'S FIRST POPE: SIMON MAGUS

By George Lujack

Simon Magus was Catholicism's first pope. Scripture records an incident that took place between Simon Magus and the apostles that began the process of apostasy infiltrating the early Christian church. Simon Magus exalted himself as the first leader of the false worldwide religious system - the Roman Catholic Church. [179][180]

After the ascension of Yeshua Messiah (Jesus Christ), Simon Peter (Kepha) left Jerusalem BRIEFLY to travel to Samaria, and then RETURNED to Jerusalem. Simon Magus met Simon Peter in Samaria and later went on to usurp Christianity under Catholicism. Simon Peter traveled to the places he wrote of (Pontus, Galatia, Cappadocia, Asia, and Bithynia), but never mentioned traveling to Rome (1 Peter 1:1). Peter NEVER served as the first pope of the Catholic Church or the bishop of Rome.

ACTS 8:9-19 (NKJV) [WITH INTERPRETATION]:

But there was a certain man called Simon [MAGUS], who previously practiced sorcery in the city and astonished the people of Samaria, claiming that he was someone great, to whom they all gave heed, from the least to the greatest, saying, "This man is the great power of God." And they heeded him because he had astonished them with his sorceries for a long time. But when they believed Philip as he preached the things concerning the kingdom of God and the name of Yeshua Messiah (Jesus Christ), both men and women were baptized. Then Simon [MAGUS] himself also believed; and when he was baptized he continued with Philip, and was amazed, seeing the miracles and signs, which were done.

Now when the apostles WHO WERE AT JERUSALEM heard that Samaria had received the word of God, they sent Peter and John to them, who, when they had come down, prayed for them that they might receive the Holy Spirit. For as yet He had fallen upon none of them. They had only been baptized in the name of the Lord Yeshua (Jesus). Then they laid hands on them, and they received the Holy Spirit.

And when Simon [MAGUS] saw that through the laying on of the apostles' hands the Holy Spirit was given, he offered them money, saying, "Give me this power also, that anyone on whom I lay hands may receive the Holy Spirit."

Simon Magus went on to deceive many, founding Roman Catholicism, usurping Simon Peter's name, and declaring Himself God on Earth and the first Catholic pope. Simon Peter returned to Jerusalem and remained there to be the apostle to the Jews (Acts 8:25; Galatians 2:7-8).

ACTS 8:20-25 (NKJV) [WITH INTERPRETATION]:

But Peter said to him, "Your money perish with you, because you thought that the gift of God could be purchased with money! You have neither part nor portion in this matter, for your heart is not right in the sight of God. Repent therefore of this your wickedness, and pray God if perhaps the thought of your heart may be forgiven you. For I see that you are poisoned by bitterness and bound by iniquity."

Then Simon [MAGUS] answered and said, "Pray to the Lord for me, that none of the things which you have spoken may come upon me."

So when they had testified and preached the word of the Lord, THEY RETURNED TO JERUSALEM, preaching the gospel in many villages of the Samaritans.

Simon Peter was never the Catholic pope of Rome. Simon Magus assumed that role. Peter NEVER traveled to Rome. Peter was the apostle to the circumcised Jews as Paul was the apostle to the uncircumcised Gentiles. Scripture records where Peter traveled to and visited, but Rome was NOT listed as one of the destinations.

GALATIANS 2:7-8 (NKJV) [WITH INTERPRETATION]:

But on the contrary, when they saw that the gospel for the uncircumcised [GENTILES] had been committed to me [PAUL], as the gospel for the circumcised [JEWS] was to Peter (for He who worked effectually in Peter for the apostleship to the circumcised [JEWS] also worked effectively in me toward the Gentiles)...

1 PETER 1:1 (NKJV):

Peter, an apostle of Yeshua Messiah (Jesus Christ), to the pilgrims of the Dispersion in PONTUS, GALATIA, CAPPADOCIA, ASIA, and BITHYNIA, elect according to the foreknowledge of God the Father, in sanctification of the Spirit, for obedience and sprinkling of the blood of Yeshua Messiah (Jesus Christ): Grace to you and peace be multiplied.

Peter did not die by being crucified upside down on a cross and his body is not buried in St. Peter's Bascilica in Rome, as Catholic Church revisionist historians proclaim. Simon Peter died in Jerusalem and his tomb has been discovered there.[181]

The Catholic Church has built itself upon a lie and anything built upon a lie will not stand. Yeshua (Jesus) did not build the Catholic Church upon the rock of Peter (Matthew 16:16-18); He built His church upon the faithful answer that Peter gave to Yeshua (Jesus), that He is the Messiah (Christ), the Son of the living God.

Simon Magus is the foundational rock, the lie upon which the Roman Catholic Church was built.

IDOLATRY: CARVED IMAGES AND LIKENESSES OF YHWH (THE LORD)

By George Lujack

A grave sin often mentioned throughout Scripture that deeply offends God is the sin of idolatry. This article will illustrate some of the ways in which man commits idolatry against God by making, serving, and praising God through artistic works and carved images of Him.

MICAH 5:13 (NKJV):

Your carved images I will also cut off, and your sacred pillars from your midst.

You shall no more worship the work of your hands.

The command to not make carved images, or any fixed images representing God, is the second commandment of the Ten Commandments, and is further mentioned and elaborated on in many other verses throughout Scripture.

EXODUS 20:4-5 (NKJV):

You shall not make for yourself a carved image - or any likeness of anything that is in heaven above, or that is in the earth beneath, or that is in the water under the earth; you shall not bow down to them nor serve them. For I, YHWH (the Lord) your God, am a jealous God…

ISAIAH 42:8 (NKJV):

I am YHWH (the Lord); that is My name. My glory I will not give to another, nor My praise to carved images.

When God gave the command to not make any images to represent Him, He also gave the reason why. He is a jealous God who will not share His praise with carved images. He views artwork, paintings, carved images, or any object representing Him as an unworthy worthless substitution for Him.

The best way to relate this in human terms would be in the following manner… A man goes on a business trip. His wife decides to surprise him and greets him at his hotel room. When the wife arrives, she discovers her husband is with a mistress or prostitute. The husband tries to beg and explain to his wife that his mistress or prostitute means nothing to him, but he just needed someone to be with, as a substitute for her, while he went away on his business trip. The wife, who loves her husband, is rightfully angry, appalled, and jealous. All the apologetic words of love coming from her husband cannot comfort her.

This is how God views man when he makes artistic or carved images of Him and sets up those images, serves those images, and praises, reveres, and worships those images.

The Catholic Church is the greatest violator of the second commandment that prohibits making and setting up images of God. The Catholic Church, from its early foundation, never had any intention of obeying God's second commandment. The Catholic Church changed its version of the Ten Commandments to accommodate its use of artwork images and carved statues of Yeshua (Jesus) and others.[182] The Catholic Church hid the second commandment as part of the first; essentially omitting it, then split the tenth commandment against coveting in two, to make the ninth and tenth commandments. Catholicism's ninth commandment is against coveting your neighbor's wife and its tenth commandment is against coveting your neighbor's property.

A Catholic argument used to defend its use of images of God is that its members are not actually 'worshiping' God through artwork or carved images; they know that the images are not actually God. The second commandment actually prohibits the use of *any likeness* of God. Even if people fully know that an image is not God, but is just a likeness of God, they are still breaking the second commandment if they set up, serve, and praise any image likenesses of God.

After the Hebrews departed Egypt in the Exodus, they decided to make themselves a golden calf representation of God (Exodus 32). Moses' brother Aaron made the calf, so he and the Hebrews surely knew that the golden calf *was not actually* God. Aaron knew he could not make God into a golden calf. Scripture records this as a great sin that angered God and God brought judgment to about three thousand people for this sin (Exodus 32:28).

Another Catholic argument used to defend its use of artistic and carved images of God (and others) is that people have photographs displayed throughout their homes, and having artistic images and statues of Messiah (Christ) is just like having photos displayed of loved family members.

This is not the case. Photos are *actual images*, capturing an *actual likeness* of an *actual moment* in time, not artistic paintings or the work of a sculptor's hands. Imagine if you entered a person's home and instead of seeing family photographs, this person had nothing but paintings and statues of his family in his home. That might be a little creepy.

Hypothetically, if Yeshua (Jesus) could be photographed, His photo would represent an actual image of Him, not the work of a craftsman's hands. If in the future, Yeshua (Jesus) allows people to photograph Him, and place a picture of Him in their homes, He would certainly NOT allow people to bow down and pray before a photographic image of Him.

The Roman Catholic Church is by no means the only violator of the second commandment. Many denominational Christian churches set up images of Yeshua (Jesus) in their places of worship and individual people of many denominational faiths have artwork or statues of Messiah (Christ) set up somewhere prominently in their home.

During the pagan holiday Christmas season, Christians set up images of Messiah (Christ) in manger scenes and set up Christmas tree idols of worship in their homes. Sacrifices of labor and money are used to purchase gifts, and the gift giver bows down and places the sacrificial gifts under the decorated Christmas tree idol.

Christmas tree idols must be set up, served (decorated), and then carried away from the home, because they cannot go by themselves (Jeremiah 10:1-6).

JOHN 4:24 (NKJV):

"God is Spirit, and those who worship Him must worship in spirit and truth."

Yeshua (Jesus) commands us to worship God in spirit and in truth, not through artistic images or carved statues. We cannot worship God in a manner of our choosing. We cannot worship God through breaking the second commandment.

1 CORINTHIANS 6:9-10 (NKJV) (HSV†):

Do you not know that the unrighteous will not inherit the reign of Elohim (kingdom of God)? Do not be deceived. Neither fornicators, nor IDOLATORS, nor adulterers, nor effeminate, nor homosexuals, nor thieves, nor covetous (†greedy of gain), nor drunkards, nor revilers, nor swindlers will inherit the kingdom of God (†reign of Elohim).

GALATIANS 5:19-21 (NKJV) (HSV†):

Now the works of the flesh are evident, which are: adultery, fornication, uncleanness, lewdness, IDOLATRY, drug sorcery, hatred, quarrels, jealousies, fits of rage, selfish ambitions, dissensions, heresies, envy, murders, drunkenness, revelries, and the like; of which I tell you beforehand, just as I also told you in time past, that those who practice such things will not inherit the kingdom of God (†reign of Elohim).

REVELATION 21:7-8 (NKJV):

He who overcomes shall inherit all things, and I will be his God and he shall be My son. The cowardly, untrustworthy, abominable, murderers, sexually immoral, drug sorcerers, IDOLATORS, and all liars shall have their part in the lake which burns with fire and brimstone, which is the second death.

Catholics and other believers who engage with artistic images and carved statues of YHWH (the Lord) are playing a dangerous game with their salvation. Setting up and serving images of God might seem like a harmless activity that actually honors Him, but Scripture repeatedly declares it to be a great sin, a sin that could cause a believer to not inherit the kingdom of God.

KEYS TO THE KINGDOM

By George Lujack

What are the keys to the kingdom of heaven? What can be bound and loosed on Earth and in heaven? What church did Yeshua (Jesus) build that the gates of hell shall not prevail against? This article will answer these theological statements made by Yeshua (Jesus) as recorded in Matthew 16:17-19.

MATTHEW 16:17-19 (NKJV):

Yeshua (Jesus) answered and said to him, "Blessed are you, Simon Bar-Jonah, for flesh and blood has not revealed this to you, but My Father who is in heaven. And I also say to you that you are Peter, and on this rock I will build My church, and the gates of hell shall not prevail against it. And I will give you the keys of the kingdom of heaven, and whatever you bind on earth will be bound in heaven, and whatever you loose on earth will be loosed in heaven."

Matthew 16:17-19 are the primary Scripture verses upon which the Roman Catholic Church uses to declare itself as the one true church established by Jesus Christ through the Apostle Peter.

Catholics interpret and proclaim Matthew 16:17-19 in the following way:

MATTHEW 16:17-19 (NKJV) [WITH INTERPRETATION]:

Yeshua (Jesus) answered and said to him, "Blessed are you, Simon Bar-Jonah, for flesh and blood has not revealed this to you, but My Father who is in heaven. And I also say to you that you are Peter, and on this rock [PETER] I will build My [CATHOLIC] church, and the gates of hell shall not prevail against it [THE CATHOLIC CHURCH].

And I will give you the keys of the kingdom of heaven [THE CATHOLIC CHURCH], and whatever [LAWS] you [AS POPE] bind on earth will be bound in heaven [WILL BECOME LAW ON EARTH AND IN HEAVEN], and whatever [OF GOD'S LAWS] you loose on earth will be loosed [ABOLISHED ON EARTH AND] in heaven."

The Catholic Church is a deceiving church that was founded upon a lie. Yeshua (Jesus) did not declare or establish a papacy through Peter, start a Catholic Church, issue literal keys to Peter, or give Peter the authority to bind new laws or unbind God's eternal laws.

JOHN 16:25 (NKJV):

"These things I have spoken to you in FIGURATIVE LANGUAGE; but the time is coming when I will no longer speak to you in FIGURATIVE LANGUAGE, but I will tell you plainly about the Father."

Yeshua (Jesus) often spoke to His disciples in figurative or parabolic language (Matthew 13:13-15,34-35; Mark 3:23, 4:2-13, 12:1; Luke 8:10).

Yeshua (Jesus) spoke to Peter in figurative, parabolic language in Matthew 16:17-19. Yeshua (Jesus) responded to Peter, who faithfully answered His question.

MATTHEW 16:13-16 (NKJV):

When Yeshua (Jesus) came into the region of Caesarea Philippi, He asked His disciples, saying, "Who do men say that I, the Son of Man, am?"

So they said, "Some say John the Baptist, some Elijah, and others Jeremiah or one of the prophets."

He said to them, "But who do you say that I am?"

Simon Peter answered and said, "You are the Messiah (Christ), the Son of the living God."

The true meaning of Yeshua's (Jesus') response to Peter is as follows:

MATTHEW 16:18 (NKJV):

"And I also say to you that you are Peter, and on this rock I will build My church, …"

Why did Yeshua (Jesus) say, "… you are Peter?" This was Yeshua (Jesus) responding in kind to what Peter just said to Him, which was, "You are the Messiah (Christ), the Son of the living God (Matthew 16:16)." Yeshua (Jesus) did not declare Peter to be some special kind of rock on which He was going to build His church upon by merely calling him by his name.

MATTHEW 16:18 (NKJV) (continued):

"… and on this rock I will build My church,"

What rock is "this rock?" Yeshua (Jesus) was replying to Peter's statement, "You are the Messiah (Christ), the Son of the living God (Matthew 16:16)." This faithful answer is the rock that Yeshua (Jesus) built His church on.

Peter was not a reliable rock. Shortly after these statements were made, Peter would go on to lose faith and deny Yeshua (Jesus) three times (Matthew 26:69-75; Mark 14:66-72; Luke 22:54-62).

MATTHEW 16:18 (NKJV) (continued):

"… I will build My church,"

Yeshua (Jesus) said that He would build His church, not the church of Peter.

What is the church that Yeshua (Jesus) built? It was not the Roman Catholic Church or any other denomination. It was not an actual church building.

COLOSSIANS 1:24 (NKJV):

I now rejoice in my sufferings for you, and fill up in my flesh what is lacking in the afflictions of Messiah (Christ), for the sake of HIS BODY, WHICH IS THE CHURCH,…

'Church' is more properly translated 'assembly.' His body of believers who have faith in Yeshua (Jesus) and congregate together are the church, are the assembly. Even when just two or three believers are gathered in His name, He is there in the midst of them (Matthew 18:20).

MATTHEW 16:18 (NKJV) (continued):

"... I will build My church, and the gates of hell shall not prevail against it."

The Catholic Church has applied Yeshua's (Jesus') words to itself, "The gates of hell shall not prevail against *the Catholic Church.*"

The Catholic Church has persecuted millions of Messianic and Christian believers throughout millennia during the Dark Middle Ages in Europe. The actual amount of people killed by the Catholic Church during the medieval period is not fully known, but it is estimated to be between 100 - 150 million people. The Catholic Church has functioned as the gates of hell in its inquisitions, persecutions, and executions of believers in Yeshua Messiah (Jesus Christ) during its bloody history.

Although Satan has used the Catholic Church to persecute true believers in Yeshua (Jesus), it shall not prevail against them (Revelation 17:6). The Catholic Church did not prevent the true gospel from going forth. The gates of hell (death) will not prevail against the martyred saints, who will be resurrected to eternal life in the age to come.

As for the Roman Catholic Church, it is Mystery Babylon - the harlot woman (church), and the gates of hell (the nations of the beast) will prevail against it as a judgment from Yeshua (Jesus) (Revelation 17).

MATTHEW 16:19 (NKJV):

"And I will give you the keys of the kingdom of heaven…"

Peter was not handed literal keys to open the doors of the Catholic Church.

The keys to the kingdom of heaven is the gospel (good news) of Yeshua Messiah (Jesus Christ) that Peter and the other apostles were entrusted with to share with all the nations (Matthew 28:18-20). The keys open the door, which is Yeshua (Jesus), by which we enter heaven.

JOHN 10:7-9 (NKJV):

Then Yeshua (Jesus) said to them again, "Most assuredly, I say to you, I AM THE DOOR of the sheep. All who ever came before Me are thieves and robbers, but the sheep did not hear them. I AM THE DOOR. If anyone enters by Me, he will be saved..."

JOHN 14:6 (NKJV):

Yeshua (Jesus) said to him, "I am the way, the truth, and the life. No one comes to the Father except through Me."

MATTHEW 16:19 (NKJV) (continued):

"… and whatever you bind on earth will be bound in heaven, and whatever you loose on earth will be loosed in heaven."

We are not permitted to bind or unbind God's eternal, everlasting, perpetual laws. Yeshua (Jesus) did not come to destroy His laws (Matthew 5:17-18), so neither can any denominational church, government institution, or man. The Catholic Church has declared that it has the authority to change God's laws based upon the authority given to Peter to "bind and loose."

DANIEL 7:25 (NKJV) [WITH INTERPRETATION]:

He [THE CATHOLIC POPE] shall speak pompous words against the Most High, shall persecute saints of the Most High, and shall *intend* to change times and law.

Catholic popes past, present, and future are referenced in Daniel 7:25. It is the Catholic pope and the Catholic Church that have persecuted true biblical Messianic and Christian saints throughout their history, while hypocritically proclaiming that they are the persecuted ones and that the gates of hell shall not prevail against them.

It is the Catholic pope who shall *intend* to change God's times and law. Scripture says "shall intend," because no Catholic pope can change God's times or God's law. God's times and law will not change by the edict or encyclical of a Catholic pope. God's times and laws are eternal and will not be abolished by any man (Matthew 5:17-18).

CATHOLIC CHURCH QUOTES:

"Perhaps the boldest thing, the most revolutionary change the church ever did happened in the first century. The holy day, the Sabbath, was changed from Saturday to Sunday not from any directions noted in the Scriptures, but from the Catholic Church's sense of its own power."
- Saint Catherine Catholic Church Sentinel, May 21, 1995.

"The Pope is of so great authority and power that he can modify, change, or interpret even divine laws."
- The Catholic Ferraris' Ecclesiastical Dictionary.

"We confess that the Pope has the power of altering Scriptures, or increasing and diminishing it, according to his will. We confess that the Holy Scripture is imperfect and a dead letter, until it is explained by the Supreme Pontiff and permitted by him to be read by lay people."
- Confessio Romano - Catholica, 'The Hungarian Confession of Faith' Art IV, I, and XXI.

"We frankly say, yes, the Catholic Church made this change, made this law [the Sunday Sabbath], as she made many other laws, for instance, the Friday abstinence, the unmarried priesthood, the laws concerning mixed marriages, the regulation of Catholic marriages and a thousand other laws."
- Peter R. Kraemer, Catholic Church Extension Society (1975), Chicago, IL.

"The authority of the church could therefore not be bound to the authority of the Scriptures, because the church had changed the Sabbath into Sunday, not by command of Christ, but by its own authority."
- Canon and Tradition Pg 263.

MATTHEW 5:17-18 (NKJV):

"DO NOT THINK THAT I CAME TO DESTROY THE LAW or the Prophets. I did not come to destroy but to fulfill. For assuredly, I say to you, till heaven and earth pass away, one jot or one tittle WILL BY NO MEANS PASS FROM THE LAW..."

Regarding binding and unbinding, what we are permitted to do is bind and unbind agreements, settle accounts, forgive debts, and forgive sins and trespasses committed against us.

DEUTERONOMY 15:1 (NKJV):

"At the end of every seven years you shall grant a release of debts. And this is the form of the release: Every creditor who has lent anything to his neighbor shall release it; he shall not require it of his neighbor or his brother, because it is called YHWH's (the Lord's) release..."

MATTHEW 18:18-35 (NKJV):

"Assuredly, I say to you, whatever you bind on earth will be bound in heaven, and whatever you loose on earth will be loosed in heaven.

Again I say to you that IF TWO OF YOU AGREE on earth concerning anything that they ask, it will be done for them by My Father in heaven. For where two or three are gathered together in My name, I am there in the midst of them."

Then Peter came to Him and said, "Lord, how often shall my brother sin against me, and I forgive him? Up to seven times?"

Yeshua (Jesus) said to him, "I do not say to you, up to seven times, but up to seventy times seven. Therefore the kingdom of heaven is like a certain king who wanted to SETTLE ACCOUNTS with his servants. And when he had begun to SETTLE ACCOUNTS, one was brought to him who owed him ten thousand talents. But as he was not able to pay, his master commanded that he be sold, with his wife and children and all that he had, and that payment be made. The servant therefore fell down before him, saying, 'Master, have patience with me, and I will pay you all.' Then the master of that servant was moved with compassion, released him, AND FORGAVE HIM THE DEBT.

"But that servant went out and found one of his fellow servants who owed him a hundred denarii; and he laid hands on him and took him by the throat, saying, 'Pay me what you owe!' So his fellow servant fell down at his feet and begged him, saying, 'Have patience with me, and I will pay you all.' And he would not, but went and threw him into prison till he should pay the debt. So when his fellow servants saw what had been done, they were very grieved, and came and told their master all that had been done. Then his master, after he had called him, said to him, 'You wicked servant! I FORGAVE YOU ALL THAT DEBT because you begged me. Should you not also have had compassion on your fellow servant, just as I had pity on you?' And his master was angry, and delivered him to the torturers until he should pay all that was due to him.

"So My heavenly Father also will do to you if each of you, from his heart, does not forgive his brother his trespasses."

MATTHEW 6:9-12 (NKJV):

"Our Father who is in heaven, holy is Your name. Your kingdom come, Your will be done on earth as it is in heaven. Give us this day our daily bread and FORGIVE US OUR DEBTS AS WE FORGIVE OUR DEBTORS."

LUKE 11:4 (NKJV):

"Our Father who is in heaven, holy is Your name. Your kingdom come, Your will be done on earth as it is in heaven. Give us this day our daily bread and FORGIVE US OUR SINS AS WE FORGIVE OUR DEBTORS."

In conclusion, a proper interpretation of Matthew 16:17-19 should be understood in the following manner:

MATTHEW 16:17-19 (NKJV) [WITH INTERPRETATION]:

Yeshua (Jesus) answered and said to him, "Blessed are you, Simon Bar-Jonah, for flesh and blood has not revealed this to you, but My Father who is in heaven. And I also say to you that you are Peter, and on this rock [FAITHFUL ANSWER] I will build My church [FOLLOWING], and the gates of hell [DEATH] shall not prevail against it. And I will give you the keys [GOSPEL] of the kingdom of heaven, and whatever [AGREEMENTS, DEBTS] you bind on earth will be bound in heaven, and whatever [AGREEMENTS, DEBTS, SINS, TRESPASSES] you loose on earth will be loosed in heaven."

SOLA SCRIPTURA, BY SCRIPTURE ALONE, IS SCRIPTURALLY SOUND DOCTRINE

By George Lujack

The Roman Catholic and Orthodox Churches teach that the Scriptures are not the only infallible source of Christian doctrine. In their view, 'the Church,' their denominational church, does not derive her certainty about all revealed truths from the Holy Scriptures alone. Both Scripture and tradition must be accepted and honored with equal sentiments of devotion and reverence. The Catholic Church actually elevates itself above the Scriptures, claiming to have authority over the Scriptures. No one or no church gets to decide the truth of Scripture. The truth is what it is. The leaders of the Catholic Church and Orthodox churches are the blind leading the blind (Matthew 15:14; Luke 6:39).

2 TIMOTHY 3:16-17 (NKJV):

ALL SCRIPTURE is given by inspiration of God, and is profitable for doctrine, for reproof, for correction, for instruction in righteousness, THAT THE MAN OF GOD MAY BE COMPLETE, thoroughly equipped for every good work.

complete:
Whole, having all that is necessary.[183]

ACTS 17:11 (NKJV):

They received the word with all readiness, and SEARCHED THE SCRIPTURES DAILY to find out whether these things were so.

Wise men of God today still search the Scriptures daily to find out whether the things being taught in Catholic and Protestant churches are true. Most often, they are NOT true. If men in the book of Acts searched the Scriptures daily to verify the truth of the preaching of the Apostle Paul, men today should likewise search the Scriptures daily to verify the truth of their local denominational church teachers.

ROMANS 16:25-27 (NKJV):

Now to Him who is able to establish you ACCORDING TO MY GOSPEL AND THE PREACHING OF YESHUA MESSIAH (JESUS CHRIST), according to the revelation of the mystery kept secret since the world began but now made manifest, AND BY THE PROPHETIC SCRIPTURES MADE KNOWN TO ALL NATIONS, ACCORDING TO THE COMMANDMENT OF THE EVERLASTING GOD, for obedience to the faith - to God, alone wise, be glory through Yeshua Messiah (Jesus Christ) forever.

Can tradition alter or overturn the commandments of Scripture?

Can we add laws and commandments to Scripture?

PROVERBS 30:6 (NKJV):

Do not add to His words, lest He rebuke you and you be found a liar.

MATTHEW 15:3,6,9 (NKJV):

He answered and said to them, "Why do you also transgress the commandment of God because of your tradition? …

Thus you have made the commandment of God of no effect by your tradition. …

And in vain they worship Me, teaching as doctrines the commandments of men."

COLOSSIANS 2:8 (NKJV):

Beware lest anyone cheat you through philosophy and empty deceit, according to the tradition of men, according to the basic principles of the world, and not according to Messiah (Christ).

Untaught and unstable lawless-minded persons twist the Scriptures to their own destruction (2 Peter 3:16). By Scripture alone is sound doctrine, but taking verses out of context and twisting Scripture is not sound. Scripture must be properly discerned by a precept upon precept (Isaiah 28:13), in context proper understanding, without twisting it to support a certain opinion. It is then that Scripture will make one wise for salvation.

SURROGATE MOTHER;
MARY WAS MESSIAH'S SURROGATE MOTHER

By George Lujack

"Hail Mary, *mother* of God?" Miriam (Mary) was NOT the biological mother of Yeshua (Jesus). Mary served God as a surrogate mother for the Messiah (Christ). This article will show that Yeshua (Jesus) was born into the world, without sin, through a surrogate birth to Mary.

LUKE 3:23 (NKJV):
Now Yeshua (Jesus) Himself began His ministry at about thirty years of age, being (as was supposed) the son of Joseph.

It has also (been supposed) by many that Yeshua (Jesus) was the biological Son of Mary.

The Catholic Church claims Jesus was born without original sin, because Mary was also free from the stain of original sin. 'Surro-gate' is one of the original false doctrines of the early Catholic Church. Referring to Mary as the 'Holy Mother of God,' as Catholics do, is bestowing undue honor and reverence upon Mary. God does not have a mother and God alone is holy. Scripture never refers to Mary as the "Holy Mother of God," and anyone who does so adds to Scripture.

Medical science has confirmed that a woman can serve as a surrogate mother, giving birth to a child who she is not related to. Yeshua (Jesus) did not inherit original sin, as all men do, because He was not the biological Child of Mary, but instead Mary was a righteous virgin - a maidservant (virgin-servant), who God chose to deliver the Messiah through by means of surrogate birth.

Mary was a sinner in need of a Savior. If Mary were the Immaculate Conception, a woman free from sin, then she herself would not need a Savior.

LUKE 1:46-48 (NKJV):
And Mary said: "My soul magnifies the Lord, and my spirit has rejoiced in God my Savior. For He has regarded the lowly state of His maidservant;"

Yeshua (Jesus) is the Immaculate Conception, a title that He does not go by in Scripture, which is a title that the Catholic Church wrongfully bestowed upon Mary. Yeshua (Jesus) was immaculately conceived by the Holy Spirit that overshadowed Mary and placed Yeshua (Jesus) inside of her. Mary served God as a SURROGATE MOTHER maidservant (virgin-servant). Scripture fully supports Yeshua's (Jesus') surrogate birth.

MATTHEW 1:18-20 (NKJV):

Now the birth of Yeshua Messiah (Jesus Christ) was as follows: After His mother Mary was betrothed to Joseph, before they came together, she was found with Child of the Holy Spirit. Then Joseph her husband, being a just man, and not wanting to make her a public example, was minded to put her away secretly. But while he thought about these things, behold, an angel of YHWH (the Lord) appeared to him in a dream, saying, "Joseph, son of David, do not be afraid to take to you Mary your wife, FOR THAT WHICH IS CONCEIVED IN HER IS OF THE HOLY SPIRIT."

TRANSLATION (Message to Joseph):

Do not be concerned to take Mary, your wife. The Child inside her is not hers; it was placed inside her by the Holy Spirit and is of God, not of another man, or of Mary.

God the Father through the Holy Spirit did NOT fertilize Mary's egg. If God the Father through the Holy Spirit fertilized Mary's egg, that would make God the Father an adulterer, for Mary was the BETROTHED WIFE of Joseph (Matthew 1:18; Luke 1:26-27, 2:4-5). Even if one considered Joseph and Mary not officially married at that point, it still would make God the Father a fornicator and Yeshua (Jesus) would have been born a bastard, the product of a union between 2-unmarried beings and a crossbreed between God and man.

The Holy Spirit did not impregnate Mary. Some falsely believe that the Holy Spirit is a being of the Trinity and the spiritual husband of Mary. Catholics have traditionally taught that the Holy Spirit was Mary's husband and Joseph and Mary were married, but remained celibate throughout their marriage. Joseph knew Mary after Yeshua (Jesus) was born and they had other children together, which proves this belief to be false.

SON OF GOD AND SON OF MAN

1 CORINTHIANS 15:45,47 (NKJV):

And so it is written, "The first man Adam became a living being." The LAST ADAM became a life-giving spirit. The first man was of the earth, made of dust; the second Man is the Lord FROM HEAVEN.

Yeshua (Jesus) was miraculously placed inside Mary and was born to her as the last Adam. Yeshua (Jesus) was not born as other men are born. He was in existence before His birth and came down from His heavenly glory to be born into the world (John 3:13,31,6:33,38,41,42,51,58).

Adam had no mother. Adam was from the Earth and the Lord was from heaven, not Miriam (Mary).

SON OF MAN, NOT THE BIOLOGICAL SON OF MAN

An objection made by some people is that if Yeshua (Jesus) was not the biological Child of Mary, then He was not fully man. This is an illegitimate assumption.

Scripture clearly proclaims that Yeshua (Jesus) was the last Adam. Adam was fully man, yet he was not biologically descended from mankind. Yeshua (Jesus) was the last Adam, and like Adam, He also was not biologically descended from man as the biological offspring of Mary. Scripture does NOT say that Yeshua (Jesus) was the *biological* Son of Man, but does state that He came into the world to be born *as* a Son of Man. Yeshua (Jesus) could not have been the biological Child of Mary, for then He would have inherited original sin from Mary, as Mary was a sinner in need of a Savior. Mary was not a sinless being.

MARY WAS NOT MADE SINLESS TO DELIVER YESHUA (JESUS)

A sinless Mary is unscriptural. There were no special graces bestowed upon Mary in order for her to deliver Yeshua (Jesus). Mary was a chosen righteous virgin (Luke 1:26-48). God did not remove sin from Mary in order for her to deliver Yeshua (Jesus), and He did not need to. The Holy Spirit alone, NOT the Holy Spirit *and* Mary, conceived the Child who was inside Mary (Matthew 1:20). Yeshua (Jesus) was delivered by a righteous virgin, who was a sinner in need of a Savior (Luke 1:48). Yeshua (Jesus) entered into a sinful world through a righteous, but not free from sin, vessel. It was not necessary that Mary be sinless in order for her to deliver a sinless being, as she served God as a surrogate mother in delivering the Savior into the world.

If, hypothetically, sin was miraculously removed from Mary, before she bore Yeshua (Jesus) as His biological mother, then God could remove sin from all sinners and Yeshua (Jesus) would have suffered and died needlessly as a Savior for mankind. Yeshua (Jesus) prayed to the Father, asking Him before His arrest, torture, and crucifixion if it were possible to let the cup pass from Him - the cup to pay the penalty for the sins of man. It was not possible for God to save mankind without Yeshua's (Jesus') atonement sacrifice and Yeshua (Jesus) carried out His Father's will (Matthew 26:39-42). It was likewise not possible that Mary was created free from original sin, or that sin was miraculously removed from her in order for her to be the biological mother of Yeshua (Jesus).

YESHUA (JESUS) EXERTED GODLY AUTHORITY OVER MARY AND DID NOT VERBALLY ACKNOWLEDGE HER AS HIS MOTHER

MATTHEW 12:46-50; MARK 3:31-35; LUKE 8:19-21 (NKJV):

While He was still talking to the multitudes, behold, His mother and brothers stood outside, seeking to speak with Him. Then one said to Him, "Look, Your mother and Your brothers are standing outside, seeking to speak with You." But He answered and said to the one who told Him, "Who is My mother and who are My brothers?" And He stretched out His hand toward His disciples and said, "Here are My mother and My brothers!

For whoever does the will of My Father in heaven is My brother and sister and mother."

JOHN 2:4, 19:26-27 (NKJV):

Yeshua (Jesus) said to her [MARY], "Woman, what does your concern have to do with Me? My hour has not yet come."

...

When Yeshua (Jesus) therefore saw His mother, and the disciple whom He loved standing by, He said to His mother, "Woman, behold your son!" Then He said to the disciple, "Behold *your* mother!"

YESHUA (JESUS) WAS MELCHIZEDEK

HEBREWS 7:1-3 (NKJV):

For this Melchizedek, king of Salem, priest of the Most High God, who met Abraham returning from the slaughter of the kings and blessed him, to whom also Abraham gave a tenth part of all, first being translated "king of righteousness," and then also king of Salem, meaning "king of peace," WITHOUT FATHER, WITHOUT MOTHER, WITHOUT GENEALOGY, having neither beginning of days nor end of life, but made unto the Son of God, remains a priest continually.

Melchizedek literally means King of Righteousness in the Hebrew language. Yeshua (Jesus) is identified as Melchizedek, without father, without mother, without genealogy. Yeshua (Jesus) has a spiritual biological Father (God the Father), of whom He was begotten from (John 1:14,18, 3:16,18; Hebrews 11:17; 1 John 4:9), but not an earthly biological father or mother.

Yeshua's (Jesus') first appearance on Earth was not as the Messiah (Christ). Yeshua (Jesus) is YHWH (the Lord God) and He walked in the Garden of Eden with Adam and Eve (Genesis 3:8). Yeshua (Jesus) said, "Before Abraham was, I Am" (John 8:58), clearly indicating that He was in existence as YHWH (the Lord). Yeshua (Jesus) was Melchizedek, priest of the Most High God, and met with Abraham (Genesis 14:18-19).

There were only 2-beings among all mankind who have appeared on Earth that had no earthly biological father, no earthly biological mother, and no earthly genealogy: Adam and Yeshua (Jesus). Eve was created from Adam's rib so she shares Adam's genealogy, as she was bone of his bones and flesh of his flesh (Genesis 2:21-23).

Yeshua (Jesus) chose to enter the world through the lineage of the house of David (Matthew 1:1-17), but DENIES His mistaken BIOLOGICAL genealogy, declaring that He is NOT a biological descendant of King David:

MATTHEW 22:41-45; MARK 12:35-37; LUKE 20:41-44 (NKJV):

While the Pharisees were gathered together, Yeshua (Jesus) asked them, saying, "What do you think about the Messiah? Whose Son is He?"

They said to Him, "The Son of David." He said to them, "How then does David in the Spirit call Him 'Lord,' saying: 'The Lord said to my Lord, "Sit at My right hand, till I make Your enemies Your footstool"'? If David then calls Him 'Lord,' HOW IS HE HIS SON?"

Translation:

"If David then calls Him "Lord," HOW IS HE HIS DESCENDANT?"

Yeshua (Jesus) is the Son of God and NOT the biological Son of Mary. Yeshua (Jesus) didn't have half-brothers and half-sisters as many believe. Yeshua's (Jesus') brothers and sisters mentioned in Scripture (Matthew 12:46-47, 13:55-56; Mark 3:31-32, 6:3; Luke 8:19-20; John 2:12; Acts 1:14) are the sons and daughters of Joseph and Mary, the earthly stepbrothers and stepsisters of Yeshua (Jesus) and not His biological siblings.

WHAT IS THE BREAD OF LIFE?

By George Lujack

This article will argue that Yeshua (Jesus) Himself is the bread of life and that the bread of life is NOT some man-made circular communion disc wafer, blessed by a priest, that believers consume.

JOHN 6:35 (NKJV):

And Yeshua (Jesus) said to them, "I AM the bread of life. He who comes to Me shall never hunger, and he who believes in Me shall never thirst."

JOHN 6:53 (NKJV):

Then Yeshua (Jesus) said to them, "Most assuredly, I say to you, unless you eat the flesh of the Son of Man and drink His blood, you have no life in you."

Are the words of Yeshua (Jesus) from John 6:53 to be taken figuratively or literally?

The Catholic Church and some of her daughter Protestant churches take these words literally. This literal interpretation forms the foundation for the Catholic Church's Transubstantiation Doctrine - the miraculous changing of bread and wine into the actual flesh and blood of Jesus Christ (Yeshua Messiah), consumed by the believer who partakes in communion.

The Catholic priest is proclaimed to have the power to call Jesus Christ (Yeshua Messiah) down from heaven into the communion wafer during Catholic mass. Catholics are told to believe that when they consume the man-made communion wafer and drink a goblet of wine during their mass, they are actually eating the miraculously transformed literal flesh and blood of Jesus Christ (Yeshua Messiah). This belief is a central tenet of the Catholic faith.

If consuming the LITERAL body and blood of Yeshua Messiah (Jesus Christ) is necessary for salvation, as Catholics claim, then the whole world must become Catholic if they wish to be saved and to escape the wrath of God. On the other hand, if Yeshua Messiah (Jesus Christ) was speaking in figurative language, which He often did, then the Transubstantiation Doctrine is nothing more than a deceptive hoax imposed upon Catholics for the purpose of keeping them in bondage and servitude to the Catholic Church.

JOHN 16:25 (NKJV):

"These things I have spoken to you in FIGURATIVE LANGUAGE; but the time is coming when I will no longer speak to you in figurative language, but I will tell you plainly about the Father."

Yeshua (Jesus) spent much of His Messianic mission speaking in figurative language.

Yeshua's (Jesus') statement that one must eat His flesh and drink His blood MUST be understood in a figurative sense.

LEVITICUS 11:4 (NKJV):

Among the animals, whatever divides the hoof, having cloven hooves and chewing the cud - that you may eat.

Yeshua Messiah (Jesus Christ) did not have divided hooves and He did not chew the cud. We cannot eat His flesh according to His own dietary law. To eat human or divine flesh would make us cannibals.

LEVITICUS 3:17 (NKJV):

It shall be a PERPETUAL STATUTE for your generations throughout all your dwellings, that you shall eat neither fat nor blood.

What part of perpetual do people not understand? We are never permitted, throughout all our generations, to consume blood. To do so, to literally consume human or divine blood, would make people vampires. Yet the Catholic Church would have us believe that we must consume the literal blood of Jesus Christ (Yeshua Messiah).

The Transubstantiation Doctrine has been modified by the Catholic Church to mean that the communion wafer sacrifice is a 'bloodless' sacrifice. The Catholic Church offers up the Eucharist as a bloodless sacrifice.

God does not respect bloodless sacrifices to atone for sin.

GENESIS 4:3-4 (NKJV):

And in the process of time it came to pass that Cain brought an offering of the fruit of the ground to YHWH (the Lord). Abel also brought of the firstborn of his flock and of their fat. And YHWH (the Lord) respected Abel and his offering, but He did not respect Cain and his offering.

YHWH (the Lord) rejected Cain's offering because it did not meet God's sacrificial requirements for atonement, while YHWH (the Lord) respected Abel's offering because it met God's sacrificial requirements for atonement (Genesis 8:20; Leviticus 1, 17:11).

A Catholic priest offers the Eucharist up as a bloodless offering, in the same manner that Cain brought an offering of fruit to YHWH (the Lord). YHWH (the Lord) did not respect Cain and his bloodless offering and YHWH (the Lord) does not respect the bloodless offering known as the Eucharist.

LUKE 22:19-20 (NKJV):

And He took bread, gave thanks and broke it, and gave it to them, saying, "This is My body which is given for you; DO THIS IN REMEMBRANCE OF ME." Likewise He also took the cup after supper, saying, "This cup is the new covenant in My blood, which is shed for you…"

At His last Passover meal with His disciples, commonly called the Last Supper, Yeshua (Jesus) declared, "Do this in remembrance of Me." Do what in remembrance of Him? Celebrate the Passover in remembrance of Him!

1 CORINTHIANS 5:7 (NKJV):

For indeed Messiah (Christ), our Passover, was sacrificed for us.

Yeshua the Messiah (Jesus the Christ) IS the New Passover. In God's final plague against the Egyptians in the Exodus from Egypt, the Hebrews were commanded to cover their doorposts with sacrificed lamb's blood, so that the angel of death would 'pass over' their households (Exodus 12:21-27).

ROMANS 3:23-26 (NKJV):

For all have sinned and fall short of the glory of God, being justified freely by His grace through the redemption that is in Messiah Yeshua (Christ Jesus), whom God set forth as a propitiation BY HIS BLOOD, through faith, to demonstrate His righteousness, because in His forbearance God had PASSED OVER the sins that were previously committed, to demonstrate at the present time His righteousness, that He might be just and the justifier of the one who has faith in Yeshua (Jesus).

We honor and remember the Lord Yeshua's (Jesus') sacrifice for us, and accept His shed blood for our sins, as His blood covers our transgressions. Yeshua (Jesus) took the righteous punishment of God for our sins upon Himself. His shed blood covers our transgressions, so that God's judgment 'passes over' us, so that we can attain eternal life.

Animal sacrifices, the killing of Scripturally clean mammals and birds and spilling of their blood, was a measure to temporarily atone for sin, but could never permanently take away sin (Leviticus 1). It was a temporary measure, a foreshadowing of the shedding of the blood of Yeshua the Messiah (Jesus the Christ), who permanently took away the sins of the world. We don't sacrifice animals today, as this measure has been rendered obsolete (Hebrews 10).

The grain offerings that temple priests prepared and ate of was symbolic of Yeshua's (Jesus') body shed for us and was a foreshadowing of the true Bread of Life who would offer His body for us (Leviticus 2).

JOHN 6:48-51 (NKJV):

"I am the bread of life. Your fathers ate the manna in the wilderness, and are dead. This is the bread which comes down from heaven, that one may eat of it and not die. I AM THE LIVING BREAD which came down from heaven. If anyone eats of this bread, he will live forever; and the bread that I shall give is My flesh, which I shall give for the life of the world."

What is this living bread that Yeshua Messiah (Jesus Christ) spoke of? What is this 'bread' we should eat to have life? Is it a weekly man-made communion wafer? NO! Yeshua (Jesus) is the 'bread' and His words are life, not some man-made communion wafer that Catholics and Protestants bow down to and receive before unscriptural priests, pastors, and reverends. Yeshua (Jesus) is the bread that came down from heaven. It is this spiritual bread, His words, which we must eat (believe and walk in) to have life.

JOHN 6:63 (NKJV):

"It is the Spirit that gives life; the flesh profits nothing. THE WORDS THAT I SPEAK TO YOU ARE SPIRIT, AND *THEY* ARE LIFE."

Yeshua the Messiah (Jesus the Christ) declares that the flesh profits nothing, yet many falsely believe that they must consume a man-made communion wafer and receive Him *AS* FLESH.

The Eucharist communion wafer is NOT the living bread that we must eat to have eternal life. Yeshua (Jesus) is the Bread of Life; His words are life.

PURGATORY DEBUNKED

By George Lujack

Purgatory, according to Catholic Church doctrine and theology, is an intermediate place or state after physical death in which those destined for heaven "undergo purification, so as to achieve the holiness necessary to enter the joy of heaven." This article will debunk the purgatory myth and expose the real deceitful reasons that the Catholic Church teaches purgatory.

The word 'purgatory' does not appear in Scripture. Purgatory is simply a made up doctrine of the Roman Catholic Church.

1 JOHN 1:7,9 (NKJV):

If we walk in the light as He is in the light, we have fellowship with one another, and the blood of Yeshua Messiah (Jesus Christ) His Son CLEANSES US FROM *ALL* SIN. …

If we confess our sins, He is faithful and just to forgive us our sins and to CLEANSE US FROM *ALL* UNRIGHTEOUSNESS.

The theology of purgatory denies the all-sufficient and once and forever sacrificed blood of Yeshua (Jesus) to atone for us and cleanse us from *all* sin and *all* unrighteousness (Hebrews 7:27, 9:12).

MATTHEW 23:14 (NKJV):

Woe to you, scribes and Pharisees, hypocrites! For you devour widows' houses, and for a pretense make long prayers. Therefore you will receive greater condemnation.

MARK 12:38-40; LUKE 20:45-47 (NKJV):

Then Yeshua (Jesus) said to them in His teaching, "Beware of the scribes, who desire to go around in long robes, love greetings in the marketplaces, the best seats in the synagogues, and the best places at feasts, who devour widows' houses, and for a pretense make long prayers. These will receive greater condemnation."

Yeshua (Jesus) was addressing the Jewish religious leaders of His time, but the substance of His words applies to Catholic priests and bishops throughout millennia. Catholic clergy love going around in long robes, love being greeted at the marketplaces, and love the best seats in churches, and the best places at events and feasts. Using the Catholic doctrine of purgatory, they devour widows' houses, incomes, and inheritances.

The Catholic Church teaches that the fate of those suffering in purgatory can be affected by the actions of the living.

What is purgatory?

Purgatory is the state of those who die in God's friendship, assured of their eternal salvation, but who still have need of purification to enter the happiness of heaven.

How can we help the souls being purified in purgatory?

Because of the communion of saints, the faithful who are still pilgrims on earth are able to help the souls in purgatory by offering prayers in suffrage for them, especially the Eucharistic sacrifice. They also help them by almsgiving, indulgences, and works of penance.
- Catechism of the Catholic Church, 1992

Many deceived Catholics, widows, and other grieving family members, have forked over substantial sums of money to the Catholic Church, and continue to do so to this day, to spare their loved ones from the torment and purification of purgatory and buy their way into heaven instead.

Silly Cathodes! The blood of Yeshua (Jesus) purifies us from all sin. No one can be purified of sin in a place or state called purgatory, nor can one atone for his or her sins through penance, nor can someone else purchase another's entrance into heaven by giving alms (cash) to the Catholic Church.

1 CORINTHIANS 15:50-52 (NKJV) (HSV†):

Now this I say, brethren, that flesh and blood cannot inherit the kingdom of God (†reign of Elohim); nor does corruption inherit incorruption.

Behold, I tell you a mystery: We shall not all sleep, but WE SHALL ALL BE CHANGED - in a moment, in the twinkling of an eye, at the last trumpet. For the trumpet will sound, and the dead will be raised incorruptible, and WE SHALL ALL BE CHANGED.

Scripture rejects a place or a state called purgatory to perfectly purify the souls of the righteous saints before entering heaven. The dead in Messiah (Christ) are in a state of sleep (unconsciousness), not in a state of purgatory. At the last trumpet, the dead in Messiah (Christ) will be raised and the living saints will be raptured and miraculously changed from corrupted beings into incorruptible beings, without the use of the flames of purgatory, in an instant, in the twinkling of an eye.

COMMON CATHOLIC AND PROTESTANT PRAYERS AND HOW TO PRAY PROPERLY

By George Lujack

This article will address some common Catholic and Protestant (protesting Catholic) prayers and will offer critical analysis and commentary on them. The article will also show believers how Scripture instructs them to pray.

THE SERENITY PRAYER:

God grant me the serenity to accept the things I cannot change;
Courage to change the things I can;
And wisdom to know the difference.
Living one day at a time;
Enjoying one moment at a time;
Accepting hardships as the pathway to peace;
Taking, as He did, this sinful world as it is, not as I would have it;
Trusting that He will make all things right if I surrender to His Will;
So that I may be reasonably happy in this life and supremely happy with Him
Forever and ever in the next. Amen.
- Reinhold Niebuhr, Protestant (1892-1971)

The portion of the Serenity Prayer asking God for acceptance, courage, and wisdom is most commonly excerpted from the prayer and shared:

God grant me the serenity to accept the things I cannot change;
Courage to change the things I can; and wisdom to know the difference.

Prayers for wisdom are proper and excerpting this section from the whole of the Serenity Prayer is prudent.

SCRIPTURE DECLARES:

King Solomon requested wisdom from God.

2 CHRONICLES 1:7-12 (NKJV):

On that night God appeared to Solomon, and said to him, "Ask! What shall I give you?"

And Solomon said to God: "You have shown great mercy to David my father, and have made me king in his place. Now, O YHWH (Lord) God, let Your promise to David my father be established, for You have made me king over a people like the dust of the earth in multitude. Now give me wisdom and knowledge, that I may go out and come in before this people; for who can judge this great people of Yours?"

Then God said to Solomon: "Because this was in your heart, and you have not asked riches or wealth or honor or the life of your enemies, nor have you asked long life - but have asked wisdom and knowledge for yourself, that you may judge My people over whom I have made you king - wisdom and knowledge are granted to you; and I will give you riches and wealth and honor, such as none of the kings have had who were before you, nor shall any after you have the like."

The whole of the Serenity Prayer, apart from the excerpted prayer for wisdom, is a defeatist, give up, faithless, white flag surrender prayer. It denies the power of God through His Holy Spirit to do wondrous things.

Here are some excerpts from the prayer:

* *"God grant me the serenity to accept the things I cannot change,"*
* *"Accepting hardships as the pathway to peace,"*
* *"Taking, as He did, this sinful world as it is, not as I would have it;"*
* *"So that I may be reasonably happy in this life."*

Comparing the Serenity Prayer with Scripture:

SERENITY PRAYER:

"God grant me the serenity to accept the things I cannot change…"

It is unclear what the author meant here in asking God for serenity in things he could not change.
If he was asking to be at peace for the loss of a loved one due to death, or to accept other things decreed by God through Scripture, then this is understandable. If the author was asking God for serenity to accept bad circumstances that he felt he *or God* could not change, then this is a weak, faithless request of God.

Why would any believer in God pray to accept bad things that they, or God, supposedly could not change?

SCRIPTURE DECLARES:

MARK 10:27 (NKJV):

For with God all things are possible.

MATTHEW 17:20 (NKJV):

So Yeshua (Jesus) said to them, "Because of your unbelief; for assuredly, I say to you, if you have faith as a mustard seed, you will say to this mountain, 'Move from here to there,' and it will move; and nothing will be impossible for you."

PHILIPPIANS 4:13 (NKJV):

I can do all things through Messiah (Christ) who strengthens me.

SERENITY PRAYER:

"Accepting hardships as the pathway to peace,"

The acceptance of hardships as a pathway to peace is the acceptance of bondage, not a path to peace at all.

The acceptance of hardships is a hindrance to peace. Should believers not pray to God and not try to solve their hardships, to free themselves from burdens? If we accept hardships, how can we expect God to deliver us from them? When the Hebrew people were living in slavery to the Egyptians, they prayed for a deliverer to free them from their hardships and bondage (Exodus 3:7,6:5,18:8).

SCRIPTURE DECLARES:

MATTHEW 11:28 (NKJV):

"Come to Me, all you who labor and are heavy laden, and I will give you rest."

LUKE 1:78-79 (NKJV):

Give light to those who sit in darkness and the shadow of death, to guide our feet into the way of peace.

SERENITY PRAYER:

"Taking, as He did, this sinful world as it is, not as I would have it;"

Did Yeshua (Jesus) merely take this sinful world as it is and not as He would have it? In one sense He did when He declared, "My kingdom is not of this world" (John 18:36). When Yeshua (Jesus) came as the Messiah, He did not come to take the world as it is, He came to change it. He called on people to repent. He came to change the state of the world, to die to atone for the sins of mankind, and to bear witness to the truth. We, as believers, have been given the Great Commission to spread the Gospel. We, as believers, should not be wallowing around in misery over the state of the sinful world, but instead we should be acting as positive agents, as the lights of the world to be fishers of men's souls.

SCRIPTURE DECLARES:

MATTHEW 4:17 (NKJV):

From that time Yeshua (Jesus) began to preach and to say, "Repent, for the kingdom of heaven is at hand."

JOHN 18:37 (NKJV):

Yeshua (Jesus) answered, "You say rightly that I am a king. For this cause I was born, and for this cause I have come into the world, that I should bear witness to the truth. Everyone who is of the truth hears My voice."

MATTHEW 28:19-20 (NKJV):

"Go therefore and make disciples of all the nations, baptizing them in the name of the Father and of the Son and of the Holy Spirit, teaching them to observe all things that I have commanded you; and lo, I am with you always, even to the end of the age."

MATTHEW 5:14-16 (NKJV):

"You are the light of the world. A city that is set on a hill cannot be hidden. Nor do they light a lamp and put it under a basket, but on a lampstand, and it gives light to all who are in the house. Let your light so shine before men, that they may see your good works and glorify your Father in heaven."

MATTHEW 4:19; MARK 1:17 (NKJV):

Yeshua (Jesus) said, "Follow Me, and I will make you fishers of men."

SERENITY PRAYER:

"So that I may be reasonably happy in this life."

Should believers be *reasonably happy* in this life? As believers in Yeshua Messiah (Jesus Christ), having knowledge of the Scriptures and knowing our destiny as future sons and daughters of the Most High God (2 Corinthians 6:18), we should be bursting with joy and overwhelmed with happiness!

Bad circumstances happen to believers. Sometimes God's people are unlawfully imprisoned or martyred. Yet even so, the Apostle Paul declared that if he were to die, he knew he would gain the kingdom and in his next conscious moment he would be standing before God in glory. For Him to live was joy in Messiah (Christ) and if he were to die he knew he would gain the kingdom (Philippians 1:21).

SCRIPTURE DECLARES:

PSALM 144:15 (NKJV):

Happy are the people whose God is YHWH (the Lord)!

PROVERBS 3:13 (NKJV):

Happy is the man who finds wisdom, and the man who gains understanding.

PROVERBS 29:18 (NKJV):

Happy is he who keeps the law.

JOHN 10:10 (NKJV):

I have come that they may have life, and that they may have it more abundantly.

'The Serenity Prayer,' the entirety of it, should be more aptly named, 'The *Surrender* Prayer.'

THE SINNER'S PRAYER:

Dear Lord Jesus, I know that I am a sinner, and I ask for your forgiveness.
I believe you died for my sins and rose from the dead.
I turn from my sins and invite You to come into my heart and life.
I want to trust You as my Lord and Savior.
In Your Name. Amen.

The problem with the Sinner's Prayer is not so much the prayer itself; it is fine. It acknowledges that one is a sinner in need of a Savior and it confirms that the person praying it promises to turn from his or her sins.

The problem with the Sinner's Prayer is with the false assurances many people give with it concerning the prayer. Many ministers say, "If you prayed the Sinner's Prayer, it means you are saved and are now part of the family of God." Many use the Sinner's Prayer to promote the 'Once Saved, Always Saved' false doctrine. Many people falsely assume that by merely reciting the Sinner's Prayer salvation is attained and guaranteed.

One must continue in the walk called for by the Sinner's Prayer, which means to turn from one's sins and live righteously.

SCRIPTURE DECLARES:

MATTHEW 10:22, 24:13; MARK 13:13 (NKJV):
"But he who endures to the end will be saved."

No one is saved the moment they recite the Sinner's Prayer, as no one is yet saved. He or she who endures in righteousness to the end, of the age or his or her life, will be (shall be - future tense) saved. If we live righteously and believe upon Yeshua (Jesus) for our salvation, we can live with the assurance that we will be saved.

2 CORINTHIANS 13:4 (NKJV):
Examine yourselves as to whether you are in the faith. Test yourselves. Do you not know yourselves, that Yeshua Messiah (Jesus Christ) is in you?

1 JOHN 2:3-6 (NKJV):
Now by this we know that we know Him, if we keep His commandments. He who says, "I know Him," and does not keep His commandments, is a liar, and the truth is not in him. But whoever keeps His word, truly the love of God is perfected in him. By this we know that we are in Him. He who says he abides in Him ought himself also to walk just as He walked.

Another commentary made by many ministers is that we are all hopeless sinners. While we all would be hopeless sinners if it were not for the free gift of salvation provided for us by God, the phrase 'hopeless sinner(s)' does not appear in Scripture. We should not look upon ourselves as hopeless sinners, but hopeful saints, former sinners looking forward to the promises of Almighty God.

SCRIPTURE DECLARES:

ROMANS 8:23-24 (NKJV):

Not only that, but we also who have the firstfruits of the Spirit, even we ourselves groan within ourselves, eagerly waiting for the adoption, the redemption of our body. For we were saved in this hope.

1 PETER 3:15 (NKJV):

But sanctify the Lord God in your hearts, and always be ready to give a defense to everyone who asks you a reason for the hope that is in you.

As faithful believing saints of Almighty God, we should not think of ourselves as being hopeless and of things as being impossible. He has empowered us to conquer obstacles in our life and to have power over our spiritual enemies.

MATTHEW 17:20 (NKJV):

So Yeshua (Jesus) said to them, "Because of your unbelief; for assuredly, I say to you, if you have faith as a mustard seed, you will say to this mountain, 'Move from here to there,' and it will move; and nothing will be impossible for you."

LUKE 10:19-20 (NKJV):

"Behold, I give you the authority to trample on serpents and scorpions, and over all the power of the enemy, and nothing shall by any means hurt you. Nevertheless do not rejoice in this, that the spirits are subject to you, but rather rejoice because your names are written in heaven."

CATHOLIC PRAYERS

Some of the most anti-Scriptural prayers are those that were introduced by the Roman Catholic Church. A complete list of man-made Catholic prayers is far too vast to cover in a single article, but many of the same errors recur throughout the Catholic faith, which is reflected in its repetitive prayers, as shown in the following examples. Catholics pray to Mary, angels, and dead saints. Catholics glorify and praise their church and declare it to be the holy institution that Jesus Christ founded.

ANIMA CHRISTI:

Soul of Christ, make me holy, Body of Christ, be my salvation
Blood of Christ, let me drink your wine
Water flowing from the side of Christ, wash me clean
Passion of Christ, strengthen me, Kind Jesus, hear my prayer
Hide me within your wounds, And keep me close to you
Defend me from the evil enemy, And call me at the hour of my death
To the fellowship of your saints, That I may sing your praise with them for all eternity. Amen.

The Catholic Church through the Anima Christi prayer teaches that when believers die they go straight to heaven to have communion and fellowship with the saints.

SCRIPTURE DECLARES:

JOHN 6:39-40 (NKJV):

"This is the will of the Father who sent Me, that of all He has given Me I should lose nothing, but should raise it up AT THE LAST DAY. And this is the will of Him who sent Me, that everyone who sees the Son and believes in Him may have everlasting life; and I WILL RAISE HIM UP AT THE LAST DAY."

Righteous believers who die in this age will not be going straight to heaven to have fellowship with others and sing praises to God. All are believers going to the grave and will remain unconscious in death until the resurrection of the dead, which will occur at the last day of grace, at the final trumpet (1 Corinthians 15:51-54; 1 Thessalonians 4:15-17).

THE APOSTLES' CREED:

I believe in God, the father Almighty, Creator of heaven and earth;

and in Jesus Christ, His only Son, Our Lord,

Who was conceived by the Holy Spirit, born of the Virgin Mary,

suffered under Pontius Pilate, was crucified, died, and was buried.

He descended into Hell. The third day He arose again from the dead;

He ascended into Heaven, sitteth at the right hand of God, the Father Almighty;

from thence He shall come to judge the living and the dead.

I believe in the Holy Spirit, the holy Catholic Church, the communion of saints, the forgiveness of sins, the resurrection of the body, and the life everlasting. Amen.

The Apostles' Creed was not written or recited by the apostles of Yeshua Messiah (Jesus Christ); it is a creation of the founders of the Roman Catholic Church. The Catholic Church is not holy, and the mention of it being so in the Apostles' Creed is a self-serving, self-glorifying statement.

SCRIPTURE DECLARES:

1 CORINTHIANS 3:16-17 (NKJV):

Do you not know that you are the temple of God and that the Spirit of God dwells in you? If anyone defiles the temple of God, God will destroy him. For the temple of God is holy, which temple you are.

We believers are the temple of God. The Spirit of God dwells in us and makes us holy, not the Catholic Church, an institution of men.

GLORY BE:

Glory be to the Father, and to the Son, and to the Holy Spirit,

as it was in the beginning, is now, and ever shall be, world without end. Amen.

The world is not the same now, as it was in the beginning, nor shall it remain as it is now.

SCRIPTURE DECLARES:

2 PETER 3:3-7 (NKJV):

Scoffers will come in the last days, walking according to their own lusts, and saying, "Where is the promise of His coming? For since the fathers fell asleep, ALL THINGS CONTINUE AS THEY WERE FROM THE BEGINNING OF CREATION." For this they willfully forget: that by the word of God the heavens were of old, and the earth standing out of water and in the water, by which the world that then existed perished, being flooded with water. But the heavens and the earth which are now preserved by the same word, are reserved for fire until the day of judgment and perdition of ungodly men.

REVELATION 21:1 (NKJV):

Now I saw a new heaven AND A NEW EARTH, for the first heaven AND THE FIRST EARTH HAD PASSED AWAY. Also there was no more sea.

The Earth will be restored to its state before it was flooded in the great flood of Noah, in the Genesis account. The age of lawlessness and sin will end, when Yeshua (Jesus) returns to establish His Millennium Kingdom.

CATHOLIC PRAYERS TO MARY

THE ANGELIS:

The Angel of the Lord declared unto Mary.

And she conceived by the Holy Spirit. (Hail Mary....)

Behold the handmaid of the Lord.

Be it done unto me according to thy word. (Hail Mary....)

And the Word was made flesh. And dwelt among us. (Hail Mary....)

Pray for us, O Holy Mother of God.

That we may be made worthy of the promises of Christ.

LET US PRAY: Pour forth, we beseech Thee, O Lord, Thy Grace into our hearts; that, we to whom the Incarnation of Christ, Thy Son, was made known by the message of an Angel, may by His Passion and Cross, be brought to the glory of His Resurrection through the same Christ our Lord. Amen.

HAIL HOLY QUEEN:

Hail Holy Queen, Mother of Mercy, our life, our sweetness and our hope. To thee do we cry, poor banished children of Eve: to thee we send up our sighs, mourning and weeping in this valley of tears. Turn then, most gracious Advocate, thine eyes of mercy toward us, and after this our exile, show us the blessed fruit of thy womb, Jesus.

O clement, O loving, O sweet Virgin Mary! Amen.

HAIL MARY:

Hail Mary, full of grace. The Lord is with thee. Blessed art thou amongst women, and blessed is the fruit of thy womb, Jesus. Holy Mary, Mother of God, pray for us sinners, now and at the hour of our death. Amen.

MEMORARE:

Remember, O most gracious Virgin Mary, that never was it known that any one who fled to thy protection, implored thy help or sought the intercession, was left unaided. Inspired by this confidence, We fly unto thee, O Virgin of virgins my Mother; to thee we do come, before thee we stand, sinful and sorrowful; O Mother of the World Incarnate, despise not our petitions, but in thy mercy hear and answer them. Amen.

MIRACULOUS MEDAL PRAYER:

O Mary, conceived without sin, pray for us who have recourse to thee, and for those who do not have recourse to thee, especially the enemies of the Church and those recommend to thee. Amen.

Mary did not conceive a Child, Yeshua (Jesus). That which was inside her, Yeshua (Jesus) was conceived *of the Holy Spirit*. Mary served God as a handmaiden, a virgin surrogate mother. Mary is not declared to be holy in Scripture, and she herself declared that she was in need of the Savior who she bore.

Mary is dead. She is not a goddess to be prayed to, nor will she pray for us, nor can she hear prayers or petitions, as only God can. If one wishes to be made worthy of the promises of Messiah (Christ), praying to Mary is an act of worthless futility. Salvation is a free gift and to be worthy of the free gift, we are to obey the will of Yeshua (Jesus) and obey His commandments.

Mary is not a queen, either on Earth or in heaven. She herself said she was a maidservant of a lowly state, not a queen. The false belief in a queen of heaven is of pagan origin and was applied by the Catholic Church and bestowed upon Mary with no Scripture justification.

Mary is not the source of our hope and dispenser of mercy, God is. Mary was not sinless, nor was she conceived without sin as the Immaculate Conception. Yeshua (Jesus) was without sin and was immaculately conceived (Matthew 1:18-23). Catholics incorrectly pray to Mary as a goddess, a sinless perpetual virgin, an Advocate / Intercessor / Mediator, and a woman who was without sin.

SCRIPTURE DECLARES:

JEREMIAH 7:18 (NKJV):
The children gather wood, the fathers kindle the fire, and the women knead dough, to make cakes for THE QUEEN OF HEAVEN; and they pour out drink offerings to other gods, that they may provoke Me to anger.

MATTHEW 1:20 (NKJV):
An angel of the Lord appeared to him in a dream, saying, "Joseph, son of David, do not be afraid to take to you Mary your wife, FOR THAT WHICH IS CONCEIVED IN HER IS OF THE HOLY SPIRIT."

MATTHEW 10:37-38 (NKJV):
"He who loves father or mother more than Me is not worthy of Me. And he who loves son or daughter more than Me is not worthy of Me. And he who does not take his cross and follow after Me is not worthy of Me."

LUKE 1:46-47 (NKJV):

And Mary said:

"My soul magnifies the Lord, and my spirit has rejoiced in God my Savior. For He has regarded the lowly state of His maidservant."

JOHN 14:15 (NKJV):

"If you love Me, keep My commandments."

EPHESIANS 2:4-5 (NKJV):

But God, who is rich in MERCY, because of His great love with which He loved us, even when we were dead in trespasses, made us alive together with Christ (by grace you have been saved).

1 TIMOTHY 1:1 (NKJV):

Paul, an apostle of Yeshua Messiah (Jesus Christ), by the commandment of God our Savior and the Lord Yeshua Messiah (Jesus Christ), OUR HOPE.

JUDE 1:21 (NKJV):

Keep yourselves in the love of God, looking for the MERCY of our Lord Yeshua Messiah (Jesus Christ) unto eternal life.

Mary was a sinner, is dead awaiting the resurrection, and she has not been assumed into heaven. She is not a goddess to be prayed to, nor can she hear prayers or petitions, only God can. If one wishes to be made worthy of the promises of Messiah (Christ), praying to Mary is an act of worthless futility. Salvation is a free gift and to be worthy of the free gift, we are to obey the will of Yeshua (Jesus), love Him, and obey His commandments.

SCRIPTURE DECLARES:

EXODUS 20:3; DEUTERONOMY 5:7 (NKJV):

You shall have no other gods before Me.

1 TIMOTHY 2:5 (NKJV):

For there is one God and ONE MEDIATOR between God and men, the Man Messiah Yeshua (Christ Jesus).

1 JOHN 2:1 (NKJV):

My little children, these things I write to you, so that you may not sin. And if anyone sins, we have AN ADVOCATE with the Father, Yeshua Messiah (Jesus Christ) the righteous.

SAINT MICHAEL PRAYER:

Saint Michael, the Archangel, defend us in battle. Be our protection against the wickedness and snares of the devil. May God rebuke him, we humbly pray; and do thou, o Prince of the heavenly host, by the power of God cast into hell Satan and the evil spirits who prowl throughout the world seeking the ruin of souls. Amen.

Catholics pray to angels for defense and worship them. God does not command us to pray to anyone but Him alone for our defense against the spiritual forces of wickedness and we are instructed to not worship angels.

SCRIPTURE DECLARES:

PSALM 59:9,17 (NKJV):

I will wait for You, O You his Strength; for God is my defense.

…

To You, O my Strength, I will sing praises; for God is my defense.

1 CORINTHIANS 6:3 (NKJV):

Do you not know that we shall judge angels?

COLOSSIANS 2:18 (NKJV):

Let no one cheat you of your reward, taking delight in false humility and worship of angels.

REVELATION 22:8-9 (NKJV):

Now I, John, saw and heard these things. And when I heard and saw, I fell down to worship before the feet of the angel who showed me these things.

Then he said to me, "See that you do not do that. For I am your fellow servant, and of your brethren the prophets, and of those who keep the words of this book. Worship God."

YESHUA (JESUS) TELLS US HOW TO PRAY:

MATTHEW 6:5-13; LUKE 11:1-4 (NKJV):

"And when you pray, you shall not be like the hypocrites. For they love to pray standing in the synagogues and on the corners of the streets, that they may be seen by men. Assuredly, I say to you, they have their reward. But you, when you pray, go into your room, and when you have shut your door, pray to your Father who is in the secret place; and your Father who sees in secret will reward you openly.

And when you pray, do not use vain repetitions as the heathen do. For they think that they will be heard for their many words. Therefore do not be like them. For your Father knows the things you have need of before you ask Him. In this manner, therefore, pray:

Our Father in Heaven, hallowed be Your name.

Your kingdom come. Your will be done on earth as it is in heaven.

Give us this day our daily bread.

And forgive us our debts (sins), as we forgive our debtors.

And do not lead us into temptation, but deliver us from the evil one.

For Yours is the kingdom and the power and the glory forever. Amen."

The Lord's Prayer covers many areas.

"Our Father in heaven, hallowed be Your name."

It is a prayer to God the Father in heaven who is holy.

"Your kingdom come. Your will be done on earth as it is in heaven."

God's kingdom is coming to Earth and Yeshua (Jesus) will establish righteousness and rule the nations with a rod of iron (Revelation 19:15, 20:4).

"Give us this day our daily bread."

We should pray for our daily needs.

"And forgive us our debts (sins), as we forgive our debtors."

If we forgive others, God will forgive us (Matthew 6:14).

"And do not lead us into temptation, but deliver us from the evil one."

Believers battle Satan and his demons in the spiritual realm. Pray for God's power and put on the full armor of God to defeat Satan and His spiritual hosts (Ephesians 6:10-13).

"For Yours is the kingdom and the power and the glory forever."

God's kingdom will last forever and there will be no end to it.

Believers have leeway when praying to God in asking for their daily needs, seeking His strength in overcoming evil and sin, for help in forgiving others, and for meeting other spiritual needs in general. However, many church or faith-based institutionalized prayers are defeatist, faithless, repetitive, unscriptural, and therefore ineffective. The purpose of this article is to make believers aware of what they are praying, so that they carefully consider and comprehend the words that are said in prayer, as prayer is supernatural communication with Almighty God.

THE RAPTURE(S): PRE-TRIB, MID-TRIB, POST-TRIB, OR NO RAPTURE AT ALL?

By George Lujack

Many have wondered about the resurrection of the dead and the timing of the rapture of the saints, or if there is a rapture at all. The resurrection(s) of the dead and the rapture(s) of the saints will be discussed in this article.

THE STATE OF THE DEAD

All who have ever lived and died are currently in a state of unconsciousness. No one's dead relatives are in heaven. Unlike what many have been taught to believe through traditional church teachings, no one has ascended to heaven other than Yeshua (Jesus). The dead know nothing and do not go to heaven when they die, nor do they serve God in death. The spirits of the dead rest unaware in unconsciousness, in God's care, and will be resurrected to life on the last day.

ECCLESIASTES 9:5 (NKJV):
... the dead know nothing.

Martha knew Lazurus did not go to heaven when he died. She also believed Lazarus would live again at the "last day," at the resurrection.

JOHN 11:20-24 (NKJV):
Now Martha, as soon as she heard that Yeshua (Jesus) was coming, went and met Him, but Mary was sitting in the house. Now Martha said to Yeshua (Jesus), "Lord, if You had been here, my brother would not have died. But even now I know that whatever You ask
of God, God will give You."
Yeshua (Jesus) said to her, "Your brother will rise again."
Martha said to Him, "I know that he will rise again IN THE RESURRECTION AT THE LAST DAY."

When Yeshua (Jesus) resurrected Lazarus, He didn't summon him down from heaven and back into his body, but from sleep (death). Yeshua (Jesus) said that no one has ascended to heaven, except Himself who had come down from heaven.

JOHN 3:13 (NKJV):
"NO ONE has ascended to heaven but He who came down from heaven, that is, the Son of Man."

Some will cling to the idea that their deceased loved ones do go to heaven, despite what Yeshua (Jesus) clearly stated in John 3:13, citing Mark 12:25-27.

MARK 12:25-27 (NKJV):

"FOR WHEN THEY RISE FROM THE DEAD, they neither marry nor are given in marriage, but are like angels in heaven. BUT CONCERNING THE DEAD, that they rise, have you not read in the book of Moses, in the burning bush passage, how God spoke to him, saying, 'I am the God of Abraham, the God of Isaac, and the God of Jacob'? HE IS NOT THE GOD OF THE DEAD, but the God of the living. You are therefore greatly mistaken."

These verses have been misunderstood being twisted upside down and backwards. God was the God of Abraham, Isaac, and Jacob. Abraham, Isaac, and Jacob are dead awaiting the resurrection. God is not the God of the dead (referring to Abraham, Isaac, and Jacob), but the God of the living. God will resume being the God of Abraham, Isaac, and Jacob after they are resurrected to life. God does not rule over or govern the dead.

THE COMING OF YESHUA (JESUS) THE LORD

Many have wondered when Yeshua (Jesus) the Lord will be returning to Earth. The Lord is NOT returning to the Earth at first, as He will be coming to the clouds to meet His saints in the air, where the Lord and His saints will congregate and wait until the end of the great tribulation concludes and then return to Earth.

1 THESSALONIANS 4:15-17 (NKJV) [WITH INTERPRETATION]:

For this we say to you by the word of the Lord, that we who are alive and remain until THE COMING OF THE LORD will by no means precede those who are asleep [DEAD]. For the Lord Himself will descend from heaven with a shout, with the voice of an archangel, and with the trumpet of God. And the dead in Messiah (Christ) will rise first. Then we who are alive and remain shall be caught up together with them in the clouds TO MEET THE LORD IN THE AIR. And thus we shall always be with the Lord.

THE RESURRECTION OF THE DEAD AND THE RAPTURE

1 CORINTHIANS 15:51-53 (NKJV):

Behold, I tell you a mystery: We shall not all sleep, but we shall all be changed - in a moment, in the twinkling of an eye, at the last trumpet. For the trumpet will sound, and the dead will be raised incorruptible, and we shall be changed. For this corruptible must put on incorruption, and this mortal must put on immortality.

1 CORINTHIANS 15:51-53 (NKJV) [WITH INTERPRETATION]:

Behold, I tell you a mystery: We shall not all sleep [DIE*], but we shall all be changed [INTO INCORRUPT SPIRIT BEINGS] - in a moment, in the twinkling of an eye, at the last trumpet. For the trumpet will sound, and the dead will be raised [FROM THE GRAVE] incorruptible, and we [WHO ARE ALIVE AT THE TIME OF HIS RETURN] shall be changed [INTO INCORRUPTIBLE SPIRIT BEINGS]. For this corruptible must put on incorruption, and this mortal must put on immortality.

*DIE. Believing saints who are alive when the rapture occurs will not die the first death, but will be instantly transported to the clouds to be with the Lord.

1 THESSALONIANS 4:15-17 (NKJV):

For this we say to you by the word of the Lord, that we who are alive and remain until the coming of the Lord will by no means precede those carried up who are asleep. For the Lord Himself will descend from heaven with a shout, with the voice of an archangel, and with the trumpet of God. And the dead in Messiah (Christ) will rise first. Then we who are alive and remain shall be caught up together with them in the clouds to meet the Lord in the air. And thus we shall always be with the Lord.

1 THESSALONIANS 4:15-17 (NKJV) [WITH INTERPRETATION]:

For this we say to you by the word of the Lord, that we who are alive and remain until the coming of the Lord will by no means precede those who are asleep [DEAD]. For the Lord Himself will descend from heaven with a shout, with the voice of an archangel, and with the trumpet of God. And the dead in Messiah (Christ) will rise first. Then we who are alive and remain shall be caught up [RAPTURED] together with them [THE DEAD] in the clouds to meet the Lord in the air. And thus we shall always be with the Lord.

The saints as well as all of mankind throughout history have died. The saints who are alive when Messiah (Christ) returns, will never die the first death, but will instead be instantly transported, in the twinkling of an eye, to the clouds to be forever with the Lord. Yeshua (Jesus) also spoke of the first resurrection and rapture event and summed it up in two verses...

JOHN 11:25-26 (NKJV):

Yeshua (Jesus) said to her, "I am the resurrection and the life. He who believes in Me, though he may die, he shall live. And whoever lives and believes in Me shall never die."

JOHN 11:25-26 (NKJV) [WITH INTERPRETATION]:

Yeshua (Jesus) said to her, "I am the resurrection and the life. He who believes in Me, though he may die [THE FIRST DEATH], he shall live. And whoever lives [IS ALIVE WHEN I RETURN] and believes in Me shall never die [SHALL BE RAPTURED TO THE CLOUDS AND WILL NEVER EXPERIENCE DEATH]."

YESHUA (JESUS) WAS 'CARRIED UP,' 'CAUGHT UP,' 'RECEIVED UP,' OR IN OTHER WORDS 'RAPTURED,' TO HEAVEN

MARK 16:19 (NKJV):

So then, after the Lord had spoken to them, He was RECEIVED UP into heaven, and sat down at the right hand of God.

LUKE 24:51 (NKJV):

Now it came to pass, while He blessed them, that He was parted from them and CARRIED UP into heaven.

ACTS 1:2 (NKJV):

He was TAKEN UP, after He through the Holy Spirit had given commandments to the apostles whom He had chosen.

1 TIMOTHY 3:16 (NKJV):

God was manifested in the flesh, justified in the Spirit, seen by angels, preached among the Gentiles, believed on in the world, RECEIVED UP in glory.

REVELATION 12:5 (NKJV) [WITH INTERPRETATION]:

And her Child [YESHUA / JESUS] was CAUGHT UP to God and His throne.

Believers will be, in like manner, caught up (raptured) to meet Yeshua (Jesus) in the clouds, before returning with Him to Earth to establish His Millennium Kingdom, and we will be forever with Him.

1 THESSALONIANS 4:17 (NKJV):

Then we who are alive and remain shall be CAUGHT UP together with them in the clouds to meet the Lord in the air. And thus we shall always be with the Lord.

Yeshua (Jesus) is a Shepherd who protects His faithful flock. He protected Noah and his family from the worldwide flood, above the floodwaters, in the ark. He will protect the first-fruit faithful saints from the Antimessiah (Antichrist) through the rapture to the clouds. The rapture is the saints' ark.

THE RESURRECTIONS OF THE SAINTS

There have been numerous resurrections recorded in Scripture. Yeshua (Jesus) resurrected Lazarus and a little girl from the dead (Mark 5:41-42; Luke 8:54-55; John 11:43-44;). Yeshua (Jesus) Himself was resurrected and many also with Him, to bear witness of Him (Matthew 27:51-53). All who were resurrected, such as Lazarus, died again, but Yeshua (Jesus) went to heaven to sit at His Father's right hand (Mark 16:19; Hebrews 10:12).

There are two righteous witnesses of God prophesied to appear during the mid-tribulation years (Revelation 11:3-12). Scripture does not reveal the identity of these two witnesses, but proclaims that that they will be clothed in sackcloth and bear witness to the truth (Revelation 11:3). When their testimony is finished, they will be killed. Then, after three-and-a-half days, the two witnesses will be resurrected to life and raptured to heaven (Revelation 11:11-12).

The resurrection of the dead in Messiah (Christ) will precede the worldwide harvest (rapture) of the saints (1 Thessalonians 4:15-16).

THE LEFT BEHIND

Those who are left behind, who are not raptured in the worldwide rapture, will have to face the Antimessiah (Antichrist). They will have to either accept the mark of the beast (Revelation 13:16-18) or refuse to do so and be beheaded.

REVELATION 20:4 (NKJV):

Then I saw the souls of those who had been beheaded for their witness to (Yeshua) Jesus and for the word of God, who had not worshiped the beast or his image, and had not received his mark on their foreheads or on their hands. And they lived and reigned with Messiah (Christ) for a thousand years.

Those left behind (in the world, outside of Israel) after the rapture occurs, will not be under the protection of God, but will still have an opportunity to repent and bear witness to the Yeshua (Jesus) and Scripture. Many of those left behind will be martyred (beheaded) for their testimony and will be counted worthy to be rewarded and be part of the first resurrection.

REVELATION 14:9-13 (NKJV):

Then a third angel followed them, saying with a loud voice, "If anyone worships the beast and his image, and receives his mark on his forehead or on his hand, he himself shall also drink of the wine of the wrath of God, which is poured out full strength into the cup of His indignation. He shall be tormented with fire and brimstone in the presence of the holy angels and in the presence of the Lamb. And the smoke of their torment ascends forever and ever; and they have no rest day or night, who worship the beast and his image, and whoever receives the mark of his name."

Here is the patience of the saints; here are those who keep the commandments of God and the faith of Yeshua (Jesus).

Then I heard a voice from heaven saying to me, "Write: 'BLESSED ARE THE DEAD WHO DIE IN THE LORD FROM NOW ON.'"

How are those 'blessed' who die in the Lord from that point on?

REVELATION 20:4 (NKJV):

Then I saw the souls of those who had been beheaded for their witness to Yeshua (Jesus) and for the word of God, who had not worshiped the beast or his image, and had not received his mark on their foreheads or on their hands. And they lived and reigned with Messiah (Christ) for a thousand years.

The dead who are killed during the great tribulation guillotine beheadings will NOT be going to the grave, but will instead be instantly raptured to be with the Lord in the clouds and will afterward reign with Messiah (Christ) for a thousand years during His Millennium Kingdom. All who have ever lived and died previously were not so blessed, but went to the grave after death. The left behind beheaded martyred saints will be instantly raptured, blessed, and will reign with Messiah (Christ) for a thousand years.

As human nature would have it, the resurrected beheaded saints, dwelling in the clouds with the Lord, will begin to grow impatient for justice...

REVELATION 6:9-10 (NKJV):

When He opened the fifth seal, I saw under the altar the souls of those who had been slain for the word of God and for the testimony which they held. And they cried with a loud voice, saying, "How long, O Lord, holy and true, until You judge and avenge our blood on those who dwell on the earth?"

REVELATION 6:11 (NKJV) [WITH INTERPRETATION]:

Then a white robe was given to each of them; and it was said to them that they should rest a little while longer, until both the number of their fellow servants and their brethren, who would be killed as they were [BY GUILLOTINE], was completed.

The raptured left behind who repent, become saints, and refuse the mark of the beast will grow impatient as to when the Lord will return to Earth to avenge their deaths. They will be given white robes, and be instructed to wait. When there are no more faithful believers left on Earth, Yeshua (Jesus) will return to save the Jews of Israel, who will call upon Him as they face annihilation (Luke 18:8; Matthew 23:37-39; Luke 13:34-35).

THE RAPTURES

The first rapture will be pre-tribulation. This will be the rapture of the American saints. The destruction of Babylon the great (America) will mark the beginning of the great tribulation (Revelation 14:8, 18). Before America is destroyed, God will rapture the American saints out from America (Isaiah 18:5-7; Jeremiah 51:45; Revelation 18:4). God provides a separate American rapture for the American saints, as to spare them from the destruction, judgment, and plagues that will come upon America.

ISAIAH 18:5-7 (NKJV) [WITH INTERPRETATION]:

For before the harvest [BEFORE THE WORLDWIDE HARVEST (RAPTURE) OF THE SAINTS], when the bud [TIMING] is perfect and the sour grape [THE SIN OF HOMOSEXUALITY] is ripening in the flower [AMERICA], then He will both cut off the twigs [THE UNRIGHTEOUS] with pruning hooks and cut down and take away [RAPTURE] the branches [THE RIGHTEOUS]. They [THE UNRIGHTEOUS] will be left [BEHIND] together for the mountain birds of prey [REVELATION 18:2] and for the beasts of the earth. The birds of prey [REVELATION 18:2] will summer on them, and all the beasts of the earth will winter on them [EAT THEM].

In that time [OF THE DESTRUCTION OF BABYLON (AMERICA)] a present [THE RAPTURED AMERICAN SAINTS] will be brought to YHWH (the Lord) of hosts from a people tall and smooth-skinned [AMERICA], and from a people awesome from their beginning onward [AMERICA] - a nation powerful and trampling [AMERICA], whose land [AMERICA] the rivers divide - to the place of the name of YHWH (the Lord) of hosts, to Mount Zion [NEW JERUSALEM].

THE FIRST-FRUITS ARE OF THE FIRST RESURRECTION

REVELATION 20:4-6 (NKJV):

And I saw thrones, and they sat on them, and judgment was committed to them. Then I saw the souls of those who had been beheaded for their witness to Yeshua (Jesus) and for the word of God, who had not worshiped the beast or his image, and had not received his mark on their foreheads or on their hands. And they lived and reigned with Messiah (Christ) for a thousand years. But the rest of the dead did not live again until the thousand years were finished. This is the first resurrection. Blessed and holy is he who has part in the first resurrection. Over such the second death has no power, but they shall be priests of God and of Messiah (Christ), and shall reign with Him a thousand years.

REVELATION 20:4-6 (NKJV) [WITH INTERPRETATION]:

And I saw thrones, and they [THE SAINTS OF THE FIRST RESURRECTION AND RAPTURE] sat on them, and judgment was committed to them. Then I saw the souls of those who had been beheaded [THE LEFT BEHIND PEOPLE WHO REPENTED AFTER THE RAPTURE] for their witness to Yeshua (Jesus) and for the word of God, who had not worshiped the beast or his image, and had not received his mark on their foreheads or on their hands. And they lived and reigned with Messiah (Christ) for a thousand years. But THE REST OF THE DEAD DID NOT LIVE AGAIN UNTIL THE THOUSAND YEARS WERE FINISHED. This is the first resurrection. Blessed and holy is he who has part in the first resurrection. Over such the second death has no power, but they shall be priests of God and of Messiah (Christ), and shall reign with Him a thousand years.

Upon His return to Earth, Yeshua (Jesus) will resurrect the dead righteous Jews, who have been deceived into rejecting Him as their Messiah, and upon their resurrection they will know that He is the Lord (Ezekiel 37). The people of the first resurrection comprise the dead in Messiah (Christ), the raptured saints, the left-behind beheaded martyrs who refuse the mark of the beast, and the resurrected Jews and the righteous living Jews who will be saved from annihilation when Yeshua (Jesus) returns to Earth to save them. The first-fruits of the first resurrection will reign with Messiah (Christ) during His thousand-year millennium reign on Earth. All the atheists, faithless, unrepentant sinners, lawless-living Christians, and others, will be raised *after* the one thousand years. Some will be judged to hell and others will repent of their sins and / or disbelief and will be given a chance at redemption.

RAPTURE DENIERS

There are many who do not believe in the rapture event. The first thing they will say is that 'rapture' is not in Scripture. While the word 'rapture' does not appear in Scripture, it is simply a word used to describe the 'twinkling of an eye' moment (1 Corinthians 15:52) in which the living saints will avoid the great tribulation and be 'caught up' to the clouds to meet Yeshua (Jesus) in the air (1 Thessalonians 4:17).

Many rapture deniers cite Matthew 24 and Luke 21 as Scriptural proof that the saints do not get raptured, but must endure through the great tribulation and that Messiah (Christ) will return for the saints AFTER the tribulation.

MATTHEW 24:15-22 (NKJV):

"Therefore when you see the 'abomination of desolation,' spoken of by Daniel the prophet, standing in the holy place (whoever reads, let him understand), then let those who are in Judea flee to the mountains.

Let him who is on the housetop not go down to take anything out of his house. And let him who is in the field not go back to get his clothes.

But woe to those who are pregnant and to those who are nursing babies in those days!

And pray that your flight may not be in winter or on the Sabbath. For then there will be great tribulation, such as has not been since the beginning of the world until this time, no, nor ever shall be. And unless those days were shortened, no flesh would be saved; but for the elect's sake those days will be shortened."

MATTHEW 24:29-31 (NKJV):

"Immediately after the tribulation of those days the sun will be darkened, and the moon will not give its light; the stars will fall from heaven, and the powers of the heavens will be shaken. Then the sign of the Son of Man will appear in heaven, and then all the tribes of the earth will mourn, and they will see the Son of Man coming on the clouds of heaven with power and great glory. And He will send His angels with a great sound of a trumpet, and they will gather together His elect from the four winds, from one end of heaven to the other."

LUKE 21:20-28 (NKJV):

"But when you see Jerusalem surrounded by armies, then know that its desolation is near. Then let those who are in Judea flee to the mountains, let those who are in the midst of her depart, and let not those who are in the country enter her.

For these are the days of vengeance, that all things which are written may be fulfilled.

But woe to those who are pregnant and to those who are nursing babies in those days!

For there will be great distress in the land and wrath upon this people."

"And they will fall by the edge of the sword, and be led away captive into all nations. And Jerusalem will be trampled by Gentiles until the times of the Gentiles are fulfilled.

And there will be signs in the sun, in the moon, and in the stars; and on the earth distress of nations, with perplexity, the sea and the waves roaring; men's hearts failing them from fear and the expectation of those things which are coming on the earth, for the powers of the heavens will be shaken. Then they will see the Son of Man coming in a cloud with power and great glory. Now when these things begin to happen, look up and lift up your heads, because your redemption draws near."

Rapture deniers err in their understanding of Matthew 24 and Luke 21. Yeshua (Jesus) was NOT addressing the entire elect of the world. Yeshua (Jesus) was specifically addressing the elect Torah-observant Judaic Jews living in Israel and Judea, who will miss the rapture due to their denial of Yeshua (Jesus) as their Messiah. There is no way to eternal life except through accepting Yeshua (Jesus) as Messiah and Savior (John 14:6). This applies to both Jews and Gentiles. The Torah-observant, Messiah-denying Jews are still God's elect chosen people and are the lost sheep of Israel. Yeshua (Jesus) addresses them in the Matthew 24 and Luke 21 verses.

MATTHEW 24:15-22 (NKJV) [WITH INTERPRETATION]:

"Therefore when you see the 'abomination of desolation,' [THE ANTIMESSIAH / ANTICHRIST] spoken of by Daniel the prophet [DANIEL 7:24-25], standing in the holy place" [THE REBUILT TEMPLE ***IN JERUSALEM***] (whoever reads, let him understand), "then let those who are ***IN JUDEA*** flee to the mountains. Let him who is on the housetop not go down to take anything out of his house. And let him who is in the field not go back to get his clothes. But woe to those who are pregnant and to those who are nursing babies in those days! And pray that your flight may not be in winter or on the Sabbath [MANY TALMUDIC JEWS WILL NOT USE MOTORIZED VEHICLES ON THE SABBATH]. For then there will be great tribulation, such as has not been since the beginning of the world until this time, no, nor ever shall be. And unless those days were shortened, no flesh would be saved; but for the elect's [JEWS'] sake those days will be shortened."

MATTHEW 24:29-31 (NKJV) [WITH INTERPRETATION]:

"IMMEDIATELY AFTER THE TRIBULATION OF THOSE DAYS the sun will be darkened, and the moon will not give its light; the stars will fall from heaven, and the powers of the heavens will be shaken. THEN THE SIGN OF THE SON OF MAN WILL APPEAR IN HEAVEN [THE TRUMPET RETURN OF MESSIAH (CHRIST)], and then all the tribes of the earth will mourn [THE UNREPENTANT SINNERS LEFT BEHIND ON EARTH], and they will see the Son of Man (YESHUA / JESUS) coming on the clouds of heaven with power and great glory. And He will send His angels with a great sound of a trumpet, and they will gather together His elect [THE MESSIANIC AND CHRISTIAN SAINTS] from the four winds [CLOUDS], from one end of heaven [THE SKY] to the other."

LUKE 21:20-28 (NKJV) [WITH INTERPRETATION]:

"But when you see ***JERUSALEM*** surrounded by armies, then know that ITS DESOLATION is near. Then let those who are ***IN JUDEA*** flee to the mountains, let those who are IN THE MIDST OF HER [ISRAEL] depart, and let not those who are in the country enter her [CITIES OF ISRAEL]."

"For these are the days of vengeance, that all things which are written may be fulfilled.

But woe to those who are pregnant and to those who are nursing babies in those days!

For there will be great distress in the land and wrath upon this people. And they will fall by the edge of the sword, and be led away captive into all nations. And ***JERUSALEM*** will be trampled by Gentiles until the times of the Gentiles are fulfilled.

And there will be signs in the sun, in the moon, and in the stars; and on the earth distress of nations, with perplexity, the sea and the waves roaring; men's hearts failing them from fear and the expectation of those things which are coming on the earth, for the powers of the heavens will be shaken. Then they will see the Son of Man coming in a cloud with power and great glory. Now when these things begin to happen, look up and lift up your heads, because your redemption [REDEMPTION OF THE JEWS] draws near."

A POST-TRIBULATION RAPTURE?

Rapture deniers make the mistake in believing that Yeshua (Jesus) will send His angels TO THE EARTH to gather His elect (Messianic and Christian saints) IMMEDIATELY AFTER THE TRIBULATION. That is not the case at all and that is NOT what Matthew 24:29-31 nor Luke 21:28 states.

The ELECT JEWS will endure through the tribulation years. THEY will miss the rapture event due to their not accepting Yeshua (Jesus) as their Messiah. NEAR THE END OF THE GREAT TRIBULATION the angels will gather (organize) the already-raptured Messianic and Christian saints along with the dead in Messiah (Christ) FROM the FOUR WINDS, FROM one end of HEAVEN (the sky) to the other. The raptured saints and those who died in Messiah (Christ) will be gathered together by the angels and will join the Lord in His trumpet return to Earth! Yeshua (Jesus) will gather His saints who were raptured FROM the four winds, FROM one end of heaven (THE CLOUDS) to the other. He will NOT gather His saints TO the four winds, but FROM the four winds. The saints will be raptured TO the clouds, will await the Lord's return to Earth, and then He will gather them FROM the clouds and return with them TO Earth.

REVELATION 6:9-11 (NKJV):

When He opened the fifth seal; I saw under the altar the souls of those who had been slain for the word of God and for the testimony that they held. And they cried with a loud voice, saying, "How long, O Lord, holy and true, until You judge and avenge our blood on those who dwell on the earth?" Then a white robe was given to each of them; and it was said to them that they should rest a little while longer, until both the number of their fellow servants and their brethren, who would be killed as they were, was completed.

The saints and resurrected dead will be raptured to the clouds and wait there with Yeshua (Jesus) for the final repentance during the great tribulation. Many of the martyred saints throughout the ages will grow impatient and ask Yeshua (Jesus) to judge the Earth and avenge their deaths. Yeshua (Jesus) will give them white robes and tell them to be patient, until the great tribulation and those who are to be killed during it, is completed.

LUKE 18:7-8 (NKJV):

"And shall God not avenge His own elect who cry out day and night to Him, though He bears long with them? I tell you that He will avenge them speedily. Nevertheless, when the Son of Man comes, will He really find faith on the earth?"

Yeshua (Jesus) will avenge His beheaded saints of the great tribulation, but when He does return to Earth post-tribulation there will be no one of faith, with the exception of righteous Jews, living on Earth for Him to rapture. There will be no one for Yeshua (Jesus) to rapture post-tribulation, because all the left behind, who repented and became saints, are to be beheaded before He returns (Revelation 6:11).

MESSIAH (CHRIST) FIRST COMES AS A THIEF TO RAPTURE HIS SAINTS

1 THESSALONIANS 5:2-4 (NKJV):

For you yourselves know perfectly that the day of the Lord so comes AS A THIEF IN THE NIGHT. For when they say, "Peace and safety!" then sudden destruction comes upon them, as labor pains upon a pregnant woman. And they shall not escape. But you, brethren, are not in darkness, so that this Day should overtake you AS A THIEF.

2 PETER 3:10 (NKJV):

But the day of the Lord will come as a thief in the night...

REVELATION 3:3 (NKJV):

"Remember therefore how you have received and heard; hold fast and repent. Therefore if you will not watch, I WILL COME UPON YOU AS A THIEF, and you will not know what hour I will come upon you."

REVELATION 16:15 (NKJV):

"Behold, I AM COMING AS A THIEF. Blessed is he who watches, and keeps his garments, lest he walk naked and they see his shame."

Yeshua (Jesus) declares that He will come like a thief in the night, in an hour that is not expected (Matthew 24:36-44). A thief in the night does not sound a trumpet. This "thief in the night" return is a SEPARATE EVENT from His trumpet return, when every eye shall see Him (Revelation 1:7).

When Yeshua (Jesus) returns as a thief references the time when He comes to rapture the saints. A thief comes unannounced and unexpected, to take goods out of a house. The first part of the return of Yeshua (Jesus) will be to the clouds, where He will raise the dead in Messiah (Christ) and rapture the saints (the goods of the Earth). This first return, to the clouds, will occur in a time of relative world peace, when the world is enjoying a time of "Peace and safety!" (1 Thessalonians 5:3). Yeshua (Jesus) will come to take (raise) the saints out from the Earth just as He came in the days of Noah, to raise Noah and the ark above the floodwaters of the Earth. We do not know when Yeshua (Jesus) will come like a thief to rapture the saints, but it will be at an hour we do not expect (Matthew 24:36-44). We are warned to be ready therefore, living righteously as good servants, so when He does come as a thief He will bless us (rapture us) to His kingdom and not curse us (cut us off) from His presence and leave us to fend for ourselves during the great tribulation (Matthew 24:45-51).

Messiah's (Christ's) trumpet return to Earth will occur when the Antimessiah (Antichrist) enters the rebuilt Jerusalem temple and the Jews in Israel and Judea have fled to the mountainous wilderness. His trumpet return to Earth will be for the elect Jews' sake, the lost sheep of Israel, to shorten those days lest there would be no flesh saved alive (Matthew 10:6, 15:24, 24:22; Luke 15:4-6). Messiah's (Christ's) trumpet return will occur when the Jews know that He is their Messiah and cry out to Him for their salvation (Ezekiel 39:27-28).

CHRONICLE OF END-TIME RAPTURES AND RESURRECTIONS

PRE-TRIBULATION

1. The American saints will be raptured out of Babylon the great (America) before it is completely destroyed and be brought before the Lord as a present (Isaiah 18:5-7; Jeremiah 51:45; Revelation 18:4). Those left behind in America will be killed in its destruction and become food for scavenger birds and animals (Isaiah 18:6; Revelation 18:2).

2. The seventh and last trumpet will blow (first blast) and the Lord Yeshua (Jesus) will descend from heaven to the clouds (1 Corinthians 15:52; 1 Thessalonians 4:16-17).

MID-TRIBULATION

3. The dead all throughout history, in Messiah (Christ), will be resurrected to meet the Lord in the clouds (1 Corinthians 15:52; 1 Thessalonians 4:16).

4. The saints who are alive at the time of Messiah's (Christ's) return (to the clouds) will be caught up (raptured) shortly after the resurrection of the dead saints. The saints of the worldwide rapture will meet with the Lord, the raptured American saints, and the resurrected saints in the clouds (1 Corinthians 15:52; 1 Thessalonians 4:15-17).

5. The people left behind on Earth who repent and become worthy saints *after* the worldwide rapture, who live through the great tribulation and are martyred (beheaded) for refusing to accept the mark of the beast, will be counted righteous and resurrected immediately upon their deaths (Revelation 14:13, 20:4).

6. The righteous-living Jews of Israel will flee to a place of safety near the end of the great tribulation (Joel 3:17; Revelation 12:14).

POST TRIBULATION

7. The righteous Jews of Israel, the lost sheep, will call on Yeshua (Jesus) the Lord to save them as they face annihilation from the Gentile armies who will conquer and trample the land of Israel (Matthew 23:37-39; Luke 13:34-35). Yeshua (Jesus) will return to Earth, at the seventh and last trumpet - final blast, and save the Jews of Israel from annihilation (Revelation 1:7, 17:14).

8. The righteous dead Jews, who were deceived into rejecting Yeshua (Jesus) as their Messiah during their lifetime, will be resurrected to life and then they will know that He is their Messiah, Lord, and Savior (Ezekiel 37).

POST MILLENNIUM REIGN OF MESSIAH (CHRIST)

9. The rest of the dead will be raised in the second resurrection (Revelation 20:5). Everyone not of the first resurrection, (the faithless, unbelievers, unrepentant, and unrighteous), will die and rise in the second resurrection, after the millennium reign of Messiah (Christ).

PRAY TO ESCAPE THE GREAT TRIBULATION AND COMFORT EACH OTHER WITH THE HOPE AND PROMISE OF THE RAPTURE

LUKE 21:34-36 (NKJV):

"But take heed to yourselves, lest your hearts be weighed down with carousing, drunkenness, and cares of this life, and that Day come on you unexpectedly.

For it will come as a snare on all those who dwell on the face of the whole earth.

WATCH THEREFORE, AND PRAY ALWAYS THAT YOU MAY BE COUNTED WORTHY TO ESCAPE ALL THESE THINGS THAT WILL COME TO PASS, AND TO STAND BEFORE THE SON OF MAN."

1 THESSALONIANS 3:12-13 (NKJV):

And may the Lord make you increase and abound in love to one another and to all, just as we do to you, so that He may establish your hearts blameless in holiness before our God and Father at the coming of our Lord Yeshua Messiah (Jesus Christ) WITH ALL HIS SAINTS.

1 THESSALONIANS 4:17-18 (NKJV):

Then we who are alive and remain shall be caught up together with them in the clouds to meet the Lord in the air. And thus we shall always be with the Lord. THEREFORE COMFORT EACH OTHER WITH THESE WORDS.

1 THESSALONIANS 5:9-11 (NKJV):

For God did not appoint us to wrath, but to obtain salvation through our Lord Yeshua Messiah (Jesus Christ), who died for us, that whether we wake or sleep, we should live together with Him. Therefore COMFORT EACH OTHER and edify one another, just as you also are doing.

JUDE 1:14-15 (NKJV):

"Behold, the Lord COMES WITH TEN THOUSANDS OF HIS SAINTS, to execute judgment on all, to convict all who are ungodly among them of all their ungodly deeds which they have committed in an ungodly way, and of all the harsh things which ungodly sinners have spoken against Him."

Luke 21:36 instructs us to watch the end-time events unfold and to pray that we may be counted worthy to ESCAPE ALL THESE THINGS THAT WILL COME TO PASS. We are to pray to escape the great tribulation through the rapture, not live through it. 1 Thessalonians 4:17 describes the rapture event pertaining to the saints who are alive and are "caught up" to the clouds, followed by verse 18 that commands believers to COMFORT EACH OTHER WITH THESE WORDS. Living and enduring through the great tribulation years is not comforting and is against what Luke 21:36, 1 Thessalonians 4:18, and 55:11 instructs.

Jude 1:14-15 proclaims that the Lord is coming with ten thousands of His saints (not angels) when He returns to Earth to execute judgment.

Believers should always strive to do the perfect will of God to be acceptable and blessed of the first resurrection (Romans 2:12; 1 Timothy 2:3). There will be greater and lesser saints in the kingdom of heaven, so desire to be great (Matthew 5:19). Blessed are they of the rapture and of the first resurrection who will dwell with Messiah (Christ) in the clouds and will return to reign with Him during His Millennium Kingdom rule (Revelation 12:12, 20:6).

MODERN WARFARE;
SCRIPTURE PROPHECY FULFILLED AND PROPHECIES YET TO OCCUR

By George Lujack

Revelation Scripture prophecies that have been fulfilled regarding World Wars I, II, other wars, as well as prophecies concerning future global conflicts that are foretold to yet occur will be [INTERPRETED] in this article.

WORLD WARS I AND II

REVELATION 8:7-9 (NKJV) [WITH INTERPRETATION]:

The first angel sounded: And hail [BULLETS] and [MUSKET] fire followed, mingled with [SOLDIERS'] blood, and they [THE SOLDIERS] were thrown to the earth [SHOT AND KILLED]. And a third of the trees were burned up, and all green grass was burned up [RETREATING ARMIES' SCORCHED EARTH FIRES].

Then the second angel sounded: And something like a great mountain burning with fire [ATOMIC BOMB DETONATION] was thrown into the sea [SURROUNDING THE ISLAND NATION OF JAPAN], and a third of the sea became blood. And a third of the living creatures in the sea died, and a third of the ships were destroyed [A THIRD OF ALL THE WORLD'S SEA SHIPS WERE DESTROYED IN WWII].

2014-2015 AMERICAN-LED GLOBAL COALITION 'WAR' ON ISIS: THE TORMENT OF MUSLIM MEN WHO DO NOT HAVE THE SEAL OF GOD ON THEIR FOREHEADS

REVELATION 9:1-4 (NKJV) [WITH INTERPRETATION]:

Then the fifth angel sounded: And I saw a star [SATAN] fallen from heaven to the earth [REVELATION 12:12,17:10]. To him was given the key to the bottomless pit. And he opened the bottomless pit, and smoke arose out of the pit like the smoke of a great furnace. So the sun and the air were darkened because of the smoke of the pit. Then out of the smoke locusts [ARMORED HELICOPTERS, MILITARY JET PLANES, AND DRONES] came upon the earth. And to them was given power, as the scorpions of the earth have power. They were commanded not to harm the grass of the earth, or any green thing, or any tree [DUE TO GLOBAL WARMING CONCERNS], but only those men who do not have the seal of God on their foreheads [MUSLIM MEN].

REVELATION 9:5-6 (NKJV) [WITH INTERPRETATION]:

And they [AMERICAN COMMANDERS] were not given authority to kill them [MUSLIM MEN OF ISIS WERE WARNED BEFORE THEY WERE BOMBED, SO THEY WOULD NOT BE KILLED], but to torment them for five months [MUSLIM MEN OF ISIS WERE ENRAGED AND TORMENTED AS THEIR BUILDINGS AND EQUIPMENT WERE DESTROYED].[184] Their torment was like the torment of a scorpion when it strikes a man. In those days men will seek death and will not find it; they will desire to die, and death will flee from them.

THE APOSTLE JOHN'S DESCRIPTION OF ARMORED HELICOPTERS

REVELATION 9:7-12 (NKJV) [WITH INTERPRETATION]:

The shape of the locusts [ARMORED HELICOPTERS] was like horses prepared for battle. On their heads were crowns of something like gold [ROTOR HELICOPTER BLADE TOPS], and their faces were like the faces of men [THE HELMETED PILOTS IN THE HELICOPTER COCKPITS]. They had hair like women's hair [HELICOPTER ROTOR BLADES RESEMBLE STRANDS OF WOMEN'S HAIR], and their teeth [MACHINE GUNS / ROCKETS] were like lions' teeth. And they had breastplates [STEEL COCKPITS] like breastplates of iron, and the sound of their wings [ROTOR BLADES] was like the sound of chariots with many horses running into battle. They had tails [RUDDERS] like scorpions, and there were stings [ROCKETS] in their tails. Their power was to hurt men five months. And they had as king over them the angel of the bottomless pit, whose name in Hebrew is Abaddon [DESTROYER], but in Greek he has the name Apollyon [DESTROYER]. One woe is past. Behold, still two more woes are coming after these things.

ARMORED TANK GROUND WARFARE DURING THE GREAT TRIBULATION PERIOD

REVELATION 9:13-19 (NKJV) [WITH INTERPRETATION]:

Then the sixth angel sounded: And I heard a voice from the four horns of the golden altar which is before God, saying to the sixth angel who had the trumpet, "Release the four angels who are bound at the great river Euphrates." So the four angels, who had been prepared for the hour and day and month and year, were released to kill a third of mankind. Now the number of the [CHINESE AND NORTH KOREAN] army of the horsemen [ARMORED TANK AND MILITARY VEHICLE OPERATORS] was two hundred million; I heard the number of them. And thus I saw the horses [ARMORED TANKS] in the vision: those who sat on them had breastplates of fiery red, hyacinth blue, and sulfur yellow [NATIONAL FLAG AND MILITARY COLORS OF CHINA AND NORTH KOREA]; and the heads of the horses [ARMOURED TANKS] were like the heads of lions; and out of their mouths [MUZZLES] came fire, smoke, and brimstone. By these three plagues a third of mankind was killed [EASTERN ASIAN REGIONS HAVE THE HIGHEST POPULATION OF PEOPLE IN THE WORLD, OF WHICH A THIRD OF THE WORLD'S POPULATION WILL BE KILLED] - by the fire and the smoke and the brimstone that came out of their [ARMORED TANKS] mouths [MUZZLES]. For their power is in their mouth [MUZZLES] and in their tails [BARRELS]; for their tails [BARRELS] are like serpents, having heads; and with them they do harm.

THE BATTLE OF ARMAGEDDON

REVELATION 16:12-20 (NKJV) [WITH INTERPRETATION]:

Then the sixth angel poured out his bowl on the great river Euphrates, and its water was dried up, so that the way of the kings from the east [CHINA AND HER ALLIES] might be prepared. And I saw three unclean spirits like frogs coming out of the mouth of the dragon [SATAN], out of the mouth of the beast [ANTIMESSIAH (ANTICHRIST)], and out of the mouth of the false prophet [FINAL CATHOLIC POPE]. For they are spirits of demons, performing signs, which go out to the kings of the earth and of the whole world, to gather them to the battle of that great day of God Almighty.

"Behold, I am coming as a thief. Blessed is he who watches, and keeps his garments, lest he walk naked and they see his shame."

And they gathered them together to the place called in Hebrew, Armageddon.

Then the seventh angel poured out his bowl into the air, and a loud voice came out of the temple of heaven, from the throne, saying, "It is done!" And there were noises and thunderings and lightnings; and there was a great earthquake, such a mighty and great earthquake as had not occurred since men were on the earth. Now the great city was divided into three parts, and the cities of the [OTHER] nations fell. And great Babylon [AMERICA] was remembered before God, to give her [AMERICA] the cup of the wine of the fierceness of His wrath.

Then every island fled away, and the mountains were not found.

SATAN'S FINAL REBELLION: SATAN LEADS A WORLD ARMY *AFTER* MESSIAH'S (CHRIST'S) THOUSAND YEAR MILLENNIUM KINGDOM REIGN

REVELATION 20:7-10 (NKJV) [WITH INTERPRETATION]:

Now when the thousand years have expired, Satan will be released from his prison and will go out to deceive the nations which are in the four corners of the earth, Gog and Magog, to gather them together to battle, whose number is as the sand of the sea. They went up on the breadth of the earth and surrounded the camp of the saints and the beloved city [JERUSALEM]. And fire came down from God out of heaven and devoured them.

The devil, who deceived them, was cast into the lake of fire and brimstone where the beast [ANTIMESSIAH (ANTICHRIST)] and the false prophet [FINAL CATHOLIC POPE] are. And they will be tormented day and night forever and ever.

Artwork by Pat Marvenko Smith, ©1982/1992 - www.revelationillustrated.com

THE FOUR HORSEMEN OF THE APOCALYPSE

By George Lujack

This article will identify and [INTERPRET] the Revelation prophecy verses that speak of the Four Horsemen of the Apocalypse, commonly referred to as Conquest, War, Famine, and Death, respectively.

THE FOUR HORSEMEN OF THE APOCALYPSE

REVELATION 6:1-2 (NKJV) (THE WHITE HORSE) [WITH INTERPRETATION]:

Now I saw when the Lamb [YESHUA (JESUS)] opened one of the seals; and I heard one of the four living creatures saying with a voice like thunder, "Come and see."

And I looked, and behold, a white horse [NATO - THE NEW WORLD ORDER].

He [AMERICA] who sat on it [LED NATO] had a bow [STRONG MILITARY]; and a crown [LEADER OF THE FREE WORLD - LADY LIBERTY - THE LADY OF KINGDOMS (ISAIAH 47:5)] was given to him [AMERICA], and he [AMERICAN-LED NATO - THE NEW WORLD ORDER] went out conquering and to conquer [TOPPLING REGIMES AND TO NATION BUILD].

REVELATION 6:3-4 (NKJV) (THE RED HORSE) [WITH INTERPRETATION]:

When He opened the second seal, I heard the second living creature saying, "Come and see." Another horse, fiery red [RUSSIA - REVELATION 9:17], went out. And it was granted to the one who sat on it to take peace from the earth [BY DESTROYING AMERICA - THE WORLD'S PEACEKEEPER], and that people should kill one another [IN THE GREAT TRIBULATION WARS THAT FOLLOW]; and there was given to him a great sword [THE NUCLEAR ARSENAL USED TO DESTROY AMERICA].

REVELATION 6:5-6 (NKJV) (THE BLACK HORSE) [WITH INTERPRETATION]:

When He opened the third seal, I heard the third living creature say, "Come and see." So I looked, and behold, a black horse, and he who sat on it had a pair of scales [REPRESENTING ECONOMIC HARDSHIP AND RATIONED FOOD] in his hand. And I heard a voice in the midst of the four living creatures saying, "A quart of wheat for a denarius, and three quarts of barley for a denarius [A LOAF OF BREAD FOR A DAY'S WAGES]; and do not harm the oil and the wine."

REVELATION 6:7-9 (NKJV) (THE PALE HORSE) [WITH INTERPRETATION]:

When He opened the fourth seal, I heard the voice of the fourth living creature saying, "Come and see." So I looked, and behold, a pale horse. And the name of him who sat on it was Death, and Hades followed with him. And power was given to them over a fourth of the earth, to kill with sword [THE GREAT TRIBULATION WARS], with hunger [FAMINE], with death, and by the [MICROSCOPIC] beasts of the earth [THROUGH PLAGUES].

REVELATION 6:9-11 (NKJV) (THE BEHEADED SAINTS) [WITH INTERPRETATION]:

When He opened the fifth seal, I saw under the altar the souls of those who had been slain for the word of God and for the testimony which they held [THOSE WHO REFUSED THE MARK OF THE BEAST - REVELATION 13:16-18, 20:4]. And they cried with a loud voice, saying, "How long, O Lord, holy and true, until You judge and avenge our blood on those who dwell on the earth?" Then a white robe was given to each of them; and it was said to them that they should rest a little while longer, until both the number of their fellow servants and their brethren [THE LEFT BEHIND WHO REPENTED AFTER THE WORLDWIDE RAPTURE], who would be killed as they were [BY GUILLOTINE], was completed.

REVELATION 6:12-17 (NKJV) (THE RETURN) [WITH INTERPRETATION]:

I looked when He opened the sixth seal, and behold, there was a great earthquake; and the sun became black as sackcloth of hair, and the moon became like blood. And the stars of heaven [A THIRD OF THE ANGELS - REVELATION 8:12, 12:4] fell to the earth, as a fig tree drops its late figs when it is shaken by a mighty wind. Then the sky receded as a scroll when it is rolled up, and every mountain and island was moved out of its place.

And the kings of the earth [POLITICAL LEADERS], the great men, the rich men, the commanders, the mighty men, every slave and every free man, hid themselves in the caves and in the rocks of the mountains, and said to the mountains and rocks, "Fall on us and hide us from the face of Him who sits on the throne and from the wrath of the Lamb [YESHUA (JESUS) AT HIS RETURN]! For the great day of His wrath has come, and who is able to stand?"

The Four Horsemen of the Apocalypse, as well as the rest of Revelation 6, is a parabolic, prophetically worded synopsis of the end-time events that are repeatedly told in various ways throughout the chapters of Revelation and in other Scripture prophecies.

SUMMATION

The first horseman, who sits on the white horse commonly referred to as Conquest, is American-led NATO - the New World Order, which is the military alliance of America and Europe. This beast empire goes out conquering and to conquer: to topple regimes and to nation build.

The second horseman, who sits on the fiery red horse commonly referred to as War, is Russia. Fiery red is the national color of Russia. Russia will take peace from the Earth by delivering a deadly wound to one of the heads of the beast empire (Revelation 13:3). The deadly wound to one of the heads of the beast empire is the destruction of Babylon the great - America (Revelation 14:8, 18). The New World Order beast empire will survive the deadly wound it receives to its empire, the destruction of America, and rapidly mobilize, reemerge, and rise as a superpower (Revelation 13:12). The horseman who sits on the fiery red horse, Russia, will take peace from the Earth as a result of destroying Babylon the great - America, the world's peacekeeping nation. The destruction of Babylon the great - America, marks the beginning of the great tribulation as peace is taken from the Earth by Russia, the horseman who sits on the fiery red horse.

The third horseman, who sits on the black horse commonly referred to as Famine, carries a pair of scales in his hand representing economic hardship and rationed food. A global economic collapse will occur after the destruction of Babylon the great - America. Merchants worldwide will not be able to sell their goods to the world's greatest importer, America (Revelation 18:10-11). Factories around the world will close. Many millions of people will suddenly become unemployed. All American foreign aid will cease being paid to governments around the world. All American foreign debts will be wiped out instantly, as all the money owed to foreign governments and investors will never be repaid. All foreign reserve holdings of U.S. currency will become instantly worthless, as no world bank will accept American dollars. People will work a day's pay for a loaf of bread.

The fourth horseman, who sits on the pale horse commonly referred to as Death, represents the death of one third of the world's population that occurs during the great tribulation (Revelation 9:15). People will die by the sword in war, through hunger in famine, and through diseases and plagues of microorganisms during the great tribulation years.

THE SEVEN TRUMPETS OF REVELATION

By George Lujack

The seven trumpets of Revelation are revealed in this article (the visions which appeared to the Apostle John who described them):

REVELATION 8:7 (NKJV):

The first angel sounded: And hail and fire followed, mingled with blood, and they were thrown to the earth. And a third of the trees were burned up, and all green grass was burned up.

THE FIRST TRUMPET - Revelation 8:7:

"Hail and fire mingled with blood" refers to the ground warfare of WWI and WWII. "Hail" (bullets) and "fire" (exploded gunpowder fire) "followed" and the bullets "mingled with the blood" of soldiers engaged in ground warfare. "They," the soldiers, were "thrown to the earth," after being shot and killed. A third of the trees and green grass that was burned up refers to the scorched earth policy of WWI and WWII in which retreating armies would burn anything that could be useful to the enemy.

REVELATION 8:8-9 (NKJV):

Then the second angel sounded: And something like a great mountain burning with fire was thrown into the sea, and a third of the sea became blood. And a third of the living creatures in the sea died, and a third of the ships were destroyed.

THE SECOND TRUMPET - Revelation 8:8-9:

The "great mountain burning with fire cast into the sea" was the atomic bombing of Japan. Japan is an island nation surrounded by sea and the atom bombs detonated on Japan appeared as inverted mountains of fire. A third of the world's warships were lost (sunk) in WWII. Nuclear bombs were detonated by the United States in the Bikini Atoll waters from 1948-1958.

REVELATION 8:10-11 (NKJV):

Then the third angel sounded: And a great star fell from heaven, burning like a torch, and it fell on a third of the rivers and on the springs of water. The name of the star is Wormwood. A third of the waters became wormwood, and many men died from the water, because it was made bitter.

THE THIRD TRUMPET - Revelation 8:10-11:

Wormwood was the 1986 Russian Chernobyl nuclear power plant disaster, where the waters were poisoned. Radiation from Chernobyl has poisoned many people and estimates vary that 100,000 to 250,000 people have acquired various cancers as a result of the Chernobyl (translated: Wormwood) disaster.

The 2011 Japanese Fukushima nuclear plant accident is a further fulfillment of the third trumpet, as it is the same type of disaster that Chernobyl was and it is affecting the waters of the Pacific.

REVELATION 8:12-13 (NKJV):

Then the fourth angel sounded: And a third of the sun was struck, a third of the moon, and a third of the stars, so that a third of them were darkened. A third of the day did not shine, and likewise the night. And I looked, and I heard an angel flying through the midst of heaven, saying with a loud voice, "Woe, woe, woe to the inhabitants of the earth, because of the remaining blasts of the trumpet of the three angels who are about to sound!"

THE FOURTH TRUMPET - Revelation 8:12:

In the fourth trumpet, "a third part of the sun was smitten, and the third part of the moon, and the third part of the stars; so as the third part of them was darkened, and the day shone not for a third part of it, and the night likewise."

In the Middle East region, a third of the sky was darkened at the conclusion of the First Gulf War in 1991. Saddam Hussein's scorched earth policy burning of the Kuwaiti oil fields upon his loss in the First Gulf War was the fulfillment the fourth trumpet.

REVELATION 9:1-11 (NKJV):

Then the fifth angel sounded: And I saw a star fallen from heaven to the earth. To him was given the key to the bottomless pit. And he opened the bottomless pit, and smoke arose out of the pit like the smoke of a great furnace. So the sun and the air were darkened because of the smoke of the pit. Then out of the smoke locusts came upon the earth. And to them was given power, as the scorpions of the earth have power. They were commanded not to harm the grass of the earth, or any green thing, or any tree, but only those men who do not have the seal of God on their foreheads. And they were not given authority to kill them, but to torment them for five months. Their torment was like the torment of a scorpion when it strikes a man. In those days men will seek death and will not find it; they will desire to die, and death will flee from them. The shape of the locusts was like horses prepared for battle. On their heads were crowns of something like gold, and their faces were like the faces of men. They had hair like women's hair, and their teeth were like lions' teeth. And they had breastplates like breastplates of iron, and the sound of their wings was like the sound of chariots with many horses running into battle. They had tails like scorpions, and there were stings in their tails. Their power was to hurt men five months. And they had as king over them the angel of the bottomless pit, whose name in Hebrew is Abaddon, but in Greek he has the name Apollyon.

THE FIFTH TRUMPET - Revelation 9:1-11:

The "locusts" coming up from the "bottomless pit" are a first century description of armored helicopters, fighter jet planes, and drones as seen by the Apostle John. Coming from the bottomless pit indicates that these armored aircrafts are of Satan's end-time beast army.

There was no word for 'helicopter' in the first century, so John described these flying machines that brought destruction in the best descriptive way that he could. To him they appeared as locusts in formation - like horses lined up for battle. They had "crowns" like gold (steel rotors/roofs), their "faces" were like human faces (the helmeted pilots), their "hair" was the helicopter blades that appeared like strands of women's hair, their "teeth" were their automatic machine guns and rockets, their "breastplates" were the steel cage cockpits the pilots fly in, and a helicopter makes the sound of many chariot horses running into battle. The stings in their tails are rockets. These end-time armored war helicopters and other fighter aircraft did not harm the grass (global warming concerns), but only persons who do not have the seal of God on their foreheads, those persons who are NOT of God.

Revelation 9:1-11 describes the global warming environmentally minded 'war' the American-led coalition waged on Islamic terrorists.

REVELATION 9:4-5 (NKJV):

They were commanded not to harm the grass of the earth, or any green thing, or any tree, but only those men who do not have the seal of God on their foreheads. And they were not given authority to kill them, but to torment them for five months.

"They were commanded not to harm the grass of the earth, or any green thing, or any tree ..."

They (U.S. led Coalition armed forces) were commanded with global warming (climate change) concerns in mind, not to harm the grass, green things, or any trees. American President Barack Obama, in his environmentally-minded "war" on ISIS, did not order the bombing of ISIS oil infrastructure due to environmental impact concerns.[185]

"... but only those men who do not have the seal of God on their foreheads."

Islamic men do not have the seal of God, figuratively speaking, on their foreheads (minds). Muslims reject Yeshua (Jesus) as their Messiah - the seal of God, and believe in their prophet Muhammad as the messenger of their god, Allah.

"And they were not given authority to kill them, but to torment them for five months."

They (Coalition commanders) did not have authority to kill Islamic terrorist men. When American and Coalition commanders actually did order the bombing of ISIS buildings and oil tankers, they first ordered their pilots to drop leaflets giving their Islamic terrorist combat enemies at least 45-minutes of advance warning notice to flee for their lives. Muslim men knew that their buildings or oil tankers were about to be destroyed, which gave them ample time to escape before the bombs dropped.

REVELATION 9:1-11 *FULFILLED*

The torment of Muslim men by American-led Coalition forces is fulfillment of Scripture prophecy Revelation 9 through verse 11, reflecting the date of the 9-11-2001 Islamic terrorist attacks against America.

REVELATION 9:12 (NKJV):

One woe is past. Behold, still two more woes are coming after these things.

The destruction of Damascus, Syria (Isaiah 17:1), followed by the destruction of Babylon the great (America) (Revelation 14:8, 18) are the two woes of Revelation 9:12.

REVELATION 9:13-21 (NKJV):

Then the sixth angel sounded: And I heard a voice from the four horns of the golden altar which is before God, saying to the sixth angel who had the trumpet, "Release the four angels who are bound at the great river Euphrates." So the four angels, who had been prepared for the hour and day and month and year, were released to kill a third of mankind. Now the number of the army of the horsemen was two hundred million; I heard the number of them. And thus I saw the horses in the vision: those who sat on them had breastplates of fiery red, hyacinth blue, and sulfur yellow; and the heads of the horses were like the heads of lions; and out of their mouths came fire, smoke, and brimstone.

By these three plagues a third of mankind was killed - by the fire and the smoke and the brimstone which came out of their mouths.

For their power is in their mouth and in their tails; for their tails are like serpents, having heads; and with them they do harm. But the rest of mankind, who were not killed by these plagues, did not repent of the works of their hands, that they should not worship demons, and idols of gold, silver, brass, stone, and wood, which can neither see nor hear nor walk. And they did not repent of their murders or their sorceries or their sexual immorality or their thefts.

THE SIXTH TRUMPET - Revelation 9:13-21:

The sixth trumpet is the great tribulation, which begins with the destruction of America, followed by a third of mankind killed and the rise of the Antimessiah (Antichrist), who will impose the mark of the beast (Revelation 14:8-10).

REVELATION 9:15-19 (NKJV):

So the four angels, who had been prepared for the hour and day and month and year, were released to kill a third of mankind. Now the number of the army of the horsemen was two hundred million; I heard the number of them. And thus I saw the horses in the vision: those who sat on them had breastplates of fiery red, hyacinth blue, and sulfur yellow; and the heads of the horses were like the heads of lions; and out of their mouths came fire, smoke, and brimstone. By these three plagues a third of mankind was killed - by the fire and the smoke and the brimstone, which came out of their mouths. For their power is in their mouth and in their tails; for their tails are like serpents, having heads; and with them they do harm.

Fire, smoke, and brimstone (via conventional and nuclear wars) are going to be the means of death of one third of the world's population. Fire comes forth from the barrels (tails) and out the muzzles (mouths) of tanks.

Fiery red, hyacinth blue, and sulfur yellow (Revelation 9:17) are the national colors of the flags and emblems of the Russian, Chinese, and North Korean peoples. Asia is home to some of the most heavily populated regions in the world. During the great tribulation, one third of the world's population will be killed through war.

REVELATION 9:20-21 (NKJV):

But the rest of mankind, who were not killed by these plagues, did not repent of the works of their hands, that they should not worship demons, and idols of gold, silver, brass, stone, and wood, which can neither see nor hear nor walk. And they did not repent of their murders or their sorceries or their sexual immorality or their thefts.

Revelation 9:20-21 is a reference to the Western democratic nations and the Catholic and Protestant people within these countries who survive the great tribulation. The Catholic Church possesses the Scriptures, yet it has always sought to change the laws of God (Daniel 7:25), most notably, it houses, makes, and worships carved image idols. Protestants (Protesting Catholics) may believe that they do not serve or worship idols, but during their Christmas festival season they set up and serve Christmas tree idols in their homes (Jeremiah 10:1-6) and set up and serve manger scene idol displays.

Most people in the Western Christian democratic nations do not rampantly murder one another, with the exception of abortion, in which many do freely murder. Most often, people do not repent of abortion murder afterward, but simply seem to want to forget it. Many people who do not commit actual abortion murder, still support the 'right' of a woman to kill her child, thus support murder and are not repentant over it.

The Western democracies are home to many types of sorceries (astrology, pharmaceutical and illegal drugs, and new age religions) and are extremely sexually immoral (through adultery, fornication, homosexuality, and pornography). The Western Christian democratic nations, with the exception of Americans killed who are not raptured, are among the "rest of mankind" that will not be primarily killed by the plagues of Revelation 9:15-19, but are the ones who will not repent of their national sins of idolatry, murder, sorceries, sexual immorality, or thefts (Revelation 9:20-21).

REVELATION 11:15-19 (NKJV):

Then the seventh angel sounded: And there were loud voices in heaven, saying, "The kingdoms of this world have become the kingdoms of our Lord and of His Messiah, and He shall reign forever and ever!" And the twenty-four elders who sat before God on their thrones fell on their faces and worshiped God, saying:

"We give You thanks, O Lord God Almighty, the One who is and who was and who is to come, because You have taken Your great power and reigned. The nations were angry, and Your wrath has come, and the time of the dead, that they should be judged, and that You should reward Your servants the prophets and the saints, and those who fear Your name, small and great, and should destroy those who destroy the earth."

Then the temple of God was opened in heaven, and the ark of His covenant was seen in His temple. And there were lightnings, noises, thunderings, an earthquake, and great hail.

THE SEVENTH TRUMPET - Revelation 11:15-19:

The seventh trumpet is the final trumpet and signals the resurrection of the dead in Messiah (Christ), the worldwide rapture of the saints, and the return of Messiah (Christ) (1 Thessalonians 4:15-17; 1 Corinthians 15:51-52). Yeshua (Jesus) will set up His Millennium Kingdom and reign with His first fruit saints for a thousand years (Revelation 20:4-6).

MYSTERY BABYLON, WHO IS IT?

By George Lujack

REVELATION 17:5 (NKJV):

And on her forehead a name was written:

MYSTERY, BABYLON THE GREAT, THE MOTHER OF HARLOTS AND OF THE ABOMINATIONS OF THE EARTH.

The identity of Mystery Babylon is often hotly debated between Messianics, Christians, and Catholics. Messianics and Christians are generally split between believing Israel or Roman Catholicism is Mystery Babylon, while Catholics believe Mystery Babylon to be Israel. Judaism rejects the B'rit Hadashah (New Testament), so Judaic Jews outright dismiss any belief in Mystery Babylon.

TWO ROADS TO BABYLON

EZEKIEL 21:19,21 (NKJV):

And son of man, appoint for yourself TWO WAYS for the sword of the king of Babylon to go. ...

For the king of Babylon stands at the parting of the road, at the fork of the TWO ROADS, to use divination...

Elohim (God) often addresses two entities simultaneously through Scripture prophecy. Concerning the identity of Mystery Babylon, it is a duel-identity. Mystery Babylon is both of Pharisaic Talmudic Judaism and Roman Catholicism. Both entities fit the descriptions of Mystery Babylon in somewhat different yet similar ways. Pharisaic Talmudic Judaism and Roman Catholicism are the two Babylonian-inspired entities that share the title of Mystery Babylon.

TWO HARLOTS

HOSEA 4:15,17-18 (NKJV):

Though you, Israel, play the harlot. ...

Ephraim is joined to idols; let him alone. Their drink is rebellion and they commit harlotry continually.

EZEKIEL 23:4-5 (NKJV):

Samaria is Oholah, and Jerusalem is Oholibah. Oholah (Samaria) played the harlot even though she was Mine.

EZEKIEL 23:11 (NKJV):

Now although her sister Oholibah (Israel) saw this, she became more corrupt in her lust than she, and in her harlotry more corrupt than her sister's harlotry.

Israel has played the harlot, committing spiritual adultery, in worshiping the gods of its surrounding nations and adopting their pagan practices onto God's word (Jeremiah 3:8-9; 5:7, 7:9-10, 23:14; Hosea 3:1).

The Gentile nations (Ephraim and Samaria) historically have committed idolatry with images. Catholicism has adopted idolatry into its church and worships images of Yeshua (Jesus), Miriam (Mary), and other figures in continual spiritual harlotry (Revelation 9:20).

WHAT IS A JEW ACCORDING TO SCRIPTURE?

The Scripture definition of a Jew is quite different than the ethnic worldly definition of a Jew.

ROMANS 2:28-29 (NKJV):

For he is not a Jew who is one outwardly, nor is circumcision that which is outward in the flesh; but he is a Jew who is one inwardly; and circumcision is that of the heart, in the Spirit, not in the letter; whose praise is not from men but from God.

Jew (noun):
A member of the people and cultural community whose traditional religion is Judaism who traces his or her origins through the ancient Hebrew people of Israel to Abraham.

Scripture defines Jews as God's spiritual people, whereas a secular definition defines a Jew as a descendant of the Hebraic descendants of Abraham.

MYSTERY BABYLON DEFINED

To understand the identity of Mystery Babylon, it is essential to understand, as best as possible, what is meant by the term, 'Mystery Babylon.'

'Mystery' refers to something that is difficult to understand and whose identity is mysterious, secretly hidden, or unknown.

'Babylon' refers to a place of confusion and wickedness. The Hebrew word for 'confused,' is babal, a word from which Babylon is derived.

'Mystery Babylon' refers to a mysterious, wicked entity, full of lies, deceptions, and confusion, secretly operating, mixing God's word in the Scriptures with pagan religion, traditions, and false doctrines.

PARALLEL SCRIPTURE REFERENCES IDENTIFYING PHARISAIC TALMUDIC JUDAISM AND ROMAN CATHOLICISM AS MYSTERY BABYLON

IMPOSTOR JEWS

REVELATION 2:9 (NKJV):

I know your works, tribulation, and poverty (but you are rich); and I know the blasphemy of those who say they are Jews and are not, but are a synagogue of Satan.

REVELATION 3:9 (NKJV):

Indeed I will make those of the synagogue of Satan, who say they are Jews and are not, but lie -indeed I will make them come and worship before your feet, and to know that I have loved you.

The scriptural definition of a Jew is that of one inwardly circumcised in heart and Spirit (Romans 2:28-29). The Jew of the New Covenant is not the same as a descendant from Abraham, but one who believes in Yeshua Messiah (Jesus Christ) through faith and obeys His commands (1 John 2:4).

The Pharisaic Talmudic Jews have added to Scripture with their Babylonian-inspired doctrines and heavy burdens that they place upon Judaic Jews from their Talmud (Matthew 23:4). They make the word of God of no effect through their traditions (Mark 7:13). In the synagogues of the Pharisaic Talmudic Jews, they have rejected the true Messiah, and seek to punish and revile Jews who accept Yeshua (Jesus) (Acts ·17:1-5).

Impostor, non-spiritual, unrighteous Jews do lie, deny Yeshua (Jesus) as the Messiah, add to and nullify Scripture with their Talmud teachings, and are a synagogue of Satan.

THE CATHOLIC CHURCH - THE NEW ISRAEL?

The Catholic Church, with all her unscriptural doctrines, pagan-inspired teachings, additions and changes to the word of God, makes a bold and self-serving claim to be the New Israel.

Excerpts from the Catholic Encyclopedia:

* The Catholic Church is the Messianic Kingdom. It is the Kingdom of God (on Earth).

* Christ during His ministry affirmed not only that the prophecies relating to the Messiah were fulfilled in His own person, but also that the expected Messianic kingdom was none other than His (Catholic) Church.

* A characteristic feature of the Messianic kingdom, as predicted, is its UNIVERSAL extent.

* The (Catholic) Church is regarded as the new People of God, the new Israel, the new Zion.

The Catholic Church claims to be the new Israel (replacement theology, the new Jews); and they are not, but are a synagogue of Satan (Revelation 2:9, 3:9).

REVELATION 17:4 (NKJV):

The woman was arrayed in purple and scarlet, and adorned with gold and precious stones and pearls, having in her hand a golden cup full of abominations and the filthiness of her fornication.

Judaism is historically associated with purple and scarlet dress garments, linens, and woven materials (Exodus 25:4, 26:1,31,36, 27:16, 28:5-8,15,33, 35:6, 23-25,35, 36:8,35-37, 38:18,23, 39:1-8,24,29).

The Roman Catholic Church's clergy dress colors are purple and scarlet. Catholic bishops and archbishops wear purple while Catholic cardinals wear scarlet. In Scripture, the word 'woman' is often figuratively used to represent a church. Catholics have adorned their churches with gold and all manner of precious stones. The golden cup in the woman's hand is a reference to the Catholic Church's weekly Eucharist mass. The Catholic Church priest holds up a golden cup in his hand and offers Christ as a continual sacrifice, rather than a completed work, along with countless other false and pagan-inspired doctrines that they practice. God calls these abominable Babylonian-adopted religious practices spiritual fornication against Him and His word.

THE PARABLE OF THE RICH MAN AND LAZARUS - LUKE 16:19-31

Yeshua (Jesus) described, in the parable of the rich man and Lazarus, the rich man being clothed in purple (Luke 16:19). Yeshua (Jesus) was addressing the rich Pharisee Jews, who were lovers of money (Luke 16:14). The rich man refused to provide any welfare or food to Lazarus, a poor beggar, who was so impoverished that he desired to be fed with the crumbs that fell from the rich man's table (Luke 16:20-21). At the conclusion of the parable, the rich man is sent to a place of torment. The rich man could see Lazarus in paradise being embraced by Abraham. The rich man pleaded with Abraham, that he might send a resurrected Lazarus as a messenger to his father's house - to warn his five brothers to prevent them from receiving his fate. The rich man believed a resurrected Lazarus could testify to his five brothers, and that his brothers would believe Lazarus, repent and not go to the place of torment that he was in. Abraham denied the formerly rich man his request, telling him that his five brothers have Moses and the prophets, and if they do not believe them, they will not believe in one who is raised from the dead.

The parable prediction of Yeshua (Jesus), that the rich man's brothers would not be persuaded to believe and repent – even if one were raised from the dead, came to pass through the resurrection of Lazarus of Bethany. Yeshua (Jesus) resurrected Lazarus and the Pharisees and chief priests would not believe the testimony of those who witnessed the resurrection of Lazarus, nor would they repent of their murderous mindset as they sought to kill Lazarus (John 11:1-48; 12:1-11,17-19).

The Pharisee Jews, chief priests, and the Pharisaic Talmudic Jews of today reject Yeshua Messiah (Jesus Christ), even though He bore witness to the truth, performed wondrous miracles, and He was raised from the dead.

Pharisaic Talmudic Judaism elitists run the world's banking and economic systems, live in lavish wealth, have little concern for their fellow man, and often believe that they are ethnically superior to Gentiles.

The Roman Catholic Church's global spending matches the revenues of the world's largest firms. Yet the majority of monies spent by the Catholic Church are not done so to help the poor and impoverished of the world, but mostly to further empower and enrich its church through business, political, and religious institutions.

The Roman Catholic Church is one of the wealthiest institutions in the entire world. It owns vast wealth through cash flow donations from its over 1-billion member flock and though its investments. Its assets include incalculable amounts of gold, land, priceless art, and real estate.[186]

REVELATION 17:5 (NKJV):

And on her forehead a name was written:

MYSTERY, BABYLON THE GREAT, THE MOTHER OF HARLOTS AND OF THE ABOMINATIONS OF THE EARTH.

Mystery Babylon is a mother church. This mother church gives birth to other harlot churches. There are two roads that trace back to Babylon: Pharisaic Talmudic Judaism and Roman Catholicism.

Babylonian-inspired Pharisaic Talmudic Judaism is the mother of the Roman Catholic Church. Talmudic Judaism mixes its Babylonian-inspired Talmud writings and traditions with the Holy Scriptures.

The Roman Catholic Church is a harlot mother church. Babylonian-inspired Roman Catholicism mixes its traditions with God's word and places its church authority above the Scriptures.

The Protestant churches were born out of Roman Catholicism. Protestants, as their name suggests, are Protesting Catholics who protest some, but not all, of Catholicism. Protestants adhere to their mother Catholic Church in many of their false doctrines including the Sunday Sabbath, pagan adopted feasts and festivals, the abolishing of God's dietary laws, and the overall general practice that the law (Torah) has been done away with and has been replaced by the New Covenant. Protestantism is not Mystery Babylon; it is the offspring of Mystery Babylon. Protestants do not adhere to the whole truth of God's eternal laws (Torah) and they obey their Roman Catholic mother church in many of her false doctrines, feasts, festivals, and traditions.

REVELATION 17:6 (NKJV):

I saw the woman, drunk with the blood of the saints and with the blood of the martyrs of Yeshua (Jesus).

The Jewish scribes and Pharisees (religious leaders) are responsible for the deaths of the righteous. Yeshua (Jesus) accused the Jewish religious leaders of being hypocrites and a brood of vipers, responsible for and approving of the murdered righteous prophets, scribes, and wise men (Matthew 23:29-37; Luke 11:47-51). Yeshua (Jesus) identifies Jerusalem as the one who kills the prophets and the righteous sent to her (Luke 13:33-34).

The Roman Catholic Church is responsible for the deaths of millions of saints and innocents during its bloody history. It is estimated that the Catholic Church killed between 100-150 million people during the Dark Middle Ages in its crusades, inquisitions, trials, and executions.

REVELATION 17:9 (NKJV):

The seven heads are seven mountains on which the woman sits.

Israel is the land that God brought the Hebrews to possess. Before taking possession of the land of Israel, God delivered seven nations greater and mightier than the Hebrews into their hands. Israel sits on the location of seven nations that were cast out before them (Deuteronomy 7:1; Acts 13:19). Israel also sits on seven hills: Scopus, Nob, Olivet/Mount of Corruption/Mount of Offense, Mount Zion, Ophel Mount, The Rock/Fort Antonia, and Southwest Hill/New Mount Zion. The seven mountains of Revelation 17:9 represent the seven nations that the Hebraic Jews dispossessed and cast out before establishing the Israelite nation and also the seven hills upon which Israel sits.

The Vatican, headquarters of the Roman Catholic Church, physically sits on seven hills. Rome is the city that was built on seven hills and is also called "The City of Seven Hills." The seven hills that Rome sits on are Aventine Hill, Caelian Hill, Capitoline Hill, Esquiline Hill, Palatine Hill, Quirinal Hill, and Viminal Hill. Vatican City is a city within Rome. The seven mountains of Revelation 17:9 are symbolic of the Seven Hills of Rome on which the Roman Catholic Church sits.

REVELATION 17:15 (NKJV):

The waters that you saw, where the harlot sits, are peoples, multitudes, nations, and tongues.

Israeli Jews have been dispersed to all the nations and many have returned to Israel in these last days (Ezekiel 11:14-21, 20:33-44, 34:11-16). They have returned as international Jews and as different peoples, with many languages and customs adopted from the countries from where they were dispersed.

The Roman Catholic Church is established in many nations as they send out missionaries all over the world and they communicate with multitudes of people in many languages.

REVELATION 17:16-18 (NKJV):

And the ten horns which you saw on the beast, these will hate the harlot, make her desolate and naked, eat her flesh and burn her with fire. For God has put it into their hearts to fulfill His purpose, to be of one mind, and to give their kingdom to the beast, until the words of God are fulfilled. And the woman whom you saw is that great city which reigns over the kings of the earth.

The ten horns are an alliance of 10-kingdom nations within the European Union that will be led by the final Antimessiah (Antichrist) beast superpower (Revelation 17:12-13). This Antimessiah (Antichrist) Euro-Empire will hate the harlot (the Vatican / Catholic Church) and make her desolate and will also invade Israel and trample the Pharisaic Talmudic Jews in Jerusalem and Judea (Luke 21:20-24). God will put it into the hearts of the kings and rulers of the Gentile nations, to give their authority to this European beast superpower, so that the prophesy of God's punishment against Mystery Babylon will be fulfilled.

Israel reigns over the kings of the Earth through its banking institutions and its political alliances throughout the world. The beast superpower and the armies of the world will surround Jerusalem, in the last days, and Jerusalem will be trampled and made desolate. The Gentile armies will conquer Jerusalem, as God will use the armies of the Gentiles to extract His vengeance upon the Pharisaic Talmudic Jews of Israel (Lamentations 4:12-13; Matthew 24:15-22; Luke 21:20-24).

The Vatican is a sovereign state that reigns over the kings of the Earth through world politics, its vast wealth, and by using its religious influence in the world. The Vatican will ride the beast superpower. The Vatican is the little horn (Daniel 7:8, 8:9) that fornicates (politically and religiously aligns) with the beast superpower (Revelation 17:1-2, 19:19-21). The final Roman Catholic pope will act as the false prophet, uniting world politics with a one-world religion. The false prophet final Catholic pope will be cast alive into a lake of fire

(Revelation 19:20, 20:10). Vatican City and the Roman Catholic Church will be hated and destroyed by fire by the Antimessiah (Antichrist) beast empire in judgment (Revelation 17:16-18).

REVELATION 18:24 (NKJV) [WITH INTERPRETATION]:

"And in her was found the blood of the prophets, and saints, and all who were slain on the earth [WITHIN AMERICA RESIDED THE OFFSPRING PRESENCE OF MYSTERY BABYLON: PHARISAIC TALMUDIC JUDAISM AND THE ROMAN CATHOLIC CHURCH, WHICH WERE RESPONSIBLE FOR THE DEATHS OF THE PROPHETS, SAINTS, AND MANY OTHERS OF THE WORLD]."

Mystery Babylon's two entities (Revelation 17), which both dwell within America and exert a strong political and religious influence over the culture, were responsible for killing the prophets and the saints. The Pharisaic Talmudic Jews were responsible for killing the prophets (Matthew 23:37; Luke 13:34) and Roman Catholics were responsible for killing the saints during the Dark Middle Ages.

LUKE 13:34-35 (NKJV):

"O Jerusalem, Jerusalem, the one who kills the prophets and stones those who are sent to her! How often I wanted to gather your children together, as a hen *gathers* her brood under *her* wings, but you were not willing! See! Your house is left to you desolate; and assuredly,

I say to you, you shall not see Me until the time comes when you say, *'Blessed is He [YESHUA / JESUS] who comes in the name of [YHWH] (the Lord)!'*"

LUKE 21:20-24 (NKJV):

"But when you see Jerusalem surrounded by armies, then know that its desolation is near. Then let those who are in Judea flee to the mountains, let those who are in the midst of her depart, and let not those who are in the country enter her. For these are the days of vengeance, that all things which are written may be fulfilled. But woe to those who are pregnant and to those who are nursing babies in those days!

For there will be great distress in the land and wrath upon this people. And they will fall by the edge of the sword, and be led away captive into all nations. And Jerusalem will be trampled by Gentiles until the times of the Gentiles are fulfilled."

Pharisaic Talmudic Messiah-denying Judaism is the dominant faith of secular Israel. Israel will be judged by Yeshua (Jesus) for its national sins, killing of the prophets, and for its rejection of Him, their Messiah. Yeshua (Jesus) will return to save the righteous Jews of Israel when they call on Him in their darkest hour to save them from annihilation.

REVELATION 19:1-2 (NKJV) [WITH INTERPRETATION]:

After these things I heard a loud voice of a great multitude in heaven, saying, "Alleluia! Salvation and glory and honor and power belong to the Lord our God! For true and righteous are His judgments, because He has judged the great harlot [THE ROMAN CATHOLIC CHURCH] who corrupted the earth with her fornication; and He has avenged on her the blood of His servants shed by her."

In Catholic traditional teachings, they twist Yeshua's (Jesus') words to Peter in Matthew 16:18, and declare, "The gates of hell shall not prevail against [the Catholic Church]." Ironically, the Catholic Church is the great harlot 'gates of hell' church that will be judged by Yeshua (Jesus) to destruction and He will prevail against it.

Who is the 'loud voice of a great multitude in heaven' that cheers at the Catholic Church's judgment? They are the resurrected raptured saints throughout millennia who were slain by the Catholic Church and those of the end times who were beheaded by it.

REVELATION 6:10-11 (NKJV):

And they cried with a loud voice, saying, "How long, O Lord, holy and true, until You judge and avenge our blood on those who dwell on the earth?" Then a white robe was given to each of them; and it was said to them that they should rest a little while longer, until both the number of their fellow servants and their brethren, who would be killed as they were, was completed.

THE END OF MYSTERY BABYLON (FALSE RELIGION)

REVELATION 19:15 (NKJV):

Now out of His mouth goes a sharp sword, that with it He should strike the nations. And He Himself will rule them with a rod of iron.

REVELATION 22:14-15 (NKJV):

Blessed are those who do His commandments, that they may have the right to the tree of life, and may enter through the gates into the city. But outside are dogs and sorcerers and sexually immoral and murderers and idolaters, AND WHOEVER LOVES AND PRACTICES A LIE.

The word of God is truth and is sharper than and two-edged sword (Hebrews 4:12-13). Yeshua's (Jesus') truths shall reveal all the lies of Mystery Babylon. When Yeshua (Jesus) returns, He will rule with a rod of iron and put an end to all false religion.

REVELATION 9:1-11 *FULFILLED;* GLOBAL WARMING AND TORMENTED MUSLIM MEN

By George Lujack

Western political leaders agreed, by general consensus, that global warming (climate change) was settled science while they simultaneously coddled, fostered, imported, monitored, and policed radical Islamic terrorist entities at home and abroad, and did everything they could to avoid killing them through war.

In Rome, Catholic Pope Francis issued an encyclical on global warming, entitled, "ON CARE FOR OUR COMMON HOME" on May 24, 2015. The chapter on "POLLUTION AND CLIMATE CHANGE" proclaims the opinion that global warming is a settled scientific fact:

"A very solid scientific consensus indicates that we are presently witnessing a disturbing warming of the climatic system. In recent decades this warming has been accompanied by a constant rise in the sea level and, it would appear, by an increase of extreme weather events, even if a scientifically determinable cause cannot be assigned to each particular phenomenon. Humanity is called to recognize the need for changes of lifestyle, production and consumption, in order to combat this warming or at least the human causes which produce or aggravate it."[187]

The Catholic Church's embrace of global warming has a pagan religious component to it known as Gaia worship: the worship of the creation (mother earth) over the Creator and the priority of caring for the Earth over the concern and welfare of human beings.[188]

In America, U.S. President Barack Obama was widely believed to be a Muslim himself, and if not, certainly a Muslim sympathizer. Obama has stated, "No challenge poses a greater threat to future generations than climate change."[189] Meanwhile, as commander-in-chief of America's armed forces, Obama did not actively wage an effective war for America to defeat its Muslim terrorist enemies abroad, but instead was concerned with containing, protecting, and even importing them through immigration.[190][191]

During the preceding years, under the spiritual approval of Catholic Pope Francis, the military direction of U.S. President Barack Obama and many others in the socio-political and scientific community, the acceptance of global warming (climate change) as scientific fact and the proliferation of Muslim-based terrorism have gone hand-in-hand.

The Scripture prophecy of Revelation 9:1-11 was fulfilled through the global warming environmentally minded 'war' America waged on Islamic terrorists.

REVELATION 9:4-5 (NKJV):

They were commanded not to harm the grass of the earth, or any green thing, or any tree, but only those men who do not have the seal of God on their foreheads. And they were not given authority to kill them, but to torment them for five months.

SCRIPTURE PROPHECY ANALYSIS AND INTERPRETATION

REVELATION 9:4 (NKJV):

"They were commanded not to harm the grass of the earth, or any green thing, or any tree, ..."

They (American-led coalition armed forces) were commanded with global warming (climate change) concerns in mind, not to harm the grass, green things, or any trees. Obama, in his environmentally minded 'war' on ISIS, did not order the bombing of Syria's oil infrastructure, because of environmental impact concerns.[192]

REVELATION 9:4 (NKJV):

"... but only those men who do not have the seal of God on their foreheads."

Muslim men do not have the seal of God, figuratively speaking, on their foreheads (minds). They reject Yeshua (Jesus) as their Messiah - the seal of God, and believe in their so-called prophet Muhammad as the messenger of their god Allah.

REVELATION 9:5 (NKJV):

"And they were not given authority to kill them, but to torment them for five months."

They (American-led coalition forces) did not have the authority to kill Islamic terrorist men. When American commanders authorized the bombing of ISIS buildings and oil tankers, they first ordered their pilots to drop leaflets giving their Islamic terrorist combat enemies at least 45-minutes of advance warning notice to flee for their lives. Muslim men knew that their buildings or oil tankers were about to be destroyed, which gave them ample time to escape, before the bombs were dropped.

Coalition forces, while protecting the lives of Islamic combatants, *tormented* them. ISIS Muslim terrorists, who did not have the seal of God on their foreheads, were not grateful for the leaflets that American and coalition armed forces dropped on them to spare them their lives, but were enraged and tormented as their buildings and supplies were destroyed.

America's policy of containing ISIS Muslim combatant terrorists, and not destroying them, while putting on a show-war was torment to Muslim men. The 'locusts' of Revelation 9 represent armored helicopters and jet fighter planes (drones also), which were the instruments of the torment to those Muslim men.

An interesting side note is that the torment of Muslim men by American armed forces was fulfillment of Scripture prophecy Revelation chapter 9 through verse 11, reflecting the date of the 9-11 Islamic terrorist attacks against America that occurred on 9-11-2001.

The American-led coalition intervention in Syria began on September 22, 2014 and the bombings ended 6-months later on April 08, 2015. During the first month of intervention, ISIS resistance fighters were killed. In the ensuing five months, ISIS Muslim men were tormented, as their military equipment, supplies, and buildings were destroyed, but they were not targeted to be killed, nor were they killed, by U.S.-led coalition forces.[193]

The Scripture prophecy of Revelation 9:5 was fulfilled, which states those men who do not have the seal of God on their foreheads (Muslims) would be tormented for five months.

Many prophecy watchers were looking at Israel during the tetrad (set of 4) blood moons that occurred on God's feast days between April 15, 2014 and September 28, 2015, anticipating a major prophetic event to be fulfilled. Many prophecy scholars noted that these events landed on 'Jewish' feast days and thus they were expecting something monumental to occur in Israel.

During previous tetrad blood moon cycles that fell on God's feast days in 1493-1494, 1949-1950, and 1967-1968, significant events surrounding the Jewish people did take place. In 1492, during the Spanish Inquisition, the Jews in Spain were issued the Alhambra Decree, also known as the Edict of Expulsion, by the joint Catholic Monarchs of Spain, ordering practicing Jews of Spain to leave Spain within four months. In 1948, the State of Israel was born and Jews around the world once again had a homeland. In 1967, Israel expanded its territory and secured its country winning the Six-Day War.

Many prophecy watchers naturally expected that the tetrad blood moons of 2014-2015, which also fell on 'Jewish' feast days, would also bring about a prophetic event in Israel. That didn't happen. Many Scripture scoffers have since mocked the tetrad blood moons as inconsequential.

LEVITICUS 23:2 (NKJV):

The feasts of YHWH (the Lord), which you shall proclaim to be holy convocations, these are My feasts.

The feast days, which are rightly observed by the Jews, are actually God's feast days, not Jewish feast days. Therefore, blood moons that fall on God's feast days could signal a prophetic event to occur anywhere on God's Earth.

A historic event of Scripture prophecy occurred during the 2014-2015 tetrad blood moons. Revelation 9:1-11 was fulfilled. The American-led coalition intervention in Syria began on September 22, 2014 and ended 6-months later on April 08, 2015, dates that fell within the 2014-2015 tetrad blood moon cycle. During the blood moons of 2014-2015, Muslim men, those without the seal of the true God on their forehead, were tormented for 5-months (Revelation 9:4-5).

The world stage is now set for the two more woes of Revelation 9:12 to be fulfilled, which are the destruction of Damascus, Syria (Isaiah 17:1), followed by the destruction of Babylon the great (America - Revelation 14:8, 18). These two woe events precede the great tribulation, which will bring about the death of a third of the world's population (Revelation 9:15).

DAMASCUS, SYRIA WILL CEASE FROM BEING A CITY AND IT WILL BE A RUINOUS HEAP

By George Lujack

ISAIAH 17:1 (NKJV) [WITH INTERPRETATION]:

"Behold, Damascus [SYRIA] will cease from being a city, and it will be a ruinous heap."

Damascus is the capital of Syria and currently its largest city with a population of just over 1.5 million as of 2016. Located in southwestern Syria, Damascus is a major cultural and religious region and the center of a large metropolitan area, which is perhaps the oldest, continually inhabited city in the world.

Scripture prophecy declares that Damascus will cease from being a city and it will be a ruinous heap.

WARS AND RUMORS OF WARS

MATTHEW 24:6-7; MARK 13:7-8 (NKJV):

"And you will hear of wars and rumors of wars. See that you are not troubled; for all these things must come to pass, but the end is not yet. For nation will rise against nation, and kingdom against kingdom."

American and Russian tensions have been high during the months leading up to October, 2016. American and Russian politicians have been saber rattling over Syria. Russia is backing Syrian President Assad and is seeking to destroy the ISIS terrorists who cause instability around the world. America wants the Assad regime toppled and has even been willing to back ISIS terrorists to help them achieve that goal.

The American - Russian political disagreements over Syria have led many pundits, the American mainstream media excluded, to conclude that the current American - Russian tensions may lead to World War III. Scripture prophecy foretells that there will be no WWIII between America and Russia, but instead a great tribulation of numerous regional wars throughout the world *after* America (Babylon the great) is destroyed (Revelation 11:12-19, 14:8, 18). Events will unfold that will lead to the destruction of Damascus, Syria, which will cease to be an inhabited city.

One of four forces is most likely to destroy Damascus, to make it a ruinous heap: America, Russia, civil warring factions within Syria, or Israel.

DAMASCUS, SYRIA WILL BE DESTROYED BEFORE AMERICA IS SIMILARLY DESTROYED

JEREMIAH 50:18 (NKJV) [WITH INTERPRETATION]:

Thus says YHWH (the Lord) of hosts, the God of Israel:

"Behold, I will punish the king of Babylon [PRESIDENT OF AMERICA] and his land [AMERICA], as I have punished the king of Assyria [PRESIDENT OF SYRIA]."

There will be wars and rumors of wars. The talk of America and Russia going to nuclear war in World War III is a rumor of a war. Damascus, Syria will cease from being a city and it will be a ruinous heap. Sometime after the destruction of Damascus comes to pass, Russia will lead a great assembly of nations (Jeremiah 50:3,9,41-46), will disable America with a cyber / EMP attack (Jeremiah 51:32), and then destroy America in one hour (Revelation 18:10,17,19). America will not retaliate (Jeremiah 51:56; Revelation 18:9-11). Russia will destroy America as Damascus was destroyed. America and Russia will not go to war before Damascus is destroyed, nor will Russia destroy America before Damascus becomes a ruinous heap and an uninhabited city. America will also have a sitting male president (king of Babylon), not a female president, when it is destroyed.

This is the order of things according to Scripture prophecy and Scripture will be fulfilled, as it is written.

THE DAY AMERICA STOOD STILL

By George Lujack

The title of this article is taken from the 1951 science fiction film, "The Day the Earth Stood Still." In the movie, an alien lands his spaceship on Earth and issues a warning to mankind to not bring its wars into outer space. Klaatu, the alien messenger, explains that the people of the other planets have safety concerns now that humanity has developed rockets and a rudimentary form of atomic power. To demonstrate that the members of the other planets mean business and will destroy the Earth if humanity does not change its warring ways, Klaatu neutralizes all electricity everywhere on Earth, except where human safety would be compromised, such as at hospitals and on aircraft in flight. Suddenly, all motorized vehicles and all electric power were inoperative and the Earth stood still for thirty minutes.

Mankind has now developed a weapon that can make the Earth literally stand still.

Electromagnetic pulse bombs, EMPs, are weapons that can fry a nation's electric grids and the electric circuitry used in everyday electronic equipment such as automobiles, computers, household appliances, lighting, radios, televisions, and all other electronic devices that people rely on for convenience. EMPs can also cripple a nation militarily, as national defense relies on machinery and weapons that are totally dependent on electric components.

Scripture prophecy declares that America, the great end-time nation referred to as 'Babylon the great,' will be crippled by an EMP attack, will stand still for a time, and then afterward will be completely destroyed by a full-scale nuclear attack.

JEREMIAH 51:32 (NKJV) [WITH INTERPRETATION]:

The reeds they have burned with fire [THE ELECTRONIC CIRCUITS AND ELECTRIC GRID OF THE NATION HAVE BEEN FRIED BY EMPs - ELECTROMAGNETIC PULSE BOMBS], and the [AMERICAN] soldiers are terrified.

reed:

An electrical contact used in a magnetically operated switch or relay.[194]

After the EMP attack, America will not be able to function or defend itself militarily. America's soldiers, rendered defenseless and recognizing their helplessness, will be terrified of an impending military attack.

JEREMIAH 50:43 (NKJV) [WITH INTERPRETATION]:

"The king of Babylon [THE AMERICAN PRESIDENT] has heard the report about them [RUSSIA AND HER ALLIES], and his hands grow feeble; anguish has taken hold of him, and pangs as of a woman in childbirth."

After the EMP attack on America, the president, his generals, and the whole U.S. military will sit defenseless as Russia and her allies surround the United States and ready themselves to destroy it.

JEREMIAH 50:41-42 (NKJV):

Behold, a people shall come from the north, and a great nation [RUSSIA] and many kings [RUSSIA'S ALLIES] shall be raised up from the ends of the earth. They shall hold the bow and the lance [NUCLEAR MISSILE LAUNCHERS]; they [RUSSIA AND HER ALLIES] are cruel and shall not show mercy. Their [RUSSIA'S AND HER ALLIES'] voice shall roar like the sea. They [RUSSIA AND HER ALLIES] shall ride on horses [MILITARY VEHICLES], set in array, like a man [SOLDIER] for the battle, against you, O daughter of Babylon [AMERICA - SPIRITUAL OFFSPRING NATION OF BABYLON (CONFUSION)].

JEREMIAH 51:1-4 (NKJV):

Thus says YHWH (the Lord): "Behold, I will stir up the spirit of a destroyer against Babylon [AMERICA], against those who dwell in Leb - My opponents [ISLAMIC NATIONS]. And I will send winnowers to Babylon [AMERICA], who shall winnow in her [AMERICA'S] empty land. For they [RUSSIA AND HER ALLIES] shall be against her [AMERICA] all around in the day of doom. Against her [AMERICA] let the archer bend his bow [LET THE MISSLE LAUNCHER AIM HIS NUCLEAR MISSILES], and stand ready in his armor [MILITARY VEHICLES AND SHIPS]. Do not spare her [AMERICA'S] young men; utterly destroy all her [AMERICA'S] army. Thus the slain shall fall in the land of the Chaldeans [AMERICAS], and those pierced through in her [AMERICA'S] streets."

Russia and her allies will destroy America without mercy, as America stands still and cannot defend itself after being neutralized by an EMP bomb attack.

PRE-TRIB, MID-TRIB, OR POST-TRIB RAPTURE?

There will be two major raptures, the American rapture and the worldwide rapture. Many Scripture scholars understand that there will be a rapture of the saints of God, but get hung up on the timing and are short-sighted in limiting God, believing that the rapture will be a single event.

ISAIAH 18:5-6 (NKJV):

For before the harvest [BEFORE THE WORLDWIDE HARVEST (RAPTURE) OF THE SAINTS], when the bud [TIMING] is perfect and the sour grape [HOMOSEXUAL GENERATION] is ripening [AGING / MATURING] in the flower [MAINSTREAM CULTURE], then He will both cut off the twigs [THE UNRIGHTEOUS] with pruning hooks and cut down and take away [RAPTURE] the branches [THE RIGHTEOUS]. They [THE UNRIGHTEOUS] will be left [BEHIND] together for the mountain birds of prey [REVELATION 18:2] and for the beasts of the earth. The birds of prey [REVELATION 18:2] will summer on them, and all the beasts of the earth will winter on them [EAT THEM].

ISAIAH 18:7 (NKJV):

In that time [OF THE DESTRUCTION OF BABYLON (AMERICA)] a present [THE RAPTURED AMERICAN SAINTS] will be brought to YHWH (the Lord) of hosts from a people tall and smooth-skinned [AMERICA], and from a people awesome from their beginning onward [AMERICA] - a nation powerful and trampling [AMERICA], whose land [AMERICA] the rivers divide - to the place of the name of YHWH (the Lord) of hosts, to Mount Zion [NEW JERUSALEM].

Isaiah 18:5 indicates that there will be two harvests, which are two raptures. There will be the American harvest (pre-trib rapture) and then afterward the world harvest (mid-trib rapture).

JEREMIAH 50:44-46 (NKJV) [WITH INTERPRETATION]:

"Behold, he [RUSSIA] shall come up like a lion from the floodplain of the Jordan against the dwelling place of the strong [OF FAITH - THE AMERICAN SAINTS], but I [YHWH - THE LORD] will make them [THE AMERICAN SAINTS] suddenly run away [BE RAPTURED - ISAIAH 18:1-7] from her [AMERICA]. And who is the Chosen One that I may appoint over her [AMERICA - FOR JUDGMENT]? For who is like Me? Who summons Me? And who is that Shepherd that will withstand Me? Therefore hear the counsel of YHWH (the Lord) that He has taken against Babylon [AMERICA], and His purposes that He has proposed against the land of the Chaldeans [AMERICAS]: Surely the least of the flock [LEAST OF THE SAINTS] [GOD] shall draw [RAPTURE] them out; He will make their [AMERICAN SAINTS'] dwelling place desolate before them. At the noise [NUCLEAR BOMB EXPLOSIONS] of the overtaking of Babylon [AMERICA] the earth trembles [FROM NUCLEAR BLAST SHOCKWAVES], and the outcry shall be heard among the nations."

The American rapture will be pre-tribulation. The destruction of Babylon the great (America) will mark the beginning of the great tribulation. American saints who are raptured will be raptured before the great tribulation, before the Antimessiah (Antichrist) rises, and before the implementation of the mark of the beast (Isaiah 18:5-7; Jeremiah 50:44-46). The worldwide rapture will be mid-tribulation. Worldwide saints who are raptured will be raptured after the great tribulation is underway, after the Antimessiah (Antichrist) reveals himself to the world, but before the mark of the beast is implemented (1 Corinthians 15:51-53; 1 Thessalonians 4:16-17; 2 Thessalonians 2:1-4).

DOOMSDAY PREPPERS OF THE ECONOMIC CRASH AND EMP ATTACK

Some economic doomsday preppers believe that the American economy will completely collapse. Scripture reveals that this will not be the case.

REVELATION 18:11 (NKJV) [WITH INTERPRETATION]:

"And the merchants of the earth will weep and mourn over her [AMERICA], for no one buys their merchandise anymore."

America will be buying and importing the world's goods right up until the day that it is destroyed. *After* America is destroyed, merchants around the world will no longer be able to sell their merchandise. As a result of the destruction of America, there will be a worldwide economic crisis as merchants around the world who supply America's goods will not be able to sell their merchandise anymore and they will shut down their factories.

There are people who are storing up stockpiles of food and weapons to protect themselves and their families in preparation for an act of war in which America will be struck by EMP weapons that will cause the country to go into an economic and electrical power crash - for years.

The EMP doomsday preppers are wasting their time, planning in futility. Scripture prophecy indicates that America will be struck by an EMP weapon (Jeremiah 51:32) and goes on to say that America will be completely destroyed by fire in one hour (Revelation 18), so there will be no prolonged years of surviving in an apocalyptic America in the aftermath of an EMP attack.

JEREMIAH 50:42 (NKJV) [WITH INTERPRETATION]:

They shall hold the bow and the lance [NUCLEAR MISSILE LAUNCHERS]; they [RUSSIA AND HER ALLIES] are cruel and shall not show mercy.

Do the doomsday preppers really believe that Russia, who will be aligned with many Muslim nations that are opponents of the God of Scripture (Jeremiah 51:1), is going to launch an EMP attack on America and allow America to survive and one day recover and retaliate? That is extremely naïve wishful thinking. Russia is not going to do an EMP hit-and-run on America, like Japan did when they bombed America's naval fleet at Pearl Harbor. Shortly after the EMP attack, Russia will use its nuclear arsenal and totally destroy its longtime rival, the United States of America.

Muslim nations, whose leaders routinely declare among their citizenry, "Death to America," are finally going to have an opportunity to deliver a deathblow to America. These Muslim nations are cruel and will show no mercy to America as they join Russia in the attack on the United States.

THE ANTIMESSIAH (ANTICHRIST) AND THE GREAT TRIBULATION

REVELATION 13:16-18 (NKJV):

He causes all, both small and great, rich and poor, free and slave, to receive a mark on their right hand or on their foreheads, and that no one may buy or sell except one who has the mark or the name of the beast, or the number of his name.
Here is wisdom. Let him who has understanding calculate the number of the beast, for it is the number of a man: His number is 666.

The worldwide economic crash will give rise to the Antimessiah (Antichrist), who will impose his mandatory mark on everyone in order to solve the world's economic problems. No one will be able to buy or sell anything without receiving the computer chip implant offered by the Antimessiah (Antichrist). Americans will never know the identity of the Antimessiah (Antichrist) and Americans will not be forced to take the mark of the beast, because America will be completely destroyed before the Antimessiah (Antichrist) rises.

WHY WILL GOD ALLOW AMERICA TO BE DESTROYED?

JEREMIAH 49:18, 50:40 (NKJV):

"As in the overthrow of Sodom and Gomorrah and their neighbors," says YHWH (the Lord), "No one shall remain (reside) there, nor shall a son of man dwell in it."

America will be destroyed for same reason and in the same manner that Sodom and Gomorrah were. America will be completely destroyed due to its widespread national sin of homosexuality and the broad acceptance of it.

WHAT SHOULD PEOPLE DO AFTER THE EMP ATTACK, AND BEFORE THE DAY OF DOOM – THE DESTRUCTION OF AMERICA?

JEREMIAH 51:2 (NKJV) [WITH INTERPRETATION]:

For they [RUSSIA AND HER ALLIES] shall be against her [AMERICA] all around in the day of doom.

After the EMP attack on America, Russia and her allies will gather their warships all around America along the east coast, west coast, and the Arctic. The United States will be crippled, defenseless, and paralyzed, unable to do anything as America's day of doom, the day of the nuclear annihilation of the land, approaches.

What are believers to do?

God would not destroy Sodom for the sake of ten righteous persons (Genesis 18:32), nor would He bring cataclysmic judgment upon America for the sake of ten righteous persons. He will provide an escape, an American rapture, for the sake of the righteous Americans before bringing judgment upon the land.

God did not destroy Sodom, until He first escorted righteous Lot and his family out of Sodom (Genesis 19:12-25). God will not destroy America until He first escorts, via the American rapture, the righteous out of America (Isaiah 18:5-7; Jeremiah 50:44-45, 51:33,45; Revelation 18:4).

JEREMIAH 51:31-32 (NKJV) [WITH INTERPRETATION]:

One runner will run to meet another, and one reporter to meet another, to report to the king of Babylon [PRESIDENT OF AMERICA] that his [THE PRESIDENT'S] city [NATION] is overtaken on all sides, the passages are blocked, the reeds they have burned with fire [THE ELECTRONIC CIRCUITRY / GRIDS OF THE NATION HAVE BEEN FRIED BY EMPs - ELECTROMAGNETIC PULSE BOMBS], and the soldiers are terrified.

After the day that causes America to stand still, many will be running to and fro, seeking assistance from the government to fix the problem, as many American people typically run to their government providers for assistance.

LUKE 21:28 (NKJV):

"Now when these things begin to happen, look up and lift up your heads, because your redemption draws near."

Luke 21:28 is not a reference to the redemption of Americans, but the same redemption principle applies. The U.S. government will not be able to prevent America's EMP attack, fix it, or prevent America's destruction that will soon follow the EMP attack. After the EMP attack, American believers should begin to call upon the name of YHWH (the Lord) for their salvation (Joel 2:32; Romans 10:13).

There are two destinies for most Americans: live faithfully and righteously to be counted worthy to escape the American nuclear annihilation through the American rapture (Luke 21:36), or be caught up in sin and unrighteousness to be left behind to die in the American nuclear holocaust and become food for the birds of prey and the beasts of the Earth (Isaiah 18:6; Revelation 18:2). Some Americans may be on foreign soil during business trips or vacations and there may be a select few Americans in deep underground bunkers who may be able to survive the nuclear detonations, who would have otherwise been killed during the nuclear attack.

Many Americans, including many professing believers, will not make the American rapture. Many professing believers are actively engaged in sins that can and will keep them from God's presence. The day America stands still will be the final sign and warning given days or hours before America's destruction occurs. Americans will have one last chance to repent and seek God for their redemption through the American rapture, before America's destruction occurs.

DESTRUCTION OF AMERICA AND SEPARATE AMERICAN RAPTURE

By George Lujack

This article will affirm that America is Babylon the great of Revelation 18, a great superpower nation that is destined to lead the end-time nations, but based on the Revelation 14 prophesy timeline, will refute the widely held belief of many Scripture prophecy watchers that America is destined to be destroyed at the end of the end times, and will argue that the destruction of Babylon the great (America the great) will begin the great tribulation. This article will also proclaim that American saints will be raptured in a special American rapture that is a separate event from the worldwide rapture.

Revelation 9:1-11 has been fulfilled. The American-led international coalition against ISIS, during a five-month bombing campaign (Sept. 2014-April 2015) against Islamic military equipment and supplies, tormented the lives of Muslim men, but did not kill these men who did not have the seal of God (Messiah / Christ) on their foreheads.

Revelation 9:15 is the next event to occur on the Revelation timeline.

REVELATION 9:15 (NKJV):

So the four angels, who had been prepared for the hour and day and month and year, were released to kill a third of mankind.

As of January 2017, the world's population was estimated to be at 7.5 billion people and rising. If Revelation 9:15 were to be fulfilled beginning in January 2017, a third of 7.5 billion people killed would equate to 2.5 billion deaths.

Many Scripture prophecy watchers believe that America will be an end-time nation and Americans will witness the rise of the Antimessiah (Antichrist.) Many believe that the United States' runaway deficit will bring about a worldwide economic crash, and in the aftermath of the economic crash, the Antimessiah (Antichrist) will rise and offer the 666 mark of the beast economic solution (Revelation 13:16-18). The Revelation Scripture prophecy timeline that many have accepted is that the Antimessiah (Antichrist) is revealed in Revelation 13, and the destruction of Babylon the great (America) does not occur until much later on in Revelation 18. That timeline of America's destruction is about to be hereby disputed.

THE SIXTH TRUMPET (WHERE HUMANITY IS TODAY):

REVELATION 9:13-17 (NKJV):

Then the sixth angel sounded: And I heard a voice from the four horns of the golden altar which is before God, saying to the sixth angel who had the trumpet, "Release the four angels who are bound at the great river Euphrates." So the four angels, who had been prepared for the hour and day and month and year, were released TO KILL A THIRD OF MANKIND. Now the number of the army of the horsemen was TWO HUNDRED MILLION; I heard the number of them. And thus I saw the horses in the vision: those who sat on them had breastplates of FIERY RED, HYACINTH BLUE, AND SULFUR YELLOW; and the heads of the horses were like the heads of lions; and out of their mouths came fire, smoke, and brimstone.

A third of mankind today is currently 2.5 billion people. In 2017, the U.S. population is slightly over 320 million people. If the United States were to be wiped out by a massive nuclear attack, and the deaths of 300 million were to occur, that would roughly equal 12.5% of the required deaths necessary to fulfill the Scripture prophecy of Revelation 9:15.

In order for the world's armies to wipe out over 2.5-billion people, the world's peacekeeper and policeman, America, must first be destroyed. Russia is the great power from the north (Jeremiah 50:3,9,41,51:48) that is prophesied to lead a great assembly of nations (from China and North Korea) to destroy America. Revelation 9:17 reveals that these nations' breastplate colors are fiery red, hyacinth blue, and sulfur yellow. These are the national colors of the Russian, Chinese, and North Korean countries.

REVELATION 14: A TIMELINE SEQUENCE SYNOPSIS OF EVENTS

REVELATION 14:8 (NKJV) (AMERICA'S FALL) [WITH INTERPRETATION]:

And another angel followed, saying, "Babylon [AMERICA] is fallen, is fallen, that great city, because she has made all nations drink of the wine of the wrath [MADNESS] of her fornication [SEXUAL IMMORALITY]."

Then *AFTER* the fall of Babylon (America) (Revelation 14:8) the mark of the beast is implemented *in the next verses*...

REVELATION 14:9-12 (NKJV) (THE 666 MARK) [WITH INTERPRETATION]:

Then a third angel followed them, saying with a loud voice, "If anyone worships the beast and his image, and receives his mark on his forehead or on his hand, he himself shall also drink of the wine of the wrath of God, which is poured out full strength into the cup of His indignation. He shall be tormented with fire and brimstone in the presence of the holy angels and in the presence of the Lamb [YESHUA (JESUS)]. And the smoke of their torment ascends forever and ever; and they have no rest day or night, who worship the beast and his image, and whoever receives the mark of his name."

Here is the patience of the saints; here are those who keep the commandments of God and the faith of Yeshua (Jesus).

Then *AFTER* the fall of Babylon (America) (Revelation 14:8) and *AFTER* the revealing of the Antimessiah (Antichrist) and introduction of his mark (Revelation 14:9-12), the worldwide rapture will occur *in the next verses...*

REVELATION 14:14-16 (NKJV) (WORLD RAPTURE) [WITH INTERPRETATION]:

Then I looked, and behold, a white cloud, and on the cloud sat One like the Son of Man, having on His head a golden crown, and in His hand a sharp sickle. And another angel came out of the temple, crying with a loud voice to Him who sat on the cloud, "Thrust in Your sickle and reap [RAPTURE], for the time has come for You to reap [RAPTURE], for the harvest [SAINTS] of the earth is ripe." So He who sat on the cloud thrust in His sickle on the earth, and the earth was reaped [RAPTURED].

The worldwide rapture, according to Revelation 14:14-16, occurs *after* the destruction of Babylon (America) the great (Revelation 14:8). What happens to the saints living in Babylon (America)? Will they be destroyed along with America?

Scripture declares that God will provide a separate rapture for the American saints, a rapture that will precede the worldwide rapture. There will be two harvests (raptures), one for Americans and another for the rest of the world. Isaiah 18:5-7 are the key verses which reveal that *BEFORE* the worldwide rapture occurs, there will be an American rapture of American saints, who will be brought before the YHWH (the Lord).

ISAIAH 18:5-7 (NKJV) (THE AMERICAN RAPTURE) [WITH INTERPRETATION]:

For before the harvest [BEFORE THE WORLDWIDE HARVEST (RAPTURE) OF THE SAINTS], when the bud [TIMING] is perfect and the sour grape [HOMOSEXUAL GENERATION] is ripening [AGING / MATURING] in the flower [MAINSTREAM CULTURE], then He will both cut off the twigs [THE UNRIGHTEOUS] with pruning hooks and cut down and take away [RAPTURE] the branches [THE RIGHTEOUS]. They [THE UNRIGHTEOUS] will be left [BEHIND] together for the mountain birds of prey [REVELATION 18:2] and for the beasts of the earth. The birds of prey [REVELATION 18:2] will summer on them, and all the beasts of the earth will winter on them [EAT THEM].

In that time [OF THE DESTRUCTION OF BABYLON (AMERICA)] a present [THE RAPTURED AMERICAN SAINTS] will be brought to YHWH (the Lord) of hosts from a people tall and smooth-skinned [AMERICA], and from a people awesome from their beginning onward [AMERICA] - a nation powerful and trampling [AMERICA], whose land [AMERICA] the rivers divide - to the place of the name of YHWH (the Lord) of hosts, to Mount Zion [NEW JERUSALEM].

JEREMIAH 51:5-6 (NKJV) [WITH INTERPRETATION]:

For Israel is not forsaken, nor Judah [SPIRITUAL ISRAEL AND JUDAH - THE SAINTS], by his God, YHWH (the Lord) of hosts, though their [AMERICA'S] land was filled with sin against the Holy One of Israel." Flee [IN THE AMERICAN RAPTURE] from the midst of Babylon [AMERICA], and every one save his life! Do not be cut off [LEFT BEHIND] in her [AMERICA'S] wickedness, for this is the time of YHWH's (the Lord's) vengeance, the recompense He is paying her [AMERICA].

JEREMIAH 50:8 (NKJV) [WITH INTERPRETATION]:

Flee [IN THE AMERICAN RAPTURE] from the midst of Babylon [AMERICA], go [BE RAPTURED] out of the land of the Chaldeans [AMERICAS]...

JEREMIAH 51:33 (NKJV) [WITH INTERPRETATION]:

For thus says YHWH (the Lord) of hosts, the God of Israel: "The daughter of Babylon [AMERICA] is like a threshing floor when it is time to thresh her; Yet a little while and the time of her harvest [RAPTURE] will come.

JEREMIAH 51:45 (NKJV) [WITH INTERPRETATION]:

"Come out of her [AMERICA'S] midst, My people! And let everyone deliver himself [THROUGH THE AMERICAN RAPTURE] from the fierce anger of YHWH (the Lord).

REVELATION 18:4 (NKJV) [WITH INTERPRETATION]:

And I heard another voice from heaven saying, "Come out [BE RAPTURED] of her [AMERICA], My people, lest you share in her [AMERICA'S] sins, and lest you receive of her [AMERICA'S] plagues..."

The sour grape (homosexuality and all the perversions that go along with it) is ripening in the flower (mainstream culture) and proliferating as never before in United States (Isaiah 18:5). America's embrace of the sin of homosexuality will bring God's judgment upon the land.

The destruction of America marks the beginning of the great tribulation. Americans, who are not raptured, will be the first of the one third of mankind to be killed from the great tribulation (Revelation 9:15)

After America falls, there will be no superpower peacekeeping nation able to prevent the other nations from engaging in war. Nations will make war and kill one third of the world's population (Revelation 9:15).

After America falls, the global banking systems and all international reserve currency holdings of American dollars will become worthless (Ezekiel 7:19; Revelation 13:16-18,14:9-12).

After America falls (Revelation 14:8, 18), and after the deaths of one third of the world's population (Revelation 9:15), and after the global economic collapse (Ezekiel 7:19), this will be a perfect opportunity and time for the Antimessiah (Antichrist) to appear on the world stage to offer peace to the nations and introduce the economic mark of the beast (Revelation 13:16-18,14:9-12).

Americans are not prophesied to survive through the great tribulation of the end times (Jeremiah 49:18, 50:3,39-40). The destruction of America will bring about the beginning of the great tribulation and will give rise to and provide an opportunity for the Antimessiah (Antichrist) to appear on the world stage.

THE THREE WOES OF REVELATION 9

REVELATION 9:12 (NKJV):

One woe is past. Behold, still two more woes are coming after these things.

The fifth trumpet has been fulfilled (Revelation 9:1-11). The fifth trumpet was the first 'woe' of Revelation 9 that has passed, and two more 'woes' are coming after the fifth trumpet (Revelation 9:12).

Revelation 9:12 speaks of two more woes before the sixth trumpet blasts, signaling the beginning of the great tribulation. The two woes are the destruction of Damascus, Syria (Isaiah 17:1) and then sometime afterward the destruction of America (Babylon the great) (Jeremiah 50:18; Revelation 14:8, 18).

The sixth trumpet signals the start of the great tribulation, which begins with the destruction of America, that will be followed by the death of one third of mankind (Revelation 9:12-19).

America will be destroyed by fire in one hour (Revelation 18:10,17,19) in the same manner and for the same national sins of Sodom (Jeremiah 49:18,50:40). On June 26, 2015, the United States Supreme Court legalized homosexual marriage, legitimizing sodomy as the law of the land in America. Thus, the Scripture requirement for America to be destroyed has been fulfilled and it is only a matter of time before it is.

The saints of America have been promised a special American rapture, separate from the worldwide rapture, to escape the plagues that are soon coming upon America (Babylon the great) (Isaiah 18:5-7; Jeremiah 50:8, 51:5-6,33,45; Revelation 18:4).

AMERICA WILL BE COMPLETELY DESTROYED BY RUSSIA (IN 1-HOUR)

By George Lujack

'Alas, alas, that great city [NATION] Babylon [AMERICA], that mighty city [NATION]! For in one hour your [AMERICA'S] judgment has come.' ... 'Alas, alas, that great city [NATION] ... For in one hour such great riches came to nothing.' Every shipmaster, all who travel by ship, sailors, and as many as trade on the sea, stood at a distance and cried out when they saw the smoke of her burning, saying, 'What is like this great city [NATION]?' ... 'Alas, alas, that great city [NATION], in which all who had ships on the sea became rich by her [AMERICA'S] wealth! For in one hour she [AMERICA] is made desolate.'
-REVELATION 18:10,16-19 (NKJV) [WITH INTERPRETATION]

Is America 'Babylon the great' of Revelation 18? Many scoffers of that idea are quick to point out that 'America' is not mentioned in Scripture. Is it really plausible to believe that Scripture would remain silent on the greatest country that has ever existed and not mention this country in end-times prophesies? Many err in that they comprehend and read Scripture with twenty-first century glasses on, failing to take into account that Scripture prophecy was written in the first century, often using apocalyptic or prophetic language.

DANIEL 12:8-9 (NKJV):

Although I heard, I did not understand. Then I said, "My Master (Lord), what shall be the end of these things?" And he said, "Go your way, Daniel, for the words are closed up and sealed *till the time of the end...*"

The prophets were shown visions of the *time of the end* that they themselves did not understand. Throughout millennia no one has understood many of the prophetic visions of Scripture. No one could possibly understand sealed end-time prophesies that could only be understood by end-time prophets in light of yet to unfold end-time world events. In the twentieth through twenty-first centuries, the meanings of these end-time prophecies have been unsealed. This now is *the time of the end*.

'MYSTERY BABYLON' AND 'BABYLON THE GREAT' ARE TWO DIFFERENT BABYLONS

REVELATION 18:1 (NKJV) (HSV†) [WITH INTERPRETATION]:

After these things [THE JUDGMENT OF MYSTERY BABYLON - REVELATION 17]
I saw *another angel (†messenger)* coming down from heaven...

Many Scripture observers lump the 'Mystery Babylon' of Revelation 17 with 'Babylon the great' of Revelation 18 together and consider them the same entity. 'Mystery Babylon' and 'Babylon the great' are two different Babylons. Mystery Babylon is a harlot (Revelation 17:1,5) that is a worldwide multinational institution that sits on many waters and that speaks in many languages (Revelation 17:15). Mystery Babylon is a 'mother' church of all the Protestant denominations (Revelation 17:5). Mystery Babylon has persecuted the true saints of Yeshua (Jesus) (Revelation 17:6). Mystery Babylon is a woman (a church) that has a city (Vatican City) that reigns over the kings of the Earth (Revelation 17:18). Pharisaic Talmudic Judaism is a branch of Mystery Babylon. Mystery Babylon is spiritual Babylon - a false, perverted religious system. Mystery Babylon is the Roman Catholic Church and Pharisaic Talmudic Judaism.

Babylon the great is a country that spreads its spiritually wicked culture, such as abortion, evolution 'science' theory, pornography, and homosexuality tolerance. Babylon the great has made merchants around the world rich (Revelation 18:3). Babylon the great has a mother country, Great Britain (Jeremiah 50:12), and is referred to as the daughter of Babylon (Isaiah 47:1,5; Jeremiah 50:42, 51:33), a spiritual reference to America's affiliation with the Catholic Church. Babylon the great is a great city (country) (Revelation 18:10,16,18-19,21). After Babylon the great is destroyed, merchants around the world will no longer be able to sell their merchandise (Revelation 18:11-18). Babylon the great is a wealthy nation (Revelation 18:19) with a mighty military (Jeremiah 50:23, 51:20-23). Babylon the great is America the great.

Why didn't the prophets mention the Roman Catholic Church and America by name in their writings? The Roman Catholic Church did not exist in the first century, nor did the nation that would become America, so the prophets who saw visions of and wrote about these two end-time entities didn't know the names of who they were. 'Babylon' is a term that connotes confusion, greatness, wealth, and wickedness. The prophets saw visions of a powerful worldwide religious organization and called it, "Mystery Babylon," and also saw visions of a great and powerful end-time nation that they referred to as "Babylon the great."

ISAIAH 47:1-5 (NKJV) [WITH INTERPRETATION]:

"Come down and sit in the dust, O virgin daughter of Babylon [SPIRITUAL OFFSPRING NATION OF ORIGINAL BABYLON]. Sit on the ground without a throne, O daughter of the Chaldeans [SPIRITUAL OFFSPRING NATION OF ORIGINAL BABYLONIANS]! For you [AMERICA] shall no more be called tender and delicate. Take the millstones and grind meal. Remove your [AMERICA'S] veil, take off the skirt, uncover the thigh, pass through the rivers. Your [AMERICA'S] nakedness shall be uncovered, your [AMERICA'S] shame will also be exposed; I will take vengeance, and I will not arbitrate with a man." Our Redeemer, YHWH (the Lord) of hosts is His name, the Holy One of Israel. "Sit silent, and go into darkness, O daughter of the Chaldeans [SPIRITUAL OFFSPRING NATION OF ORIGINAL BABYLONIANS]! For you [AMERICA] shall no longer be called The Lady of Kingdoms [LADY LIBERTY - THE LEADER OF THE FREE WORLD]."

ISAIAH 47:8 (NKJV) [WITH INTERPRETATION]:

"Therefore hear this now, you [AMERICANS] who are given to pleasures, who dwell securely, who say in your [AMERICA'S] heart, 'I [AMERICA] am, and there is no one else besides me [AMERICA]. I [AMERICA] shall not sit as a widow, nor shall I [AMERICA] know the loss of children' ['I AMERICA INDEPENDENTLY RULE THE NATIONS, I AMERICA AM NO HELPLESS WIDOW, AND WILL NOT SEE DESOLATION'].

ISAIAH 47:9-11 (NKJV) [WITH INTERPRETATION]:

But these two things shall come to you [AMERICA] in a moment, in one day: the loss of children [DESOLATION], and widowhood [HELPLESSNESS]. They shall come upon you [AMERICA] in completeness, because of the multitude of your [AMERICA'S] sorceries [CULTURAL INFLUENCES]; for the great abundance of your [AMERICA'S] enchantments [SEXUAL ENTICEMENTS]. For you [AMERICA] have trusted in your [AMERICA'S] wickedness; you [AMERICA] have said, 'No one sees me [AMERICA].' [Your [AMERICA'S] wisdom and your [AMERICA'S] knowledge have led you [AMERICA] astray. And you [AMERICA] have said in your [AMERICA'S] heart, 'I [AMERICA] am, and there is no one else besides me [AMERICA]. 'But evil shall come upon you [AMERICA], and you [AMERICA] shall not know from where it arises, and trouble shall fall upon you [AMERICA], and you [AMERICA] will not be able to put it off, and desolation [NUCLEAR ANNIHILATION] shall come upon you [AMERICA] suddenly, which you [AMERICA] shall not know."

BABYLON (AMERICA) WILL BE DESTROYED BY A NATION FROM THE NORTH (RUSSIA)

JEREMIAH 50:1-3 (NKJV) [WITH INTERPRETATION]:

The word that YHWH (the Lord) spoke against Babylon [AMERICA] and against the land of the Chaldeans [AMERICAS] by Jeremiah the prophet. "Declare among the nations, proclaim, and lift up a banner and let it be heard - do not conceal it - Say, 'Babylon [AMERICA] is overtaken, ... Her [AMERICA'S] images [STATUE OF LIBERTY, ET AL.] shall be put to shame, Her [AMERICA'S] idols are broken in pieces.' For a nation [RUSSIA] shall come up against her [AMERICA] from the north, which shall make her [AMERICA'S] land desolate, and no one shall dwell in it.

JEREMIAH 50:9-14 (NKJV) [WITH INTERPRETATION]:

"For behold, I will raise and cause to come up against Babylon [AMERICA] an assembly of great nations from the north country [RUSSIA], and they [RUSSIA AND HER ALLIES] shall array themselves against her [AMERICA]; from there she [AMERICA] shall be taken [DESTROYED]. Their arrows [NUCLEAR MISSILES] shall be like those of an expert warrior [PRECISE]; none shall return in vain. And Chaldea [AMERICA] shall become plunder; all who plunder her [AMERICA] shall be satisfied," says YHWH (the Lord). "Because you [AMERICA] were glad, because you [AMERICA] rejoiced [IN SIN], you [ATHEISTIC SECULAR HUMANIST] destroyers of My heritage [JUDEO-CHRISTIAN FOUNDED NATION], because you have grown fat [OBESE AMERICANS] like a heifer threshing grain and you bellow like bulls [COMPLAIN CHRONICALLY]. Your mother [GREAT BRITAIN] shall be deeply ashamed; she [GREAT BRITAIN] who bore you [AMERICA] shall be humiliated. Behold, the least [YOUNGEST] of the [END-TIME] nations [AMERICA] shall be a wilderness, a dry land and a desert [NUCLEAR WASTELAND]. Because of the wrath of YHWH (the Lord) she [AMERICA] shall not be inhabited, but she [AMERICA] shall be wholly desolate. Everyone who goes by Babylon [AMERICA] shall be horrified and hiss at all her [AMERICA'S] plagues. Put yourselves in array against Babylon [AMERICA] all around, all you who bend the bow [FIRE THE MISSILES]; shoot at her [AMERICA], spare no arrows [NUCLEAR MISSILES], for she [AMERICA] has sinned against YHWH (the Lord).

JEREMIAH 50:15 (NKJV) [WITH INTERPRETATION]:

Shout against her [AMERICA] all around; she [AMERICA] has given her [AMERICA'S] hand, her [AMERICA'S] foundations [JUDEO-CHRISTIAN] have fallen, her [AMERICA'S] walls [SKYSCRAPERS] are thrown down; for it is the vengeance of YHWH (the Lord). Take vengeance on her [AMERICA] as she [AMERICA] has done [TO OTHER NATIONS], so do to her [AMERICA]."

JEREMIAH 50:18 (NKJV) [WITH INTERPRETATION]:

Therefore thus says YHWH (the Lord) of hosts, the God of Israel: "Behold, I will punish the king of Babylon [PRESIDENT OF AMERICA] and his land [AMERICA], as I have punished the king of Assyria [PRESIDENT OF SYRIA]."

JEREMIAH 50:22-32 (NKJV) [WITH INTERPRETATION]:

"A sound of battle is in the land [AMERICA], and of great destruction. How the hammer of the whole earth [THE WORLD'S SUPERPOWER] has been cut apart and broken! How Babylon [AMERICA] has become a ruin among the nations! I have laid a snare for you [AMERICA]; you [AMERICA] have indeed been overtaken, O Babylon [AMERICA], and you [AMERICA] were not aware [SURPRISE ATTACKED]. You [AMERICA] have been found [GUILTY] and also caught [OFF GUARD], because you [AMERICA] have contended [DEFIANTLY SINNED] against YHWH (the Lord). YHWH (the Lord) has opened His armory, and has brought out the weapons of His indignation; for this is the work of YHWH (the Lord) GOD of hosts [GOD USING RUSSIA TO DESTROY AMERICA] in the land of the Chaldeans [AMERICAS]. Come against her [AMERICA] from the farthest border, open her [AMERICA'S] storehouses, cast her [AMERICA] up as heaps of ruins, and destroy her [AMERICA] utterly; let nothing of her [AMERICA] be left. Slay all her [AMERICA'S] bulls, let them go down to the slaughter. Woe to them! For their [AMERICANS'] day has come, the time of their [AMERICANS'] punishment. The voice of those who flee and escape [THROUGH THE RAPTURE] from the land of Babylon [AMERICA] declares in Zion [NEW JERUSALEM] the vengeance of YHWH (the Lord) our God, the vengeance of His temple. "Call together the archers [MISSILE LAUNCHERS] against Babylon [AMERICA]. All you who bend the bow [FIRE THE MISSILES], encamp against it [AMERICA] all around; let none of them [AMERICANS] escape. Repay her [AMERICA] according to her work [EVILS], according to all she [AMERICA] has done [TO OTHER NATIONS], do to her [AMERICA]; for she has been proud (IN SIN) against YHWH (the Lord), against the Holy One of Israel. Therefore her [AMERICA'S] young men shall fall in the streets, and all her [AMERICA'S] men of war [SOLDIERS] shall perish in that day," says YHWH (the Lord). "Behold, I am against you [AMERICA], O most proud one [NATION]!" says YHWH (the Lord) GOD of hosts; "For your [AMERICA'S] day has come, the time that I will punish you [AMERICA].

The most proud [NATION] shall stumble and fall, and no one will raise him [AMERICA] up. I will kindle a fire in his [AMERICA'S] cities, and it will devour all around him [AMERICA]."

JEREMIAH 50:35-36 (NKJV) [WITH INTERPRETATION]:

"A sword is against the Chaldeans [AMERICANS]," says YHWH (the Lord), "Against the inhabitants of Babylon [AMERICA], and against her [AMERICA'S] princes and her [AMERICA'S] wise men. A sword is against the liars, and they will be fools. A sword is against her [AMERICA'S] mighty men [SOLDIERS], and they will be dismayed.

JEREMIAH 50:37-46 (NKJV) [WITH INTERPRETATION]:

A sword is against their [AMERICA'S] horses [MILITARY VEHICLES], against their chariots [MILITARY SHIPS], and against all the mixed peoples [IMMIGRANTS, LEGAL AND ILLEGAL] who are in her [AMERICA'S] midst; and they [AMERICANS] will become like women. A sword is against her [AMERICA'S] treasures, and they will be robbed. A drought is against her [AMERICA'S] waters, and they will be dried up. For it [AMERICA] is the land of carved images [STATUES AND TELEVISIONS], and they boast about their idols [CELEBRITIES]. Therefore the wild desert beasts shall dwell there with the jackals, and the ostriches shall dwell in it [AMERICA]. It [AMERICA] shall be inhabited no more forever, nor shall it [AMERICA] be dwelt in from generation to generation. As God overthrew Sodom and Gomorrah and their neighbors," says YHWH (the Lord), "So no one shall reside there [IN AMERICA], nor son of man dwell in it [AMERICA]. Behold, a people shall come from the north, and a great nation [RUSSIA] and many kings [RUSSIA'S ALLIES] shall be raised up from the ends of the earth.

They shall hold the bow and the lance [NUCLEAR MISSILE LAUNCHERS]; they [RUSSIA AND HER ALLIES] are cruel and shall not show mercy. Their [RUSSIA'S AND HER ALLIES'] voice shall roar like the sea.

They [RUSSIA AND HER ALLIES] shall ride on horses [MILITARY VEHICLES], set in array, like a man [SOLDIER] for the battle, against you, O daughter of Babylon [AMERICA - SPIRITUAL OFFSPRING NATION OF BABYLON]."

"The king of Babylon [THE AMERICAN PRESIDENT] has heard the report about them [RUSSIA AND HER ALLIES], and his hands grow feeble; anguish has taken hold of him, and pangs as of a woman in childbirth. Behold, he [RUSSIA] shall come up like a lion from the floodplain of the Jordan against the dwelling place of the strong [OF FAITH - THE AMERICAN SAINTS], but I [YHWH - THE LORD] will make them [THE AMERICAN SAINTS] suddenly run away [BE RAPTURED - ISAIAH 18:1-7] from her [AMERICA]. And who is the Chosen One that I may appoint over her [AMERICA - FOR JUDGMENT]? For who is like Me? Who summons Me? And who is that Shepherd that will withstand Me? Therefore hear the counsel of YHWH (the Lord) that He has taken against Babylon [AMERICA], and His purposes that He has proposed against the land of the Chaldeans [AMERICAS]: Surely the least of the flock [LEAST OF THE SAINTS] [GOD] shall draw [RAPTURE] them out; He will make their [AMERICAN SAINTS'] dwelling place desolate before them. At the noise [NUCLEAR BOMB EXPLOSIONS] of the overtaking of Babylon [AMERICA] the earth trembles [FROM NUCLEAR BLAST SHOCKWAVES], and the outcry shall be heard among the nations."

JEREMIAH 51:1-3 (NKJV) [WITH INTERPRETATION]:

Thus says YHWH (the Lord): "Behold, I will stir up the spirit of a destroyer against Babylon [AMERICA], against those who dwell in Leb - My opponents [ISLAMIC NATIONS]. And I will send winnowers to Babylon [AMERICA], who shall winnow in her [AMERICA'S] empty land. For they [RUSSIA AND HER ALLIES] shall be against her [AMERICA] all around in the day of doom. Against her [AMERICA] let the archer bend his bow [LET THE MISSILE LAUNCHER AIM HIS NUCLEAR MISSILES], and stand ready in his armor [MILITARY VEHICLES AND SHIPS].

Do not spare her [AMERICA'S] young men; utterly destroy all her [AMERICA'S] army.

JEREMIAH 51:4-13 (NKJV) [WITH INTERPRETATION]:

Thus the slain shall fall in the land of the Chaldeans [AMERICAS], and those pierced through in her [AMERICA'S] streets. For Israel is not forsaken, nor Judah [SPIRITUAL ISRAEL AND JUDAH - THE SAINTS], by his [THE SAINTS'] God, YHWH (the Lord) of hosts, though their [AMERICA'S] land was filled with sin against the Holy One of Israel." Flee [IN THE AMERICAN RAPTURE] from the midst of Babylon [AMERICA], and every one [AMERICAN SAINT] save his life! Do not be cut off [LEFT BEHIND] in her [AMERICA'S] wickedness, for this is the time of YHWH's (the Lord's) vengeance, the recompense He is paying her [AMERICA]. Babylon [AMERICA] was a golden cup [MOST BLESSED NATION] in (YHWH's) the Lord's hand, that made all the earth drunk [WITH WEALTH]. The nations drank her [AMERICA'S] wine [CULTURE], that is why the nations are deranged. Babylon [AMERICA] has suddenly fallen and been destroyed. Wail for her! Take balm for her pain - perhaps she [AMERICA] may be healed. We would have healed Babylon [AMERICA - 2 CHRONICLES 7:14], but she [AMERICA] is not healed. Forget her [AMERICA], and let us go everyone to his own land, for her [AMERICA'S] judgment reaches to heaven and is lifted up to the skies [THE SMOKE OF AMERICA'S BURNING]. YHWH (the Lord) has revealed our righteousness. Come and let us declare in Zion [NEW JERUSALEM] the work of YHWH (the Lord) our God.

Polish the arrows [NUCLEAR MISSILES]! Put on the shields [MILITARY ARMOR]! YHWH (the Lord) has raised up the spirit of the kings of the Medes. For His plan is against Babylon [AMERICA] to destroy it, because it is the vengeance of YHWH (the Lord), the vengeance for His temple. Set up a banner on the walls of Babylon [AMERICA], strengthen the watch [UNDERSTANDING OF END-TIME PROPHECIES], station the watchmen [END-TIME PROPHETS], prepare the ambushes. For YHWH (the Lord) has both planned and done what He spoke concerning the inhabitants of Babylon [AMERICA]. You [AMERICA] who dwell by many waters, abundant in treasures, your [AMERICA'S] end has come, the measure of your [AMERICA'S] greedy gain.

JEREMIAH 51:19-23 (NKJV) [WITH INTERPRETATION]:

The Portion of Jacob [AMERICAN SAINTS OF GOD] are not like them [SECULAR SINFUL AMERICANS], For He is the Maker of all, and Israel [SPIRITUAL ISRAEL - THE SAINTS] are the tribe [PEOPLE] of His inheritance. YHWH (the Lord) of hosts is His name. "You [RIGHTEOUS AMERICA] are My battle-ax and weapons of war, for with you [RIGHTEOUS AMERICA] I will break nations in pieces, and with you [RIGHTEOUS AMERICA] I will destroy reigns. With you [RIGHTEOUS AMERICA] I will break in pieces the horse [MILITARY VEHICLE] and its rider [OPERATOR], and with you [RIGHTEOUS AMERICA] I will break in pieces the chariot [MILITARY SHIP] and its rider [OPERATOR]. And with you [RIGHTEOUS AMERICA] also I will break in pieces man and woman [CIVILIAN WAR CASUALTIES], and with you [RIGHTEOUS AMERICA] AMERICA] I will break in pieces old and young [CIVILIAN WAR CASUALTIES], and with you [RIGHTEOUS AMERICA] I will break in pieces the young man and the maiden [CIVILIAN WAR CASUALTIES]. And with you [RIGHTEOUS AMERICA] I will break in pieces the shepherd and his flock [CIVILIAN WAR CASUALTIES], and with you [RIGHTEOUS AMERICA] I will break in pieces the farmer and his yoke of oxen [CIVILIAN WAR CASUALTIES]. And with you I will break in pieces governors and rulers.

JEREMIAH 51:24-32 (NKJV) [WITH INTERPRETATION]:

And I will repay Babylon [AMERICA] and all the inhabitants of Chaldea [AMERICA] for all the evil they [AMERICA] have done in Zion [JERUSALEM] before your [RIGHTEOUS AMERICAN SAINTS'] eyes," says YHWH (the Lord). "Behold, I am against you, O destroying mountain [AMERICA], who destroys all the earth," says YHWH (the Lord). "And I will stretch out My hand against you [AMERICA]. And I shall roll you down from the rocks, and make you [AMERICA] a burnt mountain [NUCLEAR WASTELAND]. They shall not take from you [AMERICA] a stone for a corner nor a stone for a foundation [A TERRITORY TO OCCUPY NOR A TERRITORY TO ANNEX], but you [AMERICA] shall be desolate forever," says YHWH (the Lord). Lift up up a banner in the land, blow the trumpet among the nations! Prepare the nations against her [AMERICA], call the kingdoms together against her [AMERICA]: Ararat, Minni, and Ashkenaz. Appoint a commander against her [AMERICA], bring up horses [MILITARY VEHICLES] to come up like the bristling locusts [BLITZKRIEG AIR ATTACK]. Prepare against her [AMERICA] the nations, with the kings of the Medes, its governors and all its rulers, all the land of his rule, so that the land [AMERICA] will tremble and writhe in pain. For every plan of YHWH (the Lord) shall be performed against Babylon [AMERICA], to make the land of Babylon [AMERICA] a ruin without inhabitant. The mighty men [SOLDIERS] of Babylon [AMERICA] have ceased to fight, they [AMERICAN SOLDIERS] have remained in their strongholds. Their [AMERICA'S] might [MILITARY MIGHT] has failed, they became like women, they [RUSSIA AND HER ALLIES] have burned her [AMERICA'S] dwelling places. The bars of her [AMERICA'S] gate are broken.

One runner will run to meet another, and one reporter to meet another, to report to the king of Babylon [PRESIDENT OF AMERICA] that his [THE PRESIDENT'S] city [NATION] is overtaken on all sides, the passages are blocked, the reeds they have burned with fire [THE ELECTRONIC CIRCUITRY / GRIDS OF THE NATION HAVE BEEN FRIED BY EMPs - ELECTROMAGNETIC PULSE BOMBS], and the soldiers are terrified. For thus says YHWH (the Lord) of hosts, the God of Israel: "The daughter of Babylon [SPIRITUAL OFFSPRING NATION OF ORIGINAL BABYLON] is like a threshing floor at the time it is trodden. Yet a little while and the time of her [AMERICA'S] harvest [RAPTURE] will come."

JEREMIAH 51:37 (NKJV) [WITH INTERPRETATION]:

Babylon [AMERICA] shall become a heap [NUCLEAR WASTELAND], a habitation of jackals, an astonishment and a hissing, without inhabitant.

JEREMIAH 51:41-43 (NKJV) [WITH INTERPRETATION]:

Oh, how the praise of the whole earth [AMERICA] is seized! How Babylon [AMERICA] has become a ruin among the nations! The sea [OF NUCLEAR MISSILES] has come up Babylon [AMERICA], she [AMERICA] is covered with the roaring of its waves over [NUCLEAR BLAST SHOCKWAVES]. Her [AMERICA'S] cities have become ruins, a dry land and a wilderness, a land where no one dwells, through which no son of man passes by it.

JEREMIAH 51:45 (NKJV) [WITH INTERPRETATION]:

Come out of her [AMERICA'S] midst, My people! And let everyone deliver himself [THROUGH THE RAPTURE] from the fierce anger of YHWH (the Lord).

JEREMIAH 51:47-48 (NKJV) [WITH INTERPRETATION]:

"Therefore behold, the days are coming that I will bring judgment on the carved images [STATUE OF LIBERTY, ETC.] of Babylon [AMERICA], and all her [AMERICA'S] land shall be put to shame, and all her [AMERICA'S] slain shall fall in her [AMERICA'S] midst. Then the heavens and the earth and all that is in them shall sing joyously over Babylon [AMERICA], for the ravagers [RUSSIA AND HER ALLIES] shall come to her [AMERICA] from the north," says YHWH (the Lord).

JEREMIAH 51:53-58 (NKJV) [WITH INTERPRETATION]:

"Though Babylon [AMERICA] were to mount up to heaven [ORBIT SATELLITES IN SPACE], and though she [AMERICA] were to fortify the height of her strength [MAINTAIN A MASSIVE MILITARY], ravagers [RUSSIA AND HER ALLIES] would come to her [AMERICA] from Me," says YHWH (the Lord). The sound of a cry comes from Babylon [AMERICA], and great destruction from the land of the Chaldeans [AMERICAS], because YHWH (the Lord) is ravaging Babylon [AMERICA] and silencing her [AMERICA'S] loud voice [WORLD INFLUENCE], and her [AMERICA'S] waves [NUCLEAR BLAST SHOCKWAVES] roar like great waters, and the noise of their voice [DETONATIONS] is uttered [SOUNDED], because the ravager [RUSSIA AND HER ALLIES] comes against her [AMERICA], against Babylon [AMERICA], and her [AMERICA'S] mighty men [SOLDIERS] are overtaken. Every one of their [AMERICA'S] bows [NUCLEAR MISSILE SILOS] shall be broken, for YHWH (the Lord) is the God of recompense; He will surely repay.

"And I will make drunk her [AMERICA'S] princes and wise men, her [AMERICA'S] governors, her [AMERICA'S] deputies, and her [AMERICA'S] mighty men [SOLDIERS] and they [AMERICANS] shall sleep a perpetual sleep [DIE] and not awake," says the King, whose name is YHWH (the Lord) of hosts. Thus says YHWH (the Lord) of hosts: "The broad walls [MANY CITY SKYSCRAPERS] of Babylon [AMERICA] shall be utterly broken, and her [AMERICA'S] high gates [SKYSCRAPERS] shall be burned with fire. The people [AMERICANS] will labor in vain, and the nations [OTHER NEIGHBORING NATIONS], because of the fire shall be weary."

JEREMIAH 51:60-64 (NKJV) [WITH INTERPRETATION]:

So Jeremiah wrote in a book all the evil that would come upon Babylon [AMERICA], all these words that are written against Babylon [AMERICA]. And Jeremiah said to Seraiah, "When you arrive in Babylon and see it, and read all these words, then you shall say, 'O Lord, You have spoken against this place [AMERICA] to cut it off, so that none shall remain in it, neither man nor beast, but it [AMERICA] shall be desolate forever.' Now it shall be, when you have finished reading this book, that you shall tie a stone to it and throw it out into the Euphrates. Then you shall say, 'Thus Babylon [AMERICA] shall sink and not rise from the catastrophe [NUCLEAR HOLOCAUST] that I will bring upon her [AMERICA]...'"

REVELATION 14:8 (NKJV) [WITH INTERPRETATION]:

And another angel followed, saying, "Babylon [AMERICA] is fallen, is fallen, that great city [NATION], because she has made all nations drink of the wine of the wrath of her fornication [MADNESS OF HER SEXUAL IMMORALITY]."

REVELATION 18:1-18 (NKJV) [WITH INTERPRETATION]:

After these things [THE JUDGMENT OF MYSTERY BABYLON - REVELATION 17] I saw *another angel* [MESSENGER] coming down from heaven, having great authority, and the earth was illuminated with his glory. And he cried mightily with a loud voice, saying, "Babylon [AMERICA] the great is fallen, is fallen, and has become a dwelling place of demons, a prison for every foul spirit, and a cage for every unclean and hated bird, because all the nations have drunk [BEEN INFLUENCED] of the wine [CULTURE] of the wrath [MADNESS] of her [AMERICA'S] fornication [SEXUAL IMMORALITY], and the kings of the earth have committed fornication [SPIRITUAL AND SEXUAL IMMORALITY] with her [AMERICA], and the merchants of the earth have become rich through the abundance of her [AMERICA'S] luxury."

And I heard another voice from heaven saying, "Come out of her [AMERICA], My people, lest you share in her [AMERICA'S] sins, and lest you receive of her [AMERICA'S] plagues. For her [AMERICA'S] sins have reached to heaven, and God has remembered her [AMERICA'S] unrighteousness. Render to her [AMERICA] just as she [AMERICA] rendered to you [OTHER COUNTRIES], and repay her double according to her works [EVILS]; in the cup which she has mixed, mix double for her. In the measure that she [AMERICA] glorified herself and lived luxuriously, in the same measure give her torment and sorrow; for she [AMERICA] says in her heart, 'I [AMERICA] sit as queen, and am no widow, and will not see sorrow' ['I, AMERICA, RULE OVER THE NATIONS AS A QUEEN, AND AM NO HELPLESS WIDOW, AND WILL NOT SEE THE DESOLATION OF WAR']. Therefore her [AMERICA'S] plagues will come in one day - death and mourning and famine. And she [AMERICA] will be utterly burned with fire, for strong is the Lord God who judges her [AMERICA].

The kings of the earth who committed fornication [SPIRITUAL AND SEXUAL IMMORALITY] and lived luxuriously [PROFITABLY] with her [AMERICA] will weep and lament for her [AMERICA], when they see the smoke of her [AMERICA'S] burning, standing at a distance for fear of her torment [MILITARY RETALIATION], saying, 'Alas, alas, that great city Babylon [AMERICA], that mighty city [NATION]!

For in one hour your [AMERICA'S] judgment has come.' And the merchants of the earth will weep and mourn over her [AMERICA], for no one buys their merchandise anymore: merchandise of gold and silver, precious stones and pearls, fine linen and purple, silk and scarlet, every kind of citron wood, every kind of object of ivory, every kind of object of most precious wood, bronze, iron, and marble, and cinnamon and incense, fragrant oil and frankincense, wine and oil, fine flour and wheat, cattle and sheep, horses and chariots, and bodies and souls of men. The fruit that your [AMERICA'S] soul longed for has gone from you [AMERICA], and all the things, which are rich and splendid have gone from you [AMERICA], and you [AMERICA] shall find them no more at all. The merchants of these things, who became rich by her [AMERICA], will stand at a distance for fear of her [AMERICA'S] torment [MILITARY RETALIATION], weeping and wailing, and saying, 'Alas, alas, that great city [NATION] that was clothed in fine linen, purple, and scarlet, and adorned with gold and precious stones and pearls! For in one hour such great riches came to nothing.' Every shipmaster, all who travel by ship, sailors, and as many as trade on the sea, stood at a distance and cried out when they saw the smoke of her [AMERICA'S] burning, saying, 'What is like this great city [NATION]?'

REVELATION 18:19-24 (NKJV) [WITH INTERPRETATION]:

They threw dust on their heads and cried out, weeping and wailing, and saying, 'Alas, alas, that great city [NATION], in which all who had ships on the sea became rich by her [AMERICA'S] wealth! For in one hour she [AMERICA] is made desolate.' Rejoice over her, O heaven, and you holy apostles and prophets, for God has avenged you on her [AMERICA]!" Then a mighty angel [MESSENGER] took up a stone like a great millstone and threw it into the sea, saying, "Thus with violence the great city [NATION] Babylon [AMERICA] shall be thrown down, and shall not be found anymore. The sound of harpists, musicians, flutists, and trumpeters shall not be heard in you [AMERICA] anymore. No craftsman of any craft shall be found in you [AMERICA] anymore, and the sound of a millstone shall not be heard in you [AMERICA] anymore. The light of a lamp shall not shine in you [AMERICA] anymore, and the voice of bridegroom and bride shall not be heard in you [AMERICA] anymore. For your [AMERICA'S] merchants were the great men [BUSINESSMEN] of the earth, for by your [AMERICA'S] sorcery [CULTURAL INFLUENCE] all the nations were deceived. And in her was found the blood of the prophets, and saints, and all who were slain on the earth [WITHIN AMERICA RESIDED THE PRESENCE OF MYSTERY BABYLON: PHARISAIC TALMUDIC JUDAISM AND THE ROMAN CATHOLIC CHURCH, WHICH WERE RESPONSIBLE FOR THE DEATHS OF THE PROPHETS, SAINTS, AND MANY OTHERS OF THE WORLD]."

America will be judged to destruction, because America has spread its sinful culture lifestyle to all the nations and rulers of the Earth. All the nations have been influenced by the sinful culture and the rage of America's sexual immorality through the American government, the Internet, movies, pornography, and television programs. The merchants of the Earth have become rich through the abundance of America's luxuries (America's consumerism, materialism, and high standard of living - Revelation 18:2-3).

AMERICA IS THE ONLY END-TIME NATION THAT FITS THE DESCRIPTION OF BABYLON IN ISAIAH 18, 47; JEREMIAH 50-51; AND REVELATION 18

* America is a mighty, powerful nation that has been the world's superpower and God's hammer (weapon of war) that He has used to punish the nations (Isaiah 18:2,7; Jeremiah 50:23, 51:20-23).

* America is a land 'shadowed' by 'whirring wings' (commercial airplanes). America has the heaviest domestic fight air traffic above its skies in the world (Isaiah 18:1).

* America is a land that has many rivers running through it (Isaiah 18:2,7).

* America has a Judeo-Christian heritage that has been taken over and destroyed by its atheistic, secular humanist counter-culture that has changed America into a land of sin (Jeremiah 50:11, 51:5).

* America has a large overweight population that chronically complains and depends upon the social welfare state (Jeremiah 50:11).

* America has a mother nation: Great Britain (Jeremiah 50:12), is a daughter nation (Isaiah 47:1,5; Jeremiah 50:42, 51:33), and is the youngest of the end-time nations (Jeremiah 50:12).

* America has many waters with seaports through which merchants of the Earth ship their goods (Jeremiah 51:13; Revelation 18:15-19).

* America has made itself and other nations rich through foreign trade and by the importing of merchandise (Revelation 18:3,15,19,23).

* America is a land of many great musicians whose music is heard worldwide (Revelation 18:22).

There are three social tenets, a trinity of evil, that have led to the upheaval of America as the great Judeo-Christian nation that it once was to the one that it has transformed itself into: an atheistic, secular-humanist nation. They are:

EVOLUTION THEORY (a godless creation). The national secular teaching that God is not the creator and that the creation created itself as the result of a great big bang cosmic accident. Molecules eventually arranged themselves into the first simple life forms and then evolved into all the various kinds of life on Earth.

ABORTION (infanticide). The heavily propagandized movement proclaiming that women should have full reproductive rights to do what they desire with 'their' body, including exterminating children in their womb. The U.S. Supreme Court guaranteed women the right to abort their children on January 22, 1973.

HOMOSEXUALITY (sexual immorality). The national sexual liberation movement that rejects the necessity for marriage to have sex. A culture that promotes birth control, fornication, adultery, and pornography has culminated in the right to engage in homosexual sex and has institutionalized same-sex 'marriage.' The U.S. Supreme Court granted gays the right to wed on June 26, 2015.

Babylon (AMERICA) is prophesied to be destroyed by a great nation and an assembly of nations from the north (Jeremiah 50:3,9,41, 51:48). Israel is generally the starting compass point in Scripture. Directly north of Israel is Moscow, Russia. Also, if you draw a line from mid-America due north, past Canada and the Arctic Ocean, you wind up directly in mid-Russia. Russia is the great nation of the north that has been America's longtime adversary.

Why would Russia destroy America? There are a few worldly reasons:

GLOBAL DOMINANCE. Russia is tired of its position as the number two world power, behind America, after having lost the Cold War. America interferes with Russia's global ambitions, cultural, economic, trade, and world affairs.

AMERICAN DECADENCE. America has embraced homosexuality and gay marriage at home and promotes it abroad. Russia is appalled, disgusted, and repulsed by America's embrace and promotion of homosexuality. On June 11, 2013, Russian lawmakers passed anti-gay propaganda legislation criminalizing gay propaganda by a 436-0 vote.

HOMELAND SECURITY. Russia does not view the Western NATO nations, constantly aiming their ICBMs at their country, as merely a deterrent to Russian military aggression, but as threatening acts of provocation. With America destroyed, Russia will feel more secure in their homeland.

ISAIAH 17:1 (NKJV):

Behold, Damascus will cease from being a city, and it will be a ruinous heap.

Either America or Russia will likely eventually destroy Damascus, Syria, with a nuclear bomb or destroy it through repeated conventional carpet-bombing. It is not conceivable, at this time, that another power would attack Syria with a nuclear weapon. A unilateral nuclear strike against Syria, by either America or Russia, would certainly escalate tensions between the two great superpowers. This escalation of tension could also lead Russia into an eventual decision to attack America with a massive nuclear strike. America will be destroyed in the same way that Damascus, Syria is to become a ruinous heap (Jeremiah 50:18).

NEVER SCRATCH A TIGER

America, the world's greatest superpower, is a tiger nation. At times during America's brief history it has been a fierce tiger, while at other times it has acted like a paper tiger, but it has always been a tiger.

Nations that have made the mistake of scratching the American tiger, but not killing it, have paid a heavy price for doing so.

"I fear all we have done is to awaken a sleeping giant and fill him with a terrible resolve."
-Japanese Naval Marshal General Isoroku Yamamoto, 1941

In 1941, Japan attacked the United States Pearl Harbor naval base. Many of Japan's military leaders actually thought that America would surrender to Imperial Japan, but General Yamamoto knew in his heart differently. On September 11, 2001, Islamist terrorist group al-Qaeda launched a coordinated series of terrorist attacks by flying hijacked commercial planes into the World Trade Center buildings and Pentagon. Russia has certainly studied these attacks and knows that if they were ever to conduct warfare with the United States, and hope to survive, they would have to deliver America a decisive, crippling, knockout blow. America has been surprise attacked before and Scripture declares that America will be surprise attacked again, one final time…

JEREMIAH 50:24 (NKJV) [WITH INTERPRETATION]:

I have laid a snare for you; you have indeed been overtaken, O Babylon [AMERICA], and you were not aware [SURPRISE ATTACKED].

AMERICA WILL NOT LAUNCH A RETALIATORY NUCLEAR MISSILE STRIKE AGAINST RUSSIA

JEREMIAH 51:56 (NKJV) [WITH INTERPRETATION]:

Every one of their [AMERICA'S] bows [NUCLEAR MISSILE SILOS] shall be broken…

REVELATION 18:9-10 (NKJV) [WITH INTERPRETATION]:

The kings of the earth who committed fornication [SPIRITUAL AND SEXUAL IMMORALITY] and lived luxuriously [PROFITABLY] with her [AMERICA] will weep and lament for her [AMERICA], when they see the smoke of her [AMERICA'S] burning, standing at a distance for fear of her [AMERICA'S] torment [MILITARY RETALIATION]. …

REVELATION 18:15 (NKJV) [WITH INTERPRETATION]:

The merchants of these things, who became rich by her [AMERICA], will stand at a distance for fear of her [AMERICA'S] torment [MILITARY RETALIATION].

For many years, America and Russia lived under a general understanding of M.A.D. (Mutual Assured Destruction). Neither side was likely to initiate a full-scale nuclear war with the other, for if they did, they could be assured that a retaliatory nuclear strike would occur. New advanced weapon technologies have changed things.

JEREMIAH 51:32 (NKJV) [WITH INTERPRETATION]:

The reeds they have burned with fire [THE ELECTRONIC CIRCUITRY AND GRID OF THE NATION HAVE BEEN FRIED BY EMPs - ELECTROMAGNETIC PULSE BOMBS], and the soldiers are terrified.

reed:

An electrical contact used in a magnetically operated switch or relay.[195]

Russia has been developing electromagnetic pulse (EMP) bombs. These weapons can fry the electronic circuitry of a city and also the guidance and launch systems of intercontinental ballistic missiles (ICBMs). Computer cyber attacks can also interfere with missile launch operating systems. An electromagnetic pulse bomb attack, coupled with a cyber attack and a surprise massive nuclear attack, will render America defenseless. Russia will first cripple America with an EMP bomb attack, then destroy a helpless America, which will be unable to defend itself. When America is struck with an EMP attack, followed by a full-scale massive nuclear attack, even if America was able to retaliate, it is becoming increasingly unlikely that American leadership would do so (Jeremiah 51:57). At that point, there would be no America left to defend. If American political leaders were able to survive the Russian-led nuclear attack, they would likely be concerned only with their own survival, seeking to relocate to other nations as refugees.

WHAT SHOULD AMERICAN BELIEVERS DO?

As believers, we must remember that while it is Russia that will destroy America, its military is the weapon that the Lord will use to judge America. God will judge secular America with total devastation as He once judged Sodom and Gomorrah (Jeremiah 49:18,50:40). It is the Lord Himself who claims that He is responsible for the judgment that is to come to America for her sins (Jeremiah 50:9,18,24-25,31,45, 51:53; Revelation 18:8,10,20). What should believers who live in America do? Should we flee the country now, before the nuclear bombs drop? While there are reportedly some believers who have already done that, it is not feasible for most people and impossible for many others to flee America.

AMERICAN SAINTS WILL BE RAPTURED BEFORE AMERICA'S DESTRUCTION

ISAIAH 18:1-2 (NKJV) [WITH INTERPRETATION]:

Woe to the land [AMERICA] shadowed with whirring wings [COMMERCIAL AIRPLANES], which is beyond the rivers of Ethiopia [ATLANTIC OCEAN], which sends ambassadors by sea, even in vessels of reed [USS BATTLESHIPS] on the waters.

ISAIAH 18:2-7 (NKJV) [WITH INTERPRETATION]:

"Go, swift messengers [ANGELS], to a nation tall and smooth of skin [AMERICA], to a people terrible from their beginning onward [AMERICA], a nation powerful and treading down, whose land [AMERICA] the rivers divide. All inhabitants of the world and dwellers on the earth: When a banner is lifted up on the mountains, look! And when a trumpet [REVELATION 9:13-15] is blown, hear!" For thus YHWH (the Lord) said to me, "I am still and I watch from My dwelling place [HEAVEN] like dazzling heat in sunshine, like a cloud of dew in the heat of harvest." For before the harvest [BEFORE THE WORLDWIDE HARVEST (RAPTURE) OF THE SAINTS], when the bud [TIMING] is perfect and the sour grape [HOMOSEXUAL GENERATION] is ripening [AGING / MATURING] in the flower [MAINSTREAM CULTURE], then He will both cut off the twigs [THE UNRIGHTEOUS] with pruning hooks and cut down and take away [RAPTURE] the branches [THE RIGHTEOUS]. They [THE UNRIGHTEOUS] will be left [BEHIND] together for the mountain birds of prey [REVELATION 18:2] and for the beasts of the earth. The birds of prey [REVELATION 18:2] will summer on them, and all the beasts of the earth will winter on them [EAT THEM]. In that time [OF THE DESTRUCTION OF BABYLON (AMERICA)] a present [THE RAPTURED AMERICAN SAINTS] will be brought to YHWH (the Lord) of hosts from a people tall and smooth-skinned [AMERICA], and from a people awesome from their beginning onward [AMERICA] - a nation powerful and trampling [AMERICA], whose land [AMERICA] the rivers divide - to the place of the name of YHWH (the Lord) of hosts, to Mount Zion [JERUSALEM].

JEREMIAH 50:8 (NKJV) [WITH INTERPRETATION]:

"Flee [IN THE AMERICAN RAPTURE] from the midst of Babylon [AMERICA], go [BE RAPTURED] out of the land of the Chaldeans [AMERICAS]..."

JEREMIAH 51:5-6 (NKJV) [WITH INTERPRETATION]:

"For Israel is not forsaken, nor Judah [SPIRITUAL ISRAEL AND JUDAH - THE SAINTS], by his God, YHWH (the Lord) of hosts, though their [AMERICA'S] land was filled with sin against the Holy One of Israel." Flee [IN THE AMERICAN RAPTURE] from the midst of Babylon [AMERICA], and every one save his life! Do not be cut off [LEFT BEHIND] in her [AMERICA'S] wickedness, for this is the time of YHWH's (the Lord's) vengeance, the recompense He is paying her [AMERICA].

JEREMIAH 51:33 (NKJV) [WITH INTERPRETATION]:

For thus says YHWH (the Lord) of hosts, the God of Israel: "The daughter of Babylon [AMERICA] is like a threshing floor when it is time to thresh her; Yet a little while and the time of her harvest [RAPTURE] will come."

JEREMIAH 51:45 (NKJV) [WITH INTERPRETATION]:

"Come out of her [AMERICA'S] midst, My people! And let everyone deliver himself [IN THE AMERICAN RAPTURE] from the fierce anger of YHWH (the Lord)."

REVELATION 18:4 (NKJV) [WITH INTERPRETATION]:

And I heard another voice from heaven saying, "Come [BE RAPTURED] out of her [AMERICA], My people, lest you share in her [AMERICA'S] sins, and lest you receive of her [AMERICA'S] plagues."

Revelation 18:4 is a widely misunderstood verse by many. This misunderstanding goes back to confusing Mystery Babylon (the Catholic Church - Revelation 17) with Babylon the great (America - Revelation 18). Many who mix the two Babylons believe God is warning Catholics to "Come out of the Catholic Church, *My people...*" This explanation does not make sense once you realize "God's people" are not Catholics falsely worshiping in a Catholic cult church that God was about to destroy.

Revelation 18:4 is NOT a command from God; it is a declaration. It is the same "Come out of her, My people," declaration found in Jeremiah 51:45. God is about to judge America with nuclear annihilation via Russia, and His voice from heaven will announce the rapture of the Messianic and Christian saints in America. God will say, "Come out of her (AMERICA), My people, lest you share in her (AMERICA'S) sins and lest you receive of her (AMERICA'S) plagues..." and then He will rapture the saints out from America before its destruction.

As we live in these end times, know that God loves and protects the righteous. He loves the righteous more than He hates the wicked. God's desire to protect His people is greater than His desire to punish evil. God once promised Abraham that He would not destroy Sodom and Gomorrah for the sake of ten righteous people living there (Genesis 18:32). God will not forget or leave behind His righteous saints to suffer His judgment and plagues that He is bringing upon America (Jeremiah 51:5).

Many cannot accept or believe that America is Babylon the great of Scripture and that it will be completely destroyed in 1-hour. Somehow people believe that America will always be here, a great country right till the very end of the age. People should not place American patriotism and love of country above the prophetic words of Scripture. America is no longer the Judeo-Christian nation of its founding. America is a nation that officially, at the government national level, rejects God through the adoption of atheistic evolution theory, abortion infanticide, homosexuality, and all other forms of sexual immorality.

Yeshua Messiah (Jesus Christ) is the same yesterday, today, and forever, and so are His judgments (Hebrews 13:8). America's national sins are the same that Sodom and Gomorrah were committing and America will be judged in a similar manner (Jeremiah 50:40).

MATTHEW 24:22; MARK 13:20 (NKJV):

"And unless those days were shortened, no flesh would be saved; but for the elect's sake those days will be shortened."

America is not exempted from the prophesies of the end times. The United States will be completely destroyed and the rest of the world will be on the verge of extinguishing all flesh upon the Earth before the Lord Yeshua (Jesus) returns.

It is prophesied that Babylon (America) will fall, but there is good news. The righteous are going to be taken away, via the American rapture, from the destruction of Babylon (America). We will be taken to a place of peace, prosperity, and security and be presented as a present to Yeshua (Jesus) the Lord (Isaiah 18:1-7). We are commanded to rejoice at the destruction of the wickedness of Babylon (America) (Jeremiah 51:48; Revelation 18:20).

LUKE 21:36 (NKJV):

"Watch therefore, and pray always that you may be counted worthy to escape all these things that will come to pass, and to stand before the Son of Man."

Have faith in God (Matthew 11:22). Live righteously (Titus 2:11-14). Watch and pray that you may be counted worthy to escape America's judgment (Luke 21:36). Do not store up for treasures on this Earth, for neither the treasures of this Earth nor America will remain (Matthew 6:19-20; Luke 12:33-34).

GLOBAL ECONOMIC COLLAPSE AND THE GREAT TRIBULATION

By George Lujack

Many societal observers view the American economy as unsustainable and destined to crash due to the U.S. runaway federal deficit, the interest on this debt, and federal and state governments' unfunded liabilities. If America were to continue on uninterrupted, then an American economic crash would likely happen, but that is not what is prophesied to occur. This article will discuss the global economic collapse that will occur, which will be accompanied by the great tribulation.

THE GLOBAL ECONOMIC COLLAPSE

REVELATION 18:10-11 (NKJV) [WITH INTERPRETATION]:

'Alas, alas, that great city [COUNTRY] Babylon [AMERICA], that mighty city [COUNTRY]! For in one hour your judgment has come.' And the merchants of the earth will weep and mourn over her [AMERICA], for no one buys their merchandise anymore.

In the day that Babylon the great (America) is destroyed, global merchants will mourn, because America will no longer be buying their merchandise. The logical conclusion of these verses is that up until the day that America is destroyed, it will be purchasing the world's merchandise. Therefore, there will be no crippling American economic crash before America is destroyed.

A *global* economic collapse will occur *after* the destruction of America. The worldwide economic ramifications of the complete destruction of America will devastate the world economy. Global merchants will no longer be able to sell their goods to America, the world's greatest importer of global merchandise. With no demand for their products, manufacturers around the world will lay off their factory employees and shut down their factories. Many millions of people will suddenly become unemployed. All American foreign aid will cease being paid to governments around the world. All American foreign debts will be wiped out instantly, as all the money owed to foreign governments and investors will never be repaid. All foreign reserve holdings of U.S. currency will become instantly worthless, as no world bank will accept American dollars.

After the demise of America, the hardest-hit manufacturing merchants will be in the countries of Canada, China, Germany, Japan, and Mexico. These countries sell autos, electronics, and all sorts of merchandise to America. After America is destroyed, these America-dependent countries will not be able to sell their products and no one will buy their merchandise anymore.

China and Japan are the top holders of U.S. debt, which will never be repaid to them after America is destroyed.[196]

After Russia and a great assembly of nations destroy America (Jeremiah 50:9), global economic collapse and worldwide regional wars will break out. America will no longer be there to police the world's nations and restrain rivals like North and South Korea, China and Japan, India and Pakistan, and numerous other countries in the Middle East and elsewhere from waging war against each other. These countries, which had been prevented by America from waging war in the past, will now be free to wage war without any interference or repercussions from the United States.

EZEKIEL 7:19 (NKJV):

They will throw their silver into the streets, and their gold will be like refuse; Their silver and their gold will not be able to deliver them in the day of the wrath of YHWH (the Lord).

Worldwide holdings of precious metals will also become worthless, as world banking systems adjust to the global economic collapse that follows the destruction of America.

THE GREAT TRIBULATION

MATTHEW 24:21-22 (NKJV):

"For then there will be great tribulation, such as has not been since the beginning of the world until this time, no, nor ever shall be. And unless those days were shortened, no flesh would be saved; but for the elect's sake those days will be shortened."

The destruction of America will mark the beginning of the great tribulation. One third of the world's population will be killed during the great tribulation years (Revelation 9:15), beginning with the death of all the American people killed when the United States is annihilated. The great tribulation will be tribulation on a worldwide scale that starts with the destruction of America. Unless Yeshua (Jesus) returns to interrupt and shorten the days of man's earthly reign, to end the great tribulation, man would annihilate himself and no flesh on Earth would be saved alive (Matthew 24:21-22).

BEAST RISING OUT OF THE SEA; THE EUROPEAN UNION, ITS DEADLY WOUND THAT HEALS, AND THE WOMAN WHO RIDES THIS BEAST

By George Lujack

The identity of the beast of Revelation 13 has been one of the most difficult mysteries for theologians to comprehensively interpret. Due to recent end-time events that have unfolded, and related Revelation mysteries unsealed, a more complete understanding of these verses can now be decoded, more so than ever before. This article will decipher [WITH INTERPRETATION] the prophesies of Revelation 13 and related prophecies concerning the beast rising out of the sea, its deadly wound, and the woman who sits on the beast.

REVELATION 13:1-3 (NKJV) [WITH INTERPRETATION]:

Then I stood on the sand of the sea. And I saw a beast [EMPIRE] rising up out of the sea [OF NATIONS], having seven heads [THE SEVENTH REVIVAL OF THE HOLY ROMAN EMPIRE - THE EUROPEAN UNION] and ten horns [MONARCH COUNTRIES WITHIN THE EUROPEAN UNION], and on his horns ten crowns [WORN BY THE TEN KINGS / QUEENS OF THE MONARCH COUNTRIES WITHIN THE EUROPEAN UNION], and on his heads a blasphemous name [VICARIUS FILII DEI (LATIN: VICAR OF THE SON OF GOD) - THE INSCRIPTION OF THE CROWN OF THE CATHOLIC POPE, WHO SITS ON THE BEAST (THE REVIVED HOLY ROMAN EMPIRE) - REVELATION 17:3]. Now the beast [EMPIRE] which I saw was like a leopard [AGILE / SWIFT], his feet were like the feet of a bear [STRONG], and his mouth like the mouth of a lion [ROARING].

The dragon [SATAN] gave him [THE ANTIMESSIAH (ANTICHRIST)] his power, his throne, and great authority. And I saw one of his heads [ONE NATION OF THE EMPIRE, AMERICA (BABYLON THE GREAT), DESTROYED] as if it [THE EMPIRE] had been mortally wounded [AFTER AMERICA (BABYLON THE GREAT) WAS DESTROYED], and his [THE EMPIRE'S] deadly wound [AMERICA'S DESTRUCTION - A NEAR DEATH BLOW TO NATO AND THE NEW WORLD ORDER] was healed [THE EUROPEAN UNION WILL QUICKLY MOBILIZE AFTER THE DESTRUCTION OF AMERICA, WILL HEAL, AND WILL BECOME A SUPERPOWER OF ITS OWN].

And all the world marveled and followed the beast [ANTIMESSIAH (ANTICHRIST)].

REVELATION 13:4 (NKJV) [WITH INTERPRETATION]:

So they worshiped the dragon [SATAN] who gave authority to the beast [ANTIMESSIAH (ANTICHRIST)]; and they worshiped the beast [ANTIMESSIAH (ANTICHRIST)], saying, "Who is like the beast [ANTIMESSIAH (ANTICHRIST)]? Who is able to make war with him [THE ANTIMESSIAH (ANTICHRIST) AND HIS EUROPEAN UNION EMPIRE]?"

In the Revelation 13:1-4 passages, Scripture is speaking in a dual prophecy concerning 'the beast.' In some verses the beast is a beast empire; in others the beast refers to the political leader known as the Antimessiah (Antichrist).

THE DEADLY WOUND - THE FALL OF BABYLON THE GREAT (AMERICA)

Many prophesy scholars have falsely believed that the deadly wound spoken of is a deadly wound delivered to the Antimessiah (Antichrist) and that the Antimessiah (Antichrist) will be miraculously resurrected by Satan and healed of his deadly wound.

REVELATION 13:1,3 (NKJV) [WITH INTERPRETATION]:

And I saw a beast [EMPIRE] rising up out of the sea [OF NATIONS], having seven heads and ten horns, and on his horns ten crowns, and on his heads a blasphemous name. ... And I saw ONE OF HIS HEADS as if it had been mortally wounded, and his deadly wound was healed.

The Antimessiah (Antichrist) is a human political leader who has only one head, not multiple heads. Satan does not have the power to resurrect people, only God does. The deadly wound is to *one of the heads* of the New World Order - NATO. The deadly wound is the destruction of America (Babylon the great - Revelation 14:8, 18). Once Russia and her allies destroy America, Europe will be vulnerable, as it will no longer be under the military umbrella protection of the United States. Europe will rapidly mobilize, reemerge, and rise as a military superpower in the wake of the destruction of America. The European Union (revived Holy Roman Empire) will survive the deadly wound to its empire, the fall of Babylon the great (America), and heal.

SEVEN HEADS AND TEN HORNS WITH CROWNS

There have been seven historic risings (seven heads - Revelation 13:1, 17:3) of the Holy Roman Empire:

1. IMPERIAL RESTORATION - Justinian, 554 A.D.

2. FRANKISH KINGDOM - Charlemagne, 774 A.D.

3. GERMAN KINGDOM - Otto the Great, 962 A.D.

4. HABSBURG DYNASTY - Charles V, 1530 A.D.

5. FRENCH KINGDOM - Napoleon, 1804 A.D.

6. GERMAN ITALIAN AXIS - Garibaldi, Hitler, Mussolini, 1870 - 1945

7. THE EUROPEAN UNION - 1993 – Present[197]

In 1993 the Holy Roman Empire, through the European Union, reared its head for the seventh and final time.

There are currently twelve (12) sovereign monarch countries in Europe represented by kings (or queens).

1. The Principality of Andorra
2. The Kingdom of Belgium
3. The Kingdom of Denmark
4. The Principality of Liechtenstein
5. The Grand Duchy of Luxembourg
6. The Principality of Monaco
7. The Kingdom of the Netherlands
8. The Kingdom of Norway
9. The Kingdom of Spain
10. The Kingdom of Sweden
11. The Sovereign Military Order of Malta
12. The United Kingdom of Great Britain and Northern Ireland

BREXIT REFERENDUM

On June 23, 2016, the United Kingdom voted to exit the European Union. The United Kingdom European Union membership referendum was a non-binding referendum that took place on June 23, 2016. The referendum resulted in an overall vote for the UK to leave the EU by 51.9%. In order to start the process of the United Kingdom leaving the European Union, which may take several years, the British government will have to act to remove itself via a treaty agreement (Article 50) with the European Union, but it has not yet done so.[198][199][200][201]

Most of the monarchies in Europe are constitutional monarchies, which means that the monarch does not influence the politics of the state, nor wield any significant political power. Of the twelve countries of Europe represented in some manner by a crown-wearing monarch, currently seven of them are members of the European Union: Belgium, Denmark, Luxembourg, the Netherlands, Spain, Sweden, and the United Kingdom as of 2017.

REVELATION 17:12-13 (NKJV) [WITH INTERPRETATION]:

The ten horns which you saw are ten kings who have received no kingdom as yet, but they receive authority for one hour as kings with the beast [EUROPEAN UNION]. These are of one mind, and they will give their power and authority to the beast [EUROPEAN UNION].

As of 2017, the European Union consists of 28 member states that make up its union. Whether or not the United Kingdom leaves the European Union or returns to it is still yet to be determined, but when the Antimessiah (Antichrist) takes control of the last revived Holy Roman Empire - the European Union, a total of ten monarch European countries represented by kings will be a part of the European Union. These kings will formally abdicate their monarchical sovereignty, fully relinquishing their authority and power to the European Union and the Antimessiah (Antichrist).

REVELATION 12:1-6 (NKJV) [WITH INTERPRETATION]:

Now a great sign appeared in heaven: a woman [NATIONAL ISRAEL] clothed with the sun, with the moon under her feet, and on her head a garland of twelve stars [TWELVE TRIBES]. Then being with child, she cried out in labor and in pain to give birth.

And another sign appeared in heaven: behold, a great, fiery red dragon [SATAN] having seven heads and ten horns, and seven diadems on his heads [THE SEVENTH HOLY ROMAN EMPIRE - EUROPEAN UNION]. His tail [EVIL INFLUENCE] drew a third of the stars [ANGELS] of heaven and threw them to the earth [TO BE RESERVED FOR THEIR JUDGMENT - 2 PETER 2:4]. And the dragon [SATAN] stood before the woman [ISRAEL] who was ready to give birth, to devour her Child [YESHUA (JESUS)] as soon as it was born [BY KING HEROD'S DECREE - MATTHEW 2:13-16]. She [ISRAEL] bore a male Child [YESHUA (JESUS)] who was to rule all nations with a rod of iron. And her Child [YESHUA (JESUS)] was caught up [RAPTURED] to God and His throne. Then the woman [ISRAEL] fled into the wilderness, where she has a place prepared by God, that they should feed her there one thousand two hundred and sixty days [DURING THE GREAT TRIBULATION].

The flag of the European Union consists of twelve gold stars on a blue background. Officially they stand for the ideals of unity, solidarity, and harmony among the peoples of Europe. The twelve stars of the European Union's flag represent a more sinister agenda and purpose. Satan will use the European Union to invade Israel, and he will want to imitate and replace God's chosen people, represented by twelve tribes, with the European Union's twelve stars.

THE LITTLE HORN - VATICAN CITY

DANIEL 7:7-8 (NKJV) [WITH INTERPRETATION]:

After this I saw in the night visions, and behold, a fourth beast [THE SEVENTH HOLY ROMAN EMPIRE - THE EUROPEAN UNION], dreadful and terrible, exceedingly strong. It had huge iron teeth; it was devouring, breaking in pieces, and trampling the residue with its feet. It was different [MORE POWERFUL] from all the beasts [HOLY ROMAN EMPIRES] that were before it, and it had ten horns [TEN MONARCH COUNTRIES]. I was considering the horns [MONARCH COUNTRIES], and there was another horn [MONARCH STATE], a little one [VATICAN CITY], coming up among them, before whom three of the first horns [MONARCH COUNTRIES] were plucked out by the roots. And there, in this horn [MONARCH STATE], were eyes like the eyes of a man, and a mouth speaking pompous words [THE FALSE PROPHET - CATHOLIC POPE].

DANIEL 7:24-25 (NKJV) [WITH INTERPRETATION]:

The ten horns are ten kings who shall arise from this kingdom [EUROPEAN UNION]. And another [LITTLE HORN] shall arise after them. He [VATICAN CITY] shall be different from the first ones, and shall subdue three kings. He [THE FALSE PROPHET] shall speak pompous words against the Most High, and shall intend to change times and law [GOD'S HOLY DAYS AND COMMANDMENTS]. Then the saints shall be given into his hand for a time and times, and a half time [DURING THE GREAT TRIBULATION].

DANIEL 8:5,8-9,11-12 (NKJV) [WITH INTERPRETATION]:

And as I was considering, suddenly a male goat [NEW WORLD ORDER - NATO] came [PRIMARILY] from the west [AMERICA], across the surface of the whole earth, without touching the ground [BY AIR AND SEA]; and the goat [NEW WORLD ORDER - NATO] had a notable horn [COUNTRY - AMERICA] between his eyes. …

Therefore the male goat [NEW WORLD ORDER - NATO] grew very great; but when he became strong, the large horn [AMERICA] was broken [DESTROYED - REVELATION 14:8, 18], and in place of it four notable ones came up [FRANCE, GERMANY, ITALY, SPAIN] toward the four winds of heaven. And out of one of them [ITALY] came a little horn [VATICAN CITY] which grew exceedingly great toward the south, toward the east, and toward the Glorious Land [ISRAEL]. …

He [THE ANTIMESSIAH (ANTICHRIST)] even exalted himself as high as the Prince [YESHUA (Jesus)] of the host [OF HEAVEN]; and by him [THE ANTIMESSIAH (ANTICHRIST)] the daily sacrifices [IN THE REBUILT TEMPLE IN JERUSALEM] were taken away, and the place of His [YESHUA'S (JESUS')] sanctuary [REBUILT TEMPLE] was cast down. Because of transgression [SINS OF NATIONAL ISRAEL], an army was given over to the horn [VATICAN CITY] to oppose the daily sacrifices [IN THE REBUILT TEMPLE IN ISRAEL]; and he [THE FALSE PROPHET - FINAL CATHOLIC POPE] cast truth down to the ground. He [THE FALSE PROPHET - FINAL CATHOLIC POPE] did all this and prospered.

REVELATION 17:14-18 (NKJV) [WITH INTERPRETATION]:

"These [THE EU ANTIMESSIAH (ANTICHRIST) ARMY] will make war with the Lamb [YESHUA (JESUS)], and the Lamb will overcome them, for He is Lord of lords and King of kings; and those who are with Him are called, chosen, and faithful."

Then he said to me, "The waters which you saw, where the harlot [CATHOLIC CHURCH] sits, are peoples, multitudes, nations, and tongues. And the ten horns [MONARCH COUNTRIES] which you saw on the beast [EUROPEAN UNION], these will hate the harlot [CATHOLIC CHURCH], make her desolate and naked, eat her flesh and burn her with fire [SECULAR EUROPE WILL HATE THE VATICAN AND WILL TAKE PART IN ITS DESTRUCTION].

For God has put it into their [MONARCHS'] hearts [PROVERBS 21:1] to fulfill His purpose, to be of one mind, and to give their kingdom to the beast [EUROPEAN UNION], until the words of God are fulfilled. And the woman [CATHOLIC CHURCH] whom you saw is that great city [VATICAN CITY] which reigns over the kings of the earth."

Vatican City is a walled enclave within the city of Rome. It is the smallest state in the world in both area and population. Its area is approximately 110 acres with a population of less than a thousand people. Vatican City is the 'little' horn, a tiny elective monarch state, whose sovereign is the pope.

SUMMATION

The rise of the beast empire, the European Union, is the revived Holy Roman Empire through the New World Order and NATO (Revelation 13:1-2). The deadly wound this beast empire receives is the destruction of its main supporting horn (nation): America (Babylon the great). The European Union will survive the deadly wound that threatens its empire, mobilize its people, and emerge as a world superpower (Revelation 13:3).

Ten kings representing ten kingdom nations will be a part of the final European Union (Revelation 13:1). The little horn is a little sovereign state, Vatican City, that will sit on (align with) the beast empire as the religious arm of the European Union superpower, as it has done in all previous Holy Roman empires before (Daniel 7:8, 8:9). The European Union will be taken over by the Antimessiah (Antichrist), a charismatic political leader who will work together with the false prophet (final Catholic pope) and will lead the European Union beast superpower into Israel and conquer it for a time, during the great tribulation (Daniel 8:9-12, 11:31, 12:11; Matthew 24:15-16; Mark 13:14; Revelation 13:4-6).

The European Union beast superpower will ultimately grow to hate the Vatican controlling and influencing its affairs and will partake in its destruction (Revelation 17:16). Yeshua Messiah (Jesus Christ) will return as King of kings to save His people in Israel when they call on Him for their salvation (Luke 13:35). The EU Antimessiah (Antichrist) army will make war with the Lamb (Yeshua / Jesus) and He will defeat them (Revelation 17:14).

666 - THE MARK OF THE BEAST; CALCULATING AND IDENTIFYING IT

By George Lujack

Satan's 666-numerical signature is represented in various manifestations. This article will present some examples in which Satan's 666-signature is already present in this world, and how to calculate and identify his number.

REVELATION 13:18 (NKJV):

Here is wisdom. Let him who has understanding *calculate the number* of the beast, for it is the number of a man: His number is 666.

Scripture instructs those with wisdom to CALCULATE the number of the beast.

The Antimessiah (Antichrist) and the beast will rule from Rome. These are all the Roman numbers: MDCLXVI. Add up (calculate) all the different Roman numerals and the total = 1,666. Exclude the Roman numeral M = 1,000 and the total equals 666.

D (500) + C (100) + L (50) + X (10) + V (5) + I (1) = 666

REVELATION 13:1 (NKJV):

Then I stood on the sand of the sea. And I saw a beast rising up out of the sea, having seven heads and ten horns, and on his horns ten crowns, and on his heads a blasphemous name.

What is this "blasphemous name" on the "heads" of the beast? It is the crown worn upon the heads of the Catholic popes throughout the ages that bears a blasphemous inscription with a Roman numerical equivalent that equals 666. Vicarius Filii Dei (Latin: Vicar or representative of the Son of God) is inscribed on the Catholic pope's crown and is the blasphemous name spoken of in Revelation 13:1. The Catholic pope is not Messiah's (Christ's) vicar or representative on Earth. The Roman numerals in VICARIVS FILII DEI are (CAPS) VICarIVs fILII DeI. Remove the Roman numerals from the Roman letters: VICIV ILII DI. 'V' is substituted for 'U,' as U is used in English, but not in the Roman alphabet. If you add up (calculate) the Roman numerical value inscribed upon the Catholic pope's crown, you come up with 666.

VICARIVS FILII DEI = 5+1+100+1+5+1+50+1+1+500+1 = 666.

The roulette wheel, representing coveting through gambling, has a numerical equivalent of 666. If you add up (calculate) all the numbers of the roulette wheel, they = 666.

0+00+1+2+3+4+5+6+7+8+9+10+11+12+13+14+15+16+17+18+19+20+21+22+23+24+25+26+27+28+29+30+31+32+33+34+35+36 = 666.

666 symbols are present in many business designs and logos, in subtle and not-so-subtle places in this world. 666 patterns appear on every barcode used in retail buying and selling of merchandise. The barcodes are marked with the first bar, middle bar, and last barcode line marked by a 6, and the three bar lines together represent 666.

Scripture prophecy reveals that the day will come when all people will have to receive a mark or implant representing 666 in order to buy and sell. Believers are required to refuse this mark of the beast, even if it means martyrdom death.

REVELATION 13:16-18 (NKJV):

He causes all, both small and great, rich and poor, free and slave, to receive a mark on their right hand or on their foreheads, and that no one may buy or sell except one who has the mark or the name of the beast, or the number of his name. Here is wisdom. Let him who has understanding calculate the number of the beast, for it is the number of a man: His number is 666.

REVELATION 14:9-11 (NKJV):

"If anyone worships the beast and his image, and receives his mark on his forehead or on his hand, he himself shall also drink of the wine of the wrath of God, which is poured out full strength into the cup of His indignation. He shall be tormented with fire and brimstone in the presence of the holy angels and in the presence of the Lamb. And the smoke of their torment ascends forever and ever; and they have no rest day or night, who worship the beast and his image, and whoever receives the mark of his name."

REVELATION 20:4 (NKJV):

Then I saw the souls of those who had been beheaded for their witness to Yeshua (Jesus) and for the word of God, who had not worshiped the beast or his image, and had not received his mark on their foreheads or on their hands. And they lived and reigned with Messiah (Christ) for a thousand years.

THE TIMES OF THE GENTILES

By George Lujack

What is meant by the 'times of the Gentiles'? This article will explain what Yeshua (Jesus) spoke of when He said that the armies of the world would surround Israel and this would be the time of the Gentiles.

EZEKIEL 30:1-3 (NKJV):

The word of YHWH (the Lord) came to me again, saying, "Son of man, prophesy and say, 'Thus says YHWH (the Lord) God: "Wail, 'Woe to the day!' For the day is near, even the day of YHWH (the Lord) is near; It will be a day of clouds, THE TIME OF THE GENTILES."

LUKE 21:20-28 (NKJV):

"But when you see Jerusalem surrounded by armies, then know that its desolation is near. Then let those who are in Judea flee to the mountains, let those who are in the midst of her depart, and let not those who are in the country enter her. For these are the days of vengeance, that all things which are written may be fulfilled. But woe to those who are pregnant and to those who are nursing babies in those days! For there will be great distress in the land and wrath upon this people. And they will fall by the edge of the sword, and be led away captive into all nations. And Jerusalem will be trampled by Gentiles until the TIMES OF THE GENTILES are fulfilled. And there will be signs in the sun, in the moon, and in the stars; and on the earth distress of nations, with perplexity, the sea and the waves roaring; men's hearts failing them from fear and the expectation of those things which are coming on the earth, for the powers of the heavens will be shaken. Then they will see the Son of Man coming in a cloud with power and great glory. Now when these things begin to happen, look up and lift up your heads, because your redemption draws near."

The world's armies will surround Israel and its occupation and desolation (abandonment) will occur near the end of the times of the Gentiles. At the conclusion of the times of the Gentiles, Yeshua (Jesus) will return to Earth with His raptured and resurrected saints, who He will gather from the clouds, as the redemption of Israel (the Messiah-denying Jews of the nation of Israel) draws near.

LUKE 13:34-35 (NKJV) [WITH INTERPRETATION]:

"O Jerusalem, Jerusalem, the one who kills the prophets and stones those who are sent to her! How often I wanted to gather your children together, as a hen gathers her brood under her wings, but you were not willing! See! Your house [LAND] is left to you [ISRAEL] desolate; and assuredly, I say to you [ISRAEL], you [ISRAEL] shall not see Me until the time [OF THE GENTILES] comes when you [ISRAEL] say, *'Blessed is He [YESHUA (JESUS)] who comes in the name of [YHWH] (the Lord)!'*"

Yeshua (Jesus) will not return until the Messiah-denying Jews of Israel and Judea accept Him and call upon Him to save them from their annihilation. Ever since the gospel has gone into the world, for the most part, the Judeo-Christian nations have lived freely in civilized societies with human rights and dignity, free from tyrannical government oppression. There have been world wars and communist expansions, but the Judeo-Christian countries have remained free and have been the most influential and powerful nations on Earth. On a global scale, the Judeo-Christian nations have ruled the world through banking, business, finance, governments, innovation, invention, as well as militarily, philosophically, and spiritually.

The times of the Gentiles are prophesied to come, in which the Westernized Judeo-Christian nations will not be the primary force in charge of the world. The times of the Gentiles are prophesied to occur near the end of the age, preceding the return of Yeshua (Jesus). The times of the Gentiles will be the times of the great tribulation, when the communist, Muslim, and other non-Judeo-Christian nations will be running the affairs of the world.

Many prophecy watchers believe that the United States' federal deficit will one day cause a crash of America's and the world's economic systems. That is not going to happen...

REVELATION 18:11 (NKJV):

And the merchants of the earth will weep and mourn over her, for no one buys their merchandise anymore...

When Babylon the great (America) is destroyed, it will be a time when America is still buying goods from China and all other countries from around the world. The global merchants will mourn because America will not be buying their merchandise anymore *after* it is destroyed.

REVELATION 14:8-10 (NKJV) (HSV†) [WITH INTERPRETATION]:

And another angel (†messenger) followed, saying, "Babylon [AMERICA] is fallen, is fallen, that great city, because she has made all nations drink of the wine of the wrath of her fornication."
THEN [AFTERWARD] a third angel (†messenger) followed them, saying with a loud voice, "If anyone worships the beast and his image, and receives his mark on his forehead or on his hand, he himself shall also drink of the wine of the wrath of God, which is poured out full strength into the cup of His indignation."

The destruction of Babylon the great (America - Revelation 14:8) will change the world in one hour. The Judeo-Christian nations that depend on America for military protection will no longer have it. The destruction of America will mark the beginning of the great tribulation (one third of the world's population killed - Revelation 9:18).

Revelation 14:8 (the destruction of America) is followed by Revelation 14:9-10, the implementation of the mark of the beast, which comes *after* the destruction of America.

When Babylon the great (America) is destroyed (Revelation 14:8), this will cause a global economic crisis. All worldwide reserve currencies held in dollars will become immediately worthless. Factories around the world will close, because America will not be there to buy any merchant's goods anymore.

Americans are never going to face receiving the mark of the beast on American soil. The destruction of Babylon the great (America) will cause a worldwide economic collapse and the world will make war without America, the world's military policeman, there to stop them. A third of mankind will be killed during the times of the Gentiles (Revelation 9:18). The rise of the Antimessiah (Antichrist) will follow the destruction of America and the death of a third of mankind. He will impose his mark upon the economically collapsed war-torn world (Revelation 13:16-18, 14:9-11).

The times of the Gentiles begin when Babylon the great (America) is destroyed and will be fulfilled (end) when Yeshua (Jesus) returns to Earth.

THE ABOMINATION OF DESOLATION

By George Lujack

There are four prophetic Scripture verses that speak of the "abomination of desolation." This article will analyze those four verses and reveal what the abomination of desolation is, which is spoken of by the prophet Daniel and later referenced by Yeshua (Jesus).

DANIEL 11:31 (NKJV):

And forces shall be mustered by him, and they shall defile the sanctuary fortress; then they shall take away the daily sacrifices, and place there the ABOMINATION OF DESOLATION.

DANIEL 12:11 (NKJV):

And from the time that the daily sacrifice is taken away, and the ABOMINATION OF DESOLATION is set up, there shall be one thousand two hundred and ninety days.

MATTHEW 24:15-16 (NKJV):

"Therefore when you see the 'ABOMINATION OF DESOLATION,' spoken of by Daniel the prophet, standing in the holy place" (whoever reads, let him understand), "then let those who are in Judea flee to the mountains..."

MARK 13:14 (NKJV):

"So when you see the 'ABOMINATION OF DESOLATION,' spoken of by Daniel the prophet, standing where it ought not" (let the reader understand), "then let those who are in Judea flee to the mountains..."

The Antimessiah (Antichrist) and his forces will invade Israel, will cause the Jews to flee Israel and Judea, and will make their Jewish homeland desolate (Matthew 23:38; Luke 13:35).

The Antimessiah (Antichrist) will enter the rebuilt Temple in Jerusalem, where he will declare himself to be God and will set up his clone there to be worshiped as God.

The abomination 'of' desolation is the abominable spawn cloned life form 'of' the one who causes global and Israeli desolation. The abomination of desolation is the clone of Antimessiah (Antichrist).

REVELATION 13:15 (NKJV) [WITH INTERPRETATION]:

He [THE ANTIMESSIAH (ANTICHRIST)] was granted power to give breath to the image [CLONE] of the beast [ANTIMESSIAH (ANTICHRIST)], that the image [CLONE] of the beast [ANTIMESSIAH (ANTICHRIST)] should both speak and cause as many as would not worship the image [CLONE] of the beast [ANTIMESSIAH (ANTICHRIST)] to be killed.

The Antimessiah (Antichrist) will be a world political leader and he will have the world worship his image (clone) in the rebuilt Temple in Jerusalem, after he invades Israel and the Israeli Jews are either captured or forced to flee their homeland (Matthew 24:15-20; Mark 13:14-19; Luke 21:20-24).

The image of the beast (Antimessiah / Antichrist) is a human clone of himself. Stone idols or robots do not breathe; clones do. The image of the beast (Antimessiah / Antichrist) breathes.

Yeshua (Jesus) was begotten of God the Father (Psalm 2:7; John 1:14,18, 3:16,18; 1 John 4:9, 5:1). Satan often likes to imitate God as a counterfeit. The Antimessiah (Antichrist) will imitate God by making a clone begotten of himself. The Antimessiah (Antichrist) will 'set up,' 'place,' and have the cloned image 'stand' in the 'holy place' (the rebuilt Israeli Temple in Jerusalem). The image (clone) of the Antimessiah (Antichrist) is an abomination to God.

DANIEL 12:11-12 (NKJV) [WITH INTERPRETATION]:

And from the time that the daily sacrifice is taken away [JEWISH ANIMAL SACRIFICES TO ATONE FOR SIN IN THE REBUILT TEMPLE IN JERUSALEM], and the abomination of desolation [ANTIMESSIAH (ANTICHRIST) CLONE] is set up, there shall be one thousand two hundred and ninety days. Blessed is he who waits, and comes to the one thousand three hundred and thirty-five days.

REVELATION 14:11 (NKJV) [WITH INTERPRETATION]:

And the smoke of their torment ascends forever and ever; and they have no rest day or night, who worship the beast [ANTIMESSIAH (ANTICHRIST)] and his [CLONED] image, and whoever receives the mark of his name.

When Israel is initially invaded by the Antimessiah (Antichrist) and his forces (Daniel 11:31), after 45-days (1,335-days minus 1,290-days) the Antimessiah (Antichrist) will place, set up, and have stand the cloned image of himself in the rebuilt Temple in Jerusalem. Blessed are the righteous Jews and others who do not worship the abomination of desolation (clone of Antimessiah/Antichrist) and wait upon the return of Yeshua (Jesus) for their redemption (Luke 21:28).

THE RESURRECTION AND SALVATION OF THE JEWS (EZEKIEL 37)

By George Lujack

Throughout the ages, many Christian ministers have declared that the Jews who have rejected Yeshua Messiah (Jesus Christ) and have died will all be judged to hell. This is not the truth, as Yeshua (Jesus) came to save His chosen people of Israel, and they will be resurrected to life and saved. This article will analyze and [INTERPRET] the prophecies of Ezekiel 37 regarding the resurrection and salvation of the Jews.

EZEKIEL 37:1-11 (NKJV) [WITH INTERPRETATION]:

The hand of YHWH (the Lord) came upon me and brought me out in the Spirit of the Lord, and set me down in the midst of the valley; and it was full of bones [GRAVES].

Then He caused me to pass by them all around, and behold, there were very many in the open valley; and indeed they were very dry. And He said to me, "Son of man, can these bones live?"

So I answered, "O YHWH (Lord) GOD, You know."

Again He said to me, "Prophesy to these bones, and say to them, 'O dry bones, hear the word of YHWH (the Lord)! Thus says YHWH (the Lord) GOD to these bones: "Surely I will cause breath to enter into you, and you shall live. I will put sinews on you and bring flesh upon you, cover you with skin and put breath in you; and you shall live. Then you [WHO I HAVE RESURRECTED] shall know that I [YESHUA (JESUS)] am YHWH (the Lord).'"

So I prophesied as I was commanded; and as I prophesied, there was a noise, and suddenly a rattling; and the bones came together, bone to bone. Indeed, as I looked, the sinews and the flesh came upon them, and the skin covered them over; but there was no breath in them.

Also He said to me, "Prophesy to the breath, prophesy, son of man, and say to the breath, 'Thus says YHWH (the Lord) GOD: "Come from the four winds, O breath, and breathe on these slain, that they may live."'"

So I prophesied as He commanded me, and breath came into them, and they lived, and stood upon their feet, an exceedingly great army.

Then He said to me, "Son of man, THESE BONES ARE THE WHOLE HOUSE OF ISRAEL. They indeed say, 'Our bones are dry, our hope is lost, and we ourselves are cut off! [THE JEWS HAD BEEN CUT OFF FOR REJECTING YESHUA (JESUS) AS THEIR MESSIAH].

EZEKIEL 37:12-28 (NKJV) [WITH INTERPRETATION]:

Therefore prophesy and say to them, 'Thus says YHWH (the Lord) GOD: "Behold, O My people [ISRAEL], I will open your graves and cause you to come up from your graves, and bring you into the land of Israel. Then you shall know that I am YHWH (the Lord), when I [YESHUA (JESUS)] have opened your graves, O My people [ISRAEL], and brought you up [RESURRECTED YOU] from your graves. I will put My Spirit in you, and you shall live, and I will place you in your own land [ISRAEL]. Then you shall know that I, YHWH (the Lord), have spoken it and performed it," says YHWH (the Lord).'"

Again the word of YHWH (the Lord) came to me, saying, "As for you, son of man, take a stick for yourself and write on it: 'For JUDAH and for the CHILDREN OF ISRAEL, his companions.' Then take another stick and write on it, 'For Joseph, the stick of Ephraim, AND FOR ALL THE HOUSE OF ISRAEL, his companions.' Then join them one to another for yourself into one stick, and they will become one in your hand.

And when the children of your people [ISRAEL] speak to you, saying, 'Will you not show us what you mean by these?' - say to them, 'Thus says YHWH (the Lord) GOD: "Surely I will take the stick of Joseph, which is in the hand of Ephraim, AND THE TRIBES OF ISRAEL, his companions; and I will join them with it, with the stick of JUDAH, and make them one stick [UNITE THE DIVIDED KINGDOMS OF ISRAEL: ISRAEL AND JUDAH], and they will be one [NATION] in My hand."' And the sticks on which you write will be in your hand before their eyes.

"Then say to them [ISRAEL], 'Thus says YHWH (the Lord) GOD: "Surely I will take the CHILDREN OF ISRAEL from among the nations, wherever they have gone, and will gather them from every side and bring them into their own land [ISRAEL]; and I will make them one nation in the land, on the mountains of Israel; and one king shall be king over them all; they shall no longer be two nations [ISRAEL AND JUDAH], nor shall they ever be divided into two kingdoms again.

They shall not defile themselves anymore with their idols, nor with their detestable things, nor with any of their transgressions; but I will deliver them from all their dwelling places in which they have sinned, and will cleanse them. Then they shall be My people, and I will be their God.

"David [RESURRECTED KING DAVID] My servant shall be king over them, and they shall all have one shepherd [YESHUA (JESUS)]; they shall also walk in My judgments and observe My statutes, and do them. Then they shall dwell in the land [ISRAEL] that I have given to Jacob My servant, where your fathers dwelt; and they shall dwell there, they, their children, and their children's children, forever; and My servant David shall be their prince forever. Moreover I will make a covenant of peace with them [THE JEWS], and it shall be an everlasting covenant with them; I will establish them and multiply them, and I will set My sanctuary in their midst forevermore. My tabernacle also shall be with them; indeed I will be their God, and they [ISRAEL] shall be My people. The nations also will know that I, YHWH (the Lord), sanctify Israel, when My sanctuary is in their midst forevermore.'"

EZEKIEL 37:5-6 (NKJV) [WITH INTERPRETATION]:

Thus says YHWH (the Lord) GOD to these bones: "Surely I will cause breath to enter into you, and you shall live. I will put sinews on you and bring flesh upon you, cover you with skin and put breath in you; and you shall live. Then you [WHO I HAVE RESURRECTED] shall know that I [YESHUA (JESUS)] am YHWH (the Lord)."

The resurrection and salvation spoken of in Ezekiel 37 is of the righteous-living Jews who had been deceived about accepting Yeshua (Jesus) as their Lord and Savior. The commandment-keeping, righteous-living, Messiah-rejecting Jews, upon their resurrection, will know Yeshua (Jesus) as their Lord and Savior.

1 CORINTHIANS 15:51-52 (NKJV) [WITH INTERPRETATION]:

Behold, I tell you a mystery: We shall not all sleep [DIE], but we shall all be changed - in a moment, in the twinkling of an eye, at the last trumpet. For the trumpet will sound, and the dead [IN MESSIAH (CHRIST)] will be raised incorruptible, and we shall be changed.

1 THESSALONIANS 4:15-16 (NKJV) [WITH INTERPRETATION]:

For this we say to you by the word of the Lord, that we who are alive and remain until the coming of the Lord will by no means precede those who are asleep [DEAD]. For the Lord Himself will descend from heaven with a shout, with the voice of an archangel, and with the trumpet of God. And the dead in Messiah (Christ) will rise first.

The resurrection of the Messianic and Christian saints is a different event than the resurrection of the righteous, Messiah-rejecting Jews. Messianic and Christian believers, who have died and are to be resurrected, ALREADY KNOW that Yeshua (Jesus) is their Lord and Savior. Ezekiel 37 does not address the resurrection of the dead in Messiah (Christ), but is a reference to the deceived, commandment-keeping, righteous-living, Messiah-denying Jews who shall THEN know, IN THAT DAY, He is their Messiah, Lord, and Savior.

Not all Jews, just because they are Jewish, will be saved.

MATTHEW 8:10-12 (NKJV) [WITH INTERPRETATION]:

When Yeshua (Jesus) heard it, He marveled, and said to those who followed, "Assuredly, I say to you, I have not found such great faith, not even in Israel! And I say to you that many [GENTILES] will come from east and west, and sit down with Abraham, Isaac, and Jacob in the kingdom of heaven. But the sons of the kingdom [JEWS] will be cast out into outer darkness. There will be weeping and gnashing of teeth."

LUKE 13:23-29 (NKJV) [WITH INTERPRETATION]:

And Yeshua (Jesus) said to them, "Strive to enter through the narrow gate, for many, I say to you, will seek to enter and will not be able. When once the Master of the house has risen up and shut the door, and you begin to stand outside and knock at the door, saying, 'Lord, Lord, open for us,' and He will answer and say to you, 'I do not know you, where you are from,' then you will begin to say, 'We ate and drank in Your presence, and You taught in our streets [IN ISRAEL].' But He will say, 'I tell you I do not know you, where you are from. Depart from Me, all you workers of iniquity.' There will be weeping and gnashing of teeth, when you see Abraham and Isaac and Jacob and all the prophets in the kingdom of God, and yourselves [EVIL JEWS] thrust out. They [RIGHTEOUS GENTILES] will come from the east and the west, from the north and the south, and sit down in the kingdom of God."

Evil Jews and evil Gentiles will be shut out from the kingdom of God.

EZEKIEL 39:21-22 (NKJV) [WITH INTERPRETATION]:

I will set My glory among the nations; all the nations shall see My judgment which I have executed, and My hand which I have laid on them. So the house of Israel shall know that I [YESHUA (JESUS)] am YHWH (the Lord) their God from that day [OF MY RETURN] forward.

ZECHARIAH 9:16 (NKJV) [WITH INTERPRETATION]:

YHWH (the Lord) their God will save them [THE JEWS] in that day [OF HIS RETURN] as the flock of His people [ISRAEL]. For they shall be like the jewels of a crown, lifted like a banner over His land [ISRAEL].

MARK 14:61-62 (NKJV) [WITH INTERPRETATION]:

Again the [JEWISH] high priest asked Him, saying to Him, "Are You the Messiah (Christ), the Son of the Blessed?"

Yeshua (Jesus) said, "I am. And you [THE RESURRECTED HOUSE OF ISRAEL] will see the Son of Man sitting at the right hand of the Power, and coming with the clouds of heaven."

When Yeshua (Jesus) returns, everyone, both Jew and Gentile, will know Him as the Messiah (Christ), the Son of the living God, and we will all serve Him in one accord (Zephaniah 3:9).

WHEN IS YESHUA (JESUS) RETURNING?

By George Lujack

This article will address the events that must occur before Yeshua (Jesus) returns to Earth to establish His Millennium Kingdom.

LUKE 21:8 (NKJV):

And Yeshua (Jesus) said: "Take heed that you not be deceived. For many will come in My name, saying, 'I am He' and, 'THE TIME HAS DRAWN NEAR.' THEREFORE DO NOT GO AFTER THEM."

Some false prophets have predicted the exact day of the return of Yeshua (Jesus), deceiving some believers, and anyone who has ever done so has either been unstudied in the word of God or a deceiver.

MATTHEW 24:36; MARK 13:32 (NKJV):

"But of that day and hour no one knows, not even the angels in heaven, nor the Son, but only the Father."

All preachers who have ever declared the exact date of Messiah's (Christ's) return are false prophets whose predictions should never have been believed in the first place. Scripture is crystal clear that no one, not even Yeshua (Jesus) Himself, knows the day or the hour of His return, but only the Father in heaven knows. How then can any mere mortal man defiantly proclaim that he knows the day of Yeshua's (Jesus') return? There are yet many things that must happen, many prophecies yet to be fulfilled, before Messiah (Christ) will return. Anyone who proclaims that Yeshua (Jesus) could return today or tomorrow has not studied the prophetic events that Scripture declares must occur first before He returns.

THE FOLLOWING PROPHETIC EVENTS MUST OCCUR BEFORE YESHUA (JESUS) RETURNS TO EARTH TO ESTABLISH HIS MILLENNIUM KINGDOM:

ISRAELI JEWS HAD TO BE GATHERERED FROM AMONG THE NATIONS AND BROUGHT BACK TO THEIR OWN LAND, ISRAEL. YESHUA (JESUS) MUST RETURN BEFORE THE GENERATION THAT WITNESSED ISRAEL BECOME A NATION DIES OFF (EZEKIEL 34:13, 37:21; LUKE 21:29-32).

EZEKIEL 37:21 (NKJV):

Then say to them, 'Thus says the Lord GOD: "Surely I will take the children of Israel from among the nations, wherever they have gone, and will gather them from every side and bring them into their own land;"

LUKE 21:29-32 (NKJV):

Then He spoke to them a parable: "Look at the fig tree, and all the trees. When they are already budding, you see and know for yourselves that summer is now near. So you also, WHEN YOU SEE THESE THINGS HAPPENING, know that the kingdom of God is near. Assuredly, I say to you, THIS GENERATION WILL BY NO MEANS PASS AWAY TILL ALL THINGS TAKE PLACE."

The Jews of Israel (the fig tree) were gathered from all the nations and once again became a nation on May 14, 1948, in fulfillment of Scripture prophesy. The generation that saw Israel bud as a nation in the 1967 Six-Day War will not pass away before Yeshua (Jesus) returns. The return of Jews to their homeland of Israel, and Israel budding as a nation once again, set the clock in motion for the return of Yeshua Messiah (Jesus Christ).

The maximum time span of a generation of people is 120-years (Genesis 6:3). The latest date therefore, that Yeshua (Jesus) will return is up to 120-years after 1967, or 2087. Assuming that there will be more than a few centenarian plus twenty-year-old witnesses to His return (of the generation that will not pass away) Yeshua (Jesus) will likely return some decades before 2068.

WARS AND RUMORS OF WARS MUST HAPPEN BEFORE YESHUA (JESUS) RETURNS (MATTHEW 24:6; MARK 13:7; LUKE 21:9).

LUKE 21:9 (NKJV):

"But when you hear of wars and rumors of wars, do not be troubled; for such things must happen, BUT THE END IS NOT YET."

Many wars have been fought since those words of Yeshua (Jesus) were spoken. World Wars I and II have been waged. There have been rumors of war (or wars that have been avoided) such as the near war between Russia and the USA during the Cuban Missile Crisis. Many more wars will be fought before Yeshua (Jesus) returns. Yeshua (Jesus) will not return to prevent war, which must happen. Wars will not mark the end of the age or signal His return (Luke 21:9).

THE 'FALLING AWAY' MUST OCCUR AND GOD'S RESTRAINTS AGAINST THE LAWLESS, FOR THE SAKE OF THE SAINTS, MUST BE TAKEN OUT OF THE WAY BEFORE YESHUA (JESUS) RETURNS (2 THESSALONIANS 2:1-4).

2 THESSALONIANS 2:1-4,7-8 (NKJV):

Now, brethren, concerning the coming of Yeshua Messiah (our Lord Jesus Christ) and OUR GATHERING TOGETHER TO HIM, we ask you, not to be soon shaken in mind or troubled, either by spirit or by word or by letter, as if from us, as though the day of Messiah (Christ) had come. Let no one deceive you by any means; for THAT DAY WILL NOT COME UNLESS THE FALLING AWAY comes first, and THE MAN OF SIN IS REVEALED, THE SON OF PERDITION, who opposes and exalts himself above all that is called God or that is worshiped, so that HE SITS AS GOD IN TEMPLE OF GOD, showing himself that he is God. ...

For the mystery of lawlessness is already at work; ONLY HE WHO NOW RESTRAINS WILL DO SO UNTIL HE IS TAKEN OUT OF THE WAY. And then the lawless one will be revealed, whom the Lord will consume with the breath of His mouth and destroy with the brightness of His coming.

The 'falling away' is currently well in progress. The falling away is a societal falling away of nations once governed by Judeo-Christian moral principles that have lost their way, transformed into secular godless societies. The falling away pertains to the Christianized Western nations that have known the true God, not the Gentile, Muslim, pagan, or secular nations that have never known the God of the Scriptures. A nation cannot 'fall away' from the truth, unless they were a nation that once knew the truth in the first place and received national blessings from God. When such nations 'fall away' from upholding the godly values that made them great nations, national curses follow.

Societal morality in the Western Christianized nations has been in a rapid state of decline during the last few decades. Today, there is much evil that is called good, and much good that is called evil (Isaiah 5:20). Abortion on demand - the death of innocent children in the womb, and homosexuality - including gay 'marriage,' have been embraced by Western society, while there is an ever-growing intolerance of traditional Judeo-Christian values. Any type of prayer or mention of God in public schools, on college campuses, or in other public (and sometimes private) places is heavily frowned upon or not allowed. Even the act of bringing a bible to school, to read in one's free time, is getting children in trouble with their school teachers in these end times.

THE DESTRUCTION OF BABYLON THE GREAT (AMERICA) MUST OCCUR BEFORE YESHUA (JESUS) RETURNS (REVELATION 14:8, 18).

Russia and an alliance of many nations will first cripple America with an EMP attack (Jeremiah 51:32), then destroy America in one hour through a massive nuclear attack (Revelation 14:8, 18).

JEREMIAH 51:32 (NKJV) [WITH INTERPRETATION]:

The reeds they have burned with fire [THE ELECTRONIC CIRCUITS AND ELECTRIC GRIDS OF THE NATION HAVE BEEN FRIED BY EMPs - ELECTROMAGNETIC PULSE BOMBS], and the [AMERICAN] soldiers are terrified.

REVELATION 18:19 (NKJV) [WITH INTERPRETATION]:

'Alas, alas, that great city [NATION], in which all who had ships on the sea became rich by her [AMERICA'S] wealth! For in one hour she [AMERICA] is made desolate.'

The American saints will be taken in a rapture, before the nuclear bombs drop, and be presented to YHWH (the Lord) (Isaiah 18:5-7).

ISAIAH 18:5-6 (NKJV) [WITH INTERPRETATION]:

For before the harvest [BEFORE THE WORLDWIDE HARVEST (RAPTURE) OF THE SAINTS], when the bud [TIMING] is perfect and the sour grape [THE SIN OF HOMOSEXUALITY] is ripening in the flower [AMERICA], then He will both cut off the twigs [THE UNRIGHTEOUS] with pruning hooks and cut down and take away [RAPTURE] the branches [THE RIGHTEOUS]. They [THE UNRIGHTEOUS] will be left [BEHIND] together for the mountain birds of prey [REVELATION 18:2] and for the beasts of the earth. The birds of prey [REVELATION 18:2] will summer on them, and all the beasts of the earth will winter on them [EAT THEM].

ISAIAH 18:7 (NKJV) [WITH INTERPRETATION]:

In that time [OF THE DESTRUCTION OF BABYLON (AMERICA)] a present [THE RAPTURED AMERICAN SAINTS] will be brought to YHWH (the Lord) of hosts from a people tall and smooth-skinned [AMERICA], and from a people awesome from their beginning onward [AMERICA] - a nation powerful and trampling [AMERICA], whose land [AMERICA] the rivers divide - to the place of the name of YHWH (the Lord) of hosts, to Mount Zion [NEW JERUSALEM].

WORLDWIDE ECONOMIC COLLAPSE AND THE COMPULSORY IMPLEMENTATION OF THE MARK OF THE BEAST MUST OCCUR BEFORE YESHUA (JESUS) RETURNS (EZEKIEL 7:19; REVELATION 13:16-18, 20:4).

The destruction of America will cause a worldwide economic collapse that will usher in the new economic system of the Antimessiah (Antichrist).

REVELATION 13:16-18 (NKJV):

He causes all, both small and great, rich and poor, free and slave, to receive a mark on their right hand or on their foreheads, AND THAT NO ONE MAY BUY OR SELL EXCEPT ONE WHO HAS THE MARK or the name of the beast, or the number of his name. Here is wisdom. Let him who has understanding calculate the number of the beast, for it is the number of a man: His number is 666.

The technology for the mark is already here and is being further refined. Most pets sold in the USA and many Western nations are marked or 'chipped' with a computer-tracking device. It is just a matter of time and circumstance before the governments of the world, led by the Antimessiah (Antichrist), force impose the mark of the beast on the entire human population.

EZEKIEL 7:19 (NKJV):

They will throw their silver into the streets and their gold will be like refuse; Their silver and gold will not be able to deliver them in the day of the wrath of the Lord;

There are many today who, fearing the inevitable economic collapse, believe that they can avoid it by investing in gold and silver to protect themselves. Their gold and silver will not be of any value when the Antimessiah (Antichrist) implements his new economic system requiring that they receive his mark. Gold and silver will become worthless assets.

THE TEMPLE OF GOD IN ISRAEL MUST BE REBUILT BEFORE YESHUA (JESUS) RETURNS (2 THESSALONIANS 2:1-4).

Financial resources are in place and plans are well underway for the Temple to be rebuilt by Israeli Jews on the Temple Mount in Jerusalem. The problem and delay in rebuilding the Temple is not a money issue, but the fact that the Dome of the Rock, Muslims' holiest shrine, currently stands at the platform of the Temple Mount.

One way or another, Scripture prophecy will be fulfilled. The Dome of the Rock will come down from the Temple Mount and be replaced with the Temple. The Dome of the Rock will either come down by Israelite Jews or by an act of God Himself (such an earthquake). Either that or the Israelite Jews will build their Temple on a nearby site, but that is unlikely.

The possibility should not be ruled out that the Antimessiah (Antichrist) could soon come on the world scene and make a peace agreement between the Jews and Muslims that would include the rebuilding of the Temple in Jerusalem. The Jews would like this and see him as their Messiah, if he could make a peace treaty that gave them added security and allowed them to rebuild their Temple. In back-room political dealings with the Muslim powers, who would theoretically go along with this peace pact, he (the Antimessiah / Antichrist) could assure them (the Palestinians and other Muslim leaders) that he will double-cross Israel and make war to annihilate the Jews. The Palestinians would therefore willingly approve of this peace agreement deal, even if it meant the tearing down of their Dome of the Rock mosque. The desire of the Palestinians and their neighboring Muslim countries to wipe Israel off the map is stronger to them than any religious shrine that they may claim to hold sacred.

THE MAN OF SIN / SON OF PERDITION / ANTIMESSIAH (ANTICHRIST) MUST BE REVEALED BEFORE YESHUA (JESUS) RETURNS (2 THESSALONIANS 2:1-4,7-8).

The identification of the world leader known as the Antimessiah (Antichrist) will not be a mystery or a matter of guesswork. There are many antimessiahs (antichrists) living among us today, such as U.S. President Barack Obama, who are paving the way for the arrival of the Antimessiah (Antichrist) (Matthew 24:24; 1 John 2:18). Believers will be able to positively identify the man of sin / the man of perdition / the Antimessiah (Antichrist) because He will be the popular charismatic world leader who will declare himself to be God and will seat himself in the rebuilt Temple in Jerusalem, Israel, as God.

God will remove Himself from restraining evil in the world. An unrestrained Antimessiah (Antichrist), led by Satan, will unleash complete evil, destruction, and lawlessness upon the world (2 Thessalonians 2:7-8).

THE GATHERING TOGETHER TO HIM IN THE CLOUDS (THE RESURRECTION OF THE DEAD SAINTS AND WORLDWIDE RAPTURE OF LIVING BELIEVERS) MUST OCCUR BEFORE YESHUA (JESUS) RETURNS (1 CORINTHIANS 15:51-53; 1 THESSALONIANS 4:15-17; 2 THESSALONIANS 2:1-4).

The gathering to Him in the clouds (the resurrection of the dead saints and rapture of believers) must occur before that Day (the Day of His return) comes.

THE TIME OF THE GENTILE NATIONS, A TIME THE WORLD IS NOT GOVERNED, POLICED, OR RULED BY AMERICA AND HER ALLIES MUST OCCUR BEFORE YESHUA (JESUS) RETURNS (EZEKIEL 30:3).

EZEKIEL 30:3 (NKJV):

For the day is near; Even the day of YHWH (the Lord) is near; It will be a day of clouds, THE TIME OF THE GENTILES.

Before Yeshua (Jesus) returns, the Gentile nations will be ruling the Earth. America (the hammer of the Earth) will have fallen by then and been destroyed as the world superpower (Jeremiah 50:23). The Gentile nations will include the nations that have historically not been Christian nations: Russia, China, and a conglomerate of Middle East and African Muslim nations.

THE ANTIMESSIAH (ANTICHRIST) WILL ERECT AN IMAGE OF HIMSELF AND DEMAND THAT THE WORLD WORSHIP HIS IMAGE BEFORE YESHUA (JESUS) RETURNS (REVELATION 13:14-15, 14:9-11, 15:2, 16:2, 19:20, 20:4).

REVELATION 13:14-15 (NKJV):
And he deceives those who dwell on the earth by those signs which he was granted to do in the sight of the beast, telling those who dwell on the earth to MAKE AN IMAGE TO THE BEAST who was wounded by the sword and lived. He was granted power to give breath to the IMAGE OF THE BEAST, that the IMAGE OF THE BEAST should both speak and cause as many as would not worship the IMAGE OF THE BEAST to be killed.

Much of the left-behind world will be deceived and will worship the image of the beast. Many of those who don't worship the beast's image will be killed. The Judaic Jews will reject the Antimessiah (Antichrist) as their Messiah, because he will make an image of himself, a clone, and demand that the world worship his image. (Revelation 13:14-15, 14:9-11, 15:2, 16:2, 19:20, 20:4). The Hebrews (Jews) learned their lesson from the golden calf incident at Mt. Sinai and will not worship an image of God (Exodus 32).

THE ANTIMESSIAH (ANTICHRIST) WILL RULE FROM THE TEMPLE IN ISRAEL FOR A LITTLE LESS THAN 3 ½ YEARS (ONE THOUSAND TWO HUNDRED AND NINETY DAYS) BEFORE YESHUA (JESUS) RETURNS (DANIEL 11:31, 12:11-12; MATTHEW 24:15; MARK 13:14).

DANIEL 11:31 (NKJV):
And military forces shall be mustered by him, and they shall defile the sanctuary fortress; then they shall take away the daily sacrifices, and place there the abomination of desolation.

DANIEL 12:11-12 (NKJV):
And from the time that the daily sacrifice is taken away, and the abomination of desolation is set up, there shall be one thousand two hundred and ninety days. Blessed is he who waits, and comes to the one thousand three hundred and thirty-five days.

The abomination of desolation, the abomination (Antimessiah / Antichrist) that brings desolation (through nuclear warfare), will use military force to drive the Israelite Jews from their sanctuary fortress (their Temple in Jerusalem where they will be offering daily animal sacrifices). The Antimessiah (Antichrist) will sit as God in the Israeli Temple acting as God for 1,290 days (Daniel 11:31, 12:11-12). Jews who come to be believers during those tribulation years, reject the Antimessiah (Antichrist), and are able to survive will be blessed to see the return of Yeshua (Jesus) 45-days or so (1290-days + 45-days = 1,335-days) after the Antimessiah (Antichrist) leaves the Temple (Daniel 12:11-12).

THE JUDAIC JEWS OF ISRAEL MUST COME TO BELIEVE IN YESHUA (JESUS) BEFORE YESHUA (JESUS) RETURNS (EZEKIEL 39:27-28).

EZEKIEL 39:27-28 (NKJV):

When I have brought them back from the peoples and gathered them out of their enemies' lands, AND I AM HALLOWED IN THEM IN THE SIGHT OF MANY NATIONS, then they shall know that I am YHWH (the Lord) their God, who sent them into captivity among the nations, but also brought them back to their land, and left none of them captive any longer.

MATTHEW 23:38-39; LUKE 13:35 (NKJV) [WITH INTERPRETATION]:

"Your house is left to you desolate; for I say to you, you shall see Me no more till you say, *'Blessed is He* [YESHUA / JESUS] *who comes in the name of* [YHWH] *(the Lord)!'"

The Judaic Messiah-denying Jewish people will come to believe in Yeshua (Jesus) as their Messiah and Savior during the tribulation years. It is then that they will openly worship and call upon Yeshua (Jesus) as their Messiah and Savior in the sight of many nations (Ezekiel 39:27-28).

THE WORLD WILL EXPERIENCE NUCLEAR WAR AND WILL BE AT THE BRINK OF TOTAL ANNIHILATION (NO FLESH WOULD BE SAVED) BEFORE YESHUA (JESUS) RETURNS (ISAIAH 17:1; JEREMIAH 50-51; EZEKIEL 30:7; MATTHEW 24:22; MARK 13:20; REVELATION 18).

The Antimessiah (Antichrist) is also referred to as the abomination of desolation (Daniel 11:31, 12:11; Matthew 24:15; Mark 13:14). He is the abomination (who calls himself God) that brings desolation (through nuclear warfare).

Damascus, Syria will cease to be a city and become a ruinous heap (Isaiah 17:1). Many other cities and countries will be destroyed through desolation (nuclear warfare) during the reign of the Antimessiah (Antichrist) (Ezekiel 30:7).

Babylon the great (America) will be completely destroyed in one hour by arrows that bring fire (intercontinental ballistic nuclear missiles) from the north (Russia) (Jeremiah 50-51; Revelation 18).

MATTHEW 24:22; MARK 13:20 (NKJV):

"And unless those days were shortened, no flesh would be saved; but for the elect's sake those days will be shortened."

Yeshua (Jesus) will return to shorten the days of man's rule, to prevent the total annihilation of all human life - for the sake of the elect Jews of Israel (Matthew 24:22; Mark 13:20).

SIGNS IN THE HEAVENS OF YESHUA'S (JESUS') IMMINENT RETURN (EZEKIEL 32:7; JOEL 2:10,31, 3:15; MATTHEW 24:29; MARK 13:24; LUKE 21:25; ACTS 2:20; REVELATION 6:12, 8:12).

JOEL 2:31; ACTS 2:20 (NKJV):

The sun shall be turned into darkness, and the moon into blood, before the great and awesome day of YHWH (the Lord).

WHEN WILL YESHUA (JESUS) RETURN?

A blood moon is a total lunar eclipse in which a full moon passes directly behind the Earth leaving the Moon with just enough light to appear red in the wake of the Earth's shadow. Previous major prophetic events of Scripture have been fulfilled during tetrad (sets of four) blood moons. Assuming God does not intervene and realign the heavenly bodies Himself, to cause the Moon to turn to blood and the Sun to not give its light, and allows the Sun, Earth and Moon to travel on their projected courses; future tetrad sets of blood moons are set to occur in 2032-2033, 2043-2044, 2050-2051, 2061-2062, 2072-2073 and 2090-2091.

As previously stated in this article, Yeshua (Jesus) must return before the generation that witnessed Israel become a nation dies off; the absolute latest date 2068. That would therefore rule out His return occurring following the blood moons of 2072-2073 and 2090-2091.

The aforementioned prophecies cited in this article must occur before Yeshua (Jesus) returns. During the tetrad blood moons of 2014-2015 the first woe of Revelation 9:1-12 was fulfilled, which was the torment of Muslim men without the seal of God on their foreheads. The second woe is the destruction of Damascus, Syria (Isaiah 17:1), which should coincide with the tetrad blood moons of 2032-2033. The third woe is the destruction of Babylon the great (America – Jeremiah 50:18; Revelation 18), which should occur during the tetrad blood moons of 2043-2044. A prediction of the year and season of Yeshua Messiah's (Jesus Christ's) return to Earth to establish His Millennium Kingdom, based on the signs of the times and the upcoming signs in the heavens (scheduled tetrad blood moons), is that He will return during the Feast of Trumpets, in the fall, during the tetrad blood moons of 2061-2062.

LUKE 21:36 (NKJV):

"Watch therefore, and pray always that you may be counted worthy to escape all these things that will come to pass, and to stand before the Son of Man."

As more and more Scripture prophecy is fulfilled, the imminent year of His return will become more evident. As believers, we are to watch for the signs of the times and the signs in the heavens, and pray that we are counted worthy to escape the tribulation events (through the rapture) that will come to pass.

THE MILLENNIUM KINGDOM; THE FIRST FRUITS, SATAN'S FINAL REBELLION, AND THE PENITENT OF THE SECOND RESURRECTION (ZECHARIAH 8)

By George Lujack

This article will cover and [INTERPRET] Zechariah 8, which is a prophetic synopsis of the Millennium Kingdom through the second resurrection.

ZECHARIAH 8:1-10 (NKJV) [WITH INTERPRETATION]:

Again the word of YHWH (the Lord) of hosts came, saying,

"Thus says YHWH (the Lord) of hosts: 'I am zealous for Zion with great zeal; with great fervor I am zealous for her.'

Thus says YHWH (the Lord): 'I will return to Zion, and dwell in the midst of Jerusalem [WHEN HE RETURNS, DURING THE MILLENNIUM KINGDOM REIGN]. Jerusalem shall be called the City of Truth, the Mountain of YHWH (the Lord) of hosts, the Holy Mountain.'

"Thus says YHWH (the Lord) of hosts: 'Old men and old women shall again sit in the streets of Jerusalem, each one with his staff in his hand because of great age. The streets of the city shall be full of boys and girls playing in its streets.'

"Thus says YHWH (the Lord) of hosts: 'If it is marvelous in the eyes of the remnant of this people in these days, will it also be marvelous in My eyes?' says YHWH (the Lord) of hosts.

"Thus says YHWH (the Lord) of hosts: 'Behold, I will save My people from the land of the east [ASIA] and from the land of the west [THE AMERICAS -ISAIAH 18:5-7]; I will bring them back, and they shall dwell in the midst of Jerusalem. They shall be My people and I will be their God, in truth and righteousness.'

"Thus says YHWH (the Lord) of hosts: 'Let your hands be strong, you who have been hearing in these days these words by the mouth of the prophets, who spoke in the day the foundation was laid for the house of YHWH (the Lord) of hosts, that the temple might be built [THE TEMPLE IN JERUSALEM WILL BE REBUILT]. For before these days there were no wages for man nor any hire for beast [DURING THE GLOBAL ECONOMIC CRISIS OF THE GREAT TRIBULATION]; there was no peace from the enemy [ENEMIES OF ISRAEL] for whoever went out or came in; for I set all men, everyone, against his neighbor [DURING THE GREAT TRIBULATION WARS].

ZECHARIAH 8:11-23 (NKJV) [WITH INTERPRETATION]:

But now I will not treat the remnant of this people as in the former days,' says YHWH (the Lord) of hosts. 'For the seed shall be prosperous, the vine shall give its fruit, the ground shall give her increase, and the heavens shall give their dew – I will cause the remnant of this people to possess all these. And it shall come to pass that just as you were a curse among the nations, O house of Judah and house of Israel, so I will save you [YESHUA (JESUS) WILL PROTECT THE FIRST FRUITS OF THE FIRST RESURRECTION LIVING IN THE BELOVED CITY JERUSALEM, FROM SATAN'S FINAL REBELLION – REVELATION 20:7-10], and you shall be a blessing. Do not fear, Let your hands be strong.'

"For thus says YHWH (the Lord) of hosts: 'Just as I determined to punish you when your fathers provoked Me to wrath,' says YHWH (the Lord) of hosts, 'And I would not relent, so again in these days I am determined to do good to Jerusalem and to the house of Judah. Do not fear. These are the things you shall do: Speak each man the truth to his neighbor; give judgment in your gates for truth, justice, and peace; let none of you think evil in your heart against your neighbor; and do not love a false oath. For all these are things that I hate,' says YHWH (the Lord)."

Then the word of YHWH (the Lord) of hosts came to me, saying,

"Thus says YHWH (the Lord) of hosts: 'The fast of the fourth month, the fast of the fifth, the fast of the seventh, and the fast of the tenth, shall be joy and gladness and cheerful feasts for the house of Judah [THE FEASTS OF YHWH (THE LORD) WILL BE OBSERVED - LEVITICUS 23]. Therefore love truth and peace.'

"Thus says YHWH (the Lord) of hosts: 'Peoples shall yet come, inhabitants of many cities; the inhabitants of one city shall go to another, saying, "Let us continue to go and pray before YHWH (the Lord), and seek YHWH (the Lord) of hosts. I myself will go also." [PEOPLE OF THE SECOND RESURRECTION, THOSE WHO WERE PENITENT AND REFUSED TO JOIN SATAN'S FINAL REBELLION AGAINST THE BELOVED CITY OF JERUSALEM, WILL TRAVEL TO JERUSALEM TO SEEK YHWH (THE LORD)]. Yes, many peoples and strong nations shall come to seek YHWH (the Lord) of hosts in Jerusalem, and to pray before YHWH (the Lord).'

"Thus says the Lord of hosts: 'In those days ten men from every language of the nations shall grasp the sleeve of a Jewish* man, saying, "Let us go with you, for we have heard that God is with you" [PENITENT MEN OF THE SECOND RESURRECTION, FROM EVERY NATION, WILL SEEK RIGHTEOUS MEN OF THE FIRST RESURRECTION TO PREPARE AND GUIDE THEM IN ALL TRUTH AND UNDERSTANDING, SO THAT THEY CAN MAKE THEMSELVES ACCEPTABLE TO ENTER THE KINGDOM OF GOD].

---

*Many in Judaism and Messianic Judaism have incorrectly used Zechariah 8:23 to declare that only ethnic Jews will be first fruits of God's kingdom, and in order for Gentiles to be able to enter, they will need to be led in by Jewish men. This ethnic Jew self-gratifying belief is incorrect for a few reasons. It would mean that God judges people by their Jewish ethnicity, not by their righteousness and faith.

Non-ethnic Jewish Gentiles will be raptured and resurrected to eternal life and will dwell with Yeshua (Jesus) in Jerusalem during the Millennium Kingdom (Matthew 8:11). So, if a non-Jewish Gentile, who lived 90-years as an American, were resurrected or raptured and then spent a thousand years in Jerusalem with Yeshua (Jesus), for all intents and purposes the American would be grafted in to the kingdom, becoming Jewish over the Millennium Reign through culture, faith, *and* immigration.

ACTS 10:34 (NKJV):

Then Peter opened his mouth and said: "In truth I perceive that God shows no partiality. But in every nation whoever fears Him and works righteousness is accepted by Him."

ROMANS 2:11,28-29 (NKJV):

For there is no partiality with God. …

For he is not a Jew who is one outwardly, nor is circumcision that which is outward in the flesh; but he is a Jew who is one inwardly; and circumcision is that of the heart, in the Spirit, not in the letter; whose praise is not from men but from God.

The word Hebrew means to cross over; to cross over from man-made traditions and lies into Scripture truth. During the Millennium Kingdom, Gentiles from many nations will cross over from the countries they dwelled in to live with Yeshua (Jesus) in Jerusalem for a thousand years (Revelation 20:4-6). The people of the second resurrection will think of both Gentiles and ethnic Jews, who are first fruits of the kingdom, as Jerusalem-dwelling Jews.

ENDNOTES

[1] Batchelor, Doug, "Determining the Will of God," Amazing Facts Ministries,
< http://www.amazingfacts.org/media-library/book/e/24/t/determining-the-will-of-god >.

[2] "Amazing Facts of Faith - Port Royal & Lewis Galdy," YouTube, April 25, 2015,
< https://www.youtube.com/watch?v=B3kQZllkcBQ >.

[3] "The False Doctrine of the Trinity," SureWordProphecy, YouTube, May 2, 2014,
< https://www.youtube.com/watch?v=MTB69DY6HAs >.

[4] "God the Father, Jesus Christ and the Holy Spirit," United Church of God, Jan 12, 2011
< https://www.ucg.org/booklet/fundamental-beliefs/god-father-jesus-christ-and-holy-spirit >.

[5] 'Biunial,' Merriam-Webster, 2016, < http://www.merriam-webster.com/dictionary/biunial >.

[6] 'Triune,' Merriam-Webster, 2016, < http://www.merriam-webster.com/dictionary/triune >.

[7] 'Both,' Oxford Dictionaries, Oxford University Press, 2016,
< http://www.oxforddictionaries.com/us/definition/american_english/both >.

[8] *"Was 1 John 5:7 Added To The Bible? The Bible truth on the Godhead explained,"* September/08/2016,
< http://www.trinitytruth.org/was1john5_7addedtext.html >.

[9] 'Nature,' Dictionary.com, 2016, < http://dictionary.reference.com/browse/nature >.

[10] DRWard0804, "YHWH Apologetix with Lyrics," YouTube Song Parody Video,
< https://www.youtube.com/watch?v=mdRbywMH7kw >.

[11] 'Fulfill,' Oxford Dictionaries, Oxford University Press, 2016,
< https://en.oxforddictionaries.com/definition/us/fulfill >.

[12] 'Abolish,' Oxford Dictionaries, Oxford University Press, 2016,
< https://en.oxforddictionaries.com/definition/us/abolish >.

[13] 'Destroy,' Oxford Dictionaries, Oxford University Press, 2016,
< https://en.oxforddictionaries.com/definition/us/destroy >.

[14] 'Perpetual,' Oxford Dictionaries, Oxford University Press, 2016,
< https://en.oxforddictionaries.com/definition/us/perpetual >.

[15] 'Remission,' Oxford Dictionaries, Oxford University Press, 2016,
< http://www.oxforddictionaries.com/us/definition/american_english/remission >.

[16] 'Father,' Oxford Dictionaries, Oxford University Press, 2016,
< http://www.oxforddictionaries.com/us/definition/american_english/father >.

[17] 'Rabbi,' Oxford Dictionaries, Oxford University Press, 2016,
< http://www.oxforddictionaries.com/us/definition/american_english/rabbi >.

[18] 'Reverend,' Oxford Dictionaries, Oxford University Press, 2016,
< http://www.oxforddictionaries.com/us/definition/american_english/reverend >.

[19] 'Brother,' Oxford Dictionaries, Oxford University Press, 2016,
< http://www.oxforddictionaries.com/us/definition/american_english/brother >.

[20] 'Minister,' Oxford Dictionaries, Oxford University Press, 2016,
< http://www.oxforddictionaries.com/us/definition/american_english/minister >.

[21] 'Pastor,' Oxford Dictionaries, Oxford University Press, 2016,

< http://www.oxforddictionaries.com/us/definition/american_english/pastor >.

[22] 'Teacher,' Oxford Dictionaries, Oxford University Press, 2016,

< http://www.oxforddictionaries.com/us/definition/american_english/teacher >.

[23] 'Teach,' Oxford Dictionaries, Oxford University Press, 2016,

< http://www.oxforddictionaries.com/us/definition/american_english/teach >.

[24] 'Fornication,' Oxford Dictionaries, Oxford University Press,

< http://www.oxforddictionaries.com/us/definition/american_english/fornication >.

[25] 'Adultery,' Oxford Dictionaries, Oxford University Press,

< http://www.oxforddictionaries.com/us/definition/american_english/adultery >.

[26] 'Denomination,' Oxford Dictionaries, Oxford University Press, 2016,

< http://www.oxforddictionaries.com/us/definition/american_english/denomination >.

[27] 'Grace,' Oxford Dictionaries, Oxford University Press,

< http://www.oxforddictionaries.com/us/definition/american_english/grace >.

[28] "Antinomianism," Encyclopaedia Britannica, Inc., 2016,

< https://www.britannica.com/topic/antinomianism >.

[29] Grider, Geoffrey, "THE CHARISMATIC PROSPERITY MOVEMENT IS NOTHING MORE THAN A 'CHRISTIAN' CULT," NOW THE END BEGINS, FEBRUARY 1, 2016,

< http://www.nowtheendbegins.com/the-charismatic-prosperity-movement-is-nothing-more-than-a-christian-cult/ >.

[30] Gan, Richard, "The Serpent Seed The Original Sin," 1974,

< http://www.propheticrevelation.net/original_sin/the_serpent_seed_3.htm >.

[31] George, Andreas, "In The Footsteps Of St. Nicholas"

< http://www.johnsanidopoulos.com/2011/11/facts-prove-existence-of-st-nicholas-of.html >.

[32] Watkins, Terry, Dr. Th.D., "Santa Claus The Great Imposter," Dial-the-Truth Ministries.

< http://www.av1611.org/othpubls/santa.html >.

[33] 'Rebuke,' Oxford Dictionaries, Oxford University Press, 2016,

< https://en.oxforddictionaries.com/definition/us/rebuke >.

[34] 'Judge,' Oxford Dictionaries, Oxford University Press, 2016,

< https://en.oxforddictionaries.com/thesaurus/judge >.

[35] 'Rainbow flag (LGBT movement),' Wikipedia, 3 September 2016,

< https://en.wikipedia.org/wiki/Rainbow_flag_%28LGBT_movement%29 >.

[36] 'Gilbert Baker (artist),' Wikipedia, 3 September 2016,

< https://en.wikipedia.org/wiki/Gilbert_Baker_%28artist%29 >.

[37] "Testing the Star of David," 119 Ministries, YouTube, Jul 19, 2016,

< https://www.youtube.com/watch?v=-d7q2hzkG3s >.

[38] "The Flag and the Emblem," Israel Ministry of Foreign Affairs, 28 Apr 2003, "According to Sholem, the motive for the widespread use of the Star of David was a wish to imitate Christianity. During the Emancipation, Jews needed a symbol of Judaism parallel to the cross, the universal symbol of Christianity." <*http://www.mfa.gov.il/mfa/aboutisrael/israelat50/pages/the%20flag%20and%20the%20emblem.aspx >.

[39] Vance, Laurence M. Ph.D., "The Origin of King James Onlyism," King James, His Bible, and Its Translators, Vance Publications, < http://www.av1611.org/vance/kjv_only.html >.

[40] Scripture 4 All, Hebrew Interlinear Bible (OT)

< http://www.scripture4all.org/OnlineInterlinear/Hebrew_Index.htm >.

[41] Scripture 4 All, Greek Interlinear Bible (NT)

< http://www.scripture4all.org/OnlineInterlinear/Greek_Index.htm >.

[42] Ribak Gal and Weihs, Daniel, "Jumping without Using Legs: The Jump of the Click-Beetles (*Elateridae*) Is Morphologically Constrained," DOI: 10.1371/journal.pone.0020871, June 16, 2011

< http://journals.plos.org/plosone/article?id=10.1371/journal.pone.0020871 >.

[43] The Interactive Bible, "Were the KJV Translators Inspired?,"

< http://www.bible.ca/b-kjv-only.htm >.

[44] "What is the Hebrew Roots Movement?," Our Father's Festival!, June 25, 2016,

< http://www.ourfathersfestival.net/hebrew_roots_movement >.

[45] "What is Hebrew Roots exactly," House of David Fellowship, 2012,

< http://houseofdavidfellowship.com/qanda.htm >.

[46] Vander Els, Matthew, "What is Hebrew Roots," FOUNDED IN TRUTH MINISTRIES, Jan 31, 2016, < https://www.youtube.com/watch?v=MNWOqOzqIB4 >.

[47] 'Cult,' Oxford Dictionaries, Oxford University Press, 2016

< http://www.oxforddictionaries.com/us/definition/american_english/cult >.

[48] 'Denomination,' Oxford Dictionaries, Oxford University Press, 2016,

< http://www.oxforddictionaries.com/us/definition/american_english/denomination >.

[49] 'Transfigure,' Oxford Dictionaries, Oxford University Press 2016,

< http://www.oxforddictionaries.com/us/definition/american_english/transfigure >.

[50] Got Questions Ministries, "What was the meaning and importance of the transfiguration?"

< www.gotquestions.org/transfiguration.html >.

[51] Creation Science Evangelist Dr. Kent Hovind - "Where Do Different Races Come From?," YouTube, < https://www.youtube.com/watch?v=OLvTIrgmPrI >.

[52] Creation Science Evangelist Dr. Kent Hovind - "Theories about Pre-Flood Life, Humans, Animals, Earth and Atmosphere - Noah's Flood," YouTube,

< https://www.youtube.com/watch?v=JXM73ohfFDE >.

[53] "Noah, Could He Eat All Things,"? 119 Ministries,

< http://119ministries.com/noah-could-he-eat-all-things >.

[54] Peter R. Kraemer- Catholic Church Extension Society (1975), Chicago, Illinois: "We frankly say, yes, the Church made this change, made this law, as she made many other laws, for instance, the Friday abstinence, the unmarried priesthood, the laws concerning mixed marriages, the regulation of Catholic marriages and a thousand other laws."

[55] 'Scales,' International Standard Bible Encyclopedia, Bible Hub,

< http://biblehub.com/topical/s/scales.htm >.

[56] 'Scale,' Collins English Dictionary – Complete and Unabridged, HarperCollins Publishers 2016,

< http://www.collinsdictionary.com/dictionary/english/scale >.

[57] Clinton, Cliff, "Parasitic Worm in Sushi," YouTube video,

< http://www.youtube.com/watch?v=EE-jpYCh2Og >.

* Tuna sushi (the red piece) with parasitic worm. The salmon sushi, a clean fish (the orange piece), has no worms. Parasitic worms are likewise found in unclean swine (pork).

[58] Burros, Marian, "High Mercury Levels Are Found in Tuna Sushi," The New York Times, Jan. 23, 2008,< http://www.nytimes.com/2008/01/23/dining/23sushi.html?pagewanted=all&_r=0 >.

[59] Melnick, Merideth, "Bluefin Tuna Radiation: Is There A Health Risk?" HUFFPOST May 29, 2012, < http://www.huffingtonpost.com/2012/05/29/bluefin-tuna-radioactive-radiation-health_n_1552838.html >.

[60] Lopez, Joseph "Flounder," YouTube video, July 29, 2012,

< http://www.youtube.com/watch?v=OW7b6FK4P4c >.

The video depicts a flatfish (flounder) swimming. They swim horizontally not vertically, alone - not in schools, and can camouflage themselves rapidly like the unclean octopus, cuttlefish, and chameleon. They feed as a predatory fish by lying in wait for prey on the sea floor and also as scavengers that eat fish carcasses and other remains of sea creatures that they come across on the sea floor.

[61] 'Grouper,' Wikipedia, < https://en.wikipedia.org/wiki/Grouper >.

[62] "Nassau Grouper Epinephelus striatus," Florida Museum of Natural History, University of Florida, < http://www.flmnh.ufl.edu/fish/discover/species-profiles/epinephelus-striatus/# >.

[63] 'Crop,' Wikipedia, < https://en.wikipedia.org/wiki/Crop_%28anatomy%29 >.

[64] "How many edible/poisonous mushrooms are there?" Mushroom, the Journal of Wild Mushrooming,< http://www.mushroomthejournal.com/greatlakesdata/TopTen/Quest19.html >.

[65] "Food poisoning / Mushroom poisoning," American Academy of Family Physicians, 04/2014, < http://familydoctor.org/familydoctor/en/diseases-conditions/food-poisoning/mushroom-poisoning.html >.

[66] Walther, Jonathan, "GOD'S FOOD LAWS IN TODAY'S WORLD," December 29, 2003, < http://loveandtruth.net/food-laws.html >.

[67] "Fungal Infections Also called: Mycoses," MedlinePlus, January 15, 2016, < https://www.nlm.nih.gov/medlineplus/fungalinfections.html >.

[68] "Blue-green algae products testing - only Spirulina found Microcystin-free," Health Canada news release, Sept 17, 1999.

[69] Carrington, Damian, "Insects could be the key to meeting food needs of growing global population," The Guardian, August 01, 2010, < http://www.theguardian.com/environment/2010/aug/01/insects-food-emissions >.

[70] Ramos-Elorduy, Julieta; Menzel, Peter, "Creepy Crawly Cuisine: The Gourmet Guide to Edible Insects," Inner Traditions / Bear & Company, p. 5. ISBN 978-0-89281-747-4, Feb 01, 1998, < https://books.google.com/books?id=Q7f1LkFz11gC&hl=en >.

[71] 'Alcohol,' Oxford Dictionaries, Oxford University Press, 2016, < http://www.oxforddictionaries.com/us/definition/american_english/alcohol >.

[72] 'Coffee,' Oxford Dictionaries, Oxford University Press, 2016, < http://www.oxforddictionaries.com/us/definition/american_english/coffee >.

[73] 'Tea,' Oxford Dictionaries, Oxford University Press, 2016, < http://www.oxforddictionaries.com/us/definition/american_english/tea >.

[74] Cloud, John, "Why Do Heavy Drinkers Outlive Nondrinkers?" TIME, Aug. 30, 2010, < http://content.time.com/time/magazine/article/0,9171,2017200,00.html >.

[75] Hearn, C. Aubrey. Alcohol the Destroyer (Nashville: Sunday School Board, 1943).

[76] Hailey, David J. "Beverage Alcohol and the Christian Faith," 1992.

[77] National Highway Traffic and Safety Administration – 2008.

[78] "Russia Raises Price of Cheap Vodka," Article, p.4A, St. Petersburg Times, January 2, 2010.

[79] 'Drunkard,' Oxford Dictionaries, Oxford University Press, 2016, < https://en.oxforddictionaries.com/definition/us/drunkard >.

[80] "Alcohol and coffee linked to reduced risk of Alzheimer's," BT, 24 August 2015, < https://home.bt.com/lifestyle/wellbeing/alcohol-coffee-could-reduce-alzheimers-risk-11363999359381 >.

[81] Rakhmilevich, Tanya, "Could Coffee Help Protect Your Liver From Alcohol?" < http://www.thealternativedaily.com/coffee-protect-liver-from-alcohol/ >.

[82] World Health Organization International Agency for Research on Cancer "IARC Monographs evaluate consumption of red meat and processed meat," PRESS RELEASE #240, 26 October 2015, < http://www.iarc.fr/en/media-centre/pr/2015/pdfs/pr240_E.pdf >.

[83] Professor Hans-Heinrich Reckeweh, M.D., "The Adverse Influence of Pork Consumption on Health," Biological Therapy Vol.1 No.2 1983, < https://healthmasters.com/blog/adverse-influence-pork-consumption-health >.

[84] Snyder, Michael, "Yes, The Scientific Evidence Says That Eating Pork Does Cause Cancer," October 26, 2015, < http://endoftheamericandream.com/archives/yes-the-scientific-evidence-says-that-eating-pork-does-cause-cancer >.

[85] FOX News Report, "Doctors Remove Worm From Woman's Brain," November 22, 2008, < https://www.youtube.com/watch?v=4_GeNwi0bTg >.

[86] California Department of Public Health, "CDPH Warns Consumers Not to Eat Sport-Harvested Bivalve Shellfish from Monterey or Santa Cruz Counties," Number: 14-036, April 4, 2014, < http://www.cdph.ca.gov/Pages/NR14-036.aspx >.

[87] FDA U.S. Food and Drug Administration, "FDA warns consumers not to eat shellfish from Oyster Bay Harbor, Nassau County, NY," July 20, 2012,

< http://www.fda.gov/NewsEvents/Newsroom/PressAnnouncements/ucm312977.htm >.

[88] Bonfield, Tim, "Health department may recommend shellfish menu warning / Death from vibrio prompts concerns," The Cincinnati Enquirer, August 31, 1999,

< http://www.enquirer.com/editions/1999/08/31/loc_health_department.html >.

[89] Burros, Marian, The New York Times, "High Mercury Levels Are Found in Tuna Sushi," Jan. 23, 2008,< http://www.nytimes.com/2008/01/23/dining/23sushi.html?pagewanted=all&_r=0 >.

[90] Melnick, Merideth, "Bluefin Tuna Radiation: Is There A Health Risk?" HUFFPOST May 29, 2012, < http://www.huffingtonpost.com/2012/05/29/bluefin-tuna-radioactive-radiation-health_n_1552838.html >.

[91] People Magazine, "Enduring Spirit. Despite Declining Health, Pope John Paul II Proves He's Still in Charge as He Turns 84." By Susan Schindehette, Vol. 61 – No. 20 – May 24, 2004,

< http://www.people.com/people/archive/article/0,,20150148,00.html >.

[92] MD Anderson Cancer Center (TV ad),

< https://www.youtube.com/watch?t=1&v=bqzOKRQUqoI >.

[93] SayersBrook American Gourmet, "Bison Facts," 11820 Sayersbrook Road, Potosi, MO 63664 1-888-472-9377.

[94] The Watchtower, June 15, 2004, p. 21.

[95] "How Can Blood Save Your Life," Watch Tower Bible and Tract Society, 1990, p. 24.

[96] The Watchtower, June 1, 1969, pp. 326, 327.

[97] The Watchtower, February 1, 1997, p. 29.

[98] "Instructions for Filling in The Advance Decision Document," Watch Tower Bible and Tract Society, 2005, p.1.

[99] The Watchtower, October 15, 2000, pp. 30-31.

[100] Awake!, August 2006, p. 11.

[101] The Watchtower, September 1, 1986, p. 25.

[102] Statement to the media, Jehovah's Witnesses Public Affairs Office, June 14, 2000.

[103] The Watchtower, January 15, 1961, p. 63.

[104] The Watchtower, July 15, 1982, p. 20.

[105] Jehovah's Witness media release dated June 14, 2000.

[106] Peter R. Kraemer- Catholic Church Extension Society (1975), Chicago, Illinois: "We frankly say, yes, the Church made this change, made this law, as she made many other laws, for instance, the Friday abstinence, the unmarried priesthood, the laws concerning mixed marriages, the regulation of Catholic marriages and a thousand other laws."

[107] Summary of Meeting of Advisory Committee on the Microbiological Safety of Blood and Tissues and Organs for Transplantation (MSBTO), 28 June 2005.

[108] "World Blood Donor Day 2006" World Health Organization.

[109] Eckstein, Yechiel, "Shabbat: A Day of Delight," International Fellowship of Christians and Jews, 2015, < http://www.ifcj.org/assets/pdfs/limmud_oct_sabbath_final.pdf >.

[110] "Was Enoch Taken to Heaven?," Heaven & Hell What Does the Bible Really Teach?, Beyond Today, United Church of God, January 25, 2011, < http://www.ucg.org/bible-study-tools/booklets/heaven-and-hell-what-does-the-bible-really-teach/was-enoch-taken-to >.

[111] "The Thief on the Cross," Heaven & Hell What Does the Bible Really Teach?, Beyond Today, United Church of God, January 25, 2011, < http://www.ucg.org/bible-study-tools/booklets/heaven-and-hell-what-does-the-bible-really-teach/the-thief-on-the-cross >.

[112] 'Parable,' Oxford Dictionaries, Oxford University Press 2016,

< http://www.oxforddictionaries.com/us/definition/american_english/parable >.

[113] 'Destroy,' Oxford Dictionaries, Oxford University Press 2016,

< http://www.oxforddictionaries.com/us/definition/american_english/destroy >.

[114] 'Death,' Oxford Dictionaries, Oxford University Press 2016,

< http://www.oxforddictionaries.com/us/definition/american_english/death >.

[115] 'Torment,' Oxford Dictionaries, Oxford University Press 2016,
< http://www.oxforddictionaries.com/us/definition/american_english/torment >.

[116] 'Torture,' Oxford Dictionaries, Oxford University Press 2016.
< http://www.oxforddictionaries.com/us/definition/american_english/torture >.

[117] 'Revile,' Oxford Dictionaries, Oxford University Press, 2016,
< http://www.oxforddictionaries.com/us/definition/american_english/revile >.

[118] Thompson, Bert, Ph.D., "Biblical Accuracy and Circumcision on the 8th Day," Apologetics Press, 1993, < http://apologeticspress.org/apcontent.aspx?category=13&article=1118 >.

[119] World Health Organization International Agency for Research on Cancer "IARC Monographs evaluate consumption of red meat and processed meat," PRESS RELEASE #240, 26 October 2015. < http://www.iarc.fr/en/media-centre/pr/2015/pdfs/pr240_E.pdf >.

[120] Pere'rah, Rodney "The Power of Linen – The Most Amazing Facts About Linen," NEW2TORAH, < http://www.new2torah.com/2011/11/the-power-of-linen/ >.

[121] Ghose, Tia, "Genetic 'Adam & Eve Chromosome Study Traces All Men To Man Who Lived 135,000 Years Ago," LiveScience / The Huffington Post, 08/01/2013,
< http://www.huffingtonpost.com/2013/08/01/genetic-adam-eve-chromosome-men-man_n_3691084.html >.

[122] Highfield, Roger, "DNA survey finds all humans are 99.9pc the same," The Telegraph, 20 DEC 2002, < http://www.telegraph.co.uk/news/worldnews/northamerica/usa/1416706/DNA-survey-finds-all-humans-are-99.9pc-the-same.html >.

[123] Segall, Marshall, "ALL OF US ARE RELATED, EACH OF US IS UNIQUE," Syracuse University, 2002, < http://allrelated.syr.edu/fulltext.html >.

[124] "How Life On Earth Began," *Reader's Digest*, p. 116, November 1982.

[125] Paulien, Gunther B. Ph.D., "The Divine Prescription, p. 107, July 01, 1995.

[126] Hovind, Kent, "Where Did God Come From?,"
< https://www.youtube.com/watch?v=nWITp1RFOb0 >.

[128] 'Big Bang Theory,' Merriam-Webster, 2017,
< https://www.merriam-webster.com/dictionary/big%20bang%20theory >.

[129] Hovind, Kent, "Genesis 1:1: A Trinity of Trinities," YouTube, 2004,
< https://www.youtube.com/watch?v=Hi8ouoD06Bk >.

[130] "Check This Out: Evolution Refuted," Answers in Genesis, YouTube, Feb 3, 2014,
< https://www.youtube.com/watch?v=sWecPwrQv2c&index=13&list=PLFB298F25EE9B8EAC >

[131] Sherwin, Frank M.A., "Just How Simple Are Bacteria?," 2001,
< http://www.icr.org/article/just-how-simple-are-bacteria >.

[132] Bergman, Jerry, "Human-Ape hybridization: A Failed Attempt to Prove Darwinism," ICR, 2009, < http://www.icr.org/article/human-ape-hybridization-failed-attempt/ >.

[133] Moore, Jeffrey I., "27 Stephen Hawking Quotes Explain The Theory of Everything,"
< https://www.google.com/webhp?sourceid=chrome-instant&ion=1&espv=2&ie=UTF-8#q=stephen+hawking+quotes+theory+of+everything >.

[134] "Shayim," BibleStudyTools,
< http://www.biblestudytools.com/lexicons/hebrew/nas/shamayim.html >.

[135] Is Carbon Dating Accurate? Summary: Radiometric dating is a technique used to date materials using known decay rates. Are radiometric dating methods accurate? Amazing Discoveries, Professor Walter J. Velth, PhD, Feb. 19, 2009,
< http://amazingdiscoveries.org/C-deception-carbon_dating_radiometric_decay_rates >.

[136] "Is Carbon Dating Reliable?" Fryman, Helen, < http://carm.org/carbon-dating >.

[137] "ERRORS ARE FEARED IN CARBON DATING," The New York Times, Browne, Malcom W., May 31, 1990,
< http://www.nytimes.com/1990/05/31/us/errors-are-feared-in-carbon-dating.html >.

[138] Lavett Smith, C.; Rand, Charles S.; Schaeffer, Bobb; Atz, James W. (1975). "Latimeria, the Living Coelacanth is Ovoviviparous." *Science* 190 (4219): 1105-6,
< http://www.sciencemag.org/content/190/4219/1105 >.

[139] "T-rex bone blood not 70mil years old," YouTube, 2008,
< https://www.youtube.com/watch?v=97jYngUaepA >.

[140] Fields, Helen, "Dinosaur Shocker," Smithsonian Magazine, MAY 2006,
< http://www.smithsonianmag.com/science-nature/dinosaur-shocker-115306469/ >.

[141] "Soft tissue in dino fossils - nothing in science can allow this to be millions of years old," MSNBC, YouTube, 2016,
< https://www.youtube.com/watch?v=ynXwAo9V_pY >.

[142] 'Geocentrism,' Wordnik, 2016 < https://www.wordnik.com/words/geocentrism >.

[143] 'Geocentrism,' RationalWiki, 2016< http://rationalwiki.org/wiki/Geocentrism >.

[144] Heliocentrism,' Wikipedia, 2016, < https://en.wikipedia.org/wiki/Heliocentrism >.

[145] "Hammer vs. Feather - Physics on the Moon," YouTube, 1971,
< https://www.youtube.com/watch?v=KDp1tiUsZw8 >.

[146] "The helic model - our solar system is a vortex," YouTube, 2012,
< https://www.youtube.com/watch?v=0jHsq36_NTU >.

[147] 'Pillar,' Oxford Dictionaries, Oxford University Press, 2016,
< https://en.oxforddictionaries.com/definition/us/pillar >.

[148] Encyclopedia Articles, "WHY DO EARTH'S CONTINENTS MOVE?," 2007 Dorling Kindersley, < http://www.factmonster.com/dk/encyclopedia/continents.html >.

[149] "VISIBLE EARTH A catalog of NASA images and animations of our home planet,"
< http://visibleearth.nasa.gov/ >.

[150] NASA Captures "EPIC" Earth Image, July 20, 2015,
< https://www.nasa.gov/image-feature/nasa-captures-epic-earth-image >.

[151] Mashable, "Father and Son Launch iPhone Into Space [VIDEO]," OCT 17, 2010,
< http://mashable.com/2010/10/17/iphone-space-launch-video/#ktReCYGe8Pqt >.

[152] Clover, Julie, MacRumors, "iPhone 6 Gets Sent Into Space by Urban Armor Gear," January 15, 2015, < http://www.macrumors.com/2015/01/15/iphone-6-goes-to-space/ >.

[153] "T-rex bone blood not 70mil years old," YouTube, 2008,
< https://www.youtube.com/watch?v=97jYngUaepA >.

[154] Fields, Helen, "Dinosaur Shocker," Smithsonian Magazine, MAY 2006,
< http://www.smithsonianmag.com/science-nature/dinosaur-shocker-115306469/ >.

[155] "Soft tissue in dino fossils - nothing in science can allow this to be millions of years old," MSNBC, YouTube, 2016,
< https://www.youtube.com/watch?v=ynXwAo9V_pY >.

[156] Cohen, Tamara, "Dinosaurs DIDN'T rule the earth: The huge creatures 'actually lived in water' – and their tails were swimming aids," Daily Mail, 3 April 2012,
< http://www.dailymail.co.uk/sciencetech/article-2124420/Dinosaurs-DIDNT-rule-earth-The-huge-creatures-actually-lived-water--tails-swimming-aids.html >.

[157] Turvill, William "Africa as you've never seen it before: Clever comparison shows it's really as big as China, India, the United States AND most of Europe put together," Daily Mail, 5 October 2013, < http://www.dailymail.co.uk/news/article-2445615/True-size-Africa-continent-big-China-India-US-Europe-together.html >.

[158] "News about dinosaurs dead and maybe alive," The Fairservice Pages Christian Community Creation, < http://www.fairservicenz.com/dinosaur/dinosaur-1.html#New_expedition >.

[159] Line, Brett; "Asteroid Impacts: 10 Biggest Known Hits." National Geographic News, February 14, 2013, < http://news.nationalgeographic.com/news/2013/13/130214-biggest-asteroid-impacts-meteorites-space-2012da14/ >.

[160] Martin, Charles; "Flood Legends: Global Clues of a Common Event," New Leaf Press, 2009,
< http://www.amazon.com/Flood-Legends-Charles-Martin/dp/0890515530/ref=sr_1_1?ie=UTF8&qid=1448380031&sr=8-1&keywords=flood+legends >.

[161] "Archaeologists: Ancient Writings Confirm Noah's Ark," CBN NEWS, January 28, 2014,
< http://www.cbn.com/cbnnews/world/2014/January/Archaeologists-Ancient-Writings-Confirm-Noahs-Ark/ >.

[162] "Worldwide Flood, Worldwide Evidence," Answers in Genesis, 2014,
< https://answersingenesis.org/the-flood/global/worldwide-flood-evidence/ >.

[163] Prickrell, John, "Two New Dinosaurs Discovered in Antarctica," National Geographic News, March 9, 2004,
< http://news.nationalgeographic.com/news/2004/03/0309_040309_polardinos.html >.

[164] "NOVA: Arctic Dinosaurs: Warm-Blooded creatures of the Cretaceous?" PBS broadcast July 27, 2011, < http://www.pbs.org/wgbh/nova/nature/arctic-dinosaurs.html >.

[165] Pappas, Stephanie, "First Long-Necked Dinosaur Fossil Found In Antarctica," Livescience, November 04, 2011,
< http://www.livescience.com/16883-sauropod-dinosaur-fossil-antarctica.html >.

[166] Hovind, Kent; "The Age of the Earth," Creation Science Evangelism, YouTube,
< https://www.youtube.com/watch?v=AOPcr1N6NvQ >.

[167] "Richard Dawkins Knows Nothing About Nothing?," YouTube,
< https://www.youtube.com/watch?v=v34QjYPuiEA#t=22 >.

[168] Stein, Ben; "EXPELLED: No Intelligence Allowed," 2008 documentary film, "Richard Dawkins admits to Intelligent Design," < https://www.youtube.com/watch?v=BoncJBrrdQ8 >.

[169] "Stellar evolution," Wikipedia, 2016, < http://en.wikipedia.org/wiki/Stellar_evolution >.

[170] "Chemical evolution," Dictionary.com, 2016,
< http://dictionary.reference.com/browse/chemical+evolution >.

[171] Essert, Matt; News.Mic, "Cambridge Study Reveals How Life Could Have Started From Nothing," April 26, 2014,
< http://mic.com/articles/88441/cambridge-study-reveals-how-life-could-have-started-from-nothing >.

[172] "Check This Out: Evolution Refuted," Answers in Genesis, YouTube, Feb 3, 2014,
< https://www.youtube.com/watch?v=sWecPwrQv2c&index=13&list=PLFB298F25EE9B8EAC >

[173] Sherwin, Frank M.A., "Just How Simple Are Bacteria?," 2001,
< http://www.icr.org/article/just-how-simple-are-bacteria >.

[174] 174. 9. "Suspension of disbelief," Wikipedia, 2016,
< http://en.wikipedia.org/wiki/Suspension_of_disbelief >.

[175] "Wilson Bentley," Wikipedia, The Free Encyclopedia, 29 June 2016.
<https://en.wikipedia.org/wiki/Wilson_Bentley >.

[176] Zhen Yan, MD, PhD, Nathalie C. Lambert, PhD, Katherine A. Guthrie, PhD, Allison J. Porter, BA, Laurence S. Loubiere, PhD, Margaret M. Madeleine, PhD, Anne M. Stevens, MD, PhD, Heidi M. Hermes, BS, J. Lee Nelson, MD, "*Male microchimerism in women without sons: Quantitative assessment and correlation with pregnancy history*," THE AMERICAN JOURNAL of MEDICINE, August 2005, Volume 118, Issue 8, Pages 899-906,
< http://www.amjmed.com/article/S0002-9343%2805%2900270-6/abstract >.

[177] Moe, "Women May Carry the DNA of All Their Sexual Partners," GNOSTIC WARRIOR, May 5, 2015, < http://gnosticwarrior.com/women-may-carry-the-dna-of-all-their-sexual-partners.html >.

[178] Borik, Julie, "CATHOLIC RUNAWAY ESCAPES THE CATHOLIC CHURCH," Catholic Runaway, YouTube, Aug 3, 2016, < https://www.youtube.com/watch?v=9Y3EGT6JnOQ >.

[179] "The Actual First Pope," Presents of God ministry,
< http://www.remnantofgod.org/pope1.htm >.

[180] "The Real First Pope, Simon!" YouTube,
< https://www.youtube.com/watch?v=eUJX_UQSD1M&feature=youtu.be >.

[181] Peterson, F. Paul, "Peter's Tomb Recently Discovered in Jerusalem," 1971,
< http://www.aloha.net/~mikesch/peters-jerusalem-tomb.htm >.

[182] "Catholic Religion Purposely takes out one of God's Ten Commandments,"
< http://www.jesus-is-savior.com/False%20Religions/Roman%20Catholicism/tencomma.htm >.

[183] 'Complete,' Oxford Dictionaries, Oxford University Press, 2016,
< http://www.oxforddictionaries.com/us/definition/american_english/complete >.

[184] "American-led intervention in Syria," Wikipedia, The Free Encyclopedia, 4 April 2016.

< https://en.wikipedia.org/wiki/American-led_intervention_in_Syria >.

[185] McGuire, Katie, "Obama Didn't Bomb ISIS Oil Because of the Environmental Impact," RIGHT WING News, 26 Nov, 2015. < http://rightwingnews.com/top-news/obama-didnt-bomb-isis-oil-because-of-the-environmental-impact-watch/ >.

[186] Yglesias, Matthew, "How Rich Is the Catholic Church?," Slate, March 14, 2013,

<.http://www.slate.com/articles/business/moneybox/2013/03/catholic_church_and_pope_francis_religious_institutions_are_exempted_from.html >.

[187] Francis, Catholic Pope, "ON CARE FOR OUR COMMON HOME," Encyclical Letter LAUDATO SI,' 24 May 2015.

< http://w2.vatican.va/content/francesco/en/encyclicals/documents/papa-francesco_20150524_enciclica-laudato-si.html >.

[188] Zilinsky, Sheila, "GREEN GOSPEL The New World Religion," Chapter 10: "The Heart of the Green Gospel: Gaia Worship," 2015.

[189] Park, Madison, "Obama: No greater threat to future than climate change," CNN January 21, 2015. < http://www.cnn.com/2015/01/21/us/climate-change-us-obama/index.html >.

[190] "Obama on ISIS: 'We Have Contained Them'," RealClear Politics November 13, 2015.

< http://www.realclearpolitics.com/video/2015/11/13/obama_on_isis_we_have_contained_them.html >.

[191] "White House: Obama wants to admit 10,000 Syrian refugees in 2016," FOX News Politics, Associated Press, September 11, 2016., < http://www.foxnews.com/politics/2015/09/10/white-house-obama-wants-to-admit-more-syrian-refugees.html >.

[192] McGuire, Katie, "Obama Didn't Bomb ISIS Oil Because of the Environmental Impact," RIGHT WING News, 26 Nov, 2015. < http://rightwingnews.com/top-news/obama-didnt-bomb-isis-oil-because-of-the-environmental-impact-watch/ >.

[193] "American-led intervention in Syria," Wikipedia, The Free Encyclopedia, 4 April 2016.

< https://en.wikipedia.org/wiki/American-led_intervention_in_Syria >.

[194] 'Reed,' Oxford Dictionaries, Oxford University Press, 2016,

< http://www.oxforddictionaries.com/us/definition/american_english/reed >.

[195] Reed,' Oxford Dictionaries, Oxford University Press, 2016,

< http://www.oxforddictionaries.com/us/definition/american_english/reed >.

[196] Zhang, Moran, "Top 10 Foreign Holders Of US Debt: China, Japan Still In The Lead," International Business Times, 12/17/2013,

< http://www.ibtimes.com/top-10-foreign-holders-us-debt-china-japan-still-lead-1511752 >.

[197] "The Seven Resurrections of the Holy Roman Empire," The Trumpet, July 2004,

< https://www.thetrumpet.com/article/1078.24.64.0/world/government/the-seven-resurrections-of-the-holy-roman-empire >.

[198] Wheeler, Brian & Hunt, Alex, "Brexit: All you need to know about the UK leaving the EU," BBC, 10 August 2016, < http://www.bbc.com/news/uk-politics-32810887 >.

[199] Manson, Rowena; Watt, Nicholas; Traynor, Ian; Rankin, Jennifer, "EU referendum to take place on 23 June, David Cameron confirms," The Guardian, 20 February 2016,

< http://www.theguardian.com/politics/2016/feb/20/cameron-set-to-name-eu-referendum-date-after-cabinet-meeting >.

[200] Erlanger, Steven, "Britain Votes to Leave E.U.; Cameron Plans to Step Down," The New York Times, 23 June 2016, < http://www.nytimes.com/2016/06/25/world/europe/britain-brexit-european-union-referendum.html?_r=0 >.

[201] Goodman, Peter S., "Turbulence and Uncertainty for the Market After 'Brexit'," The New York Times, 23 June 2016,

< http://www.nytimes.com/2016/06/25/business/international/brexit-financial-economic-impact-leave.html >.